The North Atlantic Treaty Organisation

Facts and Figures

The North Atlantic Treaty Organisation, Facts and Figures
Published by the NATO Information Service, NATO, 1110 Brussels

NATO Facts and Figures is published under the authority of the Secretary General of NATO and is not a formally agreed document. It does not therefore necessarily represent the official opinion or position of individual member governments on all policy issues discussed.

First edition published in 1955 under the title "NATO — The First Five Years" by Lord Ismay, Secretary General of NATO 1952-1957.

Subsequent editions published under the present title:

First edition	1957
Second edition	1959
Third edition	1962
Fourth edition	1965
Fifth edition	1969
Sixth edition	1970
Seventh edition	1971
Eighth edition	1976
Ninth edition	1978
Tenth edition	1981
Tenth edition (revised)	1984
Eleventh edition	1989

(fully revised and re-set with new graphics and an extended alphabetical index)

The NATO Emblem, which appears on the cover of this book, was adopted as the symbol of the Atlantic Alliance by the North Atlantic Council in October 1953. The circle is the symbol of unity and cooperation and the compass rose suggests the common direction towards peace taken by the 16 member countries of the Atlantic Alliance. The blue background represents the Atlantic Ocean.

Acknowledgement

The Editor wishes to acknowledge with thanks the contributions of all those whose criticisms and suggestions have helped in the preparation of this edition as well as those who in other ways have contributed to this production.

Editorial Note

In this first impression of the current edition of "The North Atlantic Treaty Organisation: Facts and Figures", the main description of events and developments in the different spheres of Alliance activity covers the period 1949 to 1988. However, the opportunity has been taken to add to and update relevant sections of the book in order to take account as far as possible of major developments occurring during 1989. The Summit Meeting of the North Atlantic Council in Brussels at the end of May 1989, as well as a number of subsequent developments, are thus included in the Chronicle of Main Events (Chapter 4), in the description of progress in the field of arms control and disarmament (Chapter 11), and in the Chronology (Appendix IV). Developments in Eastern Europe occurring after mid November 1989, end-of-year Ministerial meetings of NATO Foreign and Defence Ministers, and the NATO Summit Meeting held in Brussels on December 4, 1989, are not covered in this edition.

Enquiries concerning this and other NATO publications should be addressed to:

NATO Information Service
B-1110 Brussels
Belgium

Tel.: (02) 728.41.11
Telex: 23867 OTAN/NATO
Telefax: (02) 728.45.79

ISBN: 92-845-0041-9
Printed by Ceuterick, Leuven, Belgium

Contents

Appendix III Appointments

List of Illustrations and Figures

MANFRED WÖRNER

Chairman of the North Atlantic Council and Secretary General of NATO.

Manfred Wörner was born in Stuttgart on September 24, 1934. He attended the Universities of Heidelberg and Paris and then pursued legal studies at the University of Munich. He received a doctorate in international law in 1958, his dissertation having dealt with the defence relations of allied countries.

Mr. Wörner worked as an administrator in the State of Baden-Württemberg, before becoming parliamentary adviser at the State Diet of Baden-Württemberg in 1962. Elected to the German Bundestag in 1965, he remained a member of parliament until becoming Secretary General of NATO. His special interests as an elected representative have been parliamentary reform and security policy.

Chairman of the Working Group on Defence of the Christian Democratic Union/Christian Social Union (CDU/CSU) parliamentary party until 1976, Mr. Wörner was Chairman of the Defence Committee of the German Bundestag until 1980; and Deputy Chairman of the CDU/CSU parliamentary party with special responsibility for foreign policy, defence policy, development policy and internal German relations until 1982. During this period he was also a member of the Federal Executive of the CDU and Deputy Chairman of the Konrad Adenauer Foundation.

From October 1982 until May 1988, Mr. Wörner was Minister of Defence of the Federal Republic of Germany. He took up his appointment as Secretary General of NATO on July 1, 1988.

Figure 1

Preface

The North Atlantic Alliance has played a vital role over 40 years in ensuring that democracy and the national heritage of each of its member countries have been properly protected through sound defence policies and the maintenance of political solidarity. The same Alliance now has a vital role to play in managing the process of change and ensuring that it is a lasting and secure one. We are living at a time of new opportunities—perhaps even at a historic turning point in East-West relations.

Two major Alliance policy documents were published at the conclusion of the remarkable May 1989 Summit Meeting of the North Atlantic Council—a Comprehensive Concept of arms control and disarmament and a political Summit Declaration. Through these documents, the Heads of State and Government of the member countries of the Alliance expressed their common vision of a more just, humane and democratic world—one in which there are open borders and contacts across them; more freedom; fewer weapons; guaranteed security; and respect for the rule of law. This is a vision which has long underpinned the policies of the Alliance but is now the basis for intensified efforts to shape a future in which the painful division of Europe may be overcome and its peoples can exercise their inherent right of self-determination.

The Alliance can be justly proud of its record in developing the strengths and building on the accomplishments of democracy and freedom. This has been achieved on the basis of the guiding principles derived from the Harmel doctrine—adequate provision for defence combined with constructive dialogue. These principles remain the underlying basis for progress in East-West relations and their steadfast application has now brought the Alliance closer to its ultimate goals: spreading the benefits of peace and stability throughout the world; making military aggression an option which no government can rationally contemplate or hope successfully to undertake; and establishing a new pattern of relations between East and West in which ideological and military antagonism are replaced by cooperation, trust and peaceful competition, and in which human rights and political freedoms are guaranteed and enjoyed by all.

Maintaining adequate defence is the prerequisite for the progress being sought and, when combined with realistic arms control initiatives, offers an approach which fully defends our Western interests while paying due regard to the legitimate security concerns of the Soviet Union and its allies. Moreover, the Alliance has issued a challenge to the Warsaw Treaty countries to join it in accelerating efforts to sign and implement agreements which would promote progress by reducing levels of nuclear and conventional forces in return for enhanced security.

The Allies also recognise the need at the outset of NATO's fifth decade to meet the challenge of reshaping their own interrelationships in a way which corresponds to the new political and economic realities of the 1990's. Both close cohesion between the countries of Europe and North America and the evolution of an increasingly strong and coherent European identity will have a vital importance. Measures have been taken to reinforce the process of political consultation and to ensure that respective approaches to problems affecting the common security are complementary and mutually supportive. Steps are also being taken to improve support for the economically less favoured partners in the Alliance and to increase the level of cooperation and assistance for these countries. And greater commercial, monetary and technological cooperation is being sought.

Central to the process of overcoming the division of Europe, strengthening the security and stability of all its states and guaranteeing lasting peace on the continent, is the need to address the underlying political causes of that division. In their Summit Declaration, Alliance Heads of State and Government looked to the contribution which the CSCE process can make in this respect and examined an agenda of measures to ensure that, within the framework of the Alliance, the Western nations play a constructive role in promoting steps towards genuine political and economic reform in Eastern Europe. The Declaration's "Design for Cooperation" also addresses the global challenges from which none of the other issues can be isolated and reflects the determination of member countries to pursue their work across the spectrum of Alliance activity. This includes its "Third Dimension", through which cooperation on environmental matters and in the fields of science and technology benefits all Alliance members. Above all else the Heads of State and Government of the 16 countries reaffirmed that in the future, as in the past 40 years, the Alliance remains the cornerstone of their security, peace and freedom.

During the last ten years we have faced serious and difficult challenges. The INF-debate, Afghanistan and Poland put Alliance policies to serious tests. Yet, by persevering with our complementary policies of defence and dialogue, we have been able to transform the political landscape. The Soviet Union has come to realise that the Allies are prepared to take the lead in energetically pursuing imaginative arms control, but will refuse to sacrifice security in order to conclude over-hasty and flawed agreements. East-West negotiations have often been arduous and slow. Yet if we now face brighter prospects, it is because the Allies have always heeded an important lesson: if they maintain their cohesion and purpose, despite setbacks and disappointments, their efforts will produce results.

It is on this basis that we are meeting the new opportunities in East-West relations with confidence. The first results are already behind us. Apart from the INF Treaty, the process of improving prospects for lasting peace and security has been furthered by the Stockholm Document on Confidence and Security-Building Measures, and the Concluding Document of the Vienna Follow-up Meeting to the Conference on Security and Cooperation in Europe. Each of these have represented achievements breaking new ground in East-West relations and milestones on which we are building a better future.

The improvements of which we have seen the beginnings give us much hope, both for further arms control success and for the spreading of Western values in the East. We seek not only to encourage but to actively assist such positive developments. Yet they do not in themselves remove the military capabilities which we find threatening, nor do they provide guarantees of irreversible progress towards a more peaceful international order. Thus while the Alliance will be striving to be first and foremost an instrument of peaceful political change, it will be operating in a more fragile and unpredictable international environment. For as long as the reform movement in the East is in the hands of a very few men and thus depends entirely on their political dexterity, the countries of the Alliance cannot place their trust in intentions alone. These can change suddenly, as can the leaders themselves, but the military capabilities over which they hold sway are, in the case of the Soviet Union, still impressive. Even with the most optimistic outcome of current East-West arms control negotiations, that country will possess enormous military power overshadowing Europe for many years to come. This is a power which we must continue to balance, and indeed such a prudent policy will have the added benefit of persuading the Soviet leaders that there is no alternative to domestic reform, no easy return to the Cold War diplomacy of the past.

As a result the second and related task of NATO must be to function as a framework of stability and assurance in a world increasingly gripped by dramatic change and uncertainty. Defence is the essential ingredient of such a framework. A diminishing threat in the short term should not make us lose sight of the long term dangers that such uncertainty may produce. In an age of durable and far-reaching détente, it is tempting for governments and populations alike to relax their vigilance and allow their defences to decline through structural disarmament. If we do so we will be like the driver who allows his insurance policy to lapse because he has not yet had an accident. Political courage and determination will be required as never before to convince our publics that Western structural disarmament is not a contribution to irreversible reform in the East, but a weakening of the Alliance's stability framework that can only increase the uncertainty they seek to guard against. Defence without a forward-looking strategy will not transform the status quo; but neither will a forward looking strategy without defence. With both we can maximise our opportunities, yet minimise our risks.

For the foreseeable future Europe and North America will continue to depend upon each other for the stability and security of the European continent and of Western society. Allied security is and will remain indivisible; the security of each of the 16 countries is of vital importance to the security of them all, whether they are geographically located in the centre of Europe or on its flanks, and on whichever side of the Atlantic they may be. The North Atlantic Treaty was created to defend a democratic political system and a way of life which offers freedom and choice to them all. The defence policies of their governments, and their efforts to secure more stable East-West relations and reductions of armed forces, bear witness to the fact that each of the member countries is determined to preserve its sovereignty, freedom and territorial independence. Deterrence based on the appropriate mix of nuclear and conventional capabilities continues to be the very expression of Alliance solidarity. It alone spreads the risks and responsibilities of providing for the common defence in the most equitable manner. Yet at the same time, because deterrence is a strategy that cannot be used to carry out an attack but only to defend against attack, it expresses as no other strategy can, the peaceful intentions of all the NATO member states.

So whatever its past achievements, the Alliance clearly is not resting on its laurels; it is on the move, indispensable as the only body that brings the combined weight of North America and Western Europe to bear on today's challenges. These remain considerable and our success cannot be automatic. Yet provided we remain united, maintain a strong defence and work hard to ensure the support of public opinion for what is after all the only realistic method of managing change with stability, I am convinced that at our fiftieth anniversary in 1999 we will have more and greater successes to report. Our problems are the problems of success, so they cannot be impossible to solve. Our societies are more humane and fair, our peoples more creative, our economies more dynamic. As long as the NATO member states continue to build a stability and security whose benefits are enjoyed far beyond their boundaries, the future will belong to the Western democracies.

In today's fast moving and complex world there is a glut of information and opinion. Yet to my mind "NATO Facts and Figures" remains an objective, detailed and reliable reference book for all those who wish to follow Alliance activities, review the past and assess the prospects for the future. I therefore heartily welcome the publication of this eleventh edition and wish it the wide readership that it deserves.

Part 1

The Historical and Institutional Framework

1 Origins of the Alliance

2 The Principles and Scope of the North Atlantic Treaty

3 European and Transatlantic Defence Cooperation

Chapter 1

Origins of the Alliance[1]

In the closing phase of the Second World War, seven weeks after the capitulation of Nazi Germany and six weeks before the Hiroshima bomb, representatives of 50 nations signed the United Nations Charter in San Francisco. The date was June 26, 1945. The world hoped that the lessons of the past had finally been learned and that, in the United Nations, a viable framework for peace had at last been found. However, within four years Europe found itself facing a new threat against which the United Nations Charter alone could not offer adequate protection. The Charter nevertheless contains a provision (Article 51) stipulating the right of its members, individually or collectively, to defend themselves against possible armed attack. Ten European countries, acting in accordance with this Article, turned to the United States and Canada to underwrite a pledge of mutual security, and, on April 4, 1949, they met in Washington to sign the North Atlantic Treaty.

What had happened in the space of three years and not quite nine months to convince those 12 countries of the need for a regional defensive alliance?

The defeat of the two great military and industrial powers, Germany and Japan, had left an immense vacuum to the East and West of the Soviet Union. Taking advantage of such exceptionally favourable circumstances, the Soviet Union made full use of the strength of the Red Army to conduct an expansionist policy which was soon to threaten peace and collective security. Even in 1945, the most confirmed optimist could not claim that the international sky was unclouded. The British Prime Minister, Sir Winston Churchill, in his telegram of May 12 addressed to President Truman, expressed his anxiety in the following terms: "What will be the position in a year or two when the British and American armies have melted, and the French have not yet been formed on any major scale, and when Russia may choose to keep 200 or 300 divisions on active service?" And he added: "An iron curtain is being drawn down upon their front. We do not know what is going on behind....".

Demobilisation of forces

After the German surrender, the Western democracies fulfilled their wartime pledges and began to demobilise. Most American and British forces

[1] This historical chapter, for the most part, is based on Lord Ismay's book: "NATO — the First Five Years".

were withdrawn from the continent of Europe and disbanded. The other nations of Europe addressed themselves to the complex task of reconstruction.

The armed strength of the Allied forces in Europe, at the time of the surrender of Germany, was about five million men. A year later, following demobilisation, their armed strength amounted to no more than 880,000. The strengths of American, British and Canadian forces in Europe before and after demobilisation were as follows:

	1945	1946
United States	3,100,000	391,000
United Kingdom	1,321,000	488,000
Canada	299,000	0

The Soviet Union kept its war industries going and its armed forces on a war footing. In 1946 their strength still amounted to six million men.

Wartime cooperation comes to an end

The Yalta Conference of February 1945, attended by Roosevelt, Churchill and Stalin, had taken place at a time when Britain, the United States and the Soviet Union were allied against an all-but defeated Germany and when some in the West still entertained illusions that this war-time alliance would be translated into peacetime cooperation. It was in this optic that agreement was obtained on a Charter for the future United Nations Organisation. Often incorrectly regarded as the event which legalised the division of East and West Europe, the Yalta Conference laid the ground for the disarmament and post-war administration of Germany and dealt with a number of more immediate concerns: Poland was to be reestablished with new frontiers; disputed Japanese islands would be ceded to the Soviet Union; the independence of Korea would be reestablished after a predetermined period of joint US/Soviet military occupation; and, most important of all, democratic governments would be established in all liberated countries on the basis of free elections.

When the United Nations Charter was signed in San Francisco in June 1945, Poland was not represented at the conference table because the Soviet Union and the Western powers were unable to agree on the composition of a provisional Polish Government. The Potsdam Conference of July and August 1945 followed the surrender of Germany and addressed the need for the demilitarisation of Germany, the transfer of certain territories to the Soviet Union and Poland, and the unconditional surrender of Japan. Attended by Truman, Churchill and Stalin, it did little to inspire optimism in the future intentions of the Soviet Union. In November 1945 the Soviet Union was persuaded to agree to a procedure for framing peace treaties with Italy, Finland, Bulgaria, Hungary and Romania but it was not until February 1947 that they were signed.

In March 1947, the Foreign Ministers met in Moscow to discuss the drafting of peace treaties with Germany and Austria, but they were unable to agree on Germany's future status. A new Foreign Ministers' Conference was held in

London in November 1947, but it did no more than confirm the impossibility of agreement. Proposals were made by the United Kingdom for an impartial enquiry into the situation in Romania and Bulgaria. Vyacheslav Molotov, the Soviet Foreign Minister, refused to discuss them. Shortly afterwards, Soviet representatives ceased to take part in the Allied Control Council in Berlin. The Foreign Ministers met once more in Paris in May 1949, to discuss anew the problem of Germany and Austria and, in 1951, their deputies spent 109 days at the Palais Rose Conference in Paris vainly trying to draw up an agenda for a new meeting at Ministerial level.

For all practical purposes, the stalemate at the 1947 Moscow Conference finally put an end to the cooperation which had developed between the USSR and the Western democratic countries during the war. The signing of the United Nations Charter on June 26, 1945, had raised hopes, but the Soviet Union used its right of veto repeatedly to block effective action by the United Nations Security Council. One such example was the commission of enquiry appointed by the UN Security Council in 1947 to look into incidents which had taken place between Greece, Albania and Bulgaria. The report prepared by this commission established the responsibility of both Albania and Bulgaria, but all draft resolutions recommending action by the United Nations were systematically vetoed by the Soviet Union. Western efforts to reach agreement with the Soviet Union and to make the United Nations an effective instrument for preserving peace met with nothing but obstruction.

Soviet expansion

Soviet territorial expansion under Stalin had already begun during the war with the annexation of Estonia, Latvia and Lithuania, and parts of Finland, Romania, Poland, North-Eastern Germany and Eastern Czechoslovakia, a total area of about 180,000 square miles of territory and a population of more than 23 million people. It was this expansion that moved Paul-Henri Spaak, who was at the time the Belgian Prime Minister and Minister of Foreign Affairs, to state in the General Assembly of the United Nations in 1948: "There is but one Great Power that emerged from the war having conquered other territories, and that Power is the USSR".

This territorial expansion continued after the defeat of Germany and was supplemented by policies consolidating control over the countries of Eastern Europe. The presence of the victorious Soviet armies in the heart of Europe and Communist infiltration into "popular front" governments effectively compelled Albania, Bulgaria, Romania, Eastern Germany, Poland, Hungary and Czechoslovakia to fall within the sphere of Soviet domination.

The "Conquest without war"

In Hungary, from the beginning of 1947, the Communist Party opened a violent campaign against the Smallholders Party, and as a result of its denunciations many arrests were made. The government under Ferenc Nagy had to resign on May 29. New elections did not produce an absolute majority for the Communist Party but made it the largest group in Parliament. The Communists quickly formed a new government and formally dissolved the opposition parties on November 21, 1947.

In Bulgaria, the operation was carried out along similar lines. Nikola Petkov, leader of the Opposition Agrarian Party, was accused of plotting a military coup d'état, sentenced to death on August 16, 1947, and hanged on September 23. On August 24 the Opposition Agrarian Party was dissolved on grounds of being "fascist" and on November 22, the national administration was organised along Soviet lines. On December 11, 1947, Georgi Dimitrov, former Secretary of the Comintern, assumed leadership and formed a predominantly Communist cabinet.

In Romania, after elections in November 1946 which were widely regarded as invalid, members of the opposition were accused of plotting the overthrow of the government bloc. The Peasant Party was dissolved on October 10, 1947, and its leader, Luliu Maniu, was sentenced to life imprisonment on October 29. King Michael was forced to abdicate on January 1, 1948. Shortly afterwards, a Communist-controlled government was set up, led by the Foreign Minister, Anna Pauker, who had served in Moscow during the war as adviser to the Soviet government on Romanian affairs.

In Poland, Stanislaw Mikolajczyk, head of the Peasant Party, was compelled to leave the country in November 1947 after constant threats to his life. His Party had to relinquish its role as opposition, and was finally dissolved on November 21, 1947.

In Czechoslovakia, Soviet interference steadily increased. In July 1947, soon after the Marshall Plan for a European Recovery Programme was announced, the Prague Government, which favoured participation, was obliged to reverse its decision after a hasty visit to Moscow by Klement Gottwald, the Prime Minister, and Jan Masaryk, the Foreign Minister. The Communists, by means of a campaign of denunciation, secured the arrest and trial of many members of the six democratic opposition parties. Following a government crisis in February 1948, attempts by the democratic parties to force the resignation of the Communists finally failed, and in June 1948 President Benes was compelled to resign, leaving a Communist-dominated government in place. On March 10, 1948, Jan Masaryk was found dead in a courtyard of the Foreign Ministry.

In less than a year, Moscow had thus succeeded in gaining control over the governments in Budapest, Sofia, Bucharest, Warsaw and Prague. Communist parties ruled alone, or nearly alone, in each of these capitals. All opposition had been removed. It only remained to coordinate the activities of these governments on the international level and thus establish a bloc of satellite nations.

Soviet political pressure in other parts of the world

The Soviet Union also exerted pressure, directly or indirectly, in other parts of the world.

By supporting the separatist movement in Iran's northern province of

Azerbaijan, the Soviet Union vainly sought to establish a foothold as a means of extending its influence in the Middle East as a whole. The provisions of the Treaty of Teheran and the protests of the United Nations were disregarded.

In Turkey, government and people resisted Soviet attempts at intimidation, territorial claims on Kars and Ardahan, and demands for a share in the defences and control of the Turkish Straits. In Greece, the guerrilla campaign which began in 1944 took on the aspect of real war in 1946, when the rebels received reinforcement from bases in neighbouring states within the Soviet sphere of influence. In Asia, the Soviet Union considerably extended its influence by occupying the greater part of Manchuria and Northern Korea in 1945.

Communist agitation was also intensified throughout the whole of South-East Asia. In Indochina, France and the Associated States were engaged in extensive operations against a Communist-directed rebellion. Substantial British forces were tied down by Communist-inspired guerrillas in Malaya. Communist parties fomented strikes and unrest in Burma. Communist insurgents engaged in constant guerrilla warfare in the Philippines.

At the end of 1947, a concerted and virulent campaign of opposition took place throughout Western Europe. Political agitation, subversion and orders to strike combined with persistent attempts to infiltrate all branches of activity in the West, particularly the trade unions, and especially in France and Italy.

Gravely threatened by Soviet expansionism and subversion, the free countries of Europe recognised the need to seek the means of guaranteeing their freedom and security. It was natural that, sooner or later, they should turn towards the United States, which alone was powerful enough to impress the USSR. The reaction of the United States was prompt and decisive.

Truman Doctrine

The United States had been having its own difficulties with the Soviet Union. President Truman, who had expressed his views on the dangers of isolationism as a Senator as early as 1943, took office in April 1945, convinced that the United States would merely be sowing the seeds of a future war if it turned its back on the world. In particular, he was determined that no power hostile to the United States and to democratic institutions should be allowed to dominate Europe. Nevertheless, it appeared to be happening. Contrary to the United Nations Charter and the principle of self-determination, the Soviet Union was imposing its will on the European continent. The ravages of war made easy prey of many countries. Although Truman persisted in his belief that the conflicts could be resolved, he continued to oppose Soviet expansionist policies. Aware of the consequences of a totally subservient and crippled Germany, for example, he firmly rejected exaggerated Soviet demands for war reparations.

The deterioration in relations between the Soviet Union and the Western powers reached crisis proportions by the beginning of 1947. Attempts to introduce greater stability and security, for example through the United States proposal to bring nuclear energy under international control (the Baruch plan), had failed. Previous agreements designed to remove the causes of future conflict, such as the Yalta Agreement safeguarding the status of Poland, had been ignored. It was clear that actions beyond words would soon be needed.

In Europe, Soviet pressure was nowhere stronger than in Greece and Turkey. In February 1947, the United States Government was alerted by London that Britain would be unable to provide the economic and military aid necessary to assist these two countries to resist a Communist takeover. In fact, British aid would have to be suspended from the end of March. On March 12, 1947, in the speech which gave birth to the "Truman Doctrine", President Truman showed that he no longer had any illusions about resolving differences with Stalin. He told the United States Congress: "It must be the policy of the United States of America to support free peoples who are resisting attempted subjugation by armed minorities, or by outside pressure". Congress acted fast and authorised the appropriation of $ 400 million of aid to Greece and Turkey and the despatch of American civilian and military missions to Athens and Ankara.

Marshall Plan

Although the "Truman Doctrine" was designed to deal with the specific threat to Greece and Turkey, the situation in Western Europe generally was no less alarming. In spite of the aid provided by the United States to relieve post-war shortages, the mechanism of the European economy remained badly jammed and Western Europe was likely to find itself on the brink of economic collapse. On June 5, 1947, in a speech at Harvard University, the Secretary of State of the United States, General George C. Marshall, initiated the idea of a Programme for European Recovery. He proposed that the United States should come to the help of Europe and suggested that the European countries should examine their requirements and draw up a common programme agreed by a number, if not all, of the European nations. He added that this policy was "directed not against any country or doctrine but against hunger, poverty, desperation and chaos".

This offer of economic assistance, which, in the next few years, contributed largely to the economic recovery of the Western countries, was also open to the Soviet Union and the countries behind the Iron Curtain. Stalin refused all American aid for the USSR and, despite initial interest on the part of both Czechoslovakia and Poland, forced satellite governments to do likewise.

Cominform

In September 1947, Stalin set up the Cominform, one of whose alleged aims was to fight the Marshall Plan as "an instrument of American imperialism". Its members were the leaders of the Communist parties in the USSR, Poland, Bulgaria, Czechoslovakia, Romania, Hungary, Yugoslavia,

France, Italy, and later, the Netherlands. Its chief purpose was to coordinate the activities of the Communist movement in various countries—including the armed struggle in Greece—as opposed to the Marshall Plan which was geared to the economic recovery of all European countries devastated by the Second World War.[2]

Europe thus found itself split into two blocs. The nature and extent of Soviet intentions were henceforth clearly perceived. As regards the free countries of Europe, the only way they could begin to re-establish a balance of forces was to come together. A number of statesmen, particularly Winston Churchill, the former British Prime Minister, and Louis St. Laurent, the Canadian Secretary of State for External Affairs, had already contemplated in 1946 the idea of a defensive alliance within the framework of the United Nations.

On January 22, 1948, Ernest Bevin, the United Kingdom Foreign Secretary, suggested a formula for Western Union consisting of a network of bilateral agreements on the lines of the Dunkirk Treaty. This Treaty had been signed on March 4, 1947 by France and the United Kingdom. It was a "Treaty of alliance and mutual assistance" of 50 years' duration, according to which the two countries would unite in the event of any renewed attempt at aggression by Germany. Under its terms, they were also bound, by means of continuing consultation on problems bearing on their economic relations, to take all measures necessary to increase their prosperity and economic stability, and thus enable them to make a more effective contribution to the economic and social aims of the United Nations. The idea was warmly welcomed. However, the Dunkirk Treaty had been aimed expressly against renewed German aggression. A more appropriate model was perhaps the Treaty of Rio de Janeiro, signed on September 2, 1947, by the United States and 20 Latin American countries (excluding Nicaragua and Ecuador). This Inter-American Treaty of Reciprocal Assistance was essentially a collective, defensive alliance against aggression, and provided an example of "regional grouping" within the framework of the United Nations Charter.

While these problems were under discussion, the Communist coup d'état of February 1948 drew Czechoslovakia into the Soviet orbit. This came as a sharp reminder to the Western allies that common defensive action was needed.

Brussels Treaty

On March 4, 1948, representatives of Belgium, France, Luxembourg, the Netherlands and the United Kingdom met in Brussels to consider the terms of a treaty of mutual assistance. Their efforts soon met with success. Under the Brussels Treaty, signed on March 17, 1948, these five countries pledged themselves to build up a common defence system and to strengthen their economic and cultural ties.

---

[2] Two years later, following the Moscow Treaty of January 25, 1949, the Council for Mutual Economic Assistance (CMEA) was established by the Soviet Union as a direct response to the Marshall Aid programme.

Article IV of the Brussels Treaty states that, should any of the contracting parties be the object of an "armed aggression in Europe", the other signatories to the Treaty would afford the attacked party "all the military aid and assistance in their power". The Treaty, with a duration of 50 years, provided for the creation of a supreme body in the "Western Union", known as the Consultative Council, consisting of the five Foreign Ministers. Under it was a Western Defence Committee consisting of the Defence Ministers.

Berlin blockade

On April 30, 1948, the Defence Ministers and Chiefs-in-Staff of the five Brussels Treaty signatory Powers met in London to discuss their countries' military equipment needs and to see how far they could be met from their own production resources and how much additional aid would have to be requested from the United States. From July 1948 onwards, United States and Canadian experts attended these meetings as observers.

Soon after the Brussels Treaty was signed, the Soviet Union started the blockade of West Berlin. It began on June 24, 1948, and was to last 323 days. It was countered by the organisation of an air lift by the Western Powers and was finally lifted on May 9, 1949. The process of organising Western defence was hastened as a result.

Western Union Defence Organisation

In September 1948, a military body was created within the framework of the Brussels Treaty known as the Western Union Defence Organisation. Field Marshal Montgomery was appointed Chairman of the Commanders-in-Chief Committee and set up his Headquarters at Fontainebleau, France. Commanders-in-Chief were appointed: General de Lattre de Tassigny (France) for the Land Forces; Air Chief Marshal Sir James Robb (United Kingdom) for the Air Forces; Vice-Admiral Jaujard (France) for the Naval Forces.

Vandenberg Resolution

The creation of a defence organisation by the free countries in Europe could not fail to awaken a response from the United States.

On April 11, 1948, the United States Secretary of State, General George C. Marshall and the Under-Secretary, Robert M. Lovett, opened preliminary talks with Senators Arthur H. Vandenberg and Tom Connally on the problems of security in the North Atlantic area.

The idea of a single mutual defence system, including and superseding the Brussels Treaty, was publicly put forward by Louis St. Laurent in the Canadian House of Commons on April 28, 1948. It was warmly welcomed one week later by Ernest Bevin. However, if the idea was to succeed, it was essential that the United States should be able, constitutionally, to join this "Atlantic Alliance". To this end, in consultation with the State Department,

Senator Vandenberg drew up a Resolution[3] which recommended, in particular, "the association of the United States, by constitutional process, with such regional and other collective arrangements as are based on continuous and effective self-help and mutual aid"; it also recommended that it should be an objective of the United States Government to contribute to the maintenance of peace by making clear its "determination to exercise the right of individual or collective self-defence under Article 51 (of the United Nations Charter) should any armed attack occur affecting its national security".

This Resolution, thanks to the timely initiative of Senators Vandenberg and Connally, was adopted on June 11, 1948, by the United States Senate. Constitutionally the road was now clear. Preliminary talks opened in Washington on July 6, 1948, between the State Department and the Ambassadors of Canada and the Western Union Powers. They ended on September 9, 1948, with a report to governments. This report was favourably received and enabled the Consultative Council of the Brussels Treaty to announce, at the end of October 1948, complete identity of views on the principle of a defensive pact for the North Atlantic area.

The text of the North Atlantic Treaty was published on March 18, 1949[4]. Even before that, on March 15, 1949, the signatories of the Brussels Treaty, together with Canada and the United States, officially invited Denmark, Iceland, Italy, Norway and Portugal to accede to the new Treaty.

April 4, 1949—Signature of the North Atlantic Treaty

On April 4, 1949, in spite of the pressure brought to bear by the Soviet Union on the Parties to the Treaty (notably a memorandum addressed to the twelve original signatories alleging the hostile nature of their action), the North Atlantic Treaty was signed in Washington. It was ratified by the Parliaments of the member countries within five months.

Subsequently, four other countries joined the 12 original signatories: Greece and Turkey were invited to join the Alliance in September 1951, and formally acceded to the Treaty on February 18, 1952.[4] The Federal Republic of Germany was invited to accede to the Treaty following the signature of the Paris Agreements[5] in October 1954, and officially became a member of the North Atlantic Treaty Organisation on May 9, 1955. The Protocol of Accession of Spain to the North Atlantic Treaty was signed on December 10, 1981 and, after its ratification in all member countries, Spain formally became a member of NATO on May 30, 1982.

---

3 The text of the Vandenberg Resolution is reproduced in "NATO Basic Documents" published by the NATO Information Service.

4 The texts of the North Atlantic Treaty and the Protocols on the Accession of Greece, Turkey, the Federal Republic of Germany and Spain are reproduced in Appendix I.

5 The texts of the Paris Agreements are reproduced in "NATO Basic Documents" published by the NATO Information Service.

Chapter 2

The Principles and Scope of the North Atlantic Treaty

The North Atlantic Treaty is the political framework for an international alliance designed to prevent aggression or to repel it, should it occur. It provides for continuous cooperation and consultation in political, economic and military fields. It is of indefinite duration.

The signatory countries state their desire to live in peace with all peoples and all governments. Reaffirming their faith in the principles of the United Nations, they undertake in particular to preserve peace and international security and to promote stability and well-being in the North Atlantic area.

To achieve these goals, they sign their names to a number of undertakings in different fields. They agree, for example, to settle international disputes by peaceful means, in order to avoid endangering international peace, security and justice. They also agree to refrain from the threat or use of force in any way which would not be consistent with the purpose of the United Nations. They undertake to eliminate conflict in their international economic policies and to encourage economic collaboration between their countries.

Under this Treaty, the member countries therefore adopt a policy of security based on the inherent right to individual and collective self-defence accorded by Article 51 of the United Nations Charter (Appendix I), while at the same time affirming the importance of cooperation between them in other spheres.

The text of the Treaty (Appendix I) consists of 14 Articles, and is preceded by a Preamble which emphasises that the Alliance has been created within the framework of the United Nations Charter and outlines its main purposes.

Article 1 defines the basic principles to be followed by member countries in conducting their international relations, in order to avoid endangering peace and world security.

Article 2, inspired by Article 1 of the United Nations Charter, defines the aims which the member countries will pursue in their international relationships, particularly in the social and economic spheres, and their resulting obligations.

In Article 3, signatories state that they will maintain and develop their ability, both individually and collectively, to resist attack.

Article 4 envisages a threat to the territorial integrity, political independence or security of one of the member countries of the alliance and provides for joint consultation whenever one of them believes that such a threat exists.

In practice, this consultation takes place in the North Atlantic Council and its subordinate committees.

Article 5 is the core of the Treaty whereby member countries agree to treat an armed attack on any one of them, in Europe or North America, as an attack against all of them. It commits them to taking the necessary steps to help each other in the event of an armed attack.

Although it leaves each signatory free to take whatever action it considers appropriate, the Article states that, individually and collectively, the member nations must take steps to restore and maintain security. Joint action is justified by the inherent, individual and collective right of self-defence embodied in Article 51 of the United Nations Charter; but it is agreed that measures taken under the terms of the Article shall be terminated when the Security Council has acted as necessary to restore and maintain international peace and security.

Article 6 defines the area in which the provisions of Article 5 apply. However it does not imply that events occurring outside that area cannot be the subject of consultation within the Alliance. The preservation of peace and security in the North Atlantic Treaty area can be affected by events elsewhere in the world, and the North Atlantic Council must therefore, as a matter of course, consider the overall international situation.

In Articles 7 and 8, member nations stipulate that none of their existing international commitments conflict with the terms of the Treaty and that they will not enter into any commitments in the future which do so. In particuar, they state that rights and obligations pertaining to membership of the United Nations are unaffected by the Treaty, as is the primary role of the United Nations Security Council in the sphere of international peace and security.

Under Article 9, the parties to the Treaty establish a Council, on which each of them shall be represented, which shall be able to meet promptly at any time. The Council in turn is charged with the creation of such subsidiary bodies as may be necessary to implement the provisions of the Treaty. This is the basis on which the North Atlantic Treaty Organisation has been gradually built up.

Article 10 provides the possibility of accession to the Treaty by any other European state in a position to further the principles of the Treaty. In 1952, Greece and Turkey, in 1955, the Federal Republic of Germany and in 1982, Spain acceded to the Treaty under the terms of this Article.

Article 11 describes the process of ratification of the Treaty, in accordance with the constitutional processes of the signatories, and the manner in which the Treaty is to enter into force.

Articles 12 and 13 deal with the possibility of revision of the Treaty after a period of ten years, and renunciation of the Treaty by any party to it, after 20 years. They have never been invoked.

Article 14 gives equal authority to the English and French texts of the Treaty, and arranges for their safe deposit in Washington DC.

Chapter 3

European and Transatlantic Defence Cooperation

At different intervals since the creation of the Alliance new initiatives have been taken and institutional arrangements made to facilitate greater cooperation in the defence efforts of the European and North American member countries of the Alliance, better consultation between them on security issues and improved coordination of their defence planning arrangements. The result of such initiatives has been to reinforce cooperation within the Alliance as a whole and to provide a more effective collective input to defence, to the benefit of the entire Alliance.

The Treaty of Brussels

Even before the North Atlantic Treaty was signed in April 1949, five European countries—Belgium, France, Luxembourg, the Netherlands and the United Kingdom—had come together on March 17, 1948 to sign the Treaty of Brussels, which promised a system of common defence against outside aggression. The Brussels Treaty of Economic, Social and Cultural Collaboration and Collective Self Defence represented the first formal step in the direction of the North Atlantic Treaty by establishing what became known as the Western Union. It emerged as the first multilateral regional arrangement for the security of Western Europe to be established under the United Nations Charter, in preference to the network of bilateral treaty arrangements (modelled on the lines of the 1947 Dunkirk Treaty between France and the United Kingdom) which had originally been proposed by Ernest Bevin, Foreign Secretary of the United Kingdom, in January 1948. The immediate effect of the Brussels Treaty was to provide the United States administration with the evidence it needed to convince the American Congress of Europe's determination and ability to organise itself for defence— a prerequisite for American involvement in the future Atlantic Alliance. The Brussels Treaty powers established a political structure, consisting of a Consultative Council of Foreign Ministers and a Permanent Commission, and a Military Committee. Each of these played a significant role in the further negotiations leading to the North Atlantic Treaty. The Military Committee of the Brussels Treaty powers was in fact created in response to an American request for information on European military plans and actual and potential sources of military supplies. This information was to be used to assist in preparing Congress and United States public opinion for American participation in the North Atlantic Treaty by demonstrating that the role expected of the United States was not to act alone but to lend support to a common endeavour which already had its own momentum.

Following the creation of NATO itself, the French National Assembly adopted, on October 26, 1950, a plan outlined by René Pleven, Prime Minister of France, for the creation of a unified European army, including German contingents, to be established within the framework of NATO. The plan was put forward in the context of a wide-ranging discussion concerning the contribution of the Federal Republic of Germany to the future defence of Western Europe. At the request of the North Atlantic Council the plan was further discussed in the Petersberg negotiations between the French, British and American High Commissioners in Germany and the Government of the Federal Republic. These negotiations began in December 1950 but were superseded in February 1951 by the convening of the Paris conference on the establishment of a European Defence Community (EDC).

At the instigation of the French Prime Minister, negotiations opened in Paris in February 1951 for the creation of a European Defence Community consisting of France, Italy, the Benelux countries and the Federal Republic of Germany. Negotiations continued until May 1952, when the European Defence Community Treaty was signed. The EDC came firmly within the framework of the North Atlantic Treaty and other NATO member countries such as Britain, which had participated in the EDC negotiations as an observer, were directly involved both through NATO and additional multilateral arrangements. The detailed EDC Treaty was signed by France, Italy, the Federal Republic of Germany, Belgium, the Netherlands and Luxembourg, i.e. all the members of the embryonic European Coal and Steel Community established under the 1950 Schuman plan, which was the forerunner of the European Communities later to be established by the Treaty of Rome.

The proposed EDC was enthusiastically supported by the United States, and the process of parliamentary ratification, which was needed before the Treaty could be implemented, was soon completed by all countries except Italy and France. However, on August 29, 1954, the French National Assembly decided against ratification of the Treaty, and this ambitious scheme collapsed.

Meanwhile, the Alliance's European pillar had already been reinforced by the decision by the Government of Turkey to make formal application to accede to the North Atlantic Treaty, followed by invitations extended by the North Atlantic Council to the Governments of both Turkey and Greece to be associated with the military agencies of NATO in Mediterranean defence planning. The formal accession of both countries to the North Atlantic Treaty took place in February 1952.

The Paris Agreements and the Early Development of NATO

In September 1948 a military body known as the Western Union Defence Organisation had been created within the framework of the Brussels Treaty.

Commanders-in-Chief were named for Land, Air and Naval forces. Field-Marshal Montgomery was appointed Chairman of the Commanders-in-Chief with his headquarters at Fontainebleau. Following the signing of the North Atlantic Treaty in April 1949, the Brussels Treaty powers agreed to merge the military structure of the Western Union with those being developed within NATO. The responsibilities of the Western Union Commanders-in-Chief Committee were transferred to General Eisenhower in April 1951 when he became NATO's first Supreme Allied Commander Europe, and the staff and facilities of the land, sea and air commands of the Western Union were placed at his disposal. At the same time the Western Union Infrastructure Programme, consisting primarily of cost-sharing arrangements for airfields and signals networks for the use of the five Brussels Treaty powers, also passed to NATO (see Chapter 12). Under the Paris Agreements of October 1954, the Federal Republic of Germany and Italy acceded to the Brussels Treaty and the Western Union became the Western European Union (WEU).

The Paris Agreements were the culmination of work undertaken at the conferences which had taken place earlier in the year both in London and in Paris, principally to formalise arrangements resulting from the changed status of the Federal Republic of Germany. They consisted of a complex set of documents relating to bilateral and multilateral arrangements required to provide the juridical and institutional framework within which the common defence of the 15 countries by then involved was to take shape. Different groupings of the countries concerned appended their signatures to a series of some 20 separate documents comprising agreements relating to the resolution of bilateral, cultural, economic and territorial issues between France and Germany; arrangements concerning German sovereignty in the context of the Four Power Conference (France, the Federal Republic of Germany, the United Kingdom and the United States); a declaration by the five powers inviting Italy and the Federal Republic of Germany to accede to the Brussels Treaty; protocols signed by the seven parties relating to the revised Brussels Treaty; and protocols and resolutions signed by the 14 existing members of NATO relating to the accession of the Federal Republic of Germany to the North Atlantic Treaty.

By the end of 1954 the remaining anomalous situations facing Western Europe as a result of the Second World War had therefore been largely resolved. The pattern of future relationships between former allies and adversaries had been laid down and the basic insititutional structures for multilateral defence cooperation had been established. NATO had taken on the role of an organisation politically dedicated and militarily structured to meet the needs of collective defence in the spirit of Article 51 of the United Nations Charter, and had passed the test of its first five years. Its consultative, decision-making and operational machinery had evolved at a breathless pace during the first three years, but at the Lisbon meeting of February 1952 member countries had taken stock and had begun to plan for a more orderly future. The Council Deputies, created in May 1950 to meet the need for a permanent body to undertake the task of building progressively and systematically the necessary organisational infrastructure, were transformed by the Lisbon decisions into the permanent North Atlantic Council, with full powers irrespective of the level of its meetings. The position of the Secretary General had been created to preside over the Council at all levels. In the words of the Belgian Permanent Representative of the time, André de Staerke, who was later to become the Dean of the Council, the Alliance moved from improvised arrangements to institutional forms, retaining the operating flexibility which made it "an incomparable instrument in which member states can demonstrate their solidarity without sacrificing their sovereignty".

The Lisbon reforms faced up to the impracticalities of the geographical separation between a Military Committee located in the United States, a Supreme Command (SHAPE) situated in France and the Council Deputies in London, and brought them closer together. They addressed the pressing question of the economic arrangements and controls needed to provide a stable basis for defence planning and introduced the annual review procedures which remain the basis for planning today—an assessment of the military threat, identification of requirements to meet it, and proportional contributions by the member countries based on their economic and social capabilities. Mutual examination of the force proposals of each nation enabled goals to be worked out and firm commitments made. The Alliance continued to evolve in this way but the foundation had been laid.

More recent years

With the signature of the Paris agreements many of the tasks of the Western Union passed to NATO. In the reconstituted Western European Union, like NATO, the basic structures needed to fulfill the functions expected of each organisation by their respective member governments were in place. The Alliance had been able to rectify the largest remaining anomaly and on May 5, 1955, the Federal Republic of Germany had formally acceded to the North Atlantic Treaty. No further major developments occured as far as the institutions themselves were concerned until the 1980s. In December 1981, however, a development of major significance for European defence cooperation in the institutional, political and military fields took place when the Government of Spain applied to join the Atlantic Alliance. Spain formally acceded to the Treaty on May 30, 1982. In 1986, in a referendum organised by Prime Minister Felipe González, Spanish voters supported the continued membership of Spain in the Atlantic Alliance without participation in NATO's integrated military structure.

In the political sphere, cooperation continued within the broad framework of the various treaty obligations incumbent upon the different member countries of the Alliance. Within the European Economic Communities the member countries instituted a process known as European Political Cooperation (EPC) as a practical step towards fulfilling the goals of the 1957 Treaty of Rome, those formulated in the Solemn Declaration on European Union of

June 1983, and later, those of the Single European Act of December 1985. Although notionally this form of cooperation in the field of foreign affairs includes all spheres of political activity, in practice European Political Cooperation has not confronted the security and defence-related dimension of inter-European affairs in any direct sense. Work in this sphere has to date moved ahead cautiously and tentatively. Political and economic aspects of security are discussed in European Political Cooperation, but security in its widest sense poses greater difficulties. Discussion of a European concept of security as a whole has not therefore been possible in this forum.

Bilateral and Multilateral Arrangements

Throughout the history of the Alliance, collective defence structures within the Alliance framework have been complemented by a number of bilateral and multilateral agreements and specific cooperative projects, especially in the field of armaments production. A number of such projects are described in Chapter 15. Particular efforts have also been made to enhance cooperation in the field of standardization of equipment, for example within FINABEL (France, Italy, the Netherlands, Belgium, Luxembourg and the United Kingdom), an organisation which seeks to promote standardization of equipment and material for land forces (the subject of standardization in the Alliance as a whole is discussed in Chapter 16).

Within the military organisation of the Alliance, through the structural arrangements of regional commands such as Allied Forces Northern, Central and Southern Europe (AFNORTH, AFCENT and AFSOUTH), and through their subordinate commands, groupings occur which bring together two or more member countries in cooperative, functional roles underpinning the wider multinational basis of the common defence. Likewise, in the various civilian and military agencies created by the Alliance to carry out specific tasks, such as the production and logistics agencies referred to in Chapter 22, different groupings of member nations come together to share more closely in the benefits and responsibilities of arrangements which ultimately serve the overall interests of the Alliance. The same applies in the role sharing which characterises specialised forces such as the two Standing Naval Forces (STANAVFORLANT and STANAVFORCHAN), the Naval On-Call Force for the Mediterranean (NAVOCFORMED), and the Allied Mobile Force (AMF). These are all functional arrangements in which some but not all NATO countries participate, through regional considerations or because of the suitability of the forces available, which serve to strengthen Allied deterrence as a whole. Such arrangements may be organised through the Alliance structures. They may also be organised independently and bilaterally. Thus, in the military context, within the broader strategic framework of overall Western security, the United States and Canada have since 1958 participated jointly in institutionalised command and control arrangements for the air defence and aerospace defence of North America known as NORAD—the North American Aerospace Command (formally the North American Air Defense Command).

Additional bilateral arrangements have been set in train by a number of European governments to further strengthen European defence cooperation. On January 22, 1988, France and the Federal Republic of Germany signed a protocol establishing a Defence and Security Council to strengthen and oversee bilateral cooperation in spheres such as arms control and disarmament, the organisation of joint exercises, the establishment of mixed units including the formation of a joint Franco-German brigade, and cooperation in the armaments field. Plans have also been announced by Italy and Spain for closer bilateral cooperation with their Alliance partners in different military spheres. New forms of cooperation between France and the United Kingdom have been under examination by both governments and an Anglo-German Study Group has been considerering ways of further enhancing defence cooperation between these two countries. In the development sphere, bilateral and multilateral equipment projects continue to bring together many European member countries as well as the United States and Canada in cooperative programmes designed to meet their common requirements.

The EUROGROUP

In 1968, an informal multilateral initiative designed to strengthen the European pillar of the Alliance found expression in the creation of the Eurogroup. The Eurogroup is a grouping of European governments within the framework of NATO, open to all European members of the Alliance. Its basic aim is to help strengthen the whole Alliance by seeking to ensure that the European contribution to the common defence is as strong and cohesive as possible. It does this in two ways: by providing an informal forum in which European Defence Ministers can exchange views on major political and security issues; and by fostering practical cooperation through the work of specialist sub-groups.

Eurogroup's working arrangements are flexible and pragmatic. Meetings of Defence Ministers provide the focal point for its work. They meet twice a year, just before the regular half-yearly Ministerial session of NATO's Defence Planning Committee, to discuss important defence issues and to consider reports from the chairmen of the specialist sub-groups. The chairmanship of the Eurogroup rotates each year. The work is overseen and Ministerial meetings prepared by an ad hoc committee of Eurogroup Ambassadors at NATO Headquarters. For day-to-day affairs, the main working body is the Staff Group, which is composed of officials from the national delegations at NATO Headquarters. A Secretariat is provided by the United Kingdom.

Activities aimed at increasing understanding within NATO and especially in the United States of the scale of the European defence effort are an important element of the Eurogroup's work. The Eurogroup regularly sends panels to North America for this purpose. Arrangements are made for groups of North

American legislators and journalists to see European defence forces at first hand. Briefings are given at NATO Headquarters to a wide range of visitors and a number of other public relations initatives are undertaken. In 1988 the Eurogroup published a booklet setting out the European contribution to the common defence effort and giving information on the military forces of each of the Eurogroup nations. The booklet is being widely distributed in North America.

The Sub-Groups

Eurogroup has established a number of specialist sub-groups to foster greater defence cooperation at a practical level. These sub-groups are manned by experts from national Ministries of Defence. In each of them one country takes the lead, providing a chairman and any necessary staff support. The chairman of each group reports on progress in his group to Eurogroup Defence Ministers at their twice-yearly meetings. NATO military authorities and allies who are not members of Eurogroup sometimes participate in the work of the sub-groups.

EUROCOM

EUROCOM promotes interoperability between the tactical communications systems of the land forces of the European nations. Liaison is maintained with the North American allies and with France. The operational requirements and basic systems parameters defined by EUROCOM constitute the most widely accepted standards for tactical communications within the Alliance. By 1995 Eurogroup nations will have in service equipment built to these standards, opening up growth potential to meet requirements into the next century.

EUROLOG

EUROLOG fosters closer cooperation among Eurogroup nations in the field of logistic support for their armed forces. It has been successful in harmonising common logistics philosophies and procedures in improving interoperability and mutual logistic assistance and identifying opportunities for collaboration in the logistics field. One of EUROLOG's main concerns is sustainability; through discussion and the implementation of practical measures, it is assisting in the efforts being made within the Alliance to bring about improvements in this area.

EUROLONGTERM

EUROLONGTERM develops concepts of operation for European forces in years to come. A wide range of concepts have been agreed and these provide a common baseline for national planning and for the development of collaborative equipment. Although EUROLONGTERM concentrates on areas of conceptual work of particular interest to European forces, care is taken to ensure that its work is closely linked to that of the NATO military authorities.

EUROMED

EUROMED's objective is to encourage cooperation in the field of military medicine. Among EUROMED's successes have been the development of common philosophies and procedures, the organisation of joint training courses, the establishment of arrangements for exchanging information and the introduction of joint studies in a number of important technical areas.

EURONAD/Armaments Cooperation

Through this sub-group the Eurogroup laid the foundation for close cooperation in the procurement of defence equipment. This resulted in the creation of the Independent European Programme which is now the principal European forum for work in this area.

EURO/NATO Training

EURO/NATO Training (see also Chapter 23) has been remarkably successful in its aim of developing joint training facilities. A good example of a European initiative leading to strengthened Alliance cooperation, this sub-group now includes full United States and Canadian participation. Under its auspices some 50 collaborative training programmes have been established, such as the International Long Range Reconnaissance Patrol School, the Basic Helicopter Pilot Training School and the Joint Jet Pilot Training Programme. Among other schemes under consideration are three major projects which, if realised, will greatly improve facilities for training NATO's air and land forces in Europe.

Independent European Programme Group[1]

The Independent European Programme Group (IEPG) is the principal institution through which the European members of NATO seek greater cooperation in armaments procurement. All the European Allies except Iceland are members. The IEPG is independent of both NATO and the Eurogroup. It was formed in 1976 following a call by Eurogroup Ministers for a new forum in which all the European Allies could make practical progress in collaboration. The objectives of the IEPG are:

— to permit the most efficient use of funds for research, development and procurement;

[1] See also NATO Review No 4, August 1989.

— to increase standardization and interoperability of equipment;
— to maintain a healthy European defence industrial and technological base;
— to encourage a better balanced two-way street in armaments cooperation between Europe and North America.

International collaboration in the procurement field has not been without its problems. Nevertheless, there have been many successful bilateral and multilateral equipment projects in Europe in recent years outside the IEPG framework. In one ambitious collaborative venture Germany, Italy and the United Kingdom combined to develop and produce the Tornado multi-role combat aircraft. The Tornado provides NATO commanders in Europe with their only true all-weather combat aircraft designed to operate in European conditions. European Defence Ministers, meeting for the first time under IEPG auspices in November 1984, undertook to extend the range of collaborative programmes and to give new impetus to the IEPG. As a result a structured comprehensive review of national equipment requirements has been undertaken to identify new areas offering scope for collaboration. Defence Ministers have agreed to examine all projects of significance at an early stage to ensure that the potential for international collaboration is fully considered from the outset.

To encourage more efficient use of resources by Europe's defence industries, Eurogroup Defence Ministers have agreed to show greater readiness to adopt equipment already in production in Europe, to apply competition in managing European collaborative projects and to encourage the formation of inter-European industrial relationships. A major European Defence Industry Study (EDIS)[2] was undertaken in 1985 and 1986 into the possibilities for improving the conditions which favour a more rational organisation of industrial resources. The resulting report sets out a framework for new initiatives towards greater European equipment collaboration. Its central features include a transnational open and competitive market; closer coordination of research; and encouragement of the Developing Defence Industry natons. A number of organisational and structural changes were introduced, including the assignment of new responsibilities to the three Panels which constitute the IEPG and the establishment of a permanent International Secretariat in Lisbon. Under an Action Plan adopted by IEPG Defence Ministers in November 1988 to implement proposals of the Report, the IEPG has embarked on a cooperative programme covering all aspects of defence procurement, from long-term military planning, through the formulation of operational requirements and research and development, down to actual production. The most radical feature of the plan is the opening up of the European defence equipment market to contractors from all IEPG nations.

---

[2] The Report based on this study entitled "Towards a Stronger Europe" was published in two volumes in December 1986. The Report was adopted by IEPG Defence Ministers at their meeting on June 22, 1987 as a basis for their future work in this field.

Emphasis was also given to means of developing cooperation in the critical technologies needed to preserve Europe's defence technological base.

The IEPG seeks to encourage cooperation between Europe and North America in specific areas of defence production and procurement, for example, by removing protectionist obstacles. It provides a forum in which a common European view can be developed and expressed and important emerging technologies can be exploited on a cooperative basis between Europe and North America.

The Western European Union

As far as the Western European Union is concerned, just as its military organisation (the Brussels Treaty Organisation) and its principal responsibilities in the defence field were transferred to NATO in 1951, so its primary economic, social and cultural responsibilities passed to the Organisation for European Economic Cooperation (OEEC), the Council of Europe and the European communities as and when these bodies came into being. However the Western European Union retained more limited functions arising from the revised Brussels Treaty in a number of specific areas and continued to handle these in a routine manner throughout the 1950s, 1960s and 1970s. Its tasks were mainly concerned with monitoring, through the Agency for the Control of Armaments, compliance with the voluntary arms limitations agreements agreed by the contracting parties under the revised Brussels Treaty and the 1954 Paris Agreements, and, through the Standing Armaments Committee, harmonising positions among the seven member nations and coordinating their efforts with a view to increasing the effectiveness of cooperative activity in the armaments field. The WEU Council also provided the focus for the work of its Parliamentary Assembly, which continued to demonstrate its attachment to the gradual establishment of a more coherent European security dimension.

In addition to these functions, the Western European Union served as an informal forum until 1973, when the United Kingdom acceded to the Treaty of Rome, for contacts between the United Kingdom and the six original signatories of the 1957 Treaty of Rome.

The 30th anniversary of the Brussels Treaty in 1984 was marked by a joint meeting of WEU Foreign and Defence Ministers in Rome and by a decision to reactivate the WEU. This was both a means of strengthening the European contribution to the Atlantic Alliance and an affirmation of the need for a more vigorous security dimension to the process of European construction, alongside the economic dimension vouchsafed by the European Communities and the foreign policy dimension evolving through European Political Cooperation. Given the limitations on the use which could be made of European Political Cooperation for the purposes of discussing European security issues as a whole, the seven Western European Union member countries decided to use the WEU for regular discussions of defence and security issues affecting Europe with a view to developing its role as a centre for reflection and harmonisation of views on relevant issues. Emphasis was also given to improving public information on defence in Europe and to increasing the role of the WEU Parliamentary Assembly.

The basis for the decision to reactivate the Western European Union was described in the Rome Declaration adopted by the Foreign and Defence Ministers of the seven member states on October 27, 1984. The Declaration emphasised the indivisibility of security within the North Atlantic Treaty area and stressed the necessity of close concertation with other allies who are not members of the WEU. Two other important objectives of the initiative to reactivate the organisation were also given prominence. Firstly, the Declaration called for better use of the WEU framework with a view to increasing cooperation and encouraging consensus in order to preserve peace, strengthen deterrence and defence and consolidate stability. It stated that better utilisation of the WEU would contribute not only to the security of Western Europe but to an improvement in the common defence of all the countries of the Alliance, which remains the foundation of Western security. Secondly, the Declaration recognised that increased cooperation in maintaining adequate military strength and political solidarity in Europe provided the basis for achieving a more stable relationship between the countries of East and West.

A number of specific measures were adopted by WEU Ministers in Rome including the identification of those fields in which particular efforts to harmonise views were required, institutional reforms, activation of the WEU Council, measures relating to the role of the WEU Assembly, the work of the WEU Agency for the Control of Armaments (ACA) and the Standing Armaments Committee (SAC), measures dealing with the interrelationship between the work of the Independent European Programme Group, the NATO Conference of National Armaments Directors (CNAD) and FINABEL, and finally measures dealing with liaison with non WEU member states. A three year transitional period was set for transforming the various WEU institutions to suit their new role.

Foreign and Defence Ministers of the WEU met in Bonn in 1985 and in Venice in 1986 to review progress in the revitalisation of the Organisation, and, in October 1987, met again in the Hague. On this occasion they published a consolidated "Platform on European Security Interests" laying out the basis for their future work. This important new development reflected the conviction of the WEU countries that the construction of an integrated Europe would remain incomplete as long as it did not include security and defence.

The Hague Platform examines a number of areas offering opportunities, especially in the fields of arms control and disarmament and East-West dialogue and cooperation, for Western European Union members to pursue European integration including security and defence. The development of a more cohesive European defence identity represents a major goal of the Hague Platform and is seen by the countries concerned as a prerequisite for making their joint contribution to the common defence of the West more effective.

The Western European Union has underlined the continued relevance of the Alliance's Harmel doctrine combining political solidarity with adequate military strength. In a key statement underlying the overall approach of the Hague Platform, the importance of retaining the essence and vitality of the Atlantic partnership is also recognised:

"The security of the Western European countries can only be ensured in close association with our North American allies..... Just as the commitment of the North American democracies is vital to Europe's security, a free, independent and increasingly more united Western Europe is vital to the security of North America."

The document spells out the criteria on which European security must be based, including the need to maintain cooperative arrangements between some member countries and the United States with regard to nuclear weapons, and the role of the independent nuclear forces of France and the United Kingdom in this respect.

The process of revitalisation of the Western European Union is as yet incomplete, but can be expected to reinforce efforts within the Atlantic Alliance to achieve progress both in terms of political cohesion and in terms of maintaining adequate deterrence and defence. It has also provided a viable European forum for coordination in specific areas. This has been demonstrated in a number of ways, including the use of the WEU to consult on and coordinate naval operations carried out under national auspices to protect shipping in the Gulf area, where many European countries have active shipping. Other WEU and NATO nations have been concerned with practical or financial measures to compensate for gaps thus created and to share the burden.

After a meeting of WEU Foreign and Defence Ministers in the Hague in April 1988, an invitation was extended to Portugal and Spain to become members. They signed the Treaty of Accession on November 14, and become full members once the process of ratification is complete. The possibility of further enlargement remains. Other countries, including Greece and Turkey, have also expressed interest in becoming members.

From the above broad survey of the main developments which have to date influenced the course of transatlantic and European cooperation in the defence field, it is clear that for each of the countries participating in one or more of the endeavours described, a balance of interests and obligations is involved. There is considerable interplay between the various fora and institutional arrangements created to deal with different aspects of cooperation in relation to security policies. However, political constraints, geographical factors and other national considerations can result in real or apparent differences of perspective. The limitations and prerogatives of each of the institutional bodies involved are generally well defined, in line with the undertaking of each NATO nation "not to enter into any international engagement in conflict with this Treaty".

This undertaking reflects a fundamental conviction on the part of the member countries of the Alliance: the condition both for maintaining adequate military strength and political solidarity to deter aggression, and for pursuing the search for progress towards a more stable relationship with the Soviet Union and Eastern Europe, is embodied in the transatlantic partnership and the political, economic and cultural interests and values which the United States and Canada and their European allies hold in common. It is in this perspective that efforts to strengthen the Alliance can be seen to underpin the relationship between Europe and North America which constitutes the primary focus of their common security.

Part 2

The Evolution of the Atlantic Alliance

Chapter 4

Chronicle of Main Events 1949-1989

The evolution of the Atlantic Alliance has been characterised by successive phases, each one contributing a fresh aspect to its policies and activities. The immediate task following the Treaty's signature in April 1949 was the construction of an effective system of collective defence. The Allies have, from the outset, always consulted together on political issues but in the early years their main efforts were directed towards defence problems including their economic and financial consequences. This early period also saw the enlargement of the Alliance; in 1952 the twelve original signatories were joined by Greece and Turkey, and in 1955 by the Federal Republic of Germany. It was not until 1982, with the accession of Spain, that any further enlargement took place.

A second phase in the history of the Alliance began in 1956, with the adoption by the Council of the Report on Non-Military Cooperation in NATO, better known as the Report of the Committee of Three. In the previous period, Soviet political and military pressure had been directed mainly at Europe and South East Asia as a means of consolidating and building on its post-war gains. By 1956, in the early post-Stalin period, it was apparent that the Soviet Union intended to challenge the West in many other regions of the world, employing a greater variety and sophistication of methods. In adopting the Three Wise Men's Report on Non-Military Cooperation in NATO[1] at the end of 1956, the Council gave new impetus to political consultation between member countries on all aspects of relations between East and West. Today consultation remains the life blood of the Alliance. It covers practically every subject of common interest and takes place whenever possible during the formative stages of national policies.

The third phase in the Alliance's development is associated with the Council's approval, in December 1967, of the Report on the Future Tasks of the Alliance, or Harmel Report. Although the members of the Alliance have consistently declared themselves, both individually and collectively, in favour of measures to reduce tensions in Europe, in adopting the Harmel Report the fifteen member governments undertook to pursue simultaneously a policy of maintaining both adequate military capabilities for defence and deterrence and a positive approach to East-West relations aimed at bringing about realistic solutions to existing problems and, ultimately, the removal of the underlying causes of tension between East and West. As a result, and as a

[1] The Committee of Three — Dr. Gaetano Martino (Italy), Mr. Halvard Lange (Norway), and Mr. Lester Pearson (Canada) — became known as the "Three Wise Men".

means of meeting both objectives, studies in the field of disarmament and practical armaments control measures were intensified.

These developments did not take place in a political vacuum. On the wider stage of international relations much was happening. In December 1969, with the adoption by the Federal Republic of Germany, supported by its allies, of the policy which came to be known as "Ostpolitik", a new period in East-West relations began.

Following a series of negotiations and treaties between the Federal Republic of Germany and its neighbours in Eastern Europe—the Soviet Union, Poland, the German Democratic Republic and, later, Czechoslovakia—East and West gradually edged towards a relaxation of tensions. This was to be the era of "détente". At the centre of Europe, the process was underpinned by the Quadripartite Agreement on Berlin of September 1971. It was further encouraged by the Conference on Security and Cooperation in Europe (CSCE) which culminated in the signing of the Helsinki Final Act in 1975 by the 33 European participating states, together with the United States and Canada; and by talks on mutual and balanced conventional force reductions in Central Europe (MBFR) which opened in Vienna in 1973. These developments gave rise to considerable optimism in the West. The atmospherics of the United States-Soviet relationship also took on a more positive tone and accomodations seemed possible in a number of spheres where interests coincided. The first strategic arms limitations agreement (SALT 1) and the accompanying agreement on the limitation of anti-ballistic missile systems (the ABM Treaty) were signed in 1972, and a further interim SALT agreement was concluded in 1974. Though overshadowed by the subsequent deterioration in East-West relations in the second half of the 1970s and early 1980s (caused in part by the Soviet invasion of Afghanistan and by events in Poland), these were significant and, in most cases, lasting achievements which fully vindicated the Alliance policy of dialogue and negotiation with the East. Their evolution is described later in this chapter. With regard to the CSCE process, the Alliance played a key role in coordinating Western positions and the subsequent monitoring of Eastern compliance with the undertakings and code of conduct laid down in the Final Act has remained a major topic of consultation within the Alliance. In the case of MBFR, the Council not only provided a forum for inter-allied consultation, but also assumed a management role in the development of the negotiating position of the Western participants.

One important milestone in the internal life of the Alliance during this period was the signature, in June 1974, of the Ottawa Declaration on Atlantic Relations, which reaffirmed the strong ties between the North American and European allies. While the international situation had continued to undergo profound changes since the signing of the Washington Treaty in 1949, these ties have remained fundamental to the Alliance and are its single most important asset.

The 1956 Report of the Committee of Three on Non-Military Cooperation gave rise to a range of new initatives within the Alliance including cooperation in the scientific field. In fact, since 1957, an elaborate programme of collaborative scientific activities has been conducted under the auspices of the NATO Science Committee. 1969 brought with it a new, related, initiative in the environmental field. Drawing up the future pattern of the Alliance's work in this area was another aspect of the busy work programme which occupied the 1970s. The North Atlantic Council's continuing concern with the urgent challenges to mankind arising from problems of the human environment has enabled the scientific community to build on the imaginative foundations for this work laid down at that time.

Numerous other issues also arose which the Alliance attempted to tackle with the same determination to cooperate for the common good, either formally, using Alliance channels of communication and procedures, or on a more informal basis. Disaster relief, the menace of terrorism, energy problems, long term defence requirements—examples are to be found in the relevant chapters of this book.

However, from the mid-1970s, the hopes which had been aroused about the future of East-West relations gave way to serious doubts. The achievement of Helsinki was offset by the East's unwillingness to honour its obligations under the Final Act, especially in the humanitarian field. At the same time, Soviet activities in southern Africa and the Horn called in question the nature of Moscow's policy of "peaceful co-existence" with the West and the seriousness of its undertaking to apply the CSCE principles to its dealings with all states. It soon became clear that the Soviet Union, while continuing to call for further détente in East-West relations, did not regard this as a constraint on interventionist policies in other areas. The indivisibility of détente proved to be illusory. This was finally confirmed by the Soviet invasion of Afghanistan in December 1979—an event which brought the limitations of the détente process sharply into focus.

At the same time, an accelerated build-up of Soviet military forces across the board, and in particular the deployment from 1977 onwards of large numbers of SS-20 intermediate-range nuclear missiles in the European part of the USSR, gave rise to a major new threat to the security of Alliance members and cast doubt on the credibility of the Alliance's deterrent strategy and on the indivisibility of Allied security. The North Atlantic Council recorded its grave concern at this threat during a period which proved a severe test of the Alliance's political and military cohesion. However, NATO's "dual-track" decision of December 12, 1979 was a clear demonstration of the principles on which the Alliance operates. The first track was a call for negotiations between the United States and the Soviet Union to achieve a balance in intermediate-range nuclear forces at the lowest possible level. The second track—in the absence of such an agreement—was the decision to modernise NATO's intermediate-range nuclear forces by deploying ground-launched Cruise and Pershing II missiles in Western Europe. The ability of the Alliance to take this bold decision and to see it through to a successful conclusion was proof of its determination both to surmount external and internal challenges to its security and to continue unswervingly on its course towards preserving peace through dialogue and negotiation. The essence of the Harmel doctrine—deterrence and dialogue—was manifest in the dual-track decision itself and subsequently in the Alliance's approach to East-West relations throughout the 1980s. NATO's INF deployment programme proceeded as planned, while the United States-Soviet negotiations on intermediate-range nuclear forces in Geneva, despite their interruption by the Soviet side between December 1983 and March 1985, eventually culminated in the INF Treaty of December 8, 1987 and its subsequent ratification. Thus the United States and its partners in the Alliance succeeded in achieving the first arms control agreement to remove globally an entire category of nuclear weapons.

Throughout this period, Allied efforts to put East-West relations on a healthier and less destabilising footing called for a shift from 'détente' for its own sake to a more concerted effort to achieve meaningful, durable measures to eliminate military imbalances, and to build up confidence between East and West. The term "confidence-building" had entered the vocabulary of negotiations.

Although hopes of genuine progress were repeatedly raised and dashed, and the Alliance subjected to serious strains, the period was also characterised by the challenge it presented in terms of the ability of the Alliance to implement its own decisions without yielding to pressures to divert it from its course. The Alliance was strengthened as a result and emerged from the experience having vindicated its approach, and with the principles governing its arms control policies— meaningful, assymetric, verifiable agreements—firmly enshrined in a historic treaty.

Apart from the INF issue, there were other storm-clouds in the early 1980s which cast a heavy shadow on East-West relations. The continuing Soviet occupation of Afghanistan, the imposition of martial law in Poland in December 1981 and the uncertainties surrounding Soviet foreign policy during the transition from the Brezhnev to the Gorbachev era—often marked by signs of nervousness in Moscow—kept the Alliance constantly on its guard. From the mid-1980s onwards, the atmosphere began steadily to improve. More frequent high-level contacts between Allied governments and the new Soviet leadership, including at the Summit level, started to bear fruit. This was particularly true in the arms control field, where the Stockholm Conference on Disarmament in Europe introduced a new era in military confidence-building measures. The United States-Soviet negotiations in Geneva also not only produced the INF Treaty but made substantial progress towards a 50% reduction in strategic nuclear arsenals. In the field of conventional forces, NATO and Warsaw Treaty countries began negotiations in Vienna on a mandate for conventional stability talks. Important developments took place in other spheres, and in particular, in May 1988, Soviet troops began to withdraw from Afghanistan. At the same time, however, the Soviet Union showed little sign of reducing, changing the posture, or even slowing the rate of increase of its offensive miitary capabilities. This remained a matter of major concern to the Alliance, as was made clear in the NATO Summit declaration of March 2, 1988 and in its separate statement on conventional arms control. By the end of the year more encouraging developments were to take place. Although such concerns had by no means been removed and serious imbalances in conventional forces remained, steps had been taken by the Soviet Union, including the annoucement by President Gorbachev of significant unilateral conventional force reductions, which held out the prospect of real progress in future negotiations. These developments, and those which occurred during the early months of 1989, are described later in this chapter.

* * *

First Results (1949-1950)

Opposition to the Alliance on the part of the Soviet Union was to be expected. However, far from leading to increased tension between East and West, as implied by the Soviet Union's memorandum to member governments on the eve of the signature of the North Atlantic Treaty on April 4, 1949, the creation of the Alliance was followed by a slight retrenchment by the Soviet Union leading to a perceptible easing of the East-West situation. On May 9, 1949, the USSR lifted its blockade of Berlin, which had lasted nearly a year. On May 23, 1949, the French, British, American and Soviet Foreign Ministers, meeting in Paris, achieved agreement on a limited number of practical problems arising in respect to Germany and Berlin, particularly concerning communications and commercial relationships with other countries, as well as on the question of a peace treaty with Austria. Finally, with the withdrawal in October 1949 of the Albanian and Bulgarian-based support given by the Soviet Union to the Communist insurrection in Greece, peace also returned to that country.

The Treaty came into force on August 24, 1949, duly ratified by member countries. They were then faced with two immediate tasks, namely the creation of a structure capable of implementing the Treaty, and the elaboration of a common defence policy.

The structural framework

Meeting for the first time in Washington on September 17, 1949, the North Atlantic Council began to build a civilian and military framework. The Council itself, composed of Foreign Ministers of member countries, decided to meet annually in normal circumstances but to convene more frequently should this prove desirable. Furthermore, an extraordinary session could be convened at any time if any member were to invoke Article 4 or 5 of the Treaty.

In accordance with Article 9 of the Treaty, the Council created a Defence Committee composed of the Defence Ministers of member countries, responsible for drawing up coordinated defence plans for the North Atlantic area. It was agreed that this Committee would also meet at least once a year.

A number of permanent military bodies were set up: a Military Committee, consisting of Chiefs-of-Staff of member countries, responsible for advising the Council in military matters; a Standing Group[2], the Military Committee's executive body, composed of representatives of France, the United Kingdom and the United States, and responsible for strategic guidance in areas in which NATO forces operated; and five Regional Planning Groups, for Northern Europe[3] (Denmark, Norway, United Kingdom); Western Europe[4] (Belgium, France, Luxembourg, Netherlands, United Kingdom); Southern Europe/Western Mediterranean[5] (France, Italy, United Kingdom); Canada/United States[6], and the North Atlantic Ocean[7] (all countries except Italy and Luxembourg). These Groups were to develop defence plans for their respective areas.

Civilian and military bodies

At its first session, the Council had recognised that such questions as military production and supply, and the economic and financial repercussions of the defence effort, as well as the prospects for coordinated production, standardization and technical improvement with respect to armaments, required detailed study. Meeting again in Washington on November 18, 1949, it decided to set up two further bodies to carry out this task, namely, the Defence Financial and Economic Committee, composed of Finance Ministers of the member countries; and the Military Production and Supply Board, reporting to the Defence Committee.

First defence plan

Some ten weeks after its creation, the Defence Committee, meeting in Paris on December 1, 1949, agreed upon a strategic concept for the integrated defence of the North Atlantic area, as well as on methods of working out a programme for the production and supply of arms and equipment. Their recommendations were approved by the Council during a meeting in Washington on January 6, 1950. Meeting again at The Hague on April 1, 1950, the Defence Committee approved the first draft of a four-year "medium-term defence plan".

The control and supervision of the civilian and military agencies of the Alliance could no longer effectively be undertaken by the Council in the course of its infrequent meetings. The Council therefore decided, at its meeting in London in May 1950, to set up a civilian body to carry out its directives, to coordinate the work of the Alliance's civilian and military bodies and to act as a forum for regular political exchanges between member governments.

---

2 Dissolved in 1966.

3 Dissolved August 1, 1951.

4 Dissolved September 10, 1951.

5 Dissolved April 10, 1952.

6 The Canada/United States Regional Planning Group remains responsible for developing plans for the defence of the North American area.

7 The functions of the North Atlantic Ocean Group were taken over by the Atlantic Command (ACLANT) when the latter was established on January 31, 1952.

Council Deputies

The new body was composed of Deputies to the Foreign Ministers of the member countries meeting in continuous session in London. In addition to coordinating the work of the NATO bodies, the Council Deputies were made responsible for co-ordinating programmes developed to support defence plans; recommending to governments steps to ensure that the plans were given effect; promoting and coordinating public information in furtherance of the objectives of the Treaty; and considering any further action to be taken under Article 2 of the Treaty, which defined the aims and obligations of member countries with regard to their international relationships in economic and other spheres.

From July 1950 to April 1952, the Council Deputies, and the small central international staff formed in 1951 to serve them, were housed at 13 Belgrave Square, London. On April 16, 1952 new provisional headquarters were opened at the Palais de Chaillot in Paris, in an annex erected for the United Nations General Assembly in 1951. On April 28, 1952, in accordance with the decisions taken in February, NATO became a permanent organisation but continued to occupy its temporary headquarters until more permanent arrangements could be made. In January 1960 it moved to new buildings at the Porte Dauphine where it remained until the move to Brussels in 1967.

The Korean War

Soon after this Council session, in June 1950, an event occurred which had a far-reaching effect on the evolution of NATO, namely, the Communist attack upon South Korea. The United Nations Security Council, denouncing North Korea for the aggression, decided upon economic and military sanctions. All member countries of the United Nations were requested to go to the assistance of the South Korean Republic.

Forward strategy

When the North Atlantic Council met again, in New York on September 15 to 18, 1950, its discussions centred on the problem of how to defend the NATO area against an aggression similar to that in Korea. It was agreed that a forward strategy must be adopted for Europe; that is to say that any aggression must be resisted as far to the East as possible, in order to ensure the defence of all the European member countries. Such a strategy, however, demanded forces far exceeding those available to NATO at the time. The Council accordingly requested the Defence Committee as a matter of urgency to plan for the creation of an integrated force under centralised command, adequate to deter aggression. The Standing Group was to be responsible for strategic direction of the force, which was to be placed under a supreme commander appointed by NATO.

Participation of the Federal Republic of Germany

The New York session was then adjourned to enable Ministers to consult their governments. On reconvening, on September 26, 1950, the Council, recognising that a forward strategy implied the defence of Europe on German soil, decided to study the problem of the political and military participation of the Federal Republic of Germany. This raised difficulties of principle for some member countries and for France in particular, and it was four years before a solution was found.

However, the principle of German participation in the common defence was established when the Council, meeting again in Brussels on December 18, 1950, recognised that such participation "would strengthen the defence of Europe without altering in any way the purely defensive character of the North Atlantic Treaty Organisation". The Ministers then invited the three Occupation Powers in the Federal Republic of Germany—France, the United Kingdom and the United States—to explore, in cooperation with the Federal Republic of Germany itself, ways of achieving this participation.

First Supreme Allied Commander

At Brussels the Council also took important decisions on military matters. It approved the Defence Committee's recommendation for the creation of an integrated European force under centralised command, adequate to deter aggression and to ensure the defence of Western Europe; and it approved the recommendation for appropriate steps to be taken to reorganise the NATO military structure. It also decided to request President Truman to make available General Dwight D. Eisenhower to serve as Supreme Allied Commander for Europe (SACEUR). The President agreed, and on December 19, 1950, the Council officially announced that it had made the appointment and that the Supreme Commander would establish his Headquarters in Europe in the New Year.

On December 29, 1950, the Standing Group issued the first terms of reference for SACEUR. These directed that the NATO forces made available by member nations for the defence of Western Europe would, in the event of an emergency, be organised, equipped, trained and ready to implement agreed plans. It was agreed to establish a Supreme Headquarters in Europe early in 1951 and that SACEUR would be supported by an international staff drawn from the nations contributing to the integrated force[8]. General Eisen-

---

[8] The different categories of national forces participating in NATO's integrated military structure are described in Chapter 23. With few exceptions, the forces of NATO countries remain under national control in peacetime. The Integrated Military Structure itself, in which all member countries of the Alliance participate with the exception of France, Iceland (which has no military forces) and Spain, is also sometimes referred to as the Integrated Defence Programme and the Integrated Military Command Structure. All three terms are synonymous.

hower's Command, Allied Command Europe (ACE), and the Supreme Headquarters Allied Powers Europe (SHAPE), were set up at Rocquencourt near Paris, France, on April 2, 1951.

Also at the December 1950 meeting in Brussels, the Council approved a Defence Committee recommendation to replace the Military Production and Supply Board by a Defence Production Board, with wider powers than its predecessor. This new Board was given the task of increasing production and facilitating the joint use of industrial installations in the member countries.

New structure of NATO

In May 1951, the Council Deputies in London announced some important changes in the NATO structure. The Defence Committee and Defence Financial and Economic Committee were abolished, leaving the North Atlantic Council as the Alliance's one Ministerial body. A Financial and Economic Board was established in Paris, where the Organisation for European Economic Cooperation (OEEC) could provide it with assistance. (The OEEC had been set up in 1948 to channel Marshall Plan aid.) The task of this Board was to advise both the Council Deputies and the other NATO bodies under their control on the economic and financial aspects of the defence programme. It could, in certain specific cases, also approach member governments direct.

One result of reorganisation was to increase the status of the Council Deputies, who now represented all Ministers in their government concerned with NATO matters, where previously they had represented Foreign Ministers alone. The Council Deputies became in effect the permanent working organisation of the North Atlantic Council, and, to service their needs, an International Staff, paid for out of a budget to which all member countries contributed, was set up under the direction of their Chairman, Charles M. Spofford (United States).

The Council Deputies now tackled certain legal and financial problems arising out of the establishment of the new civil and military bodies. On June 19, 1951, an 'Agreement between the Parties to the North Atlantic Treaty regarding the Status of their Forces'[9] was signed, which determined the legal status of military personnel of one member country called upon to serve under NATO command in another. A protocol to this agreement defined the status of military headquarters. A further 'Agreement on the Status of the North Atlantic Treaty Organisation, National Representatives and International Staff'[9] was signed in September 1951, covering the civilian side of the Organisation. The Deputies also settled the question of the joint financing of military headquarters and, in August, 1951, a cost-sharing formula was agreed for SHAPE and its subordinate headquarters.

---

9 These Agreements are reproduced in "NATO Basic Documents" published by the NATO Information Service.

While the efforts made since the creation of the Alliance had reduced the danger of aggression in Europe, continued tensions between East and West, the wars in Korea and Indo-China, and the United Nations deadlock on disarmament and the control of atomic energy, made it clear that the NATO countries could not relax their defence preparations. But their attention was increasingly to be occupied by the economic and financial problems involved in a sustained military effort.

Economic problems and the Temporary Council Committee

At the Council meeting held in Ottawa from September 15 to 20, 1951, Foreign Ministers were joined by Defence and Finance Ministers. The Alliance's military needs as assessed by the Military Committee called for financial contributions far greater than those which the member states considered themselves able to make. The effectiveness of the defence effort was further threatened by rising prices, the danger of inflation, imbalance of payments, and difficulties in the distribution of raw materials. The Ministers accordingly set up a Temporary Council Committee (TCC) whose task it was to reconcile requirements of collective security with the political and economic capabilities of the member countries.

In addition, the Council at Ottawa was informed by the three Occupying Powers that they supported a plan for a European Defence Community to include the Federal Republic of Germany.

Accession of Greece and Turkey

Also at Ottawa, the Council formally recommended to member governments that Greece and Turkey should be invited to accede to the Treaty. At the same time, it decided to examine the possibility of extending NATO's non-military activities, and established a ministerial committee composed of representatives of Belgium, Canada, Italy, the Netherlands and Norway to consider means of strengthening the Atlantic Community and implementing Article 2 of the Treaty.

The Temporary Council Committee started work immediately after the Ottawa meeting. Consisting of representatives of the twelve member countries, its detailed work was delegated to a three-man Executive Board: Averell Harriman (United States), the Committee's Chairman; Jean Monnet (France); and Sir Edwin Plowden (United Kingdom). The report submitted by the TCC on December 18, 1951, was in the nature of a first comprehensive review of the military capacity of the member countries under peacetime conditions. It was the forerunner of the Defence Review procedures subsequently adopted for determining the contributions individual member countries could and should make to the common defence effort.

Sharing the defence burden

Based on the principle that the burden of defending the West should be shared equitably among the member countries, the report recognised that the defence build-up must rest on a foundation of social and economic stability and that the latter demanded expanded production through concerted action. In the light of these considerations, and of the Committee's assessment of the capabilities of individual countries, the report indicated the maximum force build-up required for which the Alliance could realistically plan, and ways and means of attaining it.

Specifically, in the latter context, there were recommendations for relieving balance of payments difficulties and on the different forms of American participation in Europe's military expenditures, particularly through its contributions to common infrastructure costs and offshore procurement. This was a procedure whereby the United States purchased equipment produced by a European member country and then offered it to that country or to another member country as aid under the 1949 Mutual Defence Assistance Programme.

The TCC set the pattern for a continuing process of appraising defence programmes in the light of economic and political development, through the Annual Review, which remains a fundamental part of the defence planning procedures of the Alliance.

The Lisbon decisions—February 1952

At the top of the agenda when the Council met in Lisbon from February 20 to 25, 1952, was the Temporary Council Committee's detailed analysis of the defence capabilities of each member country. The Ministers adopted the firm force goals proposed by the TCC calling for a total of 50 divisions, 4,000 aircraft and strong naval forces by the end of 1952, as well as the TCC's provisional estimates for 1953 and 1954.

Endorsing the plans then under negotiation in Paris for the establishment of a European Defence Community (EDC), Ministers recommended that a protocol should be added to the North Atlantic Treaty, specifying the guarantees to be given to members of the proposed Community. This was to be signed at the same time as the EDC Treaty, which was due for signature in May 1952.

At the same meeting, the Council formally welcomed the accession of Greece and Turkey, who had meanwhile signed and ratified the North Atlantic Treaty.

Also in Lisbon, in response to recommendations by the Council Deputies and the Temporary Council Commitee, the Council completely reorganised the Alliance's civilian agencies, starting with itself. While continuing to be a council of governments, represented by Foreign, Defence, Finance and other competent Ministers according to the requirements of its agenda, the North Atlantic Council was to become a permanent body with headquarters in Paris. To enable it to function continuously, with effective powers of decision, irrespective of the presence or otherwise of Ministers, each government

LORD ISMAY (1952-1957)

Lord Ismay was born in India in 1887. He was educated in the United Kingdom at Charterhouse School and the Royal Military College of Sandhurst, and in 1907 returned to India where he began a distinguished military career serving initially on the North West Frontier. During the First World War he saw active service in Somaliland. He returned to India again after the war and served on the staff of the Commander-in-Chief of the British Forces. At the outbreak of the Second World War in 1939, Lord Ismay was made Deputy Secretary to the British War Cabinet, becoming Chief of Staff to Winston Churchill and later to Clement Attlee when the latter became Prime Minister and Minister of Defence in 1945. He participated in many important international conferences, including Moscow, Tehran and Yalta, and in 1946 was made Chief of Staff to Lord Mountbatten in the negotiations for India's independence.

Lord Ismay was the first Secretary General of NATO. He was appointed to the post on March 13, 1952, and took up office both as Secretary General of the Organisation and as Vice-Chairman of the North Atlantic Council on April 4, 1952, the third anniversary of the signing of the North Atlantic Treaty. The functions he was to assume had been carried out since 1951 by Charles Spofford, Chairman of the Council Deputies. The chairmanship of the Council itself continued to be held by the Foreign Minister of one of the member countries rotating annually, until 1956 when the Secretary General of NATO became the Chairman of the North Atlantic Council at whatever level of government representation it chose to meet. Foreign Ministers continue to act as honorary Presidents of the Council whenever it meets at Ministerial level.

Lord Ismay retired from his post as Secretary General in May 1957 and was succeeded by Paul-Henri Spaak, Foreign Minister of Belgium. Lord Ismay died in 1965.

Figure 2

would appoint a permanent representative who would be supported by a national delegation of advisers and experts[10].

Permanent Council and first Secretary General

The Permanent Council was to take over the tasks of the Council Deputies, Defence Production Board and the Financial and Economic Board, which were to be dissolved. Its chairmanship was entrusted to a newly appointed Vice-Chairman[10] of the Ministerial Council who would serve as Secretary General of the North Atlantic Treaty Organisation. He was to be an international civil servant, rather than a member of any one delegation, and was to organise the work of the Council and to direct the activities of an International Staff. The task of the latter would be to prepare matters for Council action and to implement Council decisions.

The Council was in future to work more closely with the military authorities of the Alliance. This would be facilitated by the move from London to Paris which placed the civilian headquarters within easy distance of the Supreme Command. The responsibilities of the Standing Group (the executive body for the Military Committee) and of the Supreme Allied Commander were increased, particularly with respect to setting priorities for the equipment of forces and to planning for their logistic support.

Creation of new commands—1952

The military structure was extended by the setting up of two new commands: Atlantic Command was established at Norfolk, Virginia (United States) in January, 1952, and Channel Command was established at Portsmouth in the United Kingdom the following month.

The remainder of the year 1952 was largely occupied by putting into effect the organisational decisions reached in Lisbon. On March, 12, 1952, Lord Ismay, Secretary of State for Commonwealth Relations in the United Kingdom Government, was appointed Vice-Chairman of the Council and Secretary General of NATO. Captain R.D. (later Lord) Coleridge was appointed Executive Secretary (Secretary to the North Atlantic Council). The International Staff of the Organisation was installed in Paris, where it was joined by all the Permanent Representatives and their national delegations.

Holding its first meeting on April 28, 1952, the Permanent Council appointed General Matthew B. Ridgway to the post of Supreme Allied Commander to succeed General Eisenhower, who had asked to be released in order to enter United States politics.

Lord Ismay's first report

At a Ministerial meeting in Paris on December 15 to 18 1952, the Secretary General submitted his first report on the progress of work in NATO. In

[10] Permanent Representatives to the North Atlantic Council and Chairmen and Presidents of the North Atlantic Council are listed in Appendix III.

adopting it, the Council voted a resolution calling for further detailed economic study with a view to promoting progress in application of Article 2 of the Treaty, and agreed that member governments should try to strengthen their countries both politically and economically by seeking solutions to balance of payments and other problems[11]. The Military Committee also reported on progress achieved, in particular in the training and effectiveness of national forces assigned to the Supreme Commanders, in cooperation between units and staffs demonstrated during combined manoeuvres, and in the standardisation of procedures.

This meeting was the occasion for the Council's first resolution on the international situation outside the NATO area. It stated that the campaign then being waged in Indo-China by the forces of the French Union deserved the support of the NATO governments.

At the two Ministerial meetings in 1953, the Council drew up long-term defence plans and arrangements for improving the quality of NATO forces. It also established a three-year, cost-sharing formula for infrastructure expenditures.

The Paris Agreements[12]

The main task for 1954 was to settle the question of German participation in Western defence. The formula approved at the Lisbon Conference was invalidated when, on August 29, 1954, the French National Assembly decided against ratification of the Treaty establishing the European Defence Community. After a period of intense diplomatic activity an alternative solution was found.

The London Conference, held from September 28 to October 3, 1954, brought together the Foreign Ministers of the five Brussels Treaty powers and of the Federal Republic of Germany, Italy, the United States and Canada. The Conference formulated a series of decisions to form part of a general settlement which concerned, directly or indirectly, all the NATO powers. It also recorded the view of all governments represented "that the North Atlantic Treaty should be regarded as being of indefinite duration".

These decisions were approved at a further meeting held in Paris from October 20 to 22, 1954, and the Paris Agreements were signed on October 23, 1954[13]. Concluded nearly 10 years after the end of hostilities with Germany, and with no early prospect of agreement with the USSR on a final peace settlement, the Agreements regularised relations between the NATO allies and the Federal Republic of Germany, brought the latter into the Western

---

11 Both resolutions are reproduced in "NATO Final Communiqués, 1949-1974", published by the NATO Information Service.

12 See also Chapter 3.

13 The Paris Agreements are reproduced in "NATO Basic Documents" published by the NATO Information Service.

alliance framework and supplied guarantees concerning European force and armament levels.

Briefly, the provisions of the Paris Agreements were as follows:

— France, the United Kingdom and the United States terminated the occupation regime in the Federal Republic of Germany and recognised it as a sovereign State. The Federal Republic of Germany undertook to authorize the maintenance on its territory of foreign forces at least at the strength obtaining at the date the Agreements came into force.
— The Federal Republic of Germany and Italy acceded to the Brussels Treaty, and the Western Union became the Western European Union (WEU). There was to be extremely close cooperation between the WEU and NATO.
— The Federal Republic of Germany was invited to join NATO, contributing a national army to be integrated into the forces of the Alliance. Machinery was set up to limit the strength of forces and quantities of armaments which could be created within the WEU.
— The United States and the United Kingdom (the latter with certain reservations in case of overseas emergency or financial difficulties) undertook to maintain their forces on the European continent for as long as necessary. (President Eisenhower publicly confirmed this undertaking on March 5, 1955). A unified military formation was to be established by assigning to the Supreme Allied Commander Europe all member countries' forces, with certain exceptions, stationed within the area of his Command.

Accession of the Federal Republic of Germany

The accession of the Federal Republic of Germany to the North Atlantic Treaty became effective on May 5, 1955[14]. Two days later, the USSR renounced its treaties with France and the United Kingdom. On May 14, 1955, the USSR concluded the Warsaw Treaty with its European satellites, presenting it as a response to the Paris Agreements.

On May 15, 1955, the Austrian State Treaty was signed, ending the Four-Power occupation regime in that country. The moment appeared ripe for a fresh attempt at resolving the problem of Germany. On June 7, 1955, the United States, France and the United Kingdom invited the USSR to attend a Four-Power summit conference in Geneva from July 18 to 21, to be prepared by a meeting of Foreign Ministers.

Failure of the Geneva Summit Conference

The Summit Conference ended on July 21 without any agreement of substance having been reached, but the Heads of Government instructed their Foreign Ministers to continue to study the problems at issue. Before the

[14] The Protocol to the North Atlantic Treaty on the Accession of the Federal Republic of Germany is reproduced in Appendix I.

second Geneva Conference, which convened on October 27, the NATO Council held a Ministerial meeting to discuss proposals by the Foreign Ministers of the United States, France and the United Kingdom. Their position was that Germany's reunification should take place under terms permitting her to remain in the Western Alliance. The Soviet Union rejected this view, and the Foreign Ministers concluded their talks on November 11 without results. The proposals that the Three Powers planned to put forward to the USSR had been the subject of extensive exchanges of views at two Ministerial meetings in July and October, and of consultations in the Council during the intervening months.

At the Ministerial Meeting in December 1955, the Council declared that the negative outcome of the Geneva Conference had in no way halted the efforts of the North Atlantic Powers to secure the reunification of Germany in freedom. It urged the importance of further consultation within NATO on this question and on that of Berlin.

Hungarian uprising and Suez crisis

While the Geneva Conference produced no result, it had shown that there were new opportunities for exchanges of views between East and West. This was no doubt due primarily to the nascent Soviet policy of peaceful co-existence which was cautiously welcomed by the Atlantic powers to the extent that it involved a certain easing of tension. But this was to be shortlived. The year 1956 witnessed the stamping out by the Soviet Union of the Hungarian revolution and a systematic campaign to counter Western influence in the Middle East. The latter progressed through Czechoslovakia's arms sales to Egypt, and the USSR taking over financing of the Aswan Dam and culminated in President Nasser's nationalisation of the Suez Canal and Franco-British military intervention. The end of the year saw a return to the cold war. Meanwhile, at a Ministerial meeting in May 1956, the NATO Council had recognised that progress towards a final European settlement could only be achieved on the basis of the unity, solidarity and cooperation of peoples sharing common ideals. In this connection it considered it timely to endeavour to extend its activities in the non-military field, as called for by Article 2 of the Treaty. In particular it appointed a committee of three Foreign Ministers to recommend ways in which the Council could better perform its task as a forum for consultation.

The Committee of Three

The three Ministers—Gaetano Martino of Italy, Halvard Lange of Norway and Lester B. Pearson of Canada—submitted their report[15] to the Ministerial Meeting in December 1956. The Council approved their recommendations,

---

[15] The Report of the Committee of Three on Non-Military Cooperation in NATO is reproduced at Appendix I.

PAUL-HENRI SPAAK (1957-1961)

Paul-Henri Spaak was born at Schaerbeek (Brussels) in 1899 and took a degree in jurisprudence at Brussels University. He became a Socialist member of Parliament for Brussels in 1932 and subsequently Minister of Transport and of P.T.T. He moved from the Ministry of Foreign Affairs to become Prime Minister from 1938 to 1939. After the war, which he spent with the Belgian Government in exile in London, he was again Minister of Foreign Affairs and Prime Minister from 1947 to 1949. In 1949 he presided over the first General Assembly of the United Nations.

In 1949 he was Chairman of the first session of the Consultative Assembly of the Council of Europe and from 1952 to 1953 President of the General Assembly of the European Coal and Steel Community. In 1956 he was chosen by the Council of the North Atlantic Treaty Organisation to succeed Lord Ismay as Secretary General. He resigned from the post in March 1961 in order to resume his political career in the service of his own country and again became Foreign Minister of Belgium. Paul-Henri Spaak was also President of the Royal Belgian Academy of French Language and Literature. He was succeeded as Secretary General of NATO in April 1961 by Dirk Stikker. He died in 1972.

Figure 3

chief among which were that member governments were to inform the North Atlantic Council of any development significantly affecting the Alliance so that effective political consultation could be held on the action to be taken; each spring the Foreign Ministers were to make an appraisal of the political progress of the Alliance, based on a review prepared by the Secretary General; disputes among members which could not be settled directly in accordance with Article 1 of the Treaty should be submitted to good offices procedures within NATO, and the Secretary General was empowered, with the consent of the parties, to initiate procedures to settle such disputes.

At the same meeting, the Council approved a directive for future military plans based on an assessment of the continued rise in Soviet capabilities and the various types of new weapons available for NATO defence. It reaffirmed the concept of forward defence in NATO strategy.

Retirement of Lord Ismay—appointment of Paul-Henri Spaak

At this time, Lord Ismay announced his desire to retire as Secretary General in the spring of 1957 and the Council appointed Paul-Henri Spaak, Foreign Minister of Belgium, to succeed him. Mr. Spaak took office on May 15, 1957.

Ministerial Meeting in Bonn—May 1957

One recommendation of the Committee of Three had been that the Council should meet from time to time in different member capitals, and the Ministerial meeting in May 1957, was held in Bonn. NATO's defence policy was discussed in the light of the campaign launched by the Soviet Union, aimed at inducing public opinion in various member countries to oppose the modernisation of Western defence forces. The Council agreed that one object of this campaign was to ensure that Soviet forces had a monopoly of nuclear weapons on the European continent and that, in the face of this threat, the Atlantic Alliance must be in a position to meet any attack which might be launched against it. No power, it stated, could claim the right to deny the Alliance the modern arms needed for its defence. At this meeting a question was raised which was to occupy the military planners for many years to come, namely, the correct balance between nuclear and conventional arms. The Council stated that there was a continuing need for a powerful shield of land, sea and air forces to protect the territory of member states.

Ministers also determined to intensify their efforts for German reunification through free elections, since the prolonged division of Germany and anomalous situation in Berlin constituted a continuing threat to world peace.

Defence and disarmament problems

At the Bonn meeting, Ministers had pointed out that a remedy existed for fears professed by the Soviet Union with regard to the availability to NATO's defence forces of nuclear weapons. This remedy was the acceptance of a general disarmament agreement embodying effective measures of control and inspection. Disarmament was frequently discussed by the Council in the following months, during which the United Nations Disarmament Sub-Committee was meeting in London with the participation of four NATO countries—Canada, France, the United Kingdom and United States. These four countries made a habit of consulting their NATO partners about any proposals they intended submitting to the Sub-Committee and informing them on the progress of the London Talks. In addition to such routine consultation, Harold Stassen and Jules Moch, the respective representatives of the United States and France at the talks, on two occasions reported personally to the Council.

The Western proposals, put forward to the London Conference on August 29, 1957, were based on advice given by the military authorities of the Alliance and reflected a viewpoint common to all the NATO member countries. The proposals comprised measures to be carried out under international control. These were: reduction of all types of armaments and military forces; cessation of production of fissionable material for military purposes; reduction of existing stocks of nuclear weapons; suspension of nuclear weapon tests; and adoption of protective measures against the risk of surprise attack. These proposals were rejected by the USSR, but later approved by a considerable majority of the General Assembly of the United Nations. Subsequently the General Assembly set up a new disarmament commission which the USSR announced it would boycott.

First space satellite launched

Other factors contributed to the increased international tensions brought about by this boycott. Firstly, the launching of the first space satellite ("Sputnik") on October 4, 1957, foreshadowed the Soviet Union's emergence as a world power with a technological capability matching that of the United States. Further it implied future military superiority, particularly in the field of long-range missiles. The significance of this development was seen at the time as a factor which introduced a new spatial dimension to the military relationship between the Soviet Union and the United States, placing the arms race on a new and potentially unlimited scale. With hindsight it is also possible to regard this event as the beginning of Soviet research into space-based defensive systems—a subject which was to play a major role, first in negotiations leading to the 1972 Anti-Ballistic Missile (ABM) Treaty, and subsequently in the discussions resulting from the announcement in 1983 of the United States Strategic Defence Initiative.

The international situation was further complicated by Western fears that Syria—with its strategic control over the pipeline outlet from the Iraqi oil fields—was in the process of becoming a Soviet satellite. This appeared to be confirmed when Moscow suddenly claimed that Turkey, backed up by the United States and United Kingdom, was preparing to invade Syria.

Meeting of Heads of Government—December 1957

In October 1957, President Eisenhower and Prime Minister Macmillan met in Washington to consider action to be taken to combat the new aspects of the Soviet threat. The Secretary General of NATO, Paul-Henri Spaak, was invited to join them for part of these talks, at the close of which the President of the United States and the Prime Minister of the United Kingdom issued a declaration of common purpose. This stressed, in particular, the fact that the countries of the free world were interdependent and must increase their cooperation, pool their resources and share tasks essential to their security and well-being. Following the Washington talks, it was decided that, in order to mark with particular solemnity the unity of the Alliance, the North Atlantic Council would meet for the first time at the level of Heads of Government.

The Heads of Government met in Paris from December 16 to 19, 1957. In a solemn declaration the Council re-dedicated itself to the principles and purposes of the Alliance, and reaffirmed the common position of its members regarding the maintenance of peace and security.

In the field of defence, the Council stressed that NATO must possess the most effective military defensive strength, taking into account recent developments in weapons and technology. To this end, it was necessary to establish stocks of nuclear warheads readily available for the defence of the Alliance in case of need. In view of Soviet policies in the field of new weapons, the Council also decided that intermediate-range ballistic missiles should be put at the disposal of the Supreme Allied Commander Europe. The deployment of these stocks, as well as arrangements for their use, was to be decided in agreement with the countries directly concerned.

Political and military recommendations

Recognising the growing interdependence of the nations of the free world, the Council recommended closer coordination in the organisation of forces to enable each NATO country to make the most effective contribution to the requirements of the Alliance. It also pointed out that better use of the Alliance's resources and greater efficiency for its forces would be obtained through as high a degree of standardization and integration as possible.

In the political field, the Heads of Government recognised the need for fuller consultation and for a broad coordination of policies.

They reaffirmed their unity regarding the problem of German reunification and the security and freedom of Berlin. In the field of disarmament, they emphasised the need for adequate international control and agreed to establish a technical group to advise on problems of arms control arising out of new technical developments. They stated their willingness to promote any negotiations with the USSR which would lead to the controlled reduction of armaments within the limits imposed by security. They proclaimed that they were prepared to examine any proposal, from whatever source, for general or partial disarmament.

Scientific and economic affairs

In the course of this same meeting, the foundations were laid for cooperation in the field of scientific and technological matters.

Recognising that progress in this field depended on vigorous action within each member country, and also on the cooperation of teachers and scientists, the Heads of Government stressed their desire to increase the effectiveness of national efforts by pooling scientific facilities and information and by sharing out the tasks. They therefore decided to establish immediately a Science Committee on which all NATO countries would be represented by experts who could speak authoritatively on scientific policy. They also recommended the appointment of an outstanding scientist as Science Adviser to the Secretary General of NATO.

The Heads of Government reaffirmed the need for closer economic association between the countries within the Atlantic Community and in the free world as a whole. They decided that the North Atlantic Council should, from time to time, in the spirit of Article 2 of the Treaty and without duplicating the work of other agencies, review economic trends, assess economic progress and make suggestions for improvements.

Soviet reactions

Before the Heads of Government Meeting began in Paris, the Soviet Union launched a diplomatic offensive which continued long after the Ministerial session. It took the form of an avalanche of letters to the various member governments; most of them were signed by Marshal Bulganin, the Soviet Prime Minister. These messages raised a number of issues such as the calling of a summit meeting; the suspension of nuclear tests; the renunciation of the use of nuclear weapons; the institution of a denuclearised zone in Europe; and the signing of a non-aggression pact. The messages were aimed at creating dissension, which could then be exploited with a view to persuading the countries of the Alliance to negotiate separately with the Soviet Union.

The NATO partners found in political consultation the answer to this attack. By agreeing to discuss within the Council both the contents of the Soviet letters and the draft replies prepared by each of the governments, the members of NATO were able to achieve a remarkable degree of harmony in their views, and in preparing subsequent positions.

East-West relations

The new military capabilities achieved by the USSR in both nuclear and conventional terms made it all the more necessary to find a peaceful solution to the potentially explosive situation created by the continued division of Germany. Accordingly, while pursuing plans for long-term defence, the Alliance directed considerable effort towards the organisation of a Summit conference to discuss a European settlement with the USSR.

At its Spring 1958 Ministerial Meeting in Copenhagen, the Council received for the first time a political report prepared by the Secretary General in accordance with the recommendations of the Committee of Three. This document emphasised the progress made by the Alliance in the field of political cooperation.

The Council approved in principle the idea of a summit conference, with the proviso that such a meeting should offer prospects of reaching settlements on important questions; it should, in other words, be properly prepared and take place in a favourable atmosphere. The Foreign Ministers emphasised that the questions of German reunification and controlled disarmament should be discussed.

With regard to the latter point, the Council demonstrated its willingness to negotiate by proposing partial measures which could serve as test cases and might later be applied on a wider scale. It pointed out that agreement on measures which might, for example, prevent surprise attacks or detect nuclear explosions would go far towards demonstrating the prospects for reaching agreement on disarmament.

Negotiations for a summit conference continued during the summer of 1958, but the USSR appeared to lose interest in the idea when it failed to obtain agreement to a conference on its own terms.

The North Atlantic Council, however, continued to be the forum for Western consultation on matters involving relations with the Soviet Union, including the suspension of nuclear weapons tests and the prevention of surprise attacks.

Declaration on Berlin—December 1958

Towards the end of 1958 it was the question of Germany's future, and that of Berlin in particular, which dominated the scene. On November 10, 1958 the Soviet leader, Nikita Khrushchev, declared that the USSR wished to terminate the present status of Berlin and on November 27, 1958, the Soviet Government confirmed this intention. It announced that it proposed to transfer to the East German authorities, within six months, all the powers it exercised in East Berlin by virtue of the 1945 agreements, as well as the control of communications between the Federal Republic of Germany and Berlin.

The North Atlantic Council held its regular Ministerial session in Paris from December 16 to 18, 1958. It gave special attention to the question of Berlin and associated itself fully with the views previously expressed on the subject by the Governments of the United States, the United Kingdom, France and the Federal Republic of Germany. It stressed, in particular, that the NATO countries could not approve a solution of the Berlin question which would jeopardise the right of the three Western Powers to remain there as long as their responsibilities so required, and which would not assure freedom of access and communication between Berlin and the free world. It emphasized that the Soviet Union would be held responsible for any action which would have the effect of hampering free access and communication. The Council stated that the question of Berlin could only be settled in the context of an agreement with the USSR on Germany as a whole. It recalled that the Western Powers had always been and still were ready to discuss this problem, as well as those of European security and disarmament.

The Council also examined a report on political cooperation in the Alliance submitted by the Secretary General, and stressed that consultation could be improved by more systematic study of long-term political questions.

Within two weeks of the Paris meeting, supported by the firm stand taken by the Alliance as a whole in the face of the new threat to Germany, the three Western Governments chiefly concerned sent formal replies to the Russian Notes on November 27, 1958. They reaffirmed their intention to stand their ground in Berlin and rejected the proclaimed Russian decision to transfer to the East German regime Moscow's responsibility for Berlin and the access routes. The Soviet bluff had failed. During the first three months of 1959, Mr. Khrushchev set about a strategic withdrawal from the apparently unyielding position he had adopted. A detente, based on 'peaceful co-existence', which he himself had defined as 'the continuation of the struggle between the two social systems, but by peaceful means', suggested itself as a more fruitful course than threats of nuclear conflict.

On March 5, Mr. Khrushchev said in a speech at Leipzig that there was no question of an ultimatum over Berlin or of regarding May 27, when the six-month period would expire, as an irrevocable deadline for the transfer of Soviet control to the German Democratic Republic. That date could be moved to June, July or even later. A few days later, speaking in East Berlin, he announced that the Soviet Union was prepared to accept the maintenance of troops in West Berlin by the Western Governments, and on March 19, Mr. Khrushchev said at a press conference that the United States, the United Kingdom and France had a legal right to remain in Berlin. The threat to that city was thus lifted—albeit temporarily—and the stage set for a form of detente.

Possibilities of detente

The Western Powers examined the prospects of genuine agreement which such a detente might offer. With this in mind, personal contacts were resumed in February 1959 between Soviet and Western leaders, as a result of which it was agreed in principle to hold a conference of the four Foreign Ministers to deal primarily with the German question.

Tenth Anniversary meeting (April 2-4, 1959)

The preparation of this Conference naturally took pride of place on the agenda of the Ministerial Meeting in Washington. The Council made a point of recalling that the unity of action and policy rendered possible by the Alliance was the best guarantee of success in negotiations with the Soviet Government and in finding genuine solutions to the problems which divided the East and the West.

The Four-Power Ministerial Meeting was held in Geneva from May 11 to

DIRK U. STIKKER (1961-1964)

Dirk Stikker was born in 1887. Having studied law at the University of Gröningen in the Netherlands, he held various appointments in banking and industry between 1922 and 1948. In 1946 he founded the Party for Freedom and Democracy (of which he became Chairman) and from 1946 to 1948 he was a member of the First Chamber of the States General (Senate). From 1948 to 1952, he was Minister of Foreign Affairs and in 1949 represented the Netherlands at the Round Table Conference on the status of Indonesia and the Netherlands West Indies. In 1950 he became Political Mediator of the Organisation for European Economic Cooperation (OEEC) and later Chairman of this Organisation. He was Ambassador in London from 1952 to 1958, and later Ambassador to the Republic of Iceland.

Mr. Stikker was appointed Permanent Representative of the Netherlands to the North Atlantic Council and to the OEEC in July 1958. In April 1961 the North Atlantic Council chose him to succeed Paul-Henri Spaak as Secretary General of NATO and Chairman of the North Atlantic Council. He relinquished this post in 1964 and was succeeded by Manlio Brosio. Dirk Stikker died in 1979.

Figure 4

August 5, with one break. The Council was kept closely informed of progress, in particular through personal reports by Couve de Murville and Selwyn Lloyd. Later it was also briefed on developments in the disarmament negotiations which had reopened in Geneva on March 15, 1960, within the framework of the Ten Power Committee[16]. At the Ministerial Meeting in December 1959, which marked the inauguration of the new NATO Headquarters at Porte Dauphine in Paris, and at the Spring 1960 Meeting in Istanbul, Ministers devoted all their attention to a review of the 'common position' of the United States, France and the United Kingdom, worked out in consultation with their Allies.

Although these negotiations between Foreign Ministers had revealed that the Western and Soviet positions concerning Germany were still irreconcilable, the discussions between President Eisenhower and Mr. Khrushchev at Camp David opened the door to further negotiation, undertaken this time at the level of Heads of Government.

In the communiqué issued at the May 1960 Istanbul meeting, the Council restated the Western position on Germany (reunification on the basis of self-determination) and on Berlin, declared itself in favour of "general and complete disarmament, to be achieved by stages under effective international control", and denounced Soviet propaganda attacks on certain NATO countries.

Breakdown of Summit

The day after the Istanbul meeting an incident occurred which was to undo all the careful planning for the Summit Conference; Mr. Khrushchev announced that an American plane had been shot down over Soviet territory. This was one of the U-2 high-altitude reconnaissance planes used by the United States to obtain the kind of strategic data which Soviet intelligence, operating in open Western societies, could gather without resorting to such methods. Such flights had provided, for example, clear photographic evidence of the existence of an extensive Soviet research programme on missile defence technology and a major test installation at Sary-Shagan—facts which were later confirmed in claims made by Soviet military officials regarding missile capabilities.

President Eisenhower acknowledged the facts of the U-2 incident and assumed personal responsibility for it. Moscow had been aware all along that U-2 flights were taking place but they flew too high and too fast to be intercepted. The capture of the plane and its pilot provided tangible evidence. As soon as the Summit Conference opened, on May 16, Mr. Khrushchev announced he would go ahead with the meeting only on condition the United States condemned the action of its air forces and punished those directly responsible. President Eisenhower replied that the flights had been sus-

[16] Participants included five Western countries (Canada, France, Italy, United Kingdom, United States) and five Eastern countries (Bulgaria, Czechoslovakia, Poland, Rumania, USSR).

pended and were not to be resumed, but this did not satisfy Mr. Khrushchev, who promptly broke up the meeting.

Summit meeting of Communist countries—'peaceful co-existence'

A few weeks later, on June 27, the Communist bloc countries suddently left the Geneva Disarmament Conference, claiming that the disarmament talks could only be usefully continued within a wider framework[17]. The only surprising factor in the cessation of the talks was its suddenness. It was, in fact, a logical step in the hardening of Soviet policy noted since the abortive Summit Conference of May 16. Moreover, it was the forerunner of a spectacular initiative by Mr. Khrushchev, who personally attended the General Assembly of the United Nations at New York in September and succeeded in inflaming the debates by his vehement interventions and extravagant behaviour. In November, in Moscow, a conference of the 81 Communist parties in the world approved Mr. Khrushchev's views on peaceful co-existence.

Resignation of Paul-Henri Spaak—appointment of Dirk Stikker

On February 1, 1961, the Secretary General, Paul-Henri Spaak, informed the Council of his decision to resume political life in his own country. He left office on March 5 and was succeeded by Dirk U. Stikker, Netherlands Permanent Representative to the North Atlantic Council, who took up his appointment on April 21.

At the Ministerial session held in Oslo in May 1961, the Council expressed regret at the lack of progress on the reunification of Germany and in the United States-Soviet negotiations on disarmament. Referring to 'the often repeated threat by the Soviet Union to sign a separate peace treaty', the Ministers reaffirmed their view that Soviet denunciation of the inter-allied agreements on Berlin would in no way deprive the other parties of their rights or relieve the Soviet Union of its obligations. They regretted the negative attitude of the Soviet Union with regard to the comprehensive draft treaty prepared by the United States and the United Kingdom for an agreement on the suspension of nuclear tests.

Soviet ultimatum on Berlin

President John F. Kennedy visited the North Atlantic Council in Paris on June 1, 1961. On June 2 and 3, he met Mr. Khrushchev in Vienna to establish personal contact and exchange views. This meeting was not expected to have immediate results and, in fact, brought out the divergent views separating East and West, particularly on the subject of Berlin. These

---

[17] Discussions on this subject were taken up on March 15, 1962, within the Conference of the Committee on Disarmament.

differences were promptly confirmed when, on June 15, Mr. Khrushchev delivered an address in Moscow. As in November 1958, he issued an ultimatum to the West. The Soviet Union would conclude a separate peace treaty with East Germany by the end of the year. This would terminate the West's rights of access to Berlin. The crisis built up rapidly. On July 8, Mr. Khrushchev announced that the USSR was abandoning a projected reduction in its armed forces and increasing its defence expenditure by over a third. On July 25, President Kennedy called for a substantial build-up of NATO forces. "We cannot and will not permit the Communists to drive us out of Berlin, either gradually or by force", he said.

Berlin Wall

On August 7, Mr. Khrushchev threatened to increase the strength of the Soviet Army on the Western frontiers and call up reserves. The mounting crisis prompted increasing numbers of East Germans to escape to the Federal Republic of Germany. During the first six months of the year over 103,000 had fled to the West. But during the night of August 13, the East German regime barricaded the Soviet sector of Berlin and, despite the protest by the three Allied Powers, started the building of the Berlin Wall.

Soviet nuclear tests

By tacit agreement, the United States, the United Kingdom and the Soviet Union had, since November 1958, discontinued nuclear test explosions. On August 31, 1961, however, claiming that the United States was threatening war as a counter-measure to the proposed separate peace treaty with East Germany, the Soviet Union resumed nuclear testing on an unprecedented scale. Within two months it had produced some 50 nuclear explosions, culminating, on October 30, with a 50 megaton bomb.

Ministerial Meeting in Paris—December 1961

The West continued to show a unitedly firm front, and once again, just when the tension appeared to be reaching its height, Mr. Khrushchev did not put his June ultimatum into effect. He announced at the October Soviet Party Congress that the USSR would not insist on signing a treaty with East Germany before December 31. In all other respects, however, the Soviet position remained unchanged.

In a communiqué issued after the NATO Ministerial Meeting held in Paris in December, the Ministers deplored the fact that the Soviet Government had refused to accept effective international controls for disarmament, refused to hold serious discussions and obstructed nuclear test ban talks for over three years while secretly preparing for the longest series of tests ever held, culminating in the most powerful explosion yet known.

Once again the Ministers reaffirmed their conviction that a just and peaceful solution to the German problem, including that of Berlin, must be based on negotiations and on the principle of self-determination.

Mobile Force created

Taking stock at the end of 1961, Ministers noted the improvements which had been made in the force contributions of member countries, particularly in response to the aggravation of the military threat arising from the deterioration of the Berlin situation. A mobile force had been created from units supplied by six different countries[18]. It consisted at that time of a multinational land element of five air-transportable battalions and a multinational air element of four fighter bomber attack squadrons. The role of the force, which remains unchanged, was to demonstrate NATO solidarity and unity of purpose in any threatened area. There had also been advances in cooperative programmes for defence research and production, as well as in communications and infrastructure. In the economic field, a mission of high-ranking personalities had been set up to study ways and means of assisting Greek and Turkish efforts to speed up their development programmes.

Nuclear defence—Athens Guidelines

At their 1962 Spring meeting in the Greek capital, the Ministers adopted the 'Athens Guidelines', setting out certain broad assumptions regarding the circumstances in which NATO might be forced to have recourse to nuclear weapons in self-defence and the extent to which political consultation would be possible in the various circumstances. The United States confirmed its determination to continue to make available for the Alliance the nuclear weapons necessary for NATO defence and, with the United Kingdom, gave firm assurances that their strategic nuclear forces would continue to provide defence against threats to the Alliance beyond the capability of NATO committed forces.

Finally, the Ministers decided to institute procedures for the exchange of information among all members concerning the role of nuclear weapons in NATO's defence.

In connection with the continuing efforts to encourage the economic development of Greece and Turkey, they invited member countries to consider the establishment of consortia to coordinate the measures to be undertaken in order to secure such development.

Cuban crisis

The second half of 1962 was overshadowed by the grave dispute between the United States and the Soviet Union in the Caribbean. Although outside the NATO area, the repercussions of a crisis in Cuba would have had a direct effect on the interests of the Alliance. The situation was therefore the subject of consultations in NATO well before the second half of October when the United States became certain of the presence of Soviet missiles on the

---

[18] Allied Mobile Force (AMF).

MANLIO BROSIO (1964-1971)

Manlio Brosio was born in 1897. He studied law at the University of Turin and, during World War I, served as an artillery officer in an Alpine regiment. After graduating in 1920, he entered politics, becoming one of the leaders of the "liberal revolution" movement, but was then forbidden to take any part in politics because of his vehement opposition to fascism. During the occupation of Italy he went underground and was, from 1943 to 1944, a member of the National Liberation Committee. In 1943 he returned to the political scene, subsequently becoming Deputy Prime Minister and, from 1945 to 1946, Minister of Defence.

Italian Ambassador in Moscow from January 1947 until December 1951, Manlio Brosio took part in negotiations over the peace treaty, as well as the first post-war trade agreement between Italy and the Soviet Union. He was appointed Ambassador in London in 1952, then to the United States in 1955, and from 1961 to 1964 was Italian Ambassador in Paris. He was chosen by the North Atlantic Council to succeed Dirk Stikker as Secretary General of NATO in 1964. He resigned from the post in 1971 and was succeeded by Joseph Luns. Manlio Brosio died in 1980.

Figure 5

island. Throughout the serious crisis which ensued, the entire Alliance gave unwavering support to the position taken by the United States. At the Ministerial Meeting in Paris in December 1962, Ministers discussed the question in detail, emphasising that the Soviet action in Cuba had brought the world to the verge of war, and that the peril had only been averted by the firmness and restraint exercised by the United States, supported by the Alliance and other free nations.

Assignment of nuclear forces

On December 21, 1962, President Kennedy and Prime Minister Macmillan met in Nassau (Bahamas). The proposals contained in the communique published after their meeting introduced fresh and highly important elements into NATO's defence policy: the United States and the United Kingdom proposed in effect to set up a NATO nuclear force to which they would both commit a part of their strategic nuclear forces; they also proposed the creation of a NATO multilateral nuclear force to which submarines armed with Polaris missiles would be assigned.

The Permanent Council undertook the study of these proposals at the beginning of 1963. Its conclusions were studied by Ministers during the meeting held in Ottawa from May 22 to 24, 1963. At this session, Ministers again affirmed their unanimity with respect to the Cuba and Berlin problems, as well as the disarmament question. However, their attention was principally directed to the organisation of the Alliance's nuclear forces. Important decisions were reached, notably for the assignment to SACEUR of the United Kingdom V-bomber force, as well as three United States Polaris submarines. A deputy was appointed to the staff of the Supreme Allied Commander, responsible to SACEUR for nuclear affairs[19]. Recognising equally the need to achieve a satisfactory balance between nuclear and conventional arms, the Ministers directed the Council in permanent session to undertake, with the advice of the NATO military authorities, further studies of the interrelated questions of strategy, force requirements and the resources available to meet them.

A few weeks later, President Kennedy went to Europe and, in a speech at Frankfurt am Main, on June 25, renewed his country's pledge to Europe and reaffirmed the principle of equal partnership within the Alliance.

Limited Test Ban Treaty—August 1963

During this period, intensive diplomatic activity took place which was to lead to two conciliatory measures: the first, a US-Soviet agreement, signed in Geneva on June 20, for the installation of a 'red telephone' (hot line) between Washington and Moscow; the second, a US-UK-Soviet Treaty Banning Nuclear Weapon Tests in the Atmosphere, in Outer Space and Under Water.

[19] This post was discontinued in September 1968.

The treaty embodying this agreement was signed at the Kremlin on August 5 and entered into force on October 10. All countries who wished to support it were invited to add their signatures. It led, in particular, to a further deterioration in Sino-Soviet relations. On 21 September the USSR denounced China's determination to obtain nuclear weapons for itself and accused the Chinese of more than 5,000 violations of the Soviet frontier.

One month later the United States, anxious to demonstrate their ability in case of need to deliver reinforcements rapidly to Europe, carried out a large-scale airborne exercise entitled 'Big Lift'.

Assassination of President Kennedy

It was beginning to look as if the year 1963 would run its course without any fresh elements emerging in East-West problems when, on November 22, a dramatic event took place: the assassination in Dallas, Texas, of President Kennedy. The tragic death of the American President deeply shocked public opinion throughout the world. On November 25, the North Atlantic Council paid solemn homage to his memory. Three weeks later the new American President, Lyndon Johnson, sent a message to the Ministerial Session of the North Atlantic Council reaffirming the United States' loyal support for NATO.

Taking stock of the situation at that December meeting and expressing satisfaction, in particular, that no major East-West crisis had developed since the confrontation over Cuba, Ministers emphasised that the unity and military strength of the Alliance had largely contributed to this result. On balanace, the Alliance's activity over the previous months was satisfactory, although no relaxation of the collective effort was justified.

Departure of Dirk Stikker—appointment of Manlio Brosio

At the beginning of April 1964, NATO's Secretary General, Mr. Dirk U. Stikker, informed the Council that for health reasons he intended to relinquish his position during the summer. Meeting in Ministerial session from May 12 to 14 at The Hague, the Council paid tribute to Mr. Stikker's untiring efforts. Their choice for his successor was Mr. Manlio Brosio, at that time Italian Ambassador in Paris. Mr. Brosio took up his appointment on August 1, 1964.

Eviction of Mr. Khrushchev and China's first atom bomb

The summer went by without any major crisis developing. In South-East Asia the situation continued to be disquieting. Relations between China and the Soviet Union were still strained, without giving rise to any specific friction.

Two events, occurring one on top of the other, brought international affairs back into prominence. On October 15, Mr. Khrushchev was deprived of his office and replaced, as Head of the Government by Alexei Kosygin, and as

Secretary General of the Soviet Communist Party by Leonid Brezhnev. On October 16, China exploded its first atomic bomb. This latter event did not come entirely as a surprise, but the former occurred with startling suddenness and for a time remained shrouded in mystery. The two events were bound, sooner or later, to have repercussions on the international situation.

By the time the Council met in Ministerial session in Paris on December 15, 1964, little light had been thrown on the situation so far as it concerned future relations with the Chinese Communist leaders and the new team in power in the Kremlin. These new uncertainties on the international scene made it all the more necessary to strengthen the cohesion of the Alliance in the strategic as well as the political field. Ministers reaffirmed their positions on issues which were constantly uppermost in their minds—in particular the German question, disarmament, East-West relations and the improvement of the defence capability of the Federal Republic of Germany and of its internal cohesion—giving special attention to the need to speed up the economic development of Greece and Turkey and to the defence problems of these two countries.

Independence of Malta

The presence of NATO establishments and forces in Malta had raised a problem for the Alliance when the island attained independence on September 21, 1964. In 1965, the Council adopted a resolution[20] confirming the agreement of the Government of Malta with respect to the legal status of the installations concerned pending further discussions, and also reaffirming the interest of NATO member countries in the island's security. (In August 1968 an open-ended Working Group was created under the authority of the Council, in accordance with the 1965 Resolution, to provide a forum for consultations concerning future relations with Malta. The Government of Malta appointed its diplomatic representative in Brussels to represent Maltese interests in relations with NATO.)

The year 1965 brought few new developments in terms of progress towards solving outstanding problems. It was a year which saw no major crisis in Europe. However the Soviet Union continued to oppose any settlement of the cardinal issues between East and West and to devote an increasing share of its economic and technical resources to military purposes. This strengthened the determination of member countries to maintain the unity of the Alliance and to tighten their defence system still further, particularly through broader allied participation in nuclear force planning.

Allied participation in nuclear planning

The development by both East and West of an invulnerable nuclear second strike capability[21] and the availability to the Major NATO Commanders of

---

[20] Joint Statement of the North Atlantic Council and the Government of Malta (November 3, 1965).

[21] The capability to retaliate to an enemy's first strike.

strategic and tactical nuclear weapons had raised highly complex political and technical problems. Among these was the need to frame a nuclear policy for the Alliance, to associate non-nuclear members of NATO as closely as possible with nuclear planning, and to develop appropriate procedures for consultation and decision-making.

Various proposals for the establishment of an allied force equipped with nuclear weapons had already been put forward. Chief among these was an American proposal for the creation of a multilateral nuclear force (MLF), several versions of which, along with a British alternative proposal for an Atlantic nuclear force (ANF), were for a while under study by a number of member governments. However, neither of these projects reached the stage of actual implementation. A decisive step towards the improvement of allied cooperation in nuclear affairs was taken in the spring of 1965 when an ad hoc Special Committee of Defence Ministers was established, under whose aegis three working groups conducted studies on exchange of intelligence information and other data communications, and nuclear planning.

New procedures for defence plans

At their meeting in Paris on May 31 and June 1, 1965, the Ministers of Defence laid stress on the need to secure a closer alignment between NATO military requirements and national force plans within the agreed strategic concept of a forward defence posture. In this respect, the Ministerial Meeting of December 1965 confirmed that progress had been made, for Ministers accepted in principle the introduction of new procedures which, by projecting Alliance force goals and country plans five years ahead each year, would enhance the capacity of the Alliance to adapt its defence plans to changes both in military technology and in the international situation.

At the general political level, there had been efforts to promote better contacts and exchanges with the Soviet Union and the countries of Eastern Europe which had met with some degree of response but no real progress had been made towards overcoming the division of Germany or towards disarmament.

Withdrawal of French forces — 1966

In 1966 events occurred which were to have serious implications for the work and structure of the Organisation. In March, in a series of Notes to the Governments of the other 14 NATO member countries, the French Government announced that it intended to withdraw French personnel from the NATO integrated Military Headquarters, terminate the assignment of French forces to the international commands, and request the transfer from French territory of the International Headquarters and of allied units and installations or bases not falling under the control of the French Authorities. These announcements were not entirely unexpected, since the President of the French Republic had already given some indication of his intentions in his speeches.

The French decisions made it necessary for negotiations to be held between the French Government on the one hand and its fourteen allies on the other hand. The "fourteen" accordingly set up a group under the chairmanship of Mr. André de Staercke, the Belgian Permanent Representative and Doyen of the Council, to work out a common basis for negotiations with France.

Brussels decisions—June 1966

By the time the Council met in Ministerial session on June 7 and 8 in Brussels, a number of solutions had already been worked out. The Ministers took several important decisions. They decided to transfer the Military Headquarters of NATO from France; invited the Benelux countries to provide a new site for SHAPE; and agreed that some simplification of the Command structure should be carried out. The Council also decided that the Standing Group should be abolished and replaced by an appropriate alternative body. Furthermore, it invited Italy to provide a new home for the NATO Defense College.

The remaining related problems, such as the tasks of French forces in Germany and French participation in NATO infrastructure projects, were referred to the Council in permanent session for discussion.

During the following months, Permanent Representatives were extremely active in tackling the numerous new tasks devolving upon them by reason of the events which had occurred inside the Alliance itself. As France continued to be a member of the Alliance, but no longer took part in the integrated military command structure, the Council was obliged to find a forum in which to discuss these questions.

Defence Planning Committee

The Defence Planning Committee (DPC), which had been established in 1963, accordingly became the coordinating and decision-making body for many of the more directly defence-related issues and for all matters concerning the integrated military command structure. The Council continued, as is required by the North Atlantic Treaty under which it was established, to consider matters concerning the implementation of the Treaty, including many subjects with a direct bearing on military aspects of defence. And similarly, the mandate which evolved for the Defence Planning Committee, while including questions of integration, was more broadly based and allowed for coordination in military fields outside the framework of integration. Thus, in 1982, when Spain became a member of the Alliance, and after the 1986 referendum which led to the decision by the Spanish Government to remain in the Alliance without participating in the Integrated Military Command Structure, membership of the Defence Planning Committee enabled Spain to establish a modus vivendi within NATO's institutional arrangements for defence which could be endorsed by its Alliance partners as well as by the Spanish Government. France maintained throughout a military liaison mission with the Military Committee and with the Major NATO Commanders. Similar arrangements apply to Spain but its participation in the Defence Planning Committee, the Nuclear Planning Group and certain other committees makes its position distinct from that of France.

Many military problems had arisen, particularly owing to the transfer of the two Headquarters. Belgium had offered a site for the Supreme Headquarters Allied Powers Europe at Casteau on the outskirts of Mons, and the Netherlands had agreed to accommodate the reorganised Central Europe Command at Brunssum. The difficulties to which these transfers gave rise were complicated by the problem of communications between the military authorities and the Council which would arise if the latter remained in Paris, a point on which no decision had yet been taken. In addition, there was still the wider problem of allied participation in the formulation of NATO's nuclear strategy. Finally, there were unmistakable signs of uneasiness within the Alliance which were not due solely to the French actions.

The Alliance and public opinion

The pattern of events, the impression that the danger of aggression had receded and the coming of age of a generation which had not known the war and its aftermath and was therefore less receptive to the lessons of that experience, had caused some people in the West to question the need for the Alliance. In these circumstances, it is not surprising that the Winter Ministerial session of the Council, which was held in Paris on December 15 and 16, 1966, should have taken on special significance All unresolved issues were discussed in detail and an unusually long communique was issued after the meeting.

With reference to the general political situation, Ministers reaffirmed their position on a number of outstanding questions and on agenda items such as the draft treaty on the peaceful use of outer space and the multilateral tariff negotiations (Kennedy Round). They also associated themselves with the views expressed in the Declaration on Germany, by the Governments of France, the Federal Republic of Germany, the United Kingdom and the United States, in which these countries confirmed that they would continue to be responsible for the security of Berlin[22].

The Harmel Report—the future tasks of the Alliance

Furthermore, the Council approved a resolution whose implementation was to prove particularly fruitful for the Alliance On the proposal of the Belgian Government, following a similar initiative taken by Canada in December 1964 which called for studies in this sphere, the Council resolved 'to undertake a

---

22 The Declaration was issued by the Foreign Ministers of these four countries following their meeting on December 14, 1966. The text of the Declaration appears in an Annex to the communiqué issued by the Council on December 16, and is reproduced in "NATO Final Communiqués, 1949-1974" published by the NATO Information Service.

broad analysis of international developments since the signing of the North Atlantic Treaty in 1949', so as 'to determine the influence of such developments on the Alliance and to identify the tasks which lie before it, in order to strengthen the Alliance as a factor for a durable peace'. This study was later to be known as the Harmel Report and reference is made to it further on in this chapter.

Nuclear planning arrangements

The decisions taken in the military sphere were no less important. On December 14, Ministers in the Defence Planning Committee approved recommendations of the Special Committee of NATO Defence Ministers which had been formed in 1965. The recommendations called for the establishment of two permanent bodies for nuclear planning: the Nuclear Defence Affairs Committee, open to all member countries; and a smaller Nuclear Planning Group of seven countries[23].

The Council also approved in principle the establishment of a NATO-wide communications scheme, and agreed to study whether a NATO satellite communications programme should be established, as a cooperative effort by member nations in the new and developing field of space technology.

The last, but not the least, of the Council's decisions of immediate practical significance was to transfer the NATO Permanent Headquarters to Brussels. This city was also to be the new home of the Military Committee which had been located in Washington since its creation in September 1949.

Relocation

From the material point of view, 1967 was for the Atlantic Alliance primarily a year of moving out and settling in. The flags of the 15 NATO member countries were lowered at SHAPE (Rocquencourt) on March 30, and on March 31 General Lemnitzer and his staff officially took possession of their new Headquarters at Casteau near Mons in Belgium. The Central European Command moved to Brunssum in the Netherlands, and for several weeks long lines of military lorries were to be seen moving Allied bases from France to their new homes. During the summer, the NATO Air Defence Ground Environment system (NADGE) was transferred to Brussels and in

---

[23] For some years membership of the Nuclear Planning Group at Ministerial level rotated and the composition of the Group varied accordingly. In November 1979, it was agreed that all member countries concerned should participate in Ministerial meetings on a regular basis. Portugal and Luxembourg joined the Group in 1980 and when Spain became a member of the Alliance in 1982, membership of the Group rose to 14 countries. Between 1983 and 1985, Spain participated in an observer capacity, resuming full membership in 1986. Iceland became an observer in 1987. As a result of these changes in the composition of the Nuclear Planning Group, decisions on nuclear matters are now taken without referral to the Defence Planning Committee, as the same countries are represented on both committees.

October the Council, the Military Committee and the International Staff moved into the temporary Headquarters which had been built for them in six months on the outskirts of the Belgian capital.

In spite of all this, the North Atlantic Council neither interrupted nor slowed down its work.

Meeting in the Defence Planning Committee on May 9, 1967, Ministers gave political, strategic and economic guidance to the military authorities with a view to the adoption in December of NATO's first five-year force plan covering the period up to the end of 1972. Indirectly, this was an indication of their common resolve not to invoke Article 13 of the Treaty under which countries could cease to be party to the Treaty after it had been in force for 20 years, i.e. in August 1969.

The Middle East War

One month later, on June 14, 1967, the North Atlantic Council's regular Spring Ministerial meeting took place in Luxembourg. By then, however, the outlook had suddenly darkened in international affairs. Between the two meetings of the Council, hostilities had broken out in the Middle East between Israel and the Arab countries and a cease-fire had only just taken place. It was natural that Ministers should devote part of their exchange of views to a review of the situation in this area. They stressed the urgency of humanitarian efforts to alleviate the sufferings caused by the war and expressed their support for all efforts to establish a lasting peace in this troubled area of the world. Although hostilities had ceased, their explosive violence had suddenly made public opinion more keenly aware of the potential dangers of an international situation in which too many problems were left unsolved.

Origins of MBFR (Mutual and Balanced Force Reductions)

Against this background of uncertainties on the international scene, the questions of non-proliferation of nuclear weapons and disarmament stood out in stronger relief since European security depends on both of them. Ministers accordingly made a new proposal, which was later to assume considerable importance. They suggested that, if conditions permitted, a balanced reduction of forces by the East and West should be made, adding that a contribution on the part of the Soviet Union and the Eastern European countries towards a reduction of forces would be welcomed as a gesture of peaceful intent.

The Harmel Exercise

The studies of the future tasks of the Alliance had been initiated in accordance with the Ministerial resolution of December 1966. As early as January 1967, work had started on this broad analysis known as the 'Harmel Exercise' after the Foreign Minister of Belgium who had suggested it. Four sub-groups had been set up, each working on a basic subject of interest to the Alliance: East-West Relations; Inter-Allied Relations; General Defence Policy; and Relations with Other Countries. These sub-groups were chaired by rapporteurs drawn from the political and academic world in member countries. The reports were drawn up during the summer and submitted to governments.

First meeting of the Nuclear Planning Group

In the meantime, the seven Ministers composing the Nuclear Planning Group (NPG) had held their first meeting in Washington in April 1967. Since then, NPG Ministers have met regularly, twice a year. Their initial agenda included matters of strategic defence and the possible tactical use of nuclear weapons in certain regions of Allied Command Europe. Robert McNamara, the United States Secretary of Defence, reported on the efforts made by his country to open discussions with the USSR on limitation of the nuclear arms race.

First Ministerial meetings at the Brussels Headquarters— December 1967

The first Ministerial meeting of the North Atlantic Council to be held at the new Brussels Headquarters opened on December 12. The fact that the relocation operations had scarcely disturbed the activities of the Alliance gave reason for satisfaction. The Ministerial Meeting took place in an atmosphere to which internal calm had, in large measure, been restored. While all the usual questions were examined—Germany, disarmament, non-proliferation of nuclear weapons, technological cooperation—it was in the specifically political and military spheres that major decisions were taken.

Flexible Response—revised strategic concept

In the Defence Planning Committee, Ministers adopted a revised strategic concept resulting from the first comprehensive review of NATO's strategy to be undertaken by the Military Committee since 1956. This concept, which adapted NATO's strategy to current political, military and technological developments, was based upon a flexible and balanced range of responses, conventional and nuclear, to all levels of aggression or threats of aggression. For the first time, a five-year force plan, covering the period 1968-1972, was also adopted.

Approval of the Harmel Report on 'Future Tasks of the Alliance'

From the point of view of the future of the Alliance, the political decisions taken at the December 1967 meeting were of the highest importance. The fifteen governments agreed on a document outlining certain basic principles and listing a number of tasks which the Alliance should undertake in the future. The document was entitled 'Report of the Council on the Future Tasks of the Alliance', and its text was attached to the Communiqué[24]. This document is in the tradition of the 1956 Report of the Committee of Three on Non-Military Co-operation in NATO. The Report lays emphasis on the continuing relevance of the twin political and military functions of the Alliance and the latter's ability to adapt itself to changing conditions. It sets the Alliance a general goal; the establishment of a more stable international relationship, an essential requirement for a just and lasting peaceful order in Europe. It also describes the method to be adopted, namely, a common approach to problems through greater consultation.

Finally, it defines two specific tasks, one of them of a military nature, namely, the defence of the exposed areas and particularly the Mediterranean, where events in the Middle East had led to an expansion of Soviet activity; and the other mainly political, although bearing on a military problem, namely, the formulation of proposals for balanced force reductions in East and West, a suggestion which had been advanced earlier at the Luxembourg meeting. The Harmel Report presented the Alliance with a realistic programme of work which could be carried out in phases over what would probably be a prolonged period. From the beginning of 1968, the Council began to implement this programme.

Reykjavik Meeting 1968—Declaration on MBFR

At the next Ministerial meeting in Reykjavik, Iceland, on June 24 and 25, the Council examined the progress achieved up to then in carrying out the tasks set by the Harmel Report. In a Declaration appended to the communiqué, the Foreign Ministers and representatives of countries participating in the integrated military structure affirmed their readiness to explore with other interested states specific and practical steps in the field of arms control. They invited the USSR and other Eastern European countries to study the problem of mutual and balanced force reductions (MBFR) and called on them "to join in this search for progress towards peace". This historic declaration became known as the "Reykjavik Signal"[25].

Invasion of Czechoslovakia

Two months after Reykjavik, the efforts of the Alliance to further detente in East-West relations were to receive a serious setback. On August 20, 1968, armed forces of the Soviet Union and four other Warsaw Treaty countries (Bulgaria, East Germany, Hungary and Poland) invaded Czechoslovakia. During the period that followed, the Council kept the situation under continuous close review. The unanimous conviction of member governments was that the military intervention of the Warsaw Treaty countries was a flagrant

---

[24] The text of the Report, known as the Harmel Report, is reproduced at Appendix I.
[25] Reproduced in "NATO Final Communiqués, 1949-1974" published by the NATO Information Service.

violation of the United Nations Charter and of international law. While extremely firm in their condemnation, they were careful to avoid any action which might exacerbate the situation. On September 4, the Defence Planning Committee issued a statement reaffirming "the necessity of maintaining NATO's military capability and of taking into account the implications of recent developments in Eastern Europe in the planning of their national forces".

The permanent Council immediately intiated a series of studies analysing the political, military and economic implications of the event and its repercussions on crisis management with a view to preparing a special Ministerial meeting.

Ministerial Meeting—November 1968

The date of the normal end-of-year Ministerial meeting was advanced, and it took place on November 15 and 16, 1968, at the Brussels Headquarters. The Ministers in their communique reaffirmed the inviolability of the principle that all nations are independent and that consequently any intervention by one state in the affairs of another is unlawful. In the case of Czechoslovakia, they noted that this principle had been deliberately violated by the Soviet leaders and four of their allies. They also underlined the dangers of the Soviet contention that a right exists for intervention in the affairs of other states deemed to be within a so-called "socialist commonwealth", as this runs counter to the basic principles of the United Nations Charter. The Ministers considered that grave uncertainty about the situation and the calculations and intentions of the USSR had been created by this use of force and that greater vigilance was now required on the part of the Allies, particularly with regard to Berlin and the access routes to that city, and to the situation in the Mediterranean.

Warning to the USSR

Addressing a warning to the USSR, the Alliance made it clear that any Soviet intervention directly or indirectly affecting the situation in Europe or in the Mediterranean would create an international crisis with grave consequences. Recent events had obliged the Allies participating in NATO's integrated military structure to re-assess the state of their defences, and a number of measures were announced, calculated to improve the overall NATO defence posture. Regretting the severe setback to possibilities of further measures of detente as foreseen at the June 1968 Ministerial Meeting in Reykjavik, the Ministers reaffirmed that NATO's ultimate objective remained the establishment of secure, peaceful, and mutually beneficial relations between East and West and that, towards this end, the Atlantic Alliance continued to stand as the indispensable guarantor of security and the essential foundation for the pursuit of European reconciliation.

Defence Planning Committee Meeting—Brussels, January 1969

Two months later, on January 16, 1969, the Defence Planning Committee met in Ministerial session and Ministers announced that they had taken certain measures designed to strengthen the conventional capability of NATO and that they had adopted a NATO force plan for 1969-1973.

They also approved the concept of an Allied naval force capable of being assembled on-call in the Mediterranean; a special command located in Naples had already been activated (on November 21, 1968) for the purpose of coordinating the maritime air reconnaissance operations of a number of Allied countries in the Mediterranean area.

Commemoration of the 20th Anniversary—April 1969

The year 1969 marked the twentieth anniversary of the signing of the North Atlantic Treaty. Commemorating the event on April 10 and 11 in Washington, the Council expressed satisfaction at the decisive contribution the Alliance had made to the maintenance of peace and to the security of all its members. The Alliance, it recalled, had been established to safeguard the freedom of all its peoples and also in response to a common fear that without an effective security system another war might break out in a divided Europe. The Alliance would continue as the expression of the common purposes and aspirations of the member countries.

Prospects for a Conference on European Security

Some time earlier, in February 1969, President Richard Nixon, on a visit to NATO Headquarters had voiced the hope that the period of confrontation was over and that an era of negotiation with the USSR was about to start. This hope was shared by the other member governments, who were seeking the means of recreating a climate of detente along the lines of their earlier efforts. The declaration by the Warsaw Treaty countries in Budapest in March 1969, which advocated the holding of an early Conference on European Security, thus came at a timely moment. Although this declaration contained proposals which had been made previously, its tone was more moderate.

The Washington Ministerial Meeting provided the Council with the opportunity to consider the extent to which the new situation could contribute to the relaxation of tension. The Ministers set themselves the task of exploring with the Warsaw Treaty countries what specific issues could best lend themselves to fruitful negotiation and early resolution. They instructed the Council in permanent session to draw up a list of these issues and to study how a useful process of negotiation could, in due course, be initiated.

Improvement in East-West relations

This new departure in East-West relations was henceforward to take precedence over all the other issues with which the Alliance was concerned. A searching study of its implications was carried out. As a result of this study and the diplomatic contacts with all the countries concerned, together with the additional proposals for a draft agenda for negotiations put forward by the Warsaw Treaty countries in October 1969 and May 1970, Ministers were able at ensuing meetings to spell out their ideas concerning the form and content of such negotiations.

Problems of the environment

It was also at this meeting that President Nixon formulated his idea that member countries should act jointly to tackle the problems of the environment, a suggestion which was to be taken up rapidly and one which gave rise to the establishment of the Committee on the Challenges of Modern Society (CCMS)[26].

Defence Planning Committee—May and December 1969

Shortly after the Washington meeting, the Defence Planning Committee in Ministerial session met in Brussels on May 28, 1969, and reaffirmed the continuing validity of the NATO strategy based on forward defence and appropriate response to any aggression. Ministers also reaffirmed their determination to make appropriate contributions on a collective basis to support this strategy, and to ensure that the overall military capability of NATO should not be reduced except as part of a pattern of mutual force reductions balanced in scope and timing.

At the December Ministerial Meeting, Ministers discussed the adequacy of forces in Central Europe and arrangements for the reinforcement of NATO's ready forces in times of tension. In the same period, consultations took place with the Canadian Authorities concerning Canadian forces in Central Europe[27].

Brussels Ministerial Meeting of the Council—December 1969

At the meeting of the North Atlantic Council in Brussels on December 4 and 5, 1969, Ministers recalled that the policy of the Alliance was directed wholly towards the establishment of a just and lasting peace. This must be the ultimate aim of any negotiations which, in the first instance, must be concerned with the source of tensions, namely, the fundamental problems of European security. In addition, the negotiations must be carefully prepared if they were to have any reasonable chance of success. To avoid the risk of disillusionment, moreover, an undertaking of this magnitude could only be embarked on if the parties had, from the outset, given tangible signs of their sincerity and of their determination to reach a satisfactory settlement. In this

---

[26] See Chapter 21.
[27] Canada now maintains some 7900 ground and air forces in Central Europe.

connection, the attitude of the USSR and the other East European countries in the negotiations which were about to begin (particularly those on Germany and Berlin) would show whether those countries were ready to contribute to the creation of a favourable climate, the absence of which would bode ill for the success of all subsequent talks. As for the procedure for negotiation, consideration could be given to all constructive possibilities, including a general conference or a series of conferences on European security, provided that they were not designed to ratify the present division of Europe. After defining their attitude towards the future development of East-West relations, Ministers indicated that, on this basis, they would continue and intensify their contacts, discussions and negotiations through all appropriate channels, both bilateral and multilateral.

Ministers also examined the increasing Soviet presence in the Mediterranean and agreed to study this further at their Spring 1970 meeting. They agreed that NATO's defence posture continued to be an essential stabilising factor in support of the search for a meaningful detente, and reaffirmed the principle that NATO would continue to ensure that there was no reduction in its overall military capability.

Strategic Arms Limitation Talks (SALT)

Members of the Alliance took the initiative of starting important bilateral talks, the progress of which could be indicative of the chances of making headway in other areas of East-West relations. Talks between the United States and the USSR on strategic arms limitations were begun in November 1969, and were continued either in Helsinki or in Vienna, their importance being stressed by Ministers at each of their meetings.

Ostpolitik

Soon after, in December 1969, the Federal Republic of Germany embarked on negotiations with the Soviet Union which led to the signature in Moscow, on August 12, 1970, of the German-Soviet Treaty. While these negotiations with the Soviet Government were still going on, the Government of the Federal Republic of Germany also began talks with Poland, in February 1970, with a view to normalising relations between the two countries. These talks culminated in the signature in Warsaw, on December 7, 1970, of the German-Polish Treaty. As part of its "Ostpolitik", designed to improve its relations with its Eastern neighbours, the Government of the Federal Republic of Germany likewise set itself the task of establishing a modus vivendi with the German Democratic Republic, and to this end began talks on March 19, 1970. The Allies assured the Federal Republic of Germany that all these initiatives had their sympathetic support.

Discussions on Berlin

In the past, Ministers had consistently stressed the need for improving the position of Berlin and access to that city, pointing out that a satisfactory settlement would be a major factor in the evaluation of overall prospects for East-West negotiations. The three Allied powers (United States, United Kingdom and France), acting in pursuance of their special responsibilities for Germany and Berlin as a whole, began talks with the Soviet Union to this effect on March 26, 1970.

The progress of all these talks and the results of bilateral contacts made by other member countries became the subject of continuing consultations within the Alliance.

Proposals for Multilateral Exploratory Contacts on European Security and Cooperation (Council Meeting — Rome, May 1970)

The Ministerial Meeting, held in Rome on May 26 and 27, 1970, was one of outstanding importance in the context of East-West relations. Ministers declared their willingness, insofar as progress was recorded in bilateral contacts, and in particular in the talks at that time in progress on Germany and Berlin, to enter into multilateral contacts of an exploratory nature with all the governments concerned, to establish when it would be possible to convene a conference or series of conferences on European security and cooperation. The establishment of a permanent body could be envisaged as one means, among others, of embarking upon multilateral negotiations in due course. It was emphasised that it was not sufficient to discuss European security in the abstract. Among the subjects which could be discussed within the framework of the multilateral contacts proposed were the principles which should govern relations between states, including the renunciation of force. Another subject which could be discussed concurrently was the development of international relations, with a view to contributing to the freer movement of people, ideas and information, and to developing cooperation in the cultural, economic, technical and scientific fields.

To underline the importance which they attached to their proposals, Ministers decided that for the first time the Rome Communiqué, together with the Declaration on Mutual and Balanced Force Reductions, issued simultaneously by Ministers of countries participating in NATO's integrated military structure, should be forwarded through the Foreign Minister of Italy to all other interested parties, including neutral and non-aligned governments. It was agreed that member governments would seek the reactions of other governments to the initiation of the comprehensive programme of exploration and negotiation which they envisaged.

At the same meeting in Rome, Ministers expressed their continued concern about the increased Soviet presence in the Mediterranean. As regards disarmament, they re-emphasised the importance of limiting the spread of nuclear weapons and welcomed the entry into force of the Non-Proliferation Treaty[28].

---

28 The Non-Proliferation Treaty on Nuclear Weapons was tabled by the United States and the USSR at the Geneva Disarmament Conference on January 19, 1968. It entered into force on March 5, 1970.

Rome Declaration on Mutual and Balanced Force Reductions—May 27, 1970

Despite the absence of any meaningful reaction from the Warsaw Pact countries, the Allies continued to explore the possibility of mutual and balanced force reductions. In view of the new developments in East-West relations, it was obvious that efforts to reduce the level of armed confrontation in Europe must be given priority. It was in this spirit that, in the Declaration appended to the communiqué on the Rome meeting, Ministers representing countries participating in NATO's integrated military structure invited the Warsaw Treaty countries and the other countries concerned to join in exploratory talks with a view to identifying the criteria which could serve as a starting point for fruitful negotiation.

Defence Planning Committee meetings—June and December 1970

When the Defence Planning Committee met in Brussels on June 11, 1970, Ministers expressed concern at the continuing growth of the armed forces of the Warsaw Treaty countries, inter alia in the maritime field, where the USSR's power and the range of its activity had markedly increased. They reaffirmed the determination of NATO countries to maintain the overall military capability of the Alliance at the level needed to ensure an effective deterrent and defensive posture. They underlined the special military and political role of North American forces present in Europe as an irreplaceable contribution to the common defence. They noted numerous steps taken in support of NATO's strategy of flexible response, particularly in the fields of infrastructure and cooperation in research, development and production. They also welcomed the successful testing of the first NATO Communications Satellite, which had been launched on March 20 and marked the implementation of the programme approved in 1966.

The year 1970 was important for another reason as well: it was agreed that a detailed review should be conducted of the defence problems to be overcome by the Alliance during the next decade. The resulting "AD 70" Study[29] and associated decisions made by the EUROGROUP countries[30] are described below.

Brussels Ministerial Meeting of the Council—December 1970

1970 had been a year of intensive diplomatic activity. The treaties between the Federal Republic of Germany and the USSR, and between the Federal Republic of Germany and Poland were seen as a major contribution to detente in Europe. The exchange of views between the Federal Republic of Germany and the German Democratic Republic would, it was hoped, pave the way for genuine negotiation which would necessarily take account of the

[29] Allied Defence in the Seventies.

[30] The EUROGROUP—an informal grouping of European member countries created in 1968 to coordinate European defence efforts within the Alliance. (See Chapter 3)

special features of the situation in Germany. However, no solution had as yet been found, within the framework of the quadripartite talks, to the problem of Berlin which was a potential source of trouble, and thus had a decisive effect on the political climate of Europe. Talks between the Soviet Union and the United States on strategic arms limitation had not so far produced any tangible results. At their December 1970 meeting in Brussels, Ministers reiterated their position that, as soon as the talks on Berlin had reached a satisfactory conclusion, and insofar as the other talks under way proceeded favourably, their governments would be ready to enter into multilateral contacts with all interested countries to explore when it would be possible to convene a conference, or a series of conferences, on security and cooperation in Europe. In this event, the Council would give immediate attention to the matter. As for the issues which might be discussed within the framework of exploratory multilateral talks, Ministers referred to their earlier proposals and outlined the principles governing relations between states on which any genuine and lasting improvement in East-West relations in Europe must be based.

Mediterranean issues

Since the Ministerial Meeting in Reykjavik in June 1968, Ministers were increasingly concerned with the expansion of Soviet military power and political influence in the Mediterranean area. Soviet penetration, in terms of a growing naval presence in the Mediterranean, poses a potential threat to the southern flank of the Alliance. Moreover, the Soviet Union's role as military adviser and supplier of arms to the Arab States in their confrontation with Israel had growing significance for Western political and economic interests in the area, particularly in view of the extent to which Western Europe depended upon oil supplied from the Middle East.

The Alliance frequently expressed concern over this situation, and recognised the need for constant vigilance. Ministers repeatedly stressed the importance of full and frequent consultation among the Allies and instructed the Council in permanent session to keep the situation in the Mediterranean under close review. In the framework of measures studied at the Reykjavik Meeting the previous June, Ministers of the countries participating in NATO's integrated defence structure subsequently approved, in May 1969, the establishment of the naval on-call force for the Mediterranean, which had been approved in principle in January 1969.

Allied Defence in the Seventies

In December 1970, the Defence Planning Committee approved the recommendations of the comprehensive study which it had commissioned in May 1970 on the defence problems which the Alliance would face in the seventies. Ministers confirmed that NATO's approach to security in the 1970s would continue to be based on the twin concepts of defence and detente. They reaffirmed the principle that the overall military capability should not be reduced except, as they had already stipulated, "as part of a pattern of mutual force reductions balanced in scope and timing". Allied strategic nuclear capability would remain a key element in the security of the West during the 1970s. While adequate nuclear forces existed, it was essential to ensure that this capability, which includes the continued commitment of theatre nuclear forces, was maintained. The situation in the field of conventional forces was less satisfactory, in view of imbalances between NATO capabilities and those of the Warsaw Treaty Organisation. Careful attention therefore needed to be paid to priorities in improving NATO's conventional strength in the 1970s. The AD 70 Study underlined the special military and political role of North American forces present in Europe, pointing out that, although their significance was closely related to an effective and improved European defence effort, their replacement by European forces would be no substitute.

European Defence Improvement Programme

It was with this in mind that, in December 1970, ten European countries (the EUROGROUP) had decided to launch a special European Defence Improvement Programme designed to improve Alliance capability in specific fields identified as being of particular importance in the AD 70 Study. President Nixon pledged that, given a similar approach by the other Allies, the United States would maintain and improve its own forces in Europe and would not reduce them except in the context of reciprocal East-West action.

Mutual and Balanced Force Reductions

By June 1971, when the North Atlantic Council met in Lisbon, Ministers noted that the Kremlin had now, for the first time, reacted positively to the proposals on mutual and balanced force reductions (MBFR) originally put forward by Allied governments participating in the integrated military structure at the Reykjavik Meeting in Spring 1968. So far, however, Moscow had confined itself to statements of intention, without providing enough data to permit meaningful negotiations. The positions of the USSR and its allies still had to be clarified in bilateral contacts, and it was decided that these should be intensified.

Committee on the Challenges of Modern Society

In the meantime, in a different sphere of Alliance cooperation altogether, impressive progress had been achieved by the Committee on the Challenges of Modern Society, particularly in studying solutions to the problem of the pollution of the seas by oil, and in other areas such as water pollution and disaster assistance. Moreover, after two years of existence, the framework developed to enable the Alliance to assist in improving the environment was not only benefiting the member countries themselves, but was complementing and contributing to the success of work going on in other international organisations.

JOSEPH LUNS (1971-1984)

Joseph Luns was born in Rotterdam in 1911. He attended schools in Amsterdam and Brussels and, aged 20, spent a year as an Ordinary Seaman in the Royal Netherlands Navy. He took his degree in Law from the Universities of Leiden and Amsterdam in 1937 and then studied at the London School of Economics and Berlin University before entering the Foreign Service of the Netherlands. During the war he served in Switzerland, Portugal and the United Kingdom.

From 1949 to 1952 he represented his country at the United Nations in New York, and resigned when he became joint Minister of Foreign Affairs of the Netherlands. As a member of the Catholic People's Party he was four times successful in elections to Parliament, and was Minister of Foreign Affairs in various administrations, in which capacity he signed the 1957 Treaty of Rome on behalf of his country.

He was appointed Secretary General of NATO in October 1971 and was succeeded by Lord Carrington in May 1984.

Figure 6

Resignation of Manlio Brosio—appointment of Joseph Luns

At the same Council meeting in Lisbon, Ministers expressed their regret at the impending departure of Mr. Brosio, who had informed them of his intention to resign as Secretary General of NATO. The Council invited Mr. Joseph Luns, Foreign Minister of the Netherlands, to succeed Mr. Brosio as from October 1, 1971.

NAVSOUTH leaves Malta

In July 1971, parliamentary elections caused a change in Malta's international policy. Although not a member of the Alliance, Malta had been host to a NATO military headquarters for many years (since the time when the island was a dependency of the United Kingdom), and had provided military facilities for British and other NATO forces.

After full consultation between all parties, NATO acceded to the Maltese request to withdraw the Headquarters of Allied Naval Forces Southern Europe (NAVSOUTH) from Malta and, following an invitation by the Italian Government, NAVSOUTH was transferred to Naples.

Agreement on Berlin

On September 3, 1971, the Four Power negotiations on Berlin, which had begun in March 1970, resulted in the signing of the first stage of a Quadripartite Agreement between France, the United Kingdom, the United States and the Soviet Union. This was the first written agreement on Berlin reached by the Four Powers since 1949.

The Agreement which came into effect after the conclusion of the relevant intra-German arrangements and the signature, in November 1972, of the final Quadripartite Declaration, reaffirms Four Power responsibility for Berlin, and is designed to ensure unimpeded civilian access between the Western sectors and the areas administered by the German Democratic Republic.

Increasing East-West contacts

The impending agreement on Berlin paved the way for multilateral East-West talks to gauge the prospects for a conference on security and cooperation in Europe (CSCE). Within this context, there was an increase in bilateral contacts between the Allied countries on the one hand, and the Eastern countries and neutral and non-aligned countries on the other. On the strength of these developments, at their meeting on December 9 and 10, 1971, in Brussels, Foreign Ministers renewed their instructions to the Council in permanent session to carry on with the preparation in depth of those issues which they had already indicated as being suitable for discussion at the conference. At this same meeting, they expressed their regret that the Soviet Union and its allies had not responded to their proposals for mutual and balanced force reductions (MBFR), and in particular to their suggestion, made in October 1971, that Mr. Brosio be asked to conduct an exploratory mission.

However, a series of events in the spring of 1972 provided evidence that the USSR and its allies seemed willing to adopt a cooperative stance. Within the framework of the first phase of the "Ostpolitik", the Federal Republic of Germany had ratified treaties with the Soviet Union and with Poland. The negotiations between the Federal Republic of Germany and the German Democratic Republic, in progress since March 1970, had borne fruit in the shape of a treaty on access and other arrangements supplementing the Quadripartite Agreement on Berlin. The Foreign Ministers of the Four Powers signed the Agreement on June 3, 1972. Other important events indicative of the improving climate were the official visits made by the President of the United States to Peking and Moscow in February and May respectively.

ABM Treaty and first SALT agreements

It was on May 26, 1972, during President Nixon's visit to Moscow, that arrangements were signed, recording the positive outcome of the first series of strategic arms limitation talks (SALT) begun in November 1969. These agreements, which had been reached after particularly arduous negotiations reflecting the complexity of the problems at issue, consisted, on the one hand, of a treaty of indefinite duration on the limitation of anti-ballistic missile systems (the ABM Treaty) and, on the other hand, of an interim, five-year agreement on measures relating to the limitation of offensive strategic weapons. The agreements had been preceded by the conclusion, during the previous autumn, of separate agreements to reduce the risk of accidental nuclear war and to improve communications arrangements between the United States and the Soviet Union. Further negotiations between the two parties were resumed in Geneva on November 21, 1972, for the purpose of working out more detailed means of limiting offensive strategic weapons (SALT II). The SALT negotiations had, from the beginning, been the subject of intensive consultation within the Alliance.

Bonn Ministerial Meeting—May 1972

The above events were evidence of a new climate in international relations, and were consistent with determined Allied efforts to achieve a rapprochement and to establish constructive and more broadly based contacts with the East. The preliminary conditions for such a move seemed to have been met. The numerous diplomatic efforts and initiatives had been interconnected, designed to gauge, in different spheres, the willingness of the Eastern countries to cooperate with a view to achieving tangible improvements in East-West relations based on balanced concessions. The Alliance had played an essential part in the preparation and coordination of the Western negotiating positions. It was against this background that the Spring Ministerial Meeting took place in Bonn on May 30 and 31, 1972. It was a particularly important meeting, since it gave the green light for a new phase in East-West relations. The countries of the Alliance agreed to enter into multilateral conversations concerned with the preparations for a conference on security and cooperation in Europe (CSCE), and accepted the proposal of the Finnish Government that such talks be held in Helsinki. At the same time, they made it plain that their aim at multilateral preparatory talks would be two-fold: on the one hand, to ensure that their proposals for the strengthening of security and cooperation in Europe would be fully considered at a conference and, on the other hand, to establish that enough common ground existed among the participants to warrant reasonable expectations that a conference would produce satisfactory results. In other words, there was no question at that stage of dealing with the substance of the problems dividing East and West, but of identifying them, and of ensuring that they were examined. Ministers noted the progress of studies made on possible issues for negotiation which had been undertaken on their instructions. They also expressed the opinion that, in the interests of security, the examination at a CSCE of appropriate measures, including certain military measures, aimed at strengthening confidence and increasing stability, would contribute to the process of reducing the dangers of military confrontation. As regards Mutual and Balanced Force Reductions, despite the lack of response from the Eastern countries, the nations concerned proposed that multilateral exploratory talks should start as soon as practicable either before or in parallel with multilateral preparatory talks for a Conference on Security and Cooperation in Europe.

Agreement on military facilities in Malta

The negotiations between the United Kingdom and Malta, which had followed the withdrawal of NAVSOUTH at the request of the Valletta Government, led to the signing, on March 26, 1972, of a seven-year agreement on the use of certain military facilities on the island. The Secretary General of NATO played a significant role in the preparation of the negotiations and they were the subject of particularly frequent consultation within the Council.

Intra-German relations and Four Power Declaration on Berlin—November 1972

On November 8, 1972, with the initialling of the "Basic Treaty" on relations between the Federal Republic of Germany and the German Democratic Republic, the negotiations which had begun in March 1970 came to an end. The next day, the Four Powers issued a declaration stating that they would support simultaneous applications for membership of the United Nations to be submitted by the Federal Republic of Germany and the German Democratic Republic. They affirmed that such membership must in no way affect their rights and responsibilities in Berlin, nor the corresponding Quadripartite Agreement and decisions and practices relating to it. The "Basic Treaty" was signed in East Berlin on December 21, 1972.

Multilateral Preparatory Talks in Helsinki

Multilateral preparatory talks on a possible conference on security and cooperation in Europe, attended by representatives from thirty-five states—all the European countries (except Albania), the United States and Canada—opened in Helsinki on November 22, 1972. Although the Allied countries brought with them their own national proposals, these had nonetheless been carefully coordinated within the framework of the North Atlantic Council.

Brussels Ministerial Meeting—December 1972

The December 1972 Ministerial meeting of the Council was inevitably dominated by these events. The Quadripartite Agreement on Berlin had just been concluded and the "Basic Treaty" between the Federal Republic of Germany and the German Democratic Republic was about to be signed. Allied Foreign Ministers indicated that their governments were now ready to consider the possibility of negotiations with the German Democratic Republic, with a view to establishing bilateral relations. The member countries of the Atlantic Alliance would continue to support the policy of the Federal Republic of Germany to work towards a state of peace in Europe in which the German people would regain their unity through free self-determination. At this same meeting in Brussels, Ministers referred to the opening of the multilateral preparatory talks in Helsinki and recalled that these were designed to establish whether such a conference could produce constructive results. However, the latter could be achieved only through a process of detailed negotiation without artificial time-limits.

MBFR Exploratory Talks in Vienna—January 1973

It was also at the Brussels winter Ministerial meeting that significant progress was recorded in efforts which the Allied countries had unceasingly pursued since 1968 to lower the level of military confrontation through constructive negotiations with the East. An invitation had been extended by certain NATO countries to the members of the Warsaw Treaty Organisation to join them in exploratory talks, beginning on January 31, 1973, to examine the scope for bringing about mutual and balanced force reductions in Central Europe[31]. After expressing the hope that these talks would make it possible

---

[31] The direct participants in MBFR were: Belgium, Canada, the Federal Republic of Germany, Luxembourg, the Netherlands, the United Kingdom and the United States, Czechoslovakia, the German Democratic Republic, Poland and the Soviet Union. Other participants: Denmark, Greece, Italy, Norway and Turkey, Bulgaria, Rumania and Hungary. France did not participate directly or otherwise in MBFR negotiations and its forces therefore were not a subject of discussion in this context. The Declared aim of the negotiations was "to contribute towards a more stable relationship and to the strengthening of peace and security in Europe by the mutual reduction of armed forces and armaments and associated measures in Central Europe".

to commence negotiations in the autumn of 1973—in parallel with the Conference on Security and Cooperation in Europe—the Foreign Ministers pointed out that, while it would be inappropriate to establish specific links between the two sets of negotiations, progress in one would have a favourable effect on the other.

Preparatory work had been going on within the Alliance and, in view of the new developments, the Council agreed to continue consultations in preparation for negotiations. The general principles governing such negotiations—defined at the Rome meeting in 1970 and intended primarily to ensure undiminished security at a lower level of forces—were reiterated, and it was emphasised that force reductions in Central Europe should not operate to the military disadvantage of either side, nor should they diminish security in other parts of Europe.

End of Multilateral Preparatory Talks in Helsinki (CSCE)

The multilateral preparatory talks for a Conference on Security and Cooperation in Europe ended in Helsinki on June 8, 1973, with the adoption of a series of recommendations to governments. These were concerned primarily with the conference agenda which was divided into three major chapters or "baskets": (i) questions relating to security in Europe, inter alia, principles governing relations between States and confidence-building measures; (ii) cooperation in the fields of economics, science and technology, and of the environment; (iii) cooperation in humanitarian fields, especially with regard to human contacts, information, and cultural and educational cooperation and exchanges. It was also agreed that, depending on the progress made during the conference, consideration would be given to any follow-up procedures which might be required. As for the conference itself, it was suggested that this should take place in three stages, the first at the level of Foreign Ministers of participating countries who would be required to approve and implement the recommendations as a whole.

Start of Conference on Security and Cooperation in Europe (CSCE)—Helsinki, July 1973

The progress of the preparatory talks in Helsinki provided ample proof that careful preparation by the Allies and the coordination of member countries' national positions had been well worthwhile in terms of protecting Allied interests and negotiating aims. Thus, at their Spring meeting on June 14 and 15, 1973, in Copenhagen, Ministers were satisfied that adequate arrangements had been made to ensure that their proposals would be examined fully and in depth and expressed their willingness to begin negotiations. During the first stage of the Conference, which took place in Helsinki from July 3 to 7, 1973, the Ministers of all participating States adopted the programme of work submitted to them and issued instructions to the committees and subcommittees for the preparation, during the second main working stage, of definite proposals concerning the various agenda items. A Coordinating

Committee was set up to harmonise the activities of the various conference committees. The level of representation at which the CSCE would meet for its last stage was to be decided before the end of the second main working stage on the basis of the recommendations made by the Coordinating Committee.

Atlantic relations

The passage from a period of confrontation in East-West relations to an era of negotiation meant that it was more than ever necessary to preserve cohesion between the member countries of the Alliance—a cohesion based on frequent consultation and on the support of public opinion in the West. Prospects for a relaxation of tension would inevitably have a bearing on Allied security requirements. Consultation within the Alliance had enabled member countries to bring about an improvement in East-West relations. If, however, these encouraging developments were to continue, it would have to be realised that maintenance of the defence effort and the affirmation of Western solidarity were prerequisites for further progress in the implementation of a policy of détente. It also had to be recognised that while the principles and objectives of the Alliance remained as valid as they had ever been, profound changes had taken place in every field of international activity in recent years. Problems which had been unforeseeable a generation earlier now called for new forms of action and cooperation by the West. Two issues stood out. First, it was clear that a Europe which was once again prosperous would have to increase its contribution to the common defence effort, in order to relieve the United States of part of the burden it had been carrying since the end of the Second World War. Secondly, the fact that the USSR had achieved strategic nuclear parity with the United States had implications for the defence of the European continent which could not be ignored.

It was not the first time that the Alliance was faced with the need to adapt itself to changing situations. It had done so successfully in the past, with the adoption in December 1956 of the Report of the Committee of Three on Non-Military Cooperation and, later, when it had endorsed the conclusions of the Report on the Future Tasks of the Alliance in December 1967. Without prejudicing ongoing negotiations in other fora, the time had come for member governments to re-examine their relationships in the light of new changes. The Council in permanent session was entrusted with this task.

Arab-Israeli war—October 1973

On October 6, 1973, hostilities flared up again in the Middle East between Israel on the one side and Syria and Egypt on the other, ending with a ceasefire on October 24. Indications that the attitude of the Soviet Union would not necessarily rule out some form of intervention compelled the United States to place some of its own forces on alert. This was clear evidence that the danger of a sudden crisis was still a very real one and that it was consequently important to preserve the means of dealing with it. The present limitations of détente were suddenly very apparent and the process called for a guarded approach if it was to produce any meaningful progress. These developments also fully vindicated Allied determination not to relax defence efforts. They bore out the wisdom of the Western view that détente and security are indivisible. Moreover, it could not be ignored that the Soviet Union was continuing its own steady military build-up, in particular the reinforcement of its naval power. The new crisis in the Middle East highlighted the necessity of keeping a close watch on events in this area and of continuing the practice of frequent and timely consultation to enable the Allies to compare their evaluations.

Ministerial Meeting of the Council—Brussels, December 1973

It was against this disturbing background, and the repercussions of the selective embargo on certain Allied countries enforced in the autumn by the oil-exporting countries, that the Winter Ministerial meeting was held in Brussels on December 10 and 11, 1973. In their review of world developments, Ministers recognised that international peace remained fragile and stressed once again the importance for the Alliance of maintaining to the full its defensive and deterrent military capability. They expressed their overriding concern to see a just and lasting settlement in the Middle East and reaffirmed the support of all member governments for the relevant resolutions of the United Nations Security Council. In the same context, they took note of the half-yearly report by the Council on the situation in the Mediterranean which had been kept under continuing review by the Council, in accordance with instructions first issued by Ministers in Reykjavik in June 1968. These reports, which reflected Allied concern over the Soviet naval build-up, acquired heightened relevance with the renewal of tension generated by the resumption of Arab-Israeli hostilities.

As regards East-West relations, there had been a number of positive developments in the previous months, particularly the recognition of the German Democratic Republic by the Allied countries; the admission of the two Germanies to the United Nations in September; the normalisation of relations between the Federal Republic of Germany and Czechoslovakia, Bulgaria and Hungary; and the improved dialogue represented by events such as Mr. Brezhnev's visits to Berlin in May and to Washington in June. This last visit was a particularly important one since it included the signature on June 21, 1973, within the framework of SALT II, of a declaration which crowned the United States efforts to reach a permanent agreement on the limitation of strategic offensive arms. This was the Declaration of Basic Principles of Negotiations on the Further Limitation of Strategic Offensive Arms, which included, in particular, recognition of each side's equally legitimate security interests. As regards progress in the Conference on Security and Cooperation in Europe, the second stage of which had begun in Geneva on September 18, 1973, Allied governments took stock of the progress of the committee set up by the Foreign Ministers of participating states in accordance with the programme established for the detailed examination of the various agenda items.

In a different sphere, namely, internal relations between their governments, substantial progress had been made towards agreement on a joint Declaration on Atlantic Relations.

Start of MBFR negotiations—Vienna, October 30, 1973

The MBFR negotiations, proposed by the Allies concerned, had opened in Vienna as planned. Ministers of the countries concerned considered a report by the Allied negotiators and reaffirmed the principles which they would continue to uphold during the course of these talks. In Vienna they had made specific proposals to establish approximate parity between the two sides in the form of a common manpower ceiling for overall ground forces on each side in the area in which reductions would take place. These proposals took into account the combat capability of the forces involved. They had also proposed a first phase agreement providing for reductions of Soviet and United States ground forces in the area.

Cost sharing

Allied governments had repeatedly indicated the value which they attached to the special role played by the United States forces in Europe as a means of preserving a credible deterrent based on a satisfactory balance of forces. It had been their constant conviction, since the policy of detente had first been conceived, that any reduction in Allied defence capabilities should take place only in the context of MBFR. The European countries had welcomed the renewed assurances of the United States Government in this respect. It was clear to all the Allied countries, however, that the maintenance of United States forces in Europe, at their present levels, called for a common effort on the part of the Allies to achieve a solution to the financial problems which the United States was facing. In the course of 1974, a number of steps were taken to meet this aim, among them bilateral offset agreements (e.g. between the United States and the Federal Republic of Germany) and measures taken within the Eurogroup as well as improvements in European forces assigned to NATO.

25th Anniversary—Declaration on Atlantic Relations

As far as Allied international relations were concerned, the principal feature of the Spring Ministerial meeting, which was held in Ottawa on June 18 and 19, 1974—and which marked the 25th Anniversary of the Alliance—was the adoption by Ministers of a Declaration on Atlantic Relations which had been the subject of thorough discussion in the Council for over a year[32]. This important document reaffirmed the commitment of all members to the North Atlantic Treaty and set the future course for the Alliance in the light of

---

32 The text of the Declaration on Atlantic Relations is reproduced at Appendix I.

new developments and the challenges of a rapidly changing world. It was built around certain guiding principles. The Alliance was the indispensable basis for the security of the member countries and thus made possible the pursuit of détente; the common defence was indivisible. Given that the strategic relationship between the Soviet Union and the United States had reached a point of near equilibrium, the defence of Europe had taken on a different perspective. However, the essential elements had not changed; the United States nuclear forces and the presence of North American forces in Europe remained indispensable to the security of the entire Alliance; on their side the European members undertook to make the necessary contribution to maintain the common defence; all necessary forces would be used to deny to a potential adversary the objectives he might seek to attain through armed conflict. Fulfilment of the common aims required the maintenance of close consultation and cooperation on matters relating to the common interests of the members of the Alliance. Those interests could be affected by events in other areas of the world. In particular, the member countries would work to remove all sources of conflict between their economic policies and encourage economic cooperation with one another. Finally, the members recalled their dedication to the principles of the Alliance and their responsibilities towards the world at large.

To underline the importance of the event, the Allied Heads of Government—for only the second time in the history of the Alliance—met in Brussels on June 26, 1974, for the solemn signing of the Declaration, after a meeting devoted to consultation on East-West relations shortly before the United States President was due to visit Moscow.

East-West negotiations

The Ottawa Ministerial Meeting also provided an opportunity to take stock of current East-West negotiations. The harmonisation of Allied views had continued to bear fruits at the Conference on Security and Cooperation in Europe. Despite the very moderate proposals put forward by the Allied countries, however, progress had been slow and uneven. Much work remained to be done on such key questions as the improvement of human contacts, the freer flow of information, confidence-building measures and essential aspects of the principles guiding relations between States. As regards MBFR, the Vienna negotiations had undoubtedly enabled both sides to define the general objective more closely, but there was still a big gap between the respective viewpoints. The Ministers concerned reiterated their proposals for a common ceiling for ground force manpower referred to at the previous meeting in Brussels, adding that a first phase agreement providing for the reduction of United States and Soviet ground forces would be an important initial step. In their customary review of the international situation, Ministers welcomed the progress towards the establishment of a democratic and representative government in Portugal, as well as the diplomatic efforts being made to restore peace to the Middle East where agreements had been reached for a military disengagement. They also discussed the experience gained in the application of the Quadripartite Agreement on Berlin of September 3, 1971, the strict observance of which remained a prerequisite for lasting detente.

Revision of the Iceland-United States defence agreement

At the request of the Icelandic Government, the Council had put forward recommendations concerning the renewal of the agreement of May 5, 1951, between Iceland and the United States for the use, on behalf of NATO, of the Keflavik facilities. The issue was complicated by a dispute between the United Kingdom and Iceland on fishing limits, but this was finally resolved, partly through the efforts of the Secretary General. The United States and Iceland reached an understanding on October 22, 1974, under which United States forces were to continue to be stationed at the base, subject to various adjustments to be made in the operation of the defence agreement between the two countries.

World economic developments

The effects of the energy crisis generated by the events in the Middle East in October 1973 became increasingly pronounced as the year went by. The four-fold increase in the price of oil coincided with a shortage of certain raw materials which led to a rapid increase in prices generally. This further accentuated existing inflationary pressures in Western economies and, inevitably, increased the threat of recession.

Ministerial Meeting of the Council—December 1974

It was with these economic problems very much in mind that Ministers gathered for their winter meeting, which took place in Brussels on December 12 and 13, 1974. Ministers had a broad discussion on the implications of the economic situation for the maintenance of Allied defence and reaffirmed their determination to seek appropriate solutions to the difficulties confronting the economies of the Allied countries. Turning to other international events, Ministers expressed their concern about the situation in the Middle East, which could have dangerous consequences not only for the security of the members of the Alliance but also for world peace. They reaffirmed the importance they attached to progress towards the restoration of peace in this area.

In their review of East-West relations, Ministers again noted that progress towards detente had remained uneven in the preceding months. At the CSCE, there had been enough progress to show that substantial results were possible, but there were many important questions still to be resolved.

As for MBFR, the Ministers concerned, after reaffirming their positions, were obliged to record that the Vienna negotiations had not so far produced results, and expressed the hope that a constructive response to Allied proposals would soon be forthcoming. Ministers also heard a report from the United States, within the context of the United States-Soviet SALT II negotiations, on the prospects which had emerged from the Vladivostok meeting between President Ford and Mr. Brezhnev on November 24, 1974, for the conclusion of a permanent agreement on the limitation of strategic offensive arms.

Summit Meeting — May 29-30, 1975

The Spring meeting of the Council was held in Brussels at the level of Heads of State and Government. This summit meeting, following the Ottawa Ministerial session of 1974, at which the Declaration on Atlantic Relations had been approved, emphasised the concern of the member countries to take the measure of an international situation complicated by increasingly severe economic problems and to manifest their solidarity in the face of such exceptional events. Recalling that the security provided by the Alliance is an essential condition for detente and peace, the Heads of State and Government reaffirmed their commitment to the North Atlantic Treaty, in particular Article 5, which provides for collective defence.

Conference on Security and Cooperation in Europe — Helsinki, August 1975 — Final Act

The second phase of the CSCE process took place at Geneva from September 18, 1973 to July 21, 1975. During this time, the Conference Committees completed drafting proposals relating to various items of the agenda previously approved by the Ministers of the participating countries. The third and final phase of the Conference took place at Helsinki on July 31 and August 1, 1975, at the level of Heads of State and Government, who signed the Final Act of the Conference. With regard to follow-up action, it was decided that a first follow-up meeting of participating states should be held in Belgrade in 1977 to examine the implementation of the CSCE Final Act.

Allied initiative towards Mutual and Balanced Force Reductions (MBFR)

In the months which followed, the substantial progress hoped for in East-West relations failed to materialise. Whilst it was certainly too early to expect any results from the Helsinki agreements, it was disappointing to find no forward movement in the MBFR negotiations, which had been in progress for more than two years. In another context, discussions between the United States and the USSR, within the framework of SALT II, had not produced a satisfactory agreement on a new limitation of strategic weapons.

It was against this background that the usual winter Ministerial meetings to review the state of the Alliance took place in Brussels. Of particular note in these discussions was an important initiative in the field of MBFR by the Allies concerned, envisaging the inclusion of certain United States nuclear armaments in the Allied proposals. These new negotiating proposals were presented to the Eastern negotiators in Vienna on December 16, 1975.

The Ministers also expressed their strong hopes for the full implementation in the near future of the measures contained in the Helsinki Final Act by all signatory states.

Quest for a constructive policy for detente

The adoption at Helsinki of the CSCE Final Act in 1975 had marked the beginning of a new phase in East-West relations. This Agreement laid out a set of principles, backed by concrete provisions, for the conduct of relations among participating states and henceforth represented one of the basic standards by which their actions were to be judged, and not only in the CSCE area. The way its provisions were implemented by each signatory served as a measure of their dedication to the CSCE principles. These required that its benefits should be felt not only in relations between states but also in the lives of individuals. It was in connection with this major objective that a clause was included in the Final Act stipulating that the participating states would meet at regular intervals to review its implementation.

At the same time, the Allied governments strove to make headway in their efforts to remove barriers and to produce a more stable relationship in Europe. The main focus of such efforts were the MBFR talks, strategic arms limitations and other initiatives in the field of disarmament and arms control. The ensuing period was marked by intense diplomatic activity, which was the subject of extensive consultations in the Alliance. As in the past, the Ministerial meetings of the North Atlantic Council provided an opportunity for regular reviews of the overall status of East-West relations and for spelling out Allied positions in the communiqués issued on these occasions.

The Allied governments stated that, if detente was to be productive, certain conditions had to be met. An improvement in East-West relations would depend on the extent to which all concerned showed moderation and self-restraint, both in Europe and in other parts of the world. The contest of opposing ideologies, however legitimate it might be, had to be conducted in a manner compatible with the letter and spirit of the Helsinki Final Act. Public support, essential to the detente process, could be obtained only if there were real improvements across the entire range of international relations. Detente could not be pursued selectively. Nor could the necessary confidence be established between East and West if crises and tensions were to be avoided in Europe only to appear elsewhere. In this connection, the Allies expressed growing concern over the direct or indirect actions of the Soviet Union and some of its Allies in a number of troubled areas.

CSCE—Final Act implementation

On numerous occasions since Helsinki, the Allied countries had deplored the fact that there had been a number of negative developments in the Final Act implementation, especially in the field of human rights and fundamental freedoms and in that of information.

It was against this background that the first of the Follow-up Meetings was held in Belgrade in 1977. As they had done for the CSCE negotiations themselves, the Allied governments made the greatest possible use of the Alliance's consultative machinery to prepare their positions jointly and carefully.

Although the Belgrade meeting did not produce substantial results, it nonetheless institutionalised the framework for regularly examining the implementation of the Final Act. The exchange of views to which it gave rise paved the way for a continuation of the dialogue and of the multilateral process initiated by the CSCE.

Three Expert Meetings, already agreed upon in the Final Act, were also held to consider certain issues more closely: a meeting on the peaceful settlement of disputes, which took place in Montreux at the end of December, 1978; a meeting on cooperation in the Mediterranean, held in Valletta in spring 1979; and a Scientific Forum held in Hamburg early in 1980.

Subsequently, the Allies prepared for the next Follow-up Meeting, to be held in Madrid in 1980. Confirming that they intended to approach the Madrid Meeting in a constructive frame of mind, they expressed the hope that, in the meantime, tangible progress would be achieved in the implementation of all three chapters (or "Baskets") of the Final Act. In this spirit, they would be ready to put forward new proposals aimed at improving the detente process and to discuss proposals of a similar nature from other participants. In particular, it was hoped that the Madrid meeting would allow for a more extensive discussion on military confidence-building measures.

Confidence-building measures

Confidence-building measures warrant special mention for two reasons: firstly, because, at the very outset of the CSCE preparatory talks, they had an important place in Western ideas regarding the improvement of security and the reduction of tension in Europe; secondly, because, in the late 1970s, new proposals, both by the Allies (mainly those made in the context of the French proposal for a Conference on Disarmament in Europe (CDE) (see Chapter 11), and by the Eastern and the neutral and non-aligned countries, suggested that there were reasonable prospects of progress. It is noteworthy that while, on the Western side, the agreed provisions of the CSCE Final Act for the notification of manoeuvres and the invitation of observers to manoeuvres had been implemented in a liberal fashion, the Eastern countries had confined themselves strictly to the letter of the provisions.

Vienna negotiations on Mutual and Balanced Force Reductions (MBFR)

In terms of security, the MBFR negotiations continued to represent, for the Allied countries concerned, a venture complementing the CSCE. The absence of significant progress in the Vienna negotiations, in spite of the efforts made by the Western negotiators, was a source of constant disappointment, but it did not discourage the Western governments concerned from taking new initiatives on various occasions in an effort to move the talks forward, while at the same time expressing the hope that the Eastern countries would make a positive response.

In substance, the Western participants held to their opening position that the final outcome should be to eliminate the ground force manpower disparity by means of a common collective ceiling on the manpower of each side in the area of reductions. The reductions should take place in two phases: the first comprising United States and Soviet withdrawals; the second concerning the common ceiling. The East, on the other hand, proposed equal percentage reductions on both sides, ceilings on the forces of the individual countries and a one-stage reduction process. Once included in a treaty, these proposals would have given an appearance of legality to Eastern superiority in the area and allowed the East an unacceptable *droit de regard* into NATO's integrated defence.

The offer made in December 1975 to include certain United States nuclear armaments as part of Western reductions was never taken up by the East. In 1976, after more than two years of negotiating, the Eastern participants had tabled some initial data for Eastern forces in the reduction area. However, a new source of disagreement arose as Eastern figures were substantially below Western estimates. The clarification of the data base was considered essential for substantial progress: reductions would only have an impact in terms of reducing disparities if the existing levels and therefore the starting point for reductions were first agreed. This problem continued to be a major stumbling-block, although some limited progress was recorded in other fields.

Arms Control and the balance of forces

From the outset, the Allies' position in arms control negotiations was based on the fundamental conviction that the success of détente hinges on maintaining the balance of forces. The considerable build-up, both qualitative and quantitative, in the military strength of the Warsaw Treaty countries beyond levels justified for defensive purposes, was scarcely compatible either with statements that they did not seek military superiority or with their publicly-declared intention to promote detente, particularly in the military sphere.

These legitimate concerns were expressed with a growing sense of urgency in the communiqués of successive Ministerial meetings. In the absence of any sign of reduction in the enormous Eastern armaments effort, Allied governments decided that action was needed to ensure that their defence capability was kept at an adequate level to provide effective deterrence against any danger of military aggression or political pressure. This was the aim of the wide-ranging Long-Term Defence Programme, adopted at the Washington Summit Meeting in May 1978 by the countries participating in the Alliance's integrated military structure, designed to enable NATO forces to meet the defence needs of the 1980s. At the same time, short-term measures were agreed to improve the capabilities of those forces by the end of 1978.

To back up this effort, a series of additional measures were taken, particularly in the framework of the Conference of National Armaments Directors, to promote more effective use of available resources through cooperative equipment programmes and to increase standardization and interoperability of weapon systems. In this connection, efforts designed to preserve and develop the strong industrial and technological capability vital for the defence of the Alliance as a whole continued, as well as efforts to bring about more balanced relations between the European and North American members of the Alliance in the field of the development and production of new defence equipment.

In this general context of the need to preserve the balance of forces through an adequate defensive capability, the Allied governments had occasion to declare once again that in the event of an attack on them, they could not renounce the use, as might be required for defence, of any of the means available to them. The Alliance had made its position equally clear in 1957, in the face of the Soviet campaign aimed at preventing it from holding nuclear weapons in Europe. The Council had emphasized then that the Atlantic Alliance must have modern weapons to be able to defend itself against any attack on it.

As a logical follow-up to their efforts to achieve a relaxation in tension at other levels, the Allied governments laid increasing stress on the danger to peace resulting from the constant growth in armaments. They had long attached importance to this question. In 1957, for example, the Alliance had done its utmost to ensure the success of efforts aimed at bringing about a general agreement on disarmament. More than twenty years later, the search continued for a foundation for the pursuit of serious arms control negotiations leading to the adoption of effective, balanced and verifiable measures.

Bearing in mind recent developments in East-West relations, the Alliance stressed on several occasions that cooperation on a wide range of disarmament and arms control issues was an urgent task for all countries. Progress in this direction could not but contribute to international prosperity and make easier the necessary growth in financial resources devoted to development. In this spirit, the Allies reaffirmed their determination to persevere, through negotiations and in a way consistent with the security of the Alliance, in the quest for practical measures to achieve these goals.

However, progress in this sphere depended on a constructive attitude on the part of the Soviet Union and its allies. Until such time as it proved possible to achieve a satisfactory military balance at lower levels of forces through realistic and verifiable force reduction agreements, Allied governments indicated that they would continue to devote all the resources necessary to modernising and strengthening their own forces to the minimum extent required for deterrence and defence.

Since 1975, therefore, Allied efforts in the main spheres of East-West negotiations had been based on these guiding principles. At the same time, the Atlantic Alliance continued, both in its regular consultations and at Ministerial meetings, to keep close track of a whole range of issues, progress in which was deemed by the Western governments to be of special importance for the international climate; these included the situation in Berlin and in the Mediterranean, as well as the North-South dialogue.

Status of East-West relations (1975-1980)

The regular Ministerial meetings of the Council in December 1975 (Brussels); May 1976 (Oslo); and December 1976 (Brussels), enabled Foreign Ministers to compare and contrast their evaluations of recent events in East-West relations and to arrive at a broad consensus on the way in which they should be interpreted. In the light of this initial preparatory analysis, the Allies decided to hold the 1977 spring meeting of the North Atlantic Council in London at Heads of State and Government level, in order to conduct a review of the action they had taken in the face of an increasingly complex international situation. The follow-up to several important initiatives taken in London was considered the following year in Washington, also at a summit meeting. The spring meeting in The Hague in May 1979 took on special significance, marking as it did the Alliance's 30th Anniversary. And the meetings held in Brussels in December 1979 were also an important milestone, particularly in the strengthening of the Alliance's defensive capability in the sphere of intermediate-range nuclear forces. In 1980, the traditional Spring Ministerial meeting of the Council reflected concern over the deterioration in East-West relations which had followed the Soviet invasion of Afghanistan. By the December 1980 Ministerial meeting this concern had not receded, and was accentuated by the Soviet threat hanging over Poland. The context in which each of these meetings took place, and the main decisions taken at them, are described in more detail below.

London Summit Meeting—May 1977

At the outset of this important session in London, the Allied leaders reaffirmed that the Alliance continued to play a central role as the guardian of their collective security; it provided the strength and confidence that enabled member countries to persevere in their efforts to lessen tensions between East and West and to increase progressively the areas of cooperation.

With regard to East-West relations since the adoption of the CSCE Final Act in 1975, it was clear that, although there had been some improvements, many elements of instability and uncertainty persisted. In particular, much remained to be done if the prospects opened up by the Final Act were ever to be realised, not only in terms of relations between states but also with respect to matters affecting the lives of the peoples of all the countries concerned. The Allies recognised as wholly legitimate the aspirations of people throughout the world to inherent human rights and fundamental freedoms. They were convinced that respect for these rights and freedoms, in accordance with the commitments accepted by governments in the United Nations Charter and in other international documents, including the Helsinki Final Act, was an essential requirement for peace, friendship and cooperation among nations. In the light of this analysis, Allied leaders requested the Council in permanent session to make a fresh study of long-term trends in East-West relations and to assess their implications for the Alliance.

Furthermore, impelled by their increasing concern at the constant growth in the power and offensive capability of the armed forces of the Warsaw Treaty countries, the leaders of the states participating in the Alliance's integrated defence structure asked their Defence Ministers to prepare and develop a long-term programme (LTDP) aimed at improving their defensive capability in order to meet the challenges of the 1980s.

Washington Summit Meeting—May 1978

The main purpose of this new Summit Meeting was to review the follow-up to the decisions set in train at the London Summit. The study of long-term trends in East-West relations, decided upon in London had confirmed the continuing validity of the two complementary aims of the Alliance. Trends in the USSR and the other Warsaw Treaty countries led Allied leaders to conclude that the Alliance must maintain its solidarity and vigilance, maintaining its defences at the minimum level necessary to provide an adequate deterrent, while at the same time striving to promote détente. The Allied Ministers concerned also reviewed progress achieved in the context of the Long-Term Defence Programme. To bring home the importance of this Programme, a summary of its main features was attached to the communiqué issued at the conclusion of this Summit Meeting. In the same context, Ministers welcomed the fact that most member countries had agreed in principle to an increase in defence expenditure of 3% in real terms.

30th Anniversary—The Hague, May 1979

For three decades, the Alliance had made a decisive contribution to the maintenance of peace in Europe and thereby to the security and economic and social advancement of its member countries. This gave grounds for satisfaction, but as the Alliance entered its fourth decade, efforts to live up to the goals of the North Atlantic Treaty could not be relaxed. A number of developments had taken place in East-West relations, and at the 30th Anniversary Meeting of the Council in The Hague, these were carefully examined. In broad terms, the Allies reaffirmed the positions they had previously taken, particularly with respect to the need to deepen the CSCE process and to achieve progress towards genuine disarmament. Attention was paid to recent statements by East European countries regarding the development of confidence-building measures, which Western countries had suggested at the Belgrade Meeting on the basis of recommendations contained in the CSCE Final Act. The growing activity on disarmament issues in the United Nations framework was welcomed, together with the exchange of views on the proposal made by France in May 1978, to all European countries and to the United States and Canada, to create a negotiating forum designed not only to introduce measures which would build confidence, but also to bring about limitations and reductions of conventional weapons throughout Europe. Agreement had also been reached between the United States and the Soviet Union in the Strategic Arms Limitation Talks and, while the agreement had yet to be ratified[33], it was recognised that a balanced limitation of the nuclear weapons capabilities of the Soviet Union and the United States would make an important contribution to East-West relations and security. Full consultations had been held in the Alliance on this important issue.

The "Double-track" Decision on Theatre Nuclear Forces Modernisation and Arms Control—December 12, 1979

From 1977 onwards, the Alliance had become increasingly concerned over growing Soviet theatre nuclear force capabilities, especially the development of a new mobile intermediate-range nuclear missile, the SS-20. During this period, while the Soviet Union had been reinforcing its superiority in long-range theatre nuclear forces (LRTNF), Western capabilities, which did not include land-based LRTNF systems, had remained static, increasing in age and vulnerability. It was felt that these trends, if allowed to continue, could undermine the stability achieved in inter-continental systems and cast doubt on the credibility of the Alliance's deterrent strategy by highlighting the gap in the spectrum of NATO's available nuclear response to aggression. Within the Long-Term Defence Programme, one of the task forces which had been created was to examine NATO's future requirements for modernised nuclear forces in the relevant category. The Nuclear Planning Group was subseqently entrusted with this task and established a High-Level Group to examine the question in detail.

As the work of this Group proceeded, the countries involved concluded that a major arms control effort represented the best way of achieving the basic Alliance goal of a more stable balance at lower levels of nuclear weapons. Accordingly, in April 1979, a Special Group was set up by the member countries concerned, tasked with the development of an arms control approach to parallel the work being undertaken on intermediate-range nuclear force modernisation. The reports of the two groups formed the basis for the decisions on the deployment in Europe of new United States ground-launched missile systems and on a parallel and complementary arms control effort, taken at a special meeting of Foreign and Defence Ministers on December 12, 1979, on the eve of the Council's normal winter meeting[34]. Given the special importance for the overall security of the Alliance of the negotiations on intermediate-range nuclear forces announced on December 12, a high level consultative body was constituted within the Alliance to support the United States negotiating effort. The Special Consultative Group, which followed the negotiations on a continuous basis, reporting regularly to Foreign and Defence Ministers, was to become the main forum for Alliance

---

33 The SALT II agreement was not ratified by the United States. New negotiations between the United States and the Soviet Union, aimed at achieving reductions in strategic arms (Strategic Arms Reductions Talks—START) began in Geneva on 30 June 1982.

34 The communiqué issued following the Special Meeting of Foreign and Defence Ministers held in Brussels on December 12, 1979 is reproduced at Appendix I.

consultation on matters concerning the INF negotiations until the latter were successfully concluded in December 1987.

The December 1979 decisions were designed to rectify the imbalance in the two sides' nuclear forces in order to ensure the continued effectiveness of the strategy of forward defence and flexible response on which the Alliance's policy of deterrence is based. In particular, the decisions reflected the determination of member countries of the Alliance to restore the credibility of the "triad" of forces linking conventional nuclear forces in Europe, via non-strategic nuclear forces, to NATO's strategic deterrent—and specifically to the strategic nuclear forces of the United States. The "decoupling" of Europe from the United States could not be allowed.

The two tracks of the "double-track" decision consisted, on the one hand, of deployment decisions and, on the other, of proposals for negotiations to render the deployments unnecessary. The deployments consisted of United States ground-launched systems comprising 108 Pershing II launchers, which would replace existing United States Pershing I-A launchers, and 464 Ground-Launched Cruise Missiles (GLCM), all with single warheads. All nations participating in NATO's integrated defence structure would participate and the missiles would be stationed in selected countries. The programme would not increase NATO's reliance on nuclear weapons; in fact 1,000 nuclear warheads were to be withdrawn from Europe and the 572 warheads to be deployed would be accommodated within the resulting reduced level. The announcement of these measures included details of specific proposals which had been elaborated during consultations within the Alliance for the bilateral negotiations between the United States and the Soviet Union which were to begin as soon as possible on these categories of nuclear forces.

The decisions were made in conjunction with a series of additional offers to negotiate in the field of confidence-building and arms control measures with a view to improving mutual security and cooperation in Europe as a whole. These offers were as follows:

— reductions in the level of strategic nuclear forces within the framework of SALT;
— proposals designed to give fresh impetus to the MBFR negotiations concerning, on the one hand, an interim Phase I agreement and, on the other, a number of associated measures designed to ensure compliance with the agreement and to make military activities more transparent;
— in furtherance of the CSCE process, readiness to examine far-reaching proposals concerning confidence-building measures and to work towards a conference on disarmament in Europe.

Council meeting—Brussels, December 13-14, 1979

On the day after this important special meeting, the Council began its regular Ministerial session. The events of the previous months had shown the continuing influence of trends which were hardly conducive to the consolidation of international stability and security. Concern was again expressed over instability caused by direct or indirect actions of the Soviet Union and some of its allies, and the concurrent build-up of their military strength. Allied Governments were resolved to reduce the growing imbalance of forces and to improve their defence and deterrent capabilities, as they had announced at the London and Washington Summits.

In the CSCE context, while there had been certain measures of relief—such as the granting of amnesty for some political prisoners—the situation in certain countries remained unsatisfactory and had even deteriorated with regard to respect for human rights and fundamental freedoms. In some cases, citizens were being subjected to harrassment and imprisonment for no reason other than their efforts to bring about the full implementation of the provisions of the Final Act. Implementation of provisions dealing with a freer flow of information and improved working conditions for journalists was also inadequate and, in some cases, had deteriorated.

The importance attached by the members of the Alliance to the process of developing the confidence-building measures and other provisions of the Final Act relating to security was reflected in the communiqué published at the conclusion of the December 1979 meeting. The latter referred to a number of proposals made by Western, neutral and non-aligned, and Warsaw Treaty member countries, in particular the proposal put forward by France for a Conference on Disarmament in Europe, and indicated that this was a sufficient basis for further work.

On several occasions, the Allied countries concerned had taken new initiatives in an effort to end the deadlock in the Vienna MBFR negotiations. The requirements for Soviet reductions in the first phase were modified in proposals made on April 19, 1978, and greater commitments regarding non-US Western reductions were offered. These moves were supplemented by a proposal made on December 13, 1978, providing for more specific reduction commitments by the individual Western participants. The East took some steps in the direction of Western positions in counter-proposals of June 1978 and June 1979 but although these developments brought the two sides closer conceptually, concrete obstacles stood in the path of agreement as long as the East remained unwilling to modify its stand on data.

In order to overcome this impasse over data, and as part of a series of arms control steps in the framework of the programme of negotiations finalised at the Special Meeting held on December 12, a new Western proposal was approved for a simplified interim Phase 1 agreement for mutual and balanced force reductions and a package of associated measures.

Ministers welcomed the increasing attention being paid to disarmament and arms control and, in particular, the efforts being made in the United Nations Committee on Disarmament, in which the countries of the Alliance were actively participating. Recent proposals had also been put forward by the Eastern countries which echoed in part the Western views on disarmament, and this was seen as a hopeful indication that these countries were beginning to adopt a more positive attitude in the search for common ground.

Consultations on events outside the North Atlantic Treaty Area

As members of an Alliance created within the framework of the United Nations Charter, NATO countries are active in promoting the objectives of the United Nations in furthering the cause of peaceful international relations throughout the world. Indeed Article 7 of the North Atlantic Treaty ensures that there can be no conflict of interests, stipulating that rights and obligations under the UN Charter are not affected by the NATO Treaty. The same article recognises the primary responsibility of the UN Security Council for the maintenance of international peace and security. However the Treaty also recognises implicitly that the security of member countries cannot exist in a vacuum and is inevitably affected by events outside the Treaty area. Accordingly, while the mutual commitment to provide assistance in response to attack is geographically limited, no such limitation pertains to consultations between the member countries. Both in theory and in practice, therefore, proper use of the North Atlantic Council involves consultations on developments affecting security wherever they may occur.

In December 1979 consultations in the North Atlantic Council on the situation in the Middle East led the members of the Alliance to affirm once again the importance they attached to elaborating and implementing a just, lasting and comprehensive settlement of the Arab-Israeli conflict on the basis of UN Security Council Resolutions 242 and 338, with the participation of all the parties concerned including representatives of the Palestinian people. A negotiated settlement which member nations could support would have to provide for the legitimate rights of the Palestinians and ensure the security of all states in the region including Israel.

In another area of the world where peace had been violated, there was a stronger basis for optimism. Cease-fire proposals had recently been agreed at the London Constitutional Conference on Rhodesia. Allied Foreign Ministers therefore expressed their hope that these would become effective quickly and that peace would return to the area. They looked forward to the day when Zimbabwe would take its place in the international community as an independent republic[35].

Fresh opportunities in Europe

Following the important decisions taken by Foreign and Defence Ministers in Brussels in December 1979, it was legitimate to conclude that the Alliance had initiated a large-scale programme that gave the Soviet Union and the members of the Warsaw Treaty Organisation a fresh and very significant opportunity to translate into action the interest they had signalled in improving the situation in Europe. It was hoped that the Eastern governments would react positively to the offers of negotiations, with a view to achieving substantial results which would enhance security and mutual trust, and establish more constructive relations between East and West.

---

[35] Zimbabwe became an independent republic on April 18, 1981.

However, as 1979 came to an end, uncertainty on the international field was compounded, firstly by the taking of hostages at the United States Embassy in Teheran on November 4, and subsequently by the Soviet invasion of Afghanistan on December 27.

The invasion of Afghanistan

This event prompted a fundamental re-examination of Alliance views on the East-West relationship. Whatever hopes might have existed about the improvements which the détente process could bring about were called into question by the direct use by the Soviet Union of military force to impose its will on a non-aligned country of the Third World in a way which threatened to affect the overall strategic situation. The action indicated that the Soviet Union continued to view detente in a highly restrictive sense, and was prepared to take extreme interventionist action in areas where it perceived its political, ideological or security interests to be involved, in flagrant contravention of international law.

The shock of Afghanistan was severe, and Alliance members took a number of actions which indicated that "business as usual" could not be conducted with the Soviet Union in the wake of the invasion. There was, however, a consensus that a redefined and more realistic detente process, without illusions, encompassing dialogue and negotiation with the Soviet Union and its partners, was an essential requirement for the future of Western security and for any hope of improvement in East-West relations.

The North Atlantic Council met on New Year's Day, 1980, to continue a process of consultation on the significance of the invasion and on measures to be taken by Alliance members. There was absolute consensus that the Soviet action was unacceptable and that it had to be reversed. Furthermore, it was agreed that it should be made clear to the Soviet Union that there was a price to pay for such actions in terms of the benefits accruing from good relations with the West. A whole range of areas of cooperation was affected by this decision.

The attitudes of Alliance governments, as well as those of many Third World nations, regarding the Moscow Olympics made it clear that official, social and courtesy contacts normal on such occasions could not take place in these circumstances. Some governments imposed a boycott on the Games. It was, however, decided by the Allies that their attitude of reserve would not extend to the severence of all contacts with Moscow; there was general agreement that lines of communication needed to be kept open, in order to impress upon the Soviet authorities the full extent of Western feelings about its actions in Afghanistan, and to avoid any dangerous misapprehensions or misunderstandings.

Ministerial Meeting of the Defence Planning Committee— May 1980

At their regular Spring Ministerial meeting, Defence Ministers reviewed progress on all aspects of the work programme facing the members of the integrated military command structure of the Alliance, including both near-term and longer-term measures they had set in hand to improve Allied defence capabilities. Many of these were reflected in the 1981-86 force goals endorsed by Defence Ministers on this occasion. As in the past, their meeting also provided an opportunity to hear a report from the Chairman of the Eurogroup on work undertaken in that forum to strengthen the cohesion of the Alliance and make the European contribution to collective defence as effective as possible. They examined the progress of the experimental Periodic Armaments Planning System (later "Phased Armements Programming System") and the achievements of the Armaments Planning Review which was providing a useful means of identifying opportunities for cooperative development and production of equipment and improving interoperability. The meeting also marked the 25th anniversary of the accession of the Federal Republic of Germany to NATO and Ministers recorded their appreciation of the important contribution made by the Federal Republic of Germany. However the focus of concern of the meeting continued to be related to the modernisation of intermediate-range nuclear forces rendered necessary by the continuing large-scale Soviet deployments of missiles in this category and the threat to the credibility of NATO's deterrent strategy which had developed.

Ankara Ministerial Meeting—June 1980

The Ministerial Meeting which took place in Ankara at the end of June 1980 was the first occasion for Foreign Ministers to consult together on the analysis which had been made of the significance of the Soviet invasion of Afghanistan and Allied actions in the light of the invasion. The views of Ministers were summed up in the final communiqué of that meeting: 'Ministers noted that the Soviet invasion of Afghanistan had done serious damage to detente, to which they reaffirmed their attachment... They agreed that restoration of a cooperative relationship must be based on a foundation of mutual confidence, and this has been shaken by recent Soviet actions'.

The Ankara meeting also gave the opportunity to the Ministers to discuss the approach of the members of the Alliance at the Madrid CSCE meeting scheduled for November 1980. They emphasised their adherence to the full implementation of the principles and provisions of the Helsinki Final Act, and warned that the prospects for progress at Madrid would be influenced by the course of the review of implementation of the Final Act.

The confidence necessary for progress had been seriously jeopardised by the events in Afghanistan. Nonetheless, NATO countries agreed to continue to develop a balanced group of proposals for presentation at Madrid. Thus, the Alliance continued its preparations in the sober realisation that Soviet actions, including the treatment of dissidents among its own citizens, and its apparent unwillingness to take any steps to redress the situation, did not augur well for concrete results.

Science for Stability

In addition to their normal review of progress on all the matters on the current East-West agenda, Foreign Ministers at Ankara endorsed the establishment of a special five-year programme proposed by the Science Committee to strengthen the scientific and technological capabilities of Greece, Portugal and Turkey by means of cooperation with scientific institutions in other countries of the Alliance. Entitled "Science for Stability", this programme was subsequently elaborated by the Council in permanent session, and became an important focus of the work being undertaken by NATO in the scientific field.

Expiry of the Agreement on the Use of Military Facilities in Malta

On March 31, 1979, when the seven-year agreement between the United Kingdom and Malta had expired, British forces had moved out of the facilities they had been using on the island on NATO's behalf in return for special payments by a number of Allied countries. Subsequently, member countries kept the situation on the island under close review and remained alert to any developments which could affect their security interests. Against this background, an agreement was reached through an exchange of notes on September 15, 1980, whereby Italy guaranteed Maltese neutrality and agreed to provide the island with economic assistance. One clause of this agreement denies Soviet warships access to Maltese shipyards.

Iran-Iraq War

The international situation suffered a new setback when, on September 22, 1980, war broke out in the Middle East between Iraq and Iran. The war did not directly involve either the members of the North Atlantic Alliance or the Soviet Union and the members of the Warsaw Treaty Organisation. However, as a further element of instability in an area of the world which already suffered from other potentially destabilising conflicts, it was a matter of grave international concern. It was in the interests of world peace that the war should be brought to an end as soon as possible, and it was in the interests of neither East nor West to allow themselves to be drawn into this bitter conflict. It is therefore no surprise that both the Western powers and the Soviet Union exercised restraint in their dealings with both participants in the war and in their contacts with each other. The members of the Alliance supported United Nations initiatives to bring the war to an end and pressed for full implementation of Security Council Resolution 598.

Berlin

NATO Governments regularly review the situation with respect to Berlin and Germany as a whole. On each occasion, they have reaffirmed that strict observation and full implementation of the Quadripartite Agreement of September 3, 1971, ensuring a constantly undisturbed climate in Berlin and on the access routes, remains an essential element of détente in Europe. After a period of reserve, an improved climate in relations between the two German States enabled new agreements to be concluded and negotiations to be continued. A setback in the relationship occurred in the autumn of 1980, when measures were introduced by the German Democratic Republic which substantially reduced inner-German travel. The Allies supported efforts by the Federal Republic of Germany to achieve the withdrawal of these measures.

Situation in the Mediterranean area

The Harmel Report recommendations of 1967 had already highlighted the fact that the growing Soviet naval presence in the Mediterranean called for constant vigilance in view of the potential threat it posed to the southern flank of the Alliance. Since then, the Permanent Council has accordingly kept a close watch on developments in this area and, in its half-yearly reports, has stressed that the maintenance of the balance of forces throughout the Mediterranean is a prerequisite for peace.

Similarly there were regular consultations on developments in the Middle East, where continuing instability and its potential consequences gave cause for serious concern. Paying tribute to the efforts of President Carter, President Sadat and Prime Minister Begin, which led to the Camp David Agreements of September 1978, NATO member countries underlined the importance of continuing efforts to achieve a just and durable peace. This required the resolution of the Palestinian problem in all its aspects and the achievement of the legitimate rights of the Palestinian people in the context of a settlement, negotiated on the basis of United Nations Resolutions 242 and 338, that ensured the security of all states in the region, including Israel.

As regards the problems at issue between Greece and Turkey, Ministers had, on several occasions, expressed the urgent hope that the continuation of the dialogue between the two governments would pave the way for a mutually acceptable solution that would strengthen the cohesion essential to the Alliance's southern flank. In this connection, they had expressed the hope that full cooperation among members of the Alliance in all aspects of the defence field would soon be resumed. The Secretary General, for his part, in accordance with his Watching Brief, had continued his efforts to bring about a rapprochement between Greece and Turkey. During the latter part of 1980, there were signs of a marked improvement in relations between the two countries which augured well for tangible improvements. On October 20, 1980, the Defence Planning Committee approved the return of Greek forces to the NATO integrated military structure (from which they had been withdrawn in August 1974), on the basis of a proposal developed by General Rogers, Supreme Allied Commander, Europe, which had been found acceptable both by Greece and by its NATO allies.

Bearing in mind the provisions of Article 2 of the North Atlantic Treaty and the difficulties experienced by some members of the Alliance in maintaining a sufficient and sustained economic growth to support an effective defence effort, the Allies resolved to provide economic assistance through cooperation aimed at helping countries in this situation in their development programmes and in bringing about improvements in living standards. The close relationship between defence and the economy was fully recognised, as was the relationship between economic and social progress and a stable democracy. The Secretary General of NATO is responsible for overseeing the implementation of Allied efforts to provide economic assistance to Portugal, Greece and Turkey in particular, and regularly reports to the North Atlantic Council on progress made and measures still required.

North-South Dialogue

In the course of their discussions, Ministers frequently exchanged views on the question of aid for the developing countries. They reiterated their determination to work vigorously for a more effective and equitable world economic system, pointing out that Allied governments had demonstrated the importance they attached to this objective through their own long-standing aid programmes. They invited the Warsaw Treaty countries to follow their example.

Opening of Madrid CSCE meeting—November 11, 1980

The preparatory talks for the CSCE Follow-up Meeting in Madrid began on September 9, 1980. They concluded with agreement on a two-stage agenda consisting of an initial period devoted to a review of the implementation of the Helsinki Final Act and a second phase to consider new proposals. Agreement was reached after considerable difficulties, mainly due to the fact that the Soviet Union wished to impose unacceptable restrictions on the review of implementation.

Nevertheless, on November 11, the main meeting started with a six week period during which a detailed review of implementation was conducted. In December the second phase began with the introduction by participating states of some 85 new proposals covering all aspects of the Final Act.

Nuclear Planning Group—November 1980

At the end of 1980 the Nuclear Planning Group, which regularly meets twice a year at Ministerial level, met in Brussels. In addition to a review of work in all the main spheres under its responsibility, the Group received a report by the United Kingdom Secretary of State for Defence on the decision to replace, in close cooperation with the United States, the existing Polaris nuclear force with the Trident submarine-launched ballistic missile system in the early 1990s. The contribution of United Kingdom nuclear forces capable of playing a deterrent role of their own to the overall strengthening of deterrence had been recognized by the Alliance on many occasions, notably in the Ottawa Declaration issued by Heads of Government in 1974.

Equipment Planning and Technology Transfer

The effectiveness of deterrence depends not only on the quality and readiness of the armed forces of NATO countries but also on their equipment and its interoperability. A vital area of Allied concern, particularly in view of the constant quantitative and qualitative development of the conventional forces of the Warsaw Treaty Organization, is therefore the equipment planning and project development aspects of interallied cooperation. Progress in this field depends to a great extent on the political support it receives and accordingly was reviewed extensively at successive meetings of the Defence Planning Committee. In addressing themselves to this issue in December 1980, Defence Ministers also reaffirmed the need to give close attention to decisions involving the transfer of advanced technologies to the Soviet Union.

Prospects for the new decade

At the December 1980 meeting of the Defence Planning Committee, Defence Ministers also warmly welcomed the reintegration of Greek forces into the military command structure of NATO on October 20, thereby strengthening the cohesion of the south-eastern flank of the Alliance. At the same meeting Defence Ministers noted progress in a number of areas within their responsibilities, including measures to improve the effectiveness and readiness of NATO air forces through a cooperative and cost-sharing training programme. Twelve countries signed a Memorandum of Understanding, establishing this programme.

In other spheres too, and in fields of Alliance activity relatively little known to publics in the member countries, positive developments were taking place. November 1980 had, for example, brought together Ministers of the Environment from seven countries of the Alliance, together with other senior officials, to exchange information and ideas on national planning in relation to the environment and problems posed by the utilisation of diversified energy sources and the environmental management of chemicals. Progress in these spheres continues to be a subject of close Allied attention, as well as of growing international importance.

However, further clouds were appearing on the international horizon and the end of year meeting of Foreign Ministers took place against a background of uncertainty. International tensions had again intervened to underline the fragility of world peace and the pressing need for nations to cooperate more effectively in their efforts to preserve it. Issues opposing East and West, far from diminishing, seemed to be growing in number and importance. On January 3, 1980, as a direct result of the Soviet invasion of Afghanistan, the United States President had requested the Senate to delay its consideration of the ratification of the SALT II Treaty. At the meeting of the North Atlantic Council in Ankara in June, Foreign Ministers reaffirmed their support for the Treaty and expressed regret that the current international crisis had delayed the process of ratification. But after a year of occupation, Soviet forces remained in Afghanistan and looked set to stay there. A grave threat to the security of the region, and an intolerable attempt to subjugate the Afghan people by force, this issue had rapidly become one of the most divisive in terms of the East-West relationship to have arisen outside Europe since the early post-war years.

Events in Poland

Nor was all well in Europe. As the year closed, the development of the situation in Poland was becoming a matter of increasing international concern in view of the risk of Soviet military intervention. The Alliance acknowledged that détente had brought some appreciable benefits in the field of East-West cooperation and exchange during the 1970s, but had been seriously damaged by Soviet actions. The process could not survive if the Soviet Union were again to violate the basic right of any state to territorial integrity and independence. The member countries of the Alliance, in public statements and private diplomacy, made clear that, for East-West relations, the consequences of such a course of action would be extremely grave. Poland must be free to decide its own future. The use of force, in flagrant breach of the principles enshrined in the United Nations Charter, the Universal Declaration on Human Rights, the Helsinki Final Act, and codes of international behaviour established under international law, remained unacceptable wherever it might occur. Its use in Poland would represent a setback in the process of building a more secure and stable basis for the conduct of international affairs and would cast doubt on the viability of future attempts to make progress. NATO countries appealed for respect for national sovereignty and the principle of non-intervention and announced their readiness to respond to genuine efforts by the Soviet Union to restore confidence.

The world continued to watch the unfolding of events in Poland with sympathy and hope. On August 31, 1980, under the Gdansk agreements, the Polish government authorised the establishment of the independent trade union "Solidarity" and accorded it official recognition. Its leader, Lech Walesa, became an international personality. These unprecedented developments kindled, not only in Poland but throughout the free world, a spirit of hope and optimism akin to the hopes vested in the changes which took place in Czechoslovakia in the Prague Spring of 1968—mingled with fears that the desires of the Polish people for a more open society, widely publicised through televised coverage of massive demonstrations of support for the "Solidarity" movement, could meet with the same fate as the aspirations of the Czechoslovak people 12 years previously.

Arms control

Throughout the eighties, a major focus of Alliance attention has been on positive and negative developments in the sphere of arms control and disarmament initiatives. The agreement reached in 1979 between the United

States and the Soviet Union in the Strategic Arms Limitation Talks (SALT II) was not ratified by the United States, in part because the climate of East-West relations had deteriorated as a direct result of the Soviet invasion of Afghanistan. Both the United States and the Soviet Union, however, indicated that they would respect its provisions on a reciprocal basis. (This informal agreement came to an end in May 1987 when the United States announced that in view of Soviet violations, it would no longer be bound by the terms of the unratified Treaty).

Despite the setback over SALT II and the difficulty of achieving any progress while relations between East and West continued to be subjected to the strains created by events in Afghanistan and Poland, efforts to achieve realistic and verifiable arms control agreements continued.

In one field in particular it was becoming imperative to halt a trend threatening to undermine the credibility and therefore the effectiveness of Allied deterrence, namely the steadily increasing imbalance created by continuing Soviet deployments of intermediate-range nuclear forces. It was the destabilising effect of these deployments, during the late seventies, and particularly those of the mobile SS-20 missile, combined with the threat to NATO strategy which had arisen partly as a result of such deployments, which had led to the NATO decision of 1979 to seek a solution through negotiations. By the time the 1979 "double-track" decision had been taken, some 130 SS-20 missiles with 390 warheads had been deployed. NATO had no weapons deployed in the category of INF missiles despite statements by the Soviet Union that a balance existed. At a meeting of the Nuclear Planning Group, held in Bodö (Norway) in June 1980, Defence Ministers called on the Soviet Union to respond positively and accept without delay the repeated offer by the United States, following consultations within the Alliance, to negotiate verifiable limitations on US and Soviet long-range land-based INF. The Ministers also noted that the withdrawal of 1,000 US nuclear warheads from Europe as an integral part of the LRTNF modernisation and arms control decision had begun. Agreement was reached in July 1980, following a visit by Chancellor Schmidt to Moscow, on the principle of negotiations on intermediate-range nuclear forces, but preliminary discussions in the autumn of 1980 made little headway on substance. By that time, some 200 SS-20s had been deployed with a total of 600 warheads. Again the Soviet Union spoke of "the balance which now exists".

In December 1980 the North Atlantic Council announced that the withdrawal of 1,000 US nuclear warheads from Europe decided upon 12 months earlier, had been completed.

New United States Administration

The beginning of 1981 marked the advent of the new American administration under President Reagan, who lost no time in reaffirming the strength of the United States commitment to NATO.

At the May 1981 Council Ministerial meeting in Rome, Foreign Ministers insisted on firmness in defence and persistence in the search for peaceful solutions. The nations concerned indicated, as they had at the April meeting of the Nuclear Planning Group in Bonn, that the position they had adopted in 1979 remained unchanged, and reaffirmed their commitment to the double-track decision. They were willing to negotiate but would act to modernise NATO's nuclear forces by deploying Pershing II and Ground Launched Cruise missiles if negotiations were not successful. Soviet SS-20 deployment already exceeded the total deployments planned by NATO. With regard to the moratorium which the Soviet Union had proposed, involving a quantitative and qualitative freeze on medium-range nuclear systems of both sides in Europe, including US forward-based systems, the Foreign Ministers of the 14 countries concerned spelled out their reasons for rejecting it: "The latest Soviet proposal for a moratorium on Long-Range Theatre Nuclear Forces[36] is wholly unacceptable to these Allies. It would freeze them into inferiority by blocking the NATO modernisation programme altogether. Moreover, the proposal would permit the Soviets to increase the threat to NATO by failing to limit systems capable of striking Allied territory from East of the Urals."

Questions of balance

At the Ministerial meeting of the Defence Planning Committee in May 1981, Defence Ministers had spoken, as they had on many previous occasions, of the disturbingly adverse trend in the military balance between East and West, especially in Europe, which had been developing over the past decade. Intensified action to maintain the credibility of deterrence was required. Soviet proposals for a moratorium, as Defence Ministers in the Nuclear Planning Group had pointed out when they met in Bonn in April, would not address the fundamental problem and could only serve to perpetuate the imbalance. Soviet claims that a balance existed, particularly with regard to intermediate-range nuclear forces, had no basis in fact.

The question of the growing imbalance of both nuclear and conventional forces was in fact coming under more and more intense scrutiny. The lessons of the previous decade were being digested. Unilateral restraint had not produced a response from the Soviet Union. Détente, which had created the illusion of enhanced security, had singularly failed to have an impact on the level of Soviet spending devoted to defence. Quite the reverse—the period of détente appeared to have been seen by the Soviet Union as an opportunity to increase its military potential across the board, with the reassurance that the West had not only opted to maintain its own defence spending at minimum levels, but had also postponed modernisation programmes which defence

---

36 Although the distinction between strategic and non-strategic nuclear weapons is more a question of possible employment than of weapon systems, the term "Theatre Nuclear Forces" is generally used to cover all non-strategic nuclear systems, i.e. those with less than intercontinental range. They include Intermediate-Range Nuclear Forces (INF), Short-Range Nuclear Forces (SNF) and non-strategic maritime systems. For more details, see Chapter 11.

studies had shown would be needed if the credibility of deterrence was to be preserved.

The experience of the 1970s had not diminished the commitment of NATO governments to the goal of creating an improved basis for conducting relations between East and West. However, it had enhanced their determination to ensure that détente meant substantial and genuine measures to reduce tensions, rather than one-sided restraint. Similiarly, in the military sphere, the lessons of the 1970s were being slowly translated into policies based on realistic programmes to correct imbalances and other measures to restore confidence in the defence and deterrent capabilities of the Alliance. The development did not take place in a political vacuum: it was more than ever necessary to demonstrate that the ability to make progress in the political sphere depended on backing political initiatives with a demonstrably credible ability to provide the resources needed for maintaining adequate defence and deterrence.

Three characteristics of the new climate of realism could be discerned.

3% Guideline

First, the goal of an annual increase in defence expenditure in the region of 3% in real terms, adopted by Defence Ministers and subsequently by their Heads of State and Government in 1977, was confirmed as a standard guideline for the Alliance. Performance continued to vary; not all governments were able to achieve the 3% goal and some who achieved it initially were unable to maintain expenditure at that level. However, the 3% goal brought into sharp focus the need to ensure that in addition to increases in resources for defence, better use was made of existing resources. The issue was not so much a question of measuring financial input as one of assessing output in relation to defence needs.

Reinvestment in defence

Second, if it could not be said that a programme of reinvestment in the defence capacity of the Alliance had been set in hand by all member countries, at least it could be said that the need for such a programme had been recognised by many governments. Particularly welcome to Defence Ministers were the significant efforts being made by the United States to strengthen its defence capability in the interests of the Alliance as a whole.

Common military assessments

Thirdly, members of the Alliance acknowledged that steps were urgently needed to provide a comprehensive joint assessment of the extent and nature of the potential threat posed by the military capabilities of the Soviet Union and the Warsaw Treaty countries. In particular, more information had to be made available publicly if support for maintaining the minimum levels of forces needed for deterrence was not to be eroded in parliaments and influential sectors of public opinion. At the October 1981 meeting of the Nuclear Planning Group in Gleneagles, Defence Ministers welcomed a comprehensive report on Soviet Military Power which had recently been published by the United States in response to Ministers' requests earlier in the year.

This was certainly not the first time that the Alliance had been confronted with assessments of adverse trends in the military balance. Detailed military evaluations of trends in this field and their implications, provided by national authorities and by the Major NATO Commanders and the Military Committee, precede every Ministerial meeting of the Defence Planning and Nuclear Planning Committees and are built into annual defence planning and review procedures. Decisions on all important defence issues are discussed against the background of the military risks which they must address. However, recent briefings to Defence Ministers had provided particularly stark and sobering evidence of the true extent of the Soviet build-up across the full spectrum of military capability. Detailed reports of these developments served not only to inform public opinion and to provide the context for Allied decision-making on resource allocation and use, but also to give the necessary guidance to governments in the field of arms control. At their 1981 Gleneagles meeting, for example, Ministers discussed two reports produced by the NPG High Level Group at the request of Foreign and Defence Ministers in the Spring of that year, presenting an updated assessment of the threat facing NATO and examining functional requirements for NATO's theatre nuclear forces. It was agreed that the papers represented a reliable basis for use by the United States in its forthcoming bilateral negotiations with the Soviet Union on theatre nuclear force arms control.

New arms control initiatives

In November 1981 President Reagan announced a series of major new initiatives designed to bring about greater security through significant reductions in the levels of all types of arms—nuclear and conventional. In an important policy address on November 18, he outlined the framework devised in discussions with Moscow for new bilateral negotiations aimed at making significant reductions in levels of strategic weapons (START)[37] as well as talks on Intermediate-range nuclear forces (INF). He pointed out that whereas during the previous six years the United States had deployed no new intermediate-range nuclear missiles, and had withdrawn 1,000 warheads from Europe, the Soviet Union had by then deployed 750 warheads on highly accurate and mobile SS-20 missiles. The solution proposed involved the complete dismantling of Soviet forces in this category (SS-4, SS-5 and SS-20 missiles) in return for the cancellation of all NATO's planned deployments of a similar range. It was this proposal, developed during consultations within the Alliance, which had been dubbed "the zero option". Its aim was to

[37] START: Strategic Arms Reduction Talks.

eliminate an entire class of nuclear weaponry. It remained the Alliance's goal and preferred outcome throughout the six years of negotiations which followed and was the basis on which agreement was eventually reached, resulting in the signature of the INF Treaty in December 1987.

The Alliance registered its full support for the far-reaching and constructive programme for the achievement of a stable peace put foward by President Reagan in his historic speech of 18 November. And they welcomed the four-point agenda, conveyed by President Reagan to the Soviet leader, covering proposals eliminating intermediate-range nuclear forces; new strategic nuclear arms control negotiations focussing on reductions; proposals for lowering levels of conventional forces in Europe; and lastly, proposals for building confidence and reducing the risk of surprise attack or war arising from miscalculation.

Negotiations on intermediate-range nuclear forces

Formal negotiations between the United States and the Soviet Union on intermediate-range nuclear forces began in Geneva on November 30, 1981. An assessment of the various stages of the INF negotiations and full details of the course they took between November 1981 and November 1983 are contained in a Report by the Special Consultative Group published by NATO at the end of 1983. Numerous different approaches were discussed, some made at the conference table, others launched amid much publicity in speeches and interviews by Soviet leaders but often not followed up in the negotiations. A number of stages in the saga of these negotiations can nevertheless be identified. While both sides put forward proposals, the Soviet side declined to build on mutually acceptable elements, preferring instead to reintroduce with slight variations demands known to be unacceptable to the United States and its NATO allies. Early in the negotiations, in December 1981, the Soviet Union proposed an agreement establishing an eventual ceiling of 300 "medium-range" missiles and nuclear-capable aircraft in Europe, including independent British and French nuclear forces, and continued to press for acceptance by the United States of this proposal. The United States, for its part, made plain its rejection of this suggestion. Regular consultations took place, principally in NATO's Special Consultative Group, enabling the United States negotiators to pursue their efforts to find a common basis on which to proceed with the full backing of the other members of the Alliance concerned. The December 1981 Council meeting emphasised Allied support for the stance adopted by the United States in the negotiations and reflected the high priority which would be given to continuous consultations within NATO's Special Consultative Group.

Terrorism

On November 4, 1979 the Embassy of the United States in Teheran had been seized by Islamic revolutionaries, together with 53 hostages, and for the next 14 months the treatment and imprisonment of the hostages had continued to shock the world, severely damaging relations between the government of Iran and democratic countries throughout the world.

Principally a matter dealt with in other fora, the question of terrorism and the need for coordinated action to combat all such acts of violence has nevertheless figured repeatedly in formal and informal consultations between Allied governments at the highest level. 1981 witnessed, in addition to acts of terrorism, assassination attempts against President Reagan and Pope John Paul and the assassination of President Sadat of Egypt. The abhorrence felt by public opinion throughout the world at all these events strengthened the hand of governments seeking to combat terrorism by every means at their disposal. NATO itself was frequently the subject of terrorist threats and was on some occasions more directly implicated, for example when a United States Army General serving with Allied Forces in Europe, James Dozier, was kidnapped in Italy in December 1981 and held until his rescue by Italian police at the end of January 1982. At the end of 1981, Foreign Ministers and Representatives of the Alliance issued a Declaration[38] reiterating their deep concern over the suffering inflicted on innocent people as well as the negative impact of such criminal offenses on international relations. They underlined their determination to take all necessary measures to eliminate such flagrant violations of human dignity and rights. Specific measures for effective national and collective action against terrorism resulting from initiatives taken in different international fora were supported by all NATO governments.

Berlin

Throughout this period, as at all times since the foundation of the Alliance and in particular since the accession of the Federal Republic of Germany in 1955, Allied governments continued to emphasise that the maintenance of a stable situation in and around Berlin remains an essential factor in East-West relations. The strict observance and full implementation of the Quadripartite Agreement of September 3, 1971 is regarded as vitally important for European security. At the end of 1981, the Council noted that the Agreement had made a decisive contribution to stabilising the Berlin situation during the ten years since its signature. Moreover, whenever opportunities occurred for dialogue and increased contacts between the Federal Republic of Germany and the German Democratic Republic, these were welcomed by the Alliance as measures which could lead to increased direct benefits for Berlin and for the people in the two German states.

---

[38] Declaration on Terrorism, issued by Foreign Ministers and Representatives of Belgium, Canada, Denmark, France, the Federal Republic of Germany, Greece, Iceland, Italy, Luxembourg, the Netherlands, Norway, Portugal, Turkey, the United Kingdom and the United States of America, December 10, 1981.

The Mediterranean

With no less attention and vigilance, the Alliance maintains a continuous review of the situation in the Mediterranean. Regular reports are made to Foreign Ministers on recent developments or significant changes in the area and consultations take place whenever the need arises. In December 1981 the Council again underlined the fact that the maintenance of adequate forces in the whole area was essential for security.

Economic Assistance within the Alliance

From the mid seventies, the Alliance has given increased recognition to the need for external assistance to be made available for the modernisation and support of the forces of those member countries economically less able to meet their commitments to the common defence. NATO governments have agreed that it is the responsibility of the Alliance as a whole to provide this assistance and regularly review the contributions made by their individual countries. Allied programmes to strengthen the economies of the less advanced or less industrialised member countries have continued in the spirit of Article 2 of the North Atlantic Treaty—an acknowledgement of the interdependence of member countries and the indivisibility of Allied security. Concern was expressed at Ministerial meetings at the end of the 1970s over the increasing severity of the economic difficulties facing Portugal and Turkey and the forthcoming need to take into account the needs of Greece in this respect. There was a need to give further momentum to the efforts to provide assistance to these countries.

Reports by the NATO Secretary General, who has responsibility for monitoring developments both with regard to the needs of the countries concerned and the measures already being taken to meet them, are regularly submitted to the Council. The latter has always recognised the continuing need to reinforce the economic basis on which Alliance cohesion and defence capabilities rest, especially at times of global economic recession when the less industrially developed nations are affected more than most. In such circumstances the need for bilateral and international support takes on even greater importance.

In his personal reports to the Council on this subject, the Secretary General drew attention to the large disparities still to be found in the standards of living of richer and less prosperous member countries and called for more assistance, especially in the defence industrial sector, to enable Greece, Portugal and Turkey to upgrade the technological capabilities of their defence industries and increase their availability for Allied procurements. The relationship between economic well-being and security has been well established and is explicitly acknowledged in the North Atlantic Treaty.

The ramifications of allied resolve to address the problem of economic difficulties in specific areas of the Alliance extend beyond the sphere of programmes directly related to defence requirements. The implementation in 1981 of the "Science for Stability" programme, under the auspices of the

NATO Science Committee, was a consequence of the need to provide not only effective assistance to Greece, Portugal and Turkey, but also a visible demonstration of allied solidarity in this crucial sphere. The programme, which is designed to strengthen the scientific and technological capabilities of these countries by means of cooperation with scientific institutions in other countries of the Alliance, is described in more detail in Chapter 20.

Poland

On October 19, 1981 Stanislav Kania was replaced by General Jaruzelski as leader of the Polish United Workers' Party and the effective leader of the country, and on December 13, 1981 martial law was declared, followed by acts of force against Polish workers, thousands of internments, harsh prison sentences and deaths. The move was widely condemned internationally. Allied governments, in a strongly-worded Declaration published at the conclusion of a special ministerial meeting of the North Atlantic Council[39] in January 1982, indicated that each government would act independently in accordance with its situation and laws, to put pressure on the Polish and Soviet authorities to live up to their international commitments. While the principal issue remained the massive violation of human rights and the suppression of fundamental freedoms, there was more at stake. The members of the Alliance urged the Polish authorities to end the state of martial law, release those arrested under its provisions, and to restore dialogue. In so doing they spelled out the implications of a failure to do so. While repression persisted, the political foundation for progress on the full agenda of issues dividing East and West was being eroded. Specific areas were identified in which allies could coordinate their political and economic actions in order to demonstrate the strength of their objections. It was made abundantly plain that respect for human rights and fundamental freedoms in Poland as elsewhere represents an indispensable component of security. Their suppression is incompatible with the objectives of the Alliance enunciated in particular in the Harmel doctrine of 1967. This recognises that a crisis cannot be excluded as long as the central political issues in Europe remain unresolved and defines it as the Alliance's task to search for progress towards a more stable East-West relationship in which solutions to such issues can be found. The events in Poland were seen by all the members of the Alliance as a blatant example of conduct by the Soviet Union and Eastern European régimes which hampered progress in East-West relations.

Accession of Spain

An event of major significance for the Alliance took place in 1982 when on May 30, Spain became the 16th member of NATO. Spain formally applied to join the Alliance on December 2, 1981 and the Protocol of Accession was signed on December 10 at the Ministerial meeting of the North Atlantic

[39] The text of the Declaration on Events in Poland is reproduced in "NATO Final Communiqués 1981-1985", published by the NATO Information Service.

Council[40]. Welcoming its most recent member, the North Atlantic Council recorded its satisfaction at this fresh sign of the enduring vitality of an Alliance between free countries, inspired by shared values of pluralistic democracy, individual liberty, human dignity, self determination and the rule of law.

Strategic Arms Reductions Talks (START)

At the May 1982 Ministerial Meeting of the Council in Luxembourg, the Allies also welcomed President Reagan's proposal to begin Strategic Arms Reductions Talks by the end of June and urged the Soviet Union to respond positively. The United States intention was to seek significant reductions in the strategic armaments of the two countries, particularly in the most destabilising systems. This was the first time that the two sides would try to negotiate significant reductions as opposed to limitations on new deployments. The negotiations began on June 30, 1982.

Force Comparisons

One of the consequences of the growing military imbalance between NATO forces available for deterrence and defence and the forces of the Warsaw Treaty Organisation was an increasing awareness among Allied governments that their publics needed to be better informed about efforts being undertaken to ensure their future security and about the challenges they faced. In particular, it had to be made clear that NATO could no longer take the view that qualitative advantages were a sufficient counterbalance to quantitative inferiority. During the previous two decades NATO had lost much of the technological advantage it had enjoyed previously and this had affected the conventional force ratio. In the nuclear field the Soviet Union had attained parity with the United States, surpassing it in some categories. From 1980 onwards, NATO governments began to pay increasing attention to the need to convey more information regarding the state of Alliance security to their publics.

In May 1982, a comparison of NATO and Warsaw Treaty forces giving the conclusions of an intensive study conducted over the previous ten months with the participation of all member countries in the integrated military structure, was issued both in Brussels and in other national capitals.

This was the first time that an authoritative NATO study of relative strengths had been made public. The comparison clearly showed the adverse trends which had developed and the growing numerical superiority of the forces of the Warsaw Treaty countries, especially in personnel, longer-range INF missile systems, submarines, aircraft and tanks, as well as the Soviet Union's marked advances in the field of technology and strongly increasing arms production capability.

The Force Comparison did not seek to be alarmist; the overall deterrent capacity of the Alliance continued to safeguard peace. However, the tables

[40] The Protocol to the North Atlantic Treaty on the accession of Spain is reproduced at Appendix I.

and explanations it contained revealed disturbing trends and focussed on the scale of the imbalances which had developed and of the task the Alliance faced in correcting them.

The Force Comparison also pointed out that in the nuclear field, the Soviet Union continued to deploy new longer-range "INF" missiles, despite the absence of any NATO missiles in this category and the fact that deployments called for under NATO's 1979 "double-track" decision were not scheduled to begin unless an agreement eliminating the need for them had still not been reached by the end of 1983.

NATO governments drew widely on this report in informing public opinion of the problems they faced in matching resources to requirements.

Afghanistan

The events which culminated in the armed intervention of the Soviet Union in Afghanistan at the end of 1979 had followed an all too familiar pattern. The Alliance had condemned the invasion from the outset and made clear its implications for East-West relations as a whole. The scale of the Afghan resistance, the core of which consisted of Mujahedin freedom fighters but also included other ethnic and tribal groups, appeared to exceed Soviet expectations. Airborne landings of some 5,000 troops took place in the last week of December 1979. By the end of January 1980, the number had risen to 40,000 and soon after reached 75,000. This figure was to rise during the next few years to 120,000. Subsequent events succeeded only in intensifying the violence and destruction created by repeated large-scale Soviet military offensives, compounding the appalling infringements of human rights by a repressive police state and generating a refugee population numbering more than 4 million. Successive attempts were made by the United Nations, backed by large majorities supporting resolutions censuring the Soviet Union, to translate international condemnation into effective international action to restore Afghanistan's independent and non-aligned status and the right of self-determination to the Afghan people. Indirect talks between Afghanistan and Pakistan eventually opened under United Nations auspices in June 1982.

Summit Meeting in Bonn—June 1982

The unity and cohesion of the Alliance, despite severe political and economic pressures, was underlined by the decision of Allied governments to meet at Summit level in Bonn in June 1982. The meeting provided an opportunity to express Allied determination to adhere to its decisions in the interests of maintaining peace and promoting future security in the context of improved East-West relations. The full catalogue of tasks and challenges posed in this situation was couched in firm but positive terms in the Bonn Declaration and its six-point progamme for Peace in Freedom, together with complementary published documents on Arms Control and Disarmament and Integrated NATO Defence. The Bonn Declaration reaffirmed the principles and objectives of the Alliance. It spelled out, in the clearest possible terms, the defensive nature of the Alliance: none of its weapons would ever be used except in response to attack. The programme it put forward called for greater restraint and responsibility on the part of the Soviet Union in order to permit a more constructive East-West relationship based on dialogue, negotiation and mutually advantageous cooperation. It underlined the importance of maintaining the defence capabilities of both the North American and European members of the Alliance and the need for better cooperation, use of resources, exploitation of emerging technologies and protection of militarily relevant technology. The programme also addressed the objectives sought by the Alliance in nuclear and conventional arms control negotiations and in the field of human rights issues and respect for the principles and provisions of the Helsinki Final Act. The Programme reflected the common view of the members of the Alliance that East-West security could not be treated in isolation and called for peaceful progress worldwide, including the removal of causes of instability such as under-development or tensions which encouraged outside interference. And lastly it set out the policies of the Alliance with regard to economic relations with the Warsaw Treaty countries and their role in the development of a stable overall East-West relationship.

Mutual and Balanced Force Reductions (MBFR)

In order to improve stability and security, remove the imbalance between NATO and Warsaw Treaty ground and air forces in the agreed area of reductions and establish approximate parity in ground and air force manpower on both sides, Western participants in MBFR sought to achieve a common ceiling of 700,000 ground force personnel and a combined such ceiling of 900,000 ground and air force personnel for each side.

The main obstacles to progress continued to be disagreement on data, i.e. the number of Eastern forces actually in place (Western figures are significantly higher than those officially acknowledged by the East); and satisfactory arrangements to ensure that agreed reductions can be verified.

In July 1980 Eastern participants had proposed that 20,000 Soviet and 13,000 United States troops should be withdrawn in the first stage of reductions. Under Phase II a mechanism would be established, prohibiting any of the direct participants from exceeding 50 % of the overall collective levels of 900,000 men on each side which Phase II would accomplish. This was taken a step further in February 1982 in a proposal which provided for Phase II reductions to 700,000 ground forces on each side and limitations of 200,000 on air forces. Difficulties in reaching prior agreement on the starting levels for reductions (the 'data problem'), on associated measures (primarily verification of reductions), and on the phasing of reductions continued to be the main obstacles to a satisfactory outcome to the negotiations.

A draft treaty was tabled in July 1982 by the Western negotiators calling for a single comprehensive agreement. The proposal, which was the result of intensive Allied consultations in Brussels, envisaged the assumption of contractual obligations on the part of all direct participants with major military formations in Central Europe to undertake ground force reductions to reach the common collective ceilings. The reductions would be accomplished in four fully verifiable stages within seven years.

In February and June 1983, Eastern negotiators were to table their own draft treaty proposals. The texts gave some welcome recognition to the importance of verification, but the solutions proposed for the verification problem still contained serious defects. On-site inspection, for example, considered crucial by the West, would be dependent on the permission of the host country. Moreover one of the major shortcomings of the Eastern draft was its continued failure to provide for prior agreement on data and therefore of reduction quotas themselves. It was again based on the assumption that the data issue could be disregarded and that both sides should simply agree to reduce their forces to 900,000 men on each side, within a period of three years. However a solution to the data problem continued to be regarded by the West as a fundamental prerequisite for an effective agreement.

The Falklands Conflict

From April 2 to June 14, 1982 the world witnessed a major armed conflict involving a member country of NATO resisting aggression against its territory in the South Atlantic over 12,000 kilometres away from its own frontiers. The Alliance itself was not involved since the conflict caused by the invasion of the Falkland Islands by Argentina took place well outside the area covered by the North Atlantic Treaty. Although the British ownership of these islands had long been contested by the Argentinian government, the government of the United Kingdom had insisted that the principle of self determination must be upheld no less forcefully for a small group of islands than in any other case. The invasion of the islands was therefore widely seen as an act of aggression which had to be met by a measured but firm response.

In a statement included in the communiqué issued at the end of the May 1982 Ministerial meeting of the North Atlantic Council, the Allies "condemned Argentina for its aggression against the Falkland Islands and Dependencies and deplored the fact that it had still not withdrawn its forces in compliance with Mandatory Resolution 502 of the United Nations Security Council". Calling for efforts to achieve a negotiated settlement to continue, the Allies made it clear that they attached fundamental importance to the principle that the use of force to resolve international disputes should be resolutely opposed by the international community.

During the the Falklands crisis, consultations took place in NATO, as prescribed by the Treaty, over the implications for the security of the North Atlantic area of the non-availability of units of the United Kingdom armed forces which in a crisis would form part of the forces assigned to the Alliance.

Rapid Reinforcement

In December 1982 Defence Ministers endorsed SACEUR's Rapid Reinforcement Plan for Europe which postulates the combined use of shipping and civil aviation to lift in reinforcements of troops and equipment to Europe early in a crisis. By facilitating the rapid and coordinated deployment of large numbers of United States, United Kingdom and Canadian reinforcements in times of tension and hostilities, and by ensuring that any aggression against NATO territory would thus be met with the full force of Allied resolve and political solidarity—including tangible evidence of Allied reinforcement capability and rapid response—the plan served to strengthen overall deterrence.

Progress of negotiations on intermediate-range nuclear forces

In February 1982 the United States rejected an inadequate proposal by General Secretary Brezhnev for a two-thirds cut in United States and Soviet arsenals of intermediate-range nuclear weapons deployed in Europe to be achieved by 1990. At the meeting of the Nuclear Planning Group in Colorado Springs in March, Defence Ministers reiterated their full support for the US position.

By March 1982 the Soviet Union had announced a unilateral moratorium on INF deployments. New SS-20 missile sites were nevertheless completed and brought into operation and the construction of new sites in the Asian part of the USSR (from which missiles can reach NATO territory) began. A much publicised event took place three months later when the US and Soviet chief negotiators developed an informal proposal which they agreed to submit to their governments. Known as the "Walk in the Woods" proposal of June 1982, this involved equal levels of INF missile launchers in Europe, cancelling deployment of Pershing II missiles and freezing Soviet SS-20 deployments in Asia at the level at which they then stood. The proposal was rejected.

Six months later proposals were made by the Soviet negotiators involving the limitation of the level of Soviet INF missiles to that of British and French missiles combined and the cancellation of all planned US deployments. The agreement would have no effect on Soviet deployments in Asia, which could continue unrestrained. These proposals were firmly rejected by the United States with the full support of its NATO allies on three specific grounds: first, the negotiations were on a bilateral basis: they could not involve the independent nuclear forces of other countries; second, to include such forces would be to accord the Soviet Union the right to maintain nuclear forces equal to those of all other powers combined—a notion tantamount to a Soviet demand for global military superiority and political hegemony; and third, Soviet deployments of the mobile SS-20 in Asia posed a threat to NATO countries, could be easily moved westwards to pose a still larger threat, and already represented an unacceptable threat to allies of the United States in Asia, primarily Japan. 1982 came to an end with little sign that the gap between the two parties to the negotiations would diminish.

United States INF initiatives

On January 31, 1983, in an open letter to the Soviet leadership, President Reagan proposed a meeting between himself and General Secretary Andropov to sign an agreement banning United States and Soviet land-based INF missiles "from the face of the earth". The proposal offered major advantages in terms of verification problems (the scale of which would be much reduced in the case of a total ban): strategic difficulties posed by residual Soviet INF missiles facing Asia (which would be removed in the case of a world-wide ban); and reassurances which would otherwise be needed with regard to mobility (the SS-20, as a highly mobile missile, could be redeployed rapidly from positions beyond the limits of a treaty concerned only with the European part of the USSR).

The criteria for reaching an agreement with the Soviet Union on intermediate-range nuclear forces remained those which had been established in consultation with the other members of the Alliance in November 1981. They included:

— Equality of rights and limits between the United States and the USSR.
— Exclusion of independent third country (i.e. British and French) nuclear deterrent forces from any agreement.
— The application of limits to be agreed on a global basis. (No transfer of Soviet longer-range INF missiles from the European to the Asian part of the USSR would be permitted).
— The agreement should not weaken NATO's conventional deterrent forces.
— The agreement must be subject to effective verification.

As a means of moving the negotiations forward, the United States formally presented a proposal for an interim agreement in March 1983, accepting equal global levels of US and Soviet warheads on INF missile launchers—preferably at zero levels, but failing that at the lowest level acceptable to the Soviet Union.

The proposal was rejected. Although the Soviet leader indicated willingness to count INF warheads as well as launchers in the Geneva INF talks, statements by Foreign Minister Gromyko and by General Secretary Andropov continued to proclaim not only that no US INF deployments must take place, but also that Soviet deployments in the European part of the USSR to be permitted under the treaty must be tied to British and French strategic systems, and deployments in the Asian part of the USSR, despite their mobility and the threat they posed to Asian and European countries alike, could not be taken into account.

Little headway was made during the following months, although a draft treaty was tabled by the United States negotiators, after discussion within the Alliance, on March 29, 1983. This involved the reduction of NATO's planned deployments to a level between zero and 572 (the total number of missiles planned) and Soviet reductions to an equal level. Nations concerned supported this position at the Paris Ministerial meeting in June, and undertook to examine NATO's LRINF requirements and make appropriate adjustments in the levels of deployments needed once concrete results had been achieved. New elements were added in September, when the United States offered to offset Soviet global INF deployments by reducing its own deployments in Europe but retaining the right to reach an equal global ceiling by deployments elsewhere. The United States also offered to consider proposals involving land-based aircraft. The United States President, in a speech to the United Nations General Assembly on September 26, 1983, explained these proposals and urged the Soviet Union to make a positive response. When the latter came in October, it was essentially a reiteration of earlier Soviet positions unacceptable to the Alliance, linking Soviet deployments to British and French forces, freezing existing Soviet deployments in the Asian USSR but denying the right of Asian deployments to the United States. However, small advances were being made—the proposal to freeze deployments in Asia, while unacceptable, did appear to concede the need to deal with the issue of INF missiles on a global basis.

Public Opinion

The impact of public opinion on Alliance policies was making itself felt increasingly during this period in a number of significant ways and nowhere more markedly than in the context of the 1979 double-track decision. Although public support for the Alliance as a whole and for the overall policies of the Alliance remained at a high level, as numerous studies and polls revealed, the specific issue of the need, in the event of a failure of arms control negotiations, for a modernisation of NATO's nuclear forces involving new deployments of intermediate-range forces in six European basing countries, gave rise to an intense, heated and prolonged public debate. In the United Kingdom this coincided with a similar controversy on the modernisation of the United Kingdom's independent strategic nuclear forces involving the acquisition of the United States Trident system to replace Polaris.

The public impact of the INF deployment issue revealed more clearly than in the past that more adequate explanations backed by detailed information had to be provided regarding the role of nuclear weapons in Alliance policies. While they had long represented an integral and essential part of a deterrent strategy designed to make war of all kinds, nuclear or conventional, less likely, and involved the maintenance of the minimum level of forces required to implement the strategy of flexible response against any future aggression, they were not seen by some sectors of public opinion as defensive and deterrent in effect. Many misperceptions persisted regarding their deterrent role.

The vast majority of the public in NATO countries nevertheless demonstrated through their voting behaviour that they accepted the view adopted by successive member governments of NATO, that decisions on security matters must continue to be made on the basis of a realistic assessment of the military capabilities of the Soviet Union and other Warsaw Treaty countries, combined with their record of international behaviour and declared ideological aspirations, and not on the basis of declarations of intentions which could be subject to change.

The debate on nuclear issues between 1980 and 1983 was on a scale which had not been heard for many years. The period saw the growth of the campaign for nuclear disarmament and a proliferation of protest groupings and demonstrations in several countries, attracting massive media coverage and commanding international public attention. The countries most directly affected were those where missile deployments were scheduled to begin at the end of 1983—Belgium, the Federal Republic of Germany, the Netherlands, the United Kingdom and to a lesser extent, Italy. The campaign offered opportunities to the Soviet Union to encourage opposition to the policies to which NATO governments were committed and in so doing to undermine the solidarity of the Alliance.

Within the Alliance, the wide-ranging debate which began in the early 1980s had numerous strands to it. It involved a series of key issues, including many which had long been preoccupations of Allied governments as well as a number of more recent concerns: the equitable sharing of the burden of defence between members of the Alliance and especially between the European and the North American countries; the strengthening of the European pillar of the Alliance; conventional defence improvements; better coordination of armaments and defence planning procedures; the scope for introducing measures to build confidence between East and West; problems of reinforcement; issues posed by events affecting the Alliance taking place outside the Treaty area; and the role of defence and space systems, particularly in the context of the United States Strategic Defence Initiative (SDI). While all these subjects amply filled the agenda of the Alliance throughout this period, the SDI research programme which had been announced by President Reagan in March 1983, dominated much of the debate.

In December 1982, Defence Ministers welcomed the growing debate in the West about how best to preserve peace with freedom over the coming years. They acknowledged the responsibility of democratic governments to ensure that the debate is carried forward in full recognition of the facts. And they emphasised that fundamental to any such discussion must be recognition both of the defensive nature of the Alliance and, equally, of the need for strong, modern and effective forces, if peace is to be preserved.

The United States Strategic Defence Initiative (SDI)

The question of national and international security figured strongly in the United States Presidential elections in 1981 and policies introduced by the new administration in its first two years in office focussed strongly on the need to modernise United States forces and improve their readiness. The significant efforts by the United States to strengthen US defence capability in the interests of the Atlantic Alliance as a whole were welcomed by NATO Defence Ministers.

In March 1983 the major new element which had been added to the strategy debate was the announcement by President Reagan of the United States Strategic Defence Initiative. In a speech on national security, delivered to the nation on March 23, President Reagan raised the question of whether an alternative could be found to strategic offence as a means of preserving deterrence and preventing war. His speech concentrated on two aspects of this question: first, the theoretical possibilities of moving away, in the longer term, from a basis for deterrence which depended on a threat to human life as a means of preserving peace; and second, in the shorter term, the practical measures which could be taken towards this end, through a research programme, to assess the potential of a number of principally non-nuclear technologies which might offer an effective defence against ballistic missiles. A comprehensive and intensive effort was to be made by the United States to define a long-term research and development programme towards this end.

The potentially far-reaching implications of the Strategic Defence Initiative (SDI) became a major focus of discussion and consultation within the Alliance. The initiative met with particularly strong opposition from the Soviet Union, which made repeated efforts to make cancellation of the programme a condition for progress in arms control negotiations. Concern was also expressed both in the United States and in other Alliance countries over the implications of SDI. Following consultations within the Nuclear Planning Group, Defence Ministers agreed that the research programme being conducted by the United States, the aim of which is to enhance stability and deterrence at reduced levels of offensive nuclear forces, was in NATO's security interest and they expressed the view that it should continue. In view of the Soviet Union's extensive efforts in the strategic defence field dating back to the 1960s, and continuing Soviet deployment, improvement and research programmes relating to ballistic missile defence, the United States programme represented a prudent step. The United States gave firm assurances that full consultation with its Allies with regard to SDI would continue.

Poland

Repeatedly, when the North Atlantic Council met in Bonn in June 1982, in Paris a year later, and again in Brussels in December 1983, Allied governments reaffirmed their concerns over the situation in Poland calling for a complete end to the threat of the use of force by the Soviet Union in Poland and elsewhere. Events in Afghanistan had been a sobering reminder that the threat was a real one and that ultimately the Soviet Union was still willing to resort to the use of force beyond its own frontiers. It was clear that this created serious obstacles to the normal development of relations. At the Bonn meeting, the Allies re-emphasised their own commitment to supporting genuine non-alignment and development of Third World countries and called upon all states to refrain from exploiting these nations' economic and social problems for political gain.

In July 1983 martial law was lifted and amnesty granted for most political detainees in Poland. However, this positive development was marred by the simultaneous introduction of new legislation which reinforced government controls. The Allies called on the Polish authorities to respect the aspirations of the people for reform and to abide by their commitments. They emphasised their readiness to respond to steps which created opportunities for constructive political and economic relations.

Madrid CSCE Follow-up Meeting

The CSCE Follow-Up meeting in Madrid, which had begun in November 1980, was the second such meeting to take place since the signature of the Helsinki Final Act. New proposals for strengthening the CSCE process included a French initiative for a Conference on Disarmament in Europe (CDE) aimed at achieving in an initial phase an agreement on a coherent set of militarily significant, binding and verifiable confidence-building measures applicable throughout the European continent. The Allies had reaffirmed their support for this proposal at the May 1981 Council meeting in Rome. Events in Poland after the declaration of martial law in December 1981 focused attention on new violations of the Final Act in Eastern Europe and inhibited business as usual in Madrid. Nonetheless agreement was finally reached on September 9, 1983 on a balanced concluding document including a mandate for a Conference on Confidence and Security-Building Measures and Disarmament in Europe (CDE) to take place in Stockholm in 1984. The concluding document reflected progress in important areas such as trade union rights, religious freedoms, the dissemination of information and the problem of terrorism, and provided for a series of additional meetings to be held on the peaceful settlement of disputes, Mediterranean cooperation, human rights and human contacts and, finally, for a further follow-up meeting to be held in Vienna in November 1986.

Close consultation and coordination among the members of the Alliance, throughout the three years of negotiations in Madrid, contributed decisively to a common Western approach often shared by neutral and non-aligned participants. The provisions for further negotiations agreed upon at Madrid underline the continuing importance of the CSCE process and the firm resolve of Western participants to stand by their commitment to defend the principles of the Final Act.

The Montebello Decision—October 1983

At the meeting of NPG Defence Ministers in Montebello in October 1983, further important decisions were taken, involving, on the one hand, the withdrawal of 1,400 more US nuclear warheads from Europe in addition to the 1,000 warheads withdrawn as a consequence of the 1979 "double track" decision; and on the other, a range of possible improvements which would be needed to ensure that the remaining minimum level stockpile would continue to make an effective contribution to deterrence. The new reduction brought the total number of warheads to be removed from Europe since 1979 to 2,400. LRINF deployments would not affect the reduction since the deployment decision stipulated that one warhead would be removed for each Pershing II or ground-launched cruise missile warhead introduced. This was a decision which accorded with the agreement reached by the countries concerned to maintain NATO's nuclear capability at the lowest level consistent with security and deterrence.

The Montebello Decision was based on analysis undertaken within the Alliance since 1977, aimed at ensuring that NATO's nuclear forces were held to the minimum level necessary for deterrence, taking into account developments in Soviet nuclear and conventional forces. Its impact was to reduce NATO's nuclear stockpile to the lowest level in over 20 years. Part and parcel of this decision was the instruction to the responsible military authorities to determine in accordance with the general framework established at Montebello, the precise composition of NATO's remaining nuclear stockpile and to work out and implement a programme for this purpose over a period of five to six years. Proposals were presented by the Supreme Allied Commander Europe at the Luxembourg meeting of the Nuclear Planning Group in March 1985 for improving the responsiveness, effectiveness and survivability of the remaining forces, as one of the consequences of the decision.

Implementation of the 1979 Double-Track Decision

This period reached a decisive point at the end of 1983, when implementation of the NATO countries' decision to deploy Cruise and Pershing missiles began, in accordance with the 1979 decision. It had not been possible to reach agreement with the Soviet Union on measures which would render such deployments unnecessary. On November 23, 1983 deliveries of the first ground-launched cruise missile components began in the United Kingdom and the Federal Republic of Germany. Shortly afterwards, the Soviet Union broke off the Geneva INF negotiations. In May 1984, with negotiations suspended, the Soviet Defence Ministry announced that it was deploying additional missile complexes in the German Democratic Republic. The United States announced that it was willing to resume talks without preconditions whenever the Soviet Union was willing to return. However, until January 1985 formal negotiations were to remain suspended.

On December 8, the US-Soviet strategic arms reduction talks in Geneva also ended with the Soviet delegation refusing to set a date for their resumption. And on December 15, the MBFR negotiations were similarly broken off. By the end of 1983, the Soviet Union had thus walked out of the three main negotiating fora with no apparent intention of returning.

Declaration of Brussels—December 1983

At the end of year Ministerial meeting of the Council, Foreign Ministers issued a Declaration (Appendix I) extending to the Soviet Union and the Warsaw Treaty countries the offer to work together with the members of the Alliance to bring about a long-term constructive and realistic relationship based on equilibrium, moderation and reciprocity. For the benefit of mankind, they advocated an open, comprehensive political dialogue as well as cooperation based on mutual advantage.

The Declaration of Brussels appealed to the Soviet Union for mutual respect for legitimate security interests, and repeated the commitment that none of NATO's weapons will ever be used except in response to attack. It also emphasised that NATO nations remained determined to ensure their own security on the basis of a balance of forces at the lowest possible levels. As far as intermediate-range nuclear forces were concerned, the Allies declared that NATO INF deployments could be halted or reversed by concrete results at the negotiating table but in the meantime would go forward. Denmark and Greece reserved their position on the relevant paragraph of the Declaration, as did Spain, which had not been a party to the 1979 double-track decision.

Washington Statement on East-West Relations—May 1984

At the December 1983 meeting of the Ministers of Foreign Affairs of the member countries of the Alliance, on the initative of the Foreign Minister of Belgium, it had been decided that the Council should undertake a thorough appraisal of East-West relations with a view to achieving a more constructive East-West dialogue. The resulting report provided the basis for the Washington Statement on East-West Relations (see Appendix I), issued at the Spring 1984 Ministerial meeting of the Council. The Statement was both a reaffirmation and a blueprint for the construction of a more mutually beneficial future relationship. The Alliance renewed its offers to the Soviet Union to work together to bring about improvements. The Statement emphasized that peace and stability called for a united effort and looked to the Soviet Union and the other Warsaw Treaty countries to join in an endeavour which would be of benefit to the world at large. The Allies were ready to examine any reasonable proposal. The Statement outlined the steps such an endeavour would require and the obstacles which continued to thwart progress, including the relentless Soviet campaign to breach the solidarity of the Alliance and to exploit any apparent weakness it perceived on the part of the Alliance.

The Allies indicated that they were fully committed to working for genuine detente with the Soviet Union and the countries of Eastern Europe, while maintaining effective defence and firm political resolve. Their Statement refuted the notion that confrontation between the social systems of East and West is inescapable, indicating that although neither side must seek unilateral advantage, military superiority or dominance over other states, there can be mutual respect for each other's security on the basis of equality of rights, non-use of force, restraint and respect for international rules of conduct—the prerequisites for strengthening confidence and building cooperation.

Poland

By the time the Council met in Washington in May 1984, there were few signs that the Polish situation was improving—in fact the trend was in the other direction; the number of political prisoners was again increasing in an atmosphere of unremitting repression. In late October 1984, the popular

LORD CARRINGTON (1984-1988)

Born in 1919, Lord Carrington was educated in the United Kingdom at Eton and the Royal Military College of Sandhurst. In 1946 he began to take an active part in the work of Parliament, and in 1951 became a Parliamentary Secretary at the Ministry of Agriculture. In 1954 he became Parliamentary Secretary to the Minister of Defence.

In 1956 Lord Carrington was appointed United Kingdom High Commissioner in Australia. In 1959 he returned to the United Kingdom, where he was appointed First Lord of the Admiralty and a Privy Counsellor, and in 1962 became Assistant Deputy Leader of the House of Lords. In the 1970 Conservative Government he was appointed Secretary of State for Defence, and subsequently Secretary of State for Energy. Between 1972 and 1974 he was Chairman of the Conservative Party. In May 1979 Lord Carrington was appointed Secretary of State for Foreign and Commonwealth Affairs and was Chairman of the Lancaster House Conference, which led to the solution of the Rhodesian problem and the creation of the independent Republic of Zimbabwe in 1981. He resigned in 1982 at the time of the Falklands crisis. In 1983 he became Chairman of the General Electric Company, a post which he held until his appointment to NATO in June 1984. In July 1988 Lord Carrington was succeeded as Secretary General of NATO by Manfred Wörner.

Figure 7

Polish priest, Father Popieluszko, was murdered by state police, and the subsequent trial and imprisonment of those responsible, highlighted the lengths to which the servants of the state had been prepared to go in order to deny the voice of the Polish people the right to be heard. Allied governments reinforced their bilateral and diplomatic initiatives to persuade the Soviet Union and the Polish authorities to permit genuine dialogue between the various elements of Polish society through joint statements made whenever the Atlantic Council met. They underlined the impact of strained relations caused by situations such as that in Poland on the policies of the Alliance as a whole. Full implementation of all the provisions of the CSCE process and the Helsinki Final Act, in particular in the field of human rights and contacts, remains a fundamental objective of the Alliance; Poland a forceful reminder that there was a long way to go before the objective could be fulfilled. Subsequently, against the background of the wide-ranging reform programmes associated with Mr. Gorbachev, there were grounds for cautious optimism with regard to Poland's future. However, the gulf between the government and the various sectors of Polish society, including the Church and Solidarity, remained very wide.

Force Comparisons

The publication of an official, detailed comparison of NATO and the Warsaw Treaty Organisation's forces in May 1982 had gone some way towards sensitising parliaments and public opinion to the imbalances which exist in key areas of Alliance defence capacity. The exercise was repeated in June 1984 when a second edition of the Force Comparison report was issued.

The 1984 comparison of NATO forces and those of the Warsaw Treaty Organisation demonstrated that the disparities with which NATO had lived for many years continued to exist. However, it also drew attention to the fact that without seeking or wishing to match capabilities man for man or weapon for weapon, the Alliance would have to respond to the persistent and steady growth of the Warsaw Treaty Organisation's military capability if NATO's deterrent capability was to preserve its effectiveness. The comparison differed in some respects from the 1982 publication in terms of presentation as well as substance, introducing inter alia a distinction between forces immediately or rapidly available and those which, because of their lower state of readiness or their location, would only be available over a longer time-frame, as reinforcements. The publication served to highlight the fact that regardless of imbalances in readily available forces, the ratios worsened considerably for NATO under conditions of full reinforcement on both sides.

At a period when negotiations in Geneva had been broken off by the Soviet Union, the Force Comparison also underlined the continuing disparity in intermediate-range nuclear forces and the progress of the NATO deployments in this category which had begun at the end of 1983 in accordance with the 1979 double-track decision.

Retirement of Joseph Luns—appointment of Lord Carrington

When the Council met in Washington in May 1984, Foreign Ministers paid tribute to the departing Secretary General of NATO, Dr.Joseph Luns, who was retiring after devoting a major portion of his professional life to upholding Western security through the Alliance. Ministers expressed their appreciation for Dr.Luns' services to the Alliance and to the cause of peace and freedom. During 13 years as Secretary General, Dr.Luns made uniquely important contributions to cooperation among individual Allies and to the cause of Allied unity.

In December 1983, the Council had announced the appointment of Lord Carrington, formerly Minister of Defence and later Secretary of State for Foreign Affairs of the United Kingdom, to succeed Dr. Luns. Lord Carrington took up his appointment as Secretary General of NATO on June 25, 1984.

Further aspects of flexible response

In November 1984, NATO's Defence Planning Committee approved a document entitled "Long Term Planning Guideline for Follow-on Forces Attack". Known as "FOFA", this document, prepared by the Supreme Allied Commander Europe and approved by NATO's Military Committee, was part of the process aimed at restoring full flexibility to the strategy of flexible response and forward defence by enhancing the effectiveness of its conventional component. Studies undertaken in the preceding years had recognised that numerical imbalances between NATO and Warsaw Treaty conventional forces could mean that, if deterrence were to fail and aggression against NATO countries were to take place, the first wave of attacking forces could be rapidly followed by repeated waves of so-called "follow-on" or "second echelon" forces. The aim of "FOFA" is to ensure that NATO has the capacity to move rapidly by conventional means against such follow-on forces to prevent them from securing their military objectives before NATO could either organise its own reinforcements, or take the decision through consultations to respond by other means. Forward defence has long been an integral part of NATO's strategy, the overall objective being to convince a potential aggressor that military victory in Europe could not be gained easily and that it would carry a high cost. Effective deterrence requires the potential aggressor to realise that his own territory would be at reciprocal risk and that his forces would not have a safe sanctuary away from the territory which he had chosen to attack.

Improvements sought through the "FOFA" concept draw on emerging technologies in a number of spheres and include systems for improved target acquisition, more timely processing of information and more effective engagement of fixed and mobile targets at extended ranges beyond troops in contact. FOFA capabilities therefore contribute significantly to the effectiveness of deterrence.

Sometimes confused with the "Follow-on Forces Attack" guideline is the United States army "Air-land Battle" concept. This national concept describes how commanders should deploy forces in a way which would enable them to draw on all the military means at their disposal in an integrated manner in order to perform the tasks required of them. The doctrine bears some similarities to the NATO Follow-on Forces Attack (FOFA) concept in that it addresses inter alia the effective use of conventional means to provide defence against a second or "follow-on" wave of attacking forces. NATO's "FOFA" concept has been developed and adopted as a basis for long-term collective planning to guide priorities in the development and procurement of armaments suitable for implementing the concept. The United States concept of Air-land Battle primarily addresses operational aspects of force employment.

Alliance maritime planning has, since 1981, been based on an agreed concept of maritime operations which provides for implementation at sea of the general concept of deterrence in peace and forward defence and flexible response in war. This includes the three basic operational concepts of: containment, to prevent Soviet fleets from reaching the open sea; defence in depth, including readiness to engage Soviet naval forces wherever necessary from their home ports to Allied lines of communication at sea; and maintaining the initiative, in order to speedily and decisively meet any threat posed to NATO's interests wherever it might occur.

Strategic Defence

Discussion of the implications of the US Strategic Defence Initiative continued throughout this period. Within the Alliance regular consultations took place on the different aspects of the SDI research programme, particularly on its implications for the 1972 Anti-Ballistic Missile (ABM) Treaty, and on its wider political and strategic implications.

Some of the principal questions raised by European member countries of the Alliance during the process of initial consultations on the Strategic Defence Initiative were clarified in a four-point agreement which emerged from discussions between the United Kingdom and the United States in December 1984. First, the United States and Western aim is not to achieve superiority but to maintain balance, taking account of Soviet developments; second, SDI-related deployment, in view of treaty obligations, would be a matter for negotiation with the Soviet Union; third, the overall aim is to enhance and not to undermine deterrence; fourth, East-West negotiations should aim to achieve security with reduced levels of offensive weapons on both sides. The United States has given assurances that deployment decisions would indeed be taken only after the technologies have been fully explored and the feasibility of the concepts proven, and then only after full consultation with its allies and discussions with the Soviet Union on the implications of deployment of defensive systems.

The extent of Soviet opposition to SDI, which took numerous different forms, was most apparent during the course of the Geneva discussions between the United States Secretary of State and the Soviet Foreign Minister in December 1984, when agreement was reached to resume nuclear arms control talks, encompassing defence and space systems. Soviet readiness to return to the negotiating table after an interval of two years could be attributed both to the failure of its attempts to prevent the implementation of NATO's INF deployment decision and to its determination to make progress in strategic nuclear and intermediate-range nuclear arms control conditional upon United States willingness to abandon SDI. The United States continued to reaffirm that its research programme is not negotiable.

In March 1985, Defence Ministers meeting in NATO's Nuclear Planning Group in Luxembourg, endorsed the aim of enhancing stability and deterrence at reduced levels of offensive nuclear forces and agreed that the United States research into strategic defence conducted within the terms of the 1972 ABM Treaty was in NATO's security interests and should continue. They welcomed the invitation to its allies by the United States to consider participation in the research programme. Memoranda of Understanding have since been signed and arrangements made with companies and institutions in several allied countries for information exchange and participation in different aspects of relevant research.

The United States announcement of its strategic defence initiative in 1983 opened up an important and far-reaching discussion not only of American but also of Soviet programmes and research activities in this field. The picture which emerged was seen to be at variance with the impression created, inter alia by vociferous Soviet opposition to President Reagan's initiative, that the United States programme was unique. The Soviet Union has in fact been actively researching in this field since the 1960s and already has in place both an ABM system of interceptor missiles and radars around Moscow, allowed under the terms of the ABM Treaty, and an operational anti-satellite system not yet covered by any arms control agreement. The Soviet Union has also been constructing for several years a Large Phased-Array Radar (LPAR) near Krasnoyarsk in Siberia which appears primarily designed for ballistic missile detection and tracking. Because of its location and orientation, the United States considers the Krasnoyarsk radar a serious violation of the ABM Treaty.

Conference on Confidence and Security-Building Measures and Disarmament in Europe (CDE)

The Conference on Confidence and Security-Building Measures and Disarmament in Europe, which opened in Stockholm on January 17, 1984 with the same 35 nation membership as its parent body, the Conference on Security and Cooperation in Europe (CSCE), marked a new stage in the CSCE process. Its mandate, given by the Madrid CSCE Follow-up Meeting, was to extend the scope of the security obligations under the 1975 Helsinki Final Act and thus reduce still further the risk of war arising from miscalculation or misinterpretation and the risk of surprise attack. This was to be achieved by concluding concrete, politically binding, military significant and verifiable agreements covering the whole of Europe from the Atlantic to the Urals.

The CDE was seen as an opportunity for creating the increased openness and mutual trust which could lead to progress in disarmament and thereby enhance security.

Progress towards a comprehensive strategy for resources

Recognition by Allied Governments of the gravity of the eonomic problems facing their countries has heightened awareness of the need to reinforce the economic basis on which Alliance cohesion and defence capabilities rest. Many of the initiatives set in train to address this problem have been brought into sharper focus as economic constraints have become more severe. One field which offers scope for a concerted effort within the Alliance is that of resource development and allocation.

At the December 1983 meeting of Defence Ministers, strong emphasis was placed on the importance of making the most effective use of available resources and of exploiting NATO's technological strength through coordinated efforts to make progress in seven specific areas, i.e.

— cooperation and coordination in defence planning and in research, development and production;
— improved coordination of infrastructure planning to bring support facilities more into line with the projected needs of NATO forces, at the same time as providing an appropriate level of funding to ensure their operational effectiveness;
— a more effective and balanced framework of transatlantic cooperation;
— greater emphasis on the potential offered by technologies, available or emerging, to make substantial and yet affordable improvements in the conventional defence of the Alliance particuarly within the context of the two-way street;
— the establishment of priorities based on the application of rigorous criteria of military value and cost effectiveness;
— adequate use of the industrial capabilities of member countries in the field of defence equipment;
— effective steps to restrict the transfer of militarily relevant technology to the Soviet Union and Warsaw Treaty countries.

When the Defence Planning Committee met in Ministerial Session the following Spring, Ministers had reviewed progress made towards a more comprehensive conceptual military framework within which NATO strategy could be implemented, together with closely related work to improve coordination of defence planning. The contribution these developments could make towards a comprehensive resource strategy was strongly underlined.

A year later, in December 1984, a full statement on resource guidance was published by Defence Ministers in conjunction with the communiqué issued at the conclusion of their meeting. The statement included strong emphasis on the urgency of devising appropriate methodology for measuring output performance for use in supplementary ministerial resource guidance. This marked a further stage in efforts being made within the Alliance to pull together all the various elements needed to facilitate the progress called for in the field of conventional deterrence. The agreement of specific resource guidance provided an additional valuable instrument for use by national authorities in planning their defence efforts.

Infrastructure funding

Upon NATO's Infrastructure programme, described in detail in Chapter 12, depends the ability of the Alliance to sustain its forces both in peacetime and in carrying out their tasks if deterrence were to fail. By December 1984 Defence Ministers were confronted with increasingly pressing needs to provide additional infrastructure resources for a large range of programmes. High on the list of priorities was the need for special provision to be made for programmes concerned with support for tactical air reinforcements for Allied Command Europe. The resulting decision to allocate 3,000 million Infrastructure Accounting Units (IAU)[41] for the next six-year period, more than double the funding agreed for the previous period, represented an important step forward.

Nuclear and Space Talks

June 1984 had brought the first indications that the Soviet Union was willing to resume negotiations when proposals were made for talks to prevent the militarisation of outer space. A few months later, in a speech to the 39th Session of the United Nations General Assembly, the Soviet Foreign Minister repeated many of the declaratory proposals listed in previous Soviet speeches on arms control and disarmament in an address which also suggested Soviet willingness to resume negotiations. Mr.Gromyko stated that his country was prepared for serious talks with the United States and was in favour of reductions of all types of nuclear weapons and of their subsequent global elimination. However, emphasis was again placed on a freeze as a first step, a measure which the West could not accept as this would freeze imbalances and did not offer adequate safeguards for Western deterrence.

Arrangements for Nuclear and Space Talks, announced by President Reagan on November 24, 1984, were agreed at a meeting between the United States Secretary of State and the Soviet Foreign Minister in Geneva on January 7-8, 1985. The talks, welcomed by NATO Foreign and Defence Ministers at their 1984 end of year meetings, were to cover strategic nuclear arms reduction (START), intermediate-range nuclear forces (INF) and defence and space issues. Their aim would be to work out effective agreements "preventing an arms race in space and terminating it on earth". The United States expressed its objectives as a search for radical reductions in the number and destructive power of offensive strategic arms; the elimination of longer-range INF or their reduction to the lowest possible equal global limits; and a discussion of the possibility of both sides moving away from deterrence based on the threat of nuclear retaliation toward

[41] 3,000 million IAUs equals approx. US$ 10,302 million at current (December 1989) rates.

increased reliance on non-threatening defences, whether ground or space based, against nuclear ballistic missiles. When talks got under way on March 12, both sides reiterated their previous negotiating positions on intermediate-range nuclear forces. Despite Soviet proposals for a bilateral moratorium on INF deployments and its announcement of a unilateral moratorium on European deployments until November 1985, deployments continued in the Soviet Union at sites already under construction. From the United States side any outcome which would achieve equal global limits was declared acceptable.

New leadership in the USSR

On March 11, 1985, the death of General Secretary Chernenko brought about a significant change of style in the leadership of the Soviet Union. Mikhail Gorbachev was named as his successor, and four months later the veteran Soviet Foreign Minister, Andrei Gromyko, became President of the Supreme Soviet of the USSR, a position he was to hold until November 1988 when the Presidency passed to Mikhail Gorbachev himself.

Ministerial meeting in Lisbon—June 1985

The Lisbon Ministerial meeting of the North Atlantic Council provided an opportunity for the Alliance to reaffirm the principles of the Statement on East-West Relations issued at Washington the previous year, together with its endorsement of the approach adopted by the United States in its bilateral negotiations with the Soviet Union. As on all such occasions, Foreign Ministers reviewed the status of East-West relations as a whole, including progress in the Vienna MBFR negotiations, the Stockholm CDE Conference and the Geneva Conference on Disarmament, and examined a number of crucial internal Alliance issues. In the former category, questions of terrorism, efforts to achieve progress in inner-German relations of benefit to confidence in Europe, to the German people and to the Berliners, East-West trade, concern over Afghanistan, Poland and other events outside the Treaty area, continued to figure very high in the list of problems. In the latter category, progress towards improved armaments cooperation, conventional defence improvements, economic assistance and cooperation, objectives of the NATO Science Programme and Civil Emergency Planning dominated the agenda.

Planning for the use and mobilisation of civil resources and infrastructure is an essential element of the overall deterrent and defensive concept of NATO. Its aim is to ensure support for the defence effort and support and protection for the civil population in the event of crisis or war. It is a national responsibility, but like many other aspects of Allied preparedness, calls for maximum cooperation between capitals and at NATO level. On the basis of a Report presented to them at the Lisbon meeting, Foreign Ministers issued guidance for all future Civil Emergency Planning activities within the Alliance for the period 1985-1989.

Arms Control

Some movement seemed possible in arms control negotiations in October 1985, with the announcement by General Secretary Gorbachev of elements of a counter proposal for an interim agreement involving a bilateral freeze on INF deployments and the "deepest possible" reductions thereafter. The agreement would not be linked to strategic and space defence issues. He also indicated that the Soviet SS-4 missile was being phased out and some SS-20s removed from combat status. However, Soviet insistence on linking INF nuclear force reductions to French and British systems, which had been rejected by both countries for reasons given earlier, reappeared in the form of a proposal made by Mr. Gorbachev, during his visit to Paris, that there should be a dialogue with France and Britain on medium-range nuclear weapons, in the framework of the European balance.

At the beginning of November the United States responded to these developments, building on the positive aspects of Soviet proposals and in particular on the prospect of achieving an INF agreement independent of progress in strategic or defence and space-related negotiations. Its proposal included interim limitations on missile launchers to levels provided for in NATO's planned deployments and agreed levels for warheads within that limit; proportional reductions of SS-20 launchers in Asia, and constraints on shorter-range INF (SRINF). The United States proposal included detailed conditions for agreement on strategic nuclear arms reductions and space and defence issues. By the time President Reagan and Mr. Gorbachev met at the Geneva Summit on November 21, 1985, hopes were again much higher. In a joint statement they agreed to commit their two countries to early progress at the Geneva negotiations and to focus on areas where there was common ground. A special meeting of the North Atlantic Council took place immediately afterwards, at which President Reagan reported to NATO Heads of State and Government and Foreign Ministers on the outcome of the summit.

The Summit was followed by new proposals by the Soviet leader in the form of a letter to President Reagan reiterating some of the same unacceptable conditions, but also enlarging the concept of nuclear arms control negotiations to embrace a complete elimination of nuclear weapons within a 15 year period and elimination of US and Soviet LRINF missiles in Europe within five to eight years.

The United States responded cautiously, bearing in mind conventional imbalances and the crucial role played by nuclear forces in NATO's strategy of deterrence and, without dismissing the wider goals of nuclear arms reductions across the board, placed emphasis on taking advantage of the immediate progress which could be made in the INF context.

Terrorism

The issue of terrorism and violence was one which assumed increasingly grave proportions as the decade continued. The Declaration issued by the

Alliance at Bonn in June 1982 emphasised the need for the most effective cooperation possible to defeat what had become a threat to democratic institutions and an obstacle to normal international relations. Another political assassination took place in India in October 1984, when the Prime Minister, Mrs. Gandhi, was murdered. And a number of apparently isolated acts of terrorism, as well as organised and state-sponsored terrorism by different indigenous groups, combined to create an international problem for which the only solution consisted in improved coordination between all states threatened by this situation. For 17 days in June 1985, 39 American hostages were held in Beirut by Lebanese Shiite Moslems, following their hijacking of a TWA airliner. In October, Palestinian guerillas hijacked an Italian cruise ship, the Achille Lauro, in the Mediterranean, taking 440 people hostage and murdering a US citizen. The hijackers were arrested three days later following the interception by US forces of the plane carrying them from Egypt.

Nuclear Testing

At the end of November 1985 the Soviet Union appealed to the United States to join in a moratorium on nuclear tests—a proposal which the United States rejected on the grounds that in present circumstances continued tests were required to ensure the safety and reliability of the US nuclear deterrent. However, by March 1986 President Reagan announced a new proposal for on-site monitoring of nuclear tests which could be implemented immediately and would strengthen the verification provisions of the Threshold Test Ban Treaty (TTBT) and Peaceful Nuclear Explosions Treaty (PNET). He also invited Soviet scientists to inspect the CORRTEX system at the US test site in Nevada and to monitor a US nuclear weapon test.

Conceptual Military Framework

A major objective of NATO's defence planning process is to achieve the most efficient and cost-effective use of the collective resources of the Alliance. In 1980 it had been agreed that planning should be extended through the production by NATO's Military Authorities of Long Term Planning Guidelines (LTPGs). A further important stage in the evolution of the planning process was the development of a conceptual military framework which could serve as a basis for establishing priorities in the various crucial areas of conventional force capabilities where improvements were needed to strengthen deterrence and on which the Long Term Planning Guidelines would be based. While focussing primarily on the conventional component of deterrence, the conceptual military framework takes into account the relationship between conventional and nuclear forces and their relative roles.

The origins of the conceptual military framework lie in initial discussions concerning emerging technologies and the potential they offered for improving NATO's conventional defence capabilities. It was evident that because of limitations on resources, the effective exploitation of emerging technologies required more precise and coordinated military guidance. It was also felt that this should be set in an overall planning context. A framework was needed which set out the basic requirements of Alliance strategy, principally over the longer term. It would thus allow planners to see where scarce resources could be most usefully spent. The requirement for such a framework was reinforced by the December 1984 decision of Ministers of Defence to make a special effort to improve NATO's conventional forces.

The resulting document, prepared by the Military Committee, in conjunction with the Major NATO Commanders, was considered by Defence Ministers at their December 1985 meeting. It defines the main elements of the strategy of flexible response and forward defence, analyses deficiencies in conventional forces which limit the execution of this function, and identifies the areas on which NATO should concentrate in order to enhance deterrence and defence. It is supplemented by supporting documents providing more detailed analysis for use in NATO defence planning activities and in developing long term planning guidelines, related armaments requirements and force proposals. In addition to facilitating the identification of priorities, it aims to enable resources to be allocated more effectively and long term planning to be undertaken in a coherent and coordinated manner.

Conventional Defence Improvements

The need to improve conventional defence has been examined under different perspectives at regular intervals. The monitoring of progress and development of new initiatives in this field are continuous and integral parts of NATO defence planning. However, against the background of growing conventional disparities between the forces of NATO and those of the Warsaw Treaty countries over the last two decades and warnings by NATO's military authorities of the risks of over-dependence on nuclear deterrence, there have been a number of important steps to redress the situation which stand out from the permanent and routine force planning procedures followed by the Allies participating in NATO's integrated military structure.

One such step was the initiation at the London Summit meeting of 1977 of the Long Term Defence Programme (LTDP), most of the consequences of which have now been absorbed into the normal defence planning cycle. Subsequent developments, each of which has to be seen in the context of the overall political objectives of the Alliance, brought together measures to strengthen deterrence, efforts to achieve a balance of forces at lower levels, reaffirmation of the strategy of flexible response to aggression, and the formulation of specific objectives such as those targetted in the 1984 Nunn Amendment to the United States Defense Authorisation Act. The latter postulated a more direct link between the maintenance of United States forces in Europe at approximately their existing strength and a common perception throughout the Alliance of the commitment to credible conventional defence. The Nunn Amendment and the admonitions it contained, led to a series of efforts within NATO to avert what Senator Nunn referred to as "structural disarmament"—the process whereby the growing financial burden of providing the armaments and forces needed for defence would lead automatically to diminishing inventories and reduced military capacity unless positive steps were taken. At the core of the discussion was the need to re-establish the principle of a robust conventional defence structure. The situation called for Alliance planning to take account of its reduced ability to rely on a technological advantage and to translate the scope offered by technological innovation into practical measures to meet conventional defence needs.

In December 1984 NATO Defence Ministers had called for proposals for a coherent effort to improve conventional defences. The work included that which was already being undertaken to develop a conceptual military framework and covered the establishment of priorities, the harmonisation of national efforts to improve their capabilities in this field, the encouragement of joint efforts to coordinate defence procurement, Alliance-wide efforts to make the necessary resources available, optimum use of the resources already available, and integration of the results of all the above into the planning process of the Alliance.

Six months later Defence Ministers endorsed the resulting report by the Secretary General and the Defence Planning Committee in Permanent Session, which provided a coherent and balanced approach to improvements, identifying key deficiencies on a regional and functional basis which could, if uncorrected, threaten NATO's ability to implement its strategy. In the action plan provided by the comprehensive recommendations contained in the report, they agreed to give special attention to medium and long-term measures which offered the greatest return in terms of effectiveness and improving the credibility of Alliance strategy. In essence the action plan seeks a greater focussing of national plans on collective Alliance needs by setting clear military priorities and identifying areas of deficiency where additional resources will yield the greatest return. By the end of 1985 Defence Ministers were able to welcome the first signs of progress but emphasised the need for a sustained commitment and greater convergence between Alliance and national planning.

Armaments Cooperation Improvement Strategy

In the overall context of efforts to improve allied conventional defence and of the "CDI action plan" agreed upon by Defence Ministers in May 1985, Foreign Ministers took a related decision at the December 1985 meeting of the North Atlantic Council. This took the form of a specific directive to the Conference of National Armaments Directors to implement a new Armaments Cooperation Improvement Strategy. The main elements of the strategy are described in the statement issued by Foreign Ministers on December 13, 1985. The significance of initiatives such as the introduction of the Armaments Cooperation Improvement Strategy lies, in part at least, in generating the political will to collaborate, without which little progress can be achieved.

Mutual and Balanced Force Reductions

Following agreement to resume the MBFR negotiations in March 1984, Western participants had presented a new proposal which attempted to simplify the all-important data issue which had blocked progress for so long, by calling for a preliminary exchange of data only on a portion of the ground forces of both sides—setting aside the service and support forces which were responsible for much of the discrepancy between Eastern and Western figures. Nearly two years later there was still little sign of progress.

On December 5, 1985, building on previous Western and Eastern proposals, the NATO participants tabled another important initiative in Vienna. This envisaged an initial reduction period of up to one year in which, without prior agreement on data for this step, the US and the USSR would cut their forces in the area by 5,000 and 11,500 men respectively. It would be based on satisfactory verification provisions and followed up by a collective commitment on the part of all participants not to increase their manpower within the area for three years. The 1985 proposal continued to reflect Allied thinking on the need for substantial progress towards an equitable conclusion to these long-standing negotiations.

Implementation of agreements under the CSCE process

At their December 1985 meeting Foreign Ministers also reviewed progress in the implementation of provisions of the Helsinki Final Act and the Concluding Document agreed upon at the Madrid Follow-up Meeting. They recorded their regrets that efforts to move the CSCE process forward through meetings which had taken place in Ottawa and Budapest had been only partially effective. Both the meeting on Human Rights held in Ottawa and the Budapest Cultural Forum[42] were considered useful in themselves. However, they had revealed persistant difficulties in the implementation of agreed measures, including those which concerned fundamental rights such as those of freedom of conscience and belief. These affected, inter alia, the rights of ethnic and national minorities, in certain Warsaw Treaty countries, whose plights are of particular concern to some members of the Alliance. For these and other reasons, no common conclusions were reached.

Chernobyl

The nuclear accident at Chernobyl in April 1986 had severe repercussions, not only in terms of the human suffering and environmental damage it caused over long distances, but also in political terms. The name and the event were engraved on the world's conscience as a symbol of the potential scale of threats to mankind from events beyond the boundaries and control of individual countries or continents. Occurring one year after the advent of the

---

[42] The Ottawa Experts Meeting on Human Rights was held from May 7 to June 17, 1985. The Budapest Cultural Forum took place from October 15 to November 25, 1985.

new Soviet leader, Mikhail Gorbachev, who was already becoming identified as an exponent of greater openness towards the West and closer contacts with the outside world, Chernobyl exposed the practical consequences of inadequate communications and information exchange between nations sharing the same limited environment. They cannot remain impervious to each other's actions, even when these take place outside their own territory. If the experience of witnessing the Soviet Union seeking and accepting Western assistance with the aftermath of the disaster was a new one, it was nevertheless widely interpreted by public opinion as a development which augured well for the future.

Spain

Following the accession of Spain to the North Atlantic Treaty in 1982, discussions took place between the Spanish Government and its allies to define the nature of Spanish participation in the various institutions of the Alliance, and in particular to address the question of possible integration of Spanish forces with the military structures of the Alliance. Simultaneously the public debate taking place in Spain touched on all aspects of the optimum future relationship of Spain with its allies, including the central issue of continued Spanish participation in the Alliance itself. On March 12, 1986, in a referendum[43] organised by Prime Minister Felipe Gonzalez, Spanish voters supported the continued membership of Spain in the Atlantic Alliance, without participation in NATO's integrated military structure. Under the terms of the referendum, the existing ban on the deployment or stockpiling or introduction of nuclear weapons on Spanish territory will be maintained; and the United States military presence in Spain will be gradually reduced.

The Spanish Government subsequently developed a series of nine general principles governing future Spanish participation in the Alliance. On the basis of these nine principles, presented to the Atlantic Council on May 20, 1986, Spain would continue its participation as a full member in the Atlantic Council, the Nuclear Planning Group, the Defence Planning Committee and the Military Committee. Spain would also continue its participation in the Conference of National Armaments Directors, the Senior Logisticians Conference, the Senior Civil Emergency Planning Committee, the NATO integrated Communications and Information System, and the Civil Budget. Spain also expressed willingness to participate in NATO's force planning cycle, through a system similar to that used by other members of NATO's Defence Planning Committee, and to establish coordination agreements with the Major NATO Commanders in order to develop Spain's military contribution to the common defence. Spain's participation in the NATO Infrastructure programme and its contribution to NATO's military budget would reflect its non-integration in the military command structure. In February 1988 both the North Atlantic Council and the Defence Planning Committee agreed that

[43] Out of ballots cast at the March 12, 1986 referendum in Spain, 52.55 % voted in favour of the proposal, 39.8 % voted against and 7.65 % abstained.

negotiations between Spain and its NATO partners should continue on this basis. General guidelines for the development of Coordination Agreements between the Major NATO Commanders and Spanish Military Authorities were approved later in the year.

Terrorism

In 1986 terrorism was again the subject of renewed efforts to improve international cooperation to eliminate an increasingly serious spate of attacks on individual freedom and on the security of civilian diplomatic personnel as well as state-sponsored attacks on military forces acting in a peace-keeping capacity in the Mediterranean. As such it represented a threat to the conduct of normal international relations.

In March 1986 United States forces reacted to Libyan attacks on US forces in the Mediterranean by sinking Libyan patrol boats and attacking a Libyan missile site. In April the United States again responded to terrorist attacks attributed to Libya by attacking targets in Tripoli and Benghazi. Acts of terrorism and the taking of hostages by extremist groups are of worldwide concern and despite initiatives taken by many countries and the wide condemnation of such acts internationally, they continue to damage the basis of normal international relations.

The seriousness with which the Allies viewed this problem was reflected in the Halifax Statement issued by the NATO Council in May 1986, and on several other occasions Allied governments announced that they were intensifying their fight against this scourge, whatever its form and from whatever quarter it came. Closer international cooperation remains central to this task and individual governments showed increasing determination to take whatever action was necessary.

US Strategic Defence Initiative

As during the previous two years, discussion of the United States Strategic Defence Initiative continued during 1986. It was generally agreed that it was too soon to tell whether the systems it envisaged were feasible or deployable. However, the consensus among the Allies concerned remained that it would be prudent to carry out research into strategic defence.

The US Strategic Defence Initiative is a long-term research programme. Agreements limiting research are neither practicable nor potentially verifiable and the United States has maintained its view that for these and other reasons SDI is not negotiable. However, in its proposals of November 1985, the United States stated that although it remains committed to the research programme as permitted by the 1972 ABM Treaty, it is ready to explore jointly how a cooperative transition could be accomplished, should new defensive technologies prove feasible. The offer included proposals for "open laboratories" arrangements whereby information would be provided by both sides on each other's strategic defence research and facilities made available for reciprocal visits to associated research establishments.

Statement on the Ministerial meeting of the North Atlantic Council at Halifax, Canada — May 1986

All aspects of East-West relations were again reviewed by NATO Foreign Ministers when they met in Canada in May 1986. In addition to their statement reaffirming allied policies on all the principal topics of concern, Ministers published a Statement on Conventional Arms Control. This contained the announcement that the Alliance had decided to set up a high-level task force on conventional arms control with a mandate to build on proposals made in the CDE Conference in Stockholm and the MBFR negotiations in Vienna, taking into account the statement made by Mr. Gorbachev in April — particularly with regard to Soviet readiness to pursue conventional force reductions from the Atlantic to the Urals. The task force was established immediately and has continued to work towards the Alliance's goal of achieving agreements which would strengthen stability and security in the whole of Europe. The kind of agreement at which the Alliance is aiming will take advantage of increased openness between East and West to establish a verifiable, comprehensive and stable balance of conventional forces at lower levels.

The Stockholm Conference

The Conference on Confidence and Security-Building Measures and Disarmament in Europe (known as CDE), which had opened in January 1984, ended with the adoption of the September 19, 1986 Document of the Stockholm Conference. Close consultations took place within the Alliance throughout the three year period following the presentation of a comprehensive series of proposals by Western participants designed to improve both mutual confidence and security. Not all Western aims were achieved at the Conference, but the document which was adopted nevertheless included important sections prescribing detailed measures for the notification, observation and on-site inspection of the military manoeuvres of participating countries. These took the agreements reached at Helsinki an important stage further, introducing for the first time procedures for on-site challenge inspections of military activities.

Once the agreements came into force, implementation of their provisions was generally good. Annual calendars of military activities were exchanged and details provided of military activities which have to be notified in advance. By the end of 1987 there had been a significant increase in the number of exercises attended by observers in each other's countries under the mandatory conditions laid down by the Stockholm Document, as opposed to the voluntary measures provided for by the Helsinki Final Act; and a number of inspections had also taken place. Despite the unprecedented nature of such inspections, few difficulties were encountered.

Inspection visits are governed by detailed arrangements including the submission of a report to all CSCE signatories by the State carrying out the inspection. The first such inspection to take place occurred in August 1987, when United States officials inspected a military exercise near Minsk, in the Soviet Union. This set the pattern and pace for future inspections. Turkey was the first Allied country to receive a team of Soviet inspectors within the framework of the Stockholm Document in connection with exercises held in October 1987. Further examples of the manner in which the provisions were implemented during the first year included separate inspections in the Federal Republic of Germany by officials from the USSR and from the German Democratic Republic and inspections in the German Democratic Republic by teams of Western officials. This pattern continued in 1988 involving inspections of various military activities by teams from several other Alliance and Warsaw Treaty countries.

While the limitations of the Stockholm Document have to be recognised, and there is scope for strengthening and deepening the measures agreed upon, it is clear that these developments are contributing to the process of building confidence and understanding between East and West in a manner which could scarcely have been envisaged only a few years ago.

The Reykjavik Summit Meeting—October 1986

In February 1986 President Reagan announced that US negotiators in Geneva had tabled a concrete plan for a global INF agreement which offered hopes of immediate progress. October 1986 brought President Reagan and General Secretary Gorbachev together again in a Summit Meeting in Reykjavik which was to become a landmark in the history of these negotiations, despite the fact that no conclusive agreement was reached on strategic and defence and space systems and the meeting ended in deadlock on these issues. The two sides nevertheless came close to an agreement on an INF deal based on NATO's "zero option". It was agreed to accept equal global ceilings of 100 LRINF warheads for each side, none of which would remain in Europe. 100 residual warheads would be permitted in Soviet Asia and on United States territories. Key elements of the kind of verification arrangements needed for an agreement were also agreed. However, the stumbling block was Soviet insistence on linking an INF agreement to acceptance by the United States of constraints on its Strategic Defence Initiative beyond those of the 1972 Anti-Ballistic Missile (ABM) Treaty. The talks ended in the full glare of publicity without agreement being reached, in an atmosphere of anti-climax. Constraints in the SRINF category were also unresolved. There were nevertheless positive signs.

The Reykjavik meeting was a dramatic development in other respects in that it raised the prospect, however remote it had appeared before, of major new agreements being reached at summit level which would have far-reaching implications for Allied defence policy and deterrent strategy. The United States President and the Soviet leader envisaged extensive measures of reduction of nuclear arsenals beginning with 50% reductions of strategic weapons during the first five years following an agreement, after which all Soviet and United States ballistic missiles would be eliminated during a further five-year period. The United States would agree to postpone deployment of a strategic defence system for the duration of that period.

United States Secretary of State Shultz attended a special meeting of the North Atlantic Council on October 13, at which member nations expressed appreciation to President Reagan for his efforts to achieve outstanding results at Reykjavik. They emphasised their determination to seize the opportunities for progress which had emerged from the Summit Meeting. Soon after the United States presented a new START proposal in Geneva, incorporating areas of agreement reached in Reykjavik and new solutions to problems where differences remained, followed, in May 1987, by a draft START treaty incorporating phased reductions over seven years to global ceilings on strategic nuclear delivery vehicles and sub-limits on missile warheads.

An intensive period of consultations within the Alliance followed the Reykjavik summit. However, within a short time the upsurge of optimism which aspects of the dialogue at summit level had generated, mixed with uncertainty over the profound implications which agreement could have engendered, was to take a downward turn. Proposals announced by the Soviet Union had the effect of negating some of the progress made both at the Geneva and at the Reykjavik summits. The linkage of progress in INF to the START talks and to SDI was re-established.

Nuclear Testing, Strategic Arms Reductions, and Defence and Space Systems

In advance of the October 1986 Reykjavik Summit, President Reagan put forward a number of important proposals in a speech to the United Nations General Assembly on September 22. These reflected the step by step "build-down" approach developed by the United States in conjunction with its allies in several spheres of negotiation. The main elements of this initiative were as follows: the United States was ready to move foward on ratification of the Threshold Test Ban Treaty and the Treaty on Peaceful Nuclear Explosions, once agreement was reached on improved verification procedures. Upon ratification of those treaties, and in association with a programme to reduce and ultimately eliminate all nuclear weapons, the United States was prepared to discuss ways to implement a step-by-step parallel programme of limiting and ultimately ending nuclear testing. Furthermore, if the two sides could agree on radical reductions in strategic offensive weapons, the United States would be prepared to sign an agreement with the USSR on research, development, testing and deployment of strategic defences. This agreement would be based on several elements.

First, both sides would agree to confine themselves, until 1991, to research, development and testing permitted by the ABM Treaty, to determine whether advanced systems of strategic defence were technically feasible.

Second, if after 1991 either side should decide to deploy such a system, that side would be obliged to offer a plan for sharing the benefits of strategic defence and for eliminating offensive ballistic missiles.

And third, if the two sides could not agree after two years of negotiation, either side would be free to deploy an advanced strategic defensive system, after giving six months' notice to the other.

Progress towards an INF Treaty

At the beginning of 1987 attempts by the United States to reintroduce progress led to detailed new proposals being presented at Geneva on January 15, which attempted to meet the principal concerns of both sides as far as intermediate-range nuclear forces were concerned. The proposals covered phased reductions to global ceilings, time constraints, geographical constraints which permitted limited deployments outside Europe, avoidance of linkage to other negotiations, a ban on specified SRINF development and deployments to be followed by negotiations on this category within 6 months, data exchange before and after reductions, on-site observation and effective monitoring of the agreed elimination procedures, and parallel negotiations on subsequent verification.

In February 1987 US-Soviet negotiations in Geneva were temporarily suspended while further consultations took place between the United States and its allies on the issue of the US Strategic Defence Initiative and its conformity with the ABM Treaty. The position of the United States in this context remained that which had been outlined by the US Secretary of State to the North Atlantic Assembly when it met in San Francisco in October 1985: the SDI research programme would continue to be structured and conducted in accordance with the "restrictive" interpretation of the ABM Treaty obligations—i.e. SDI deployment would be the subject of consultations with the United States allies and of discussion and negotiation with the Soviet Union. By the end of February, in a move welcomed by NATO countries as a significant breakthrough, Mr. Gorbachev announced Soviet willingness to conclude an INF Treaty without insisting that this must be linked to progress in the negotiations relating to strategic and defence and space systems.

A serious obstacle to progress towards INF reductions was thus removed. The statement made by Mr. Gorbachev on February 28 also made no reference to British and French systems—confirming Soviet recognition that "third country" systems could not be covered in the bilateral Geneva negotiations. The opportunity for progress was seized upon and a draft treaty text was tabled by the United States in Geneva on March 4, placing strong emphasis on verification. Details of the verification procedures considered necessary were tabled eight days later. However, by the time the current session of negotiations ended in Geneva on March 26, 1987, some retrograde steps had again compromised progress. The Soviet Union made demands on shorter-range INF (SRINF) missiles which would effectively allow it a monopoly in this category and render an INF agreement invalid.

Talks between the two Foreign Ministers in Moscow in April marked some advances and agreement in principle on "intrusive" verification procedures was established. Likewise it was acknowledged that Soviet SRINF deployments in the German Democratic Republic and in Czechoslovakia, increased following the beginning of NATO's INF deployments, would be withdrawn and the missiles destroyed.

The negotiations followed an uphill course during the following months, marked by occasional developments which heralded progress, however gradual. A Soviet draft treaty presented at the end of April 1987 included implicit agreement on a "zero" outcome after 5 years with limitations on LRINF deployments in Asia. It also proposed measures which would eliminate SRINF in Europe, including US-owned warheads on Pershing IA missiles in the Federal Republic of Germany. Soviet proposals made in March had failed to take account of the agreement reached in this sphere—a crucial issue since the exclusion of SRINF from the INF Treaty would not only allow the USSR a virtual monopoly of these systems but would also leave the Soviet Union free to circumvent the INF agreement by increasing its existing SRINF missile force.

On April 16, 1987 the North Atlantic Council was given a detailed report by the United States Secretary of State on his talks in Moscow. These had been firmly embedded in an Alliance context: United States Ambassador Nitze had been present in the Council only a week earlier for consultations before the visit. The Council took careful note of the Soviet offer for a phased elimination of shorter range INF missiles. It was agreed that the Council in permanent session and its appropriate subsidiary expert bodies should begin immediately to consider the implications to allied security of the proposals under negotiation. This work would take into account the complex interrelationship between the conventional and nuclear weapons of the Alliance and the Warsaw Treaty countries as well as Soviet superiority in chemical forces.

Conventional Stability

In the military sphere 1987 saw positive signs of progress in efforts to find a satisfactory basis for two new negotiations to take place within the CSCE framework. The negotiations would address, firstly, measures to strengthen stability and security in Europe principally through establishing balance at lower levels of forces, eliminating disparities and taking steps to reduce the risks of surprise attack or large-scale offensive operations; and secondly, new confidence-building and security measures in Europe, from the Atlantic to the Urals.

New negotiations on conventional stability had been called for in NATO's Brussels Declaration of December 1986. Informal consultations began in February 1987 to try to agree upon a mandate. The North Atlantic Council met on June 11-12 and reached agreement on steps which would allow an allied draft mandate to be tabled. While the new conventional stability negotiations would take place within the CSCE framework, they would retain autonomy with regard to subject matter, participation and procedures. The Brussels Declaration had also called for further discussions on confidence and security-building measures (CSBMs).

In both fields a number of important differences were revealed between the approaches advocated by NATO countries and those put forward by the

Warsaw Treaty countries. The former pressed for distinct negotiations leading to agreements which would:

— build upon and expand the results of the Stockholm Conference on Confidence and Security-Building Measures;
— eliminate existing disparities, from the Atlantic to the Urals, and establish conventional stability at lower levels, between the countries whose forces bear most immediately upon the essential security relationship in Europe, namely those belonging to the Alliance and the Warsaw Treaty countries.

The latter envisaged negotiations among all CSCE signatories leading to substantial reductions designed to "maintain" the balance of forces at the lowest possible level, including tactical or short-range nuclear weapons and aircraft.

At the Vienna CSCE Follow-up Meeting, the Allies tabled a proposal on July 10, 1987, which called for two distinct negotiations, and on July 27, put forward a draft negotiating mandate providing for autonomous conventional stability negotiations between the 23 Warsaw Treaty and NATO members within the overall CSCE framework. Other CSCE signatories would be involved in exchanges of views and information at the start of each round of the negotiations, which would cover conventional land-based forces but not nuclear forces, naval forces or chemical weapons. These proposals would thus establish the relationship between the CSCE process and the conventional stability talks on the one hand, and on the other commit all CSCE participants to new negotiations designed to further the confidence building process. During the summer and autumn of 1987, various counter proposals were also tabled by other CSCE participants, for example proposals by Sweden, addressing neutral and non-aligned country participation in talks on conventional reductions, and by Yugoslavia and Cyprus, also dealing with aspects of military security. However, the principal difficulties in formulating a mutually acceptable mandate for negotiations continued to hinge on Eastern determination to extend direct participation to neutral and non-aligned countries and to include short-range "battlefield" nuclear weapons. Neither proposal met the NATO requirement for the negotiations to focus on the countries directly concerned so that serious imbalances in conventional forces could be addressed.

By the end of the third round of the conventional stability talks, in November 1987, agreement had been reached on the formulation of the objectives for the negotiations. In the communiqué issued at the conclusion of the December 1987 Ministerial meeting of the North Atlantic Council, Foreign Ministers stated their hope that agreements on mandates for such negotiations could be achieved as part of a balanced outcome of the Vienna CSCE Follow-up Meeting so that the negotiations themselves could begin in the near future. When talks resumed at the beginning of 1988, the task was therefore to define the area and forces to be covered in the negotiations, which it was hoped would begin in the autumn. The purpose of both sets of negotiations would be to build on and expand the measures agreed upon in the Helsinki Final Act.

Developments in East-West Relations

Realistic opportunities for progress in the field of human rights and arms control are as central a focus of analysis and consultation within the Alliance as is the work needed to maintain and improve the effectiveness of military deterrence. Arms control agreements which are equitable and verifiable offer a means of enhancing security at lower levels of forces and lower costs and, with positive developments in the human rights field, contribute to progress in the East-West relationship as a whole by building confidence and reducing the risk of conflict through mistrust or miscalculation. The members of the Alliance have consistently emphasised the need to work towards meaningful agreements whose implementation contributes to these objectives in a tangible manner as opposed to measures of a purely declamatory nature. It is therefore important to maintain a clear distinction between the two.

The complexities of arms control have tended on occasion to obscure the realities. Students of East-West relations in general and of security issues in particular have seldom been exposed to such a stream of arms control and confidence-building proposals and counter proposals as they have in recent years. 1987 saw a proliferation of speeches and declarations emanating from individual leaders of East European countries or from meetings of their Foreign Ministers or government leaders, in which some additional elements were combined with reiterations of well-known positions and objectives. On a number of occasions arms control issues figured extensively in communiqués and official statements.

However, policies adopted and positions taken in negotiations by the Soviet Union and Eastern Europe governments frequently failed to reflect their public statements on arms control, confidence building and human rights issues. High levels of defence spending remained the dominant feature of Soviet security policies although there were indications that economic and political considerations are playing a greater part in foreign policy making. Arms control issues predominated both in the communiqué issued at the 1987 Warsaw Treaty Organisation Summit meeting in East Berlin and in a separate declaration calling for talks on military doctrines. However, while both documents addressed the plethora of Eastern arms control initiatives at length, they contained very little that was new on substantive issues.

At the June 1987 Ministerial meeting of the North Atlantic Council in Reykjavik, and again at their meeting in Brussels in December, Foreign Ministers noted the encouraging signs in Soviet internal and external policies but agreed that in assessing Soviet intentions, the final test would be Soviet conduct across the spectrum from human rights to arms control. The year before, in Halifax, they had stressed that having presented detailed proposals directed at enhancing stability and security, they awaited an equally constructive response at the negotiating table. Public statements alone were not enough. The Alliance regarded adequate verification measures as the key to progress in all the present negotiations and essential for building trust and openness. Any agreement should enhance confidence in compliance and strengthen the existing treaty régime. The members of the Alliance were prepared to accept comprehensive verification measures on a fully reciprocal basis, including systematic on-site inspections.

Mutual and Balanced Force Reductions

Eastern proposals made in February 1986 offered some hopes of progress in the Vienna negotiations but fell far short of Western demands on information exchange and verification. Like other areas of negotiation requiring on-site inspections following implementation of an agreement, the Eastern proposals included provisions giving the right to refuse inspection.

In November 1986, Foreign Ministers of Alliance countries participating in MBFR were present in Vienna for the opening of the CSCE Follow-up Meeting. They met under the chairmanship of the Belgian Foreign Minister to review progress in MBFR with the Heads of the Western delegations to the talks. In a declaration issued to underline the importance of the role played by the MBFR talks in achieving progress in conventional arms control in Europe, they reaffirmed the need to address conventional imbalances. Their declaration stressed the importance of verification, where there had been little positive movement and indeed some negative trends, and, in a reference to the major initiative taken by the Western side in putting forward its proposals of December 5, 1985, expressed the hope "that the East will demonstrate that it can match us in openness and imagination in the conclusion of an agreement which can give encouragement to the peoples of both East and West". The statement also reaffirmed Western readiness to make reductions, accept limitations on forces, and to disclose their size and disposition.

By the end of 1987, although the MBFR talks remained in being, there appeared to be little prospect of reaching agreement, given the inadequacy of Eastern responses to Western proposals on data and verification. The Alliance countries participating in the talks called upon the Warsaw Treaty participants to adopt a more constructive posture in the negotiations and reiterated their own desire to achieve a meaningful agreement.

Meeting of the North Atlantic Council in Reykjavik—June 1987

The June 1987 Reykjavik meeting of the North Atlantic Council resulted in a statement by the Foreign Ministers of the Alliance reaffirming their desire to obtain a "zero" outcome on intermediate-range nuclear forces and calling on the Soviet Union to drop its demand to retain a portion of its SS-20 capability. The Soviet offer on SRINF missiles was accepted subject to certain conditions. The communiqué set out a framework for a coherent and comprehensive concept of arms control and disarmament consistent with the strategy of flexible response, which would include 50% reductions in United States and Soviet strategic systems. It would also include global elimination of chemical weapons and stable and secure levels for conventional forces in the whole of Europe through the elimination of disparities; and in conjunction with both of these, it would also include tangible and verifiable reductions of

United States and Soviet land-based short-range nuclear systems leading to equal ceilings.

Statements made by Mr. Gorbachev in July 1987, following formal presentation by the United States of its proposals on SRINF systems, revealed a change in the Soviet position which would permit agreement to be reached on both LRINF and SRINF systems—in fact a "double global zero option". Verification aspects were also taken a step forward at the end of that month with proposals again being formally tabled by the United States.

In August the issue of Pershing IA missiles stationed in the Federal Republic of Germany looked set to block further progress for the time being. These missiles were presented by the Soviet Union as "the main barrier" to a successful outcome to negotiations. However, as had been made clear by the United States throughout, provisions affecting systems maintained by other allies of the United States could not form part of any bilateral US-Soviet agreement.

The same month, at a special session of the talks, revised proposals on verification were tabled by the US side. These took account of the implications of the agreement now reached to move towards a "double zero" outcome. It had long been the US view that such an agreement would be easier to verify than earlier concepts involving the retention and modernisation of a number of INF systems on each side.

The problem of the Pershing IAs, which had continued to be a contentious issue, was removed at the same time as a consequence of an important announcement by Chancellor Kohl on August 26. Although these missiles could not be the object of the negotiations in Geneva, the Federal Republic was willing to dismantle the 72 weapons concerned and to forgo replacements for them, subject to implementation of the "double zero" solution, in accordance with an agreed schedule and compliance with the Treaty. This intervention represented an important contribution to a breakthrough at a time when the negotiations were at a decisive stage. In announcing this decision, the German Chancellor also called on the Soviet Union to renounce current modernisation of missiles in the range below 500 kilometres.

Events outside the Treaty area

The members of the Alliance share a common interest in the security, stability and independence of the countries outside the NATO area. They cannot be indifferent to any development affecting peace, international equilibrium or the independence of sovereign nations. Moreover, military aggression outside the NATO area has the potential to threaten the vital interests of the West and can therefore have direct implications for the security of members of the Alliance.

The situation in the Middle East continued to be a major concern and threat to stability and security throughout this period. Several Alliance countries had sent military contingents to Beirut in 1983 and minesweepers to deal with the danger to shipping from mines in the Gulf in 1984. In all such instances the Alliance provides a forum for consultation and information exchange. The implications for the Alliance of measures taken by member countries in specific situations such as these, outside the NATO area, can thus be jointly assessed.

The extent to which events outside the Treaty area could affect the vital common interests of the Alliance was demonstrated with particular clarity during 1987, as a consequence of the war between Iran and Iraq which began in 1980. With the war in its seventh year, repeated attacks occurred on international shipping and mine-laying operations by Iranian warships rendered the passage of civilian and commercial vessels through these vital international oil shipping lanes increasingly hazardous. Various actions were taken individually, both by the United States and by several European countries, to protect shipping, and steps were taken by some of the countries concerned to coordinate their operations bilaterally and multilaterally—for example, in the framework of the Western European Union, experts convened in the Hague on August 20, 1987 to consider joint action. On September 21, France and Italy announced measures to promote exchange of information and technical coordination between naval forces operating to protect shipping in the Gulf. Bilateral consultations took place between several other Allied governments. Action taken by the United States on October 18, after attacks on convoys passing through the Gulf resulted in the destruction of two Iranian oil platforms by US naval forces. Further steps were taken by member countries of the WEU to coordinate their military presence in the Gulf following more attacks on shipping. The governments of countries involved in temporary deployments of their naval forces for mine countermeasure operations in the Gulf or other deployments out-of-area took steps to keep the Alliance fully informed of such activities, both with regard to their impact on Western interests as a whole, and with regard to any more direct implications they might have for defence planning within the Alliance.

Against the background of international conflicts such as this, the priority for the Alliance itself is to ensure that military capabilities in the Treaty area are sufficient to maintain an adequate defence posture. The Alliance machinery provides for consultations on temporary or permanent measures needed to compensate for the possible redeployment of forces normally available to the Alliance. In this context, for example, the Federal Republic of Germany announced on October 15, 1987 that it had dispatched three German warships to the Mediterranean to replace vessels of NATO allies redeployed to protect shipping lanes in the Gulf. As far as the Gulf War itself was concerned, strenuous international efforts were eventually to lead to a ceasefire on August 20, 1988, in the framework of UN Security Council Resolution 598.

Afghanistan

By January 1987, the régime in Kabul, supported by some 120,000 Soviet forces, was beginning its eighth year of unbroken conflict with the Afghan resistance forces without any sign of a solution on the horizon. Dissatisfaction on the part of both the Moscow government and the Soviet people with the seemingly endless costs of this war in lives and resources was beginning to find expression in ways which could not be ignored. On January 15, Kabul declared a unilateral ceasefire but proposals for national reconciliation were rejected and the Mujahadin announced that the armed struggle would continue. The ceasefire did not last more than a few days. Western leaders emphasized the need for Soviet withdrawal from Afghanistan at every opportunity, both in bilateral contacts and in joint communiqués.

By the end of 1987 Mr. Gorbachev had publicly accepted the principle of withdrawal within 12 months, indicating that the only question to be resolved was the timetable for withdrawals. And a few weeks later, Moscow spelled out its conditions for a total withdrawal to be completed, according to Mr. Gorbachev's statement, within 10 months. This was welcomed by the West as a positive development which would, if fully implemented, produce the desired result—the restoration of the principle of non-intervention by external forces in an independent sovereign state and of the freedom of the Afghan people themselves to determine their own future. The plan proposed by the Soviet leader depended on agreement being reached between Afghanistan and Pakistan, to which several million refugees from Afghanistan had fled, in the United Nations sponsored Geneva peace talks which had begun in June 1982. For Moscow, the proposal represented a means of reaping some political credit for bringing to an end an expensive, humiliating and ill-advised attempt at power projection abroad which had brought upon the Soviet Union international condemnation and an inglorious military failure.

The member countries of the Alliance acted bilaterally and multilaterally in the appropriate fora in support of United Nations initiatives designed to bring about a Soviet withdrawal and a peaceful settlement. They pointed out repeatedly that the situation could not but affect adversely the conduct of East-West relations across the board and was therefore damaging to the Alliance objective of bringing about a more stable relationship which would favour the solution of underlying problems affecting East and West.

World attention again focused on Afghanistan on February 8, 1988, when Soviet leader Gorbachev announced that Soviet troops would begin to withdraw from Afghanistan on May 15, 1988, provided that the Geneva talks between Afghanistan and Pakistan resulted in a settlement by March 15. Following the Geneva Accords on that date, the process of Soviet troop withdrawal finally began in mid-May, after over eight years of occupation. Subsequently postponements and delays occurred which raised questions about the future course of the withdrawal. However on February 15, 1989, the withdrawal of Soviet military forces from Afghanistan was completed in accordance with the schedule which had been announced and the undertaking given to the United Nations General Assembly by President Gorbachev in December 1988.

Reinforcement

Reinforcement of NATO forces in Europe remains a key issue for Allied defence planners. The ability to put Treaty commitments into practice, by reinforcing any area of the Alliance under threat of aggression, has long been axiomatic in terms of the credibility of deterrence. Plans for the rapid reinforcement of Europe as necessary in a crisis were approved by NATO Defence Ministers in December 1982. Such plans are regularly tested, as are other aspects of defence in multinational exercises such as "Ocean Safari"—a biannual series of exercises designed to rehearse the Alliance's ability to keep open the vital North Atlantic sea lanes in times of crisis or conflict and to demonstrate Europe's continued dependence on rapid reinforcement across the Atlantic.

Allied consultations took place during 1987 on measures needed to safeguard this reinforcement capability following the announcement by the Canadian government of its decision to redirect its commitment to the reinforcement of Europe from the Northern to the Central Region. The Canadian decision was made in the context of a major defence review and far-reaching re-examination of Canadian defence commitments summarised in the 1987 Canadian White Paper on defence. It involved the relocation of the Canadian Air-Sea Transportable Brigade (the "CAST" Brigade), together with two air squadrons, from its current commitment to the reinforcement of Northern Norway, as a means of consolidating the Canadian commitment to the central front in Southern Germany. In June 1988 NATO countries announced the formation of a Composite Force for the reinforcement of Northern Norway in periods of tension or hostility to replace the Canadian CAST Brigade, demonstrating the Alliance's full commitment to multinational defence of this critical region and to taking effective and appropriate measures to this end, based on the principle of equitable burden-sharing. Detailed planning began regarding the size of national commitments to the Composite Force and other practical aspects of its formation.

Over and above the importance of reinforcements, the continuing and undiminished presence of United States and Canadian forces in Europe is essential to NATO's defence and deterrence strategy and serves the interests of all the members of the Alliance. These forces play a unique and essential role in integrated defence and are a concrete demonstration of the cohesion and will of the Alliance. Similarly, efforts by European members of the Alliance to maintain and improve their defence capabilities are essential elements.

Short-range nuclear forces

Although public attention has tended to focus primarily on developments concerning strategic or long-range nuclear weapons and nuclear weapons in the intermediate category, the question of short-range nuclear forces (SNF) in the range below 500 kilometres has come increasingly under scrutiny as prospects for effective arms control agreements have improved. The principles governing the collective security and common defence of members of the Alliance, together with those underlying the deterrent strategy of flexible response and forward defence, are particularly crucial in developing an Alliance approach to this issue. The Soviet Union stated its willingness to eliminate battlefield or tactical short-range nuclear missiles in April 1987 and pressed for negotiations.

The members of the Alliance stated that the policy of deterrence currently necessitated the maintenance of nuclear forces in this category. This need was enhanced by significant imbalances and Soviet preponderance in important categories of conventional or non-nuclear arms compounded by other factors which distinguish the strategic position of the European members of the Alliance from that of the Warsaw Treaty countries. They emphasized that balanced conventional force reductions were the priority concern of the Alliance and should precede any further consideration of nuclear reductions beyond the implementation of the INF Treaty and the achievement of the Allied objective of 50 % reductions in strategic systems. The credibility of the Alliance's strategy for the defence of the Atlantic area, and therefore the effectiveness of deterrence, continued to depend on possession of an adequate level and appropriate mix of effective nuclear and conventional forces, including short-range nuclear systems. Arms control discussions relating to SNF missiles and nuclear artillery systems had to be considered against this background.

Conventional Defence Improvements

Force Goals for 1987-1992 and the NATO Force Plan for 1987-1991, reflecting the priorities identified in the development of Conventional Defence Improvement programmes were adopted at meetings of the Defence Planning Committee during 1986. The same determination to maintain momentum in the effort to improve conventional defences was likewise reflected in the Ministerial Guidance document approved on May 27, 1987—the major political directive for defence planning both by nations and by the NATO Military Authorities—and again in the NATO Force Plan for 1988-1992 adopted at the end of 1987 at the conclusion of the 1987 Annual Defence Review.

The close of 1987 also saw endorsement by Ministers of proposals for the establishment of a NATO Conventional Armaments Planning System (CAPS) for a two-year trial period, subject to the finalisation of the policy framework for such a system. Agreement on the framework was reached in the Council on January 20, 1988. On March 8, a new NATO body comprising national planners and armaments staffs—the NATO Conventional Armaments Review Committee (NCARC)—took the necessary detailed decisions to launch the trial. The objective of the "CAPS" was to reach agreement within NATO on a conventional armaments plan that can offer major guidance to nations in their research, development and production efforts. The system would thus relate national armaments plans, whether or not involving cooperation, to Alliance military requirements.

Nuclear testing

During 1987 the United States and the Soviet Union agreed that full-scale stage-by-stage negotiations on nuclear testing should begin by December 1st of that year. The official announcement stated that "In these negotiations, the sides, as the first step, will agree upon effective verification measures which will make it possible to ratify the US-USSR Threshold Test Ban Treaty of 1974, and the Peaceful Nuclear Explosions Treaty of 1976, and proceed to negotiating further intermediate limitations on nuclear testing, leading to the ultimate objective of the complete cessation of nuclear testing as part of an effective disarmament process".

The two sides subsequently agreed during the Washington summit meeting in December 1987 to design and conduct a joint verification experiment at their test sites in Semipalatinsk and Nevada, allowing each side an opportunity to measure the yield of explosions at the other's test sites. These visits and measurements took place in August and September 1988. United States officials indicated in December 1988 that work on a verification protocol for the Peaceful Nuclear Explosions Treaty had been substantially completed but further negotiations would be required to finalise the verification protocol for the Threshold Test Ban Treaty.

Chemical Weapons

The elimination of chemical weapons on a global basis is a long-standing Alliance objective. Proposals such as those made by the Warsaw Treaty countries in January 1984 and September 1985, limiting a ban to Europe, are inadequate for a number of reasons including the potential to reintroduce into Europe weapons stockpiled outside the area covered by such an agreement and the problem posed by verification.

A detailed draft convention for a comprehensive, worldwide, verifiable ban covering development, production, stockpiling, transfer and use of such weapons was tabled by the United States at the Conference on Disarmament in April 1984.

Significant moves on the issue of chemical weapons were contained in a declaration on arms control by Mr. Gorbachev in January 1986, and again in proposals put forward by the Soviet delegation in Geneva in April. These were energetically pursued by Western negotiators during the following months. Proposals were presented by the United Kingdom in July 1986, for example, which sought to overcome some of the problems posed by the complex issue of verification. These included practical steps needed to implement the provisions of the future Convention banning such weapons, such as the early establishment of an international inspectorate to inspect declared chemical weapons facilities, including stockpiles, weapons production lines, and certain civilian production facilities; to check the destruction of stockpiles; and to conduct challenge inspections when required.

By mid 1987 there were encouraging signs of progress following Soviet moves towards Western positions on verification. There had also been significantly more openness in discussions relating to chemical weapons. In statements by the Soviet Union in March, possession of chemical weapons was acknowledged for the first time in references to the destruction under a future agreement of both chemical weapons and of the production base for such weapons by all those possessing them, including the Soviet Union and the United States. By April, Mr. Gorbachev had spoken openly of moves made by the Soviet Union to terminate production of chemical weapons and to build installations to enable such weapons to be destroyed once an international convention had been successfully negotiated. Later in the year, the Soviet Union stated that its chemical weapons arsenal totalled about 50,000 tons. The United States had already taken steps to encourage increased openness in this sphere, disclosing detailed information on the composition of its stockpiles, and subsequently made public the locations of storage sites and production facilities.

The achievement of a complete, permanent and verifiable worldwide ban remains NATO's objective. Substantial progress could be registered on questions such as the regime for the destruction of chemical weapons and their means of production, and acceptance of the principle of verification of civil chemical production. A number of serious problems remained, however, including crucial details on the treatment of the civil chemical industry and on "challenge" inspection procedures, which would provide a means of verification of last resort.

On August 6, 1987 the Soviet Union announced its readiness to accept the principle of mandatory challenge inspections with no right of refusal, as part of the verification provisions for a chemical weapons ban.

On October 3-4, delegates from the Conference on Disarmament accepted an invitation by the Soviet Foreign Minister to visit Shikhany, one of the main Soviet chemical weapons establishments. 110 officials from 45 countries attended, plus 55 members of the press. Various types of chemical weaponry were shown and observers witnessed a live demonstration of the destruction of chemical weapons.

This was the first such visit to the Soviet Union although similar visits for delegates to the Conference have taken place in the West. The visit provided information on the Soviet chemical weapons inventory and destruction procedures. In order to build the confidence needed to underpin a comprehensive ban on chemical weapons, however, more information regarding the composition and locations of Soviet weapons would be required, on the lines of information already provided by the West.

The Geneva Conference on Disarmament summer session ended on August 28, 1987. Intersessional work on chemical weapons continued in November and December 1987 and in January 1988. The Conference itself resumed work in February 1988. Until such time as an effective and verifiable global ban has been achieved—an aim to which the Alliance as a whole is committed and to which the Soviet Union has also commited itself—the United States has said that its policy will be to maintain a retaliatory capability to deter chemical attack against US or Allied forces. Pending such a ban, during 1987 the United States government announced its decision to modernise its chemical weapons by introducing binary weapons (consisting of two chemicals which combine in flight to produce a lethal agent)—a decision for which the United States Congress had given conditional approval in July 1985. The new weapons are safer to store and handle and enable stockpiles to be significantly reduced. At the Washington summit meeting in December 1987, President Reagan and Mr.Gorbachev restated their commitment to negotiating a global and verifiable CW ban.

International Conference on Disarmament and Development

An International Conference on Disarmament and Development, postponed from 1986, took place in New York from August 24 to September 11, 1987. A French initiative, this Conference brought together 128 countries excluding the United States, which opposes the establishment of a formal linkage between the two issues. Other Allied countries participating also emphasised that there was no automatic link between the two and that the availability of resources for development cannot be dependent on progress in arms control.

The Conference adopted a Final Document containing sections dealing with philosophical aspects and with the economic and social implications of military spending. NATO countries involved in this process underline the importance of taking account of the element of security in addressing these issues. Normal consultation between the members of the Alliance takes place on these aspects.

Nuclear and Space Talks

On September 10, 1987, the North Atlantic Council was briefed by Ambassador Nitze, senior arms control adviser to President Reagan, and the three US arms control negotiators from Geneva on recent developments in those negotiations and preparations for the forthcoming meeting between Secretary of State Shultz and Soviet Foreign Minister Shevardnadze. The United States Secretary of State, embarking on his mission to Moscow to establish whether an INF agreement with the Soviet Union was now genuinely within reach, was therefore able to do so in the knowledge that he could continue to speak with the full support of the Alliance for the US negotiating position.

The way now appeared clear for final details and procedures to be worked out. An "Inspection Protocol", including a stringent verification régime, was presented by the United States at the Geneva talks on September 14, as part of a new draft treaty. It provided for extensive on-site inspection arrangements at short notice and exchange of information on locations of each side's facilities.

Four days later, at the conclusion of talks between the Soviet and United States Foreign Ministers in Washington, the announcement was made that agreement on the conclusion of an INF treaty had been reached—in principle. Plans were announced for a summit meeting at which the Treaty would be signed, and a target of Spring 1988 set for concluding a separate agreement on 50% reductions in strategic offensive missiles, but at a further meeting in Moscow it still proved impossible to set a date for the summit. The Delegations to the Geneva talks were nevertheless instructed to finalise the treaty text as quickly as possible. After a short interval, attributed to the

Soviet leadership's need to consolidate support within the Politburo, given the wide gap remaining between the United States and the Soviet Union on defence and space issues, the Soviet Union was able to confirm agreement on a summit meeting to take place before the end of the year.

As far as the Alliance was concerned, the action of the United States in putting forward the new draft and its proposals on inspection were fully endorsed by the members of the Special Consultative Group at a meeting on September 24, 1987.

On October 24, at a meeting of the North Atlantic Council, Alliance Foreign Ministers held full consultations with US Secretary of State Shultz and the US negotiating team, focussing on the meetings of Secretary Shultz with Soviet leaders in Moscow. This was the latest in the series of discussions between the members of the Alliance on these crucial arms control developments. Such meetings have become an integral part of the normal consultative process within NATO. They are an illustration of the frank manner in which the Alliance is able to move together to ensure the collective security of its member countries. Central to the process is the clear representation of their national positions and concerns by each of the sovereign nations involved, in an atmosphere which maximises the possibility of reaching consensus on policy issues. The degree of solidarity which had thus been achieved within the Alliance was demonstrably a prime factor in the successful course which the INF negotiations had begun to take.

At the end of October 1987 the details for the summit were ironed out during further discussions between the Foreign Ministers in Washington and the date of December 7 was set for the signature of what would become the first treaty to eliminate an entire class of US and Soviet nuclear missiles. Plans for the implementation of the agreement provided for elimination of SRINF missiles within one year and of all LRINF missiles within three years.

As far as strategic systems were concerned both sides envisaged a further summit to take place in Moscow in 1988 at which a treaty on 50 % reductions might be signed.

NATO Defence Ministers involved in NATO's Nuclear Planning Group met in California on November 3-4 and expressed their support for the agreement in principle on INF. They also reaffirmed their determination, consistent with NATO's arms control obligations, "to implement those measures required to maintain the effectiveness, responsiveness and survivability" of the nuclear component of deterrence.

Signature of the INF Treaty — December 1987

On December 8, 1987 President Reagan and Mr. Gorbachev signed the INF Treaty eliminating worldwide all US and Soviet intermediate-range and shorter-range land-based missiles in the 500 — 5,500 kilometre range. It is the first agreement to achieve actual reductions of nuclear weapons as opposed to limitations. Some 670 deployed Soviet missiles, including 405 SS-20s, each capable of delivering three nuclear warheads, will be destroyed, together with about 440 deployed United States missiles. The stringent verification provisions also set a good precedent for future negotiations.

In a communiqué issued following the meeting of the North Atlantic Council in Brussels on December 11, Ministers welcomed the INF Treaty. The 15 Allies concerned reaffirmed the view they had expressed at Reykjavik in June 1987, that the Treaty represented an important element in a coherent and comprehensive concept of arms control and disarmament consistent with NATO's doctrine of flexible response.

The shorter-range INF missiles covered by the Treaty will be phased out over 18 months following ratification, and the longer-range missiles over three years in accordance with an agreed timetable. NATO deployments were suspended, pending ratification of the Treaty and the beginning of its implementation. The Soviet Union initiated steps to dismantle the missiles. Full hearings took place in the United States Senate during the early part of 1988 and the Treaty was ratified by both countries immediately before the Moscow Summit meeting between President Reagan and General Secretary Gorbachev in June.

The details of the inspection arrangements are set out in the Inspection Protocol appended to the INF Treaty. At a ceremony at NATO Headquarters in Brussels on December 11, 1987, Basing Country Agreements were signed between the United States, the United Kingdom, the Federal Republic of Germany, Belgium, the Netherlands and Italy, establishing practical procedures and provisions for verification. There were subsequently exchanges of notes between the countries concerned and the Soviet Union, granting inspection rights on national territory subject to Soviet undertakings regarding compliance with each country's laws and procedures and respect for national sovereignty and security. Regular consultations on the implementation of the inspection régime will take place between the countries concerned and the United States.

Four types of inspections are involved:

(a) Baseline data exchange inspection—within 30-90 days of the treaty's entry into force.

(b) Short notice challenge inspections during the period when missiles are still deployed.

(c) Close-out inspections when all the missiles have been eliminated.

(d) Continuing short-notice challenge inspections for 10 years after the end of the three year period during which the missiles will be eliminated.

Strategic Weapons and Defence and Space Issues

While progress on the INF negotiations inevitably became the focus of attention during much of the period from 1985 to 1987, the bilateral negotiations which had opened in Geneva in March 1985 under the broad heading of Nuclear and Space Talks involved two other important spheres—strategic arms reductions and defence and space issues. The agreed aim for the talks as a whole was to work out effective arrangements for preventing an arms race in space and terminating it on earth; for limiting and reducing nuclear arms; and for strengthening strategic stability. For much of the period, the vehemence of Soviet opposition to the United States' research programme on its Strategic Defence Initiative meant that few advances were made in the strategic sphere.

In May 1987 the US had tabled a draft treaty which provided for 50% cuts in US and Soviet offensive strategic nuclear weapons over a period of seven years. The Soviet Union continued to insist that an agreement would have to be linked to constraints on the US Strategic Defence Initiative. Several other major differences between the two sides persisted, including problems concerning sub limits and difficulties over submarine-launched cruise missiles (SLCMs).

In July 1987 the Soviet Union had tabled a draft agreement on defence and space issues. The presentation of the draft was a positive development, but Soviet proposals followed the same line as previous Soviet positions, making the 50% reduction in strategic offensive arms contingent upon an accord limiting the testing and deployment of space-based missile defence systems. They also required both sides to agree not to withdraw from the ABM Treaty and to observe all its provisions strictly for ten years while a strategic arms agreement was implemented.

In a joint statement issued at the end of the December 1987 Washington Summit, President Reagan and Mr. Gorbachev announced that considerable progress had been made towards an agreement on 50% reductions in strategic nuclear weapons. They instructed their negotiators to speed up work on a treaty text, preferably in time for signature at their next Summit in the first half of 1988, building on the Joint Draft START Treaty Text being developed in Geneva. The negotiators were instructed to give priority to:

— further steps to ensure that reductions would enhance strategic stability;
— counting rules for air-launched cruise missiles on heavy bombers and ballistic missiles;
— the question of limiting long-range submarine-launched cruise missiles;
— developing verification measures on the basis of the INF Treaty provisions, to include data exchanges, baseline inspections, on-site observation and monitoring and short-notice on-site inspections.

The two sides were also instructed to discuss ways to ensure predictability in the development of the US-Soviet strategic relationship under conditions of strategic stability which would reduce the risk of nuclear war.

As regards space and defence issues, the two leaders instructed their Geneva negotiators "to work out an agreement that would commit the sides to observe the ABM Treaty, as signed in 1972, while conducting their research, development, and testing as required, which are permitted by the ABM Treaty, and not to withdraw from the ABM Treaty, for a specified period of time." Intensive discussions of strategic stability were to begin "not later than three years before the end of the specified period, after which, in the event the sides have not agreed otherwise, each side will be free to decide its course of action."

Anniversary of the Harmel Doctrine

At regular intervals throughout its history, the Alliance has commissioned thorough reviews of the state of East-West relations and the extent to which Alliance policies measure up to current demands. The focus of such reviews has sometimes been directed towards one particular aspect of Alliance policy. Thus the work of the Temporary Council Committee, analysing in detail the defence capabilities of each member country, led to the important measures and organisational changes endorsed in the 1952 Lisbon Decisions of the Council; the 1956 Report of the Committee of Three concentrated in particular on non-military aspects of cooperation within the Alliance and addressed topics such as political consultation and economic cooperation, cultural cooperation, and cooperation in the field of information policy; the comprehensive AD 70 Study looked at the tasks facing Allied Defence in the 1970s and at the relationship between the political objectives of the Alliance and the military apparatus needed to realise them; and in 1974 the conclusions of a number of studies focusing on the transatlantic relationship came together in the Ottawa Declaration on Atlantic Relations.

Of all the reviews leading to documents which have become a part of the present-day Alliance's political heritage, the 1967 Harmel Report on the Future Tasks of the Alliance is the one which has had the most enduring and fundamental effect on Allied policy-making and has provided the reference point for the more difficult collective decisions taken by Allied governments. The short text of the Report is reproduced in full in the documentation section of this book and is referred to in numerous different contexts elsewhere. It stated in essence that the essential purpose of the North Atlantic Treaty Organisation is to provide the political solidarity and military strength necessary to permit the search to be pursued for a more stable relationship between East and West in which the fundamental political issues dividing them can be resolved peacefully. It recognised that for the foreseeable future the Alliance would continue to be compelled to safeguard peace through its ability to deter aggression and to provide protection from political blackmail. And it affirmed the importance of continuing to seek ways of improving the situation.

In December 1987 the North Atlantic Council marked the 20th anniversary of the Harmel Report and highlighted the continuing validity of its balanced and complementary approach. Deterrence and defence, together with arms control and disarmament, would remain integral parts of Alliance security policy. Member countries remained committed to vigorous efforts in all appropriate fora, to achieve substantial, balanced and verifiable arms limitations and reductions. The INF Treaty which had just been signed demonstrated the effectiveness of these policies, the object of which was to achieve a stable military balance, if possible at reduced levels of forces.

Pierre Harmel was the 1987 recipient of the Atlantic Award for services to the Alliance.

Resignation of Lord Carrington—appointment of Manfred Wörner

When Foreign Ministers met in December 1987, they noted that Lord Carrington had announced his intention to relinquish his post as Secretary General. The Council invited Manfred Wörner, Minister of Defence of the Federal Republic of Germany to succeed Lord Carrington. Mr. Wörner took up his appointment on July 1, 1988.

Summit Meeting of the North Atlantic Council—March 2-3, 1988

NATO's summit meetings have always been special events for the Alliance, never a matter of routine. Together, the three meetings of the North Atlantic Council which took place at summit level in 1982, 1985 and 1988 marked the history of what has been called "the INF era". The 1982 Summit, which took place in Bonn demonstrated Allied resolve to implement its 1979 double-track decision. Faced with the Soviet refusal to enter serious negotiations which would obviate the need for NATO to deploy its own land-based intermediate INF missiles, the countries concerned proceeded with deployments in order to preserve the effectiveness and credibility of deterrence and the indivisibility of Allied security.

The second meeting attended by Heads of State and Government in this period was held in Brussels on November 21 1985. This was a time for renewed hope following the first meeting of President Reagan and Mr. Gorbachev and the advent of a more promising climate in East-West relations. The third summit meeting in this era, in March 1988, took place at a time of achievement. It also provided an opportunity for taking stock in the period following the signature of the INF Treaty, for reaffirming the fundamental tenets of Allied security in the run-up to the forthcoming Moscow Summit, and charting the way ahead.

The March 1988 Summit meeting set out the political strategy which was to guide the Alliance's work during the forthcoming challenging period in the East-West relationship. Heads of State or Government from all member countries participated, attended by some 1,200 representatives of the world's press and media. Opening this important meeting, the Secretary General, Lord Carrington, hailed the signature of the INF Treaty as a success for the Alliance. The Treaty was a milestone in the search for better security at lower levels of forces on which NATO governments had embarked many years earlier. The Alliance, however, could not rest on its laurels. The achievement of a single agreement to reduce weapons and the apparent willingness of a new Soviet leader to reduce some of the tensions, welcome as these developments were, did not in themselves remove the significance of the military capability and potential of the Soviet Union.

The March Summit Declaration[44] demonstrated the coherence of the approach taken by the Alliance towards East-West relations as a whole. It

---

[44] The Declaration of the Heads of State and Government participating in the March 1988 meeting of the North Atlantic Council in Brussels is reproduced in full at Appendix I.

stressed the continuing validity of the Alliance's balanced security policy as set out in the Harmel Report: political solidarity and adequate military strength, and on that basis, the search for constructive dialogue and cooperation, including arms control. It reaffirmed at the highest level Allied unity and common ideals and purposes; the principles and provisions of the North Atlantic Treaty; the importance of the Alliance for security; and the validity of the Alliance's strategy for peace. It reasserted the indivisibility of Allied security, the Alliance's dedication to preserving peace and freedom, to collective self-defence and to political solidarity and adequate military strength, as the basis for the search for constructive dialogue and cooperation with the East.

The Summit Declaration reaffirmed the essential components of the Alliance's policy for achieving these objectives, including the vital linkage between the security and prosperity of the European allies on the one hand and the North American allies on the other, and the significance for the transatlantic partnership of a strong European pillar.

The Summit meeting also examined the wider dimensions of Alliance polices aimed at the prevention of any kind of war or intimidation. Allied leaders emphasised that credible deterrence, which has secured peace in Europe for nearly forty years, cannot be assured by conventional defences alone. For the foreseeable future there is no alternative to the strategy of deterrence based upon an appropriate mix of adequate and effective nuclear and conventional forces kept up-to-date where necessary. The efforts to ensure the continued viability, credibility and effectiveness of these forces have to be sustained and the risks, burdens and benefits of defence fairly shared. The Alliance upholds the principles of sovereignty, territorial integrity and individual rights, seeks to overcome the unnatural division of Europe and to improve the situation in Berlin, and is dedicated to the search for improved and more stable East-West relations. The Summit Declaration again called upon the Soviet Union and other countries of Eastern Europe to join with the members of the Alliance in working for further relaxation of tensions, greater security at lower levels of armaments, more extensive human contacts and increased access to information.

The Declaration constituted not only a powerful reaffirmation of policy but a concrete prescription for the political and military steps required to translate objectives into achievements. It emphasised that signs of change in the policies of the Soviet Union and some of its Allies, holding out prospects for greater openness, were welcome, but that the Alliance looked beyond pronouncements. There was as yet no evidence of any relaxation of the Soviet military effort or assurance that it would not be used outside the borders of the Soviet Union. While this fundamental source of tension between East and West persisted, steadfastness and greater efficiency were needed in the application of resources to defence and within the Alliance practical cooperation to this end was continuing. Arms control negotiations were an integral part of the process, not for their own sake but for the contribution they make to security. The INF Treaty exemplified this approach. Progress was needed across the board, in nuclear arms control, in resolving conventional imbalances, in the field of human rights, in the implementation of the CSCE and CDE accords and the strengthening of the CSCE process, and in achieving the speedy and complete withdrawal of Soviet troops from Afghanistan and restoration of that country's sovereignty.

This was therefore the background for the forthcoming Summit meeting in Moscow, between the United States President and the Soviet leader.

Conventional Arms Control: The Way Ahead

A second document, published under the authority of the Heads of State and Government, focussed on the prerequisites for progress in the field of conventional arms control[45]. Allied governments identified military confrontation as the result, not the cause, of the painful division which burdens the European continent. The conventional imbalance remains at the core of Europe's security concerns, along with other asymmetries such as the capability for surprise attack and large-scale offensive action and the continuing shroud of secrecy over its military posture and activities of the Soviet Union and other Warsaw Treaty countries. The Alliance neither has nor aspires to such capabilities and its military activities are transparent and open to permanent public scrutiny. Allied leaders declared that the dominant military presence of Soviet forces in Europe—fifty per cent of the total forces present—serving a political as well as a military function, casts a shadow over the whole continent.

The Statement on Arms Control also focussed on the prerequisites underlying Allied negotiating proposals for achieving conventional stability, including the need to ensure that defence and arms control policies remain in harmony and make complementary contributions to Allied security.

High priority is accorded to the Alliance's objective of establishing a situation in Europe in which force postures as well as the numbers and deployments of weapon systems no longer make surprise attack and large scale offensive action a feasible option. Together with this fundamental goal, the establishment of a more stable balance of forces as a whole, and enhanced respect for human rights and fundamental freedoms throughout Europe, represent a realistic basis for bringing about lasting security and stability.

The period following the March 1988 NATO Summit Meeting saw a number of further developments of significance for East-West relations as well as progress in relation to several topics on the Alliance's internal agenda.

Burden sharing

Closely related to the issue of improvements in defence capabilities is the question of the equitable distribution both of the economic burden of defence

[45] Statement issued under the authority of Heads of State and Government participating in the March 1988 meeting of the North Atlantic Council in Brussels. Reproduced in full at Appendix I.

and of the roles, risks and responsibilities shared by member nations. This is a subject of major importance in an Alliance in which sovereign and independent nations enter into a contractual relationship with their allies based upon unity of purpose, common interests and common values. There is nevertheless room for legitimate differences of view over what constitutes equitable burden sharing. Pressures to reduce the United States trade deficit and levels of government spending has focussed renewed attention on this issue. One consequence of this, reflected in efforts made within the Alliance to develop an improved strategy for the management of resources, has been to transfer emphasis from defence expenditure to the manner in which defence budgets are translated into effective deterrent forces, equipped, trained, deployed where required, and ready to perform their task. Measuring contributions to the common security in terms of output rather than input constitutes a better basis for future discussion of burden sharing issues.

At their meeting in Brussels in May 1988, Defence Ministers reviewed other work which had been set in hand, including measures to improve the effectiveness of conventional forces and efforts to broaden Alliance participation in the provision of assistance to Greece, Portugal and Turkey. The Force Goals of these countries established under NATO's defence planning process would henceforth include a new category of Military Assistance Requirements.

US-Soviet Moscow Summit Meeting

The process of ratification of the INF Treaty, involving further contacts between Secretary of State Shultz and Soviet Foreign Minister Shevardnadze to clarify treaty provisions dealing inter alia with on-site inspections, culminated in the exchange of the instruments of ratification at the US-Soviet Moscow Summit meeting on June 1, 1988. The Summit Meeting itself provided tangible evidence that a new climate in East-West relations now prevailed.

Some progress was made towards a treaty on strategic nuclear weapons, aimed at a 50% reduction, and progress was also registered in the fields of human rights, regional conflicts and human contacts. Unprecedented prominance was accorded to human rights in the joint statement issued at the conclusion of the Summit. These developments were welcomed by Foreign Ministers of the Alliance at the June 1988 Spring Ministerial Meeting of the North Atlantic Council, both for their substance and as a portent for the future development of East-West relations.

Meeting of the North Atlantic Council in Madrid—June 1988

The Ministerial Meeting of the North Atlantic Council in Madrid, the first to be held in that city since Spain joined the Alliance in 1982, provided an opportunity to reiterate the welcome given to Spain and to emphasise the Council's support for the process under way in response to Spanish proposals for defining a significant Spanish military contribution to the common defence, outside the integrated military structure.

Other issues addressed by Foreign Ministers in Madrid included the current situation in and prospects for Eastern Europe; the outcome required from the CSCE Follow-up meeting in Vienna, and the commitment to share equitably the risks, burdens and responsibilities as well as the benefits of the partnership between the members of the Alliance.

Foreign Ministers also paid tribute to the outstanding contribution of the departing Secretary General, Lord Carrington, on completion of his term of office.

Vienna CSCE Follow-up Meeting

Since the signature of the Helsinki Final Act in 1975, Follow-up Meetings had taken place in Belgrade (1977-78) and Madrid (1980-83) and there had been a number of meetings of experts convened in accordance with mandates issued by the Helsinki, Belgrade and Madrid meetings to seek progress in specific fields. The third major Follow-up Meeting had opened in Vienna in November 1986. Hopes for the conference were high, following the relative success of the "CDE" (Conference on Security and Confidence-Building Measures and Disarmament in Europe) which had taken place from 1984 to 1986 and whose achievements the Vienna meeting would assess. Moreover, the pronouncements by General Secretary Gorbachev regarding plans for far-reaching reforms in the Soviet Union and greater openness in Soviet dealings with the West, led to the expectation that further advances building on the progress already made in the CSCE context would be forthcoming. With the end of 1988 approaching, however, agreement on a satisfactory concluding document still eluded the 35 participating countries, in large part as a result of difficulties encountered in gaining acceptance for measures designed to deepen the CSCE process in the human rights field—an area where progress is regarded by Western participants as indispensable for the success of the CSCE process as a whole. Major importance was therefore attached to specific and concrete commitments in this field.

Nuclear Matters

When NATO Defence Ministers met in the Hague in October 1988, they recorded their satisfaction that the INF Treaty had entered into force and that to date its implementation was proceeding smoothly. Their agenda included reports on progress towards measures to ensure that NATO's nuclear forces continue to provide a credible and effective contribution to the Alliance's strategy of deterrence. In the communiqué issued following their meeting, the NPG Ministers expressed continued support for the efforts of member countries to meet requirements stemming from the Montebello decision to maintain a credible nuclear deterrent posture at the minimum necessary level of weapons. While no decision was required then on the implementation of specific measures, security needs were to be kept under review in the context of the Montebello framework and in accordance with the continuing development of a comprehensive and integrated concept of security and arms control.

Conventional Forces in Europe: The Facts

On November 25, in the context of encouraging greater openness about military matters and increased transparency, the Alliance published its assessment of the strengths of the armed forces in Europe belonging to the countries of the North Atlantic Alliance and the Warsaw Treaty Organisation[46]. This information was published without prejudice to either of the forthcoming negotiations within the CSCE framework on Confidence and Security-Building Measures and on Conventional Stability. It was simultaneously transmitted to all CSCE participating states. Improved openness about military forces and their activities represents a fundamental objective of the Alliance at the talks on Confidence and Security-Building Measures. Accordingly, the Alliance simultaneously announced that they would present, as they had done at the 1984-1986 Stockholm Conference, a proposal that participating states should provide each year, on the basis of an agreed formula, information on the composition, organisation and deployment of their armed forces in Europe. At the Conventional Stability talks[47] the provision of detailed information on relevant forces and weapons systems would also be necessary in the context of a verifiable agreement on how to achieve stability at lower levels. The information published on this occasion was not a substitute for the data which all participants would need to provide in the course of the two new negotiations, nor did it seek to pre-judge the categories of forces to be covered or the degree of detail necessary.

Decisions of the Defence Planning Committee—December 2, 1988

Defence Ministers came together again early in December for the regular end-of-year Ministerial meeting of the Defence Planning Committee. Their agenda was particularly full on this occasion since the results of work initiated at earlier meetings in several key areas of concern were now available. The normal communiqué issued at the conclusion of the meeting referred to the potential for improved and progressively more stable East-West relations if current signs of change in the policies of the Soviet Union and of some of the other members of the Warsaw Treaty Organisation were to result in a relaxation in the scale of their military efforts and a more defensive doctrine. However the Ministers emphasized the need to ensure NATO's defence against the reality of the Soviet Union's actual military capabilities.

---

46 "Conventional Forces in Europe: The Facts". Copies of this publication are available from the NATO Information Service, B-1110 Brussels.

47 Renamed Negotiations on Conventional Armed Forces in Europe (CFE).

Central to the Defence Ministers' deliberations was the need for all Alliance members to share equitably the roles, risks and responsibilities, as well as the benefits of their collective defence. The results of the review on this subject commissioned in May 1988 were contained in a major report which had now been published[48]. The report addressed the perceptions and realities involved in this issue and concluded that, as the Alliance approached its 40th anniversary, its strength and cohesion remained as firm as ever, with major contributions being made by both the European and North American pillars of the Alliance. Nevertheless, the report had also shown that there are signficant variations among countries in the scale and nature of their contributions, and had identified a number of areas where further improvements could be made to strengthen the Alliance's defence capability.

Defence Ministers took several other important decisions, including the initiation of a study by the NATO Military Authorities on how to enhance the effectiveness and availability of operational capabilities of the European forces in the Northern Army Group area which would examine the feasibility of forming a multinational division. In addition, Defence Ministers examined the problem of ensuring that NATO forces continued to receive the necessary level of training while seeking to minimise the impact on their publics. The report on enhancing Alliance collective security had emphasised that sustained public support for defence and security would continue to be a determining factor in improving prospects for enhanced security, thereby strengthening peace and security.

In the context of Conventional Defence Improvements, progress in redressing key deficiencies in conventional forces was reviewed and the importance of meeting the goals which had been set in this field was reaffirmed.

Several other important topics were also addressed, including progress being made on the participation of Spain in Allied defence planning under guidelines which had been approved for the development of coordination agreements between the Major NATO Commanders and the Spanish Military Authorities for Spain's military contribution to the common defence outside the integrated military structure; the need for early results from the current examination of levels of assistance to Greece, Portugal and Turkey through research and cost-sharing arrangements within armaments projects, and opportunities to broaden the basis for such assistance; and progress in the trials going on of the NATO Conventional Armaments Planning System. Under decisions taken on infrastructure financing, it was agreed to provide additional funding to accommodate the relocation of the United States 401st Tactical Fighter Wing from Spain to Italy.

In the arms control field, conventional disparities in Europe had been highlighted in the facts and figures published by the Alliance on November 25. Defence Ministers emphasized that it was in this field that the greatest

---

[48] Report by NATO's Defence Planning Committee entitled "Enhancing Alliance Collective Security. Shared roles, risks, and responsibilities in the Alliance". Published on December 2, 1988. Progress Report published November 1989.

potential existed for enhancing security and expressed their desire to see an early commencement of Conventional Stability Talks covering Europe from the Atlantic to the Urals following a substantial and balanced outcome to the Vienna Follow-up Meeting and the Conference on Security and Cooperation in Europe.

Meeting of the North Atlantic Council in Brussels— December 8-9, 1988

Real signs of progress in relations between East and West made the setting for the end of year ministerial meeting of the North Atlantic Council more positive than had been possible for some time. Realistic expectations of further progress in the relationship, towards goals which have been at the heart of Alliance policies for many years, did not allow major concerns over such issues as Afghanistan, human rights, military postures and imbalances in military forces to be ignored. Many serious problems continued to accentuate the East-West divide and to represent actual or potential causes of tension. However, objective assessments of what had thus far been achieved in enhancing stability justified some optimism. This was reflected in the stance adopted by NATO Foreign Ministers in their public utterances.

The statement on Conventional Arms Control issued by Foreign Ministers on December 8 marked an important juncture in the search for progress towards meaningful negotiations in this field. At the March 1988 Summit Meeting, Allied governments had emphasised their concerns over the imbalance in conventional forces. This imbalance had recently been highlighted once again by the publication of an Allied assessment of conventional forces in Europe. The Alliance was now able to announce specific proposals which would be presented at the negotiating table to redress it.

Two sets of negotiations had been proposed, both to begin in the near future—one on conventional stability between the 23 members of the two military Alliances in Europe and one on confidence and security-building measures among all 35 signatories of the Helsinki Final Act.

The December statement outlined in considerable detail the principles to which member countries of the Alliance would adhere in conducting the negotiations. In the framework of progress towards stability, the emphasis would be on the most destabilising conventional systems; the very systems in which the East has such a massive preponderance—tanks, artillery and armoured troop carriers. President Gorbachev's announcement of reductions and the Soviet Union's declared readiness to adjust its force posture, made public at the 43rd United Nations General Assembly on December 7, were welcomed as a positive contribution and a very important first step towards correcting the situation. They would reduce but not eliminate conventional imbalances. The important thing now was to build on these hopeful developments at the negotiating table.

In the framework of progress towards greater transparency in military organisation and activities, and better contacts and communications, all of which are essential if real stability is to be achieved, the Alliance similarly set out the principles which would be the basis for the negotiations. The objective was to achieve steady progress on all aspects of the confrontation which has divided Europe for more than four decades. The statement emphasised that conventional arms control has to be seen as part of a dynamic process which addresses the military, political and human aspects of this division. The full text of the Statement is reproduced at Appendix I.

In the Communiqué published by Foreign Ministers on December 9, Foreign Ministers outlined the context for continued efforts to secure further progress in East-West relations across the board. There were clear signs of change in the internal and external policies of the Soviet Union and of some of its allies. Promising prospects were opening up for an improved East-West dialogue. If this trend were sustained it would offer an unprecedented opportunity to shape a better international environment. Among the most promising recent developments was the address made by President Gorbachev at the United Nations. The members of the Alliance reiterated that they were willing to work closely with the Soviet Union and its allies in the search for ways to ease and finally overcome the painful division of Europe.

While the focus of attention was naturally on the hopes and aspirations which resulted from the improved prospects for progress in all these spheres, the Communiqué stressed the need for realism. In many fields there is a long way to go before major concerns are satisfied. Pressures for movement towards political and economic reform are mounting in Eastern Europe. Progress achieved in certain areas is welcome but a realistic view of developments is called for. The Soviet Union and the other Eastern countries still have to meet fully their obligations on human rights. Important measures recently introduced or announced in this field were encouraging. In the defence area, too, it was hoped that President Gorbachev's address represented the starting point of a new approach by the Soviet Union to the size and structure of its military forces and programmes.

The Allies reaffirmed their approach to these matters. They stressed the importance of the INF Treaty whose smooth implementation they welcomed. Those participating in the MBFR talks emphasised their agreement that the talks should continue until a mandate for new negotiations on conventional stability had emerged, and be concluded before the start of new negotiations. The Alliance also remained fully committed to the goal of an early conclusion of a truly world-wide, comprehensive and effectively verifiable ban on chemical weapons and endorsed the call for a conference in Paris of the states which are party to the 1925 Geneva Protocol, and other states concerned.

As on all such occasions the Council discussed other matters high on the list of priority concerns for the Alliance as a whole. Progress on the further development of a comprehensive concept of arms control and disarmament was examined and welcomed. Those countries concerned discussed the work being done to enhance the collective security of the Alliance and noted that the report recently published on this subject broke new ground and set out a clear course for future action.

Other matters examined by the North Atlantic Council included the expected resumption of the Soviet troop withdrawal from Afghanistan to enable the February 15 deadline for completion of the process to be met; improvements needed on economic cooperation and assistance within the Alliance; the importance for the Alliance of the guidelines which had been approved for coordination agreements between the Major NATO Commanders and the Spanish Military Authorities; and Ministerial guidance for civil emergency planning and preparedness. The Council also discussed issues relating to East-West trade; the situation in the Mediterranean; armaments cooperation and planning— including in particular Canadian proposals being examined by the Conference of National Armaments Directors for assistance to countries with lesser developed defence industries; and the overall status of Allied aims and objectives just before the 40th Anniversary of the North Atlantic Treaty.

Already a year which had been punctuated by significant developments in the sphere of international affairs, 1988 thus drew to a close in a new spirit of confidence created, on the one hand, by the announcement by the Soviet Union of significant conventional force reductions and changes affecting Soviet military posture, as well as other far-reaching proposals in political, economic, technological and environmental fields; and on the other by the announcement of the Alliance initiative, to be pursued at the forthcoming negotiations in Vienna, designed to move towards an East-West relationship based on greater stability, greater transparency of military organisation and activities, and better contacts and communications. This initiative postulated a vision for Europe as a continent where military forces only exist to prevent war and to ensure self defence, not for the purpose of initiating aggression or for political or military intimidation. Its realisation may still be a long way off, but it is a vision which appeared a step nearer than could have been foreseen at the beginning of the year.

Vienna CSCE Follow-up Meeting

The Vienna CSCE Follow-up Meeting ended on January 19, 1989 with the adoption of a far-reaching concluding document extending and developing the CSCE process in many important respects. The main provisions of the document are outlined in Chapter 11. Of particular importance to the process of enhancing security and stability in the whole of Europe were agreements on mandates for two new sets of negotiations on Conventional Armed Forces in Europe (CFE), among the 23 members of NATO and the Warsaw Treaty Organisation; and on Confidence and Security-Building Measures (CSBMs) among all 35 CSCE states.

Conclusion of MBFR Negotiations

With the decision to open new negotiations within the CSCE framework, the states which had participated since 1973 in efforts to achieve Mutual and Balanced Force Reductions agreed to conclude these negotiations. They held their last meeting on February 2, 1989.

Soviet and East European force reductions

During January and February 1989, in the build-up to the opening of the new negotiations on conventional forces, the Soviet Union and several East European countries (the German Democratic Republic, Poland, Hungary, Czechoslovakia and Bulgaria) announced their intention to withdraw and cut back their conventional forces in a number of significant respects. The announcements were welcomed by Alliance leaders as an indication of the long-awaited recognition by the Warsaw Treaty countries of the need to address major disparities in Eastern and Western forces in Europe. If implemented, the cuts would contribute to the process of assymetrical reduction needed to increase stability and mutual confidence. However, even after full implementation of the measures announced, large imbalances in forces and armaments would remain. These would be addressed in far-reaching proposals to be made at the conference table in Vienna, when the new conventional force negotiations opened in March 1989.

CSCE Ministerial Meeting in Vienna — March 6-8, 1989

Foreign Ministers and other representatives of the CSCE countries met in Vienna from March 6-8, 1989 on the occasion of the opening of the two new sets of negotiations on Conventional Forces in Europe and on Confidence and Security-Building Measures. On March 6, the Western participants released detailed position papers explaining Western proposals in both negotiations.[49]

Opening of Vienna Negotiations on Conventional Armed Forces in Europe (CFE) — March 9, 1989

The negotiations on Conventional Armed Forces in Europe (CFE) formally opened on March 9, 1989. The mandate of the negotiations, the development of which is described earlier, is to strengthen stability and security in Europe through the establishment of a stable and secure balance of conventional forces at lower levels. Outline proposals tabled by NATO countries on the first day of the talks, and an initial proposal introduced by the Eastern participants are summarised in Chapter 11.

Opening of Vienna Negotiations on Confidence and Security-Building Measures (CSBMs) — March 9, 1989

The second set of negotiations agreed upon at the Vienna CSCE Follow-up Meeting also opened on March 9. Involving all 35 CSCE States, these negotiations seek inter alia to maintain the momentum of the successful implementation of the Stockholm Document agreed upon in 1986. The complementary and interactive nature of all the different endeavours currently being undertaken in the field of arms control and disarmament is fully

---

49 See NATO Review N° 2, 1989.

recognised by the Alliance and indeed the negotiations on Confidence and Security-Building Measures are seen by member countries as a key element which can favourably influence the climate for negotiating successful agreements to eliminate imbalances in specific fields of armaments and armed forces.

Meeting of NATO Heads of State and Government — May 29-30 1989

The NATO Summit Meeting held at the end of May 1989 was a singularly noteworthy occasion for the Alliance. Two major statements of Alliance policy were adopted, namely a Declaration marking the fortieth Anniversary of the Alliance and setting out goals and policies to guide the Allies during the fifth decade of their cooperation; and a Comprehensive Concept of Arms Control and Disarmament, prepared in response to the mandate given at the June 1987 Ministerial meeting in Reykjavik.

The Summit Declaration[50] contained many extremely important elements. It recognised the changes that are under way in the Soviet Union as well as in some other East European countries, and outlined the Alliance's approach to the overcoming of the division of Europe and the shaping of a just and peaceful European order. It reiterated the need for credible and effective deterrent forces and an adequate defence and endorsed in principle President Bush's arms control initiative, calling for an acceleration of the CFE negotiations in Vienna and for significant reductions in land-based combat aircraft, helicopters, and United States and Soviet military personnel stationed outside their national territory, as well as in the three categories (tanks, artillery, armoured troop carriers) included in the initial Western CFE proposal made in Vienna in March 1989. A broad agenda for expanded East-West cooperation in other areas, for action on significant global challenges, and for meeting the Alliance's long-term objectives, was also set forth.

The Comprehensive Concept[51] placed the Allies' arms control policy within the broad context of overall Alliance political and military objectives and policies. The guiding principles of arms control — security, stability and verifiability — were identified and developed, and the Allies' objectives in a number of arms control areas (conventional, nuclear and chemical weapons) were stated. The Comprehensive Concept won widespread public support, not least for its resolution of the politically difficult issue concerning short-range nuclear forces. In a key paragraph addressing this issue, the Alliance first reiterated that one of its highest priorities in negotiations with the East is reaching an agreement on conventional force reductions which would achieve the objectives formulated at Reykjavik in 1987 and reaffirmed in Brussels in 1988. The Alliance would make every effort to bring these

---

50 The Declaration of the Heads of State and Government participating in the May 1989 meeting of the North Atlantic Council in Brussels is reproduced in full at Appendix I.

51 The Comprehensive Concept of Arms Control and Disarmament is reproduced in full at Appendix I.

negotiations to an early and satisfactory conclusion. "Once implementation of such an agreement is under way", the text states, "the United States, in consultation with those Allies concerned, is prepared to enter into negotiations to achieve a *partial* reduction of American and Soviet land-based nuclear missile forces of shorter range to equal and verifiable levels". Referring to the Western proposals tabled at the CFE negotiations in Vienna, enhanced by the additional proposals by the United States mentioned above, endorsed by the Alliance, the report on the Comprehensive Concept then affirms that "the Allies concerned proceed on the understanding that negotiated reductions leading to a level below the existing level of their SNF missiles will not be carried out until the results of these negotiations have been implemented. Reductions of Warsaw Pact/SNF systems should be carried out before that date."

Ministerial Meeting of the Defence Planning Committee, June 8-9 1989

When Defence Ministers met for their normal Spring Ministerial meeting a week after the Summit, in addition to their usual review of a wide range of defence planning issues, they recognised that the CFE negotiations, and the further proposals which, as had been agreed at the Summit, would be tabled at the CFE negotiations, have important implications for NATO's collective defence planning activities. They agreed that it is essential that the Alliance's defence and arms control objectives remain in harmony in order to ensure their complementary contribution to achieving the goal of enhanced security at the lowest possible level of forces. Accordingly they tasked the Defence Planning Committee in Permanent Session to consider how Alliance defence planning can most effectively contribute to this end.

Re-opening of Strategic Arms Reductions Talks and Defence and Space Talks — June 19, 1989

In mid-June, after an interval of seven months, during which period the transition to the new Administration in the United States had taken place, bilateral negotiations between the United States and the Soviet Union re-opened in Geneva in the Strategic Arms Reductions Talks (START) and the Defence and Space Talks. Much detailed work towards agreement in START had been carried out before the previous round of negotiations had been concluded, and although the complexity of the issues to be resolved should not be underestimated, the prospects for progress are favourable. In parallel with these START negotiations, the United States is continuing its talks with the Soviet Union on defence and space matters, in order to ensure that strategic stability is enhanced.

Chemical Weapons

Difficulties and challenges notwithstanding, unprecedented progress has been achieved in the field of arms control generally. In another area of major concern, that of progress towards a global, comprehensive and effectively verifiable ban on chemical weapons, the Paris Conference on the Prohibition of Chemical Weapons, held in January 1989, reaffirmed the authority of the 1925 Geneva Protocol and gave powerful political impetus to the negotiations taking place in the Conference on Disarmament in Geneva.

The Fifth Decade

In the wider political sphere there have been positive developments and marked progress on other matters of importance to the West. Soviet troops have left Afghanistan. There has been movement towards the resolution of some, although not all, of the remaining regional conflicts in which the Soviet Union is involved. Improvements have taken place in the observance of human rights in the Soviet Union, even if serious deficiencies remain. Following the conclusion of the Vienna CSCE Follow-up Meeting, further progress in the CSCE process can be anticipated. And the intensity of high-level dialogue between East and West offers new opportunities. In all this, the Alliance has clearly had a fundamental rôle.

With the Alliance entering its fifth decade without illusions but with the resolve of its 16 member countries to pursue their common objectives through cooperation and constructive dialogue, this chronicle of events in the forty-year history of the Alliance thus concludes. The narrative is a continuing one and the pace of change is accelerating. Yet international developments in the Spring of 1989 demonstrated only too well that the stability of international relations can be all too easily undermined by oppression, despite the inherent inability of oppressive systems to fulfill the aspirations of their citizens.

The leaders of the North Atlantic Alliance could look back on a history of success when they met to mark the Alliance's fortieth anniversary. They registered the need to maintain Allied defence in a time of considerable change and to take the initiative in seeking to exploit the potential of arms control as an agent of change. In their Summit Declaration, however, it was on the Alliance's longer term objectives that they placed the focus. An enhanced partnership within the Alliance and a determination to replace confrontation with cooperation outside the Alliance offer the prospect of addressing directly the fundamental issues which have been at the heart of Allied concerns since the signing of the 1949 Treaty — overcoming the underlying political causes of the division of Europe; establishing a new pattern of relations between East and West in which ideological and military antagonisms are replaced by cooperation, trust and peaceful competition with full guarantees for human rights and political freedoms; and achieving progress in meeting global challenges not only in the security field but also in political, economic, environmental, scientific and technological spheres. The fortieth anniversary Summit Meeting provided the occasion for the Alliance to rise to these challenges with a blueprint for shaping the future and a dynamic joint agenda for its progressive implementation.

Part 3

The Political Framework

Chapter 5

Political Consultation in NATO

NATO is composed of sovereign nations which retain their independence in all fields including foreign policy. All NATO allies have equal rights and each has an equal voice at the Council table, irrespective of size, population, territory or the scope of its global or regional commitments. Decisions in the Council are therefore not taken by majority vote but by common consent. Consensus is the rule throughout the Organisation. However, the process of achieving it among 16 nations, each of which brings to any given problem its individual experience and outlook, necessarily demands patience and time. If all are fully and freely to agree, the first requirement is that they understand one another's positions.

Close political cooperation among the Allies thus depends first and foremost on all member governments being fully informed of each other's overall policies and of the underlying considerations which give rise to them. Secondly, if there is to be any coordination of foreign policies, there must be continuing consultation among member countries regarding the evolution of their thinking and their respective positions on more specific questions. These two aims are separate, but linked.

Informing member governments

Keeping the other member governments informed means regular exchanges of information on events of interest to the Alliance as a whole, and notification of decisions before they are made public. In practice this exchange of information was initially little more than a courtesy, but it has come to be established as the highly important first stage of a recognised procedure for political cooperation. If political consultation is to be effective, and is to open the way to genuine coordination of policies, it cannot stop at the mere exchange of information. Governments need to exchange views during the policy-making stage of their deliberations, before decisions are taken.

Political consultation, the evolution of which is described in more detail in Chapter 4, began as a systematic exercise in NATO when the Council Deputies first met in May 1950. One of their tasks was to exchange views on political problems of common interest within the scope of the Treaty. Member countries coordinated their points of view, particularly with respect to how Germany might best contribute to the defence of the West, and to the question of Greek and Turkish association with NATO. They also exchanged views and information on the policies of the Communist bloc countries.

When the Council began to meet in permanent session, in April 1952, it extended the field of political consultation in the light of recommendations adopted that year at the Lisbon Ministerial Meeting. The Council's powers in this field were further increased by a resolution approved in April 1954, urging member countries to submit to the Council all political information likely to be of interest to other members. It was during this period (starting in 1953), that the Council discussed replies drafted by the three Western occupying powers to various notes on Germany from the Soviet Union. It also took part in negotiation of the Paris and London agreements, approved in October 1954, and the preparatory work for the Geneva Summit Conference during the summer of 1955 and for the Geneva Foreign Ministers' Conference which followed in the autumn of the same year. Political events within the NATO framework, and the growing conviction that the Organisation should become more closely knit, led to the establishment, at the Ministerial session of May 1956, of the Committee on Non-Military Cooperation.

This Committee—more frequently referred to as the "Committee of Three" or the "Three Wise Men"—was instructed to "advise the Council on ways and means to improve and extend NATO cooperation in non-military fields and to develop greater unity within the Atlantic Community". It was this Committee's report[1] and recommendations, approved by the Council on December 13, 1956, shortly after the Suez crisis, that highlighted, for the first time, the vital importance of NATO political consultation and did much to spur its development.

Non-Military Cooperation in NATO

The Committee emphasised that NATO could only fulfil its deterrent task under certain conditions, and in particular only if there were close political and economic relations between its members. "An Alliance in which the members ignore each other's interests, or engage in political or economic conflict, or harbour suspicions of each other, cannot be effective either for deterrence or defence." In this way, the members of the Committee made clear their conviction that the two aspects of security— political and military—cannot be considered separately; NATO must "do enough to bring about that close and continuous contact between its civil and military sides which is essential if it is to be strong and enduring". The Committee specifically recommended expanded cooperation and consultation in the political field, "in the early stages of policy formation and before national positions became fixed", noting that "at best it will result in collective decisions on matters of common interest affecting the Alliance", and at least "it will ensure that no action is taken by one member without a knowledge of the views of the others".

The Committee foresaw difficulties and problems in applying these principles once they were agreed. They nevertheless thought it worthwhile to set

[1] The text of the Report is reproduced at Appendix I.

down a number of suggestions to serve as guidelines for future development. They were:

— members should inform the Council of any development significantly affecting the Alliance; they should do this not as a formality, but as a preliminary to effective political consultation;

— both individual member governments and the Secretary General should have the right to raise in the Council any subject which is of common NATO interest and not of a purely domestic character;

— a member government should not, without adequate advance consultation, adopt firm policies or make major political pronouncements on matters which significantly affect the Alliance or any of its members, unless circumstances make such prior consultation obviously and demonstrably impossible;

— in developing their national policies, members should take into consideration the interests and views of other governments, particularly those most directly concerned, as expressed in NATO consultation, even where no community of view or consensus has been reached in the Council;

— where a consensus has been reached, it should be reflected in the formation of national policies; when, for national reasons, the consensus is not followed, the government concerned should offer an explanation to the Council. It is even more important that, when an agreed and formal recommendation has emerged from the Council's discussions, governments should give it full weight in any national action or policies related to the subject of that recommendation.

These were the general guidelines. The Committee also drew up a number of more specific recommendations to strengthen the procedure, including the following:

— to strengthen the process of consultation, the Foreign Ministers, at each spring meeting, should take stock of the political progress of the Alliance on the basis of an annual political appraisal to be submitted by the Secretary General;

— to assist the Permanent Representatives and the Secretary General in discharging their responsibilities for political consultation, a Committee of Political Advisers should be constituted under the Council;

— any dispute between member countries which has not proved capable of direct settlement should be submitted to good offices procedures within the NATO framework, before resorting to any other international agency (except for disputes of a legal or an economic character for which attempts at settlement might best be made initially in the appropriate specialised organisations). The Secretary General should be empowered to offer his good offices to the countries in dispute and, with their consent, to initiate or facilitate procedures of enquiry, mediation, conciliation or arbitration.

These general guidelines and practical recommendations of the Committee of Three still form the basis of political consultation today.

Future Tasks of the Alliance

The recommendations on political consultation by the Committee of Three were redefined by the Report on the Future Tasks of the Alliance (the Harmel Report),[2] which was approved by the Council of Ministers in December 1967. The Report recognises that "As sovereign states, the Allies are not obliged to subordinate their policies to collective decision". However it emphasises that the Alliance affords an effective forum and clearing house for the exchange of information and views which enables each Ally to "decide its policy in the light of close knowledge of the problems and objectives of the others." "To this end", the Report noted, "the practice of frank and timely consultations needs to be deepened and improved ..."

The Report describes the ultimate political purpose of the Alliance as the achievement of a "just and lasting peaceful order in Europe accompanied by appropriate security guarantees", and it defines the role of the Allies—and of their consultation—in promoting an improvement in relations with the Soviet Union and the countries of Eastern Europe. Its definitions of the fundamental elements of Alliance strategy—maintaining adequate military strength and political solidarity as a necessary condition for a dialogue to reduce tensions and bring about a more stable relationship—have formed the basis of the Alliance's approach to arms control and other negotiations with the East.

Declaration on Atlantic Relations[2]

The Ottawa Declaration on Atlantic Relations of June 1974 again gave new impetus to political consultation within the Alliance. In Paragraph 11, the Allies state their conviction "that the fulfillment of their common aims requires the maintenance of close consultation, cooperation and mutual trust, thus fostering the conditions necessary for defence and favourable for detente, which are complementary." The Declaration goes on to state that the members of the Alliance "are firmly resolved to keep each other fully informed, and to strengthen the practice of frank and timely consultations by all means which may be appropriate on matters relating to their common interests as members of the Alliance, bearing in mind that these interests can be affected by events in other areas of the world."

East-West negotiations

Political consultation entered a particularly active phase as a result of the opening of broadly-based negotiations on East-West relations, which began in the early 1970s. The main focus of consultation within the NATO Council was the coordination of Allied negotiating positions on Mutual and Balanced Force Reductions and the Conference on Security and Cooperation in Europe.

---

[2] The texts of the Harmel Report and of the Declaration on Atlantic Relations are reproduced in Appendix I.

A further study was undertaken in 1978 to look at the East-West relationship in the longer term. It concluded that, while maintaining a credible level of deterrence and defence, the development of stable relations with the East was the correct policy for the future. The Soviet invasion of Afghanistan at the end of 1979 cast a shadow over East-West relations. Despite the serious setback which this caused, consultation among the Allies nevertheless led to the conclusion that there was no acceptable alternative to the continued pursuit of better East-West relations through meaningful dialogue and negotiations even if, in the circumstances, prospects for progress seemed limited. The thaw in East-West relations since then, the achievements of the INF Treaty and the prospects for further improvements, demonstrate the validity of this approach.

In the case of the negotiations on Mutual and Balanced Force Reductions, the Council took on a management role. Prior to the start of the negotiations, the Allied nations participating in MBFR (see Chapter 11) decided to negotiate on the basis of agreed positions on all questions of policy and strategy. Throughout these long drawn-out negotiations, common positions were elaborated in Brussels by the Council in permanent session, assisted by the Political Committee, on the basis of national instructions, before being transmitted as binding guidance to the Ad Hoc Group of Allied negotiators in Vienna. On the basis of this guidance, the Ad Hoc Group decided on day-to-day negotiating tactics. Representatives of the Ad Hoc Group reported to the Council in person at regular intervals.

The Council was thus involved directly in the complex negotiating process. In the case of other multilateral or bilateral arms control negotiations, the Council's involvement is generally less direct but equally crucial in enabling Allied governments to exchange views and coordinate their positions so that maximum progress can be made in achieving the goals of enhanced security and stability at lower levels of forces.

The Alliance indeed pays very special attention to a wide range of disarmament and arms control issues. They are an integral part of security policy. Extensive consultations in this field take place within NATO, with a view to reaching common positions and coordinating national decisions, taking full account of possible implications for the security of the Alliance. These consultations normally take place within the regular sessions of the Political Committee and in special meetings with disarmament experts from capitals. Thanks to these consultations, member countries have been better able to prepare for negotiations, some of which have culminated in the conclusion of important treaties, such as the 1963 Limited Test Ban Treaty; the 1968 Treaty on the Prohibition of the Emplacement of Nuclear Weapons and Other Weapons of Mass Destruction on the Sea-bed; and the 1972 Convention on the Prohibition of the Development, Production and Stockpiling of Bacteriological (Biological) and Toxin Weapons and on Their Destruction; and, in 1987, after eight years of intensive inter-Alliance consultation and bilateral US-Soviet negotiations, the Intermediate-range Nuclear Force (INF) Treaty.

The fact that arms control negotiations involving intermediate-range nuclear forces have been of such direct concern to the European Allies has meant that consultations in this area have been particularly intense. The Western position on arms control involving INF was developed by a Special Group on arms control and related issues established in April 1979. The report of this Group, along with that of the NPG High-Level Group on INF modernisation, formed the basis for the December 12, 1979, double-track decision on long-range INF modernisation and arms control.[3] The Special Consultative Group on Arms Control involving Intermediate-Range Nuclear Forces (SCG) was created as part of the December 1979 decisions for the purpose of supporting the United States negotiating effort. Consultations took place in the Special Consultative Group throughout the period leading up to the opening of preliminary talks between the United States and the Soviet Union in October 1980 and continued to provide the main forum for consultation on this subject throughout the course of the negotiations. Senior members of the United States negotiating teams continued to make regular reports in person to the NATO Council in order to keep member governments abreast of developments and to hear their views at first hand. Consultations in the latter stages of the negotiations before the INF Treaty was signed in December 1987 were particularly frequent and intensive.

Similarly, because of the importance of the bilateral United States-Soviet Strategic Arms Limitation Talks for the security of the Alliance as a whole, thorough discussions on them were held during the SALT I and SALT II negotiations (1970-1972 and 1972-1979). These consultations generally took place in the Council, with the participation of the various chief United States negotiators. They were often followed by discussions on more technical subjects among experts. This pattern of intensive consulting between the Allies continued throughout the Strategic Arms Reductions Talks (START) in 1982 and 1983 and has been the hall-mark of the so-called "umbrella" talks encompassing defence and space systems, strategic nuclear forces and intermediate range nuclear forces which began in March 1985.

Consultations take place concerning developments in other international fora such as the Conference on Disarmament in Geneva, which has focused primarily on efforts to ban chemical weapons; the United Nations Conference on prohibitions or restrictions on the use of certain inhumane conventional weapons; the United Nations General Assembly; and the United Nations Special Sessions on Disarmament. Bilateral and multilateral negotiations, like the Soviet-United States negotiations on chemical weapons and the Soviet-United Kingdom-United States negotiations for a Comprehensive Nuclear Test Ban Treaty, and specific initiatives, like the French proposal for the Conference on Disarmament in Europe which led to the signature of the Stockholm Document in September 1986, have also been the subject of thorough consultations.

Conference on Security and Cooperation in Europe (CSCE)

The question of holding a conference on security and cooperation in Europe, and what the conference should deal with, were issues which were

[3] See Appendix I.

discussed extensively within the Alliance. The member countries agreed on joint positions and aims for the preparatory conference held in Helsinki in 1972-1973. For the three phases of the Conference in Geneva and Helsinki (1973-1975), not only were major problems examined by the Council and other NATO committees, but at the Conference itself there was the closest possible day-to-day coordination of positions between the delegations of the Alliance countries. This practice of consultation while preparing positions and coordination during the negotiations themselves, by then well-established, was continued after the signing of the Helsinki Final Act as the normal pattern for multilateral CSCE matters. It has characterised the preparations for the CSCE Follow-up meetings in Belgrade (1977-1978), Madrid (1980-1983) and Vienna (1986-1989) and the coordination of Allied positions during the conduct of those meetings; and it was the nub of Allied efforts to bring the Stockholm Conference on Confidence and Security-Building Measures and Disarmament in Europe (CDE) to a successful conclusion.

Fora for political consultation

The principal forum for political consultation remains the Council which derives its authority directly from the North Atlantic Treaty. Here, under the chairmanship of the Secretary General, the Permanent Representatives of member countries raise any political issues which their governments, or they themselves, consider merit discussion. These meetings of the Council take place with a minimum of formality; discussion is frank and direct. The Secretary General may also initiate the discussion of questions and, by virtue of his chairmanship, plays an important part in the deliberations of the Council. The other fora described below derive their authority from the Council.

Because of the multiplicity of its tasks, the Council requires the assistance of the Political Committee. The latter (originally named "Committee of Political Advisers") was set up in 1957, following the recommendation of the Committee of Three. The Political Committee meets at least once a week throughout the year, either at the level of Deputy Permanent Representatives (when it is known as the Political Committee at Senior Level) or, more usually, with political counsellors of delegations. Besides keeping abreast of political trends and developments of interest to NATO in all areas of the world, the Committee prepares studies of political problems for discussion by the Council and submits reports to it. The Political Committee is also used for the regular exchange of views and information on a wide range of matters including the attitudes or intentions of member governments with regard to official visits and diplomatic contacts, political démarches made towards them by non-NATO countries and significant political developments abroad. A particularly important task of the Political Committee at Senior Level is the preparation of drafts of communiqués or declarations to be issued when the Council meets at Ministerial level or with participation of Heads of State or Government. In fact, this drafting process in itself entails intensive consultations between the 16 member states on the most important issues facing the Alliance.

Consultation also takes place within a number of ad hoc political working groups dealing with specific themes and through meetings of national regional experts which take place in preparation of the bi-annual discussions of the international situation held by Foreign Ministers in the NATO Council.

A particularly interesting development of the consultative process was the creation, in 1961, of the Atlantic Policy Advisory Group (APAG). Composed of senior planning officials from the Ministries of Foreign Affairs of NATO countries, its function is to take a longer-term and imaginative look at various aspects of the East-West relationship in the global context, as they might develop over the coming years. The Group's discussions are conducted on a personal basis, and do not commit governments. This allows officials a free rein to develop various hypotheses which can then be further reflected on by Alliance authorities. Its mandate is to provide the Council with studies on long-term policy problems, making suggestions for future action if needed and if necessary recording possible divergencies in experts' assessments. The Group submits reports to the Council on the responsibility of its Chairman, the Assistant Secretary General for Political Affairs.

There are therefore five distinct fora for formal political consultation: the Council; the Political Committee; Regional Experts Groups; Ad Hoc Political Working Groups or Special Consultative Groups; and the Atlantic Policy Advisory Group. Their activities are assisted by the International Staff. As a rule, the working papers and reports for political consultation are based on information supplied by national delegations and prepared by the Political Affairs Division.

Consultation also takes place on an informal basis in many different contexts. The different levels or categories of formal or informal consultation were summarised in an article by Sir Clive Rose[4], formerly Permanent Representative of the United Kingdom on the North Atlantic Council, as follows:

1. Exchange of views or information, with or without analysis;
2. Communication of actions or decisions which have already been taken or are imminent;
3. Advance warning of actions, or decisions, with a view to receiving the comments of allies and/or their endorsement;
4. Discussion with the aim of reaching a consensus on policies to be adopted or actions to be taken in parallel by all allies concerned;
5. Consultation for the purpose of arriving at Alliance agreement on collective decisions or action.

At one end of the scale, the process is continuous and, as a result of the colocation of all 16 national delegations within the same headquarters building, takes place with a minimum of delay or inconvenience. At the other, it enables intensive work to be carried out at short notice with the full participation of representatives from all member governments, on specific subjects calling for collective decisions or action.

The consultative machinery of the Alliance is extensively used. Member

[4] "Political Consultation in the Alliance" — NATO Review No. 1, 1983.

countries have adopted the practice of reporting directly to their partners, for example when important visits to foreign capitals have taken place. Thus Heads of Government or Ministers visiting the Soviet Union, Eastern Europe or China often share their impressions with their Alliance partners and exchange information with them on their return. It is significant that the NATO Council chamber has frequently been the first port of call for Alliance leaders after such contacts have taken place. And the consultative machinery operates through exchanges of information in the Permanent Council even when Heads of Government or Ministers are not able to be present in person. The status of the Council, either as a forum for consultation or as a decision-making body, does not vary, regardless of the level of representation on it.

Allies likewise make use of opportunities for exchanging views prior to important visits or following contacts in their own countries with visiting government leaders or officials from abroad, particularly if matters affecting Allied security or relevant to the implementation of Allied policies are involved. In addition, the process is complemented by frequent bilateral contacts between members of the Alliance and by meetings between them in other fora. Just as the rights and obligations of member countries under the United Nations Charter are unaffected by their membership of the Alliance (Article 7 of the NATO Treaty), so Allied governments ensure that their international engagements in other contexts are not in conflict with their obligations under the NATO Treaty (Article 8). Moreover in other fora in which defence and security issues are discussed—for example the Western European Union, the EUROGROUP or the Independent European Programme Group—Allies have been at pains to ensure that cooperation reinforces Allied security and cohesion within the Alliance as a whole.

Consultation in NATO therefore reflects the guidelines formulated in the 1956 Report of the Committee of Three which were designed not only to reinforce the process of consultation but to enhance its effectiveness. While the objective remains the formulation of collective decisions based on a consensus on matters of common interest affecting the Alliance, the process benefits all member countries even if its results may not always lead to consensus. Each member has the right to raise in the Council any subject of common interest; the duty to consult before adopting firm policies or making major policy pronouncements on matters affecting the Alliance and the expectation that its partners will do the same; the assurance that national views and interests will be taken into account by other member countries in the implementation of their policies even if no consensus has yet emerged; and the knowledge that a consensus within the Alliance, or an agreed and formal recommendation will indeed be reflected in national policies and actions. As befits an intergovernmental organisation which has no recourse to any supranational authority which can be invoked when practice falls short of these ideals, NATO relies on the commonality of interests among its member countries to ensure that departures from them are few and far between. In fact the Organisation has been able to achieve a high degree of success in building permanent and continuous political consultation into its normal routine.

The need for consultation is of course not limited to political subjects and there are many manifestations of regular consultation in NATO fora other than the Council. In the defence planning field, for example, wide-ranging consultation takes place in the Defence Planning and Defence Review Committees. The same applies to armaments cooperation which is the subject of consultation in a number of fora, particularly the Conference of National Armaments Directors and the Conventional Armaments Review Committee. The procedures involved are described more fully in other chapters. There are also occasions when national policies on allied defence matters may be driven by political developments outside the NATO treaty area and in such cases consultation in one context may spill over into another. Thus nations which find that their commitments to NATO may be temporarily or permanently affected by requirements for additional resources to meet their obligations elsewhere in the world, consult with their allies as a matter of course on the implications this may have for Allied defence and deterrence. The consultation is no mere formality; in such rather rare instances consideration of the need for compensatory measures is axiomatic. Consultation in the economic field is described in Chapter 6 and other chapters describe the many other spheres in which consultation is a vital element of cooperation within the Alliance.

Crisis management

As important as consultation may be in the formulation and implementation of policies over the long term, it naturally takes on a particular significance in times of crisis or tension. Moreover the defence policy of the Alliance is predicated upon a possible failure of deterrence. In such circumstances the need for rapid and decisive implementation of defence plans on the basis of consensus would call for immediate and continuous consultation between member governments. The practices and procedures involved form the Alliance's crisis management arrangements. These arrangements do not have to be activated by a formal decision of the Council. They are in place and operate on a continuous basis whether or not there is a crisis. However, in the particular circumstances foreseen by Article 4 of the North Atlantic Treaty, they must be able to move into a higher gear without delay. In this key article of the Treaty, the countries of the Alliance agree to consult "whenever, in the opinion of any of them, the territorial integrity, political independence or security of any of the Parties is threatened." The principal fora for the intensive consultation which such circumstances require are the Council or Defence Planning Committee, supported by NATO's Military Committee.

The procedures and machinery that provide the basis for these consultations have evolved with the changes of NATO strategy. The earlier concept of massive retaliation implied little or no warning and hence offered little time for consultation. The current strategy of flexible response to a progressively deteriorating political-military situation would require considerable consultation during a period of rising tension and right through the full operational spectrum of response, should deterrent measures fail. Immediate access to complete and accurate information is a prerequisite for decision-making and the strategy is therefore dependent upon effective arrangements within the Alliance for providing it.

Since 1967 these arrangements have been provided by the NATO Situation Centre, known as the SITCEN. The Situation Centre houses NATO-wide communications, automatic data processing resources, round-the-clock monitoring operations and the other facilities which comprise the physical arrangements for crisis management. The primary task of the SITCEN, which is jointly manned on a 24 hour basis by civilian and military staffs, is to assemble, collate and disseminate all intelligence and information made available by member nations and the NATO Military Authorities with regard to developing situations. It thus provides, at all times, the technical means for effective and rapid consultation, against a background of common information drawn from the same data base, among national representatives, and between them and their capitals and the NATO Military Authorities.

The Defence Planning Committee participates in exercises at regular intervals, in conjunction with national capitals and the NATO Military Authorities, to examine, test and develop procedures associated with their respective roles and responsibilities in a period of tension and crisis. The Military Committee, the Political Committee, the Senior Civil Emergency Planning Committee and the Alerts Committee provide support to the Defence Planning Committee during such exercises.

The Defence Planning Committee and the NATO Headquarters also become involved when major military exercises are being conducted under the aegis of the Major NATO Commanders in order to test the capabilities of the machinery for crisis management. The experience gained during such exercises is critically examined and analysed and, where appropriate, modifications to the procedures are introduced on the basis of the lessons learned.

The practical arrangements for crisis management and the preparation and conduct of exercises designed to test the system are coordinated by a Council Operations and Exercise Committee known as COEC. The principal responsibilities of this Committee include the development, in close liaison with the NATO Military Authorities, of the policies governing crisis management arrangements and the formulation of recommendations and procedures associated with Council or Defence Planning Committee participation in exercises. The Council Operations Directorate, which is responsible to the Executive Secretary, provides staff support for the COEC and the Executive Secretary is the Chairman of this Committee. The Directorate is also responsible for developing and revising operating procedures and procuring the physical facilities required.

Consultation, whether as part of the normal routine of a defensive organisation which bases its policies and its decisions on consensus, or as an element of crisis management, is the lifeblood of the Alliance. Subsequent chapters describe the structures and procedures which exist to facilitate consultation between member nations in different spheres relating to their common defence.

Chapter 6
Economic Cooperation

The unique feature of NATO's Economics Committee is that it is the only forum established under the North Atlantic Council concerned exclusively with consultations between members of the Alliance on economic developments with a direct bearing on allied security policy. Analyses and joint assessments of security-related economic developments in East and West, prepared by the Economics Directorate and agreed by the Economics Committee, are key ingredients in the coordination of allied security policy which takes place on a continuous basis in other NATO committees or fora. There is an obvious link between economics and security in fields directly related to defence issues such as Soviet and East European military spending or developments in Soviet defence industries. The availability of resources for the implementation of NATO's defence plans and the fulfilment of force goals is likewise an area where the relationship with security concerns is clearly apparent. Combining studies of defence-related economic developments in the East with analysis of Western trends, the Economics Committee submits an agreed "Economic Appreciation" to NATO's Defence Review Committee, which is responsible, together with the Nuclear Planning Group, for the detailed defence planning which underpins the policy of deterrence (see Chapter 10). Together with the "Military Appreciation", elaborated by NATO's Military Authorities, the Economic Appreciation forms the basis for NATO's defence resource guidance issued under the authority of NATO Defence Ministers every other year.

Studies of economic developments with primarily political implications constitute the major part of the work undertaken by NATO in the field of economics. Apart from international defence spending comparisons, a wide range of issues is examined, including balance of payments developments, industrial performance, consumer problems, and agricultural difficulties in the East; and other subjects of major importance for the Alliance such as economic aspects of the transatlantic burden-sharing debate, economic cooperation and assistance within the Alliance in support of Greece, Portugal and Turkey and economic considerations underlying allied cooperation in the field of armaments.

The work undertaken by NATO in this field has its origins in the North Atlantic Treaty itself, Article 2 of which states that the partners "will seek to eliminate conflict in their international economic policies and will encourage economic collaboration between any or all of them".

From its inception, the Alliance, while primarily concerned with coordinating the common defence of its members and facilitating political consultation between them, has recognised the need for consultation on economic matters. The 1956 Report of the Committee of Three[1] took the view that "political cooperation and economic conflict are not reconcilable" and that "in the economic as well as in the political field there must be a genuine desire among the members to work together and a readiness to consult on questions of common concern based on the recognition of common interest". In a period in which protectionist pressures are increasing, these objectives remain as valid today as in the 1950s when they were formulated.

The 1956 Report recognised that the purposes and principles of Article 2 would be pursued and implemented primarily by other organisations and international fora specifically concerned with economic cooperation and that NATO should avoid unnecessary duplication of work carried out elsewhere. It proposed, however, that such collaboration should be reinforced by NATO consultation whenever economic issues of special interest to the Alliance are involved, and particularly those which have political or defence implications or affect the economic health of the Altantic Community as a whole. Consultation within the Alliance "should seek to secure a common approach on the part of member governments where the questions are clearly related to the political and security interests of the Alliance". These principles have been reaffirmed on a number of subsequent occasions.

The Alliance therefore provides a forum in which different and interrelated aspects of political, military and economic questions—such as the economic aspects of the follow-up to the CSCE Helsinki Final Act and questions relating to economic relations with the Soviet Union and Eastern Europe—can be examined. The consultative process also provides a means of stimulating or initiating specific action in the economic field to safeguard Alliance interests when the need arises. For example in May 1978, concerned by the deepening economic crisis afflicting NATO's least prosperous member countries, the Secretary General took the initiative of drawing Allied attention to the specific economic problems of Greece, Portugal and Turkey. Recognizing that Alliance security depends on the economic stability and well-being of all its members as well as on political cohesion and military deterrence, the Council initiated a study on economic cooperation and assistance within the Alliance. It resulted in special action by member governments to assist the less prosperous members of the Alliance by means of major aid programmes implemented through the Organisation for Economic Cooperation and Development (OECD). At the request of member countries, the Secretary General continues to monitor the special economic problems and economic prospects of these countries, paying attention to financial and economic aid in general and assistance and cooperation in defence industrial fields in particular.

Economic developments in the Alliance

The provision of adequate forces to implement the agreed strategic concept involves political, military and economic considerations. Economic

[1] The text of the report of the Committee of Three on Non-Military Cooperation in NATO is reproduced in Appendix I.

consultation concerning NATO countries' economies takes place within the context of the defence planning process, described in Chapter 10. As part of the process of drawing up NATO force goals, the economic appreciation looks at future prospects for the Alliance as a whole and their implications for allied defence. A similar appraisal is made of economic prospects and their implications in the Warsaw Treaty countries. Both are taken into account in drawing up the agreed Ministerial Guidance, which provides the framework for the preparation of force proposals by NATO's military authorities. Individual economic assessments for all member countries participating in the integrated military structure are also made. These are examined during the preparation of force goals and the annual defence review. They describe recent economic developments and medium or longer term prospects for Alliance economies and provide the relevant economic background against which NATO's force plans have to be considered.

Economic developments in the Warsaw Treaty and other CMEA[2] countries

To assess the political and military potential of a nation, it is essential to evaluate its economic strengths and weaknesses. Consultation and analysis within the Alliance enable member countries to arrive at an agreed view of the main factors determining economic developments in the Warsaw Treaty and other CMEA countries—economic growth, demographic trends, industrial and agricultural performance, the energy situation, the pattern of foreign trade, the convertible currency balance of payments and planning reforms. Analyses of this kind provide a better understanding of recent economic developments and future prospects for these economies and make it possible to arrrive at a more informed assessment of the resources available for military purposes. They also contribute to a better understanding of the motives of the Soviet Union and its allies in international negotiations.

External economic relations of the Warsaw Treaty countries and other CMEA members

The NATO countries regularly consult and exchange information on the development of trade with the Soviet Union and East European countries and on problems associated with its financing. Trade, conducted on the basis of commercially sound terms and mutual advantage, that avoids preferential treatment for the Soviet Union, contributes to constructive East-West relations. However, trade with these countries can raise problems because their political aims often override economic considerations and their foreign trade is still largely run by state monopolies. It is also important to follow carefully the development of trade and financial relations between the Soviet Union and East European countries and the developing countries. Soviet arms sales are of particular significance.

---

[2] CMEA: Council for Mutual Economic Assistance (also known as COMECON).

Finally, the Alliance cannot be indifferent to the development of intra-CMEA economic relations. Indeed, the results obtained by these countries in the field of economic and technological cooperation, and the success of their efforts towards economic integration, could constitute important elements for the development of their future economic potential.

Role of the Economics Committee and Economics Directorate

The Economics Committee, on which all member countries of the Alliance are represented, was created in 1957. It meets regularly under the chairmanship of the Director of the Economics Directorate and reports directly to the Council. In addition to the preparation of reports and assessments such as those referred to above, the Committee acts as a clearing-house for the exchange of information concerning the Soviet and East European economies and their external economic relations, and as a forum for the consideration of any other economic questions raised by any member country of the Alliance or by the Council. The implications of these exchanges are discussed in the Committee, and where appropriate, may be used as guidance for member governments in framing national policies. For example, the Committee played an important role in establishing common views among member countries during the preparation of the CSCE.

The Economics Directorate is part of the Political Affairs Division of the International Staff. Its principal functions and activities are as follows:

— preparation of papers on military expenditures and internal economic developments at national and sectoral levels in the Warsaw Treaty countries and on the external economic relations of those countries with one another, with the West and with the developing countries;
— provision of macro-economic assessments of member countries and of the Alliance generally, with particular reference to medium and longer term prospects which provide the relevant economic framework for defence planning purposes;
— preparation of the economic appreciation which Ministers take into account when they issue guidance to the NATO Military Authorities for the preparation of force proposals;
— support of regular and reinforced meetings of the Economics Committee and the Defence Review Committee;
— provision of general economic advice and briefings on defence related economic problems, NATO burden-sharing, defence collaboration, etc.;
— preparation of the Secretary General's personal report to Ministers of Foreign Affairs on Economic Cooperation and Assistance within the Alliance;
— liaison with national delegations and, through appropriate channels, with other international and national economic organisations;
— organisation of an annual colloquium on a subject of topical interest relating to the Soviet Union and Eastern Europe;
— organisation of an annual workshop on a defence economic topic relating to the Alliance.

Chapter 7
NATO's Public Diplomacy

The diversity of NATO's 16 country membership poses considerable challenges when it comes to providing the public with a basic core of information about the Alliance. As a matter of policy, the explanation of national defence positions, including membership of the North Atlantic Alliance and the benefits and obligations pertaining to membership, is a national responsibility. As a consequence, the choice of the methods to be employed and the resources to be devoted to the information task is also a national prerogative. The public communications role of the 16 nations collectively, through the organisation which serves the Alliance from the Brussels headquarters of NATO, is therefore complementary to that of the nations.

The need for a centralised structure to fulfill that role was recognised soon after the Alliance was created. The Information Service was constituted in NATO's early stages with its terms of reference being based on a number of formal documents modified to some extent over the years by specific Council decisions. From the beginning, the Information Service has been expected to work directly with national authorities and national organisations at the level and in the manner which conforms to the requirements of each government. The arrangements which facilitate this work are necessarily flexible and responsive, not only to differing political, geographical, cultural or linguistic situations, but to evolving national and international concerns as well as to new developments in intra-Alliance or East-West relations.

The programmes which have been developed to meet such a diversity of tasks are based on the principle that although the nations themselves can best assess public opinion problems relating to security and address them in the national context, NATO's Information Service can also play an important role in assisting them through its own institutional information programmes. The latter draw on the full range of available information resources, applying them selectively in what is often broadly described as a "multiple approach". This concept provides the flexibility needed to meet the requirements of individual member countries and the versatility to assign the most appropriate public relations media to each of them. The multiple approach remains the basic operating principle for NATO's public information activities, the major elements of which include publications, small and large screen film production, radio, photographs, displays, seminars and conferences, an important visitor's programme, and speaking tours in different member countries.

Inevitably, a need exists for the Alliance to respond to demands for information directed at the Organisation's international Headquarters and a role has developed for centralised communication activities. A primary operational task for the NATO Information Service therefore is the creation of information materials which can be used both in NATO Headquarters programmes and in conjunction with programmes managed by national authorities and non-governmental organisations of specific interest to their own constituencies.

The Information Service, is therefore concerned with providing facts through all available media about such questions as why and how NATO was created, how it functions, and what are the broad lines of agreed NATO policy. However, apart from the provision of basic factual information about the Alliance, NATO information programmes also seek to emphasise several basic themes, the essence of which has remained constant for much of the Alliance's history. Central among these is the fact that NATO is a defensive Alliance which maintains only adequate military strength and political solidarity to deter aggression and other forms of pressure, and to defend the territory of member countries if aggression should occur. Equally important is the Alliance commitment to ensuring Western security at the lowest levels of military forces. It therefore continues to press for balanced and verifiable reductions in a wide range of nuclear weapon systems and for agreements which would result in the removal of disparities and the lowering of conventional force levels in Europe.

The major programme elements used to carry out these information tasks are described below. They complement the activities of the Press Service whose functions are primarily related to the channelling of official policy statements and announcements to journalists, and the day-to-day relations with the media, including the arrangement of interviews with senior NATO officials.

Audio-Visual Media

The TV, Films/Radio Section provides technical assistance to television companies making programmes on any aspect of NATO, and encourages the production of such programmes. A limited number of documentary films is produced to illustrate NATO activities.

As with television, radio offers a wide medium for the diffusion of information on NATO, carrying interviews and discussions for relay through the broadcast facilities of the NATO countries.

The Photo and Exhibition Unit provides the world press with photographs of NATO subjects, including news items such as Ministerial meetings and features covering various aspects of the Organisation. It also makes available display stands and materials covering a wide range of NATO subjects for use in conjunction with public events within the member countries.

Visitors Programme

One of the major activities of the NATO Information Service is its international Visitors Programme. Each year this brings about 20,000 individuals in some 700 groups to NATO Headquarters for briefing sessions with NATO experts from both the International and International Military Staffs as well as from national delegations. The topics offered to groups cover every aspect of NATO's work. Many such visits also take in SHAPE near Mons and occasionally subordinate military headquarters in Allied Command Europe.

The programme is directed principally at opinion leaders actively involved in defence and security debates within the 16 NATO member countries. The main categories of visitors are parliamentarians, party political workers, research assistants, journalists, church leaders, trade unionists and academics. In addition, an extensive network of contacts has been built up with universities throughout the NATO area which facilitates visits to NATO by students specialising in modern history, political science and international relations.

Youth Audiences

To stimulate interest in NATO affairs among the younger generation a number of projects are carried out under NATO auspices in close cooperation with international and national youth movements. In this context, courses, seminars, and exchange programmes for youth leaders, students and young politicians are regularly organised in the NATO countries and at NATO's Brussels headquarters and, every year, youth seminars take place on issues concerning the Atlantic Alliance.

Publications

Written materials are provided both to the general public and to schools and educational organisations, libraries, journalists, writers, politicians and other students of NATO affairs.

Publications and works of reference include, inter alia, "The North Atlantic Treaty Organisation: Facts and Figures"; volumes of final communiqués of the Council, Defence Planning Committee and Nuclear Planning Group; a compilation of basic NATO documents; a general purpose handbook, outlining the origins and organisation of the Alliance; and books and pamphlets on specific aspects of NATO published in a number of different languages.

In addition, NATIS supports the publishing activities of a number of non-governmental organisations by providing financial, technical and editorial assistance; contributes to international yearbooks and encyclopaedias; promotes books and publications which serve to increase public knowledge of NATO history and current security issues; and sponsors joint publishing initiatives on many topics related to aspects of East-West relations or to security problems.

A periodical magazine, the NATO Review, is published every two months in English, French, Danish, Dutch, German, Italian and Spanish, quarterly in Greek, Norwegian, Portuguese and Turkish, and annually in Icelandic. Distributed throughout the Alliance and beyond, the Review contains topical articles designed to contribute to a constructive consideration and analysis of

Atlantic issues. NATO Information Service publications are issued under the authority of the Secretary General and are free of charge[1].

NATO Research Fellowship Programme

The Information Directorate administers a programme of research fellowships which, since its inception in 1956, has awarded several hundred grants to post-graduate students and other qualified persons who are citizens of the member countries. The aim of the programme is to stimulate study and research, leading to publication of works on subjects relevant to the life of the Alliance.

During their meeting in May 1989, NATO Heads of State and Government decided to offer in addition a programme of " Democratic Institutions Fellowships " open both to citizens of Warsaw Treaty Organisation countries and those of Nato countries. The programme is designed to foster research on democratic institutions and their functioning within agreed areas of research.

The Information Service also administers an annual Atlantic Award for outstanding services to the Alliance, which is presented to private citizens, on the recommendation of an independent jury, by the Secretary General of NATO.

[1] Details of publications, films and materials mentioned above and of other information programmes described in this chapter can be obtained from the NATO Information Service, NATO B-1110 Brussels.

Part 4

Deterrence and Defence

Chapter 8

NATO and the Warsaw Treaty Organisation

NATO is a defensive alliance. Its military posture is based on the principle that the member countries must collectively maintain adequate defence to deter aggression and, should deterrence fail, to preserve their territorial integrity. The basis for NATO's assessment of the quantity and quality of forces necessary to carry out these roles is the military posture of the Soviet Union and its allies.

The Warsaw Treaty Organisation was founded on May 14, 1955 with the signature of a Treaty of Friendship, Cooperation and Mutual Assistance by eight European states (Albania, Bulgaria, Czechoslovakia, the German Democratic Republic, Hungary, Poland, Romania, and the USSR). Albania's participation lapsed in 1961 and it formally renounced the Treaty on September 12, 1968. Unlike the North Atlantic Treaty, the 1955 Warsaw Treaty reinforces a series of bilateral mutual aid treaties—many of which predate the Warsaw Treaty—commiting the signatories, inter alia, to providing mutual military assistance, and is complemented by a series of status of forces agreements between the USSR and its allies. This parallel series of agreements would continue to tie the Warsaw Treaty countries to the Soviet Union if the Warsaw Treaty Organisation itself were to be dissolved. The original Treaty remained valid until May 1975 when it was renewed for a further 10 years. In April 1985, the Treaty was extended for another 20-year period; its terms were unchanged.

Any assessment of the balance of forces between NATO and the Warsaw Treaty Organisation must take into account not only the relationship between defensive and offensive forces but also many less quantifiable factors. Differences in military strategy and structure, political organisation, cohesion, loyalty, and qualitative factors as they pertain to leadership, personnel and military equipment are all part of the equation.

Such assessments also need to take account of geographical dissimilarities between NATO and the Warsaw Treaty Organisation which have a direct bearing on the roles of their armed forces and the tasks they may have to perform. The Warsaw Treaty countries belong to one geographic entity; they can transfer land and air forces from place to place via internal and generally secure lines of communication. Many NATO countries are separated from each other by oceans, seas and in some cases by the territory of countries which are not members of the Alliance. NATO must often transfer resources over long distances via vulnerable air and sea routes. The timely reinforcement of forward areas in Europe—upon which the successful defence of all Allied territory largely depends—involving the forces of many Allied countries, including those of Canada and the United States from the other side of the Atlantic, is therefore a formidable task.

The military posture of the Warsaw Treaty countries, and in particular that of the Soviet Union, continues to exceed the legitimate needs of defensive security. The current strength of Soviet military forces has been achieved through a massive commitment of resources during the past twenty years, even in the face of a faltering economy. Measured in constant prices, estimated Soviet defence spending increased sharply by 4 to 5% a year on average during the late 1960s and early 1970s, but exhibited a lower rate of growth, just under 2% on average, over the period 1975-1987.

The level of procurement spending was sufficient to enable the Soviet Union to introduce considerable qualitative and quantitative improvements across the whole spectrum of its military capabilities. Consistent and systematic modernisation has produced formidable, well-organised and modern forces capable of conducting both defensive and offensive operations, including conventional, chemical and nuclear warfare. The introduction of new aircraft with much increased ranges, and the growth of the Soviet navy also enables Soviet military power and influence to be projected far afield over wide areas of the globe.

However, defence expenditure, which is assessed as having absorbed some 15-17% of Soviet GDP in the mid-1980s, places a heavy weight on the economy. President Gorbachev is well aware of the difficulty of reconciling high, let alone increasing, defence spending with his plans for modernising and revitalising the economy. It appears that he would like to reduce the defence burden provided this can be achieved without damaging the level of security and defence capability of the state. This may have been a factor prompting the Soviet Union to agree to the INF Treaty, and to enter into negotiation on further arms control accords. Further evidence of this is provided by Gorbachev's announcement at the United Nations on December 7, 1988 of significant reductions of Soviet conventional forces in Europe and restructuring of remaining forces—a move which, when implemented, will go some way to reduce, but not eliminate, conventional imbalances in Europe. Reductions announced by other Eastern European governments will also contribute to this process but have similar limitations.

As a defensive Alliance, NATO does not need to match the Warsaw Treaty Organisation man for man and weapon for weapon. But it must ensure that its nuclear and conventional forces are sufficient to maintain the credibility of the strategy of flexible response. They must therefore be demonstrably adequate to defend against aggression if it were to occur, and thus be able to counter and frustrate the military objectives which an opposing military force could be expected to set itself if it were to embark on an aggressive course of action. NATO's military forces must accordingly be flexible, effective and survivable and their availability must be assured.

Over the years NATO has carried out substantial improvements to the quantity and quality of its conventional forces. Underpinning these efforts were defence resources which constituted as an average 4.3% of GDP and averaged an annual growth rate of 3.8% in the period from 1978 to 1987.

The gap between the capabilities of NATO and the Warsaw Treaty Organisation nevertheless tended to widen. In order to redress the possible long term implications of this trend, which could adversely affect the flexibility of NATO's strategy, NATO Defence Ministers adopted an action plan in May 1985 known as the Conventional Defence Improvements (CDI) initiative. The adoption of this plan signalled the determination of each of their countries, working collectively within the constraints of the resources available for defence, to make every effort to secure adequate and effective conventional forces.

The sections which follow examine briefly the military posture of the Warsaw Treaty Organisation and NATO in the major areas of nuclear forces, ground forces, naval forces and air forces.

Nuclear forces are usually subdivided into strategic and theatre forces; the latter category includes intermediate-range, short-range and maritime forces. Each of these categories is described below.

Strategic nuclear forces

Strategic nuclear forces are those whose range or type of delivery system is suitable for inter-continental employment. They comprise three elements—Inter-Continental Ballistic Missiles (ICBMs), Submarine-Launched Ballistic Missiles (SLBMs), and strategic bombers. NATO's strategic nuclear forces are provided primarily by the United States, but also include SLBMs deployed by the United Kingdom. France has an independent nuclear deterrent force. The strategic forces of the Warsaw Treaty Organisation are all provided by the Soviet Union. There is broad parity between the strategic forces of the United States and the Soviet Union. Overall, the Soviet Union has a greater number of delivery vehicles, but the United States at present has more, but smaller, warheads (although the gap is diminishing with the increasing Soviet deployment of Multiple Independently-targetable Re-entry Vehicles (MIRVs)). The Soviet Union has a greater number of ICBMs which are generally newer than those of the United States, and some of which are also mobile. It also has more SLBMs, but those of the United States have a larger number of warheads. The United States has an advantage in the category of heavy bombers and air-launched cruise missiles, although this is partially offset by the large Soviet strategic air defence network which has no counterpart in the United States.

Intermediate and Short-Range Nuclear Forces

This category of nuclear forces covers systems of less than intercontinental range. Intermediate-Range Nuclear Forces (INF) include land-based nuclear missiles and nuclear-capable aircraft with ranges or combat radii between 500 and 5,500 km, i.e. capable of striking targets beyond the general region of the battlefield but not capable of intercontinental range.

INF missiles are further divided into Longer-Range INF (LRINF) missiles with ranges in excess of 1,000 km and Shorter-Range INF (SRINF) with ranges between 1,000 and 500 km. To the first category belong the SS-20, SS-4 and SS-5 Soviet missiles and the Pershing II and the BGM-109G Ground-Launched Cruise Missile (GLCM) of the United States. To the second category belong the SS-12 and SS-23 Soviet missiles and the Pershing IA on the NATO side. All United States and Soviet missiles of both categories will be destroyed with their respective launchers in the implementation of the INF Treaty, by the end of May 1991 and November 1989 respectively. As announced by the Government of the Federal Republic of Germany, the Pershing IA missiles owned by the Federal Republic, which were not subject to the INF Treaty, will also be dismantled.

A large portion of the combat aircraft of both NATO and the Warsaw Treaty countries is technically capable of delivering nuclear weapons, but not all can be assumed to be assigned nuclear missions. Force comparisons in this field are therefore particularly difficult. It can be said, however, that the Warsaw Treaty countries have a large numerical advantage in nuclear-capable aircraft in Europe. This superiority is being increased by the continuing Soviet programmes of replacement and upgrading of older aircraft and further improvements of the already highly effective Soviet air defences.

Short-Range Nuclear Forces (SNF) consist of land-based missiles, rockets and artillery capable of striking targets on the ground at ranges of less than 500 km. The Soviet Union has a decisive numerical superiority in all SNF delivery systems, particularly in nuclear capable missile launchers, and its SCUD missile has about three times the range of the only existing NATO missile, the LANCE. A shorter-range rocket, the FROG, deployed in large numbers throughout Warsaw Treaty armies, has been steadily replaced since 1986 by a modern, highly accurate missile, the SS-21.

Maritime Nuclear Forces (MNF)

Besides sea-based strategic forces, both NATO and the Warsaw Treaty countries have other Maritime Nuclear Forces (MNF) of less than intercontinental range. These weapons can be used in most areas of maritime warfare including air defence, anti-ship and anti-submarine warfare, or to strike targets ashore from platforms at sea.

The Soviet Union has operational submarines equipped with ballistic missiles with a range of less than 2,000 km. Some of these can deliver strikes against land targets in NATO Europe. In addition, Soviet warships, submarines and naval aircraft can deliver a wide variety of land-attack cruise missiles, anti-ship cruise missiles, depth bombs, surface-to-air missiles and anti-ship or anti-submarine torpedoes, many of which are capable of carrying conventional or nuclear warheads.

NATO's maritime nuclear forces include surface-to-air missiles, anti-submarine missiles, depth bombs and nuclear capable aircraft embarked in United States and United Kingdom carriers. Some surface warships and attack submarines of the United States Navy are equipped with Sea-Launched Cruise Missiles capable of nuclear strikes against land targets.

Ground Forces

During the last decade substantial improvements have been made to the combat power and offensive capability of Soviet divisions, particularly those stationed forward in Eastern Europe. Restructuring of forces, improved readiness and sustainability, more responsive command and control and new operational tactics have resulted in significantly enhanced combat potential of ground forces. Emphasis has been placed on increasing mobility, fire-power and the capability of seizing and holding territory of Soviet divisions, through the introduction of new and more capable tanks, armoured vehicles and self-propelled artillery in increasing numbers. These improvements have considerably enhanced the capacity of Soviet armed forces, in the event of conflict, to overcome NATO defences rapidly and decisively through the maximum use of surprise and the concentration of superior numbers.

The increase in artillery has been an important part of this modernisation, particularly as many of these systems have been given nuclear capability. Soviet forces also maintain a substantial stockpile of chemical weapons. Chemical warfare defensive equipment is an organic part of ground force units and training in a chemical environment is a common feature of military exercises.

The Soviet Army is therefore a modern, well-equipped force which enjoys the advantages of highly centralised command and control, rigid discipline and a substantial degree of conformity and standardization with other forces of the Warsaw Treaty Organisation. However, while it is in all senses an impressive force, the Soviet Army also suffers from a number of problems, many inherent in the nature and structure of Soviet armed forces and the Warsaw Treaty Organisation. The most evident of these are the basic standards of training of Soviet recruits, the consequent lack of flexibility and initiative displayed at lower levels and the reliability of some of the Soviet Union's allies.

NATO's ground forces in Europe and their reinforcement potential have also undergone improvements in recent years. Substantial progress has been made in redressing deficiencies in a number of areas in order to enhance the effectiveness and credibility of NATO's conventional forces. NATO countries are continuing with plans to introduce new equipment into their inventories. The most signficant measures concern the replacement and upgrading of tanks, new armoured personnel carriers, and enhancement of anti-armour and air defence capabilities, complemented by improved stocks of ammunition and spare parts. This has resulted in better overall sustainability and greater effectiveness for NATO forces.

Naval Forces

In the late 1950s the Soviet navy, whose traditional role had hitherto been confined to the close-in defence of Soviet home waters and interdiction of NATO's sea lanes of communication, was transformed to give it more offensive capabilities which could be used to support Soviet policy and strategy worldwide. By embarking on an impressive shipbuilding programme, the Soviet Union was able to bring increasingly sophisticated types of vessels into service more rapidly. Emphasis was placed on creating and protecting a strategic force at sea and building up a naval force capable of controlling large areas of the sea, projecting military power to areas remote from national territory and supporting the Soviet army. An additional and important supporting role has been played by the Soviet merchant navy.

The Soviet navy consists of four large but separate fleets: the Northern, Baltic, Black Sea and Pacific. Each of these fleets includes its own fleet air force, consisting of strike/reconnaissance and anti-submarine aircraft, with a number of transport aircraft in support. Moreover, nearly all medium-range bombers in the Soviet air force can carry anti-ship missiles with ranges of about 100 nautical miles. The Soviet Union maintains a permanent Mediterranean presence with its Mediterranean squadron, which has air cover provided by Soviet naval aviation operating out of the Ukraine. A similar squadron is also permanently present in the Indian Ocean. However, there are relatively few naval bases and facilities available to the Soviet navy outside its home waters and, except in the North Atlantic and North Pacific, it has limited access to the main ocean areas. The navies of non-Soviet members of the Warsaw Treaty Organisation are small and are equipped for operating in home waters, and forward amphibious operations.

NATO's political and military geography and the economic dependence of NATO countries on freedom of the high seas for much of their vital trade impose very different requirements for its naval forces. In this respect, their ability to defend the transatlantic and Mediterranean sea lines of communication, to preserve the integrity of the entire NATO area, especially on the flanks, and to protect shipping carrying military and industrial supplies to Europe, is of crucial importance to NATO. The Warsaw Treaty countries are essentially independent of sea lines of communication and would remain so in the event of a conflict.

The Soviet navy's emphasis on attack submarines, large surface warships, amphibious forces, and its naval air force, with the majority of these units armed with anti-ship missiles, gives it the potential to sever Western Europe from American reinforcements and to support Soviet ground and air forces in offensive operations in northern and southern Europe. NATO's naval forces have very different roles, of which the most important are to defend the European flanks, safeguard transatlantic sea lines, neutralise Soviet strategic submarines, and prevent the Soviet Union from gaining maritime supremacy in the North Atlantic. They include Carrier Battle Groups, escort vessels, submarines, amphibious forces and mine countermeasures ships and aircraft. In total they still exceed the size of Soviet naval forces, although the threat to them posed by Soviet submarines, Soviet naval aviation, and mines continues to be a major concern. At present NATO remains capable, although not without difficulties and some shortfalls, of carrying out its maritime strategy as part of the overall strategy of forward defence and flexible response, as prescribed by NATO's Concept of Maritime Operations and Conceptual Military Framework.

Air forces

The Soviet Union is carrying out a continuous and progressive modernisation programme of its tactical air forces. Soviet attack air forces facing NATO have increased considerably in recent years. The introduction of modern aircraft, many comparable in quality to those of NATO, has more than tripled the range and doubled the payload of some fighter and ground attack aircraft. A large number of well-protected airfields are available, providing the Soviet air force with a rapid development capability, and improving their flexibility, mobility and survivability. Airlift capability— the capacity to transport forces and equipment by air—continues to increase.

In general, Soviet air forces in the 1980s include large numbers of the most modern aircraft, whose ranges and firepower give them a strong offensive capability in Europe.

Because of the threat which these forces represent, NATO maintains in Europe an air defence system covering a range of altitudes. It consists of a permanently airborne early warning and control system, a belt of surface-to-air missiles, and fighter and attack aircraft capable of engaging air and ground targets at considerable ranges. Air defence is supplemented by the anti-aircraft weapons of ground and naval forces.

Although inferior in overall numbers, NATO has a higher proportion of multi-purpose aircraft of good performance with highly qualified and better trained pilots and air crew.

A more detailed assessment of the conventional ground and air forces of NATO and the Warsaw Treaty countries was published by the Alliance in November 1988 in a report entitled "Conventional Forces in Europe: The Facts"[1]. However, such assessments have to take into account the fact that the respective forces have been developed according to different requirements. Moreover, static comparisons depend on critical assumptions concerning the area and the forces under consideration. Finally, there are many factors which would be important in determining the outcome of any conflict but which cannot be quantified.

What can be said is that the Warsaw Treaty countries enjoy numerical advantages over NATO in most of the important areas. They have the potential to bring to bear a greater number of fighting men than NATO and many more of the important elements of combat power than NATO in a

[1] Copies of this document can be obtained from the NATO Information Service, B-1110 Brussels.

relatively short period. How significant these advantages would be would depend on the circumstances and conditions under which conflict occurred.

Despite these disadvantages, NATO's defence posture is kept under constant review in order to ensure that the Alliance is capable of deterring aggression and defending the NATO area should deterrence fail. Any attempt to breach NATO's conventional defences would require a massive effort, and any agressor would have to take account of the possiblity of such an attack resulting in escalation to the nuclear level. He might thus well conclude that an attack involved an unacceptable degree of risk. However, the maintenance of an adequate deterrent and defensive posture requires a continuous effort to preserve the effectiveness of all three elements of the triad of forces—strategic and theatre nuclear forces and conventional forces—and the clear linkage between them.

Chapter 9
NATO Defence Policy

Since its inception the Alliance has sought to preserve its security through the concept of deterrence, making it clear to a potential adversary that the costs of aggression would far outweigh the potential benefits. Protected by this concept, the Atlantic area has enjoyed a sustained period of peace and prosperity. Until the differences that determine the current relationship between East and West are resolved, the need for deterrence will remain.

Nuclear weapons and conventional forces are both important components of the concept of deterrence because together they confront a possible aggressor with unacceptable risks. However, the number and types of nuclear forces required, the precise role and their relationship to NATO's conventional forces have, not surprisingly, been the subject of constant discussion and adjustment. In recent years their numbers have decreased, first as a result of the withdrawals decided upon by NATO in 1979 and 1983, and subsequently as a consequence of the INF Treaty concluded at the end of 1987.

In the early years of the Alliance, in the light of the marked inferiority of NATO's conventional forces against the perceived Soviet political and military threat, a strategy that threatened massive nuclear retaliation to an attack against NATO territory was believed to provide the most effective solution. NATO's capacity to deter therefore rested heavily on the strategic nuclear superiority of the United States. However, the importance of creating more effective conventional forces was always recognised.

In 1951, in view of the continued Soviet military presence in Eastern Europe as well as the scale of the military forces in the Soviet Union itself, the most urgent task facing the Alliance was to provide Western Europe with well-equipped and well-trained forces capable of defending NATO territory against aggression. In the same year, following the Alliance decision to create an integrated command structure, the United States agreed to place its units in Germany under the command of the Supreme Allied Commander Europe (SACEUR). France, the United Kingdom and other members followed suit. By May 1952, the military objectives (the Lisbon Force Goals) proposed by the Temporary Council Committee for the period up to 1954 had been accepted; machinery for coordinating the military efforts of member countries had been set up; the command structure had been considerably improved; the forces of Greece and Turkey had been incorporated into Allied Command Europe; the strategic concept had been further developed; and the effectiveness of the armed forces in support of this strategy had increased.

In the next four years further substantial progress was made and new developments occurred. In particular, with the accession of the Federal

Republic of Germany in 1955, it became imperative as well as possible to think in terms of "forward" defence—in other words the provision of forces which could defend Europe as near to its Eastern borders as necessary, in the central region, on the flanks and at sea.

Although considerable progress was made towards fulfilling the commitments called for in the Lisbon Force Goals, the weaknesses which persisted meant that NATO's conventional forces could still not be regarded as an adequate deterrent on their own. At the same time, technological advances in East and West were changing the premises on which the strategy of massive retaliation was based. The acquisition by the Soviet Union of the means of attacking United States and Canadian territory with nuclear weapons, particularly through the development of ballistic missiles, made the concept of an all-out nuclear response by the United States to possibly limited forms of aggression against NATO territory increasingly less credible to potential adversaries and allies alike.

Strategic concept of 1957

These developments were dramatised by the launching of the first Soviet Sputnik, an event which symbolised the newly acquired technological capacity of the Soviet Union and its potential as a world power. The Heads of Governments of the NATO countries meeting soon afterwards in Paris in December 1957 decided that NATO's defence plans should take more account of recent developments in weapons and techniques; that intermediate range ballistic missiles (IRBM) should be deployed in Europe under the command of SACEUR (Thor and Jupiter missiles were subsequently deployed in the United Kingdom, Italy and Turkey); and that a stock of nuclear warheads should be established in Europe for the defence of the Alliance. Their deployment and arrangements for their use were to be decided in agreements with the nations directly involved. Since that time, the importance of nuclear weapons for NATO's defence has meant that nuclear issues have remained at the forefront of Alliance preoccupations.

Athens Guidelines—1962

An important step was taken with the adoption in 1962 of the "Athens Guidelines", which outlined in general terms the situations in which it might be necessary to use nuclear weapons in NATO's defence and the degree to which political consultation on such use might be possible. Both the United Kingdom and the United States specifically committed themselves to consult with their Allies, time and circumstances permitting, before releasing their weapons for use.

Assignment of nuclear forces

At the beginning of 1963, the nuclear forces available to NATO Commanders were strengthened by the assignment to SACEUR of the United

Kingdom's V-bomber force and of three United States Polaris submarines. The latter replaced intermediate range ballistic missiles which were becoming obsolete. At the same time, in May 1963, the North Atlantic Council at its Ottawa meeting approved the measures taken to organise the tactical nuclear strike forces assigned to SACEUR. These measures included arrangements for broader participation by officers of non-nuclear member countries in the nuclear activities of Allied Command Europe and in the coordination of operational planning at the Headquarters of the United States Strategic Air Command at Omaha (Nebraska, USA).

Review of defence policy

As the 1960s progressed it became evident that while the possibility of a large scale Soviet attack on NATO could not be ruled out, it was not the only possibility nor perhaps the most likely one. Increasing account began to be taken of the possibility and the implications of aggression with relatively limited objectives, and of attacks of a minor or probing kind which might begin through miscalculation of NATO's will to resist, but which could very rapidly expand or escalate. Moreover, it was noticeable that the Soviet Union was developing types of forces designed to enable it to deploy a significant military capability to other parts of the world. The increasing Soviet presence in the Mediterranean area in particular posed a potential threat to NATO's Southern Flank.

Furthermore, the development of the inter-continental ballistic missile as the principal means of delivering nuclear warheads, and the construction of highly protected or "hardened" launching sites, made it theoretically possible to survive a surprise nuclear attack and retaliate within a matter of minutes. This capability was enhanced by the development of an even less vulnerable weapon system in the form of nuclear-propelled submarines carrying ballistic missiles. Both sides now had forces that could survive a surprise attack and retaliate with devastating effect against the territory of the other side (the so-called second-strike capability) and were therefore mutually vulnerable.

Amid growing doubts both about the assumption that a major nuclear war was the most likely form of conflict, and about the credibility of a strategy of massive retaliation in circumstances other than a major nuclear attack, there was general recognition that greater flexibility was needed to respond to different possible forms of aggression. After a sustained period of discussion and debate within the Alliance, a new and more flexible strategy was developed and adopted by NATO Ministers in 1967.

Strategy of flexible response

France, Spain, and Iceland (which has no military forces), do not participate in NATO's integrated military structure. However, with the exception of France, all member countries base their common defence on the strategy of flexible response. The basis of this concept was and is that NATO should be able to deter, and if necessary to counter, military aggression at any level. Closely tied to the strategy of flexible response is the commitment to "forward defence".

Flexible response requires a balanced combination of both nuclear and conventional forces. These forces must be sufficient to deter aggression and, should deterrence fail, be capable of direct defence, including escalation under political control, to the level of response necessary to convince the aggressor of the defender's determination and ability to resist, thus persuading him to cease the attack and withdraw. An aggressor must therefore be convinced of NATO's readiness to use nuclear weapons if necessary, while remaining uncertain as to the precise circumstances in which they would be used.

Flexibility of response means that conventional and nuclear forces must be deployed in adequate numbers and locations, prepared to respond effectively and ready for use at short notice. NATO's readiness posture, and its capacity to mobilise, reinforce and deploy in times of tension and crisis, are critical elements of this policy, the purpose of which is to meet any level of aggression with a response designed to restore peace and deter further aggression.

NATO defence policy is therefore based on a number of separate but interdependent elements, each of which contributes to the overall policy of deterrence against all possible forms of aggression, including direct aggression against one or more of the member countries or the threat of the use of force for the purposes of coercion or intimidation. The policy is based on the maintenance of adequate forces at sufficient levels of readiness to provide a credible forward defence, thus enabling NATO to respond flexibly to any form of aggression wherever it might occur. Within the framework of the North Atlantic Treaty whereby members of the Alliance agree that an armed attack against one or more of them, in Europe or North America, shall be considered an attack against them all, the policy is both the expression of the political solidarity of the member countries and the means by which they provide for their common defence.

Should aggression occur, NATO's objective would be to preserve or restore the integrity and security of the Treaty area, restore deterrence and terminate the conflict as soon as possible. A potential aggressor must be convinced that any aggression could initiate a sequence of events which could not be determined in advance, and which would involve risks out of all proportion to any advantages which could possibly be gained.

Chapter 10
Defence Planning

NATO's defence planning, which must continuously be adapted to keep pace with changing circumstances and technological developments, is based on an evaluation of the relative force capabilities of NATO and Warsaw Treaty countries. Reference is made in Chapter 8 to the quantitative and qualitative factors which must be taken into account in order to arrive at such an evaluation. The evaluation itself is constantly extended and updated by close coordination between the International Staff, in conjunction with the countries involved in NATO's force planning process and with NATO's Military Authorities.

In determining the size and nature of their contribution to the common defence, member countries have full independence of action. Nevertheless, the collective nature of NATO's defences demands that, in reaching their decisions, governments take account of the force structure recommended by the NATO Military Authorities and of the long-term military plans of their partners. NATO's procedures for common force planning must take into account such factors as the military requirements which have to be met, the best use of the available resources, advances in science and technology, an equitable division of effort among member countries and the need for force plans to be within the countries' economic and financial capabilities.

Resources for defence

The provision of adequate forces for implementing the agreed strategic concept involves inter-related questions of strategy, force requirements and the resources available to meet them. The achievement of the appropriate balance between these three elements demands that full weight be given in defence planning to economic considerations. Economic and financial studies undertaken in this context have three main objectives: to ensure that adequate resources are devoted to the fulfilment of agreed defence programmes; to contribute to the most rational use of available resources, in particular through long-term planning and through improving cost-effectiveness and similar instruments of economic management; and to progress as far as possible towards an equitable distribution of the economic and financial burden of the common defence. Within an alliance of free sovereign states, there is an overall need to plan to achieve a fair sharing of the risks, burdens and responsibilities of the common defence, as well as the benefits.

These objectives are not easy to reach in an Alliance whose members' economic situations differ widely, particularly with regard to population factors and the stage of their economic development. Those countries whose per capita income is still low must ensure that their defence effort does not hamper economic progress. At the same time, members of the Alliance must take account of developments in Warsaw Treaty countries and, not least, of their level of expenditure on defence.

Because of the wide disparity in economic resources between members of the Alliance, concerted action is necessary on programmes of military assistance to those members who have difficulty in financing from their own resources the full range of their contributions to the common defence. Apart from direct grants, this assistance includes credits under advantageous conditions, assistance in the context of the development and production of equipment, the sharing of technology, licensing agreements and other arrangements which will enable these nations to become more self-sufficient.

Development of the NATO force planning process

The first attempt at reconciling NATO's military requirements with the economic and financial resources of member countries dates back to 1951 and was based on a report prepared for the Ministerial Meeting at Lisbon in 1952 by Averell Harriman, Sir Edwin Plowden and Jean Monnet. The report was founded on the principle that defence must be built on a sound economic and social basis and that no country should be called on to shoulder a defence burden beyond its means. This was the basic premise of the "Annual Review" examinations of countries' defence efforts carried out between 1952 and 1961. A "Triennial Review" procedure was adopted in 1961 in a step designed to improve and simplify the process.

At a meeting in Ottawa in May 1963, Ministers instructed the Council to study, with the help of the NATO Military Authorities, the inter-related questions of strategy, force requirements and available resources. As a result of this study, new procedures were introduced in 1966 and a NATO force plan for the period 1966-1970 was adopted. At the same time, it was recognised that there was a continuing need for such studies and accordingly, procedures for NATO defence planning reviews were also approved. Under these procedures, which were revised in 1971, NATO's force plans are reviewed and projected each year for a period of five years ahead. This makes it possible to modify future force plans to meet changing circumstances and also provides a firm basis on which countries can plan their force contributions. A most important aspect of this process is the development of new NATO force goals every second year. These, in the first instance, represent targets which the Alliance sets for the six years ahead and are an attempt to balance national force plans in order to meet, to the extent possible, the wider force requirements established for the Alliance as a whole. Development of the process has led to the projection of selected force goals and information on country plans beyond the six-year period. The main elements of the current procedures are described in more detail in the following paragraphs.

Ministerial Guidance

In preparing their force proposals, NATO's military authorities are guided by a document approved by Defence Ministers every second year. This takes into account the advice of the NATO Military Committee as well as other crucial factors such as the prevailing economic situation. "Ministerial Guidance" also covers the political factors affecting the development of NATO forces over the period and assesses the likely impact of all these factors on the current strategic concept of the Alliance generally, and on the preparation of the next set of force proposals in particular. The Guidance also sets objectives for the longer term, and provides direction to the relevant NATO bodies for their tasks in meeting Alliance military requirements and planning guidance for national authorities on matters under their responsibility.

Military Input to Ministerial Guidance

As part of the process leading up to the development of the next set of NATO force goals, the Military Committee prepares an assessment in strategic terms which advises the Alliance of the situation which it may face. This advice, which constitutes the military input for Ministerial Guidance, attempts to identify all military factors and considerations likely to affect force structures, deployments, and equipment, both in NATO and in the Soviet Union and Eastern Europe, during the planning period and in the longer term.

Force proposals and the adoption of force goals

Force proposals are prepared every two years by the Major NATO Commanders, proposing for each country both the level of their contribution to collective defence and specific improvements required during the planning period. These proposals are considered by the Military Committee before being forwarded to the Defence Planning Committee with a statement of the reasons underlying them and the level of strategic risk associated with the ensuing force posture. The Defence Review Committee, acting on behalf of the Defence Planning Committee, then conducts an examination of the proposals, including their financial, economic and political implications. The Defence Review Committee must satisfy itself that the force proposals are compatible with the guidance given by Ministers. In the interests of collective defence it must seek to ensure that there is a reasonable and realistic challenge in the package of force proposals which each country is being asked to accept—a challenge which goes beyond the country's supposed intentions. The Defence Review Committee then reports to the Defence Planning Committee, commenting in particular on any adjustments which it believes necessary for economic or any other reasons, and on the associated risk as assessed by the Military Committee. In the light of the reports by the Military Committee and the Defence Review Committee, the Defence Planning Committee then approves a set of proposals for adoption as NATO Force Goals which countries will use as the basis of their force plans for the five-year period under consideration, as well as for longer term planning.

Annual review

Each year, countries formulate their plans, taking into account the NATO force goals, and forward them to NATO where they are analysed by both the NATO Military Authorities and the International Staff. When differences occur between the plans and the force goals a first joint attempt to reconcile them is made by the International Staff, the International Military Staff and the Major NATO Commanders' representatives. These trilateral discussions are reported to the Defence Review Committee which conducts a further critical examination of country plans, particularly directed at eliminating as far as possible any remaining differences between country force plans and NATO force goals. On the basis of these multilateral examinations the Defence Review Committee reports to the Defence Planning Committee how far countries have been able to meet the force goals, and if and why they have fallen short. At the same time, the Military Committee reports on the military suitability of the emerging Alliance-wide, five-year force plan, and on the degree of risk associated with it. In the light of these reports, the Defence Planning Committee is in a position to recommend a five-year force plan to Ministers.

Adoption of a five-year NATO Force Plan

Each December, Ministers consider the Defence Planning Committee's report and recommendations for the NATO force plan from the viewpoint of its overall balance, feasibility and acceptability, taking into account the Military Committee's advice. The NATO five-year force plan is then adopted as a basis for national defence planning over the whole period and, most importantly, as a firm commitment of forces by each country for the first year, and a reliable basis for operational planning by the Major NATO Commanders.

Significance of the NATO force planning process

NATO's force planning process thus provides both the method and the machinery for determining the forces required for the defence of the Alliance, coordinating national defence plans, and drawing them towards the agreed force goals in the best interests of the Alliance as a whole. Actions taken by nations on the basis of specific studies, some of which may be undertaken independently of the normal procedures, can also be introduced into the process at an appropriate stage.

The collective consideration of countries' defence efforts, and the attempt to harmonise them from an Alliance-wide point of view, have contributed considerably to mutual understanding; they have provided the means for reaching agreement on steps which are both desirable and practicable; and in many cases have led to cooperative efforts for solving problems. It is significant that, to enable this to be done, the countries of the Alliance have agreed to the systematic exchange of detailed and precise information on their military, economic and financial programmes, on a scale unprecedented in peace or even in war, and have continued to submit these programmes to the examination and criticism of their partners.

Longer-term defence planning and coordination

In parallel with force planning for the medium term, NATO is constantly reviewing ways in which the defence posture of the Alliance should adapt to challenges foreseen in the years ahead. Among other things, this led to the adoption by Ministers in 1980 of new procedures designed to extend progressively the coverage and timescale of NATO defence planning. These procedures allow nations to base their longer-term projections on early NATO guidance on defence needs and a common assessment of the future military, economic and political background.

The effectiveness of NATO long-term planning was further enhanced in 1985 when Ministers agreed to the Military Committee's Conceptual Military Framework. This framework, along with supporting documents prepared by the Major NATO Commanders, is designed to provide a more detailed basis for NATO Defence Planning up to the year 2000 and beyond. The basis is further refined, where appropriate, by long-term planning guidelines which set out the need and parameters for various defence improvements. These guidelines are taken into account by nations in developing their plans and by the NATO Military Authorities in preparing force proposals for the longer term.

There are four major disciplines in NATO defence planning: force structure, armaments, logistics and infrastructure. These are all supported by specialised committees whose functions are described in other chapters of this book. To extract maximum overall value from their many activities, action has been underway since 1983 to improve coordination between them. Much has been done since then and the benefits can be seen in the improved effectiveness of planning. Nevertheless, continued emphasis needs to be placed on coordination as NATO seeks to improve its capability in longer term planning. One recent important initiative has been the introduction on a trial basis of a Conventional Armaments Planning System (CAPS) (see Chapter 15) which is designed to determine how the military needs of the Alliance can best be met by national armaments programmes, either individually or collectively, and to elaborate armaments cooperation opportunities.

Conventional Defence Improvement Initiative

Making use of and enhancing the processes described above, the Conventional Defence Improvement Initiative assessed the ability of the Allies to meet the longer-term challenges of the 1980s and 1990s and provided a special review of steps to improve conventional defence capabilities. This effort was designed to strengthen coordinated defence planning among member countries by establishing more firmly based goals both for individual nations and for the Alliance as a whole. By focussing on requirements to overcome the most significant deficiencies, steps were taken to enable military requirements to be met, through the force goals, in the most cost effective way. Included among these measures are greater cooperation in research, development and production of armaments, improvements in infrastructure planning and refinements in the force planning process itself. The overall aim for the future is to present nations with more coordinated rather than separate claims on their defence resources.

Nuclear Planning

The important role of nuclear weapons in NATO's strategy, and the ever-increasing complexity of the political and technical aspects of the deployment of nuclear weapons, made it essential for NATO member countries which do not own nuclear weapons to be closely associated with Allied nuclear planning and to participate in nuclear policy formulation. The Nuclear Planning Group, formed in 1967 to meet this requirement, operated initially on the basis of a rotating participation of member countries but is now permanently composed of all NATO countries except France. Iceland participates as an observer.

Nuclear Planning Group

The Nuclear Planning Group's activities span the full spectrum of policy and force deployment issues associated with nuclear weapons. The NPG Staff Group, in which members of the delegations of the NPG nations and representatives of the NATO Military Authorities participate, receives overall direction from meetings of the Permanent Representatives of the nations participating in the Group. The Staff Group undertakes the detailed work required for the examination of policy issues relating to nuclear weapons and the formulation of specific proposals. Defence Ministers meet regularly twice a year in NPG Ministerial sessions to consider policy matters and recommendations arising from the work undertaken by the NPG at the level of Permanent Representatives or recommendations by NATO Military Authorities or other groups created to address specific issues. Nuclear-related issues and future Alliance needs are discussed and guidance is provided for the future work of the NPG.

Close coordination takes place between national delegations to NATO and sections of Ministries in national capitals with responsibilities in the nuclear field. The work is supported by a Nuclear Planning Directorate within the International Staff's Division of Defence Planning and Policy, which coordinates the work of the Nuclear Planning Group and the preparation of NPG meetings at Ministerial or Permanent Representative level.

From the outset, a primary role of the Nuclear Planning Group has been the development of coordinated policy guidance on nuclear matters, including consultation procedures. In 1986 a comprehensive document providing General Political Guidelines for the Employment of Nuclear Weapons in Defence of NATO was approved by NPG Ministers. This document incorporates previous policy decisions and provides current guidance for use by nations and by NATO military authorities.

NATO's policy and strategy, designed to deter aggression and to prevent war, are based on the capabilities of its conventional and nuclear forces and the clear will on the part of the Alliance to use these, as necessary, in a timely and flexible fashion, should deterrence fail. This requires the maintenance of strong, diverse and flexible nuclear and conventional capabilities based on an equitable sharing among all the countries concerned of the burdens, risks and responsibilities involved as well as the benefits of the security thus provided.

At the core of this policy is the political demonstration of the Alliance's capability and resolve to deter aggression and, if necessary, to defend itself by the use of its military forces, including nuclear weapons. These forces therefore serve a fundamental political purpose in peacetime as well as in a crisis or war situation. Any decision concerning the use of nuclear weapons by NATO would involve the fullest possible consultation within the Alliance. Such consultation would permit member governments to express their views immediately on any request or proposal by the NATO Military Authorities for the use of nuclear weapons in defence of NATO and would reflect the solidarity of the whole Alliance in reaching its decisions. However, the ultimate decision to authorise the use of any nuclear weapon remains with the political authorities of the nuclear power owning it.

Nuclear forces, including intermediate- and short-range nuclear weapons of different ranges, maritime systems, and ultimately, systems at the strategic level provide NATO governments with a range of political and military options for deterrence and defence. Maintaining the credibility of this deterrent force has required the modernisation of portions of NATO's nuclear forces from time to time. For example, examination in the Nuclear Planning Group during the late 1970s led to the parallel and complementary NATO decisions of 1979 on intermediate-range nuclear force modernisation and arms control, whereby it was agreed that 1,000 United States nuclear warheads would be withdrawn from Europe and 572 ground-launched cruise missiles and Pershings would be deployed, unless a verifiable arms control agreement obviated the need for them. The withdrawal of the 1,000 warheads was completed by 1981.

On October 27, 1983, Defence Ministers meeting in the NATO Nuclear Planning Group in Montebello, Canada, in keeping with the Alliance policy of maintaining only the minimum number of nuclear weapons necessary for credible deterrence, announced their decision to withdraw a further 1,400 nuclear warheads from Europe by 1988, bringing the total of such withdrawals since 1979 to 2,400. The withdrawals were completed ahead of schedule. Ministers recognised that the remaining capabilities must be survivable, responsive and effective, and accordingly identified a range of possible improvements.

Deployment of the Cruise and Pershing missiles began in November 1983 but, with the signature of the INF Treaty in December 1987 (described in more detail in Chapter 11), and its subsequent ratification by the United States and the Soviet Union in June 1988, agreement was reached to eliminate land-based intermediate-range nuclear missiles on a global basis.

The INF Treaty represented a major achievement for the Alliance and was a vindication of the policies adopted by NATO countries. However, the proportion of nuclear weapons eliminated by the INF Treaty only amounts to some 4 % of nuclear weapons deployed. Within the framework of NATO's comprehensive concept of arms control and disarmament, every opportunity will be taken of further reducing levels of conventional and nuclear forces, through negotiations, in a manner which is commensurate with the overall objective of enhanced security. In the meantime, in accordance with the Alliance strategy of deterrence based upon an appropriate mix of adequate and effective nuclear and conventional forces, which need to be kept up-to-date where necessary, work is underway to continue those measures required to maintain the effectiveness, responsiveness and survivability of NATO's nuclear forces within the framework of the Montebello Decision. Changes in the situation such as progress achieved in arms control, new technology and the overall evolution of the nuclear and conventional military capabilities of the Soviet Union are taken into account.

Chapter 11

Arms Control and Disarmament[1]

Arms Control Policy

The fundamental purpose of the Atlantic Alliance is to safeguard peace and to search for a more stable relationship between East and West in which the underlying political issues dividing them can be resolved peacefully. To create the conditions in which progress towards these objectives can be achieved, the first function of the Alliance is to maintain adequate political solidarity and military strength to deter aggression or other forms of pressure and to defend the territory of member countries if aggression should occur. The maintenance of peace and stability and the enhancement of security depend on the continued ability of the Alliance to carry out these tasks, if possible at lower levels of military forces. Arms control is therefore an integral part of NATO's overall security policy.

The basis for NATO's security policy remains the Harmel doctrine of 1967. In accordance with this doctrine, the two objectives—maintaining a sufficient military capacity to act as an effective and credible deterrent against aggression and other forms of pressure while seeking to improve the East-West dialogue—are fully complementary. The Alliance's objectives in arms control are therefore tied to the achievement of both aims. Meaningful and verifiable arms control agreements which respect the security concerns of East and West contribute both to the improvement of the dialogue and to the credibility of deterrence. It is therefore important that defence and arms control policies remain in harmony and that their roles in safeguarding the security of the countries of the Alliance are consistent and mutually reinforcing.

Accordingly, the principal consideration of the Alliance in the context of any arms control negotiation is not whether agreement is a desirable objective in its own right, but rather whether or not it maintains and enhances security. Arms control is thus part of an overall defence policy involving many other important elements, each of which has its own relevance to the goals of peace and stability.

The numerical balance of the armed forces of NATO and the Warsaw Treaty Organisation has altered slowly but steadily over the past two to three decades. Imbalances in the sphere of conventional forces in particular have increased. The same period has witnessed a marked increase in the nuclear

---

1 This chapter describes the main features of the arms control programme on which the Alliance is engaged and outlines the progress made in each of the principal negotiating fora. The principal landmarks in the various spheres of negotiation are described in chronological sequence in Chapter 4.

force capabilities of the Soviet Union. Member countries of the Alliance have also lost some of the technological advantage which used to permit NATO to rely partially on quality to compensate for quantitative disadvantages. An important aspect of any arms control agreement, assuming that it can be successfully concluded and satisfactorily verified, is therefore the contribution it can make to reducing imbalances. Purely numerically equal reductions in the size of military forces and the extent of their armaments are inadequate. At best they perpetuate existing disparities; at worst, in circumstances of imbalance, reduced force levels can place NATO countries at a greater military disadvantage and consequently weaken deterrence, adding to insecurity and rendering war and conflict more, rather than less, likely.

There are therefore several strands involved in developing a valid arms control policy. The foremost imperative is that arms control proposals should be made in the context of enhancing security rather than in isolation from other strategic concerns. All arms control initiatives from whatever source must be judged against this yardstick. From the Alliance's point of view, this involves weighing the collective security interests of 16 different independent nations spread over a wide geographic area. Care has to be taken that measures that might have beneficial effects on one country do not have adverse effects on others.

The Alliance has always insisted that arms control agreements must also be clear and precise. The outcome must be verifiable and not open to circumvention. Mere declarations of good intent and expressions of political will, whether they are genuine or designed for propaganda purposes, are not enough.

Important progress has been made in the field of arms control, and the successful conclusion of the INF Treaty between the United States and the Soviet Union in December 1987, in particular, was an important step in the arms control process. The Treaty eliminated all United States and Soviet land-based intermediate-range missiles on a global basis. In addition to removing a whole class of weapons, it also established the principle of assymetrical reductions and provided for a stringent verification régime. Its implementation, however, will only affect a small proportion of the Soviet nuclear armoury and the Alliance continues to face a substantial array of modern and effective Soviet nuclear systems of all ranges as well as serious imbalances in conventional forces. The full realisation of the Alliance arms control agenda therefore requires further steps.

A Comprehensive Concept

In order to take account of all the complex and inter-related issues arising in the arms control context, the Alliance has developed a comprehensive concept of arms control and disarmament. Elements of the comprehensive concept include:

The Comprehensive Concept addresses the role of arms control in East-West relations, the principles of Alliance security, and a number of guiding principles and objectives governing Allied policy in the nuclear, conventional and chemical fields of arms control. The report sets out the interrelationships between arms control and defence policies and establishes the overall conceptual framework within which the Alliance is seeking progress in each area of its arms control agenda, i.e.

— a 50% reduction in the strategic nuclear weapons of the United States and the Soviet Union;
— the global elimination of chemical weapons;
— the establishment of a secure and stable balance of conventional forces in Europe at lower levels, the elimination of disparities prejudicial to stability and security, and the elimination of the capability for launching surprise attack and for initiating large-scale offensive action;
— once implementation of an agreement on conventional force reductions is under way, negotiations to achieve a *partial* reduction of American and Soviet land-based nuclear missile forces of shorter range to equal and verifiable levels, on the understanding by the Allies concerned that negotiated reductions leading to a level below the existing level of their SNF missiles will not be carried out until the results of the conventional force negotiations have been implemented.

Work on the comprehensive concept provided the foundation for progress in the arms control sphere which the Alliance has been actively seeking for many years. The Concept was formally adopted and published at the Summit Meeting held in Brussels on May 29-30, 1989. The text of the Comprehensive Concept, together with that of the Summit Declaration, is reproduced in full at Appendix I.

The Scope of Arms Control

The history of arms control, and the various fora which have been created to provide for negotiations in this field, are a reflection of the scope and complexity of the issues involved. The following paragraphs describe some of the general principles which apply and outline the main developments in bilateral and multilateral negotiations over recent years.

Arms control deals essentially with two broad categories of proposals; those for measures which build confidence and those which result in reductions and limitations of military manpower and equipment. The Alliance is actively involved in both these areas and considers that progress is needed in both, although not necessarily concurrently.

Extensive consultation takes place within NATO over the whole range of disarmament and arms control issues, so that commonly agreed positions can be reached and national positions coordinated whenever appropriate. The key body for this consultation process is the North Atlantic Council supported by the Political Committee, both in its regular sessions and in separate meetings with disarmament experts. In addition, special bodies have been created within NATO to deal with specific arms control issues. As a result of these numerous opportunities for consultations, member countries have been better able to prepare for negotiations in the many different arms control fora.

The main focus of the Alliance's interest in arms control lies in negotiations and agreements which directly affect Alliance security—in particular, the two sets of negotiations provided for in the concluding document resulting from the Vienna CSCE Follow-up Meeting which ended on January 19, 1989; namely the negotiations on Conventional Armed Forces in Europe (CFE) and the negotiations on Confidence and Security-Building Measures (CSBMs). These negotiations address the conventional imbalance which has long been a principle cause of the military instability which is at the core of Allied security concerns in Europe. Other negotiations of direct concern to the Alliance include: the bilateral talks in Geneva between the United States and the Soviet Union on reduction and limitation of strategic nuclear weapons (known as START) and on Defence and Space (DST); the successful negotiations on land-based intermediate-range nuclear weapons (INF), to which reference is made above, and the subsequent implementation of the INF Treaty; the Conference on Security and Cooperation in Europe (CSCE) and the implementation of the 1975 Helsinki Final Act; the Conference on Confidence and Security-Building Measures and Disarmament in Europe (CDE), which is itself part of the CSCE process, and the implementation of the resulting Stockholm Document of September 1986; and the implementation of all the measures agreed upon at CSCE Follow-up Meetings designed to strengthen the CSCE process, in particular those measures contained in the Concluding Document resulting from the Vienna CSCE Follow-up Meeting.

There are, however, other fora, to which members of the Alliance contribute, involving subjects which have a direct bearing on the interests of the Alliance as a whole. A good example is the Conference on Disarmament (CD), which meets under United Nations auspices in Geneva and is the principal multilateral forum for negotiations on a number of issues including a global ban on chemical weapons, where there is a wide consensus among Alliance members. Developments in all these spheres and in each of the principal negotiating fora are described below.

Bilateral United States-Soviet Negotiations

Since the beginning of bilateral negotiations between the United States and the Soviet Union on nuclear arms control in 1969, this topic has been one of the major items for consultations between the United States and its NATO allies. Negotiations have resulted in the first interim Strategic Arms Limitation Agreement (SALT I) and its companion, the Anti-Ballistic Missile (ABM) Treaty in 1972, the unratified SALT II agreement of 1979, and the recent Treaty on Intermediate-range Nuclear Forces (INF) which was signed at the end of 1987 and came into force, after ratification, on June 1, 1988. Negotiations are under way on a Strategic Arms Reductions Agreement (START) and on a Defence and Space (DST) agreement. Although each of these negotiations take place on a bilateral basis, consultations within the Alliance, often of an intensive nature, provide the opportunity for the interests of the Alliance as a whole to be fully addressed.

Strategic Arms Limitation Talks (SALT I and SALT II)

The SALT I agreement froze the number of launchers for Inter-Continental Ballistic Missiles (ICBMs) and Sea-Launched Ballistic Missiles (SLBMs) at the levels prevailing in 1972. It was to last for a five year period. The Anti-Ballistic Missile (ABM) Treaty is of unlimited duration with provision for withdrawal after 6 months notice. Its main purpose was to prevent either side from deploying an effective nation-wide ABM defence. It limited the two parties to deploying ABM defensive missile systems in no more than two (subsequently reduced to one) areas each. It also placed quantitative and qualitative limits on these systems and on ABM system components, such as radars, located elsewhere. In addition, the Treaty placed constraints on the development and testing of certain types of ABM systems or their components as well as qualitative limitations on other types of systems which could potentially be used for ABM purposes.

The SALT II agreement set equal aggregate ceilings (2400, falling to 2250) on the launchers for ICBMs and SLBMs plus heavy bombers. In addition, it provided for equal subceilings on certain categories of strategic arms, e.g.

— 1320 on the total number of launchers for "MIRVed"[2] ICBMs and SLBMs plus heavy bombers equipped with Air-Launched Cruise Missiles (ALCMs);
— 1200 on the total number of MIRVed ballistic missile launchers; and
— 820 on the total number of MIRVed ICBM launchers.

The Treaty also contained limitations on "MIRVing", an extensive set of detailed definitions and a variety of provisions to enhance verification. Although it was respected by the two sides for some years, the Treaty was not ratified and therefore never entered into force. In May 1987, the United States announced that, in view of Soviet violations, it would no longer be bound by the terms of the unratified Treaty.

Negotiations on Intermediate-range Nuclear Forces

The INF Treaty[3] was signed in Washington on December 8, 1987, and entered into force, after ratification by the Soviet Union and the United States, on June 1, 1988. In contrast to earlier agreements, which concentrated on setting limitations on further deployments, it provides for the total elimination on a global basis of an entire class of United States and Soviet nuclear systems—ground-launched missiles with ranges between 500 and 5,500 kilometres. The Treaty establishes several important precedents. In order to reach the "zero outcome" called for by the agreement, the Soviet Union must destroy many more of its systems than the United States, thus establishing the principle of asymmetric reductions to reflect asymmetries in

---

[2] MIRVed: missiles carrying "Multiple Independently-targetable Re-entry Vehicles".

[3] Treaty between the United States of America and the Union of Soviet Socialist Republics on the Elimination of their Intermediate-Range and Shorter-Range Missiles.

force levels. In addition, the Treaty provides for an unprecedented, stringent and intrusive verification regime, including provision for numerous on-site inspections to be conducted for a variety of purposes. These verification arrangements set an invaluable and vital precedent in moving towards the still more ambitious and demanding arms control objectives remaining on NATO's future arms control agenda, for example in the field of strategic nuclear weapons.

Alliance consultation was very intensive from the outset and throughout the process of negotiating the INF Treaty. A major unilateral Soviet escalation of the number and capabilities of its intermediate-range nuclear forces, and therefore in the threat they posed to Western Europe, through its deployment of the SS-20 missile system, led the Alliance countries concerned to take their "double-track" decision of December 1979. The decision involved pursuing a dual course of preparing for the deployment of approximately comparable United States systems to counter the Soviet build-up while simultaneously seeking to negotiate an agreement with the Soviet Union for the reduction or elimination of this category of weapons. Despite Soviet threats and blandishments as well as domestic political pressures, the Alliance adhered to its original decision. After intensive but unsuccessful efforts to make a breakthrough in the negotiations in Geneva, NATO deployments began on schedule in November 1983, and continued until the autumn of 1987, when agreement was finally reached and the INF Treaty was concluded. The Treaty is a major achievement which simultaneously reduces the military threat to NATO, creates greater confidence between East and West, and lays the groundwork for even more extensive arms control agreements in the future.

Strategic Arms Reductions Talks (START) and Defence and Space Talks (DST)

By early 1988 work was well underway on a START agreement which would reduce the strategic forces of the United States and the Soviet Union by 50%. In contrast to SALT I and II, the primary unit of account in the START negotiations is strategic nuclear warheads, the aim being to reduce these to 6,000. Delivery systems—ICBMs, SLBMs, heavy bombers—are to be reduced to 1,600. Such an agreement would represent a major step forward in reducing the strategic arsenals of the two sides and, more importantly, would do so in a manner which considerably enhances strategic stability. While the verification regime for the agreement has yet to be worked out, the two sides have already agreed on an extensive list of monitoring activities which are to be included in the treaty. Although the INF precedent means that much of the groundwork has been carried out, the verification requirements of START are extremely demanding and complex since the prospective agreement deals with a much wider variety of systems and will require continuous monitoring of the various levels of systems permitted, as opposed to the "zero" level involved in the INF Treaty.

Since the conclusion of the ABM Treaty in 1972, the march of technology has opened up new possibilities for defences against ballistic missile attack. This is exemplified in the United States Strategic Defence Initiative (SDI) and in its much less publicised but nonetheless extensive Soviet analogue. Both the United States and the Soviet Union have been grappling with ways of coming to terms with this new reality. Through its negotiating posture and public campaigning it became clear that the Soviet Union wished to impose severe restrictions on the United States SDI programme. The United States, however, has been determined to keep its options for strategic defence open and if possible to work cooperatively with the Soviet Union towards the development of more defensively oriented strategic postures for both sides. Negotiations have examined the possibility of an agreement foreclosing deployment of strategic defences beyond what is permitted by the 1972 ABM Treaty for a specified period. While there are points of agreement, the Soviet government has sought to place tighter constraints on the development and testing of such defences than the United States considers to be required by the ABM Treaty. To that end, the Soviet Union linked its readiness to agree to a START treaty to obtaining satisfaction in its demands at the Defence and Space Talks. The United States, for its part, emphasised the need for the Soviet Union to rectify existing violations of the ABM Treaty, in particular the Soviet large phased-array radar near Krasnoyarsk in Siberia. The United States has said that it will continue to negotiate but will not conclude a START Treaty until the Krasnoyarsk violation is satisfactorily remedied.[4]

As this review of the record demonstrates, bilateral nuclear negotiations between the United States and the USSR have been lengthy and complex but have borne fruit. The United States intends to pursue vigorously further negotiations in this sphere. In so doing it will be guided by certain fundamental principles. Any agreements must clearly enhance the security of the West. They must be verifiable, providing high certainty that Soviet non-compliance could not go undetected. Agreements must also be balanced and equitable so that neither side gains unilateral advantage from them. Finally, such agreements must work to enhance stability, in part by channelling future strategic competition into areas that make a nuclear first strike increasingly less feasible and less rational, so that the net result will be to diminish the risk of nuclear war. In the context of the Strategic Defence Initiative, the Alliance countries concerned hold to their view that research into strategic defence is a prudent measure and this is therefore reflected in the positions they have taken on arms control issues.

---

[4] Postscript: In September 1989 commitments were made by the Soviet Union relating to important obstacles to progress in the START negotiations. These included a Soviet decision to dismantle its Krasnoyarsk radar station, in response to the US objection that the station constituted a violation of the ABM Treaty; and a Soviet decision to drop its previous insistence on limitations on United States SDI research as a precondition for the conclusion of a treaty on strategic arms. Significant commitments were also made by both the US and the Soviet Union in the context of efforts to bring about a global ban on chemical weapons, as well as progress in the field of nuclear testing.

Consultations likewise take place within the Alliance as a matter of course on developments in the various multilateral negotiating fora concerned with arms control. The negotiations on Mutual and Balanced Force Reductions were an example.

Mutual and Balanced Force Reductions (MBFR)

Negotiations on Mutual and Balanced Force Reductions opened in October 1973 in Vienna. In these negotiations, participants from NATO and the Warsaw Treaty Organisation sought to reduce the heavy concentration of military forces in a specified area of Central Europe, including the Federal Republic of Germany, the Netherlands, Belgium, Luxembourg, the German Democratic Republic, Poland and Czechoslovakia. Nations with territory or forces in Central Europe were represented as direct participants, i.e. on the part of the West: Belgium, Canada, the Federal Republic of Germany, Luxembourg, the Netherlands, the United Kingdom and the United States; and on the Eastern side: Czechoslovakia, the German Democratic Republic, Poland and the Soviet Union. Other NATO nations (Denmark, Greece, Italy, Norway and Turkey) and members of the Warsaw Treaty Organisation (Bulgaria and Romania) bordering upon the area of reductions were indirect participants. The possibility of Hungary's inclusion among the direct participants was left open. France did not participate in the MBFR negotiations and its forces were not a subject of discussion in this context.

The key Western objective throughout these negotiations was to correct the potentially destabilising Eastern superiority in the area through phased reductions leading to equal collective combined manpower ceilings for NATO ground and air forces and those of the Warsaw Treaty Organisation.

While broad agreement was reached on a number of points, it was not possible, in the absence of Eastern willingness to provide adequate data or to engage in serious efforts to find a solution to the data problem, to resolve major issues such as the size of Eastern forces currently deployed in the reductions area, the treatment of armaments, or the problems associated with verification.

Following the decision to open new negotiations on Conventional Armed Forces in Vienna in March 1989, the states participating in MBFR decided to conclude these negotiations. The last meeting took place on February 2, 1989. The concluding communiqué issued at that time noted that the negotiations had served to maintain a serious dialogue between East and West on security issues and had provided the first multilateral forum for the exploration of the complex problems associated with efforts to strengthen stability and security in Europe. However, there was insufficient common ground to enable the participants to agree on a treaty. The positions of the two sides had nevertheless converged on a number of issues. Valuable experience had been gained, as well as a clearer picture of what would be necessary to achieve mutually agreeable and verifiable reductions and limitations of forces and armaments in Europe.

The Conference on Security and Cooperation in Europe (CSCE)

The Conference on Security and Cooperation in Europe is a continuous process involving 35 nations—all the nations of Europe, except Albania, including all the European members of NATO, of the Warsaw Treaty Organisation and of the so-called Neutral and Non-Aligned (NNA) states, plus the United States and Canada.

The CSCE process was launched in 1972 and initially resulted in the Helsinki Final Act of 1975. This document encompassed a wide range of agreements on principles governing relations between states; measures designed to build confidence between them; principles concerning the free movement of people, ideas and information; and cooperation in cultural, economic, technical and scientific fields. It incorporated a set of voluntary Confidence-Building Measures (CBMs) which called for the prior notification of military exercises involving more than 25,000 men and also provided for the invitation of observers from participating states to attend military exercises.

The Helsinki process has been the subject of periodic reviews or Follow-up Meetings. The second such meeting, held in Madrid between November 1980 and September 1983, created a variety of separate fora including Expert Meetings to deal with various aspects of the CSCE agenda during the period between Madrid and the next Follow-up Meeting in Vienna, scheduled for 1986.

The Conference on Disarmament in Europe (CDE)

The most important and prominent new CSCE Forum agreed upon in Madrid was the CDE which got underway in Stockholm in January 1984. Officially known as the Conference on Confidence and Security-Building Measures and Disarmament in Europe, the CDE reached agreement in September 1986 (shortly before the start of the Vienna CSCE Follow-up Meeting) on what has become known as the Stockholm Document. This embodies a comprehensive series of "CSBMs" or Confidence and Security-Building Measures which include:

— notification at least 42 days in advance of most types of military activities involving over 13,000 men;
— mandatory invitation of observers from all participating states to activities involving more than 17,000 men;
— provision in November of each year of annual calendars listing anticipated notifiable activities for the coming calendar year;
— constraining provisions which specify that activities involving over 40,000 men should be included in the annual calendar provided in the second year prior to the activity and that activities involving over 75,000 men will not be carried out unless they have been the object of communication as defined above; and
— verification provisions which, in cases of doubts about compliance, grant participating states the right to mount an on-site inspection in any other participating state. The latter has no right to refuse the inspection request.

The Stockholm Document, which is politically binding, was a considerable achievement for the Alliance. Most of its Confidence and Security-Building Measures reflect Western proposals. Several features of it are striking improvements when compared with the Helsinki Final Act, including lower thresholds, mandatory invitation of observers, on-site inspections by other participating states without right of refusal, and inclusion of all Soviet territory in Europe up to the Urals (by contrast the Helsinki Final Act included only a 200 kilometre-wide band of Soviet territory along borders facing other CSCE participants).

Compliance with the Stockholm Document has been encouraging. As for the future, there was agreement among the participating nations in Vienna that a further conference to build upon and expand the results of Stockholm would be convened in March 1989.

Progress towards Conventional Stability Talks and Negotiations on further Confidence and Security-Building Measures

In 1986 the fact that so many problems had long beset the MBFR negotiations gave rise to important new Alliance initiatives. Eastern intransigence over the data issue, the inherent problems of dealing with a limited area of reductions both from a political and military point of view, and not least the practicalities of implementing an agreement in a way which would offer adequate assurances that it would not be circumvented, all combined to render the MBFR negotiations extremely difficult. At the same time, the prospect of the successful conclusion of the INF Treaty, and possibility of further deep reductions in nuclear forces, raised the importance of addressing the conventional imbalance. For all these reasons the case became stronger for expanding the area of conventional arms control negotiations to include imbalances and asymmetries in the whole of Europe from the Atlantic to the Ural mountains.

This was the background for the decision taken by Allied Foreign Ministers at the Halifax meeting in May 1986, calling for the strengthening of security and stability in the whole of Europe through increased openness and the establishment of a stable balance of forces at lower levels. In pursuit of this objective, they established a High Level Task Force for conventional arms control. Its first report to Ministers provided the basis for the Brussels Declaration on Conventional Arms Control in which the Allies set out the basic purposes they had in mind and methods envisaged for negotiations (see Appendix I). They also expressed their readiness to launch East/West discussions on a mandate for such negotiations. Following this initiative, mandate talks between the 16 members of the Alliance and the 7 Warsaw Treaty countries began in February 1987 in Vienna, and in July 1987 the Allies tabled their draft mandate for the negotiations themselves. Talks continued with the objective of enabling conventional stability negotiations to begin as early as possible. However, as they were to be held within the framework of the CSCE process, their timing also depended on the achievement of a balanced outcome to the CSCE Follow-up meeting in Vienna.

In the declaration on "Conventional Arms Control: The Way Ahead", issued under the authority of the Heads of State and Government at the Brussels meeting of the North Atlantic Council on March 2-3, 1988, the Alliance expressed its key objectives in the conventional stability negotiations as follows:

— the establishment of a secure and stable balance of conventional forces at lower levels;
— the elimination of disparities prejudicial to stability and security;
— as a matter of high priority, the elimination of the capability for launching surprise attack and for initiating large-scale offensive action.

The Summit Meeting of the Alliance thus gave a fresh impetus to the Vienna Mandate Talks by calling for early agreement on a conventional stability mandate as part of a balanced outcome to the Vienna Follow-up Meeting of the Conference on Security and Cooperation in Europe. At the same time, the Allies sought agreement on a mandate for new negotiations on Confidence and Security-Building Measures (CSBMs), also in the framework of the Vienna CSCE Follow-up Meeting.

In a further important development, the North Atlantic Council issued a comprehensive Statement on Conventional Arms Control at its meeting on December 8, 1988. The Statement welcomed the reductions recently announced by President Gorbachev at the United Nations General Assembly as a positive contribution towards meeting allied concerns over the massive preponderance of the East in systems regarded as the most destabilising because of their relevance to large-scale offensive military operations and the seizing and holding of territory—i.e. main battle tanks, artillery and armoured troop carriers. The implementation of these measures, together with the proclaimed Soviet readiness to restructure the remaining forces, would be a very important first step towards reducing conventional imbalances.

They would not, however, eliminate imbalances. Accordingly, the Council Statement set out the broad lines of proposals which the Alliance would present in detail at the negotiating table, aimed, on the one hand, at greater stability through further reducing conventional force disparities and, on the other, at greater transparency of military organisation and military activities, and improved contacts and communications. These proposals reflected the Alliance view that conventional arms control must be seen as part of a dynamic process which addresses the military, political and human aspects of the division which has existed in Europe for more than four decades. A secure peace can only be achieved with steady progress in all these spheres.

The text of the Statement by the North Atlantic Council is reproduced in full at Appendix I.

Conclusion of the Vienna CSCE Follow-up Meeting — January 1989

The third CSCE Follow-up Meeting, which had opened in Vienna in November 1986, was formally concluded on January 19, 1989. The Concluding

Document marked a number of major advances in the level of the commitments undertaken by the participating states and was widely seen as a vindication of the intensive efforts made over more than two years of negotiations to achieve a balanced outcome which would strengthen and enhance the CSCE process.

The agreements reached in Vienna are extensive and address every aspect of the CSCE process, including questions of principle and commitment to the continuation of the process, as well as assessments of progress achieved to date; new efforts to enhance stability and security in Europe; and increased cooperation in the different areas with which CSCE is concerned.

Calendar of CSCE Meetings agreed at Vienna

6 March 1989	Opening of Negotiations on Conventional Armed Forces in Europe (23 participating nations), Vienna
	Opening of Negotiations on Confidence and Security-Building Measures (35 participating nations), Vienna
18 April – 12 May 1989	Information Forum, London
30 May – 23 June 1989	First Meeting of the Conference on the Human Dimension (CDH), Paris
16 October – 3 November 1989	Meeting on the Protection of the Environment, Sofia
19 March – 11 April 1990	Conference on Economic Cooperation in Europe, Bonn
5 June – 29 June 1990	Second Meeting of the Conference on the Human Dimension (CDH), Copenhagen
24 September – 19 October 1990	Meeting on the Mediterranean, Palma de Mallorca
15 January – 8 February 1991	Experts' Meeting on the Peaceful Settlement of Disputes, Valletta
28 May – 7 June 1991	Cultural Heritage Symposium, Cracow
10 September – 4 October 1991	Third Meeting of the Conference on the Human Dimension (CDH), Moscow
10 March 1992	Opening of Preparatory Meeting in Helsinki for Fourth CSCE Follow-up Meeting
24 March 1992	Opening of Fourth CSCE Follow-up Meeting, Helsinki

The objectives of the participating countries are set forth with regard to cooperation in the fields of economics, science, technology, the environment, trade and industry, and Mediterranean issues. Of special significance is the emphasis given to the intensification of cooperation in the humanitarian field where commitments go much further than those achieved at previous CSCE meetings in upholding individual human rights and fundamental freedoms. The Concluding Document also makes provision for continuous monitoring of standards of implementation of accords reached in the human rights sphere. This represents another new departure. These measures are supplemented by specific agreements applying to future efforts in the field of human contacts, freer and wider dissemination of information, cultural and educational cooperation, and the human dimension of the CSCE process as a whole, itself the subject of a special conference scheduled to take place in three stages; in Paris (May-June 1989), Copenhagen (June 1990), and Moscow (September-October 1991). Agreement was also reached on a meeting on Security and Cooperation in the Mediterranean, designed to follow up and strengthen aspects of earlier work, to be held in Palma de Mallorca in the Autumn of 1991. And new commitments were made to develop procedures for the peaceful settlement of disputes, including a meeting of experts on this subject early in 1991.

Many of the areas of further work identified in the Vienna Concluding Document will receive special focus during a number of other meetings scheduled to take place between 1989 and March 1992, when the fourth CSCE Follow-up Meeting will open in Helsinki. Thus progress in all the main areas of concern will remain under scrutiny, and the momentum for improvement will be maintained.

Mandates for New Negotiations on Conventional Armed Forces in Europe (CFE) and Negotiations on Confidence and Security-Building Measures (CSBMs)

Agreement was also reached in Vienna on the mandates for the negotiations beginning in March 1989 among the 23 member countries of NATO and the Warsaw Treaty Organisation on conventional armed forces, and for separate negotiations among all 35 CSCE participants on Confidence and Security-Building Measures. The latter are intended to expand and build upon the provisions of the Stockholm Document of September 1986 signed at the conclusion of the Conference on Confidence and Security-Building Measures and Disarmament (CDE).

The objective of the Negotiations on Conventional Armed Forces (CFE) is to strengthen stability and security in Europe from the Atlantic to the Urals, at lower levels of conventional armaments and equipment, through elimination of disparities and of the capacity for surprise attack and offensive action. Rigorous and effective verification measures, including detailed exchange of information as well as on-site inspections, will be needed to ensure compliance with the provisions of any agreement.

The CFE negotiations, for which the agenda, rules and arrangements have been determined by the 23 participating states, are being conducted autonomously within the framework of the CSCE process. The Helsinki Follow-up Meeting in 1992 will provide an opportunity for all 35 CSCE states to exchange views on progress achieved, as will other information exchange meetings with the European neutral and non-aligned states scheduled to take place at regular intervals during the intervening period.

Opening of Vienna Negotiations on Conventional Armed Forces in Europe and Negotiations on Confidence and Security-Building Measures — March 6-8, 1989

A meeting of CSCE Foreign Ministers and other representatives took place in Vienna on March 6-8, 1989. On March 6, Western countries released detailed position papers[5] explaining Western proposals in both these new negotiations and on March 9 both sets of negotiations got under way.

On the first day of the CFE talks, NATO tabled its outline proposals. These consisted of reduction and limitation proposals on tanks, artillery and armoured troop carriers that would result in equal holdings at levels about 5-10% below NATO's current holdings. Other provisions dealt with stationed forces and also proposed that no one participating country could have more than 30% of the total holdings in the Atlantic to the Urals area. Verification and stabilising measures would be introduced, including a regular exchange of information.

The Eastern countries also produced an initial proposal. This showed some degree of convergence with the West's proposals but was not as specific and included other elements not acceptable to the West.

At the NATO Summit Meeting on May 29, 1989, President Bush announced a major new initiative calling for an acceleration of the CFE negotiations in Vienna and for significant reductions in land-based combat aircraft, helicopters, and United States and Soviet military personnel stationed outside their national territory, as well as in the three categories (tanks, artillery, armoured troop carriers) included in the initial Western CFE proposals presented in Vienna in March. NATO Heads of State and Government endorsed this initiative in principle in the Summit Declaration issued at the conclusion of their meeting and announced that by September 1989, the beginning of the third round of the CFE negotiations, they intended to present a proposal amplifying and expanding on the position which they had tabled at the opening of the negotiations. The Alliance's High Level Task Force on Conventional Arms Control was tasked with the further elaboration of this proposal.

The main elements of the Alliance's initiative include registering agreement, based on ceilings already proposed in Vienna, on tanks, armoured troop carriers and artillery pieces, held by members of the two alliances in Europe, with all the withdrawn equipment to be destroyed; expanding the current proposal to include reductions by each side to equal ceilings 15%

---

[5] See NATO Review No. 2, 1989.

below current Alliance holdings of helicopters and of all land-based combat aircraft in the Atlantic-to-the Urals zone, with all the withdrawn equipment to be destroyed; proposing a 20% cut in combat manpower in US stationed forces, and a resulting ceiling on US and Soviet ground and air force personnel stationed outside national territory in the same Atlantic-to-Urals zone of approximately 275,000 (requiring the Soviet Union to reduce its forces in Eastern Europe by some 325,000) and demobilizing the forces withdrawn; and seeking such an agreement within six months to a year, accomplishing the reductions by 1992 or 1993.

In the negotiations on Confidence and Security-Building Measures (CSBMs) which had also opened on March 9, the Western participants took the initiative, tabling an outline of their proposals on the first day. The proposals seek a detailed exchange of information on military structures and on planned weapon deployments, backed up by a random evaluation system. Improvements to provisions of the 1986 Stockholm Document are also proposed, and a seminar for an exchange of ideas on military doctrine is envisaged. At the NATO Summit Meeting in May, Heads of State and Government emphasized the importance they attached to maintaining the momentum created by the successful implementation of the Stockholm Document.

The initial proposals by Eastern countries contrasted rather sharply with the West's approach by tending to focus on constraints of activity and seeking to apply CSBMs to independent air and naval activities outside the scope of the mandate for the negotiations, and therefore not acceptable to Western participants.

Conference on Disarmament

The Conference on Disarmament (CD) is the only multilateral disarmament negotiating forum of the international community which takes place under the auspices of the United Nations. Its membership of 40 includes all the 5 nuclear-weapon states and 35 other states. The NATO countries participating in the Conference on Disarmament are: Belgium, Canada, France, the Federal Republic of Germany, Italy, the Netherlands, the United Kingdom and the United States. The Conference was established in this configuration following the first special session of the United Nations General Assembly devoted to disarmament. It started its work in 1979 carrying forward the negotiating efforts of its predecessors: the Conference of the Ten-Nation Committee on Disarmament (1960-1962), the Conference of the Eighteen-Nation Committee on Disarmament (1962-1968), and the Conference of the Committee on Disarmament (1969-1978). From 1979 to 1983, this body was known as the Committee on Disarmament but thereafter assumed its present title.

The Conference on Disarmament is entrusted with responsibility for negotiating multilateral disarmament agreements in the framework of the United Nations. It is engaged in intensive negotiations for a ban on the development, production, stockpiling, transfer and use of chemical weapons and for their destruction. Other objectives covered by the Conference are a nuclear test ban, prevention of an arms race in outer space, effective international arrangements to assure non-nuclear weapon states against the use or threat of use of nuclear weapons, prevention of nuclear war, agreements covering new types of weapons of mass destruction, agreements on radiological weapons and a comprehensive programme of disarmament.

Intra-Alliance consultation on these matters takes place in NATO's Political Committee and, in particular, at its semi-annual meetings with national disarmament experts. During these meetings, arms control and disarmament issues which are dealt with by the Conference on Disarmament, and questions related to developments in other international fora like the United Nations General Assembly, the United Nations Disarmament Commission, and Review Conferences, are discussed, so that positions of Allied nations can be harmonised.

Multilateral and Bilateral Negotiations on Chemical Weapons

Negotiations on a Chemical Weapons Convention represent the most important area of the work of the Conference on Disarmament. The 1925 Geneva Protocol for the Prohibition of the Use in War of Asphyxiating, Poisonous or Other Gases, and of Bacteriological Methods of Warfare, which has over 115 signatories, prohibits the use in war of chemical and bacteriological weapons, but not their development, production, possession or transfer. Biological weapons are prohibited by the 1972 Biological and Toxins Weapons Convention[6]. The Geneva Protocol has been signed by all the NATO and Warsaw Treaty countries, but many States which are parties to the protocol have recorded reservations retaining a right to retaliate in kind if such weapons are used against them or their allies, and to use chemical weapons against States which are not parties to the protocol. All NATO member countries are firmly committed to the conclusion of a comprehensive, global and effectively verifiable convention, not only banning the development, production, stockpiling, transfer and use of chemical weapons but also requiring the destruction of all existing stockpiles and production plants.

Negotiations on chemical weapons have been taking place in Geneva since 1968. An Ad Hoc Committee has been working since 1980 to draw up an international agreement for a total ban. The Alliance members of the Conference on Disarmament have greatly contributed to the work of this forum.

Progress has been made in the CW negotiations over the last two years as the Soviet Union has started to accept Western positions, for example, on the need for effective verification. However, agreement on points of principle has underlined the complexity of the remaining issues— in particular, how to

[6] Convention on the Prohibition of the Development, Production and Stockpiling of Bacteriological (Biological) and Toxin Weapons and on Their Destruction.

ensure that the verification regime will be fully effective; the problems of maintaining the security of the parties to the Convention during the initial destruction period; the protection of sensitive non-CW-related technical and commercial information during inspections; and the problem of ensuring participation in a convention of CW-capable states. Until the objective of a global ban can be realised, the risk of proliferation of chemical weapons elsewhere in the world remains a major concern.

It was only in March 1987 that the Soviet Union admitted for the first time that it possessed chemical weapons, although it is known that the Soviet Union possesses the world's largest offensive CW capability. In April 1987 Mr. Gorbachev stated that the Soviet Union had ceased CW production and declared that no Soviet chemical weapons were positioned outside the borders of the Soviet Union, that other East European states had never produced chemical weapons or had them on their territories, and that the Soviet Union was building a facility to destroy chemical weapons. The validity of some of these claims is uncertain and further information is required to substantiate them. Subsequently, in August 1987, the Soviet Union announced its support at the Conference on Disarmament for mandatory on-site inspections on challenge with no right of refusal and, in December 1987, provided a figure for its chemical weapon stockpiles. The United States, for its part, provided detailed information in 1986 on the composition of its stockpiles. In April 1988, the United States presented further detailed information on the chemical weapons themselves, and in July 1988 revealed the location of its chemical weapons production facilities which would be destroyed under a future chemical weapons convention. Agreement has also been reached between countries participating in the Geneva Conference on Disarmament to conduct national trial inspections of chemical plants which would be monitored under the convention to ensure against production of chemical weapons and their components. Multilateral trial inspections have been proposed to follow the national trials. The Alliance recognises the importance of concluding a comprehensive Chemical Weapons Convention as soon as possible, both to remove the massive Soviet superiority in this field compared to NATO's limited retaliatory capability, and to curb the proliferation of chemical weapons in Third World countries.

In addition to the multilateral negotiations in the Conference on Disarmament, the United States and the Soviet Union have been actively engaged in regular bilateral talks on the prohibition of chemical weapons since January 1986. These discussions are held in accordance with the Geneva Summit agreement of November 1985 to accelerate efforts to conclude a chemical weapons ban and to intensify bilateral discussions, at expert level, on all aspects of such a chemical weapons ban, including the question of verification.

Multilateral and Bilateral Negotiations on Nuclear Testing

The issue of a nuclear test ban has also been dealt with both by the Conference on Disarmament and by the United States and the Soviet Union through bilateral talks. Progress in the Conference on Disarmament has so far been relatively modest, because the positions of participants on this issue vary considerably. In particular, some states believe that the role of nuclear weapons in maintaining deterrence means that the testing of nuclear weapons will continue to be necessary both to ensure weapon reliability and safety and as part of the process of modernising existing weapons. Other Conference on Disarmament members have expressed, to a greater or lesser extent, support for progress towards a comprehensive test ban. Members of the Alliance maintain consultations with a view to ensuring that the basic criterion of enhanced security is met by future agreements.

Since November 1987 the United States and the Soviet Union, the two major nuclear powers, have engaged in formal stage-by-stage negotiations on nuclear testing. As a first step, the United States and the Soviet Union are negotiating improved verification measures for two unratified nuclear testing treaties, the Threshold Test Ban Treaty of 1974 (TTBT) and the Peaceful Nuclear Explosions Treaty of 1976 (PNET). Once the US verification concerns have been satisfied and the two treaties ratified, the two sides have agreed to proceed with negotiations for further intermediate limitations on nuclear testing leading to the ultimate objective of the complete cessation of nuclear testing as part of an effective disarmament process. This process would pursue, as the first priority, the goal of further reducing the number of nuclear weapons deployed.

The two sides exchanged visits by experts to each other's nuclear testing sites in January 1988, in preparation for the joint verification experiments at each other's test sites which took place in August and September 1988. These successful experiments provided opportunities to measure the yield of nuclear explosions using the techniques preferred by each side. It is expected that this process will result in agreed improvements to the verification provisions of the Threshold Test Ban Treaty and the Peaceful Nuclear Explosions Treaty. United States officials said in December 1988 that work on a verification protocol for the Peaceful Nuclear Explosions Treaty was substantially completed, but that further negotiation would be necessary on a verification protocol for the Threshold Test Ban Treaty.

Chapter 12
Infrastructure

Infrastructure in the NATO context means fixed installations which are necessary for the deployment and operation of the armed forces, e.g. airfields, telecommunications installations, command, control and information systems, military headquarters, fuel pipelines and storage, radar warning and navigational aid installations, port installations, missile installations, forward storage sites and support facilities for reinforcement forces. Certain mobile facilities closely associated with these fixed installations (e.g. communications satellites) also come within the definition of NATO infrastructure.

Installations of this kind, set up at the request of Major NATO Commanders (MNCs) in close collaboration with national military authorities for the peacetime training of the forces assigned to them, and for operational use in wartime, may be designated as "NATO common infrastructure". Installations and equipments so designated are financed collectively by the governments of participating countries within agreed limits for common funding. They may be used by one or more NATO nations, but the acquisition of the sites themselves and the provision of certain local utilities remain a "host nation" responsibility.

National infrastructure, that is installations set up solely for the use of national forces, or those portions of NATO installations exceeding NATO common-funding criteria, are paid for out of national budgets.

Cost-sharing formulae

Since common installations can be used by the forces of contributing member countries of the Alliance, the country on whose territory installations are set up (referred to as the "host country") cannot and should not bear alone the cost of these installations. Furthermore, for geographical and strategic reasons, certain member countries are required to act as host to a greater number of installations than others. Contributions from the other countries, some of which may be users of the infrastructure installations, represent the only fair way of paying for these projects.

The common financing of the NATO infrastructure programme is worked out on the basis of cost-sharing formulae agreed by the participating countries for each long-term programme or "Slice Group", based loosely on gross national product and the assessed economic, industrial and financial advantages of participation.

Infrastructure cost-sharing formulae

The table on page 246 shows in column 1 the cost-sharing formula approved in 1950 by the Brussels Treaty Powers (Slice I); the cost-sharing formula approved by the Council in 1960 for Slices II to VIIa (column 2); and the cost-sharing formula at "14" and at "15" for Slices XXXI to XXXV (columns 3 and 4). Subject to the addition of ad-hoc contributions to off-set the reduction in the Belgian share, this is also applicable to Slices 36 to 41 (1985-1990).

Country	Slice I %	Slices II to VIIa[1] %	Slices XXXU to XXXV % at "14"	% at "15"
Belgium	13.18	5.462	5.5912	4.8446
Canada	—	6.021	6.3578	5.5087
Denmark	—	2.767	3.7273	3.2296
France	45.46	15.041	—	13.2209
Germany	—	—	26.5446	22.9996
Greece	—	0.750	0.7932	0.6888
Italy	—	5.681	7.9873	6.9206
Luxembourg	0.45	0.155	0.2130	0.1846
Netherlands	13.64	3.889	5.1386	4.4524
Norway	—	2.280	3.1417	2.7222
Portugal	—	0.146	0.2011	0.2011
Turkey	—	1.371	0.8045	0.8021
United Kingdom	27.27	12.758	12.0897	10.4665
United States	—	43.679	27.4200	23.7583

[1] This formula replaces the shares previously applied in Slices II, III, IVa and IVb to VIIa.

Financial arrangements

Every half year host countries submit a financial report which includes expenditure actually incurred at the end of the period under review as well as expenditure forecast for the next 6 months. On this basis the NATO International Staff establishes the quarterly contributions due to and from each member country. Both financial reports and contributions are approved by the Infrastructure Payments and Progress Committee.

Since NATO neither holds nor administers infrastructure funds, contributions are paid and offset directly between the participating countries in accordance with a multilateral compensation system. Actual payments for projects are made by the host country, using contributions from the other member countries to which its own share is added.

A record is kept of all these transactions by the NATO International Staff, which keeps track of the accounts of each host country on the basis of contributions paid and actual expenditure reported.

Long-term Infrastructure planning

Establishing priorities among projects for inclusion in the NATO Infrastructure programme is the responsibility and prerogative of the NATO Military Authorities. In accordance with the Improved Procedures for NATO Infrastructure agreed in 1983, the Major NATO Commanders (MNCs), taking into account the latest available NATO six-year force proposals and goals, develop proposals for a corresponding six year period. These Infrastructure Proposals, together with the MNCs' corresponding Impact Statements, serve as the basis for agreement by the Council/DPC on six-year financial (Slice Group) ceilings, and on revisions of those ceilings when necessary. When revised in the light of the agreed funding ceiling, the MNCs' Infrastructure Proposals become Infrastructure Goals for the coming six years and are the basis for the Allied Commander Europe Long Term Infrastructure Plan (ACELIP) and the Maritime Commanders' Long-Term Infrastructure Plan (MARCLIP). The MNCs' Infrastructure Goals are updated or "rolled forward" every two years, in parallel with the NATO force goal cycle, on the basis of updated Infrastructure Proposals and within agreed funding ceilings. The ACELIP and MARCLIP are updated continuously on the basis of changes in priorities and cost-estimates, and serve as a basis for the advance authorisation of planning funds.

Annual (Slice) programmes

Annual Slice programming is at a level equal to about one sixth, in real terms, of the Slice Group financial ceiling, less an allowance for contingencies. The first step in formulating a yearly programme or slice takes place when the subordinate commands, after consultation with nations, inform the MNCs of infrastructure work needed in their assigned areas. The MNCs coordinate these requests, after ensuring that the proposed installations are indispensable to the support of forces and that they are available for common use or have a common interest.

After a general examination carried out in cooperation with national experts, the MNCs propose an infrastructure slice for the year in question. The proposed slice is then examined by the Military Committee which, in its turn, makes recommendations to the Council or the Defence Planning Committee based on military considerations. Simultaneously, the financial, technical, political and economic aspects of the proposal are examined by the Infrastructure Committee, with the assistance of the International Staff, before the slice is sent to the Council or the Defence Planning Committee for approval.

Simplified procedures exist for the programming and authorisation of minor works (up to IAU 100,000[1] per project) and of urgent remedial works.

Implementation and control of works

Once an infrastructure slice has been approved, the execution phase begins. The entire responsibility for implementation of individual projects is

[1] IAU — Infrastructure Accounting Unit, used as a base for the conversion of different currencies (Note: The value of the IAU was initially based on that of the UK £, but is now revised semi-annually in the light of recent exchange rates; on 1 December 1989, the value of the IAU was US $ 3.434 or £ 2.113).

assumed by the host country or by NATO agencies acting in the same capacity. In such cases agencies are said to be "acting as host nation".

The host country must decide, in consultation with the NATO Military Authorities, upon the site where the works are to be carried out. It must acquire the land, if necessary, at its own expense and draw up a plan which is then sent to the relevant MNC for approval. After the plan has been approved, the host country authorities and user country(ies) prepare a detailed estimate of construction costs, which must be approved by the Infrastructure Payments and Progress Committee before any funds can be committed.

The authority to authorise "scope of works" and expenditures for all approved projects is in the hands of the Infrastructure Payments and Progress Committee, made up of members of the national delegations, which has technical assistance from experts on the International Staff. The Committee's terms of reference call for close examination of the estimates submitted and, where necessary, suggestions for alternative or more economical methods of carrying out the work to the required specifications. These estimates are called "requests for authorisation to commit funds", and they constitute the basis for calculating the amount due to host countries.

International Competitive Bidding (ICB)

Unless otherwise agreed by the Infrastructure Payments and Progress Committee the host country, in accordance with the Procedures for International Competitive Bidding, invites bids from firms of member countries participating in the funding of the project and awards the contract to the lowest compliant bidder. All member countries are informed through the International Staff of the outcome of the bidding. Civil works projects are often exempted from International Competitive Bidding because of the nature of the work.

Monitoring and controlling of Infrastructure cash flow

The Infrastructure Committee has developed a procedure for estimating annual infrastructure expenditure, thus providing a mechanism for control of infrastructure cash flow. Each country budgets for the amount it will be requested to pay as its contribution to Infrastructure funding. The NATO International Staff, on the basis of its expenditure estimates for future years, recommends annual contributions targets/ceilings for acceptance by the Infrastructure Committee. The Infrastructure Payments and Progress Committee tries to ensure that the actual contributions required are as close as possible to these amounts.

Acceptance into NATO Inventory

Upon completion, a project is inspected by a team consisting of representatives of the host country, the user country, the International Staff, and the military authorities. The team, which is chaired by a member of the

International Staff, inspects the projects and, when it is satisfied that the works are in conformity with the authorisation, standards and criteria and good engineering practice, draws up a report for the Infrastructure Payments and Progress Committee, recommending that the completed project be accepted by NATO.

International audit

Once the works have been completed and accepted by the Infrastructure Payments and Progress Committee, the International Board of Auditors for NATO, which is entirely unconnected with the host country and responsible only to the NATO Council, examines the financial statements made out by host countries and verifies the correctness of expenditure charged to NATO common funds.

The principal categories of infrastructure works are as follows:

Airfields

At present some 230 NATO airfields are operational or available for use by NATO forces in an emergency. All comply with standards laid down by the NATO Military Authorities, are suitable for different types of aircraft, and include such essential installations as fuel and weapon storage facilities, advanced maintenance facilities and ground aids which permit aircraft to operate by night and day in all weathers. As a result of the 1971-1974 European Defence Improvement Programme, 70 % of in-place aircraft and all essential components of the aircraft weapon system at each base are protected, that is to say housed in "hardened" aircraft shelters. Protected structures for reinforcing tactical aircraft are also being constructed under an important programme agreed in 1984.

As airfields are completed, communications are also established to ensure full coordination between them and the respective allied air commands.

Communications and Information Systems (CIS)

The signals networks represent an investment of more than IAU 698 million. About 50,000 kilometres of landlines, radio links and submarine cables have been built to supplement existing civilian networks. However, in spite of the considerable number of circuits available, NATO military authorities were aware that the system did not provide the safety margins necessary in time of war, particularly with regard to the security and speed of transmission. As a result the NATO Integrated Communications System (NICS) was developed.[2] This new communications system uses the most

[2] The scope of the NATO Integrated Communications System was expanded in 1985 and was renamed the NATO Communications and Information System. See Chapter 17.

modern techniques to ensure that political authorities and Major NATO Commanders can be informed of developments as rapidly as possible in any situation which might arise, a vital requirement if they are to be able to make timely decisions.

The rapidly developing technology of automatic data processing (ADP) offered NATO and, in particular, the military authorities, opportunities to introduce significant improvements in their procedures. In order to coordinate these, the Council decided in October 1970 to establish a NATO Command, Control and Information System. This has since been integrated into the infrastructure programme.

Petroleum Facilities

The petroleum portion of the infrastructure programme covers the construction aspects involved in building-up the regional networks of the NATO Pipeline System, together with other fuel storage and distribution facilities not directly linked to it. The first facilities were constructed under the Western Union Defence Organisation Programme in the early 1950s. Three decades later, more than 3 million cubic metres of storage and some 11,000 kilometres of pipelines, with numerous entry and delivery facilities, had been brought on to the NATO inventory. The development of this important resource for the support of Allied forces continues. The programme has benefited throughout from successive improvements in pipeline technology and has kept in step with modern methods of environmental protection. Its potential use for civilian purposes is also being examined.

Air Defence Systems

The NATO Air Defence Ground Environment (NADGE)[3] has been by far the largest single defence construction project so far authorised by the NATO Council. Comprising a chain of radar sites and associated command and control centres, it is concerned with the early warning of and response to any infringement of NATO airspace. Implementation of the NADGE system was managed in a manner which differs from other NATO Infrastructure programmes, and involved the creation of an integrated air defence system under the command and control of the Supreme Allied Commander Europe (SACEUR). It remains a classic example of international cooperation in an area of fundamental importance to the common defence.

The system has since been modernised and is being expanded to include air defence facilities located in the United Kingdom. Planning is well advanced for a comprehensive enhancement and extension of the NADGE system under the designation "Air Command and Control System" (ACCS).

---
[3] See Chapter 18.

Reinforcement facilities and other infrastructure projects

Infrastructure projects play a particularly important part in meeting the requirements for external reinforcement. Slice Group XXXI to XXXV saw the introduction of a significant new category of projects designed to support external reinforcement by providing for the storage of prepositioned equipment, material and ammunition for reinforcing units, together with additional support facilities for their movement, reception and maintenance. Other important infrastructure projects, such as naval installations and missile sites, are listed in the following table.

The Infrastructure Programme

	Infrastructure Accounting Units (Million)
1. NATO Common-funded Infrastructure	
A. Slices II to 37 (1986)	
— Airfields Number of airfields: 230	1,276
— Communications Network Landlines, submarine cables, radio links and NICS projects Over 50,000 km	698
— Fuel Supply Systems Pipelines: about 11,000 km Storage: about 3 million cubic metres	473
— Naval Facilities	282
— Radar Warning Installations	385
— Air Defence Ground Environment	112
— Ammunition Storage	61
— Missile Sites	269
— Reinforcement Support	173
— Other Projects, including War Headquarters, Forward Storage Sites, Training Installations, Radio Navigational Aids	669
	4,398
B. Slices 38 (1987) to 41 (1990) (Projected Programming)	1,917
2. Infrastructure funded under other arrangements	
A. Slice I (Western Union Defence Organisation Programme)	32
B. Infrastructure in Germany prior to the accession of the Federal Republic of Germany to the North Atlantic Treaty	95
C. European Defence Improvement Programme (EDIP)	150
	277
Total:	6,592

Chapter 13
Logistics

The role of logistics within the Alliance is to plan and carry out the movement and maintenance of NATO Forces. This includes several different logistic functions, each of which contributes to NATO force sustainability. These can be grouped into four functional elements:

— materiel/equipment (including vehicles, weapons, ammunition, fuel, etc.): acquisition, storage, movement, distribution, maintenance, evacuation, disposition;
— personnel: movement, evacuation, hospitalisation;
— facilities: acquisition or construction, maintenance, operation and disposition of installations;
— services: e.g. provision of food, laundry and bath facilities, graves registration.

Together these elements are termed "consumer" logistics. The other category of logistics, known as "production" logistics, is primarily concerned with the long term planning, budgeting, design, development and procurement of equipment. Unlike consumer logistics, which is concerned with providing support to military forces, production logistics in NATO is largely a civilian responsibility and is dealt with by the Conference of National Armaments Directors (CNAD)[1].

The common purpose of all consumer logistics elements is to provide sustained support for the forces of the Alliance. The specialisation reflected in the functional grouping described above is consistent with NATO's civil and military organisation, in which responsibilities for coordinated and cooperative planning in specific areas are vested in different bodies. For the most part consumer logistics falls within the responsibility of the Senior NATO Logisticians' Conference (SNLC), with the exception of common-funded NATO facilities dealt with under the NATO Infrastructure programme, which is described in the previous chapter. The Senior Civil Emergency Planning Committee (SCEPC), dealt with in the next chapter, is responsible for coordinating the use of civil resources, for example in the fields of transport, energy, and industrial facilities, to support the Alliance's overall defence effort. The various responsibilities of these two bodies are, of course, interrelated, and as a consequence there is close liaison between them and between their subordinate committees. The elements of consumer logistics which come under the responsibility of the Senior NATO Logisticians' Conference are discussed below.

---

[1] See Chapter 15.

Logistic principles

It is a basic tenet of the Alliance that each nation is responsible for the continuous support of its own forces. However, nations organise and support their forces in different ways and it is therefore the responsibility of each Major NATO Commander to identify, plan and coordinate the support required for the forces assigned to him to enable him to meet his operational commitments.

Coordinated support planning is vital in order to ensure constant logistic readiness and effectiveness. However economy in the provision of logistics support is as basic a principle in the Alliance as in individual nations. Close cooperation and collaboration and regular exchange of information between nations are therefore essential factors in ensuring efficient and economical use of logistics resources.

Ideally, from a logistics point of view, materiel, procedures and services must be standardized. Failing standardization, interoperability is the minimum requirement to enable logistics support to be applied flexibly in support of all NATO forces.

The degree of logistics support available to a commander is also a major factor in the development of combat operational plans. Requirements are regularly reviewed and updated and the reliability of logistics support is regularly tested in realistic exercises.

Coordination and cooperation in consumer logistics

The requirement for coordination and cooperation is not new. Logistics conferences have long been a feature of planning within NATO's military command structure. In 1964 the ACE Logistics Coordination Centre (LCC) was formed to meet the requirements of Allied Command Europe. This Coordination Centre has detailed emergency and wartime roles which are rehearsed and tested during exercises. The Atlantic Command (SACLANT) also has a Logistics Coordination Board. Regular meetings take place of both of these organisations.

As greater attention has come to be focussed on Alliance preparedness including logistics readiness and sustainability, so the need to concentrate on cooperation and coordination in consumer logistics has increased. The Senior NATO Logisticians' Conference (SNLC) was established in 1979 to respond to this requirement. It is the principal NATO committee dealing with consumer logistics, and its composition reflects the dependence of consumer logistics on both civil and military considerations. It therefore reports both to the North Atlantic Council or Defence Planning Committee, as appropriate, and to the Military Committee. Its meetings take the form of joint civil and military sessions attended by both civil and military representatives from national Ministries of Defence responsible for civil and military aspects of consumer logistics. The Major NATO Commands, the International Staff, International Military Staff, the NATO Maintenance and Supply Organisation

(NAMSO) and the Military Agency for Standardization (MAS)[2] are also represented. The Assistant Secretary General for Infrastructure, Logistics and Civil Emergency Planning, and the Deputy Chairman of the Military Committee are co-chairmen of the Committee. The SNLC can therefore provide an overall assessment of the logistics posture of the Alliance and address the wide range of issues involved in ensuring adequate and sustained logistic support for Alliance forces.

Amongst the many consumer logistics topics kept permanently under review are those which have a bearing, in particular, on the improvement of logistics sustainability within the conventional defence capabilities of the Alliance. Examples, in this complex area of support, are the building up of war reserve stocks of ammunition, fuels and major combat equipment, the provision of corresponding storage facilities, the improvement of Alliance preparedness in the medical field and the support provided by host nations to the forces of other nations.

NATO Pipeline System

The NATO Pipeline System was constructed to facilitate the supply of fuels to Allied forces. It is being improved and extended under the NATO Common Infrastructure Programme[3]. It is regionally based and consists of seven networks of storage facilities inter-connected by pipelines, many of which have a multi-product capability. The largest of these is in Central Europe, where more than 6,000 kilometres of pipelines have been laid. The network is operated and maintained by an integrated multinational organisation— the Central Europe Operating Agency—which is described below. The second largest network is in Turkey. This is divided into two separate parts, one for the East and the other for the West of the country. There are also networks in Greece, Italy, Denmark (covered by the North European system which reaches into North Germany), and Norway (mainly storage facilities). The United Kingdom pipeline system is a national asset containing a small number of NATO funded facilities, including both storage and pipelines. Operation and maintenance of these networks are undertaken by national pipeline organisations, acting in consultation with the NATO Military Authorities. The host nations are the normal users but other NATO nations can use the systems by arrangement.

In July 1956, the Council established the NATO Pipeline Committee to act on its behalf, in consultation with the NATO Military Authorities and other competent bodies, on all matters connected with the control, operation and maintenance of the NATO pipeline system.

Central Europe Operating Agency

The Central Europe Operating Agency (CEOA), which was established on January 1, 1958 and is based at Versailles, coordinates the operation and

[2] The MAS is described in more detail in Chapter 23. NAMSO is described later in this chapter.

[3] See Chapter 12.

maintenance of the Central Europe Pipeline System (CEPS). This is organised under seven national pipeline divisions (three in France, two in Germany, one in the Netherlands, one in Belgium). The member nations are Belgium, Luxembourg, the Netherlands, Canada, France, Germany, the United Kingdom and the United States. This was the first of a number of Production and Logistics Organisations or "NPLOs" created by NATO to manage specific aspects of the support needed on a permanent basis by NATO forces.

The CEPS has two directing bodies: one civil, the Central Europe Pipeline Policy Committee (CEPPC), which normally meets in Brussels and deals with political and financial matters; and one military, the Central Europe Pipeline Office (CEPO), which normally meets at the headquarters of Allied Forces Central Europe (AFCENT), at Brunssum in the Netherlands, and deals with military, operational and technical matters.

NATO Maintenance and Supply Organisation

In April 1958, the North Atlantic Council approved the establishment of the NATO Maintenance Supply Services System (NMSSS). This centralised organisation was renamed the NATO Maintenance and Supply Organisation (NAMSO) in 1964. It consists of a Board of Directors, subsidiary committees of the Board, and an executive element known as the NATO Maintenance and Supply Agency (NAMSA). The Board provides policy guidance to NAMSA and oversees the implementation of that policy.

The main task of NAMSA is to assist NATO nations by the common procurement and supply of spare parts and by providing the maintenance and repair facilities necessary for the support of various weapons systems in their inventories. This assistance is available whenever two or more nations have the same system and have made a conscious decision to use the facilities of NAMSA to provide support. The purpose of the Organisation is to achieve maximum effectiveness in logistics support, at a minimum cost to NATO nations, both individually and collectively. NAMSO and its main operating agency, NAMSA, are located at Capellen, Luxembourg. A separate depot has been established at Taranto, Italy, to stock spare parts for weapon systems for three southern region countries— Greece, Italy and Turkey. A further subsidiary of the Agency has been established in Paris and is responsible for HAWK logistics management[4].

Weapons systems and materiel currently supported by NAMSA include the NIKE, PATRIOT, SIDEWINDER, HAWK, LANCE and TOW Missile Systems; the Multiple Launch Rocket System (MLRS); the Forward Scatter and Satellite Communications Station; the NATO Air Defence Ground Environment (NADGE)[5]; Mark 37/44/46 Torpedoes; Drone CL-89 and the replacement CL-289; FH-70 Howitzer; the NATO Airborne Early Warning and Control System (AWACS)[5]; and other conventional equipment.

---

[4] The HAWK and other weapon systems and materiel mentioned in this chapter are described in more detail in Chapter 15.

[5] See Chapter 18.

NAMSA has an establishment of some eleven hundred personnel and stocks approximately 100,000 line items worth US$120 million. In addition to providing spare parts from stock, NAMSA also satisfies requisitions by acting as intermediary between nations. There are also arrangements for providing mutual support in emergencies and for redistributing materiel surplus to a nation's requirements.

Maintenance support may take the form of in-house maintenance programmes or contractual maintenance. In-house maintenance involving NAMSA personnel and equipment is provided, for example, in the case of an on-site calibration of field test equipment. There are also permanent workshops at Capellen equipped to repair systems such as LANCE and TOW. Contractual maintenance by external contractors working under NAMSA supervision constitutes about 95% of the maintenance provided by NAMSA.

The procurement function is concerned primarily with support for supply and maintenance activities. It involves placing contracts for the acquisition of spare parts, services and quality assurance. Consolidation of requirements and international competitive bidding procedures enable maximum cost effectiveness to be obtained on behalf of the user nations. In cases where identical equipment has had to be provided for commonly funded NATO Infrastructure projects located in different NATO countries, NAMSA may also act as a procurement agency for the countries concerned, purchasing the equipment on their behalf through international competitive bidding. NAMSA is also involved in the consolidated procurement of selected types of conventional ammunition and in maintaining munitions stocks.

Technical support provided by NAMSA includes both technical assistance and configuration management. Technical assistance covers such activities as on-site assistance, the preparation of technical specifications for maintenance contracts and the monitoring of surveillance programmes. Configuration management includes data collection and analysis on equipment failures, technical studies, evaluation of equipment modification proposals and updating of technical documentation.

NAMSA does not perform all of the foregoing tasks for all the weapon systems and equipment which it supports. User nations, in consultation with NAMSA, select those tasks which, in the interests of cost effectiveness and logistical readiness, can best be performed centrally. Apart from the advantages stemming from the consolidation of requirements and from centralised procurement, this selection takes into account the potential benefits to be obtained in each case from reduction or elimination of duplicative inventories or test equipment and from standardization of procedures as well as materiel.

Lastly, the availability through NAMSA of centralised, efficient and cost effective supply and maintenance support for all weapon systems developed or held in common by two or more nations is an important factor which nations are able to take into account at the planning stages of development or procurement.

Chapter 14
Civil Emergency Planning

The deterrent value of the strategic concept of flexible response can only be fully realised if military preparedness is complemented by credible civil preparedness. National civil resources must be capable of being rapidly mobilised to support the total defence effort, to ensure the continuity of effective democratic government, and to enable protective measures to be taken to reduce the vulnerability of civilian populations.

The scope of civil emergency planning is therefore extremely wide. It embraces such matters as the mobilisation and use to the best advantage of basic national resources (e.g.energy, manpower, food and agriculture, raw materials, transportation, industrial and telecommunications infrastructure), as well as civil defence measures, including detection and public warning, medical care and other measures aimed at minimising the consequences of military conflict for civilian populations.

In addition to maintaining the social and economic life of member nations and ensuring the survival of their populations during or after hostilities, civil emergency planning in NATO has another important function. This is to provide civil support for Allied military forces. A significant amount of the planning effort is directed, for example, towards providing civil support for the rapid reinforcement of the military forces assigned to the Supreme Allied Commander Europe (SACEUR) for the defence of the area which comes under his responsibility.

Arrangements made by member nations for providing civil support for defence constitute an important element of the overall defence capacity of the Alliance, as does the level of civil preparedness in the member countries themselves. Civil emergency planning therefore not only covers a wide variety of subjects, but also has to provide for a range of different contingencies. Some of these relate to the various types of political, economic and military pressures which the Alliance might have to face in a crisis or conflict. Others are a function of the general effects which modern weapons might be expected to have, both in conventional war, in which the possible use of chemical weapons or other weapons of mass destruction cannot be excluded, and in the case of a nuclear attack.

NATO's Role

Civil preparedness as a whole is a national responsibility and resources management is no exception. Individual member nations retain control over their own resources at all times and would continue to do so even in a crisis or war. However, since national economies are increasingly interdependent, there is considerable scope for coordination through NATO of the management of resources. The benefits of such coordination would become even more significant in a crisis or war situation than in peacetime. The economic base on which a successful defence would be heavily dependent can be considerably strengthened if national resources management planning is directed towards a common goal instead of operating in isolation or even in competition.

Whatever the contingency, there is accordingly a compelling case for active consultation and close coordination between member nations on civil emergency matters. The process of consultation and coordination enables experience to be exchanged and differing priorities to be discussed so that arrangements can be made for dealing with the many problems which would, in an emergency, call for international cooperation or have international implications.

Coordination of these aspects within a NATO framework not only facilitates national planning but also ensures that the important contribution which civil emergency preparedness can make to the overall defence of the Alliance and to the credibility of deterrence is cost-effective and well structured.

In a period of rising tension, the objective of civil emergency measures would be to facilitate the transition to crisis management arrangements within the Alliance by ensuring that the North Atlantic Council is properly and regularly informed of the level of civil preparedness of member nations. Nations can then act in harmony if it becomes necessary to increase their state of readiness.

In wartime, the task becomes one of practical coordination, both with regard to the use of vital resources for civil and military defence needs and with regard to the maintenance, recovery and, if need be, the rebuilding of national economies.

Senior Civil Emergency Planning Committee

The formulation of policy and the general coordination of civil emergency planning at NATO level is undertaken on behalf of the Council by the Senior Civil Emergency Planning Committee (SCEPC), supported by an International Staff element, the Civil Emergency Planning Directorate of the Infrastructure, Logistics and Civil Emergency Planning Division. In plenary sessions, the Committee is chaired by the Secretary General or the Assistant Secretary General for Infrastructure, Logistics and Civil Emergency Planning. The members are the national representatives responsible for coordination of civil emergency planning in the sixteen national capitals. The plenary session convenes twice a year. In between, the Committee normally meets once a month under the chairmanship of the Assistant Secretary General for Infrastructure, Logistics and Civil Emergency Planning or the Director of Civil Emergency Planning. The representatives are normally drawn from national delegations to NATO. The NATO Military Authorities are also represented.

In a crisis the Senior Civil Emergency Planning Committee is one of the NATO bodies which would be permanently convened to support the NATO

Council. Others include the Military Committee, the Political Committee, the Alerts Committee, and the NATO Maintenance and Supply Organisation. Other bodies dealing with communications functions would also be active as components of the crisis response structure.

Planning Boards and Committees

The SCEPC coordinates and guides the activities of eight Planning Boards and Committees, each of which covers a specific field of civil emergency planning. The importance of the coordinated use of resources for the defence of the Alliance has already been stressed, and it is therefore no surprise that seven out of the eight Planning Boards and Committees deal with resources, while the eighth deals with civil defence. The membership of these Planning Boards and Committees consists of representatives with specialised knowledge appointed by the member nations.

The Civil Emergency Planning Boards and Committees consist of those dealing with supplies, namely the Food and Agriculture Planning Committee; the Industrial Planning Committee; and the Petroleum Planning Committee; those concerned with transport, i.e. the Planning Board for Ocean Shipping; the Planning Board for European Inland Surface Transport; and the Civil Aviation Planning Committee; a Civil Communications Planning Committee which is concerned with the problems of maintaining civil communications in an emergency; and finally the Civil Defence Committee, which is the forum for consultation on national plans for all aspects of the protection of the public in an emergency.

NATO Civil Wartime Agencies

Under the overall guidance of their parent committee, the Planning Boards and Committees have evolved plans for setting up NATO Civil Wartime Agencies (NCWAs) which would be activated in times of emergency. The agencies vary in size, but have basically the same structure: a directing body, in which all participating member nations would be represented; an international staff of experts; and liaison officers from the NATO Military Authorities. Each agency depends on its "host nation" (currently Italy, the Netherlands, the United Kingdom and the United States) to provide operational facilities as well as communications and logistical support. The key agencies are split into East and West divisions to enhance effective coverage and ensure survivability.

Existing plans include the following NATO Civil Wartime Agencies:

- The Central Supplies Agency—responsible for ensuring the continued availability and equitable distribution for both civil and military purposes of essential supplies in the field of food, agriculture and industry.
- The NATO Wartime Oil Organisation—to provide the forum for consultation on, and coordination of, the plans of member nations to ensure the continued availability and equitable distribution, for both civil and military purposes, of essential supplies of crude oil and petroleum products.

— The Defence Shipping Authority—responsible for ensuring that the NATO pool of merchant ships is so organised and controlled as to achieve the greatest possible degree of economy in its employment and to render it readily available to meet the civil and military needs of the Alliance.
— The Interallied Insurance Organisation, which works closely with the Defence Shipping Authority and provides wartime insurance for ships participating in the NATO shipping pool.
— The Agency for the Coordination of Inland Surface Transport in Central Europe—responsible for giving guidance on and coordinating the use of roads, railroads and inland waterways for civil and military transport in Central Europe.
— The Southern Europe Transport Organisation—responsible for the coordination of sea and land transport in Southern Europe, terms of reference for which have yet to be approved.
— The NATO Civil Aviation Agency—to provide a forum for concerting the policies of all NATO member nations in the field ofcivilaviation in support of both civil and military requirements. The agency not only acts as an information-gathering centre but also coordinates the use of civil aircraft made available by one member country for use by any other.
— The NATO Refugee Agency—to provide member nations with a forum for consultation on, and coordination of, their actions to overcome problems of international significance arising out of uncontrolled population movement.

Training

All national representatives and international experts who have been designated to serve in a NATO Civil Wartime Agency are trained in peacetime for their crisis management and wartime duties. Most are volunteers from business and industry. The plans and procedures for all the Agencies are regularly tested in exercises and are subject to continuous review and updating.

Chapter 15
Armaments Cooperation

As NATO is not a supranational organisation, it has no mandatory powers over national governments, and thus the responsibility for equipping and maintaining forces remains a national one. With the exception of certain areas such as communications, airborne early warning and control, and common infrastructure works described in other chapters, NATO is not directly involved in the research, development and production of equipment. The role of NATO is one of advice and coordination, with the purpose of fostering cooperation in order to improve and strengthen the collective defence effort of the allies.

The period 1949 to 1979—organisational steps

The first attempts to rationalise defence production in NATO were made by the Military Production and Supply Board, set up in November 1949, and its successor, the Defence Production Board. Studies prepared by these Boards led to recommendations made on the best means of increasing production in fields where deficiencies were greatest. One of the responsibilities of the Temporary Council Committee, set up in 1951, and the purpose of the Annual and Triennial Review procedures adopted subsequently, was to develop proposals for reconciling military requirements, including arms and equipment, with the resources available.

A Defence Production Committee was created in 1954. Four years later, its terms of reference were broadened to enable it to deal with questions of applied research and development, and it became the Armaments Committee. A Production and Logistics Division had already formed in 1952 as part of the newly created International Staff and in October 1960, this became the Production, Logistics and Infrastructure Division. On September 1, 1967, its title was changed to the Defence Support Division as part of the reorganisation which took place upon the transfer of NATO from Paris to Brussels. This broader title now includes defence research activities.

In January 1979, as the result of a further reorganisation, the Defence Support Division assumed its present responsibilities in the area of armaments, including Command, Control and Communications, and Air Defence Systems.

Early cooperative efforts

In the first years of NATO, the emphasis in the equipment field was mainly on the provision of arms and equipment for European forces assigned to the

Alliance. North American aid, in the form of off-shore procurement orders and grants towards the cost of establishing new plants, was a significant factor in increasing allied defence production capacity. An extensive range of North American defence materiel was also made available to member nations. This ensured some degree of uniformity of equipment ("standardization"), though the importance of this was not stressed at that time. The economic pressures and operational imperatives which subsequently drove nations to study the procurement of common standard items had not yet made themselves felt.

Standardization in the early days of the Alliance was mainly confined to procedures or to equipment components or parts, which became the subject of Standardization Agreements (STANAGs) promulgated by NATO's Military Agency for Standardization. A well-known example of an equipment STANAG concerns the 7.62mm NATO basic round for small arms. Similar agreements have been reached throughout the years and they now run into hundreds. This cooperative activity within the Alliance remains extremely important, although it has now been overshadowed, as far as equipment is concerned, by efforts to agree on major items or systems.

Another early example of cooperation arose as a sequel to the acquisition by European countries of North American materiel. The need to find sources of spare parts to maintain those items, especially aircraft, caused countries to collaborate in joint procurement. This activity expanded and later gave rise to the NATO Maintenance and Supply Organisation (NAMSO) which is described in Chapter 13.

Correlated production programmes

In 1952, plans were made for correlated production programmes of major items of equipment, including aircraft, artillery, small arms, radar and wireless sets, vehicles, ships and various types of ammunition.

In April 1953 contracts for combat aircraft were signed between several countries. Already in 1949, Belgium had undertaken to manufacture Derwent jet engines for installation in British Meteor aircraft to be built in the Netherlands. France had undertaken to build Vampire aircraft and to manufacture Nene jet engines. Appropriate licensing arrangements had been negotiated with British firms. The 1953 programme embraced the production of British, French and United States aircraft in five Western European nations. Principal features of the programme were the production of Hawker Hunter and Vickers Supermarine Swift aircraft in the United Kingdom, of Dassault Mystere aircraft in France, the joint production of Hunter aircraft in Belgium and the Netherlands, and the assembly of American F 86 all-weather fighter aircraft in Italy.

As an early example of a "two-way street" in transatlantic cooperation, the United States commenced production in 1953 of the British Canberra bomber. Production was phased over a six-year period and a total of 403 B57 bombers of different versions were built.

Useful results were also obtained under correlated production programmes for electronic equipment and for ammuniton.

The correlated programme concept, however, came increasingly to be called into question. The programmes were limited in scope. No attempt was made to draw up any overall master plan for the equipment of all NATO forces which would parcel out production to the most efficient or economical sources. Such ideas, canvassed in the early days of NATO, ran into a number of obstacles. National authorities naturally tended to favour home industries and to be reluctant to finance multinational projects. Member countries were at differing stages of economic and industrial development. There were serious security problems. Furthermore, large programmes imposed upon industries would have had the effect of smothering incentive and reducing useful competition in the private industrial sector of many of the countries concerned.

Individual project approach

With the gradual abandonment of the correlated programme concept, tacit agreement was reached that any approach to production should be on the basis of individual projects. The steadily increasing complexity and cost of weapon systems gave added impetus to the need to collaborate in producing the following new major items of equipment.

Joint Aircraft production—the G.91

This first multinational venture for the development and production within NATO of a very light jet fighter for close support of ground troops began in 1954. Designs were drawn up and prototypes developed, constructed, and tested. The Italian Fiat G.91, with the British Bristol Orpheus engine, was selected for the first generation of NATO light weight tactical reconnaissance aircraft.

Over 600 aircraft were produced in Italy and, under licence, in the Federal Republic of Germany, and some of them are still in service. A twin-engined version, the G.91Y was also produced in Italy. Many useful lessons in cooperative ventures were learned from this first experience.

NATO Maritime Patrol Aircraft—the "Atlantic"

This multinational project started in 1957. Basic military requirements were formulated by the NATO Military Authorities, and a group of experts set up by the Defence Production Committee converted them into operational characteristics. Technical specifications were then circulated to aircraft companies in various countries.

The selected design was the French Breguet 1150, which was given the name "Atlantic", and cooperative arrangements were worked out between the original four European producing nations, Belgium, France, the Federal Republic of Germany, and the Netherlands, and the United States Government. Italy joined the project in 1968. Design and manufacture were entrusted to an industrial consortium, and the division of prototype work among the European countries set the pattern for the sharing of work and equipment in the production phase. Most of the electronic equipment was supplied by the United States and built under licence in Europe. 87 aircraft have been produced; 20 for the Navy of the Federal Republic of Germany, 40 for the French Navy, 9 for the Netherlands Navy and 18 for the Italian Navy. Three simulators were built for training purposes. An International Supply and Logistics Centre and an international warehouse provide for joint logistics and spare parts for European users of the Atlantic.

Advanced weapon programmes

Towards the end of 1956, the United States, aware from its own experience of the full cost and complexity of planning and producing new equipment, began to make suggestions for co-ordinated efforts for the introduction of advanced weapons.

At the Heads of Government meeting in December 1957, President Eisenhower offered to make available his country's technical knowledge and experience to further joint European weapons production. The first two projects selected by European nations were a surface-to-air and an air-to-air missile system.

HAWK Programmes

In 1958, Belgium, France, the Federal Republic of Germany, Italy and the Netherlands accepted the offer by the United States for the production in Europe of a surface-to-air missile system—the HAWK. Five European firms participated in the production under the supervision of the Board of Directors of the NATO HAWK Management Organisation. The programme was completed in 1967. In November of the same year, the participating countries embarked on the study of an improvement programme for the HAWK weapon system—the HAWK European Limited Improvement Programme (HELIP)—which was intended to enhance the capabilities of the system and prolong its useful life. The preliminary studies were completed in 1970 and were followed in 1971 by a series of trials in Europe with a United States improved battery. Greece, Denmark and Norway joined the Hawk Organisation in 1972, 1973 and 1986 respectively.

Since 1974, the participating nations have sought to increase the capabilities of the system. In 1974, the HELIP was initiated and this was followed in 1979 by a further Product Improvement Programme. More recently, the HAWK command and control capability has been improved, and the radars associated with the system are presently being upgraded.

Sidewinder Programme

The air-to-air missile SIDEWINDER was the second existing United States missile to be chosen for production in Europe, this time by Belgium,

Denmark, the Federal Republic of Germany, Greece, the Netherlands, Norway, Portugal and Turkey. A German firm—Fluggerätewerk—was selected as prime contractor. Production arrangements were agreed by the Council in December 1959, and the first missiles assembled in Europe in November 1961. Most of the flight tests were performed in Europe with the assistance of France, which ordered several hundred missiles. Production, which involved a programme of the order of 10.000 missiles, was completed in December 1966, and responsibility for logistic support transferred to the NATO Maintenance and Supply Agency (NAMSA).

Armaments Committee and advisory groups

In April 1958, the European countries submitted a proposal to a meeting of Defence Ministers for specific items which might be produced jointly. The terms of reference of the Defence Production Committee were changed to pave the way towards the establishment of the Armaments Committee. The ability of this Committee to address questions of applied research and development was in itself recognition of the fact that allied co-operation in the armaments field needed to precede the production stage. In order to help with naval equipment, a NATO Naval Advisory Group was set up in 1958, to be followed by similar Army and Air Force Groups in 1962.

Procedures for co-operation

In parallel with the introduction of the advanced weapons programmes and changes in the committee structure, attention began to be focussed on equipment planning procedures. These procedures cannot, of course, guarantee the success of co-operative ventures, but they can help to promote collaborative efforts. Although equipment development and production is the responsibilty of the member nations, NATO has an important role to play in providing, at the international level, appropriate procedures to facilitate cooperation in the interests of collective defence.

The first attempts at cooperative production had revealed the complexity of the problem. It was clear that the potential advantages of joint production were dependent upon co-operative planning at the earliest possible stage. Agreed procedures were needed to cover the entire life of a cooperative project, right from the time of its inception through to the day when the resulting equipment entered into service.

NATO Basic Military Requirements (NBMRs)

To meet this need a new system was devised, which can be described as the "NBMR" approach. Introduced in 1959, it represented a determined effort to improve cooperation. Under this system, the NATO Military Authorities established agreed NATO-wide basic military requirements, as the starting point from which operational characteristics and their technical specifications could be derived. Common equipment could then be developed to meet these requirements.

Although originally intended to be used flexibly, in practice the system became too rigid. Harmonising differing national military requirements to produce agreed NATO requirements was far from easy. Economic and political factors also came into play. Although 49 "NATO Basic Military Requirements" were in fact produced, none resulted directly in the cooperative development or production of equipment items. This underlined the difficulty of achieving NATO-wide cooperation in the face of competing national economic and trade pressures—a fact of life still relevant today.

Further cooperative programmes

Nevertheless, the "NBMR" approach did encourage the Armaments Committee and the Service Advisory Groups to look for cooperative possibilities and several cooperative programmes based on existing equipment were undertaken in the next few years. The following projects are examples:

The Starfighter Programme

In December 1960, Belgium, the Federal Republic of Germany, Italy and the Netherlands, agreed to participate in a co-ordinated production programme, in Europe, of the United States F-104G Starfighter aircraft. This became a NATO programme in June 1961 and was completed in 1966, by which time nearly 1,000 aircraft had been produced. Canada was closely associated with the programme when producing similar aircraft for the Canadian Forces. This integrated production programme, the largest of its kind, marked a major step forward for the European Aerospace industry.

Bullpup Missile Programme

Following discussions within NATO, Denmark, Norway, Turkey and the United Kingdom decided to procure the United States Bullpup air-to-surface missile for their forces from a common European production source. In May 1962, the Council set up the NATO Bullpup production organisation, with headquarters in Oslo, to produce Bullpup missiles on a cooperative basis. The production programme, the value of which exceeded US $38 million, was shared among the participating countries roughly in proportion to the orders they placed. Production of more than 5,000 missiles was completed in 1967 and the liquidation of the production organisation and the transfer to the NATO Maintenance and Supply Agency of responsibility for logistic support was completed in 1968.

AS-30 Missile Programme

In June 1962 the Council set up a NATO Steering Committee for the production of the French developed AS-30 air-to-surface missile. France, the Federal Republic of Germany and the United Kingdom committed themselves to adopting the missile and production of nearly 2,000 missiles was completed in 1966. The Steering Committee was disbanded in June 1966 and an agreement reached between the interested nations to coordinate logistic support.

M-72 Light Anti-Tank Weapon

In July 1963, the Council set up a NATO Steering Committee for the production of the M-72 US light anti-tank weapon. Canada, the Netherlands and Norway undertook to adopt the missile and production, involving expenditure of more than US$10 million, was completed in 1968.

New forms of armaments cooperation

The early efforts in armaments cooperation, described above, had brought tangible benefits but it was clear that more could and should be achieved. The "NBMR" approach had proved unsatisfactory, and the NATO Military Authorities found themselves in a situation which was both illogical and uncomfortable in that they were approving NATO Basic Military Requirements without having responsibility for developing and producing the resulting equipment and in many cases without having adequate scientific and technical advice or political and economic guidance.

It became evident, after a few years, that a fundamental reappraisal of the whole approach to cooperation was needed, and so in October 1965 an exploratory group was set up by the Council to examine the question thoroughly and propose new solutions.

This group prepared a report, setting out the principles on which cooperation should be based, the procedures which should be followed, and the proposed structure for putting them into effect. The report, approved by the Council in May 1966, became a standard reference for all matters concerning co-operation in research, development and production of military equipment.

A flexible approach

The new procedures embodied a change in philosophy based on recognition of the fact that countries cannot be compelled to co-operate nor constrained to observe rigid procedural rules. They emphasised flexibility, and the need to make cooperation as easy and as advantageous as possible. The mandatory aspects of the earlier system were abandoned. The "NBMRs" were abolished and it was agreed that co-operative action could start on the basis of proposals from any country or from the NATO Military Authorities. If at least two countries express interest in a proposal, a group can be formed to discuss it. Gradually those member countries which decide against participation in the project can drop out. The remainder draw up characteristics, plan the development and production of the equipment, and prepare cost estimates. When they are ready to make final commitments to proceed, they present a report asking for the project to be designated as a NATO project. From that point on, participating countries make their own arrangements, the only conditions being that they must make an annual report to NATO and that, if other NATO countries wish to join at a later stage, they can do so under reasonable and equitable conditions. The body managing the project is called a NATO Steering Committee and takes whatever form the participants wish. Projects can start at any point in the research, development and production process, but for completely new items of equipment, it is preferable to begin as early as possible in the research stage before firm decisions have been taken.

The Conference of National Armaments Directors (CNAD)

In 1966, a certain number of organisational changes were made by the Council to give effect to the new procedures. The Armaments Committee was disbanded, and a new high-level body, the Conference of National Armaments Directors or CNAD was established to act under the authority of the Council.

At present, there are six Main Groups operating under the Conference of National Armaments Directors. The existing three Service Advisory Groups were transformed in 1966 into Service Armaments Groups and are now called the NATO Naval Armaments Group (NNAG); the NATO Air Force Armaments Group (NAFAG); and the NATO Army Armaments Group (NAAG). At the same time a Committee of Defence Research Directors, which had been set up early in 1964 became the Defence Research Group. The two other Main Groups set up subsequently were the Tri-Service Group on Air Defence (TSGAD), and the Tri-Service Group on Communications and Electronic Equipment (TSGCEE). The latter was formed in June 1977 to deal with tactical command and control, communications, navigation and identification systems of national forces. The Tri-Service Group on Air Defence was disbanded in the Spring of 1981 when the major part of its work was taken over by the NATO Air Defence Committee. A seventh Group, not officially designated as one of the Main Groups but considered as having equal status with them, is the NATO Industrial Advisory Group (NIAG) which provides advice and assistance on industrial matters to the Conference of National Armaments Directors and to the Main Groups.

There are also bodies known as "Cadre Groups", which undertake activities of general interest to all other groups in the structure, such as the NATO Group on Acquisition Practices, the Group of National Directors on Codification, the Group of National Directors for Quality Assurance, the Group on Rationalisation of Design Principles, Test and Safety Criteria for Explosive Materials and Explosive Stores, and the Group on Materiel (ACSM) Standardization. The latter group was created to deal with materiel standardization in the areas of assemblies, components, spare parts and materiel (hence ACSM), a field described in more detail later in this chapter.

All the Main and Cadre Groups have subordinate bodies which are variously called sub-groups, panels, working groups or study groups. In many cases they in turn have their own sub-bodies, normally of an ad hoc nature.

The National Armaments Directors' Representatives (known as the "NADREPs") are members of the national delegations to NATO concerned with armaments co-operation. They meet regularly under the chairmanship of the Assistant Secretary General for Defence Support to carry out the routine tasks of the CNAD and to undertake any such additional tasks as the CNAD may direct. One of their tasks is to direct the work of the Cadre Groups on behalf of the CNAD.

The CNAD organisation not only encourages member countries to join together in equipment and research projects, and assists them in doing so, but also provides the means for exchanges of information on operational concepts, national equipment programmes and appropriate technical and certain logistical matters where cooperation can benefit NATO and the nations, even if no particular project as such is likely to materialise. It further encourages discussions on longer-term research activities, with a view to providing guidance on the possibility of meeting future military needs through the application of advanced technology or new scientific discoveries.

The initial experience with the new procedures and organisation was most encouraging. There was a new air of freedom and a greater readiness to bring forward proposals for projects and to discuss ways and means of cooperating. The fact that there no longer had to be NATO-wide agreement on requirements was instrumental in this. It was realised that even if only two countries cooperated in producing a weapon for their forces, this was better than nothing and there was the hope that one day more countries would agree to join the endeavour.

Initially, many of the proposals concerned items which were already at a late stage of development in one country or another. However, once these items had been thoroughly examined, the tendency was to look further ahead. This encouraged countries to exchange information on ideas and intentions and has been extremely valuable in helping to harmonise national concepts and practices in a variety of fields. The result has been a broader contribution to the cohesion of the Alliance than is revealed merely by lists of projects so far designated as "NATO Projects". The new procedures brought with them the prospect of an enhanced role in defence equipment cooperation for the smaller and less industrialised nations of the Alliance, whose special needs in this area have been increasingly acknowledged.

In 1985, in recognition of the growing importance of armaments cooperation as a primary means of improving NATO's conventional defence, the CNAD was directed to implement a new "Armaments Cooperation Improvement Strategy". This improvement strategy and the high level of political interest which it had already stimulated by early 1986, led to an immediate intensification of effort under the CNAD Main Groups in their endeavours to establish cooperative programmes for the acquisition of armaments equipment and systems. The increasing political importance of armaments cooperation is reflected in the participation of Deputy Defence Ministers in two meetings of the Council in 1985 and 1986 to address the issue of enhanced armaments cooperation.

Cooperative programmes under the new procedures

Many successful cooperative programmes have been undertaken since the establishment of the CNAD in 1966. Examples are given below grouped by arm of service (navy, air force, army or multi-service)[1].

Naval Projects

NATO SEASPARROW

NATO SEASPARROW is an anti-air point defence missile system fitted in ships of frigate size and above, in different NATO navies. The project is the result of multinational cooperation initiated in 1968 with the participation of Belgium, Canada, Denmark, the Federal Republic of Germany, Greece, Italy, the Netherlands, Norway and the United States.

NATO FORACS

The NATO Naval Forces Sensor and Weapon Accuracy Check Sites in Europe (NATO FORACS) programme is the result of multinational cooperation initiated in 1974 by the navies of Denmark, the Federal Republic of Germany, Greece, Italy, Norway, the United Kingdom and the United States. The aim of the programme was to acquire, equip and operate two ranges for the purpose of checking the accuracy of all sensors connected with shipborne weapon systems. The Northern Range in Stavanger, Norway was completed in 1978 and the Southern Range in Souda Bay, Crete was completed in 1984. Both are now fully operational.

NATO Frigate Replacement for the 1990s (NFR-90)

This is the largest programme ever undertaken in the naval sphere. Its objective is to design, build and support more than 60 frigate-type ships, capable of responding to the requirements of the 21st century. The programme began in the early 1980s with the participation of Canada, France, the Federal Republic of Germany, Italy, the Netherlands, Spain, the United Kingdom and the United States. The first unit is expected to be operational in 1997[2].

NATO Helicopter for the 1990s

This project aims to develop a helicopter (about 8 tons) suitable for tactical transport land operations and for shipborne employment in the anti-submarine and anti-surface warfare roles from frigate-type ships. The project involves France, the Federal Republic of Germany, Italy and the Netherlands. The planned in-service date is 1995.

---

[1] The information given reflects the status of the programmes in mid 1989.

[2] France, Italy and the United Kingdom withdrew from this project in September 1989.

NATO Link 11 Improvements (NILE)

The aim of this project is to develop and refine technical specifications for an improved Maritime Data Link 11 which will be able to communicate effectively in an electronically hostile environment. The participants in the project are Canada, France, the Federal Republic of Germany, Italy, the Netherlands, Spain, the United Kingdom and the United States.

Air Force Projects

NATO Multi-Role Combat Aircraft—TORNADO

Established as a NATO Project in September 1969, the NATO Multi-Role Combat Aircraft—TORNADO—is a two-seater, twin-engined, variable geometry aircraft developed by two international industrial consortia. The three participating countries—the Federal Republic of Germany, Italy and the United Kingdom—have agreed to an initial co-production of 809 aircraft (324 for the Federal Republic of Germany, 100 for Italy and 385 for the United Kingdom).

NATO F-16 Combat Aircraft

Established as a NATO project in October 1975, the F-16 Air Combat Fighter was developed by the General Dynamics Corporation. The aircraft was selected to meet Belgian, Danish, Netherlands, Norwegian and United States air force requirements for a fighter aircraft able to carry out an acceptable range of tactical air warfare tasks at a reasonable cost. The five nations formed a consortium and agreed to co-production, with an extremely high degree of commonality, of a total of 998 aircraft. The same nations have since ordered further aircraft. Greece and Turkey also plan to procure the F-16.

NATO European Fighter Aircraft (EFA)

Established as a NATO project in February 1987, the European Fighter Aircraft (EFA) is a twin-engined aircraft being developed by two international industrial consortia. It is being designed as an air-superiority fighter with a secondary air-to-surface attack role. It will have a short take-off and landing capability and the ability to operate from semi-prepared surfaces. The four participating countries, the Federal Republic of Germany, Italy, Spain and the United Kingdom, signed the Memorandum Of Understanding for the development phase in 1988. Deliveries of the first production aircraft are scheduled for 1996/97.

Modular Stand-Off Weapons (MSOW)

The MSOW Programme aims to develop cooperatively a familiy of air-delivered autonomous weapon dispensers with various stand-off ranges capable of attacking fixed and mobile ground targets. Five countries are involved in the programme (the Federal Republic of Germany, Italy, Spain, the United Kingdom and the United States), and the project definition phase is scheduled for 1989.

Army Projects

MILAN Guided Anti-Armour Weapon

The NATO Steering Committee on MILAN comprises Belgium, France, the Federal Republic of Germany, Greece, Italy, Spain and the United Kingdom. The Steering Committee monitors the configuration control of this weapon system which has been developed jointly by France and the Federal Republic of Germany. It also provides a forum for discussion of related logistics, training and safety matters.

Small Arms and their Munitions

Most of the member countries of the Alliance began procurement of a new generation of individual weapons during the 1980s, in order to satisfy their tactical requirements and enhance the effectiveness of portable infantry weapons. Several countries also wish to procure new support weapons.

In this area, it has long been recognised that standardization of munitions is essential and is desirable for weapons as well. In the interests of standardization, the Conference of National Armaments Directors agreed that only two calibres should be adopted for small arms, one of them being the existing NATO 7.62mm calibre.

In order to determine the second calibre, a joint weapon and munitions evaluation programme formulated in 1976 was established by Belgium, Canada, Denmark, France, the Federal Republic of Germany, Greece, Luxembourg, the Netherlands, Norway, the United Kingdom and the United States. As a result of this programme, 5.56mm has been adopted as the second standard NATO calibre for small arms and the Belgian SS 109 ammunition has been selected as a basis for standardization.

Multiple-Launch Rocket System (MLRS)

The MLRS is an all-weather, rapid fire, non-nuclear system designed to supplement other weapons available to division or corps commanders for the delivery of a large volume of fire in a very short time against critical, time-sensitive targets. A basic Memorandum Of Understanding (MOU) on a cooperative programme for a medium LRS was signed by France, the Federal Republic of Germany, the United Kingdom and the United States in July 1979. The MOU encompasses the development of a multiple-launch free-flight rocket system to satisfy the agreed tactical requirements of all four participants. Italy joined the programme in 1982. The MLRS progamme was approved as a NATO project in May 1983.

155mm Autonomous Precision Guided Munition (APGM)

Eight NATO countries (Canada, France, the Federal Republic of Germany, Italy, the Netherlands, Spain, Turkey and the United States) signed an MOU in April 1987 to conduct an Expanded Feasibility Study addressing the development of a 155mm artillery-delivered autonomous hit-to-kill anti-armour munition. The Study is scheduled for completion in 1990. Participating countries will assume funding obligations commensurate with their share of the work.

Command and Control, Communications, Navigation and Identification (C2/CNI) Projects

Since its establishment in 1977, the Tri-Service Group on Communications and Electronic Equipment (TSGCEE) has initiated a number of cooperative projects in the CNI areas. Four projects which are typical of such cooperation are described below.

NAVSTAR Global Positioning System (GPS)

In 1978, Belgium, Canada, Denmark, France, the Federal Republic of Germany, Italy, the Netherlands, Norway and the United Kingdom joined the United States programme for the establishment of a satellite-based worldwide positioning and navigation system known as the NAVSTAR Global Positioning System (GPS). Spain joined the project in 1987. The aim of the project is to foster the use of the GPS within the Alliance countries by developing suitable equipment and exchanging technical and operational information, promoting a high level of equipment standardization and interoperability within the forces, and avoiding duplication of effort. The GPS will be available for both civilian and military use and is expected to be operational in the early 1990s.

Battlefield Information Collection and Exploitation Systems (BICES)

Belgium, Canada, Denmark, France, the Federal Republic of Germany, Greece, Italy, the Netherlands, Norway, Spain, Turkey, the United Kingdom and the United States have agreed to cooperate together with the NATO Communications and Information Systems Agency (NACISA) in creating a capability for receiving, processing and rapidly combining data from a variety of sources required by military commanders as an aid to decision-making. The project is expected to enter the feasibility phase in the near future.

Multifunctional Information Distribution System (MIDS)

In 1987 Canada, France, the Federal Republic of Germany, Italy, Norway, Spain, the United Kingdom and the United States agreed to cooperate in the development of an advanced, high capacity, secure, Electronic Counter Measure (ECM)-Resistant data distribution system with a positioning and identification capability. The system is known as the MIDS Low Volume Terminal. The project definition phase has been completed and full-scale development is expected to begin in 1990.

Shipborne Inertial Navigation System

In 1987, Canada, the Netherlands, Spain and the United Kingdom agreed to the collaborative acquisition of a NATO Low Cost Shipborne Inertial Navigation System. The responses to the Request for Proposals are being evaluated and a contract is expected to be signed in 1989.

Defence Research Activities

In addition to equipment-oriented projects, there are also many joint ventures of a scientific or technical nature, initially sponsored by the Defence Research Group. Examples are given below:

Azores Fixed Acoustic Range (AFAR)

In 1967, eight NATO nations (Canada, France, the Federal Republic of Germany, Italy, the Netherlands, Portugal, the United Kingdom and the United States) took the initial step towards the construction of a deep-water acoustic range in the Atlantic Ocean off the Island of Santa Maria in the Azores. The transmitting and receiving antennae were implanted in 1970 and 1971, and the range was operational from May 1972 until May 1979, yielding a large amount of data on underwater sound propagation, and thus enhancing the Alliance's capabilities in underwater detection.

Mobile Acoustic Communications Study (MACS)

In 1976, three of the AFAR Nations—France, the Federal Republic of Germany and the United States—agreed to carry out underwater sound propagation measurements between mobile platforms in various maritime environments to complement the AFAR data, especially regarding bulk and bottom effects. Four sea trips took place in 1976 and 1977, and the project was terminated in 1979, after completion of the data evaluation.

European Transonic Windtunnel (ETW)

In 1978 France, the Federal Republic of Germany, the Netherlands and the United Kingdom embarked on the preliminary design of a large-scale transonic windtunnel of the cryogenic type, i.e. operating at very low temperature. Following the preliminary design phase, conducted by a multinational technical group in Amsterdam, it was decided to build the ETW in the Federal Republic of Germany. The project is in its Final Design Phase.

Demonstration of Advanced Radar Techniques (DART)

In 1980 Denmark, France, Italy, the Netherlands, the United Kingdom and the United States agreed to support the above project aimed at improving the survivability of future radars through demonstrations using different advanced techniques. Later Denmark withdrew from the project and the Federal Republic of Germany joined it. An Experimental Radar is under development, to be built by contractors from the participating nations. Future demonstration tests are planned.

Data Fusion Demonstrator (DFD)

In 1986, the Federal Republic of Germany proposed the establishment of a project to develop a testbed system for the investigation of techniques for fusion of battlefield sensor reports. Canada, Denmark, France, the Federal Republic of Germany, the Netherlands, the United Kingdom and the United States are currently defining the programme and developing an MOU. The programme is scheduled for completion in 1996.

Research Study Groups

The Defence Research Group also sponsors the activities of a large number of Research Study Groups (RSGs). The RSGs are involved in a range of cooperative defence research activities, including field trials for data collection and technique evaluation, model development, signal processing technique development, design methodologies, cost-effectiveness analysis, human engineering, component evaluations, materials science, and many others. The RSGs are composed of experts from the participating nations.

NATO Industrial Advisory Group

In 1968, the NATO Industrial Advisory Group (NIAG) was established by the Conference of National Armaments Directors as an industrial forum for a free exchange of views on various aspects of NATO armaments research, development and production. The purpose was to provide a means of obtaining industry's advice on how to foster government-to-industry and industry-to-industry cooperation, and to assist Main Armaments Groups in exploring opportunities for international collaboration.

Since its creation, NIAG has provided advice and suggestions for action in a number of areas covering legal, management, economic and technical problems. It has also identified a number of obstacles to cooperation and has made recommendations for overcoming them. In addition, the NIAG has undertaken "prefeasibility" studies on a wide range of subjects, with a view to establishing the technical feasibility and estimated cost of possible solutions, assessing trade-off points and the penalties involved in adopting certain courses of action and identifying areas where more detailed study was required. Subjects covered include advanced approach and landing systems, battlefield surveillance, expendable targets, compatibility of naval data handling equipment within ships, certain radar problems, anti-surface ship missiles, anti-ship missile defence, air-delivered weapons, air defence weapons, the NATO Frigate Replacement for the 1990's, a NATO helicopter autonomous precision munition, and battle tank components.

NIAG has amply demonstrated the technological capability of industry in many equipment areas and has become a significant factor in improving NATO's cooperative equipment endeavours. Member nations are becoming increasingly aware of the support it has to offer.

Work of the cadre groups

The following paragraphs describe the work of the cadre groups under the CNAD and the broad problems which they handle, ranging from general management to legal and administrative matters.

Safety and suitability for service of ammunitions and explosives

The increase in international collaboration and standardization in the weapons field and the purchase by nations of foreign weapons has given rise to problems caused by differing national approaches to design principles, safety and suitability for service.

This in turn had led to differences in national criteria and procedures for the safety appraisal of weapons and those parts of weapon systems in which explosives are used. In undertaking appraisals of foreign weapons, it is difficult to establish what test (or what equivalent to national tests) a weapon has undergone and with what result.

A group under the Conference of National Armaments Directors has therefore been tasked to establish agreed international terminology, design principles, criteria, procedures and tests to cover all aspects of the process by which assessments of safety and suitability for service are made, since it is these criteria and procedures which provide guidance for the weapon designers.

NATO Codification

An important factor in the management of support for national armed forces is the supply problem. Huge stocks with millions of individual items necessitate a system of handling that is fast, flexible and precise. The NATO Codification System provides a uniform method of supply classification and item identification and is thus an ideal tool for logistics data management. It also helps inventory managers by simplifying supply and procurement procedures and can form a basis for standardization. A particular asset is the use of one number for one item in NATO projects, regardless of origin, which is a sine qua non for efficient cross-servicing. The system has resulted in a reduction in items and stocks, a decrease in management costs and an improvement in the determination of assets.

Use of the system is spreading to the civilian departments of governments, to international organisations and also to countries outside the Alliance.

The codification system is fully computerised, and is based on the principle that the country of production codifies the item and makes the identifying data available to procuring countries. Data is exchanged between countries on computer media, which facilitates the maintenance of the data files which form the basis for materiel management systems.

The Group of National Directors on Codification, which comes under the Conference of National Armaments Directors, operates Panels which cover all codification procedures and methods and Sub-Groups which supervise the coordination of the codification of all joint NATO projects. It establishes the codification policy and supports the day-to-day operations of the fourteen national codification bureaux of the NATO nations.

Quality Assurance

As soon as NATO countries and agencies started to implement equipment programmes in which the manufacture of various components was entrusted to industries of different countries, it became clear that requirements for uniform and adequate quality standards could not be met satisfactorily unless the participants in cooperative projects followed common rules and procedures. The task of drawing these up was given to the Group of National Directors for Quality Assurance which was established specifically for this purpose. As a result of its work, the basic requirements for NATO quality assurance doctrine and policy have been established and published as NATO Allied Quality Assurance Publications (AQAPs).

The Group is continuing its work in developing quality assurance requirements in those areas related to procurement which most affect the attainment of quality targets: the preparation of software quality control system requirements and the development of the reliability and maintainability quality assurance policy. The scope and impact of NATO quality assurance policy will continue to grow, both within the Alliance and beyond.

Assemblies, Components, Spare Parts and Materials (ACSM)

A review of activities within NATO concerned with the standardization of assemblies, components, spare parts and materials indicated an urgent need for improvement in this field. Only a limited number of standardization documents related to these items had been agreed, and effective implementation had often not taken place. It was against this background that the Conference of National Armaments Directors established the Senior Cadre Group on Materiel (ACSM) Standardization in 1977, to develop an effective NATO standardization policy and programme; to further the coordination of short and long-range standardization activities in the area of ACSM; and to promote utilisation to the maximum practical extent of national and international industrial standards, military standards and specifications. The Group draws up proposals for engineering design (ACSM) standardization, monitors progress in this field and provides advice and assistance as appropriate. It also surveys the work of CNAD subsidiaries concerned with ACSM, and co-ordinates or directs the work of subsidiaries as CNAD decides.

Safety aspects of storage and transport of ammunition and explosives

A more specialised activity in which considerable success has been achieved on a NATO-wide basis is that of safety aspects of storage and transportation of ammunition and explosives. A group of experts has produced a comprehensive manual on safety principles for storage, which is the most authoritative work in existence on this important subject, and in demand worldwide. The same group has developed similar publications covering safety aspects of the various modes of transporting ammunition and explosives.

Intellectual property problems

The ever-increasing flow of technology among the members of the Alliance and their industries, in the framework of armaments cooperation, requires the adoption of measures for protecting the intellectual property rights involved and facilitating the transfer and use of proprietary information. The relevant problems are handled by the NATO Group on Intellectual Property and Cooperative Arrangements which, in the course of its 25 years of activity, has elaborated the following two agreements.

The "NATO Agreement on the Mutual Safeguarding of Secrecy of Inventions relating to Defence, and for which applications for Patents have been made", of September 21, 1960. This is one of the important legal instruments established by the Group. By committing governments to safeguard the secrecy of such inventions, this Agreement makes it possible for nations to lift prohibitions on the filing of patent applications in other countries, which, in the past, had adversely affected the promotion of NATO cooperation in research, development and production of military equipment.

The "NATO Agreement on the Communication of Technical Information for Defence Purposes", of October 19, 1970. This was prepared by the Group in order to provide adequate protection to the owners of technical information exchanged between member governments or NATO organisations, thereby encouraging industries in NATO nations to make their technology more readily available for purposes of armaments cooperation.

In an effort to increase and harmonise licensing and co-production policies in NATO nations, the Group established its "Intellectual Property Principles and Guidelines in the field of Licensing and Co-production for the purpose of Armaments Standardization and Interoperability". These were completed in 1979, after close consultation with the NATO Industrial Advisory Group, and endorsed by the Conference of National Armaments Directors.

Among other guidance papers and studies accomplished by the Group in support of NATO armaments cooperation, the following should be mentioned: "Guidance for NATO procurement authorities" and "Guidance on drafting international cooperative research and development agreements" (both published in booklet form); "National practices in NATO countries regarding proprietary rights in cooperative research and development programmes"; "Military equipment and industrial property legislation" (2 volumes); "Recoupment of research and development costs in NATO countries"; and "Regulations in NATO countries concerning employees' inventions". These have all been published in the form of NATO brochures.[3] A new brochure has been produced by the Group on "Guidance for the drafting of Memoranda of Understanding and International Cooperative Arrangements".

Acquisition Practices

The need to make more efficient use of national resources in the face of constrained defence budgets and rising costs led the Conference of National Armaments Directors in October 1981 to establish the NATO Group on Acquisition Practices. This succeeded the NATO Group on Intellectual Property and Cooperative Arrangements.

The Group is tasked to study the legal, contractual, financial and administrative mechanisms of collaborative acquisition, with a view to harmonising acquisition practices, facilitating contracting processes, reducing cost driving factors in armaments programmes, and enhancing equipment collaboration between governments and industry.

A key aspect of the Group's activities is the development of practical advice to those in charge of negotiating cooperative arrangements, mainly in the form of additional guidance to supplement the general guidelines "for the drafting of MOUs and International cooperative arrangements".[4]

In particular, the Group developed guidelines and recommended approaches on currency exchange management, price adjustments and pricing practices in cooperative programmes, as well as for the handling of liability for patent infringement and third party liability in cooperative programmes.

In furtherance of initiatives taken by the CNAD to promote short-term opportunities for exploiting emerging technologies, the Group established a number of pragmatic measures to foster early government-industry collaboration, such as a model wording for an inter-government Statement of Intent and criteria for selecting work-sharing and cost-sharing formulae. It developed a checklist for a "Programme Memorandum of Understanding", to be signed at the outset of a programme, laying down all vital principles governing collaboration over the entire life cycle of that programme.

In an effort to foster a mutual understanding between governments and industry on contractual terms to be negotiated in support of cooperative programmes, the Group, in consultation with the NATO Industrial Advisory Group, has established contracting guidelines and samples of contract provisions for cooperative programmes, covering in particular the requirements of feasibility studies.

Problems of Materiel Standardization

As is natural in an Alliance, much stress is laid on cooperation, and indeed it is often viewed as a desirable goal in itself, even though there is

---

3 These brochures may be obtained from: Defence Support Division, NATO, B-1110 Brussels.

4 Allied Publication AACP-1, published in 1981.

sometimes no clear idea or consensus as to what types of cooperation would be most advantageous. This was initially the case with the CNAD, which was established primarily with the object of improving the mechanisms for cooperation in research, development and production of military equipment within NATO. In more recent years, prompted not least by the spiralling cost and complexity of modern armaments and by the rapid build-up and increasing sophistication of the equipment of the Warsaw Treaty forces, the CNAD has focused increasing attention on defining its objectives in equipment cooperation more precisely. The emphasis on standardization has been one outcome.

Standardization covers a wide area and is dealt with in further detail in the following chapter. It may range from real equipment commonality to interoperability between military forces. Standardization in NATO often results in the development of NATO Standardization agreements (STANAGs).

Equipment interoperability has figured implicitly in cooperative programmes since the beginning of the Alliance, but only since 1975 has it been singled out as a specific object of cooperation. Particular areas where special efforts have been initiated include the cross-servicing of aircraft, fuels, ammunition and communications equipment. Associated with this has been a drive to improve the efficacy of STANAGs, both in their scope and in their implementation. A fully comprehensive range of STANAGs universally applied would solve almost all the problems of interoperability. Studies are underway to see how this can be achieved. In the meantime special efforts are being made in certain areas. Examples are given in the following paragraphs.

Procedures for Armaments Cooperation

Armaments cooperation under the CNAD is based essentially on an information exchange process which seeks agreement between nations and the Major NATO Commanders on harmonised operational requirements in order to promote cooperative equipment programmes. Because the responsibility for equipping their forces is the prerogative of individual member nations, this cooperative process can be supported but not regulated by NATO. There is therefore no formal or centralised NATO armaments planning system. However, in order to give greater coherence and structure to co-operative efforts, two formalised processes known as the NATO Armaments Planning Review (NAPR) and the Phased Armaments Programming System (PAPS) (formerly "Periodic Armaments Planning System") have been adopted to improve the management and programming of CNAD work.

The NAPR, formally established in October 1979, is primarily a review system designed to expose opportunities for cooperation more clearly. It uses, as its point of departure, equipment replacement schedules provided annually by the nations. These are examined by CNAD groups, the MNCs and the International Staff with a view to identifying standardization requirements and potential opportunities for cooperation.

The PAPS is a managerial review process for CNAD programmes structured around key milestones of a typical weapon system life cycle. The system facilitates programme reviews at key decision points. One of its major objectives is to encourage early cooperation on the basis of operational deficiencies identified before national solutions have been precisely determined. PAPS has proved a valuable managerial instrument for furthering NATO cooperative projects since its inception in 1981.

Transatlantic Equipment Cooperation

A particular aspect of the evolution of NATO cooperation in defence equipment has been the desire to improve the collaboration between the European and North American member countries of the Alliance in the interests of making more cost-effective use of the total resources of the Alliance. This has resulted in:

— General Memoranda of Understanding (MOUs) between many industrialised European nations and the United States on the reciprocal procurement of defence materiel and the removal of trade barriers;

— the dual production by interested NATO nations of systems developed by another nation (or group of nations) under fair and equitable conditions;

— a Family of Weapons approach whereby interested nations agree to develop and produce different equipments of a given family under either European or North American leadership, in such a way that duplication of research and development effort for the same equipment is minimised (e.g. in the air-to-air missile family, Europe would take the lead for a new short-range air-to-air missile, while the United States and Canada would take the lead in a new medium-range air-to-air missile).

This triple approach is designed to facilitate wider Alliance cooperation in armaments and to contribute significantly to the achievement of NATO rationalisation, standardization and interoperability (RSI) objectives.

A transatlantic dialogue between the European and North American nations is conducted on these initiatives under the aegis of the Conference of National Armaments Directors and a report is made to it at its bi-annual meetings.

A further step was taken when, at its Autumn 1987 meeting, the Conference of National Armaments Directors examined proposals drawn up by the Secretary General for the establishment of a NATO Conventional Armaments Planning System (CAPS). At the same meeting Armaments Directors discussed the relevance of these proposals to the overall effort to improve NATO's defence planning in the context of the imbalance of NATO and Warsaw Treaty Organisation conventional forces and received the first in a series of regular briefings by Major NATO Commanders on deficiencies in NATO's forces. On March 8, 1988, agreement was reached on a plan of action to launch the new system for a trial two-year period and a new committee, known as the NATO Conventional Armaments Review Committee (NCARC), was created to oversee and coordinate the testing of the mechanisms and procedures being developed. This development reflects the growing realisation of the need to make more efficient use of the resources available for defence.

Chapter 16
NATO Standardization

"Standardization" is mentioned in several chapters of this book and indeed is a subject which is of relevance to most Committees and Groups in one way or another. This may range from developing standards, applying these standards, or suggesting changes to existing standards.

Aims of NATO Standardization

The overall aim of NATO standardization is to increase the combined operational effectiveness of the military forces of the Alliance and to make better use of the economic resources available for defence. Increased cooperation and the elimination of duplication among Alliance nations in the research, development, production, procurement and support of defence systems and equipment all contribute to this end and enable Alliance nations to improve their collective defence capability and strengthen deterrence.

It is agreed policy in NATO to try to make optimum use of standardization work undertaken by other international organisations such as the International Organisation for Standardization (ISO) and the International Electrotechnical Commission (IEC).

Standardization in NATO

Standardization is the process of formulating, agreeing, implementing and updating standards for regular use throughout NATO. It is not enough simply to formulate a standard; nations have to agree to it and implement it if it is to be effective. This may involve incorporating NATO standards in national regulations, evaluating results and proposing any necessary modifications or additional standards.

From the outset, efforts to achieve standardization in NATO have been directed towards the incorporation of standard procedures or components into NATO Standardization Agreements (STANAGs). However, standardization within NATO also has wider implications and involves the process of developing concepts, doctrines, procedures and designs which will help to achieve and maintain the most effective levels of compatability, interoperability, interchangeability and commonality in the fields of operations, administration and material.

Interoperability is a minimum requirement for military effectiveness since it enables systems, units or forces to provide services to, and accept services from, other systems, units or forces and to use the services exchanged in a manner which enables them to operate effectively together. The need to be able to intercommunicate, for example, is self-evident.

NATO standards are normally classified in three categories i.e. operational standards, materiel standards and administrative standards. One standard may come into more than one of these categories. Operational standards are those which affect future and/or current military practice, procedure or format. They may apply to such matters as concepts, doctrine, tactics, techniques, logistics, training, organisations, reports, forms, maps and charts. Materiel standards are those which affect the characteristics of future and/or current materiel. They may cover production codes of practice, as well as specifications. Materiel includes complete systems, sub-systems, assemblies, components, spare parts and materials and includes consumables. Administrative standards concern terminology as well as administrative procedures and documentation.

The NATO Standardization Group

Many groups in NATO produce standards. A substantial part of the work takes place within the structure of the Conference of National Armaments Directors (CNAD), and is mainly concerned with materiel standardization. The Military Agency for Standardization (MAS) is exclusively concerned with standardization, primarily in the operational field. Specific topics are also dealt with by other groups under the Military Committee.

In 1983 the North Atlantic Council decided to establish a NATO Standardization Group (NSG) composed of national representatives from both the operational and materiel-oriented sides of defence departments, and representatives from the Major NATO Commands (MNCs), the International Staff (IS), the International Military Staff (IMS) and the MAS. The purpose of the Group is to provide a multi-national forum for the harmonisation of national views and the pursuit of NATO standardization activities. The Group is responsible to the Council for obtaining national and staff inputs with a view to the preparation of a composite NATO Standardization Programme (NSP) to be submitted to the NATO Standardization Tasking Authorities, after approval by the Council, for subsequent implementation.

The NSG is in the process of preparing a first NATO Standardization Programme. The Group agreed that in preparing this Programme, the use of automatic data processing would be essential. Since there is a need for up-to-date information on all standardization activities, the Group is therefore developing a NATO Standardization Information Base (NSIB). This will provide an imput for the preparation of the Programme, serve as a management tool for those dealing with standardization in NATO, and establish a general source of information on all standardization activities in NATO.

Chapter 17
Communications and Information Systems

Rapid and reliable communications and information systems are required by national and NATO political and military authorities for political consultations, crisis management and the command and control of assigned forces. These requirements can only be met by the utilisation of the most modern technology and the integration of strategic and tactical communications and information systems into an overall NATO Communications and Information System (CIS).

NATO Strategic Communications

In the early days of the Alliance, NATO's strategic communications were rudimentary and consisted of a series of point-to-point links mainly using national post-office (PTT) circuits. These were later supplemented by limited NATO-owned links using terrestrial line-of-sight microwave and tropo-scatter systems.

In the late 1960s, it became clear that a new approach was required to meet the needs of the new strategy of flexible response and the increased emphasis being placed upon crisis management. This, in turn, required a much wider exchange of information among NATO nations and a system which would enable nations to consult together both in normal and in crisis situations. In addition, better communications were needed to enable the political and military authorities of the Alliance to exercise command and control of NATO forces in a wide range of contingencies.

Accordingly, in 1966, plans were laid to provide direct communications between the NATO Headquarters and all the NATO capitals, as well as the three Major NATO Commanders. The move of the North Atlantic Council from Paris to its present Headquarters in Brussels provided the opportunity to establish a complex specially devised for crisis management including a modern communications centre which became operational in 1969.

In order to provide better voice as well as telegraph communications, especially to the more distant NATO areas, it was agreed that NATO should have a satellite communications system. In March 1970, the first of NATO's own satellites became operational and later in the spring of the same year the first of the large satellite ground terminals was brought into service.

For the North Atlantic Council and the Defence Planning Committee to be able to discharge their overall responsibilities for coordinating civil and military activities in the field of communications and electronics, it was clear that a forum was needed to bring together senior national military and civil representatives of the members of the Alliance on a regular basis to develop the required advice. The NATO Joint Communications-Electronics Committee (NJCEC) was established for this purpose in October 1969.

In March 1971, the North Atlantic Council agreed to establish the NATO Integrated Communications System (NICS) and to create a special agency, the NICS Management Agency (NICSMA), to be responsible for the planning and implementation of the new system.

The NICS concept was based on the development of a common user, automatically-switched network, employing sophisticated computer-driven switches for all forms of voice, telegraph and data traffic. The system had to be implemented in stages. The first involved the implementation of a series of stand-alone sub-systems to automate NATO's voice and telegraph communications. Further enhancements by stages have involved the geographical and technical expansion of these sub-systems and their welding into a single fully integrated system. The system will be completed by 1995.

The NICS is one of the largest commonly-funded infrastructure projects which the Alliance has ever undertaken. With the completion of the first stage, NATO has at its disposal a modern communications system equal to any other in the Western World, significantly improving the Alliance capability for crisis management and for the command and control of NATO forces.

The NATO Command, Control and Information System (NCCIS)

In October 1970, the North Atlantic Council established the NATO Command, Control and Information System and Automatic Data Processing Committee (NCCDPC). The activities of the Committee ranged from recommending policies concerning command, control and information and initiating the overall organisation for the NATO CCIS, to identifying and defining those aspects which require standardization. The NCCDPC reported to the North Atlantic Council or to the Military Committee as appropriate.

The NATO Communications and Information System (CIS)

Early in the 1980s it became apparent that both the communications aspects of the NICS and the information process aspects of the NCCIS had become so interdependent that they could not be dealt with in isolation. Studies were undertaken which culminated in November 1985 in the amalgamation of the former policy committees of the NJCEC and the NCCDPC, together with the former NATO Communications and Electronics Board of the Military Committee, into one single committee to deal with all NATO CIS matters. The title of this new Council Committee is the NATO Communications and Information Systems Committee (NACISC) which also provides advice to the Military Committee on military CIS aspects. The NACISC is supported by a new streamlined sub-structure which includes the Military Telecommunications and Military CIS Agencies.

The studies also concluded that in keeping with the rationalisation of policy direction, the scope of the activities of the former NICS Management Agency (NICSMA) should be progressively expanded to undertake, on a case by case basis, the management and implementation of other NATO CIS projects in addition to those associated with the evolutionary enhancements of the NATO Integrated Communications System. The agency was renamed the NATO Communications and Information Systems Agency (NACISA) and its structure was revised to reflect its expanded responsibilities.

Alliance Strategic CIS requirements, which are being formulated in a NATO Consultation, Command and Control (C3) Master Plan, take civil and military needs into account. These include military requirements to support NATO's integrated military structure established in a Tri-MNC Command and Control (C2) Plan; the civil and military requirements to support political consultation and crisis management, and the civil requirements to support emergency planning established in a "Political Consultation, NATO Civil Emergency Planning (PCNCEP) CIS Plan"; and the technical requirements of the NATO C3 Architecture. Strategic CIS requirements are implemented from common funds, primarily through the Infrastructure Programme (see Chapter 12).

Tactical Command and Control, Communications, Navigation and Identification (C2/CNI) Systems

Although the provision of the tactical C2/CNI equipment and systems for use by assigned forces is the responsibility of the individual members of the Alliance, it is essential that these forces can interoperate. A number of multinational bodies have therefore been established under the Military Committee and the NACISC with responsibility for operational and procedural matters related to standardization and interoperability. The Conference of National Armaments Directors (CNAD) and its subordinate bodies are responsible for the promotion of cooperation among the countries of NATO in the areas of research, development, production and procurement with the aim of achieving standardization or at least interoperability for such equipment and systems (see Chapter 15).

Initially C2/CNI matters were addressed by the three service armaments groups of the CNAD. However, in 1977 the Tri-Service Group on Communications and Electronic Equipment (TSGCEE) was established in order to promote cooperation, standardization and interoperability in this sphere. The work of the TSGCEE has resulted in cooperative projects on the development of a NAVSTAR Global Positioning System (GPS); a Shipborne Inertial Navigation System (SINS); a NATO Identification System; a Multifunctional Information Distribution System (MIDS) Low Volume Terminal; Battlefield Information Collection and Exploitation Systems (BICES); a Tactical Communications System for the Land Zone Post 2000; and an Ada Programming Support Environment (APSE). A Memorandum of Understanding (MOU) on a project on Internetworking Technologies and Future Data Links Architecture is under development. Furthermore, a large number of CNI equipment and systems STANAGs (Standardization Agreements—see Chapter 15) have been established as well as a series of STANAGs comprising the Single Architecture of Technical Common Interoperability Standards (SATCIS) in accordance with the NATO Reference Model for Open System Interconnection. Additional STANAGs are under development.

The Air Command and Control System (ACCS)

The special CIS requirements for NATO's air defence, including the Early Warning System, the Air Defence Ground Environment and Airborne Early Warning and Control System, are described in Chapter 18.

Civil Communications Planning

In support of NATO Civil Emergency Planning arrangements, the Civil Communications Planning Committee (CCPC), a subsidiary body of the Senior Civil Emergency Planning Committee (SCEPC), is responsible for the planning of civil communications. Its task is to determine their suitability and enable their continued use in meeting the emergency, wartime and survival period requirements in the political, economic and military fields. The CCPC is also responsible for the provision of communications for NATO Civil Wartime Agencies (see Chapter 14).

Chapter 18
Air Defence

The early warning system

The preamble to the North Atlantic Treaty reflects the resolve of the signatory nations "to unite their efforts for collective defence and for the preservation of peace and security". Article 3 of the Treaty sets out the basis for the defence of the North Atlantic Treaty area in more detail: "The Parties, separately and jointly, will maintain and develop their individual and collective capacity to resist armed attack". However, although the requirement for collective defence had been firmly established, initially there was no single coordinated air defence system within NATO. To varying degrees, each nation had the elements needed for an effective system. What was needed was the coordination of those national capabilities so that improvements could be then made on a comprehensive basis, to the overall benefit of the Alliance.

The need for such a system was recognised by all members of the Alliance by the beginning of the 50s, and in 1954 the various activities in this field culminated in the proposal "that a system be established to provide for coordination of air defence capabilities in Europe". In December 1955, the Military Committee approved the concept of a coordinated system for air defence in a document known as MC 54/1. Coordinating authority was assigned to the Supreme Allied Commander Europe (SACEUR). It was also agreed to establish an air defence component within the Supreme Headquarters Allied Powers Europe (SHAPE) and to found an Air Defence Technical Centre at The Hague in the Netherlands.

A first step towards integration was taken in 1957, when the North Atlantic Council agreed on a requirement for an early warning system covering the approaches to Allied Command Europe (ACE). This led to the creation of a chain of eighteen radar stations linked by a communications system to provide information on air activity in the airspace adjacent to the European portion of the North Atlantic Treaty area. This system was completed in 1962, and was financed in common through the Infrastructure programme. The establishment of this early warning system, which was the first cooperative effort in terms of Alliance air defence, was to provide the cornerstone for the future development of a NATO Air Defence Ground Environment.

NADGE—The NATO Air Defence Ground Environment

By the end of 1960, the North Atlantic Council had approved the creation of an integrated air defence system for Allied Command Europe under the command and control of the Supreme Allied Commander Europe (SACEUR). The nations concerned were invited to assign their air defence forces in Europe to SACEUR in peacetime. To achieve a coherent air defence capability, adequate linking of national elements of the air defence ground environment and much of the existing early warning system was required. In 1962 preparations therefore began for the implementation of an integrated air defence system in Europe and the NADGE Improvement Plan was born.

Initial planning for the NADGE system saw the development of system requirements which were to be used as the basis for system design. The NADGE Improvement Plan was financed through the NATO Infrastructure programme, and in 1966 a production and logistics organisation, known as the NADGE Management Office was established to manage the execution of the project. NADGE contracts were finally signed in 1966 for a programme involving 84 sites from the North Cape to the mountains of Eastern Turkey. When the last sites were completed in the summer of 1973, the first integrated air defence command and control system to satisfy SACEUR's operational requirements had become a reality.

The air threat to Allied Command Europe continued to grow however, and it was recognised that further improvements to the NADGE system were necessary. Thus, in Infrastructure Slices XXI to XXIV (1970-1973) (see Chapter 12) an additional ten radar sites in Greece, Italy and Turkey were updated through a Radar Improvement Plan for the Mediterranean. Since that time, there have been a number of improvements to the air defence ground environment. These consisted of the provision of modern 3-D radars and of improved computer and display systems in many locations, and the replacement of the obsolete 412 L system in Germany (GEADGE) and of the LINESMAN system in the United Kingdom (UKADGE and Improved UKADGE). The NADGE is in the process of being further extended by the implementation of a Portuguese Air Command and Control System (POACCS) and of the Iceland Air Defence System (IADS).

NATO Airborne Early Warning and Control

Until the early seventies, surveillance of airspace had been accomplished by a system of ground-based radars. The growing capability for aircraft to operate effectively at low and very low levels brought about the requirement to detect and track targets at such levels. It was clear from topographical considerations that adequate surveillance virtually from ground level up would entail the construction of an enormous number of surface stations. Attention was therefore directed to the possibility of "elevating" the surveillance system, and the Airborne Early Warning and Control System (AWACS) concept came under consideration by the Alliance. Evidently, the airborne early warning radars, with their availability to detect low flying aircraft at great distance, would have to be integrated into the existing ground environment to enhance ground radar capabilities and contribute to the control of Alliance air forces. Towards the end of 1978, thirteen NATO nations embarked on the largest common-funded acquisition programme ever undertaken by the Alliance and agreed to provide an airborne early warning system with the necessary links to the ground environment. The airborne system was to comprise eighteen E-3A Airborne Early Warning aircraft with a United Kingdom contribution of eleven NIMROD Mk 3 Airborne Early Warning aircraft. 34 ground sites were to be modified through the so-called Airborne Early Warning and Control Ground Integration Segment. Under the supervision of the NATO Airborne Early Warning and Control Programme Management Organisation, by the end of 1986 all 18 NATO E-3A aircraft were in service and in mid-1988 modification of all of the ground radar sites was completed.

Towards the end of the implementation programme, it became apparent that the deferred Electronic Support Measures capability could be reinstated, and an additional programme to achieve this is currently in progress. Since this NATO facility must remain appropriate to the Warsaw Pact threat it faces, further improvements and enhancement are currently being considered for implementation.

In December 1986, the United Kingdom authorities decided to acquire a similar version of the E-3A instead of the NIMROD as its contribution to this force. The NATO Airborne Early Warning Force is a multinational force operating under the command of the Supreme Allied Commander Europe on behalf of all three Major NATO Commanders.

Air defence programme development

The development of a programme for air defence formed one part of the Long Term Defence Programme, which resulted from directives given at a Summit Meeting of the NATO Council held in London in 1977. By the end of 1979 an air defence programme for the period 1980-1994 had been prepared. It included a fifteen year projection of air defence needs for Allied Command Europe and associated command and control requirements and was agreed by Defence Ministers as the architectural basis for the future air defence system.

Early in 1980 it was recognised that the existing committee structure for air defence was inadequate and did not allow all members of the Alliance to play an effective part in the development and approval of the future air defence programme. Thus, in November 1980, the Council agreed on a new committee structure, headed by the NATO Air Defence Committee (NADC), to advise the Council and the Defence Planning Committee on all aspects of air defence programme development for NATO and the adjacent sea areas. Not only has the air defence programme development needed to take into consideration the manned aircraft threat and countermeasures to it, but, more recently, the Council also charged the NADC with taking the lead in activities within the Alliance concentrating on one developing aspect of the overall threat, namely that of the increasing Warsaw Treaty capability in the field of tactical missiles, particularly tactical ballistic missiles. This work has also involved consideration of appropriate countermeasures in the context of the overall air defence programme development.

Initially the Committee was set up with two subordinate Panels, one on the Airspace Management and Control System (PAMCS) and one dealing with Air Defence Weapons (PADW). The PAMCS was given responsibility for advising and assisting in the planning and coordination of the overall air defence programme. Those activities directly in support of the existing air defence ground environment, the Air Defence Software Committee and the Air Defence Hardware Committee, were transferred to the PAMCS. As well as monitoring the technical and logistical effectiveness of the existing system, this Panel oversees the activities of the multinational Air Command and Control System Team. This Team, created in 1981, is charged with the preparation of a long-term costed master plan describing the transition from NADGE to an air command and control system which in future will support all air operations. Once the master plan has been completed and nations have agreed to a programme for its implementation, it will be realised over a period extending into the early 2000s.

The PADW is concerned with weapons mixes and the development of a long term weapons programme which goes into sufficient detail to identify the possible contributions of each member of the Alliance. A major objective of the Panel is the harmonisation of complementary national weapons programmes with a view to ensuring the best use of available resources to meet the overall operational requirements of the Alliance. The work of the Panel is also designed to assist in identifying possible collaborative programmes. The PADW has also been considering countermeasures to the tactical missile threat.

In 1983 a third Panel on Air Defence Philosophy (PADP) was established, responsible for advising the NATO Air Defence Committee on the possible consequences for the Alliance of proposals regarding air defence concepts and programmes. In particular, the PADP provides assessments of specific political, economic and military factors likely to have an impact on air defence. The Panel also comments upon the allocation of necessary resources. One of its first tasks has been to assess, on behalf of the NADC, the extent of the threat to the Alliance from the Warsaw Treaty countries' tactical missile capability, also taking into consideration the potential effects of arms reduction agreements such as the INF Treaty.

Air Defence Representatives act as points of contact within NATO Headquarters for the Air Defence community. This forum meets under the chairmanship of the Vice-Chairman of the NATO Air Defence Committee to exchange information, hold preliminary discussions, help to formulate positions on matters of interest to the Committee and its subordinate Panels, and generally coordinate and prepare its work.

Chapter 19

European Airspace Coordination[1]

Several thousand civil and military aircraft cruising, climbing and descending in all directions up to 60,000 feet at widely varying speeds have to be accommodated in NATO European airspace. Close coordination of civil and military use of the airspace and control of air traffic is therefore essential to ensure safety from collision and optimum freedom of movement. It is also necessary to enable a comprehensive picture of the air situation to be established and maintained and all aircraft to be accurately identified, which in turn is a prerequisite for effective defence. NATO is concerned with these problems because of its responsibilities for air defence and for the training and operation of air forces in the area—and because civil aviation is of considerable economic importance to NATO member countries.

Airspace Coordination Committee

In April 1955, the Council established a Committee for European Airspace Coordination (CEAC) with the general aim of promoting safety and economy in flying, without impinging unduly upon the requirements of military airspace users. The members of the Committee represent the civil and military aviation authorities of NATO countries. NATO Military Authorities are also represented, in particular the major commands. The International Civil Aviation Organisation (ICAO)[2], the International Air Transport Association (IATA)[3] and the European Organisation for the Safety of Air Navigation

---

[1] Although the Committee for European Airspace Coordination is concerned with matters which have a bearing on deterrence and defence, and is therefore discussed under the relevant heading in Part 4 of this book, it should be emphasised that it has a dual purpose and was set up for the joint benefit of both civilian and military users of the airspace. Its task involves a permanent effort to establish acceptable compromises which take account of civil and military requirements without jeopardising the vital interests of either.

[2] ICAO is a United Nations specialised agency set up by the Convention on International Civil Aviation (signed at Chicago on December 7, 1944), which coordinates international civil aviation. It has 157 member states.

[3] IATA includes most of the world airlines; it was set up in Havana in April 1945. Its aim is to promote safe and economical air transport, to provide means of coordination between air transport companies, and to cooperate with other international organisations such as ICAO.

(EUROCONTROL)[4] are invited to attend as observers when subjects of concern to their organisations are being studied.

One of CEAC's long-term basic tasks is to encourage better and more uniform civil/military air traffic control throughout NATO Europe. Committee studies have led to improved conditions for all airspace users by promoting the compatibility of civil and military airspace organisations and air traffic control systems and procedures; establishing joint civil/military control centres; and providing for joint civil/military use of radars. Furthermore, joint civil/military air/ground/air communications, navigational aid and associated frequency requirements are coordinated in one overall plan for the European part of the NATO area.

Air Exercises

Exercises play a fundamental role in the training and readiness of military forces. During large-scale air exercises, large numbers of sorties lead to congested airspace and necessitate special arrangements in respect of airspace organisation and control to ensure safe, economic and flexible operations for civil and military aircraft. It may, for example, be necessary to redelineate certain airways and to restrict the operating altitudes of civil aircraft, as well as restricting military operations in high density civil traffic areas. The Committee for European Airspace Coordination has established methods and procedures to effect this coordination and draws up an overall plan for each exercise which describes the area, date and time of the exercise, as well as measures to be taken by non-exercise aircraft to ensure their safe and economic passage. This plan is published by nations in Notices to Airmen in adequate time for all air crews to acquaint themselves with the conditions they will encounter and the measures to be taken. The Committee's work in this area has improved operating conditions for all airspace users and promoted safety in today's complex and congested airspace, while at the same time avoiding unacceptable penalties on airline operations and maintaining the essential training requirements of NATO air forces.

Rapid Reinforcement of Europe

One of the prerequisites for maintaining the continuous air flow which would be required for the rapid reinforcement of the European countries in times of tension and war is that national air traffic services should continue to operate effectively and to be able to respond to NATO requirements. To ensure that national plans for these situations are coherent and compatible

---

[4] EUROCONTROL is an international organisation composed of Belgium, France, the Federal Republic of Germany, Greece, the Republic of Ireland, Luxembourg, Malta, the Netherlands, Portugal, Turkey and the United Kingdom. Through the EUROCONTROL Agency the member states coordinate objectives, plans, training and research and development for air traffic services for civil aviation. The Agency itself provides air traffic services in parts of the airspace of Belgium, the Netherlands, Luxembourg and the Federal Republic of Germany.

NATO-wide, the Committee on European Airspace Coordination coordinates and promotes such plans, in close liaison with the NATO Military Commands and other agencies concerned, notably the Civil Aviation Planning Committee.

Future Challenges

There is certainly no lack of challenges in the field of European Airspace Coordination in the next decade. Air traffic management in many parts of Europe is experiencing alarming problems caused by a traffic volume which the supporting air traffic control and airport structure simply cannot handle at peak times. Efforts are being made to increase the capacity of the national systems and to improve coordination between them. However, the fact is that the increase in civil air traffic over the last few years has been in the order of 12-16% as opposed to a projected increase of 3-5%. It is therefore likely that congestion and delays to flights will be a feature of air travel at peak times for a number of years to come. While this situation is clearly of concern to the air transport industry, the potential impact on military operations is also considerable. In these circumstances, it is obvious that the closest possible civil/military coordination, both nationally and internationally, is more imperative than ever. Furthermore, the introduction of increasingly complex, automated systems both for air defence and air traffic control, involving systems like the NATO Air Command and Control System, the NATO Identification System, and the NAVSTAR GPS navigation aid, makes such coordination essential for operational as well as economic reasons.

Although current European airspace problems are essentially of a civilian character, the Committee is actively considering how it might contribute to alleviating them in terms of civil/military cooperation, both nationally and internationally. The Committee's considerations include promoting the agreed concept of flexible shared civil/military use of airspace, including temporarily reserved military airspace. Member states in the most critical area of NATO Europe have in fact increasingly implemented this concept to the extent that it is compatible with air safety and still provides the essential freedom of operation required by the military users of the airspace to carry out their missions.

Recent problems of acute air traffic congestion and delays in Europe have resulted in calls for immediate remedial action both at national and international level. While the International Civil Aviation Organisation is the worldwide organisation responsible for civil aviation matters, and EUROCONTROL plays an important part in the European planning process, the Committee for European Airspace Coordination remains the only international forum where both NATO and national military requirements can be taken fully into account in a management forum exclusively concerned with civil and military airspace matters. This forum is likely to become even more important in future in view of the dramatic surge in civil traffic following deregulation, and the fact that civil and military users will have to continue to share the European airspace in an equitable way.

Part 5

NATO's Third Dimension

Chapter 20
Scientific Cooperation

Science and security

"Security is far more than a military matter. The strengthening of political consultation and economic cooperation, the development of resources, progress in education and public understanding, all these can be as important for the protection of the security of a nation, or an alliance, as the building of a battleship or the equipping of an army". (Report of the Committee of Three on Non-Military Cooperation in NATO, December 1956).

Security is concerned as much with providing freedom from political pressure or blackmail and an ideological environment in which democracy and human rights remain sacrosanct as it is with providing defence against physical aggression. The concept of mutual security likewise includes a broad range of security concerns of a global nature, including the protection of the physical environment, the management of natural resources and the welfare of peoples. There is a vital need for international cooperation in science and technology in an increasingly interdependent world. This philosophy, upon which the work of the NATO Science Committee is based, appears even more compelling now than in 1957, when the Science Programme was established. National and international security are directly related to progress in science and technology, and it is in this awareness that NATO continues to support different types of international scientific collaboration—a task which has come to be regarded as the "third dimension" of the Alliance.

Origins of the NATO Science Programme

The 1956 report of the Committee of Three to the North Atlantic Council, from which the quotation above is taken, stated that progress in the field of science and technology "is so crucial to the future of the Atlantic community that NATO members should ensure that every possibility of fruitful cooperation is examined". Against the background of the more general need for individual member countries to adopt more positive scientific policies, the Committee of Three pointed to the central and urgent problem of improving the recruitment, training and utilisation of scientists, engineers and technicians.

The Council adopted the recommendations of the Committee of Three, and a Task Force on Scientific and Technical Cooperation was appointed in June 1957. While emphasising that national efforts must continue to form the basis of any generalised action, the Task Force believed NATO had a constructive role to play, given that "the future of the West is dependent to an ever-increasing degree on the rate at which science and technology advance". The challenge lay in encouraging member goverments to carry out national programmes to develop their scientific and technical resources; organising international activities with a view to economising national resources and stimulating exchanges; and cooperating with other agencies active in the scientific field.

The Task Force carried out its deliberations with an urgency which was given additional emphasis by the launching of the first Soviet Sputnik satellite in October 1957. The political and scientific implications of this event resulted in the Task Force Report being presented directly to the Heads of Government of the Alliance at their meeting in December 1957. Two specific recommendations were adopted. Firstly, a Science Committee was established to develop its own programme in the light of circumstances, with the broad responsiblity of advising the Council on how NATO could fulfil the role ascribed to it by the Task Force Report. Secondly the position of Science Adviser was created on the International Staff to give impetus and direction to the work of the Committee, and to act as the Secretary General's adviser on scientific questions. The work of the Science Committee rapidly increased in importance, and it was not long before the Science Adviser was made Assistant Secretary General for Scientific Affairs, with a staff of scientists forming the Scientific Affairs Division of the International Staff. With the establishment of the Committee on the Challenges of Modern Society in 1969, the Division also became involved with environmental matters and in 1973, the title was changed to Assistant Secretary General for Scientific and Environmental Affairs.

The NATO Science Committee

The NATO Science Committee, which meets three times a year, and is chaired by the Assistant Secretary General for Scientific and Environmental Affairs, is composed of national representatives qualified to speak authoritatively on science policy in the name of their respective governments. The Science Committee is charged with the overall task of stimulating and strengthening science within the Atlantic Alliance. The Assistant Secretary General for Scientific and Environmental Affairs, with the aid of his scientific staff, is responsible for promoting cooperative action and implementing the Committee's decisions, administering science programmes, and advising the Secretary General of NATO on scientific matters. He is assisted in this work by groups or panels of experts in different areas of science. The willingness of high-level scientists to put their professional expertise at the disposal of the Scientific Affairs Division has been of inestimable value in setting and maintaining a high scientific standard throughout.

The first meeting of the Science Committee was held in March 1958. During its first year of existence, the Committee examined a large number of proposals for strengthening science in the NATO countries. Three main programmes were established, which remain the backbone of NATO science activities: the Science Fellowships Programme, the Advanced Study Institutes Programme, and the Collaborative Research Grants Programme.

In 1976, the Science Committee commemorated its 20th Anniversary by organising a major conference aimed at taking stock of the impact of science and technology on Western societies and examining future challenges to the Western scientific establishment, including methods of interacting in more meaningful ways with increasingly complex societal issues. The conference was attended not only by scientists but also by Ministers of Science, senior parliamentarians, senior officials responsible for national science policy, heads of national research councils and prominent industrialists.

By 1987, the Science Committee was able to look back on 30 years of catalytic action to enhance the scientific and technological capability of the Alliance. Through periodic reviews of its purposes and methodology, it had also been able to modify its programmes and policy where necessary to keep abreast of changing scientific and social conditions. A major review was undertaken during 1988 by Deputy Permanent Representatives, following which the value and efficiency of the programmes were confirmed. A number of recommendations are now being implemented to improve the impact of the Science Programme.

The NATO Science Programme

The NATO Science Programme is the only cooperative international effort embodying multilateral government support for advancing the frontiers of modern science through high-level basic research. This activity in which scientists of both the advanced and the developing nations of the Alliance participate on an equal basis—has proved to be of real benefit in strengthening science in all the member countries of NATO. It has shown itself to be not only an extremely useful vehicle for trans-Atlantic communication in this field, but also a valuable method of fostering intra-European cooperation where there is evidence of surprising insularity.

Over 200,000 people have directly participated in the NATO Science Programme including several thousand from countries outside the Alliance. Participants are members of the international scientific community engaged in professional work of national concern who play a significant role in decision-making in their countries. The ties engendered between them, brought about by the close cooperation implicit in the NATO programmes, have endured and grown. Many more scientists have also been served by widely disseminated publications which carry the results achieved by NATO programmes well beyond the circle of their immediate participants.

Most activities under the NATO Science Programme take the form of international scientific exchange programmes which promote collaboration by encouraging mobility among scientists in an international sense. However, unlike many international scientific programmes which are institution or project oriented, the NATO programmes are focussed on individual scientists.

To implement these programmes, the Science Committee currently has an annual budget of some 780 million Belgian francs (about US $20 million), allocated as follows:

Science Fellowships Programme	51 %
Collaborative Research Grants Programme	17 %
Advanced Study Institutes Programme	17 %
Advanced Research Workshops Programme	6 %
Special Programmes	8 %
Planning and Support	1 %

In addition to its scientific exchange programmes, the Science Committee sponsors a programme of scientific and technological assistance to three Alliance countries. This programme, known as Science for Stability, was set up in 1980 in response to the Committee's deep concern about the growing disparity in scientific and technological capabilities within the Alliance. The programme, with an annual budget of approximately 145 million Belgian francs (about US$ 3.5 million), aims at strengthening national infrastructure for scientific and technological management in Greece, Portugal and Turkey.

The programmes are managed by the staff of the Scientific Affairs Division, with the assistance of panels of scientists drawn from all countries of the Alliance. Each of the programmes is described in more detail below. The Scientific Affairs Division also publishes further information brochures on the Science Programmes and a quarterly newsletter called "Science and Society".

NATO International Scientific Exchange Programmes

The Science Fellowships Programme

The need for new scientists to be trained, and for established scientists to be given the opportunity to further and renew their specialised education and scientific training, was recognised by NATO Heads of Government when, in December 1957, they agreed that more should be done to increase the supply of trained scientists in many branches of science and technology. A period of training abroad for young scientists and an opportunity to engage in research outside their own countries are recognised as normal and effective ways of pursuing a scientific career. The possibilities for obtaining scholarships for such purposes were very limited in many countries and in 1959 the Science Committee therefore established the NATO Science Fellowships Programme.

No fellowships programme on the same scale had previously been undertaken by an international organisation. Experience has also shown that the NATO programme has favourably stimulated an active national fellowships programme of at least comparable magnitude in most member countries.

During the early 1960s, some 1,000 Science Fellowships were awarded annually. As the amount of each stipend increased owing to inflation and the rising standard of living in the member countries, the number of fellowships levelled off at between 700 and 750 per year during the 1970s. Today about 1,300 fellowships are awarded each year. Since the programme started, over 19,000 scientists have benefited from NATO Science Fellowships which have enabled them to study overseas for periods of about one year or longer. The United States has received about 60 % of all the fellows, but many other NATO countries, particularly the United Kingdom, France and the Federal Republic of Germany, have also acted as host countries. The fellows study a large number of subjects. Chemistry and physics are the most popular, but biology and engineering also attract a large percentage.

The Science Committee decided at the outset to entrust the administration of its Fellowships Programme to agencies in the member countries who would be best able to judge national requirements. This mandate to the agencies concerned to manage international funds on behalf of NATO enables each country to direct support towards its chosen age range, scientific fields and professions, as well as to decide on the most appropriate level of financial support to individual fellows. Retaining overall responsibility, the Science Committee safeguards the international characteristics of the Programme. The criteria for selection and the eligibility conditions vary somewhat from country to country, but applications are considered by independent committees of specialised and senior scientists and are judged on scientific merit.

The Collaborative Research Grants Programme

Economic and social progress depend upon scientific research, which can be enhanced by pooling the capabilities and resources of different groups of scientists. This programme contributes to the advancement of fundamental knowledge by stimulating collaborative research carried out by scientists in different member countries.

NATO research grants assist projects which rely mainly on national funding, where the element of international collaboration entails costs that cannot be met from other sources. The specific research projects supported under the programme are carried out as joint efforts between teams working in university, government and other research institutes. The main support provided under this programme includes travel and living expenses for researchers working in each other's institutions abroad.

Most fields of science are eligible for support, emphasis being given to fundamental aspects rather than to technological development, although projects in the basic and applied sciences with promising areas of application are also funded. At present, in certain fields (e.g. nuclear physics, experimental high energy physics, space research, and clinical medicine) or in areas where other international agencies are already active, support is not generally provided to very large projects. Both theoreticians and experimentalists are involved in most projects, and a sizeable amount of the research is of an interdisciplinary nature.

Grants are awarded for an initial period of one year. Upon demonstration of significant progress, these may be renewed, but projects are normally supported for a limited period and after about four years are expected to have reached a conclusion.

Since its inception in 1960, this programme has funded well over 6,000 projects. At the present time, about 450 new projects receive support each year, with an average initial award of $6,000. Over 600 publications of research results made possible through NATO's support appear each year.

The Advanced Study Institutes Programme (ASIs)

A major factor in pursuing the objective of furthering national collaboration amongst scientists from member countries has been the wide-reaching and perhaps the most successful programme of the Science Committee, the Advanced Study Institutes Programme. Each year, the programme sponsors about 60 institutes, with 70-100 scientists attending each meeting. The aim of the programme is to contribute to the dissemination of advanced knowledge and to the formation of international contacts among scientists. A NATO Advanced Study Institute is primarily a high-level teaching activity, at which a carefully defined subject is presented in a systematic and coherently structured programme. The subject is treated in considerable depth by lecturers eminent in their field and normally of international standing; it is presented to other scientists specialising in the field or with an advanced general background. Advanced Study Institutes are aimed at audiences of approximately post-doctorate level, but this does not exclude post-graduate students and it may well include senior scientists of high qualifications and notable achievement in the subject of the Institute or in related fields.

Subjects treated at the institutes vary as widely as the nationality of participants. Meetings have been held on subjects ranging from mathematics and astronomy to biological and medical topics, and embracing such areas as psychological measurement theory and language programming for computers. Certain institutes are organised as interdisciplinary meetings. In such cases, the didactic aspect of the meeting consists of scientists specialised in one field teaching scientists highly qualified in a different area. The role of the teacher and the taught can then be interchanged during the meeting as themes of common interest are developed from the viewpoint of different sciences.

The Advanced Study Institutes Programme seeks to improve the general level of scientific competence throughout the NATO area, and provides the added benefit of high-level scientific exchange in interdisciplinary areas which are rarely found in university curricula. The programme is considered unique and is highly regarded in the scientific community. Since its inception in 1959, the programme has supported more than 1,600 Advanced Study Institutes, in which over 140,000 scientists have participated, many of them leaders in their fields. A further benefit of the ASIs is the publication of proceedings, of which about three-quarters appear in book form. These have been generally recognised as authoritative surveys of their subjects and have reached a very large audience, both inside and outside the Alliance. In 1973, an agreement was reached with four international publishers to publish a uniform series of NATO Advanced Study Institute Proceedings. Over 1,000 books have been published in this series, which is growing by more than 100 books a year.

The Advanced Research Workshops Programme (ARWs)

During the 1970s the Science Committee sponsored a series of conferences designed to focus attention on new scientific opportunities, seeking a consensus on assessments of past research and recommendations for future research which would be of value to the scientific community. These conferences were managed by Scientific Affairs Division staff, and it was possible to organise only two each year.

With this experience, and in an effort to respond to the many requests for support received for meetings which did not fit into the Advanced Study Institutes format, the Science Committee decided in 1981 to convene a group of experts to advise on the objectives, format and conditions for a workshop-type activity. The Advanced Research Workshops Programme was the outcome. It was agreed that this Programme would fill an obvious need, as no other organisation sponsored such a general purpose programme of workshops and more importantly no regular national funding existed within member countries to fund international working meetings of this kind.

From the eight workshops funded in 1981, the Advanced Research Workshops Programme has grown into an important and popular series of some 50 meetings a year. About 250 had been held by the end of 1988. An Advanced Research Workshop is principally distinguished from other types of scientific meeting by the accent on intensive discussions among prominent experts in a given scientific area for some five days. From 20 to 40 scientists attend each workshop. All scientific areas are considered for support and workshops have been held on such varied topics as Immunotoxicology, Ethical Issues in Preventive Medicine, Microstructures in Non Equilibrium Systems, the Undercooled Melt, Mycological Examination of Food, and Somites in Developing Embryos.

Special Programmes

To complement its basic multidisciplinary interaction programmes, the Science Committee has for many years sponsored short-term "special programmes" in specific scientific fields. In earlier years the areas studied were rather wide, for example Oceanography, Meteorology and Human Factors. More recently, however, the subjects have been much more narrowly defined, and have been selected for concentrated support for a limited period as emerging scientific areas or fields undergoing rapid change. A Special Programme has an active life of five years, and has a further year in which the work accomplished is reviewed, and recommendations are made on appropriate research directions which hold promise for the future.

The programmes supported at present are listed below. Further programmes are to be established during 1989:
— Condensed Systems of Low Dimensionality (1985-1989)
— Advanced Educational Technology (1988-1992)
— Chaos, Order and Patterns: Aspects of Nonlinearity (1988-1992)

Science for Stability

The Science for Stability Programme arose out of the political determination of member countries of the Alliance to provide concrete assistance, in the spirit of Article 2 of the North Atlantic Treaty, to the economically less prosperous members. The Programme was approved by the North Atlantic Council in June 1980, and became fully operational in 1981.

The principal objective of the Programme is to assist Greece, Portugal and Turkey in enhancing their scientific and technological infrastructures through the realisation of specific research and development projects. The projects are chosen by national authorities to fit within their priorities for economic development. Particular attention is devoted to strengthening cooperation between universities, public research institutes and private industrial companies. They are essentially joint ventures of significance to the development of the scientific, engineering and technological capabilities of these countries.

The Programme supplements national resources allocated to the projects by funding for equipment, foreign technical and managerial expertise and the training abroad of scientists and engineers.

In the first phase of the Programme, coming to an end in 1988, 15 projects—five in each country—were undertaken. Most of the projects are convincingly achieving both their organisational and economic development goals.

A second phase of the Programme was approved in 1986; a new series of multi-year projects authorised in 1987 and 1988 will continue through 1992. The entire Programme now comprises some 30 projects in agronomy, aquaculture, water resources, mining, energy, computer science, microelectronics, biotechnology, transportation, remote sensing, archeology, oceanography and food chemistry. The NATO contribution to an individual project may be spread over several years and varies between US$ 200,000 and US$ 1 million.

Science Policy

In addition to establishing scientific programmes designed to respond to the more immediate needs, the Science Committee has concerned itself with studying the long-term aspects of scientific development in the Western world. In early 1959, the Committee set up a special study group chaired by Louis Armand, and including some of the most distinguished scientists in the NATO countries, to examine the factors tending to retard the development of science in the Western world. The factors impeding science are often political and administrative, frequently resulting from a failure to appreciate the nature of science and of the conditions necessary for its growth. The Armand Report, published in 1960 under the title "Increasing the Effectiveness of Western Science", addressed itself primarily to such matters. Many of its recommendations have been translated into general practice, and it has also served the wider purpose of inspiring governments to give serious thought to the problems discussed.

Following the 20th Anniversary Commemoration Conference in 1978, the Science Committee decided to hold more frequent discussions on policy issues so as to focus on problems, needs and trends and to help bring about a more dynamic research system in NATO countries. This decision reflects the manner in which the Committee's role vis-à-vis questions of national and international science policy has evolved, as has its attitude towards the potential for influencing both policy and its effects on the development of science and technology in member countries. The Committee has instituted a series of Forum Discussions, at which a particular topic is introduced for critical debate. The resulting assessments provide the Committee with the means of advising governmental science and research organisations on the maintenance and improvement of scientific and technological capabilities, as well as assisting it in reviewing its own programme and in carrying out its advisory role to the North Atlantic Council.

The von Karman Institute for Fluid Dynamics

The NATO scientific community maintains close contact with the von Karman Institute (VKI) for Fluid Dynamics, an international non profit-making scientific organisation whose activities are dedicated to post-graduate training and research in fundamental and applied fluid dynamics. The Institute, located in Brussels, was founded in 1956 under the auspices of the Advisory Group for Aerospace Research and Development (AGARD) and with the inspiration and leadership of Dr. Theordore von Karman, who served as the Chairman of the Board of Directors until his death in 1963. The Institute has a number of closely inter-related academic and research programmes aimed at providing post-graduate education, encouraging research and contributing to the dissemination of knowledge in the field of fluid dynamics.

Chapter 21
Environmental Challenges

The creation of the Committee on the Challenges of Modern Society (CCMS) was proposed at the 20th Anniversary Meeting of the North Atlantic Alliance at Washington in April 1969. The then American President, Richard Nixon, called for the creation of "a committee on the challenges of modern society ... to explore ways in which the experience and resources of the Western nations could most effectively be marshalled toward improving the quality of life of our peoples", and to help 20th Century man learn "how to remain in harmony with his rapidly-changing world".

NATO established the Committee on the Challenges of Modern Society on November 6, 1969. Its aim was to attack practical problems already under study at the national level and, by combining the expertise and technology available in member countries, to arrive fairly rapidly at valid conclusions and make recommendations for action to benefit all.

Cooperation in NATO towards the improvement of the quality of life in modern society evolved both from the terms of the North Atlantic Treaty and from the experience of the Alliance during its first twenty years. Article 2 of the Treaty provides that member countries will contribute towards the further development of peaceful and friendly international relations by promoting conditions of stability and well-being. This Article also served as the basis for the statement in the report of the Committee of Three, established in 1956 to advise the North Atlantic Council on ways of improving and extending NATO cooperation in non-military fields, that "from the very beginning of NATO ... it was recognised that while defence cooperation was the first and most urgent requirement, this was not enough". The Committee of Three recommended that science and technology should be considered of special importance. The programme of scientific and technical cooperation undertaken by the Science Committee, which was created as a result of that report (see Chapter 20), provided an important precedent for the work of CCMS, especially in the interchange and practical application of technological and scientific information.

How the CCMS works

In creating the CCMS, the North Atlantic Council decided that the Committee would not itself engage in any research activities, and that its work would be carried out on an entirely decentralised basis, without building new bureaucratic structures within the NATO International Staff. No programme funds for CCMS activities were made available through the NATO budget. Four concepts therefore characterise the work of the Committee.

Firstly, its work is undertaken by member countries acting as pilot countries for specific projects. Working with other interested countries (including many countries not members of the North Atlantic Treaty Organisation), each pilot country is responsible for developing, conducting, and disseminating the results of a pilot study. Co-pilot countries and other participants share the workload according to the level of their interest in the particular subject. No member is required to participate in any study; on the contrary, each country is free to choose where best to apply its resources and expertise. Results, on the other hand, are available to all. In this way, nations whose priorities might prevent them from devoting large-scale resources to a particular problem can contribute to projects selectively while continuing to benefit from the programme as a whole.

Secondly, emphasis is placed on projects which can guide policy formulation and stimulate domestic and international action. While often identifying new areas for research in its "action orientation", the CCMS has sought to make the results of research accessible to policy makers and to make the latter more sensitive to environmental concerns.

Thirdly, the CCMS is an outward-looking and open organisation. On subjects that were also the concern of specialised international organisations in existence before the CCMS was formed, the Committee developed complementary pilot studies. Examples of these areas are health, meteorology, and maritime issues. In areas where the CCMS was in the vanguard of international activity— e.g. energy conservation and alternative energy sources— its studies have helped define frameworks for bilateral and multilateral international cooperation.

Finally, the CCMS has developed a follow-up procedure, which reflects the Allies' concern that the CCMS should play a positive role in national and international environmental activities. Each pilot country assumes responsibility for ensuring that its study has an effective and an appropriate role in stimulating national and international action.

These four concepts—the pilot country leadership; stimulation of national and international action; open participation and results; and follow-up— are the essential components of the CCMS approach. Together, they make the Committee unique among fora for international cooperation.

The Pilot Studies

35 CCMS pilot studies have been completed and 12 are currently underway. The studies cover a large spectrum of activities dealing with many aspects of environmental protection and the quality of life. The studies completed were devoted to:

— Advanced Health care
— Advanced Waste Water Treatment
— Air Pollution
— Air Pollution Assessment Methodology and Modelling
— Air Pollution Control Strategies and Impact Modelling
— Automotive Propulsion Systems

— Coastal Water Pollution and Ocean Oil Spills
— Conservation/Restoration of Monuments
— Contaminated Land
— Dioxin Problems
— Disaster Assistance
— Disposal of Hazardous Wastes — Phases I and II
— Drinking Water
— Environmental and Regional Planning
— Flue-Gas Desulphurisation
— Forest Fires
— Geothermal Energy
— Health and Medical Aspects of Disaster Preparedness
— Improvement of Emergency Medical Services
— Inland Water Pollution
— Integrated Pest Management
— Management of Estuarine Systems (Phase I)
— Nutrition and Health
— Plastic Wastes Recovery
— Rational Use of Energy
— Regulations concerning the Application and Production of Pheromones
— Remote Sensing for the Control of Marine Pollution
— Risk Management of Chemicals in the Environment
— Road Safety
— Role of Transportation in Urban Revitalisation
— Rural Passenger Transportation
— Seismology and Earthquake Loss Reduction
— Solar Energy
— Urban Transportation
— Utilisation and Disposal of Municipal Sewage Sludge

Current studies are concerned with:

— Aircraft Noise in a Modern Society
— Assessment of the Risk of Accidental Pollution from the Shipping of Dangerous Products
— Conservation of Historic Brick Structures
— Disaster Preparedness Plans responding to Chemical Accidents
— Estuarine Management (Phase II)
— Indoor Air Quality
— Opportunities offered by Remote Sensing in setting up Models designed to anticipate Maritime Pollution Movements
— Preservation of Historic Stained Glass
— Promotion of Environmental Awareness in the Armed Forces
— Protection of Astronomic and Geophysical Sites
— Remedial Action Technologies for Contaminated Land and Groundwater
— Training in Environmental Problems

Most of the studies consist of several components. Thus, the pilot study on geothermal energy consisted of several projects in the area of computer-based information systems, direct (i.e. non-electrical) uses, multipurpose processing and disposal of geothermal brines, small electric power-plants and hot dry rock concepts. The project on dioxin problems dealt with exposure hazards, technology and the management of accidents. The current study on aircraft noise includes sub-sections on source technology, receiver technology and aircraft operations. Both completed and on-going studies are described in more detail in other publications which can be obtained from the Scientific Affairs Division (CCMS), NATO, B-1110 Brussels.

Seminars

As an element of a defensive organisation, it is wholly appropriate that NATO's Committee on the Challenges of Modern Society should take an interest in the effect on the environment of defence activities in peacetime. This interest has taken the form of a series of international seminars—frequently attended by participants of Ministerial level—which have examined various aspects of this question. There have been six seminars in this series since it was launched in 1980:
— General effect on the environment of defence activities (Munich);
— Environmental impact assessments in the defence area (Hamburg);
— Environmental technical information systems (Heidelberg);
— Noise abatement near airfields (Utrecht);
— Land-use planning for defence purposes (Munich);
— Aircraft noise in a modern society (Mittenwald).

Environmental Round Table

Since the first Plenary Meeting of the Committee on the Challenges of Modern Society in December 1969, the organisation has served as a forum for the informal exchange of information and opinions on environmental issues. At the 1971 Autumn Plenary Meeting, this "review of national policies" officially became known as the Environmental Round Table. At a time when little relevant research and development had been carried out and national policies had not been established, the CCMS Round Table provided an opportunity for nations to compare problems, frustrations and successes.

As the CCMS reached its fifth anniversary, however, it became clear that the Round Table, to a great extent, had fulfilled its function in this area. From 1975, based on a proposal by the United Kingdom, each Environmental Round Table has been devoted to a specific topic. The resulting exchanges of information have been timely and valuable.

Their success led naturally to the first meeting of Environmental Ministers under CCMS auspices. This took place in Brussels in November 1980 when Ministers of the Environment and other senior officials from Alliance countries came together to exchange information and ideas on national planning and to review a range of environmental problems, including, in particular, problems relating to energy, chemicals and environmental planning itself.

CCMS Fellowship Programme

The CCMS sponsors a small Fellowship Programme, which provides modest grants to a number of individuals each year, to encourage studies in public policy related to the natural or social environment which are linked to the Committee's on-going pilot projects.

Publications

CCMS publications offer comprehensive and up-to-date information of a technical nature resulting from the pilot studies. They are of considerable value both to technical people and to government decision-makers. More than 170 publications have been made available under CCMS auspices.

Part 6

Organisation and Structures

Figure 8

The North Atlantic Council, the highest authority in NATO, provides a forum for wide political consultation and coordination between the allies. Military policy is discussed in the Defence Planning Committee (DPC) composed of all member countries except France. The Council and the DPC meet twice yearly in ministerial meetings when member countries are represented by Foreign and Defence Ministers. In permanent session the Council meets at least once a week at the level of Ambassadors (Permanent Representatives). The Secretary General of NATO is Chairman of the Council and the DPC and also heads the International Staff. In support of their roles, the Council and the DPC have established a number of committees covering the whole range of NATO's activities which normally meet under the chairmanship of a member of the International Staff.

The Military Committee, composed of the Chiefs-of-Staff of all member countries except France and Iceland, is the senior military authority in the Alliance. It provides advice to the Council or DPC on military matters and gives guidance to the Major NATO Commanders. Meeting at Chiefs-of-Staff level at least twice a year, the Committee in permanent session meets weekly at the level of national Military Representatives appointed by their Chiefs-of-Staff. The Chairman of the Military Committee is elected by the Chiefs-of-Staff for a period of 3 years. Implementation of the policies and decisions of the Military Committee is ensured by the International Military Staff (IMS) which acts as executive agency. The NATO defence area is divided into three separate regional Commands—Allied Command Europe, Allied Command Atlantic and Allied Command Channel—and a Regional Planning Group for the North American area. Each regional command is the responsibility of a Major NATO Commander or "MNC". These are known respectively as the Supreme Allied Commander Europe (SACEUR), the Supreme Allied Commander Atlantic (SACLANT) and the Allied Commander-in-Chief Channel (CINCHAN). Under the general guidance of the Military Committee the Major NATO Commanders are responsible for planning the defence of their areas and for conducting NATO's land, sea and air exercises.

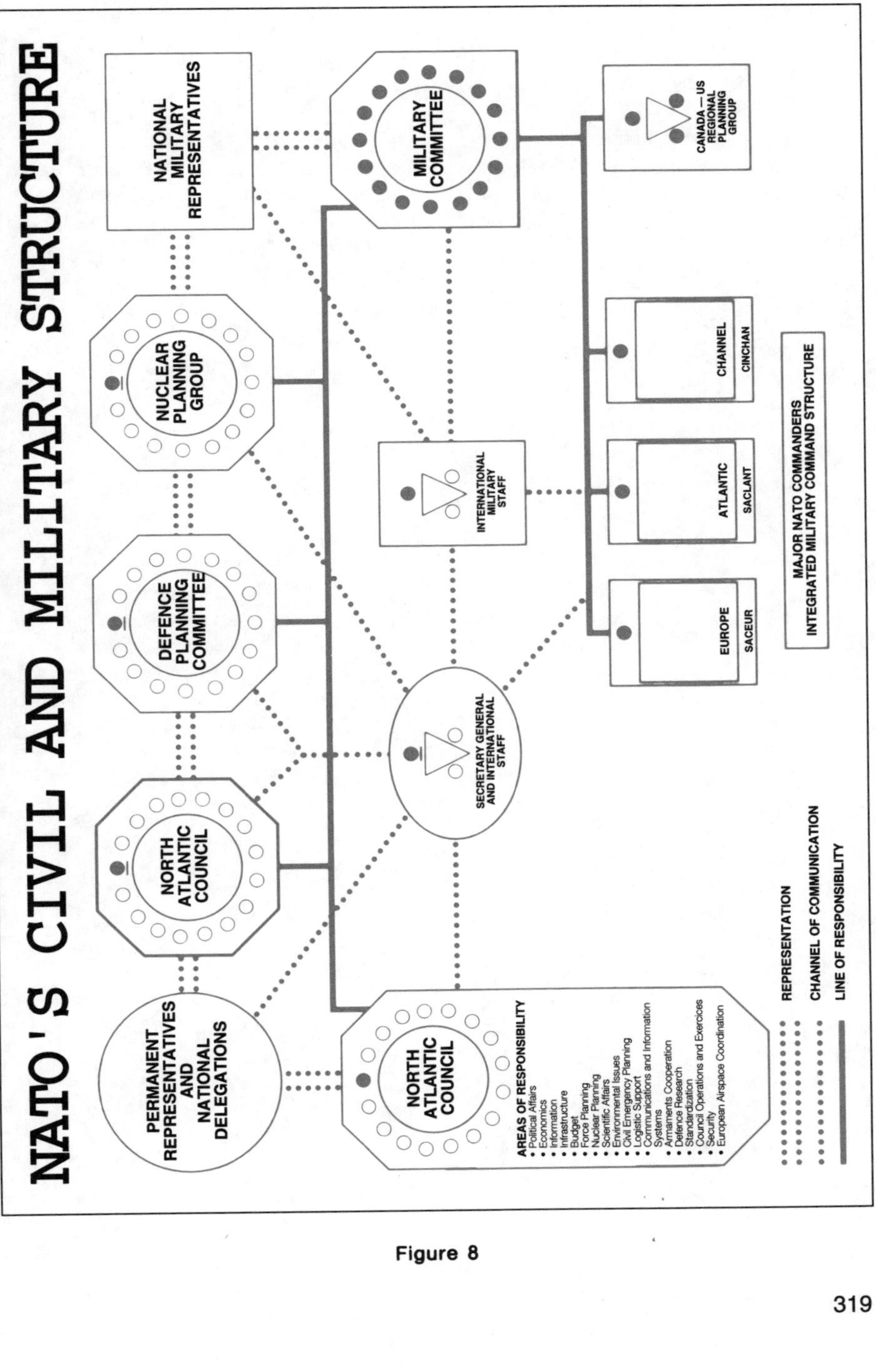

NATO'S CIVIL AND MILITARY STRUCTURE
PERMANENT REPRESENTATIVES AND NATIONAL DELEGATIONS
NORTH ATLANTIC COUNCIL
DEFENCE PLANNING COMMITTEE
NUCLEAR PLANNING GROUP
NATIONAL MILITARY REPRESENTATIVES
NORTH ATLANTIC COUNCIL
SECRETARY GENERAL AND INTERNATIONAL STAFF
INTERNATIONAL MILITARY STAFF
MILITARY COMMITTEE
AREAS OF RESPONSIBILITY
• Political Affairs
• Economics
• Information
• Infrastructure
• Budget
• Force Planning
• Nuclear Planning
• Scientific Affairs
• Environmental Issues
• Civil Emergency Planning
• Logistic Support
• Communications and Information Systems
• Armaments Cooperation
• Defence Research
• Standardization
• Council Operations and Exercices
• Security
• European Airspace Coordination
EUROPE
SACEUR
ATLANTIC
SACLANT
CHANNEL
CINCHAN
CANADA — US REGIONAL PLANNING GROUP
MAJOR NATO COMMANDERS INTEGRATED MILITARY COMMAND STRUCTURE
REPRESENTATION
CHANNEL OF COMMUNICATION
LINE OF RESPONSIBILITY

Figure 8

Chapter 22

NATO's Civilian Structure

What is the Council?

When negotiations leading to the North Atlantic Treaty culminated in April 1949 in the signature of the Treaty, the process of creating the Alliance began in earnest. Under Article 9 of the Treaty, the governments of the member countries had established a Council, on which each of them was to be represented, to consider matters concerning the implementation of the Treaty. The Council's instructions were concise and to the point: it was to be so organised as to be able to meet promptly at any time; and it was to set up "such subsidiary bodies as may be necessary". All subsequent decisions which were taken to put in place the structures needed to implement the other provisions of the Treaty flowed from this mandate. The Council remains the principal authority of the Alliance and its task is to work towards the fulfillment of the Treaty's basic objective—international peace and the security of its member countries. It has no terms of reference other than the Treaty itself.

The Council meets at various levels—Ambassadors of each of the member countries (known as Permanent Representatives), Foreign Ministers or, on occasion, Heads of State or Government—but at whatever level it meets, its status remains the same, and its decisions have equal validity. NATO is not a supranational organisation. All the sovereign member countries have equal rights. Agreement is reached by common consent. There is no voting or decision by majority. Decisions are taken on the basis of unanimity. Once adopted by the Council they become binding and can only be reversed by the Council itself.

When the Council meets at the level of Permanent Representatives, it is known as the Council in permanent session. It also meets at least twice a year at the level of Foreign Ministers, normally once in Brussels and once in the capital of a member nation. On occasion, Defence and Finance Ministers have also attended these meetings. On several occasions (1957, 1974, 1975, 1977, 1978, 1982, 1985, 1988, and twice during 1989) it has met at "summit" level (Heads of Government or State).

Each government appoints a Permanent Representative to NATO, who is supported by staffs which vary in size. The role of the Permanent Representatives is to act, under instructions from their capitals, as spokesmen for their governments. In a reciprocal way, they are also the spokesmen of the Council in reporting back to their governments. Permanent Representatives represent not only their Foreign Minister but all departments of their government concerned with Alliance business.

Figure 9

The North Atlantic Council provides a unique forum for confidential and constant intergovernmental consultation. It represents the highest level of decision-making machinery within NATO. There is no supranational element in the Organisation. All 16 sovereign member countries have an equal right to express their views round the Council table and decisions are reached on the basis of consensus and mutual consent. Governments do not adopt specific policies because NATO requires them to do so—they are all parties to the formulation of NATO policies. Consultation between them therefore plays a fundamental role. Political consultation ranges over the whole field of foreign affairs and is not limited to NATO's geographical area. The only topics excluded are those relating to the purely internal affairs of member countries. Each national delegation is headed by a Permanent Representative with the rank of ambassador supported by staffs which vary in size. All act on instructions from their capitals and represent the views of their governments in NATO fora. Conversely they report back to their national authorities on the views expressed and positions taken by other governments and inform them of developments or movement towards consensus on important issues. Under the Chairmanship of the Secretary General, the Council provides a unique type of diplomatic workshop. To attain such a high degree of constant consultation between the 16 countries through bilateral diplomatic exchanges would be quite impracticable—in fact each meeting of the Council represents the equivalent of over 120 bilateral exchanges as shown by the lines in the diagram opposite. The colocation of the Permanent Delegations of all member countries in the same headquarters in Brussels also provides opportunities for continuous and regular informal consultation between the nations.

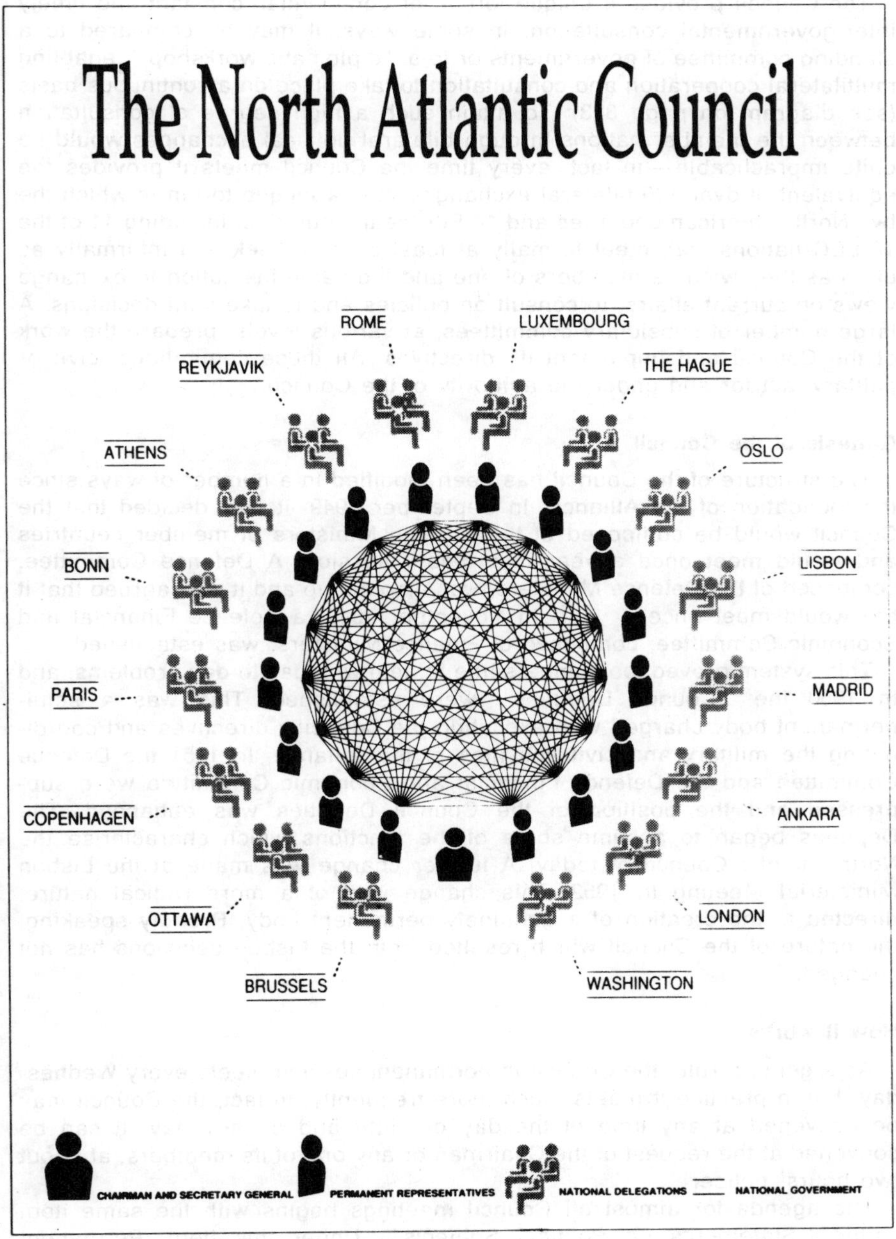
The North Atlantic Council
ROME
LUXEMBOURG
REYKJAVIK
THE HAGUE
ATHENS
OSLO
BONN
LISBON
PARIS
MADRID
COPENHAGEN
ANKARA
OTTAWA
LONDON
BRUSSELS
WASHINGTON
CHAIRMAN AND SECRETARY GENERAL
PERMANENT REPRESENTATIVES
NATIONAL DELEGATIONS
NATIONAL GOVERNMENT

Figure 9

The Council provides a unique forum for confidential, constant and timely inter-governmental consultation. In some ways, it may be compared to a standing committee of governments or to a "diplomatic workshop", enabling multilateral cooperation and consultation to take place on a continuous basis (see diagram on page 323). To attain such a high degree of consultation between the member nations through bilateral political exchanges would be quite impracticable—in fact, every time the Council meets it provides the equivalent of over 120 bilateral exchanges. It is a unique forum in which the two North American countries and 14 European countries, including 11 of the 12 EEC nations, can meet formally at least once a week and informally as often as they wish as members of one and the same institution to exchange views on current affairs, to consult on policies and to take joint decisions. A large number of subsidiary committees, at various levels, prepare the work of the Council and implement its directives. All these committees, civil or military, act for and under the authority of the Council.

Genesis of the Council

The structure of the Council has been modified in a number of ways since the foundation of the Alliance. In September 1949, it was decided that the Council would be composed of the Foreign Ministers of member countries and would meet once a year in ordinary session. A Defence Committee, composed of the Defence Ministers, was also set up and it was agreed that it too would meet once a year. In November 1949, a Defence Financial and Economic Committee, composed of Finance Ministers, was established.

This system proved too cumbersome to deal with day-to-day problems, and in 1950 the "Council Deputies" were established. This was a semi-permanent body charged with executing the Council's directives and coordinating the military and civil activities of the Alliance. In 1951 the Defence Committee and the Defence Financial and Economic Committee were suppressed and the position of the Council Deputies was enhanced. The Deputies began to assume some of the functions which characterise the North Atlantic Council of today. A further change was made at the Lisbon Ministerial Meeting in 1952. This change was of a more radical nature, directed at the creation of a genuinely permanent body. Broadly speaking, the nature of the Council which resulted from the Lisbon decisions has not changed.

How it works

As a general rule, the Council in permanent session meets every Wednesday, but in practice it meets much more frequently. In fact, the Council may be convened at any time of the day or night and on any day. It can be convened at the request of the Chairman or any one of its members, at about two hours' notice.

The agenda for almost all Council meetings begins with the same item called "Statements on Political Subjects". Under this item, Permanent Representatives are able to raise and discuss, in a restricted forum, topical

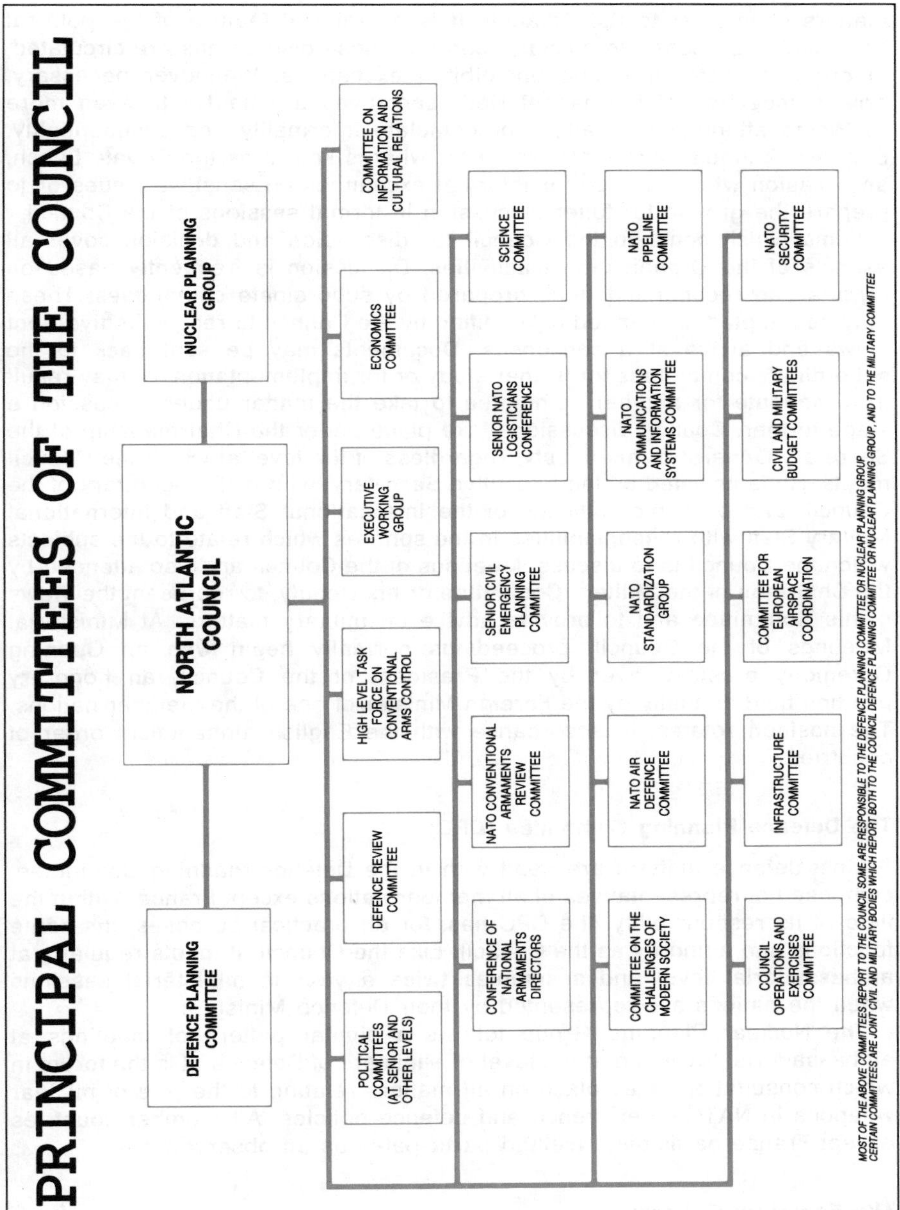
PRINCIPAL COMMITTEES OF THE COUNCIL
DEFENCE PLANNING COMMITTEE
NORTH ATLANTIC COUNCIL
NUCLEAR PLANNING GROUP
POLITICAL COMMITTEES (AT SENIOR AND OTHER LEVELS)
DEFENCE REVIEW COMMITTEE
HIGH LEVEL TASK FORCE ON CONVENTIONAL ARMS CONTROL
EXECUTIVE WORKING GROUP
ECONOMICS COMMITTEE
COMMITTEE ON INFORMATION AND CULTURAL RELATIONS
CONFERENCE OF NATIONAL ARMAMENTS DIRECTORS
NATO CONVENTIONAL ARMAMENTS REVIEW COMMITTEE
SENIOR CIVIL EMERGENCY PLANNING COMMITTEE
SENIOR NATO LOGISTICIANS CONFERENCE
SCIENCE COMMITTEE
COMMITTEE ON THE CHALLENGES OF MODERN SOCIETY
NATO AIR DEFENCE COMMITTEE
NATO STANDARDIZATION GROUP
NATO COMMUNICATIONS AND INFORMATION SYSTEMS COMMITTEE
NATO PIPELINE COMMITTEE
COUNCIL OPERATIONS AND EXERCISES COMMITTEE
INFRASTRUCTURE COMMITTEE
COMMITTEE FOR EUROPEAN AIRSPACE COORDINATION
CIVIL AND MILITARY BUDGET COMMITTEES
NATO SECURITY COMMITTEE
MOST OF THE ABOVE COMMITTEES REPORT TO THE COUNCIL SOME ARE RESPONSIBLE TO THE DEFENCE PLANNING COMMITTEE OR NUCLEAR PLANNING GROUP
CERTAIN COMMITTEES ARE JOINT CIVIL AND MILITARY BODIES WHICH REPORT BOTH TO THE COUNCIL DEFENCE PLANNING COMMITTEE OR NUCLEAR PLANNING GROUP, AND TO THE MILITARY COMMITTEE

Figure 10

matters of interest to the Alliance. It is a practical feature of the political consultation process. No official records of these discussions are circulated, in order to foster free and uninhibited exchanges. Whenever necessary, private meetings of Permanent Representatives are held with even more restricted attendance to allow for complete informality and confidentiality. Each week ambassadors also meet for what is known as the Private Lunch, an occasion which is used for informal exchanges on sensitive issues or to prepare the ground for fuller discussion in formal sessions of the Council.

Items which come to the Council for discussion and decision cover all aspects of the Organisation's activities. Discussion is frequently based on reports and recommendations prepared by subordinate committees. These may be adopted unchanged or modified by the Council to reconcile divergent views and arrive at a consensus. Documents may be sent back to the subordinate committees for further study or for implementation, or may result in a mandate for another committee to take the matter under discussion a stage further. Council discussions take place under the Chairmanship of the Secretary General or his deputy, regardless of the level at which the Council meets. He is assisted by the Executive Secretary, who is the Secretary of the Council, and by senior officials of the International Staff and International Military Staff with responsibilities in the spheres which relate to the subjects which the Council is to discuss. Meetings of the Council are also attended by the Chairman of the Military Committee or his Deputy, to represent the views of his Committee and to provide advice on military matters. At Ministerial Meetings of the Council, proceedings normally begin with an Opening Ceremony presided over by the President of the Council, an honorary position held annually by the Foreign Minister of one of the member nations. The position rotates, in accordance with the English alphabetical order of countries.

The Defence Planning Committee (DPC)

Most defence matters are dealt with in the Defence Planning Committee, composed of representatives of all member nations except France. Within the field of its responsibility, the DPC has, for all practical purposes, the same functions and authority as the Council. Like the Council, it meets regularly at ambassadorial level and assembles twice a year in ministerial sessions when the nations are represented by their Defence Ministers.

The Nuclear Planning Group follows a similar pattern of meetings at ambassadorial level and at the level of Ministers of Defence. It is the forum in which consultation takes place on all matters relating to the role of nuclear weapons in NATO's deterrence and defence policies. All member countries except France participate. Iceland participates as an observer.

The Secretary General

Chairman of the North Atlantic Council and the Defence Planning Committee, the Secretary General is also Chairman of the Nuclear Planning Group,

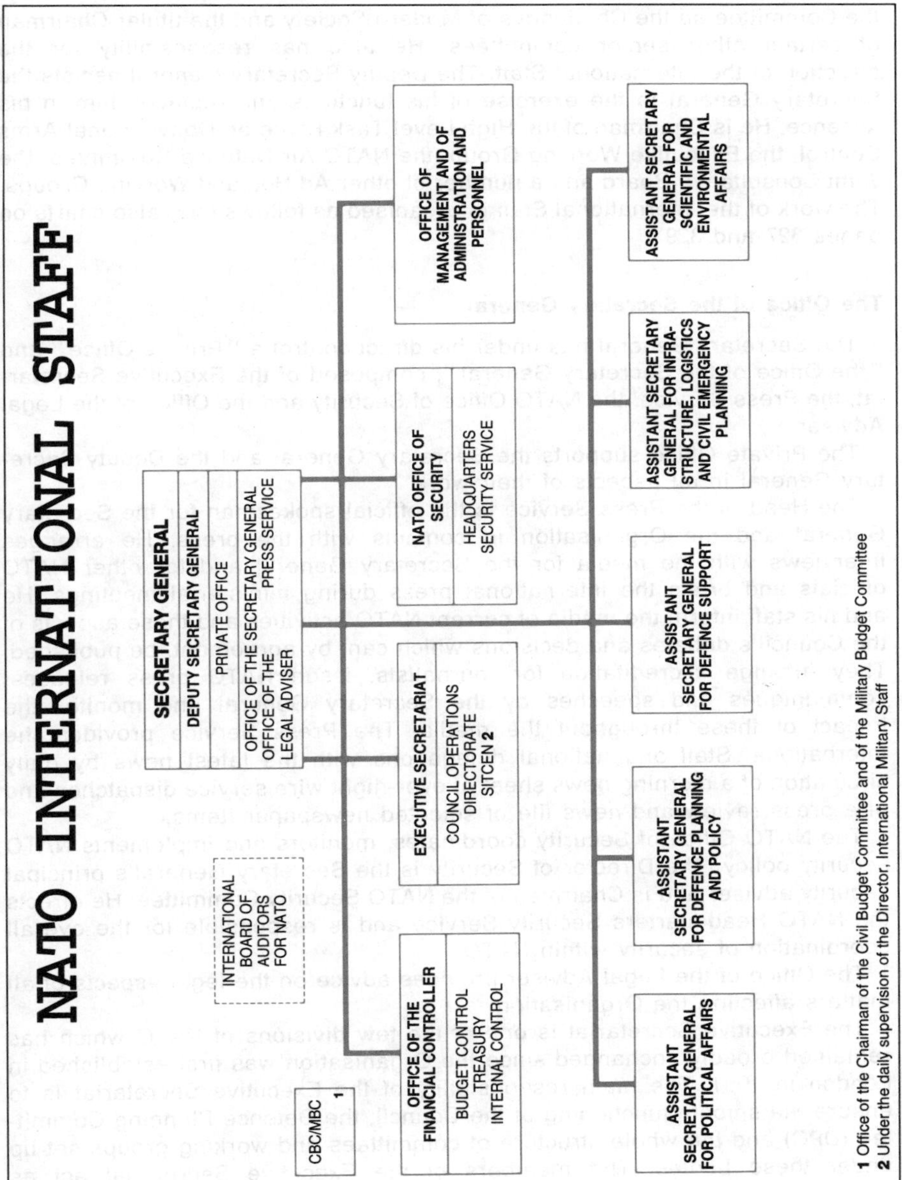
NATO INTERNATIONAL STAFF
CBC/MBC 1
INTERNATIONAL BOARD OF AUDITORS FOR NATO
SECRETARY GENERAL
DEPUTY SECRETARY GENERAL
PRIVATE OFFICE
OFFICE OF THE SECRETARY GENERAL PRESS SERVICE
OFFICE OF THE LEGAL ADVISER
OFFICE OF THE FINANCIAL CONTROLLER
BUDGET CONTROL
TREASURY
INTERNAL CONTROL
EXECUTIVE SECRETARIAT
COUNCIL OPERATIONS DIRECTORATE
SITCEN 2
NATO OFFICE OF SECURITY
HEADQUARTERS SECURITY SERVICE
OFFICE OF MANAGEMENT AND OF ADMINISTRATION AND PERSONNEL
ASSISTANT SECRETARY GENERAL FOR POLITICAL AFFAIRS
ASSISTANT SECRETARY GENERAL FOR DEFENCE PLANNING AND POLICY
ASSISTANT SECRETARY GENERAL FOR DEFENCE SUPPORT
ASSISTANT SECRETARY GENERAL FOR INFRA-STRUCTURE, LOGISTICS AND CIVIL EMERGENCY PLANNING
ASSISTANT SECRETARY GENERAL FOR SCIENTIFIC AND ENVIRONMENTAL AFFAIRS
1 Office of the Chairman of the Civil Budget Committee and of the Military Budget Committee
2 Under the daily supervision of the Director, International Military Staff

Figure 11

the Committee on the Challenges of Modern Society and the titular Chairman of certain other senior committees. He also has responsibility for the direction of the International Staff. The Deputy Secretary General assists the Secretary General in the exercise of his functions and replaces him in his absence. He is Chairman of the High Level Task Force on Conventional Arms Control, the Executive Working Group, the NATO Air Defence Committee, the Joint Consultative Board and a number of other Ad Hoc and Working Groups. The work of the International Staff is organised as follows (see also charts on pages 327 and 329):

The Office of the Secretary General

The Secretary General has under his direct control a "Private Office" and "the Office of the Secretary General", composed of the Executive Secretariat, the Press Service, the NATO Office of Security and the Office of the Legal Adviser.

The Private Office supports the Secretary General and the Deputy Secretary General in all aspects of their work.

The Head of the Press Service is the official spokesman for the Secretary General and the Organisation in contacts with the press. He arranges interviews with the media for the Secretary General and for other NATO officials and briefs the international press during ministerial meetings. He and his staff inform the media of current NATO activities and those aspects of the Council's debates and decisions which can, by agreement, be published. They arrange accreditation for journalists, issue NATO press releases, communiqués and speeches by the Secretary General and monitor the impact of these throughout the media. The Press Service provides the International Staff and national delegations with the latest news by daily circulation of a morning news sheet of over-night wire service dispatches and of a press review and news file of selected newspaper items.

The NATO Office of Security coordinates, monitors and implements NATO security policy. The Director of Security is the Secretary General's principal security adviser and is Chairman of the NATO Security Committee. He directs the NATO Headquarters Security Service and is responsible for the overall coordination of security within NATO.

The Office of the Legal Adviser provides advice on the legal aspects of all matters affecting the Organisation.

The Executive Secretariat is one of the few divisions of NATO which has remained broadly unchanged since the Organisation was first established in London in 1951. The main responsibility of the Executive Secretariat is to ensure the smooth functioning of the Council, the Defence Planning Committee (DPC) and the whole structure of committees and working groups set up under these bodies. The members of the Executive Secretariat act as Committee Secretaries and provide secretarial and administrative back-up for the Council, Defence Planning Committee and Nuclear Planning Group, and for a number of other senior committees and working groups in the fields of political and military affairs, armaments, infrastructure, logistics, civil

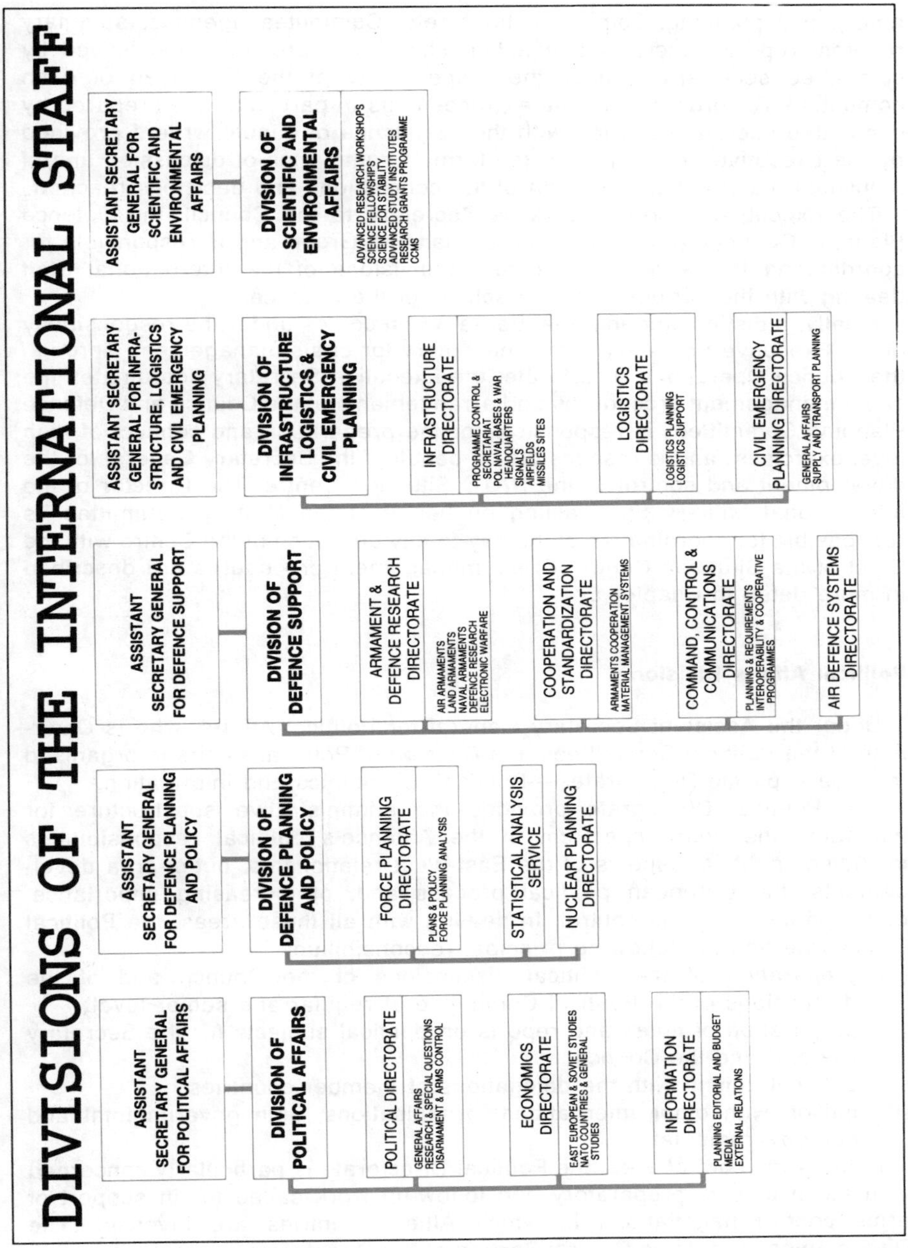
DIVISIONS OF THE INTERNATIONAL STAFF
ASSISTANT SECRETARY GENERAL FOR POLITICAL AFFAIRS
DIVISION OF POLITICAL AFFAIRS
POLITICAL DIRECTORATE
GENERAL AFFAIRS
RESEARCH & SPECIAL QUESTIONS
DISARMAMENT & ARMS CONTROL
ECONOMICS DIRECTORATE
EAST EUROPEAN & SOVIET STUDIES
NATO COUNTRIES & GENERAL STUDIES
INFORMATION DIRECTORATE
PLANNING EDITORIAL AND BUDGET
MEDIA
EXTERNAL RELATIONS
ASSISTANT SECRETARY GENERAL FOR DEFENCE PLANNING AND POLICY
DIVISION OF DEFENCE PLANNING AND POLICY
FORCE PLANNING DIRECTORATE
PLANS & POLICY
FORCE PLANNING ANALYSIS
STATISTICAL ANALYSIS SERVICE
NUCLEAR PLANNING DIRECTORATE
ASSISTANT SECRETARY GENERAL FOR DEFENCE SUPPORT
DIVISION OF DEFENCE SUPPORT
ARMAMENT & DEFENCE RESEARCH DIRECTORATE
AIR ARMAMENTS
LAND ARMAMENTS
NAVAL ARMAMENTS
DEFENCE RESEARCH
ELECTRONIC WARFARE
COOPERATION AND STANDARDIZATION DIRECTORATE
ARMAMENTS COOPERATION
MATERIAL MANAGEMENT SYSTEMS
COMMAND, CONTROL & COMMUNICATIONS DIRECTORATE
PLANNING & REQUIREMENTS
INTEROPERABILITY & COOPERATIVE PROGRAMMES
AIR DEFENCE SYSTEMS DIRECTORATE
ASSISTANT SECRETARY GENERAL FOR INFRA-STRUCTURE, LOGISTICS AND CIVIL EMERGENCY PLANNING
DIVISION OF INFRASTRUCTURE LOGISTICS & CIVIL EMERGENCY PLANNING
INFRASTRUCTURE DIRECTORATE
PROGRAMME CONTROL & SECRETARIAT
POL NAVAL BASES & WAR HEADQUARTERS
SIGNALS
AIRFIELDS
MISSILES SITES
LOGISTICS DIRECTORATE
LOGISTICS PLANNING
LOGISTICS SUPPORT
CIVIL EMERGENCY PLANNING DIRECTORATE
GENERAL AFFAIRS
SUPPLY AND TRANSPORT PLANNING
ASSISTANT SECRETARY GENERAL FOR SCIENTIFIC AND ENVIRONMENTAL AFFAIRS
DIVISION OF SCIENTIFIC AND ENVIRONMENTAL AFFAIRS
ADVANCED RESEARCH WORKSHOPS
SCIENCE FELLOWSHIPS
SCIENCE FOR STABILITY
ADVANCED STUDY INSTITUTES
RESEARCH GRANTS PROGRAMME
CCMS

Figure 12

emergency planning, communications, etc. Committee agendas, summary records, reports, decision and action sheets are prepared and issued by committee secretaries under the responsiblity of the Chairman of each committee. Records of committee proceedings in particular are prepared by committee secretaries, often with the assistance of minute writers provided by the Executive Secretariat, in the form of summaries of discussion and of individual national positions and of the conclusions and decisions reached.

The Executive Secretary acts as Secretary to the Council, the Defence Planning Committee and the Nuclear Planning Group and is responsible for coordinating the work of the different divisions of the International Staff dealing with the various areas of activity of the Alliance.

Finally, a distinct and important area which comes under the responsibility of the Executive Secretary is the machinery for crisis management. Through the Council Operations Directorate, the Executive Secretary coordinates the crisis management procedures and arrangements of the Council and Defence Planning Committee; is responsible for the preparation and conduct of high level exercises; and is responsible on behalf of the Secretary General for the development and control of the NATO Situation Centre. The Director of the International Military Staff, acting on behalf of the Military Committee, is responsible for coordination of the day-to-day operation of the Centre with the Chief of the Situation Centre. Crisis management procedures are described in more detail in Chapter 5.

Political Affairs Division

Under the Assistant Secretary General for Political Affairs, who is Chairman of the Political Committees, the Division of Political Affairs is organised in three separate Directorates—Political, Economics and Information.

The Political Directorate provides the administrative substructure for managing the entire spectrum of the Alliance's political responsibilities including: political aspects of the East-West relationship, out-of-area developments, the European political process and, of increasing importance, developments in arms control. In dealing with all these areas, the Political Directorate has the following principal responsibilities:

(a) preparation of the political discussions of the Council and of the discussions of the Political Committee at regular and senior level;
(b) preparation of notes and reports on political subjects for the Secretary General and the Council;
(c) political liaison with the delegations of member countries;
(d) liaison with other international organisations, both governmental and non-governmental.

In the arms control area, the Political Directorate is particularly concerned with the extensive preparatory and follow-up work called for in support of arms control negotiations in which Allied countries are involved. The Disarmament and Arms Control Section of the Directorate prepares the work of the High Level Task Force formed by the 16 Allies as the vehicle for political decision-making in the area of conventional arms control and, in particular, in the current negotiations in this field in Vienna.

The Economics Directorate carries out similar functions with regard to all economics questions having political or defence implications for NATO and maintains contacts with international economics organisations. It undertakes studies, on behalf of the Economics Committee, relating to economic issues in the Soviet Union and Eastern Europe and to economic aspects of security in NATO countries. It also undertakes work related to NATO defence planning and maintains close liaison with the Division of Defence Planning and Policy. The Director of the Economics Directorate is Chairman of the Economics Committee.

The Information Directorate has the task of informing public opinion about the aims and achievements of the Atlantic Alliance. It assists member governments to widen public understanding of NATO activities through the medium of publications, films, radio and television programmes, photographs and exhibitions. It also arranges for group visits to NATO Headquarters for briefings and participates in the organisation of conferences and seminars on NATO matters, particularly for young people. The Director of Information is Chairman of the Committee on Information and Cultural Relations. He takes the chair at the Conference of National Information Officials and also chairs an annual meeting of Ministry of Defence Information Officers. The Directorate includes a Library and Documentation Service.

Defence Planning and Policy Division

The Assistant Secretary General for Defence Planning and Policy is Chairman of the Defence Review Committee (DRC), Chairman of the Alerts Committee, Vice-Chairman of the Executive Working Group (EWG) and supervises the work of the Nuclear Planning Group (NPG) Staff Group.

The Division is divided into two Directorates:

The Directorate of Force Planning is responsible for the preparation, in collaboration with national delegations, of all papers and business concerned with the Defence Review, including the analysis of national defence programmes; for other matters of a politico-military and military-economic nature considered by the Defence Planning Committee; for the preparation of studies of general or particular aspects of NATO defence planning and policy on behalf of the Executive Working Group of the Defence Planning Committee; for the maintenance of a computerised data base of information on NATO and Warsaw Treaty forces; and for the organisation and direction of all statistical studies and in particular those required to assess the NATO defence effort. The Director of Force Planning is Vice-Chairman of the Defence Review Commitee.

The Directorate of Nuclear Planning is responsible for coordination of work on the development of NATO defence policy in the nuclear field and the work of the Nuclear Planning Group.

The Division of Defence Support

The Assistant Secretary General for Defence Support has two major responsibilities:

(a) advising the Secretary General, the North Atlantic Council, the Defence Planning Committee and any other NATO bodies on all matters relating to armaments research, development, production, procurement, and materiel aspects of air defence and all commmand, control and communications systems;

(b) promoting the most efficient use of the resources of the Alliance for the equipment of its forces.

The Assistant Secretary General for Defence Support serves as the Permanent Chairman of the Conference of National Armaments Directors. The Division provides liaison with NATO production and logistics organisations concerned with cooperative equipment projects and with NATO military agencies dealing with defence research and connected problems. It participates in all aspects of the NATO Defence Planning process within its resposibility and competence.

The Division consists of four Directorates:

The Directorate of Armaments and Defence Research is responsible for encouraging cooperation amongst nations in harmonising the concepts and requirements for future maritime, land and air equipment and harmonising procurement and replacement plans, so as to facilitate greater material standardization; encouraging coordination of national research, development and production programmes so as to improve the efficiency of resource utilisation; and organising systematic exchanges of information to support better national decision-making and to facilitate international cooperation in defence equipment and its support.

The Directorate of Command, Control and Commuications is responsible for encouraging cooperative programmes in communications and electronics, for the coordination of the overall policy aspects of NATO's civil and military communications, and for providing support to the NATO Communications and Information Systems Committee. (The latter also acts as the NATO Communications and Information Systems Policy Committee).

The Directorate of Air Defence is responsible for promoting and coordinating efforts to assure the continuing adequacy, effectiveness and efficiency of NATO air defence systems; for providing support to the NATO Air Defence Committee (NADC), whose role is to advise on all aspects of air defence programme development; and for liaison with the agencies responsible for the implementation of the NATO Airborne Early Warning Programme (NAPMA), the Improved HAWK requirement (NHMO), and the design of the future air command and control system (ACCS).

The Directorate of Cooperation and Standardization is responsible for general policy preparation in support of armaments cooperation, including the development of guidance for systematising and rationalising armaments collaboration, for promoting international cooperation among industries in the defence equipment field and also between government and industry, for liaison with outside bodies, and for providing guidance, coordination and staff support to the activities of all NATO committees or bodies dealing with Defence Support matters, particularly in the areas of material management, standardization, safety of transportation and storage of ammunition and explosives, intellectual property and acquisitions practices.

The Division of Infrastructure, Logistics and Civil Emergency Planning

The Assistant Secretary General for Infrastructure, Logistics and Civil Emergency Planning is Chairman of the Infrastructure Committee and the Infrastructure Payments and Progress Committee. He chairs the Senior Civil Emergency Planning Committee in plenary session and is co-Chairman of the Senior NATO Logisticians' Conference.

The Division consists of three Directorates:

The Infrastructure Directorate, under the direction of the Controller for Infrastructure, who is also the permanent Chairman of the Infrastructure Committee, and the Deputy Controller, who is also the permanent Chairman of the Infrastructure Payments and Progress Committee. The Infrastructure Directorate is responsible for supporting the Infrastructure Committees by:

(a) developing proposals on policy issues, on funding issues related to the shape and size of NATO Infrastructure programmes and on improved procedures for their management;
(b) providing technical and financial supervision of the NATO Infrastructure Programme;
(c) screening, from the technical, financial, economic and political points of view, the Major NATO Commanders' programmes for annual Infrastructure Slices and related cost estimates; and
(d) screening, from a technical and financial point of view, requests to the Payments and Progress Committee for authorisation of the scope and funding of infrastructure works.

The Logistics Directorate, under the direction of the Director of Logistics, who is also the Chairman of the NATO Pipeline Committee and deputy co-Chairman of the Senior NATO Logisticians' Conference, is responsible for:

(a) the development and coordination of plans and policies towards a coherent approach within NATO on consumer logistics matters in order to increase the combat effectiveness of Alliance forces by achieving greater logistical readiness and sustainability;
(b) providing staff support to the Senior NATO Logisticians' Conference and its subsidiary bodies;
(c) providing technical staff support to the NATO Pipeline Committee;
(d) supporting, coordinating and maintaining liaison with the NATO military authorities, NATO and other committees and bodies dealing with the planning and implementation of consumer logistics matters; and
(e) maintaining liaison, on behalf of the Secretary General, with the directing bodies of the Central Europe Pipeline System and the NATO Maintenance and Supply Organisation.

The Civil Emergency Planning Directorate, under the direction of the Director of Civil Emergency Planning, who is also the Chairman of the Senior Civil Emergency Planning Committee in permanent session, is responsible for:

(a) the coordination and guidance of planning aimed at the rapid transition of peacetime economies of the nations of the Alliance to an emergency footing;

(b) development of the arrangements for the use of civil resources in support of the Alliance defence effort and for the protection of the civil populations; and

(c) providing staff support to the Senior Civil Emergency Planning Committee and the eight civil emergency planning boards and committees established to develop crisis management arrangements in the areas of civil sea, land and air transport, energy, industry, food and agriculture, civil communications and civil defence.

Division of Scientific and Environmental Affairs

The Assistant Secretary General for Scientific and Environmental Affairs has the following responsibilities:

(a) advising the Secretary General on scientific and technological matters of interest to NATO;

(b) chairing the NATO Science Committee, directing the activities of the sub-committees created by it, implementing the decisions of the Committee and developing ways to strengthen scientific and technological capabilities of Alliance countries;

(c) serving as Acting Chairman of the Committee on the Challenges of Modern Society (CCMS), and supervising the development of pilot projects;

(d) ensuring liaison in the scientific field with the International Staff of NATO, with NATO agencies, with agencies in the member countries responsible for implementation of science policies and with international organisations engaged in scientific, technological and environmental activities.

Office of Management

The Director of Management is responsible for all matters pertaining to the organisation and structure of the International Staff. He advises the Secretary General on civilian staff policy and emoluments throughout the Organisation and is charged with the preparation, presentation and management of the International Staff budget. He supervises the activities of the Pensions Computation Unit and of the Management Advisory Unit which has responsibility for advising the Secretary General on all matters related to organisation, work methods, procedures and manpower.

The Deputy Director of Management is responsible for the general administration of the International Staff including personnel services, the maintenance of the headquarters, the provision of conference, interpretation and translation facilities and the production and distribution of internal documents.

Staff Appointments

The NATO International Staff is composed of personnel from all member countries employed either as independent specialists in their chosen field recruited directly by the Organisation or as civil servants from different spheres of national administrations seconded to NATO on a temporary basis, normally for periods of three to four years. National delegations to NATO are informed of vacancies and are invited to submit names of well-qualified candidates whom their authorities wish to propose. Members of the International Staff and agencies are also entitled to apply for vacant posts. Applications are also made by outside candidates in response to advertising and other means of recruitment. Appointing authority is vested in the Secretary General, who has overall responsibility for the professional standards of the staff and for maintaining an appropriate balance of nationalities. Appointments are made on the basis of recommendations made to the Secretary General by interview panels without appointing authority. Their recommendations are subsequently examined, depending on the level of the appointment, either by an Establishment Committee composed of senior officials or by the Director of Management acting on behalf of the Secretary General. The Office of Management is responsible for recruitment and contracts and for overseeing the general employment policy of the Organisation. The establishment of new posts or the deletion of posts no longer required is discussed by the Civil Budget Committee on the basis of recommendations made by the Director of Management acting on behalf of the Secretary General.

Financial control

A Financial Controller is appointed by the Council and is responsible for the call up of funds and the control of expenditures within the framework of the civil and military budgets (see Chapter 24).

International Board of Auditors

The accounts of the various NATO bodies and the accounts relating to commonly financed NATO Infrastructure works are audited by the International Board of Auditors for NATO (see Chapter 24).

Special agencies and steering committees

The Council has created a number of production and logistics organisations and agencies and project steering committees to carry out specific tasks. A number of projects for which such bodies have been created are described in detail in Chapter 15. Examples are also given below.

Production and Logistics Organisations

— Central Europe Operating Agency (CEOA)
— Central Europe Pipeline System (CEPS);
— NATO Maintenance and Supply Organisation (NAMSO);
— NATO HAWK Production and Logistics Organisation (NHPLO);
— NATO Multi-Role Combat Aircraft Development and Production Management Organisation (NAMMO);
— NATO Communications and Information Systems Organisation (NACISO);
— NATO Airborne Early Warning and Control Programme Management Organisation (NAPMO)
— NATO European Fighter Aircraft Development, Production and Logistics Organisation (NEFMO).

Some organisations have completed their tasks and have been disbanded:
— NATO F-104G STARFIGHTER Production Organisation;
— NATO SIDEWINDER Production and Logistics Organisation;
— NATO BULLPUP Production Organisation;
— NATO Air Defence Ground Environment Management Organisation (NADGEMO).

Project Steering Committees

Established in accordance with procedures for cooperation in research development and production of military equipment approved by the Council in May 1966, Project Steering Committees exist for the joint development and production of the following armaments equipment:
— SEASPARROW Point Defence Missile System;
— Multi-Role Combat Aircraft (MRCA);
— NATO MILAN Anti-Armour System;
— NATO FORACS (NATO Naval Forces Sensor and Weapon Accuracy Check Sites in Europe);
— Multi-national F-16 Programme;
— NATO NAVSTAR GPS Project;
— Cooperative Support of the 76/62 OTO MELARA Compact Gun;
— NATO Maritime Patrol Aircraft;
— Conventionally Powered Submarine for Employment in European Waters (dormant);
— Sea Anti-Invasion Mine;
— Sea Ground Mine (80);
— Tripartite Minehunter;
— Demonstration of Advanced Radar Techniques (DART);
— Multiple Launch Rocket System (MRLS);
— Versatile Exercise Maritime Mine (VEM);
— European Fighter Aircraft (EFA).

Chapter 23

NATO's Military Organisation

In 1949, the 12 founder members of NATO had fewer than 20 divisions[1] and their reserves of trained manpower were inadequately equipped and therefore ineffective. In Western Europe, there were fewer than 1,000 operational aircraft available, many of which were obsolete models from World War II. Airfields (fewer than 20 in all) were not equipped to handle jet aircraft and were situated in vulnerable forward areas. The greatest concentration of NATO air and ground support was located in Western Germany where it was deployed, not for defence against attack, but to carry out occupation and police duties. Supply lines ran from north to south instead of west to east. The naval position was better but many warships had been scrapped, put in reserve, or converted for use as civilian transport. The West would have been incapable of effectively resisting attack and its total fighting forces were inadequate to deter aggression.

The history of NATO since 1949 has witnessed the development of member countries' forces, and their progressive adaptation to new technology, as well as the gradual development of an allied command structure.

The integrated military command structure

The strategic area covered by the North Atlantic Treaty is divided among three Major NATO Commands (European, Atlantic and Channel) and a Regional Planning Group for Canada and the United States. This division is governed by both geographical and political factors and the authority exercised by the different Commands varies in form in relation to those factors and to the situation in peacetime or wartime. All member countries assign forces to the integrated military command structure with the exception of France, Spain and Iceland (which has no military forces).

The Major NATO Commanders are responsible for the development of defence plans for their respective areas, for the determination of force requirements and for the deployment and exercise of the forces under their command. Their reports and recommendations regarding forces and their logistic support are referred to the NATO Military Committee.

Military Committee

The NATO Military Committee is the highest military authority in the North Atlantic Treaty Organisation under the political authority of the North Atlantic

---

[1] The numerical strength of divisions in NATO countries varies. Many NATO divisions consist of more personnel than normal divisions of Warsaw Treaty countries but the latter have larger numbers of tanks and artillery, thereby obtaining similar combat power.

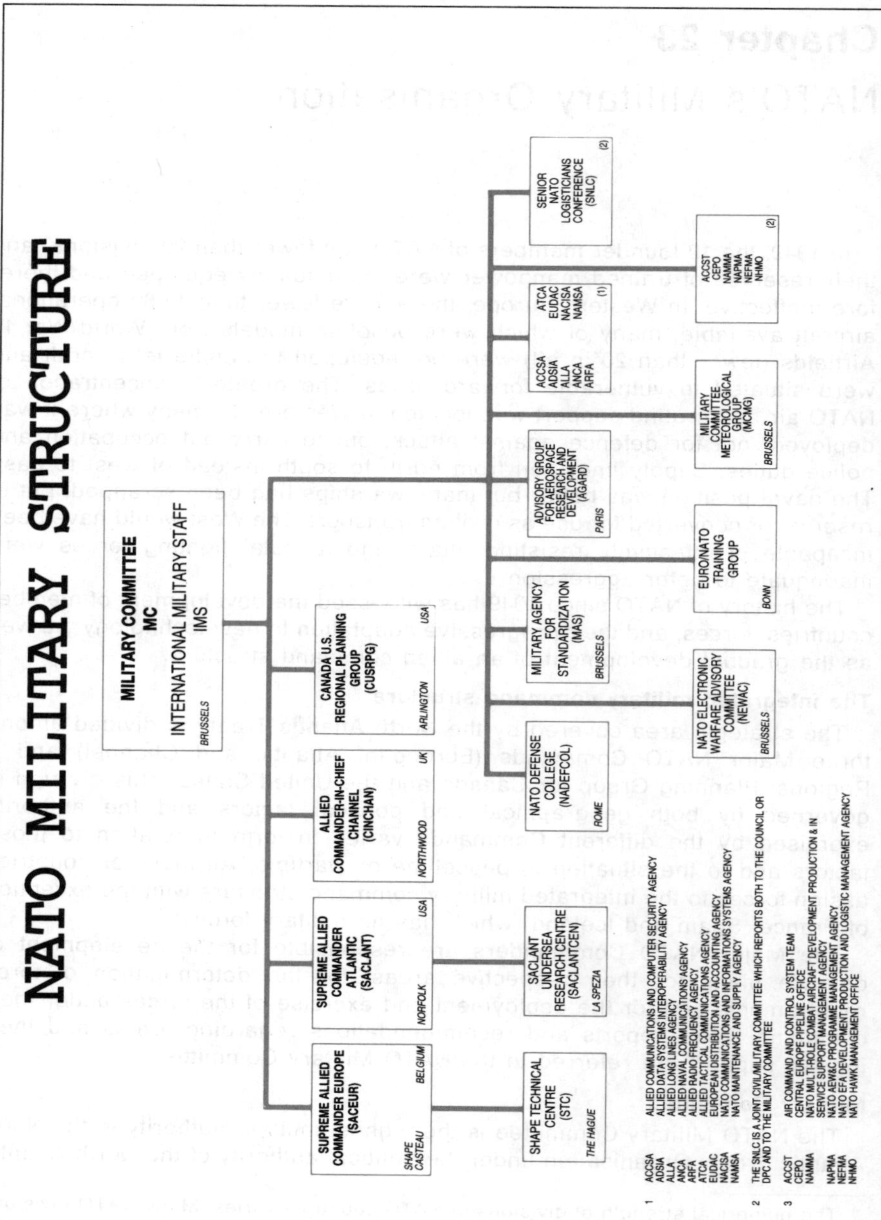
NATO MILITARY STRUCTURE
MILITARY COMMITTEE MC
INTERNATIONAL MILITARY STAFF IMS
BRUSSELS
SUPREME ALLIED COMMANDER EUROPE (SACEUR)
SHAPE CASTEAU
BELGIUM
SUPREME ALLIED COMMANDER ATLANTIC (SACLANT)
NORFOLK
USA
ALLIED COMMANDER-IN-CHIEF CHANNEL (CINCHAN)
NORTHWOOD
UK
CANADA U.S. REGIONAL PLANNING GROUP (CUSRPG)
ARLINGTON
USA
SHAPE TECHNICAL CENTRE (STC)
THE HAGUE
SACLANT UNDERSEA RESEARCH CENTRE (SACLANTCEN)
LA SPEZIA
NATO DEFENSE COLLEGE (NADEFCOL)
ROME
MILITARY AGENCY FOR STANDARDIZATION (MAS)
BRUSSELS
ADVISORY GROUP FOR AEROSPACE RESEARCH AND DEVELOPMENT (AGARD)
PARIS
ACCSA ADSIA ALLA ANCA ARFA
ATCA EUDAC NACISA NAMSA (1)
SENIOR NATO LOGISTICIANS CONFERENCE (SNLC) (2)
NATO ELECTRONIC WARFARE ADVISORY COMMITTEE (NEWAC)
BRUSSELS
EURO/NATO TRAINING GROUP
BONN
MILITARY COMMITTEE METEOROLOGICAL GROUP (MCMG)
BRUSSELS
ACCST CEPO NAMMA NAPMA NEFMA NHMO (2)
1 ACCSA ALLIED COMMUNICATIONS AND COMPUTER SECURITY AGENCY
ADSIA ALLIED DATA SYSTEMS INTEROPERABILITY AGENCY
ALLA ALLIED LONG LINES AGENCY
ANCA ALLIED NAVAL COMMUNICATIONS AGENCY
ARFA ALLIED RADIO FREQUENCY AGENCY
ATCA ALLIED TACTICAL COMMUNICATIONS AGENCY
EUDAC EUROPEAN DISTRIBUTION AND ACCOUNTING AGENCY
NACISA NATO COMMUNICATIONS AND INFORMATIONS SYSTEMS AGENCY
NAMSA NATO MAINTENANCE AND SUPPLY AGENCY
2 THE SNLC IS A JOINT CIVIL/MILITARY COMMITTEE WHICH REPORTS BOTH TO THE COUNCIL OR DPC AND TO THE MILITARY COMMITTEE
3 ACCST AIR COMMAND AND CONTROL SYSTEM TEAM
CEPO CENTRAL EUROPE PIPELINE OFFICE
NAMMA NATO MULTI-ROLE COMBAT AIRCRAFT DEVELOPMENT PRODUCTION & IN SERVICE SUPPORT MANAGEMENT AGENCY
NAPMA NATO AEW&C PROGRAMME MANAGEMENT AGENCY
NEFMA NATO EFA DEVELOPMENT PRODUCTION AND LOGISTIC MANAGEMENT AGENCY
NHMO NATO HAWK MANAGEMENT OFFICE

Figure 13

Council and the Defence Planning Committee. It is composed of the Chiefs-of-Staff of each member nation except France. France is represented by a military mission to the Military Committee. Iceland, having no military forces, may be represented by a civilian. At the level of the Chiefs of Staff, the Committee meets at least three times a year or whenever it is deemed necessary. In order for the Committee to function on a continuous basis with effective powers of decision, each Chief-of-Staff appoints a permanent Military Representative as a member of the Military Committee in permanent session.

The Military Committee is charged by the North Atlantic Council with the peacetime task of recommending those measures considered necessary for the common defence of the NATO area. It is the body to which the Supreme Allied Commander Europe, the Supreme Allied Commander Atlantic, the Commander-in-Chief Channel and the Canada-United States Regional Planning Group are responsible. In addition, a number of NATO military agencies serve under the authority of the Military Committee. These are described later in this chapter.

The Military Committee in permanent session meets regularly at NATO Headquarters in Brussels. Its members have their offices in the Headquarters complex colocated with those of the Chairman of the Military Committee and the International Military Staff. The meetings of the Military Committee in Chiefs-of-Staff session may be held at NATO Headquarters or in any one of the member countries.

The Presidency[2] of the Military Committee rotates among the nations annually in the order of the English alphabet.

The Chairman[2] of the Military Committee presides over both the Chiefs-of-Staff and permanent sessions. He is elected by the Chiefs-of-Staff for a three-year term. He directs the day-to-day business of the Committee and acts as its spokesman, attending meetings of the Council and the Defence Planning Committee to provide advice on military matters. The Chairman is assisted by the Deputy Chairman and by the Director of the International Military Staff.

The Deputy Chairman of the Military Committee is also responsible for the coordination within the Military Committee and International Military Staff of nuclear matters and of arms control and disarmament matters. He acts as military advisor to the Chairman of the High Level Task Force on Conventional Arms Control and is Co-Chairman of the Senior NATO Logisticians' Conference.

Origins of the Military Committee

The history of the Military Committee goes back to the establishment of the Organisation itself. Two days before the North Atlantic Treaty was signed on April 4, 1949, a working group began to formulate recommendations for the establishment of agencies which the treaty organisation would require if it

[2] Presidents and Chairmen of the Military Committee are listed in Appendix III.

was to operate successfully. The report of this group was approved by the NATO Foreign Ministers meeting as members of the North Atlantic Council at their first session on September 17, 1949. The working group recommended that the military organisation should include a Military Committee (composed of one military representative of each country, preferably a Chief-of-Staff). During its first session, the North Atlantic Council created a Defence Committee to consist of the NATO Defence Ministers, charged with establishing the required military organisation. The Defence Committee convened on October 5, 1949, and promptly established the NATO Military Committee, which held its first meeting on October 6, 1949, in Washington DC. In November 1988, the Military Committee held its 100th meeting attended by Chiefs of Staff.

Standing Group

To assist the Military Committee in performing its tasks, an executive agency, the NATO Standing Group, was created. This gave the Military Committee a day-to-day channel for the exchange of national viewpoints and the orderly flow of military plans, studies and recommendations. France, the United Kingdom and the United States provided permanent representatives to the Standing Group in addition to the necessary technical and staff support. Each of the remaining NATO nations with military forces appointed an accredited national representative in permanent liaison to the Standing Group. In 1950 this liaison group was officially designated as the Military Representatives Committee and re-named the Military Committee in permanent session in 1957. This mirrored parallel developments on the civilian side, leading to the creation of the North Atlantic Council in permanent session.

Also in 1957, the Standing Group was expanded by inviting each non-Standing Group nation to provide one staff planner in order to secure the input of national guidance on a working level. In 1963, the Military Committee in Chiefs-of-Staff session agreed to modify the Standing Group further by establishing an International Planning Staff, made up of members from both Standing Group and non-Standing Group nations.

The Standing Group continued to support the Military Committee until France withdrew from the integrated military command structure of the Alliance in 1966, making the concept of a three-nation military executive invalid. The North Atlantic Council directed that on July 1, 1966, the Standing Group and International Planning Staff be disestablished and their authority be transferred to the Military Committee. An International Military Staff, composed of officers of all nations except France and Iceland, was established on February 10, 1967.

International Military Staff

The International Military Staff, which comprises about 150 officers, 150 enlisted men and 100 civilian employees, is made up of military personnel

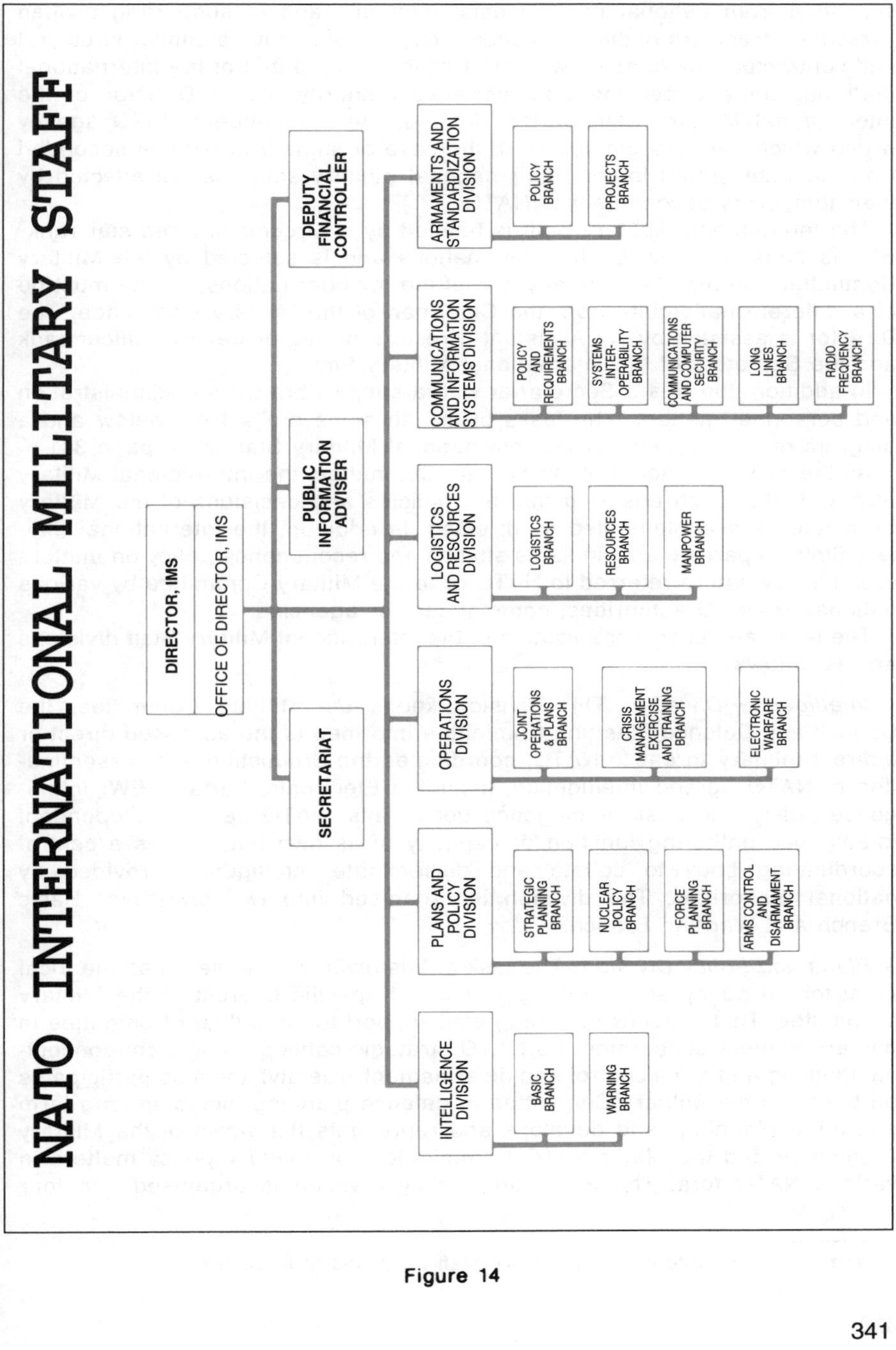
NATO INTERNATIONAL MILITARY STAFF
DIRECTOR, IMS
OFFICE OF DIRECTOR, IMS
DEPUTY FINANCIAL CONTROLLER
PUBLIC INFORMATION ADVISER
SECRETARIAT
ARMAMENTS AND STANDARDIZATION DIVISION
POLICY BRANCH
PROJECTS BRANCH
COMMUNICATIONS AND INFORMATION SYSTEMS DIVISION
POLICY AND REQUIREMENTS BRANCH
SYSTEMS INTER-OPERABILITY BRANCH
COMMUNICATIONS AND COMPUTER SECURITY BRANCH
LONG LINES BRANCH
RADIO FREQUENCY BRANCH
LOGISTICS AND RESOURCES DIVISION
LOGISTICS BRANCH
RESOURCES BRANCH
MANPOWER BRANCH
OPERATIONS DIVISION
JOINT OPERATIONS & PLANS BRANCH
CRISIS MANAGEMENT EXERCISE AND TRAINING BRANCH
ELECTRONIC WARFARE BRANCH
PLANS AND POLICY DIVISION
STRATEGIC PLANNING BRANCH
NUCLEAR POLICY BRANCH
FORCE PLANNING BRANCH
ARMS CONTROL AND DISARMAMENT BRANCH
INTELLIGENCE DIVISION
BASIC BRANCH
WARNING BRANCH

Figure 14

seconded from national military establishments and of supporting civilian personnel. Members of the International Military Staff have a similar structural and contractual relationship with the Organisation to that of the International Staff but come under the administrative authority of the Director of the International Military Staff or the Head of the independent NATO agency within which they are employed. In the case of military personnel seconded from national armed forces, their national military status is not affected by their temporary secondment to NATO.

The International Military Staff is headed by a Director of three star rank[3] who is nominated by the member nations and is selected by the Military Committee. He may be from any one of the member nations, but he must be of a different nationality from the Chairman of the Military Committee. The Director is assisted by six Assistant Directors of flag or general officer rank and the Secretary of the International Military Staff.

In addition, there is a Secretariat with a support branch for administration and personnel matters. The tasks of the divisions are set out below and a diagram of the structure of the International Military Staff is on page 341.

As the executive agent of the Military Committee, the International Military Staff is tasked with ensuring that the policies and decisions of the Military Committee are implemented as directed. In addition, the International Military Staff prepares plans, initiates studies and recommends policy on matters of a military nature referred to NATO or to the Military Committee by various national or NATO authorities, commanders or agencies.

The tasks and basic organisation of the International Military Staff divisions are as follows:

Intelligence Division: This division keeps the Military Committee, the Council and Defence Planning Committee informed of the assessed direct or indirect military threat to NATO, coordinates the production and dissemination of NATO agreed intelligence, including Electronic Warfare (EW) intelligence policy and basic intelligence documents. NATO has no independent intelligence gathering function or capacity of its own but acts as a central coordinating body to collate and disseminate intelligence provided by national authorities. The division is organised into two branches: Basic Branch and Warning Branch.

Plans and Policy Division: The task of this division is to serve as the focal point for all policy and planning matters of specific interest to the Military Committee. This includes providing staff support to the Military Committee in military matters concerning the NATO strategic concept, long term conceptual thinking and arms control and disarmament. The division also participates on behalf of the Military Committee in defence planning including long term and force planning; and develops and represents the views of the Military Committee and the Major NATO Commanders on military policy matters in various NATO fora. The Plans and Policy Division is organised into four

---

[3] Directors of the International Military Staff are listed in Appendix III.

branches: Strategic Planning, Force Planning, Nuclear Planning and Arms Control and Disarmament.

Operations Division: This division provides staff support to the Military Committee in matters concerning current operational plans; the NATO force posture and the organisational structure of NATO Commands and military headquarters; the definition and management of contingency reactions to international crises where NATO interests are involved; the promotion and coordination of multinational training and exercises; and the coordination of efforts towards an effective NATO Electronic Warfare operational capability and associated training and exercises. The Operations Division consists of the Joint Operations Plans Branch, Crisis Management, Exercises and Training Branch and Electronic Warfare Branch.

Logistics and Resources Division: This division is responsible to the Military Committee for the international military management of Allied logistics, financial, manpower and infrastructure matters. The division is organised into three branches dealing with Logistics, Resources and Manpower.

Communications and Information Systems Division: This division provides staff support to the Military Committee on Command, Control and Information Systems including the application of Automatic Data Processing (ADP) techniques to NATO functions and activities; communications and electronics; and communications and ADP security and long lines (PTT) leasing policy and practices. The division has five branches: Policy and Requirements, Systems Interoperability, Communications and Computer Security, Long Lines and Radio Frequency.

Armaments and Standardization Division: The function of this division is to provide staff support to the Military Committee on matters concerning the development and assessment of NATO military policy and procedures for armaments and related standardization activities and act as the focal point for staffing and coordination of military needs in these areas. The Division has two branches: Policy and Projects.

Allied Command Europe (ACE)

Allied Command Europe (ACE) is one of NATO's three major military commands. Its task is to safeguard the area extending from the northern tip of Norway to Southern Europe, including the whole of the Mediterranean, and from the Atlantic coastline to the eastern border of Turkey. This equates to nearly two million square kilometres of land, more than three million square kilometres of sea, and a population of about 320 million people. The command was established in 1951.

The military task of ACE is to contribute, along with the forces of the other Major NATO Commanders, to the deterrence of all forms of aggression against NATO. Should aggression occur, however, or be considered imminent, the Supreme Allied Commander, Europe will then take all required military measures to preserve the security, or restore the integrity, of Allied Command Europe.

The Supreme Allied Commander, Europe (SACEUR)[4]

In peacetime, SACEUR's main functions are to prepare and finalise defence plans for the area under his command, and to ensure the combat efficiency of the forces assigned to his command in event of war. SACEUR also makes recommendations to NATO's Military Committee on matters likely to improve the organisation of his command. He sets down standards for organising, training, equipping, maintaining and sustaining the forces he commands and he conducts exercises and evaluations to ensure that they knit together into a unified and capable force for the collective defence of NATO territory.

In wartime, SACEUR would control all land, sea and air operations in his area. Although internal defence and the defence of coastal waters remain the responsibility of the national authorities concerned, SACEUR would have full authority to carry out those operations he considered necessary for the defence of any part of the area under his command, within the framework of the political authority exercised by the North Atlantic Council or the Defence Planning Committee.

SACEUR makes recommendations to NATO's political and military authorities on any military matter which affects, or might affect, his ability to carry out his responsibilities in peace and war. He has direct access to the Chiefs-of-Staff, the Defence Ministers and Heads of Government of the NATO nations.

The Supreme Headquarters Allied Powers Europe (SHAPE)

The headquarters of Allied Command Europe is SHAPE. At SHAPE, SACEUR and his international staff of Allied officers, enlisted personnel and civilians conduct the studies, analyses, planning, coordination and exercises necessary to fulfill the missions and responsibilities assigned to the forces of Allied Command Europe in peace and war.

The coordination and integration of requirements, plans and procedures between SHAPE, other ACE Commands (see diagram on page 345) and the military staffs and commands of NATO nations are facilitated by the presence, at SHAPE, of a National Military Representative (NMR) from each NATO country which has military forces in the integrated military command structure of the Alliance (see Chapter 9). The National Military Representa-

---

[4] Supreme Allied Commanders Europe (SACEURs), Supreme Allied Commanders Atlantic (SACLANTs) and Allied Commanders-in-Chief Channel (CINCHAN) are listed in Appendix III.

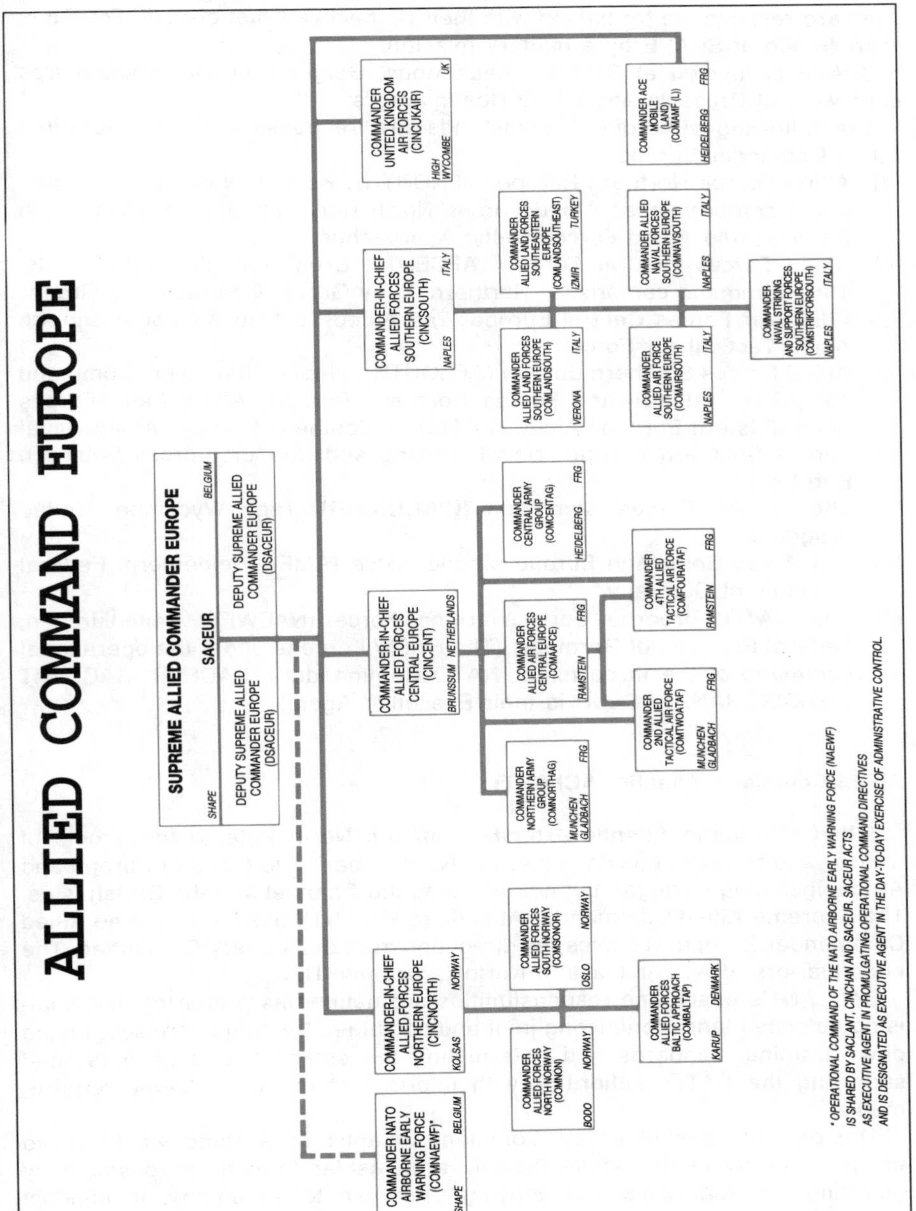
ALLIED COMMAND EUROPE
SUPREME ALLIED COMMANDER EUROPE
SHAPE
BELGIUM
SACEUR
DEPUTY SUPREME ALLIED COMMANDER EUROPE (DSACEUR)
DEPUTY SUPREME ALLIED COMMANDER EUROPE (DSACEUR)
COMMANDER NATO AIRBORNE EARLY WARNING FORCE (COMNAEWF)*
SHAPE BELGIUM
COMMANDER-IN-CHIEF ALLIED FORCES NORTHERN EUROPE (CINCNORTH)
KOLSAS NORWAY
COMMANDER ALLIED FORCES NORTH NORWAY (COMNON)
BODO NORWAY
COMMANDER ALLIED FORCES SOUTH NORWAY (COMSONOR)
OSLO NORWAY
COMMANDER ALLIED FORCES BALTIC APPROACH (COMBALTAP)
KARUP DENMARK
COMMANDER-IN-CHIEF ALLIED FORCES CENTRAL EUROPE (CINCENT)
BRUNSSUM NETHERLANDS
COMMANDER NORTHERN ARMY GROUP (COMNORTHAG)
MUNCHEN GLADBACH FRG
COMMANDER ALLIED AIR FORCES CENTRAL EUROPE (COMAAFCE)
RAMSTEIN FRG
COMMANDER CENTRAL ARMY GROUP (COMCENTAG)
HEIDELBERG FRG
COMMANDER 2ND ALLIED TACTICAL AIR FORCE (COMTWOATAF)
MUNCHEN GLADBACH FRG
COMMANDER 4TH ALLIED TACTICAL AIR FORCE (COMFOURATAF)
RAMSTEIN FRG
COMMANDER-IN-CHIEF ALLIED FORCES SOUTHERN EUROPE (CINCSOUTH)
NAPLES ITALY
COMMANDER ALLIED LAND FORCES SOUTHERN EUROPE (COMLANDSOUTH)
VERONA ITALY
COMMANDER ALLIED LAND FORCES SOUTHEASTERN EUROPE (COMLANDSOUTHEAST)
IZMIR TURKEY
COMMANDER ALLIED AIR FORCE SOUTHERN EUROPE (COMAIRSOUTH)
NAPLES ITALY
COMMANDER ALLIED NAVAL FORCES SOUTHERN EUROPE (COMNAVSOUTH)
NAPLES ITALY
COMMANDER NAVAL STRIKING AND SUPPORT FORCES SOUTHERN EUROPE (COMSTRIKFORSOUTH)
NAPLES ITALY
COMMANDER UNITED KINGDOM AIR FORCES (CINCUKAIR)
HIGH WYCOMBE UK
COMMANDER ACE MOBILE (LAND) (COMAMF (L))
HEIDELBERG FRG
* OPERATIONAL COMMAND OF THE NATO AIRBORNE EARLY WARNING FORCE (NAEWF)
IS SHARED BY SACLANT, CINCHAN AND SACEUR. SACEUR ACTS
AS EXECUTIVE AGENT IN PROMULGATING OPERATIONAL COMMAND DIRECTIVES
AND IS DESIGNATED AS EXECUTIVE AGENT IN THE DAY-TO-DAY EXERCISE OF ADMINISTRATIVE CONTROL.

Figure 15

tives are responsible for liaison with their respective Chief-of-Staff. France is represented at SHAPE by a military mission.

SHAPE is located at Casteau, near Mons, Belgium, about 45 kilometres southwest of Brussels and NATO Headquarters.

The following subordinate commands are responsible to the Supreme Allied Comander Europe:

(a) Allied Forces Northern Europe (AFNORTH): Kolsås, Norway. This Command compromises: Allied Forces North Norway; Allied Forces South Norway; and Allied Forces Baltic Approaches.

(b) Allied Forces Central Europe (AFCENT): Brunssum, the Netherlands. This Command comprises: Northern Army Group, Central Army Group; Allied Air Forces Central Europe; 2nd Allied Tactical Air Force and 4th Allied Tactical Air Force.

(c) Allied Forces Southern Europe (AFSOUTH): Naples, Italy. This Command comprises: Allied Land Forces Southern Europe; Allied Land Forces South-Eastern Europe; Allied Air Forces Southern Europe; Allied Naval Forces Southern Europe; Naval Striking and Support Forces Southern Europe.

(d) The UK Air Forces Command (CINCUKAIR): High Wycombe, United Kingdom.

(e) The Allied Command Europe Mobile Force (AMF): Heidelberg, Federal Republic of Germany.

(f) The NATO Airborne Early Warning Force (NAEWF): Geilenkirchen, Federal Republic of Germany. (The NAEW Force is under the operational command of the three major NATO Commanders, SACEUR, SACLANT and CINCHAN. SACEUR is their Executive Agent).

Allied Command Atlantic (ACLANT)

Allied Command Atlantic extends from the North Pole to the Tropic of Cancer and from the coastal waters of North America to those of Europe and Africa, including Portugal, but not including the Channel and the British Isles. The Supreme Allied Commander Atlantic (SACLANT), like the Supreme Allied Commander Europe, receives his directions from the Military Committee. The headquarters of ACLANT are at Norfolk, Virginia, USA.

SACLANT's peacetime responsibilities are defined as preparing and finalising defence plans; conducting joint and combined training exercises; laying down training standards and determining the establishment of units; and supplying the NATO authorities with information on his strategic requirements.

The primary task of Allied Command Atlantic in wartime would be to ensure security in the whole Atlantic area as far forward as possible by guarding the sea lanes and denying their use to an enemy, to conduct conventional and nuclear operations against enemy naval bases and airfields and to support operations carried out by SACEUR. SACLANT also has responsiblity for islands in his area. His authority in the event of war covers,

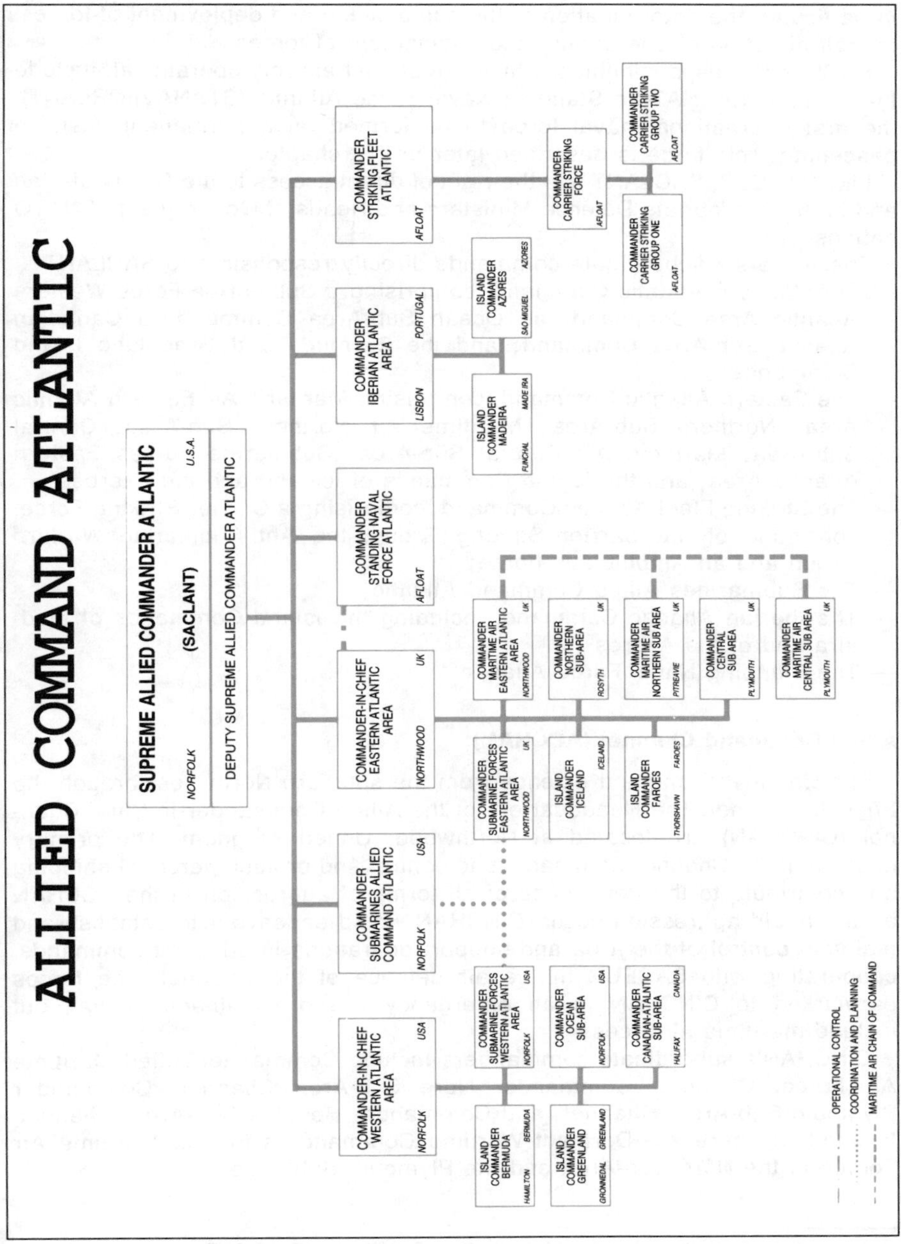
ALLIED COMMAND ATLANTIC
SUPREME ALLIED COMMANDER ATLANTIC
(SACLANT)
NORFOLK
U.S.A.
DEPUTY SUPREME ALLIED COMMANDER ATLANTIC
COMMANDER-IN-CHIEF WESTERN ATLANTIC AREA
NORFOLK
USA
COMMANDER SUBMARINES ALLIED COMMAND ATLANTIC
NORFOLK
USA
COMMANDER-IN-CHIEF EASTERN ATLANTIC AREA
NORTHWOOD
UK
COMMANDER STANDING NAVAL FORCE ATLANTIC
AFLOAT
COMMANDER IBERIAN ATLANTIC AREA
LISBON
PORTUGAL
COMMANDER STRIKING FLEET ATLANTIC
AFLOAT
ISLAND COMMANDER BERMUDA
HAMILTON
BERMUDA
ISLAND COMMANDER GREENLAND
GRONNEDAL
GREENLAND
COMMANDER SUBMARINE FORCES WESTERN ATLANTIC AREA
NORFOLK
USA
COMMANDER OCEAN SUB-AREA
NORFOLK
USA
COMMANDER CANADIAN-ATALNTIC SUB-AREA
HALIFAX
CANADA
COMMANDER SUBMARINE FORCES EASTERN ATLANTIC AREA
NORTHWOOD
UK
ISLAND COMMANDER ICELAND
ICELAND
ISLAND COMMANDER FAROES
THORSHAVN
FAROES
COMMANDER MARITIME AIR EASTERN ATLANTIC AREA
NORTHWOOD
UK
COMMANDER NORTHERN SUB-AREA
ROSYTH
UK
COMMANDER MARITIME AIR NORTHERN SUB AREA
PITREAVIE
UK
COMMANDER CENTRAL SUB AREA
PLYMOUTH
UK
COMMANDER MARITIME AIR CENTRAL SUB AREA
PLYMOUTH
UK
ISLAND COMMANDER MADEIRA
FUNCHAL
MADEIRA
ISLAND COMMANDER AZORES
SAO MIGUEL
AZORES
COMMANDER CARRIER STRIKING FORCE
AFLOAT
COMMANDER CARRIER STRIKING GROUP ONE
AFLOAT
COMMANDER CARRIER STRIKING GROUP TWO
AFLOAT
OPERATIONAL CONTROL
COORDINATION AND PLANNING
MARITIME AIR CHAIN OF COMMAND

Figure 16

in particular, the determination of the composition and deployment of forces, overall direction of operations, and assignment of forces.

SACLANT's responsibilities, which are almost entirely operational, include the command of NATO's Standing Naval Force Atlantic (STANAVFORLANT), the first international naval force to be formed on a permanent basis in peacetime. This force is described later in this chapter.

Like SACEUR, SACLANT has the right of direct access to the Chiefs-of-Staff and to the appropriate Defence Ministers and Heads of Government of NATO nations.

There are six subordinate commands directly responsible to SACLANT:

— The Western Atlantic Command, comprising a Submarine Force Western Atlantic Area Command; an Ocean Sub-Area Command; a Canadian Atlantic Sub-Area Command; and the Bermuda and Greenland Island Commands;
— The Eastern Atlantic Command, comprising Maritime Air Eastern Atlantic Area; Northern Sub-Area; Maritime Air Northern Sub-Area; Central Sub-Area; Maritime Air Central Sub-Area; Submarine Forces Eastern Atlantic Area; and the Island Commands of Iceland and the Faeroes;
— The Striking Fleet Atlantic Command, comprising a Carrier Striking Force, consisting of the Carrier Striking Group, the Anti-Submarine Warfare Group and an Amphibious Force;
— The Submarines Allied Command Atlantic;
— The Iberian Atlantic Command, including the island Commands of Madeira and of the Azores[5];
— The Standing Naval Force Atlantic.

Allied Command Channel (ACCHAN)

The Channel Command extends from the southern North Sea through the English Channel. The Headquarters of the Allied Commander-in-Chief Channel (CINCHAN) are located at Northwood, United Kingdom. The primary mission of the Channel Command is to control and protect merchant shipping and contribute to the deterrence of all forms of aggression in the ACCHAN area. Should aggression occur, CINCHAN would endeavour to establish and maintain control of the area and support operations in adjacent commands, cooperating with SACEUR in the air defence of the Channel. The forces earmarked to CINCHAN in an emergency are predominantly naval, but include maritime airforces.

CINCHAN's subordinate commanders include Commander Allied Maritime Air Force, Channel; Commander Nore Sub-Area Channel; Commander Plymouth Sub-Area, Channel; and Commander Benelux Sub-Area, Channel. In addition, there are Dormant Wartime Commanders for the Maritime Air Forces in the Nore Sub-Area and the Plymouth Sub-Area.

---

[5] The transfer of this Command from WESTLAND to IBERLANT was approved in 1988.

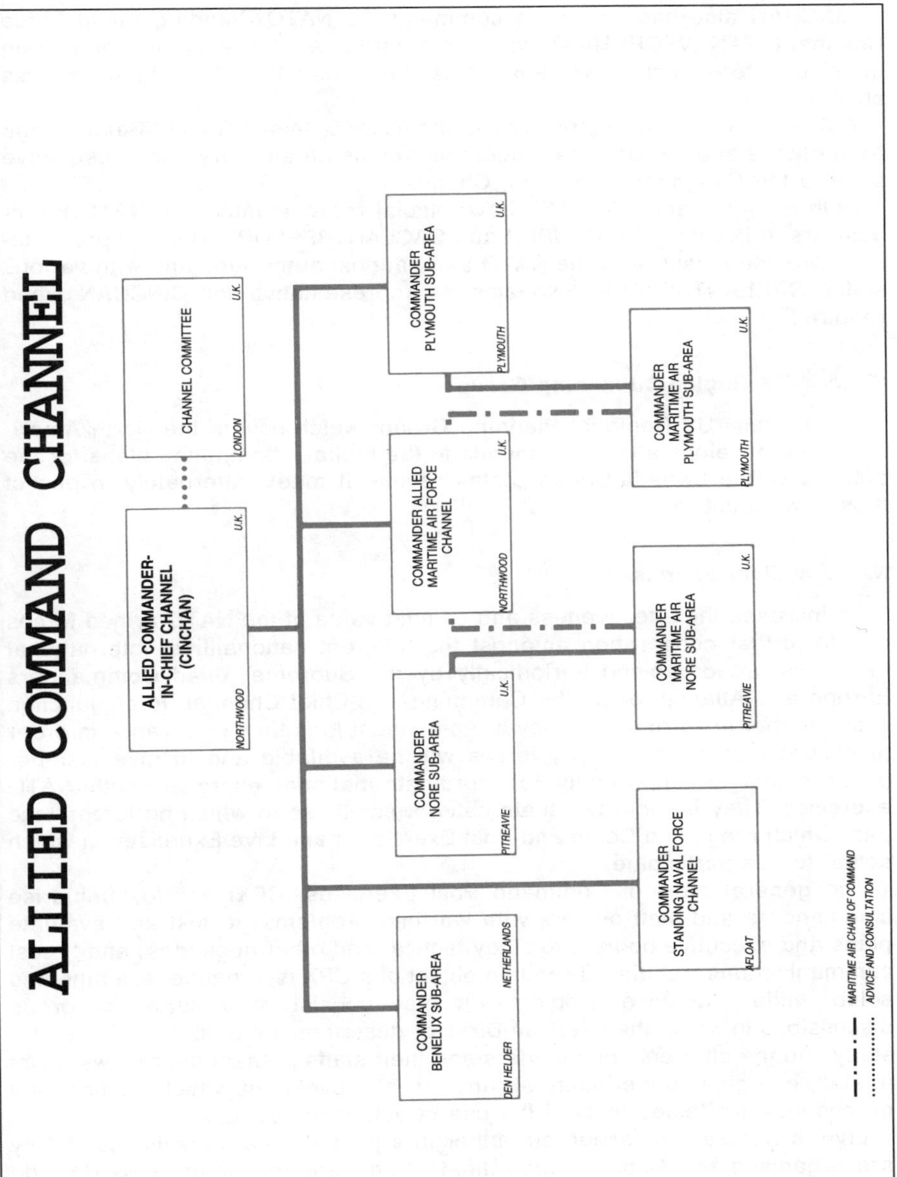
ALLIED COMMAND CHANNEL
ALLIED COMMANDER-IN-CHIEF CHANNEL (CINCHAN)
NORTHWOOD
U.K.
CHANNEL COMMITTEE
LONDON
U.K.
COMMANDER BENELUX SUB-AREA
DEN HELDER
NETHERLANDS
COMMANDER NORE SUB-AREA
PITREAVIE
U.K.
COMMANDER ALLIED MARITIME AIR FORCE CHANNEL
NORTHWOOD
U.K.
COMMANDER PLYMOUTH SUB-AREA
PLYMOUTH
U.K.
COMMANDER STANDING NAVAL FORCE CHANNEL
AFLOAT
COMMANDER MARITIME AIR NORE SUB-AREA
PITREAVIE
U.K.
COMMANDER MARITIME AIR PLYMOUTH SUB-AREA
PLYMOUTH
U.K.
MARITIME AIR CHAIN OF COMMAND
ADVICE AND CONSULTATION

Figure 17

CINCHAN also has under his command the NATO Standing Naval Force Channel (STANAVFORCHAN), which is a permanent force mainly comprising mine counter-measure vessels. This force is described later in this chapter.

A Channel Committee consisting of the naval Chiefs-of-Staff of Belgium, the Netherlands and the United Kindgom serves as an advisory and consultative body to the Commander-in-Chief, Channel.

Both SACEUR and SACLANT have official representatives at NATO Headquarters in Brussels (SACEUREP and SACLANTREPEUR). These representatives provide liaison with the NATO and national authorities and with various staffs. SACLANTREPEUR also acts as representative for CINCHAN when required.

Canada-US Regional Planning Group

The Canada-US Regional Planning Group, which covers the North American area, develops and recommends to the Military Committee plans for the defence of the Canada-United States region. It meets alternately in one of these two countries.

NATO military exercises

To increase the effectiveness and combat value of the NATO armed forces and to further cooperation amongst the different nationalities, international exercises are organised periodically by the Supreme Allied Commanders Europe and Atlantic, or by the Commander-in-Chief Channel, in conjunction with member governments. They are planned a long time in advance in order to ensure that the necessary forces will be available and to give member governments an opportunity to coordinate national exercises with NATO exercises. They fall into two main categories: those in which no forces take part, which are called Command Post Exercises; and Live Exercises in which actual forces participate.

The general aims of Command Post Exercises (CPX) are to familiarise commanders and staff officers with wartime problems; to test and evaluate plans and executive bodies; to study tactical and other questions; and to test communications facilities. The main object of a CPX is to define, examine and solve military defence problems. It may consist of a series of group discussions in which the Exercise Director describes the problems chosen for study and the different commanders and their staffs present their views; or of a staff exercise, undertaken at any or all levels, in which tactics and procedures are tested without the use of actual troops.

Live exercises are carried out either in a limited area, in which case they are organised by Major or Subordinate Commanders, or on a NATO-wide scale when they are jointly conducted by the Major NATO Commanders concerned.

There are different types of exercises, each of which is given a special name. The number of forces participating varies considerably. The purpose of the exercises is to increase cooperation between the forces of various member countries and to test plans or study strategic problems.

Forces available to NATO

The forces of member countries available to NATO's integrated military command structure are essentially in two categories. Assigned forces are those which come under the operational command or operational control of a Major NATO Commander when required, in accordance with specified procedures or at prescribed stages of alert measures approved by NATO. Earmarked forces are those which nations have agreed to assign to the operational commmand or operational control of a Major NATO Commander at a future date.

It should be noted that some of the above terms have precise military definitions. The terms "command" and "control", for example, relate to the nature of the authority exercised by military commanders over the forces assigned to them. When used internationally, these terms do not necessarily have the same implications as they do when used in a purely national context. In assigning forces to NATO, member nations assign operational command or operational control as distinct from full command over all aspects of the military operations and administration of those forces.

In general, national forces remain under national command in peacetime. Exceptions to this rule are the integrated staffs in the various NATO military headquarters; certain air defence units on constant alert such as the units manning the Airborne Early Warning and Control Force (AWACS); some communications units; and four small multinational forces created for specific tasks. These are described below.

The ACE Mobile Force (AMF)

In 1960, the first elements of a Mobile Force for Allied Command Europe were constituted. NATO announced the formation of a small, multinational task force which could be sent at short notice to any threatened part of Allied Command Europe to demonstrate the solidarity of the Alliance and its ability and determination to defend itself against aggression. Officially designated the ACE Mobile Force, the AMF is composed of land and air forces from Belgium, Canada, the Federal Republic of Germany, Italy, Luxembourg, the Netherlands, the United Kingdom and the United States of America.

Until assembled at the request of the Supreme Allied Commander Europe (SACEUR), most units assigned to the AMF are stationed in their home countries. United States units are provided by U.S. Forces already stationed in Europe.

The role of the AMF is to deter aggression. The headquarters of AMF's land component is located near Heidelberg in the Federal Republic of Germany. It has a small permanent staff drawn from most of the nations which contribute to its forces. When the full land component of the AMF is brought together, it becomes a balanced force made up of infantry battalions, artillery batteries and supporting units, with the fighting strength of a brigade group of about 5,000 men. The air component of the AMF has no permanent headquarters. The air squadrons assigned to it are placed under the control of the local Air Force commander in the area to which the force is sent.

The entire force can be deployed rapidly to any part of Allied Command Europe. The force is trained and tested every year in tough, realistic exercises held in both the northern and southern flanks of Europe. By its presence in a threatened area, it demonstrates that the NATO Allies are determined to fulfil their Treaty obligations and that they do, indeed, consider an attack against one an attack against all.

Standing Naval Forces

In a similar fashion, a Standing Naval Force Atlantic (STANAVFORLANT) was established in 1967. Composed of destroyer or frigate class ships drawn from the navies of member countries, this force, which flies the NATO flag, comes under the command of the Supreme Allied Commander Atlantic (SACLANT). Control is delegated to the Commander-in-Chief Eastern Atlantic when it is operating in European waters. The force carries out a programme of scheduled exercises, manoeuvres, and port visits. The ships composing the unit are rotated to enable national naval forces contributing to the Standing Force to gain useful experience in working as a multinational team and in command and control procedures, communications, surveillance, tactics and operations. The force can be rapidly deployed to a threatened area in times of crisis or tension. Ships from Canada, the Federal Republic of Germany, the Netherlands, the United Kingdom and the United States form the permanent membership of the force. They are joined periodically by naval units from Belgium, Denmark, Norway and Portugal.

In keeping with the same concept, a Standing Naval Force Channel (STANAVFORCHAN) was commissioned in May 1973. It consists of mine counter measure vessels and operates under the Command of the Allied Commander-in-Chief, Channel (CINCHAN). Belgium, the Federal Republic of Germany, the Netherlands and the United Kingdom are regular contributors to the force. Danish, Norwegian and United States' ships also join the force from time to time.

In addition, a Naval On-Call Force for the Mediterranean (NAVOCFORMED) was created in 1969. Similar in purpose to STANAVFORLANT and STANAVFORCHAN, this naval force is assigned to the Supreme Allied Commander, Europe. It is not permanently in being and assembles only when called upon. Between exercises, which take place at least once a year, the ships remain under national command. Italy, Greece, Turkey, the United Kingdom and the United States normally contribute ships to the force and units of other nations have also exercised with the force.

Reserve Forces

People are the most important and precious of all the resources needed for defence. However, it is in this sector of human resources that a shortage will become evident in the late eighties and in the nineties as a result of a drop in the birth rate which began in the sixties. The solution to this problem will involve making more extensive use of reserve forces. These consist of civilians who have received military training and can be called to active duty in time of need. More than 50% of the troops which NATO needs for adequate deterrence and defence are mobilisable reserves—a proportion which will increase as the effects of the demographic situation become apparent. Reserves will then become an even more important component of the resources required to implement NATO's flexible response strategy than they are at present. The ability to mobilise reserves quickly and in a timely fashion in order to provide adequate conventional response to aggression is an essential part of the policy of deterrence.

Reserve forces play an important role in the whole spectrum of NATO's defence structure. They are part of what are known as "in place forces at full strength". In the event of a crisis, units in this category would be required to take up their positions and carry out their tasks alongside regular forces.

In the event of the deployment of reinforcements to mainland Europe, reserve forces would be called upon to ensure that reinforcements, which would themselves include reservists, could be effectively moved forward to threatened areas. Their tasks would include the manning of reception facilities at ports and air bases, the provision of logistics support, traffic control, and transport. In the light of the threat posed by hostile airborne and seaborne forces in such circumstances, securing vital rear areas, transportation networks and communication centres would also depend to a large extent on the availability to NATO of well-trained and well-equipped reserve forces.

The ability to assure the timely presence of reserve forces, in sufficient strength, at the positions and in the areas most critical to NATO, is an important factor in increasing the effectiveness and the credibility of the deterrent provided by conventional forces. In the event of a prolonged crisis, their importance would increase. Ensuring the availablility of adequate reserve forces is therefore an integral part of the defence planning process of NATO nations. (See also Chapter 27— CIOR).

Military Agencies

In addition to its other responsibilities, the Military Committee is charged with the direction of a number of NATO military agencies. The structure and activities of these are described below.

The Advisory Group for Aerospace Research and Development (AGARD)

The Advisory Group for Aerospace Research and Development (AGARD) was formed in 1952 as a result of recommendations made by a conference of Aeronautical Research Directors from NATO countries organised a year earlier by Dr. Theodore von Karman. The NATO Standing Group agreed to the formation of AGARD on a trial basis of two years. At the end of this period, the experiment was considered sufficiently successful to warrant a permanent establishment for AGARD and it was designated as a Standing Group Agency, financed from NATO funds. In 1966, when the Standing Group was disbanded, it became an agency under the Military Committee which approved the Charter under which AGARD operates.

The AGARD Board of National Delegates, with the assistance of an Advisory Committee and a Steering Committee, establishes the policies and approves the programmes of AGARD. The Technical Programme of AGARD is accomplished in the Technical Panels and the Aerospace Applications Studies Committee involving 500 to 600 scientists and engineers from all the NATO nations. They are supported by the staff of the AGARD Headquarters which is composed of 31 permanent posts and 18 non-established posts supported by the nations, as additional contributions to AGARD.

AGARD's task is to foster and improve the interchange of information relating to aerospace research and development between the NATO nations in order to ensure that the advances made by one nation are available to the others. AGARD also provides scientific and technical advice and assistance to the NATO Military Committee in the field of aerospace research and development, with particular regard to military applications.

The AGARD staff provides the secretariat for nine Technical Panels[6] and for a number of Aerospace Applications Studies. Each Panel comprises 40 to 50 specialists drawn from the member nations and holds two symposia each year. The proceedings of the symposia are published and each Panel also publishes reports relating to its sphere of interest.

AGARD also sponsors six Lecture Series every year. Each series is given in at least three different countries by a team of visiting consultants; it funds many individual visits by consultants to different Alliance countries and promotes other bilateral or multi-nation interchanges between NATO nations. Particular emphasis has been given to supporting Greece, Portugal and Turkey in this respect, following a general initiative within NATO to assist these countries in strengthening the scientific and technological basis of their defence efforts (see Chapter 20).

The Headquarters of AGARD is located in Paris, but the Technical Panels meet in different member countries. This enables large numbers of the host nation's scientists to meet their counterparts from other countries.

The work of AGARD is described in more detail in a recent booklet entitled "AGARD—35 Years of Service to the Aerospace Research and Development Community of NATO"[7].

The Military Agency for Standardization (MAS)

Organised in London in 1951, the MAS is the principal military agency for standardization within NATO. The purpose of MAS is to facilitate operational,

---

[6] Aerospace Medical Panel; Avionics Panel; Electromagnetic Wave Propagation Panel; Flight Mechanics Panel; Fluid Dynamics Panel; Guidance and Control Panel; Propulsion and Energetics Panel; Structures and Materials Panel; Technical Information Panel.

[7] Available from the NATO Information Service, 1110-Brussels.

procedural and material standardization among member nations to enable NATO forces to operate together in the most effective manner. Cooperation between the international technical expert groups and the agency in regard to defence equipment is effected through the NATO Standardization Group and by liaison with the International Staff and the International Military Staff. Since January 1970 the MAS has been housed within NATO Headquarters in Brussels.

The NATO Electronic Warfare Advisory Committee (NEWAC)

NEWAC was established in 1966 to support the Military Committee, the Major NATO Commanders (MNCs) and the nations by acting as a specialist multinational body to promote on a tri-service basis an effective NATO electronic warfare capability. It monitors national and MNC progress in implementing measures which improve NATO's electronic warfare capabilities.

NEWAC is composed of representatives of each NATO country and of the MNCs. The Chairman of the Committee and the secretary are permanently assigned to the Operations Division of the International Military Staff (IMS).

The work of the NEWAC is carried out through plenary meetings, normally two per year, and by establishing working groups on specific subjects. By sponsoring symposia, NEWAC allows for a broad exchange of ideas on electronic warfare matters between nations and MNCs.

The EURO/NATO Training Group (ENTG)

Responsibility within NATO for consolidation of training on a multinational basis has been vested in the EURO/NATO Training Group (ENTG). The Group is a unique example of institutionalised linkage between the EUROGROUP[8] and NATO itself. In 1970, the EUROGROUP established the EURO-TRAINING Sub-Group, with the aim of furthering multinational training arrangements between the European member nations. To facilitate the participation of Canada and the USA, in 1971 the Military Committee set up the NATO Training Group. However, as a practical measure of collaboration and to avoid duplication, the two groups now meet in combined session as the EURO/NATO Training Group.

The Group's most important objectives are to improve and expand existing and to initiate new, multinational training arrangements between member nations and to develop these arrangements to the point where one nation can assume responsibility for training in specific areas on behalf of its partners. This enables savings to be made both in terms of personnel and costs.

The work of the Group is carried out through plenary meetings, which are normally held twice a year, and through working groups. The ENTG reports to the NATO Military Committee and to the EUROGROUP.

---

[8] The EUROGROUP is described in Chapter 3.

The Military Committee Meteorological Group (MCMG)

The MCMG acquired its present title in 1967, having been previously designated as the Standing Group Meteorological Committee created in 1950. Its task is to advise the Military Committee on meteorological matters affecting NATO and to make appropriate recommendations as required. The MCMG also acts as the coordinating agency of the Military Committee for all military meteorological policies, procedures and techniques within NATO. The MCMG has two sub-groups, a Working Group on Weather Plans and a Working Group on Weather Communications. Both were formed in 1954.

Communications and Information Systems

Nine specialised multinational Communications and Information Systems Committees, Working Groups or Agencies provide the Military Committee with expert technical advice on military matters within their own fields of competence. These are:

— NATO Communications and Information Systems Committee (NACISC)
— Allied Communications and Computer Security Agency (ACCSA)
— Allied Long Lines Agency (ALLA)
— Allied Radio Frequency Agency (ARFA)
— Allied Tactical Communications Agency (ATCA)
— Allied Data Systems Interoperability Agency (ADSIA)
— Information Systems Working Group (ISWG)
— Communications Systems Working Group (CSWG)
— Allied Naval Communications Agency (ANCA)

The permanent staffs of these bodies, with the exception of ANCA staff located in London, are drawn from the NATO International Military Staff and are co-located in Brussels.

The SHAPE Technical Centre

The SHAPE Technical Centre was conceived as early as 1954 when General Gruenther, then Supreme Allied Commander Europe, expressed concern about the relative weakness of air defence within the NATO defence system. To remedy this, he suggested that air defence be studied as a whole and organised internationally according to a general plan, each country of the Alliance putting into effect the part which concerned it.

However, the creation of such an integrated air defence system, whose operation must cut across national boundaries, entailed the solution of political, tactical and technical problems, which in turn had to be considered from the viewpoint of all the NATO countries. The political and military authorities of the Alliance therefore authorised SHAPE, as the executive command for the integrated air defence system, to secure the assistance of a technical and scientific air defence centre composed of experts to be drawn from all the member countries.

In view of the time inevitably required to agree on the organisation, structure, method of financing, and site of such a Centre, the United States Government agreed to bear the costs until NATO could take over, providing that the Centre had proved its worth. After exhaustive enquiries, the United States Government decided to entrust the establishment and control of this Centre to a non profit-making Dutch scientific research agency, RVO-TNO (Rijksverdedigings Organisatie—Toegepast Natuurkundig Onderzoek). A contract was signed between the United States and Netherlands governments on December 14, 1954, which led to the foundation on February 15, 1955, in The Hague, of the SHAPE Air Defence Technical Centre, to be administered by RVO-TNO.

Established as a non profit-making organisation, operating under the policy guidance of SHAPE, the Centre continued to be funded by the United States Government until July 1, 1960, when, following a decision taken by the NATO Council on February 24, 1960, it became eligible for international financing under the NATO Military Budget. This did not affect the way in which the Centre was organised. The Netherlands Government renewed, with respect to NATO, the undertakings it had given to the United States Government in 1954. On March 1, 1963 the Centre was established as an international military organisation in its own right, under the policy direction of the Supreme Allied Commander Europe.

The SHAPE Technical Centre's task is to provide scientific and technical advice and assistance to SHAPE. It is required to undertake research, studies, investigations, development projects and operational tests for Allied Command Europe. As a subsidiary function the Centre may render similar scientific and technical assistance, within the approved programme, to NATO nations requesting such aid. Initially the task was limited to air defence problems, but on October 23, 1963 its scope was widened to cover all military matters pertaining to Allied Command Europe. The name of the Centre was accordingly changed to SHAPE Technical Centre.

The focal point of the Centre's work has changed to keep pace with SHAPE's requirements. In the beginning it was occupied in assessing the effectiveness and compatibility of air defence systems and communications facilities provided by member nations for integration into a NATO system and proposing new and better means. The current programme is much broader and is directed towards three major areas of concern to Allied Command Europe: force capability and force structure, including the effects of new weapons technology; command and control, including application of automated data processing; and communications, including concept formulation, systems engineering and operations support.

The Centre has a complement of 106 scientists, supported by technicians, management and administration. Most of the Centre's tasks are supported by its large-scale central scientific computer accessible from terminals located throughout the Centre. Feasibility trials and simulation of new systems, e.g.

SATCOM—air command and control—special radio communications, and new techniques are performed in the Centre's electronic laboratories involving war-gaming, large computer modelling and simulation trials. Since 1968 custom-built premises leased from the Netherlands Government have brought the facilities of the Centre together.

When international funding was introduced, a new board was established, called the Scientific Committee of National Representatives. This facilitates the flow of information between nations and the Centre and avoids duplication of work.

The SACLANT Undersea Research Centre

The SACLANT Anti-Submarine Warfare Research Centre was commissioned in May 1959 at La Spezia, Italy. Nine NATO nations participated: Canada, Denmark, France, Germany, Italy, the Netherlands, Norway, the United Kingdom and the United States. Financial support for the Centre was initially provided by the United States until such time as NATO could take over.

Discussions leading to a NATO charter for the Centre began in July 1962 with the formation of a working group, authorised by the Council, with representatives from interested NATO countries and permanent military commands. The working group examined the future status of both the SACLANT Centre and the SHAPE Technical Centre. NATO charters and appropriate transition plans were worked out for both Centres.

The NATO charter, which resulted from discussions carried out in Paris during the summer and autumn of 1962, was adopted by the Council on October 20. Its provisions were based on the reorganisation of the Centre as a NATO international military organisation under the continuing policy direction of SACLANT. The transfer to NATO was completed on July 1, 1963. In December 1987 the Centre was renamed the SACLANT Undersea Research Centre.

The task of the Centre is to provide scientific and technical advice and assistance to SACLANT in the field of anti-submarine warfare, and to be in all respects responsive through SACLANT to the requirements of NATO naval forces in this field. The Centre may also render scientific and technical assistance within the approved programme to NATO nations requesting aid on anti-submarine warfare problems.

The Centre carries out research and limited development (but not engineering or manufacturing) in the field of anti-submarine warfare, including oceanography, operational research and analysis, advisory and consultant work; exploratory research and other related tasks as necessary. It is organised by a director, assisted by a deputy director and a naval adviser appointed by SACLANT. The broad scientific direction of the Centre is carried out by a scientific committee of national representatives, to which any NATO nation may appoint a member. The scientific work is conducted, under the supervision of the Director, by a staff of scientists, engineers, and technicians from the participating nations.

The headquarters and shore-based laboratories occupy buildings made available by the Italian Government in the naval base at La Spezia. The staff of the Centre includes over 200 scientists, engineers, technicians and administrators. In July 1986, under the auspices of SACLANTCEN, the first ship ever funded jointly by NATO, the 3,200-ton anti-submarine research vessel ALLIANCE, was officially launched at La Spezia. The ship became operational in May 1988 and replaces an older chartered merchant ship modified as a research vessel.

The scientific programme is divided into the following main categories: underwater acoustic research; oceanographic research; systems concept evaluations; and anti-submarine warfare studies.

About 40 scientific reports per year are distributed to NATO governments and to interested NATO Commands.

NATO Defense College

The idea of a NATO Defense College originated with General Eisenhower. Addressing the Standing Group[9] in 1951, he said: "It is highly desirable to establish in the near future a NATO Defense College for the training of individuals who will be needed to serve in key capacities in NATO organisations. It should be under the general direction of the Standing Group, or of the Council Deputies, or of both. Its students should consist of carefully selected officers of the military services, probably of the grade of colonel or equivalent, who are considered of suitable calibre for later assignment to key NATO military posts, and also of selected national civil servants who may later be made available to serve in key NATO posts. The course might include a study of military, political and economic factors which influence our NATO defence efforts, as well as a consideration of specific problems, in both the military and the political fields for which satisfactory solutions may not yet have been found". SACEUR's conclusions were accepted by the Council, and Admiral Lemonnier was appointed as the first Commandant of the College.

The French Government made available the Artillery wing of the Ecole Militaire at the southern end of the Champ de Mars, and on November 19, 1951, the College opened for its first course. It represented a novel experiment in international teaching. Over 100 graduates a year have since graduated from the College to fill key posts, not only on NATO staffs, but also in their respective national ministries.

The choice of course members, about 25% of whom are civilians, is left entirely to the governments, whose task it is to make a selection on the basis of past experience and training. It is also up to the governments to employ these same officers in suitable future appointments which make the best use of the instruction received at the College.

An important change in the history of the College occurred in the spring of 1966, when the French Government decided to cease its participation in the

---

[9] The Standing Group was disbanded in 1966, and its functions transferred to the Military Committee.

activities of the College and requested its transfer from French territory. The 29th course, the last to be held in the Ecole Militaire, came to an end on July 22, 1966. At the Ministerial Meeting in Brussels in June 1966, the Council invited Italy to provide a new site for the College, and in the autumn of 1966 the College moved to Rome[10].

When the NATO Defense College was created, some experience in developing a suitable academic programme was already available. On the national level, there were the examples of the National War College in Washington, the Imperial Defence College in London, and the Institut des Hautes Etudes de Défense Nationale in Paris. These establishments already combined the study of strictly military problems with that of social, political and economic matters, conducted in a broad national spirit and in the manner of the older western universities. The first basic elements of the academic programme of the NATO Defense College were inspired by these examples. Studies focussed on:

(a) The aim and policies of the Alliance, its strategic concept, organisation and functions.
(b) The geographical, political and military characteristics, including special defence problems and technological and economic potential, of member nations.
(c) Developments outside the NATO area and their effect on the Alliance.
(d) Defence management.
(e) English and French language studies.

Organised on a military basis, the College, which comes directly under the Military Committee, is commanded by a field officer of the rank equivalent or superior to Lieutenant General. The appointment is normally for a two to three year period.

The Commandant is assisted by a Faculty comprising three deputies (two military and one civilian) and eight Faculty advisers, one quarter of whom are civilians. The tasks of the Faculty Advisers is less to teach than to assist, guide and stimulate the course members in the study of a wide range of problems undertaken in common in a spirit of intellectual freedom and objectivity.

In April 1970, an independent Advisory Board was established to advise the Commandant individually and collectively on the continuing improvement of the College. The board meets under the chairmanship of the Chairman of the Military Committee and has up to six members, each appointed for a period of four years.

The academic activities of the College consist of lectures and discussions, team studies, examining and attempting to solve designated problems and instructional tours.

Perhaps the most valuable work of all takes place in committee meetings. Course members are grouped in committees, each with a Faculty Adviser. These committees are changed once during the course to allow members to

---

[10] The address of the NATO Defense College is: Viale della Civilta del Lavoro 38, 00144 Rome.

have the opportunity of working closely with as many of their colleagues as possible. Differing personal and national points of view are brought out, and the particular views of the various services and ministries from which the course members come can be examined.

Instructional tours and visits are also an essential part of the course. Each course involves a tour of the United States and Canada and a European tour which takes in most of the European member countries of the Alliance. In addition to visits of national capitals, the course members visit major NATO Headquarters and military and industrial installations in each country. Shorter visits are also organised in Italy. The tours include briefings by senior national officials and representatives of industry, economic institutions etc. The aim is to give course members a chance to familiarise themselves with the various member nations, and to increase their knowledge and understanding of their allies. Representatives of those countries which cannot be visited during a particular course come to the College to give national presentations.

Prospective course members have to be thoroughly competent in their own specialised field and to have sufficient breadth of vision to allow them to grasp the points of view of other members within the context of the Alliance. A very thorough knowledge of one of the two official NATO languagues is also required.

Chapter 24

Budgetary and Financial Control

The running costs of the International Staff[1], the International Military Staff, the military headquarters and the various specialised agencies are paid for by means of contributions from member countries. The funds contributed are subject to strict management and control at several levels.

Responsibility for NATO finances is vested in the North Atlantic Council, which is advised by the Military and Civil Budget Committees and by the International Board of Auditors. Budget estimates are prepared by the appropriate sections of the International Staff and International Military Staff and are scrutinised by the respective budget committees before being submitted to the Council. Budget estimates for the International Staff are examined by the Civil Budget Committee. The Military Budget Committee examines those of the International Military Staff, the Major NATO Commands and the various subordinate headquarters and specialised agencies. A nationally funded Chairman is provided by one of the nations to maintain the independence of the Budget Committees.

The NATO Financial Regulations approved by the Council cover every step in the process of commitment and expenditure of funds contributed by member countries to ensure that they are properly used for the purpose for which they were authorised. Competitive bidding procedures are followed for works and supply contracts, thus ensuring economy and at the same time offering contractors and suppliers in all member countries a chance to submit bids. There is an established system for the clearance and payment of accounts and appropriate rules apply to the maintenance of accounting records.

The responsibility for ensuring strict compliance with the Financial Regulations and for the day-to-day control of the various budgetary and financial operations devolves upon Financial Controllers, who are independent of the administrative services and combine these functions with those of treasurers. There is a Financial Controller for the International Staff and the International Military Staff and one for the headquarters of each of the Major NATO Commanders—SACEUR, SACLANT and CINCHAN. Their appointment must be approved by the Council. At subordinate headquarters, local controllers are responsible to the Financial Controllers of the respective Major NATO Commands.

It is also the responsibility of Financial Controllers to obtain contributions due from member countries, payable in instalments in the course of the year.

---

[1] Including the costs of the operational budgets for information, the science programme, defence support, etc.

Each nation's contribution is calculated on the basis of an agreed cost-sharing formula.

International Board of Auditors

The accounts of the International Staff, the International Military Staff, the military headquarters and agencies, and the accounts relating to commonly funded infrastructure works, described in Chapter 12, are audited by the International Board of Auditors for NATO. The members of the Board are government officials belonging to audit bodies in member countries or having a thorough knowledge of auditing procedures. They are selected and remunerated by their respective countries and appointed by the Council. They have independent status, and are responsible only to the Council. They are assisted by members of the International Staff.

The primary function of the Board of Auditors is to enable the Council and, through their Permanent Representatives, the governments of member countries, to satisfy themselves that common funds have been properly used for the purposes for which they have been authorised. It ensures that expenditures are within the relevant budgetary authorisations and that they have been carried out, in compliance with the financial regulations in force, as economically as possible. The Board establishes its own audit procedures, in line with modern methods.

The Board prepares annual reports on the various audits it has performed for approval by the Council. It may include in these reports whatever recommendations it deems appropriate concerning the efficiency of NATO procedures for financial control and the financial implications of administrative practices, drawing special attention to the need for adequate justification of expenses and cost-efficient use of funds.

NATO's financial management procedures are designed to ensure that the funds made available by the member countries are used effectively in the light of the requirements established in the Civil and Military Budgets and controlled by a series of management mechanisms comparable with those used by national and international administrations.

Part 7

Non-Governmental Activities

Chapter 25
The North Atlantic Assembly

The North Atlantic Assembly is the inter-parliamentary organisation of the 16 member countries of the Alliance, and as such it provides a forum where North American and European parliamentarians meet to discuss problems of common concern.

The Assembly was founded in 1955, and, until 1966, was known as the "NATO Parliamentarians Conference". Its aims are to strengthen cooperation and understanding among the countries of the Alliance, to encourage governments to take the Alliance viewpoint into account when framing legislation; and to encourage a common feeling of Atlantic cohesion in national parliaments.

Although the Assembly is completely independent of NATO, it constitutes a link between the national parliaments and Alliance officials. The highest military and civilian authorities of the Alliance address the Assembly at its bi-annual sessions where a wide range of Alliance issues are examined and discussed in detail. The Secretary General of NATO usually attends the Assembly's autumn session and answers questions from members.

The North Atlantic Assembly has 188 members and as many alternates nominated by member parliaments under different national procedures. The number of delegates from each member nation varies according to the size of its population. No minister or member of a government in office can be a member of the Assembly.

The Assembly has five committees whose activities cover a wide range of subjects. They are: the Civilian Affairs Committee; the Economic Committee; the Military Committee; the Political Committee; and the Scientific and Technical Committee. Special Committees on NATO in the 1990s and NATO Strategy and Arms Control were created in 1987 and 1988 respectively.

The committees meet twice a year during the spring and autumn sessions to discuss draft reports, and policy recommendations on the most urgent issues facing the Alliance. When the committees identify a need to analyse a specific subject in greater depth they can form sub-committees. Sub-committees currently exist on the following subjects: the free flow of information and people; public information on security and defence; transatlantic trade relations; defence cooperation; conventional defence; terrorism; Eastern Europe; advanced technology and technology transfer. These sub-committees, which meet frequently during the year, provide continuity in the work of the Assembly.

The North Atlantic Assembly convenes in plenary session twice a year. Members discuss policy recommendations and vote on resolutions. These are normally presented by the five committees following their own deliberations, but may be presented directly to the Plenary Assembly by individual members at the request of the President. Policy recommendations are forwarded to the Secretary General of NATO, who formulates a reply in consultation with the North Atlantic Council. These documents, along with the committee reports, are also sent to member governments, parliaments and relevant international organisations. At the 34th Annual Session held in Hamburg from November 13 to 18, 1988, members adopted resolutions on the "Gorbachev effect" on Western public opinion; civil defence; trade policies; strategic arms reductions; terrorism; confidence-building measures; East-West scientific, technical and environmental cooperation; nuclear non-proliferation; and the Gorbachev challenge to the Alliance.

The Assembly also organises an annual tour to a specific region in the Alliance to better acquaint member legislators with the complexities and problems associated with Alliance defence.

The contribution of the North Atlantic Assembly to the effective functioning of the North Atlantic Alliance was acknowledged in the Declaration on Atlantic Relations signed by the Heads of NATO Governments in Brussels, in June 1974, and reaffirmed in paragraph 14 of the Declaration of the June 1987 meeting of the North Atlantic Council at Reykjavik. Foreign Ministers noted that "Alliance cohesion is substantially enhanced by the support of freely elected parliamentary representatives". They therefore encouraged free debate on Alliance issues by Alliance parliamentatians including those of the North Atlantic Assembly.

The budget of the Assembly is drawn from contributions from member governments or parliaments. A grant is allocated by NATO towards the costs of the plenary sessions.

Further information on the North Atlantic Assembly may be obtained from the International Secretariat—Place du Petit Sablon 3, B-1000 Brussels. Tel.: (02) 513.28.65

Chapter 26

The Atlantic Treaty Association

Private societies in NATO countries, particularly the voluntary associations affiliated to the Atlantic Treaty Association (ATA), support the activities engaged in by the Organisation and by the governments to promote the objectives of the Treaty.

The Atlantic Treaty Association was created at at conference held in The Hague on June 18, 1954. Its objectives are:

(a) to educate and inform the public concerning the aims and goals of the North Atlantic Treaty Organisation;

(b) to conduct research in the various purposes and activities related to the Organisation;

(c) to promote the solidarity of the peoples in the North Atlantic area;

(d) to develop permanent relations and cooperation between its national member committees or associations.

An Atlantic Education Committee (AEC) and an Atlantic Association of Young Political Leaders (AAYPL) (formed in 1963) are active in their respective fields.

The following national voluntary organisations are members of that ATA:

Belgium
The Belgian Atlantic Association
24 rue des Petits Carmes
1000 Bruxelles

Canada
The Atlantic Council of Canada
15 King's College Circle
Toronto
Ontario M5S 2V9

Denmark
Danish Atlantic Association
Ved Idraetsparken 4
Postboks 2715
2100 Copenhagen O

France
French Association for the Atlantic Community
185 rue de la Pompe
75116 Paris

Federal Republic of Germany
The German Atlantic Association
Am Burgweiher 12
5300 Bonn 1

Greece
Hellenic Atlantic Association
18 Sina Street
Athens 106 72

Iceland
Association of Western Cooperation
PO Box 28
121 Reykjavik

Italy
Italian Atlantic Committee
Piazza di Firenze 27
00186 Rome

Luxembourg
Luxembourg Atlantic Association
BP 805
Luxembourg

Netherlands
Netherlands Atlantic Committee
Laan van Meerdervoort 96
2517 AR The Hague

Norway
Norwegian Atlantic Committee
Fridtjof Nansens Plass 6
0160 Oslo 1

Portugal
Portuguese Atlantic Committee
Av. Infante Santo 42, 6e
1300 Lisbon

Spain
Spanish Atlantic Association
Joaquim Costa 61-1°
28003 Madrid

Turkey
Turkish Atlantic Committee
Kuleli Sokak 44/1
Gaziosmanpaşa
06700 Ankara

United Kingdom
The British Atlantic Committee
5 St. James's Place
London SW1A INP

United States
The Atlantic Council of the United States
1616 H. Street NW
Washington DC 20006

Further information concerning the Atlantic Treaty Association may be obtained from the Secretary General of the ATA at 185, rue de la Pompe, 75116 Paris, tel.: 45532880

Chairmen of the Atlantic Treaty Association

1955-57	Umberto Morra di Lavriano (Italy)
1957-58	Lester B. Pearson (Canada) — Ralph C.M. Flynt (United States)
1958-61	Ivan Matteo Lombardo (Italy)
1961-63	W. Randolph Burgess (United States)
1963-66	Lord Gladwyn (United Kingdom)
1966-69	Paul-Henri Spaak (Belgium)
1969-72	Sir Frank Roberts (United Kingdom)
1972-76	Eugene V. Rostow (United States)
1976-79	Karl Mommer (Federal Republic of Germany)
1979-82	Muharrem Nuri Birgi (Turkey)
1982-85	Peter Corterier (Federal Republic of Germany)
1985-88	Lord Pym (United Kingdom)
1988-	Bernadino Gomes (Portugal)

Chapter 27

The Interallied Confederation of Reserve Officers (CIOR)

The reserve forces of NATO nations have to be able to operate together with the active or standing forces of NATO. There is therefore a clear need for peacetime training of these forces and of the reservists themselves. Reserve officers promote the cooperation required for such training through an organisation which brings together the national reserve officers associations of 12 NATO nations. The Interallied Confederation of Reserve Officers, a non-governmental, non-political, non-profit-making organisation, contributes to interallied solidarity and enhances NATO's deterrent and defence capacity.

Known by its French acronym CIOR, the Confederation was formed in 1948 by the reserve officers associations of Belgium, France and the Netherlands. Since then all existing national reserve officer associations of NATO-member nations have joined the Confederation. It represents more than 800,000 reserve officers and aims to inculcate and maintain an interallied spirit among its members and to provide them with information about NATO developments and activities. It also aims to contribute to the organisation, administration and training of reserve forces in NATO countries and to improve their motivation, capabilities, interoperability and mutual confidence through common and exchange training programmes.

The Confederation maintains close liaison with appropriate national defence organisations and with NATO military authorities and develops international contacts between reserve officers. Its members are active in professional, business, industrial, academic and political circles in their respective countries and contribute individually to the improvement of public understanding of NATO and the strengthening of public support for its policies.

The chief executive of the Confederation is an elected President who serves in that office for a period of two years. He is assisted by a Secretary General and an Executive Committee composed of delegates from all national member associations. The head of each national delegation is also a Vice-President of the Confederation.

The Interallied Confederation of Medical Reserve Officers (CIOMR) is affiliated to the CIOR.

Member associations of the CIOR:

Belgium	Union Royale Nationale des Officers de Réserve de Belgique (URNOR/BE), Rue des Petits Carmes 24, B-1000 Bruxelles

Canada	The Conference of Defence Associations of Canada (CDA), PO Box 893, Ottawa, Ontario K1P 5P9
Denmark	Reserve Officers Foreningen i Danmark (ROID), Svanestok, Kastellet 68, DK-2100 Copenhagen
Federal Republic of Germany	Verband der Reservisten der Deutschen Bundeswehr (VdRBw), e.V. PO Box 140361, D-5300 Bonn I
France	Union Nationales des Officiers de Réserve de France (UNOR/FR), 12 Rue Marie Laurencin, F-75012 Paris
Greece	The Supreme Pan-Hellenic Federation of Reserve Officers (SPFRO), 100 Solonos Street, GR-Athens 144
Italy	Unione Nazionale Ufficiali in Congedo d'Italia (UNUCI), Via Nomentana 313, I-00162 Rome
Luxembourg	Amicale des Anciens Officiers de Réserve Luxembourgeois (ANORL), 124 A Kiem, L-8030 Strassen
The Netherlands	Koninklijke Vereniging van Nederlandse Reserve Officieren (KVNRO), Postbus 95395, NL-2501 JE The Hague
Norway	Norske Reserveoffiserers Forbund (NROF) Oslo Mil. Akershus NO-Oslo 1
United Kingdom	The Reserve Forces Association of the United Kingdom (RFA) Centre Block, Duke of York's Headquarters, Chelsea, GB-London SW3 4SG
United States	The Reserve Officers Association of the United States (ROA), 1 Constitution Avenue N.E. Washington DC 20002

The CIOR and CIOMR are represented at NATO Headquarters by a liaison office situated within the International Military Staff. Further information about the Confederations may be obtained from this office (CIOR/CIOMR Liaison Office, NATO/IMS/P&P, B-1110 Brussels).

Appendix I
Documentation

1. Article 51 of the Charter of the United Nations (October 24, 1945)
2. The North Atlantic Treaty (April 4, 1949)
3. Protocol to the North Atlantic Treaty on the Accession of Greece and Turkey (October 22, 1951)
4. Protocol to the North Atlantic Treaty on the Accession of the Federal Republic of Germany (October 23, 1954)
5. Protocol to the North Atlantic Treaty on the Accession of Spain (December 10, 1981)
6. Text of the Report of the Committee of Three on Non-Military Cooperation in NATO (December 13, 1956)
7. The Future Tasks of the Alliance — Harmel Report (December 14, 1967)
8. Ottawa Declaration on Atlantic Relations (June 19, 1974)
9. Montebello Decision (October 27, 1983)
10. Declaration of Brussels (December 9, 1983)
11. Washington Statement on East-West Relations (May 31, 1984)
12. Halifax Statement on East-West Relations (May 30, 1986)

13. Brussels Declaration on Conventional Arms Control (December 11, 1986)

14. Statement on the Ministerial Meeting of the North Atlantic Council at Reykjavik (June 12, 1987)

15. Conventional Arms Control: the Way Ahead. Statement issued under the authority of Heads of State and Government at Brussels (March 2, 1988)

16. Declaration of the Heads of State and Government participating in the meeting of the North Atlantic Council in Brussels (March 3, 1988)

17. Statement on Conventional Arms Control issued by the North Atlantic Council in Brussels (December 9, 1988)

18. The Alliance's Comprehensive Concept of Arms Control and Disarmament adopted by the Heads of State and Government at the meeting of the North Atlantic Council in Brussels (May 29-30, 1989)

19. Declaration of the Heads of State and Government participating in the meeting of the North Atlantic Council in Brussels (May 30, 1989)

1

Article 51 of the Charter of the United Nations

San Francisco, October 24, 1945

Nothing in the present Charter shall impair the inherent right of individual or collective self-defence if an armed attack occurs against a Member of the United Nations, until the Security Council has taken measures necessary to maintain international peace and security. Measures taken by Members in the exercise of this right of self-defence shall be immediately reported to the Security Council and shall not in any way affect the authority and responsibility of the Security Council under the present Charter to take at any time such action as it deems necessary in order to maintain or restore international peace and security.

2

The North Atlantic Treaty

Washington D.C., April 4, 1949

The Parties to this Treaty reaffirm their faith in the purposes and principles of the Charter of the United Nations and their desire to live in peace with all peoples and all governments.

They are determined to safeguard the freedom, common heritage and civilisation of their peoples, founded on the principles of democracy, individual liberty and the rule of law.

They seek to promote stability and well-being in the North Atlantic area.

They are resolved to unite their efforts for collective defence and for the preservation of peace and security.

They therefore agree to this North Atlantic Treaty:

Article 1

The Parties undertake, as set forth in the Charter of the United Nations, to settle any international dispute in which they may be involved by peaceful means in such a manner that international peace and security and justice are not endangered, and to refrain in their international relations from the threat or use of force in any manner inconsistent with the purposes of the United Nations.

Article 2

The Parties will contribute toward the further development of peaceful and friendly international relations by strengthening their free institutions, by bringing about a better understanding of the principles upon which these institutions are founded, and by promoting conditions of stability and well-being. They will seek to eliminate conflict in their international economic policies and will encourage economic collaboration between any or all of them.

Article 3

In order more effectively to achieve the objectives of this Treaty, the Parties, separately and jointly, by means of continuous and effective self-help and mutual aid, will maintain and develop their individual and collective capacity to resist armed attack.

Article 4

The Parties will consult together whenever, in the opinion of any of them, the territorial integrity, political independence or security of any of the Parties is threatened.

Article 5

The Parties agree that an armed attack against one or more of them in Europe or North America shall be considered an attack against them all and consequently they agree that, if such an armed attack occurs, each of them, in exercise of the right of individual or collective self-defence recognised by Article 51 of the Charter of the United Nations, will assist the Party or Parties so attacked by taking forthwith, individually and in concert with the other Parties, such action as it deems necessary, including the use of armed force, to restore and maintain the security of the North Atlantic area.

Any such armed attack and all measures taken as a result thereof shall immediately be reported to the Security Council. Such measures shall be terminated when the Security Council has taken the measures necessary to restore and maintain international peace and security.

Article 6[1]

For the purpose of Article 5, an armed attack on one or more of the Parties is deemed to include an armed attack:

— on the territory of any of the Parties in Europe or North America, on the Algerian Departments of France,[2] on the territory of Turkey or on the Islands under the jurisdiction of any of the Parties in the North Atlantic area north of the Tropic of Cancer;

— on the forces, vessels, or aircraft of any of the Parties, when in or over these territories or any other area in Europe in which occupation forces of any of the Parties were stationed on the date when the Treaty entered into force or the Mediterranean Sea or the North Atlantic area north of the Tropic of Cancer.

Article 7

This Treaty does not affect, and shall not be interpreted as affecting in any way the rights and obligations under the Charter of the Parties which are members of the United Nations, or the primary responsibility of the Security Council for the maintenance of international peace and security.

Article 8

Each Party declares that none of the international engagements now in force between it and any other of the Parties or any third State is in conflict with the provisions of this Treaty, and undertakes not to enter into any international engagement in conflict with this Treaty.

Article 9

The Parties hereby establish a Council, on which each of them shall be represented, to consider matters concerning the implementation of this Treaty. The Council shall be so organised as to be able to meet promptly at any time. The Council shall set up such subsidiary bodies as may be necessary; in particular it shall establish immediately a defence committee which shall recommend measures for the implementation of rticles 3 and 5.

Article 10

The Parties may, by unanimous agreement, invite any other European State in a position to further the principles of this Treaty and to contribute to the security of the North Atlantic area to accede to this Treaty. Any State so invited may become a Party to the Treaty by depositing its instrument of accession with the Government of the United States of America. The Government of the United States of America will inform each of the Parties of the deposit of each such instrument of accession.

Article 11

This Treaty shall be ratified and its provisions carried out by the Parties in accordance with their respective constitutional processes. The instruments of ratification shall be deposited as soon as possible with the Government of the United States of America, which will notify all the other signatories of each deposit. The Treaty shall enter into force between the States which have ratified it as soon as the ratifications of the majority of the signatories, including the ratifications of Belgium, Canada, France, Luxembourg, the Netherlands, the United Kingdom and the United States, have been deposited and shall come into effect with respect to other States on the date of the deposit of their ratifications.

Article 12

After the Treaty has been in force for ten years, or at any time thereafter, the Parties shall, if any of them so requests, consult together for the purpose of reviewing the Treaty, having regard for the factors then affecting peace and security in the North Atlantic area, including the development of universal as well as regional arrangements under the Charter of the United Nations for the maintenance of international peace and security.

Article 13

After the Treaty has been in force for twenty years, any Party may cease to be a Party one year after its notice of denunciation has been given to the Government of the United States of America, which will inform the Governments of the other Parties of the deposit of each notice of denunciation.

Article 14

This Treaty, of which the English and French texts are equally authentic, shall be deposited in the archives of the Government of the United States of America. Duly certified copies will be transmitted by that Government to the Governments of other signatories.

---

[1] The definition of the territories to which Article 5 applies was revised by Article 2 of the Protocol to the North Atlantic Treaty on the accession of Greece and Turkey and by the Protocols signed on the accession of the Federal Republic of Germany and of Spain.

[2] On January 16, 1963, the North Atlantic Council heard a declaration by the French Representative who recalled that by the vote on self-determination on July 1, 1962, the Algerian people had pronounced itself in favour of the independence of Algeria in co-operation with France. In consequence, the President of the French Republic had on July 3, 1962, formally recognised the independence of Algeria. The result was that the "Algerian departments of France" no longer existed as such, and that at the same time the fact that they were mentioned in the North Atlantic Treaty had no longer any bearing.

Following this statement the Council noted that insofar as the former Algerian Departments of France were concerned, the relevant clauses of this Treaty had become inapplicable as from July 3, 1962.

3

Protocol to the North Atlantic Treaty on the Accession of Greece and Turkey

London, October 22, 1951

The Parties to the North Atlantic Treaty, signed at Washington on April 4, 1949,

Being satisfied that the security of the North Atlantic area will be enhanced by the accession of the Kingdom of Greece and the Republic of Turkey to that Treaty,

Agree as follows:

Article 1

Upon the entry into force of this Protocol, the Government of the United States of America shall, on behalf of all the Parties, communicate to the Government of the Kingdom of Greece and the Government of the Republic of Turkey an invitation to accede to the North Atlantic Treaty, as it may be modified by Article 2 of the present Protocol. Thereafter the Kingdom of Greece and the Republic of Turkey shall each become a Party on the date when it deposits its instruments of accession with the Government of the United States of America in accordance with Article 10 of the Treaty.

Article 2

If the Republic of Turkey becomes a Party to the North Atlantic Treaty, Article 6 of the Treaty shall, as from the date of the deposit by the Government of the Republic of Turkey of its instruments of accession with the Government of the United States of America, be modified to read as follows:

"For the purpose of Article 5, an armed attack on one or more of the Parties is deemed to include an armed attack:

i. on the territory of any of the Parties in Europe or North America, on the Algerian Departments of France, on the territory of Turkey or on the islands under the jurisdiction of any of the Parties in the North Atlantic area north of the Tropic of Cancer;

ii. on the forces, vessels, or aircraft of any of the Parties, when in or over these territories or any other area in Europe in which occupation forces of any of the Parties were stationed on the date when the Treaty entered into force or the Mediterranean Sea or the North Atlantic area north of the Tropic of Cancer."

Article 3

The present Protocol shall enter into force when each of the Parties to the North Atlantic Treaty has notified the Government of the United States of America of its acceptance thereof. The Government of the United States of America shall inform all the Parties to the North Atlantic Treaty of the date of the receipt of each such notification and of the date of the entry into force of the present Protocol.

Article 4

The present Protocol, of which the English and French texts are equally authentic, shall be deposited in the Archives of the Government of the United States of America. Duly certified copies thereof shall be transmitted by that Government to the Governments of all the Parties to the North Atlantic Treaty.

4

Protocol to the North Atlantic Treaty on the Accession of the Federal Republic of Germany

Paris, October 23, 1954

The Parties to the North Atlantic Treaty signed at Washington on April 4, 1949,

Being satisfied that the security of the North Atlantic area will be enhanced by the accession of the Federal Republic of Germany to that Treaty, and

Having noted that the Federal Republic of Germany has, by a declaration dated October 3, 1954, accepted the obligations set forth in Article 2 of the Charter of the United Nations and has undertaken upon its accession to the North Atlantic Treaty to refrain from any action inconsistent with the strictly defensive character of that Treaty, and

Having further noted that all member governments have associated themselves with the declaration also made on October 3, 1954, by the Governments of the United States of America, the United Kingdom of Great Britain and Northern Ireland and the French Republic in connection with the aforesaid declaration of the Federal Republic of Germany,

Agree as follows:

Article 1

Upon the entry into force of the present Protocol, the Government of the United States of America shall on behalf of all the Parties communicate to the Government of the Federal Republic of Germany an invitation to accede to the North Atlantic Treaty. Thereafter the Federal Republic of Germany shall become a Party to that Treaty on the date when it deposits its instruments of accession with the Government of the United States of America in accordance with Article 10 of the Treaty.

Article 2

The present Protocol shall enter into force, when (a) each of the Parties to the North Atlantic Treaty has notified to the Government of the United States of America its acceptance thereof, (b) all instruments of ratification of the Protocol modifying and completing the Brussels Treaty have been deposited with the Belgian Government, and (c) all instruments of ratification or approval of the Convention on the Presence of Foreign Forces in the Federal Republic of Germany have been deposited with the Government of the Federal Republic of Germany. The Government of the United States of America shall inform the other Parties to the North Atlantic Treaty of the date of the receipt of each notification of acceptance of the present Protocol and of the date of the entry into force of the present Protocol.

Article 3

The present Protocol, of which the English and French texts are equally authentic, shall be deposited in the Archives of the Government of the United States of America. Duly certified copies thereof shall be transmitted by that Government to the Governments of the other Parties to the North Atlantic Treaty.

5

Protocol to the North Atlantic Treaty on the Accession of Spain

Brussels, December 10, 1981

The Parties to the North Atlantic Treaty, signed at Washington on April 4, 1949,

Being satisfied that the security of the North Atlantic area will be enhanced by the accession of the Kingdom of Spain to that Treaty,

Agree as follows:

Article 1

Upon the entry into force of this Protocol, the Secretary General of the North Atlantic Treaty Organisation shall, on behalf of all the Parties, communicate to the Government of the Kingdom of Spain an invitation to accede to the North Atlantic Treaty. In accordance with Article 10 of the Treaty, the Kingdom of Spain shall become a Party on the date when it deposits its instrument of accession with the Government of the United States of America.

Article 2

The present Protocol shall enter into force when each of the Parties to the North Atlantic Treaty has notified the Government of the United States of America of its acceptance thereof. The Government of the United States of America shall inform all the Parties to the North Atlantic Treaty of the date of receipt of each such notification and of the date of the entry into force of the present Protocol.

Article 3

The present Protocol, of which the English and French texts are equally authentic, shall be deposited in the Archives of the Government of the United States of America. Duly certified copies thereof shall be transmitted by that Government to the Governments of all the Parties to the North Atlantic Treaty.

6

Text of the Report of the Committee of Three on Non-Military Cooperation in NATO

Approved by the North Atlantic Council on December 13, 1956

CHAPTER I

General introduction

The Committee on Non-Military Cooperation, set up by the North Atlantic Council at its session of May 1956, was requested: "to advise the Council on ways and means to improve and extend NATO cooperation in non-military fields and to develop greater unity within the Atlantic Community".

2. The Committee has interpreted these terms of reference as requiring it (1) to examine and re-define the objectives and needs of the Alliance, especially in the light of current international developments; and (2) to make recommendations for strengthening its internal solidarity, cohesion and unity.

3. The Committee hopes that the report and recommendations which it now submits will make NATO's purely defensive and constructive purposes better understood in non-NATO countries, thereby facilitating and encouraging steps to lessen international tension. The events of the last few months have increased this tension and reduced hopes, which had been raised since Stalin's death, of finding a secure and honourable basis for competitive and ultimately for cooperative co-existence with the Communist world. The effort to this end, however, must go on.

4. Inter-Allied relations have also undergone severe strains. The substance of this report was prepared by the Committee of Three in the course of its meetings and inter-governmental consultations last September. Subsequent events have reinforced the Committee's conviction that the Atlantic Community can develop greater unity only by working constantly to achieve common policies by full and timely consultation on issues of common concern. Unless this is done, the very framework of cooperation in NATO, which has contributed so greatly to the cause of freedom, and which is so vital to its advancement in the future, will be endangered.

5. The foundation of NATO, on which alone a strong superstructure can be built, is the political obligation that its members have taken for collective defence: to consider that an attack on one is an attack on all which will be met by the collective action of all. There is a tendency at times to overlook the far-reaching importance of this commitment, especially during those periods when the danger of having to invoke it may seem to recede.

6. With this political commitment for collective defence as the cornerstone of the foreign and defence policies of its members, NATO has a solid basis for existence. It is true, of course, that the ways and means by which the obligation is to be discharged may alter as political or strategic conditions alter, as the threat to peace changes its character or its direction. However, any variations in plans and strategic policies which may be required need not weaken NATO or the confidence of its members in NATO and in each other; providing, and the proviso is decisive, that each member retains its will and its capacity to play its full part in discharging the political commitment for collective action against aggression which it undertook when it signed the Pact; providing also—and recent events have shown that this is equally important—that any changes in national strategy or policy which affect the coalition are made only after collective consideration.

7. The first essential, then, of a healthy and developing NATO lies in the whole-hearted acceptance by all its members of the political commitment for collective defence, and in the confidence which each has in the will and ability of the others to honour that commitment if aggression should take place.

8. This is our best present deterrent against military aggression, and consequently the best assurance that the commitment undertaken will not be engaged.

9. However, this deterrent role of NATO, based on solidarity and strength, can be discharged only if the political and economic relations between its members are co-operative and close. An Alliance in which the members ignore each other's interests or engage in political or economic conflict, or harbour suspicions of each other, cannot be effective either for deterrence or defence. Recent experience makes this clearer than ever before.

10. It is useful, in searching for ways and means of strengthening NATO unity and understanding, to recall the origin and the aims of the Organisation.

11. The Treaty which was signed in Washington in 1949 was a collective response—we had learned that a purely national response was insufficient for security—to the fear of military aggression by the forces of the USSR and its allies. These forces were of overwhelming strength. The threat to Greece, the capture of Czechoslovakia, the blockade of Berlin, and the pressure against Yugoslavia showed that they were also aggressive.

12. While fear may have been the main urge for the creation of NATO, there was also the realisation—conscious or instinctive—that in a shrinking nuclear world it was wise and timely to bring about a closer association of kindred Atlantic and Western European nations for other than defence purposes alone; that a partial pooling of sovereignty for mutual protection should also promote progress and cooperation generally. There was a feeling among the government and peoples concerned that this close unity was both natural and desirable; that the common cultural traditions, free institutions and democratic concepts which were being challenged, and were marked for destruction by those who challenged them, were things which should also bring the NATO nations closer together, not only for their defence but for their development. There was, in short, a sense of Atlantic Community, alongside the realisation of an immediate common danger.

13. Any such feeling was certainly not the decisive, or even the main impulse in the creation of NATO. Nevertheless, it gave birth to the hope that NATO would grow beyond and above the emergency which brought it into being.

14. The expression of this hope is found in the Preamble and in Articles 2 and 4 of the Treaty. These two Articles, limited in their terms but with at least the promise of the grand design of an Atlantic Community, were included because of this insistent feeling that NATO must become more than a military alliance. They reflected the very real anxiety that if NATO failed to meet this test, it would disappear with the immediate crisis which produced it, even though the need for it might be as great as ever.

15. From the very beginning of NATO, then, it was recognised that while defence cooperation was the first and most urgent requirement, this was not enough. It has also become increasingly realised since the Treaty was signed that security is today far more than a military matter. The strengthening of political consultation and economic cooperation, the development of resources, progress in education and public understanding, all these can be as important, or even more important, for the protection of the security of a nation, or an alliance, as the building of a battleship or the equipping of an army.

16. These two aspects of security—civil and military—can no longer safely be considered in watertight compartments, either within or between nations. Perhaps NATO has not yet fully recognised their essential interrelationship, or done enough to bring about that close and continuous contact between its civil and military sides which is essential if it is to be strong and enduring.

17. North Atlantic political and economic cooperation, however, let alone unity, will not be brought about in a day or by a declaration, but by creating over the years and through a whole series of national acts and policies, the habits and traditions and precedents for such cooperation and unity. The process will be a slow and gradual one at best; slower than we might wish. We can be satisfied if it is steady and sure. This will not be the case, however, unless the member governments—especially the more powerful ones—are willing to work, to a much greater extent than hitherto, with and through NATO for more than purposes of collective military defence.

18. While the members of NATO have already developed various forms of non-military cooperation between themselves and have been among the most active and constructive participants in various international organisations, NATO as such has been hesitant in entering this field, particularly in regard to economic matters. Its members have been rightly concerned to avoid duplication and to do, through other existing international organisations, the things which can best be done in that way.

19. Recently, however, the members of NATO have been examining and re-examining the purposes and the needs of the Organisation in the light of certain changes in Soviet tactics and policies which have taken place since the death of Stalin, and of the effect of the present turmoil in Eastern Europe on this development.

20. These changes have not diminished the need for collective military defence but they have faced NATO with an additional challenge in which the emphasis is largely non-military in character. NATO must recognise the real nature of the developments which have taken place. An important aspect of the new Soviet policies of competitive co-existence is an attempt to respond to positive initiatives of the Western nations aimed at improving, in an atmosphere of freedom, the lot of the economically less-developed countries, and at establishing a just and mutually beneficial trading system in which all countries can prosper. The Soviet Union is now apparently veering towards policies designed to ensnare these countries by economic means and by political subversion, and to fasten on them the same shackles of Communism from which certain members of the Soviet bloc are now striving to release themselves. The members of NATO must maintain their vigilance in dealing with this form of penetration.

21. Meanwhile some of the immediate fears of large-scale all-out military aggression against Western Europe have lessened. This process has been facilitated by evidence that the Soviet Government has realised that any such all-out aggression would be met by a sure, swift and devasting retaliation, and that there could be no victory in a war of this kind with nuclear weapons on both sides. With an increased Soviet emphasis on non-military or paramilitary methods, a review is needed of NATO's ability to meet effectively the challenge of penetration under the guise of coexistence, with its emphasis on conflict without catastrophe.

22. Certain questions now take on a new urgency. Have NATO's needs and objectives changed, or should they be changed? Is the Organisation operating satisfactorily in the altered circumstances of 1956? If not what can be done about it? There is the even more far-reaching question: "Can a loose association of sovereign states hold together at all without the common binding force of fear?"

23. The Committee has been examining these questions in the light of its firm conviction that the objectives which governments had in mind when the Pact was signed remain valid; that NATO is as important now to its member states as it was at that time.

24. The first of these objectives—as has already been pointed out—is security, based on collective action with adequate armed forces both for deterrence and defence.

25. Certainly NATO unity and strength in the pursuit of this objective remain as essential as they were in 1949. Soviet tactics may have changed; but Soviet armed might and ultimate objectives remain unchanged. Moreover, recent events in Eastern Europe show that the Soviet Union will not hesitate in certain circumstances to use force and the threat of force. Therefore the military strength of NATO must not be reduced, though its character and capabilities should be constantly adapted to changing circumstances. Strengthening the political and economic side of NATO is an essential complement to—not a substitute for—continuous cooperation in defence.

26. In spite of these recent events Soviet leaders may place greater emphasis on political, economic and propaganda action. There is no evidence, however, that this will be permitted to prejudice in any way the maintenance of a high level of military power in its most modern form as a base for Soviet activity in these other fields.

27. We should welcome changes in Soviet policies if they were genuinely designed to ease international tensions. But we must remember that the weakening and eventual dissolution of NATO remains a major Communist goal. We must therefore remain on guard so long as Soviet leaders persist in their determination to maintain a preponderance of military power for the achievement of their own political objectives and those of their allies.

28. This brings us again to the second and long-term aim of NATO: the development of an Atlantic Community whose roots are deeper even than the necessity for common defence. This implies nothing less than the permanent association of the free Atlantic peoples for the promotion of their greater unity and the protection and the advancement of the interests which, as free democracies, they have in common.

29. If we are to secure this long-term aim, we must prevent the centrifugal forces of opposition or indifference from weakening the Alliance. NATO has not been destroyed, or even weakened, by the threats or attacks of its enemies. It has faltered at times through the lethargy or complacency of its members: through dissension or division between them; by putting narrow national considerations above the collective interest. It could be destroyed by these forces, if they were allowed to subsist. To combat these tendencies, NATO must be used by its members, far more than it has been used, for sincere and genuine consultation and cooperation on questions of common concern. For this purpose, resolution is more important than resolutions; will than words.

30. The problem, however, goes deeper than this. NATO countries are faced by a political as well as a military threat. It comes from the revolutionary doctrines of Communism which have by careful design of the Communist leaders over many years been sowing seeds of falsehood concerning our free and democratic way of life. The best answers to such falsehoods is a continuing demonstration of the superiority of our own institutions over Communist ones. We can show by word and deed that we welcome political progress, economic advancement and orderly social change and that the real reactionaries of this day are these Communist regimes which, adhering to an inflexible pattern of economic and political doctrine, have been more successful in destroying freedom than in promoting it.

31. We must, however, realise that falsehoods concerning our institutions have sometimes been accepted at face value and that there are those, even in the non-Communist world, who under the systematic influence of Communist propaganda do not accept our own analysis of NATO's aims and values. They believe that while NATO may have served a useful defensive deterrent role in the Stalinist era, it is no longer necessary even for the security of its members; that it is tending now to become an agency for the pooling of the strength and resources of the "colonial" powers in defence of imperial privileges, racial superiority, and Atlantic hegemony under the leadership of the United States. The fact that we know these views to be false and unjustified does not mean that NATO and its governments should not do everything they can to correct and counteract them.

32. NATO should not forget that the influence and interests of its members are not confined to the area covered by the Treaty, and that common interests of the Atlantic Community can be seriously affected by developments outside the Treaty area. Therefore, while striving to improve their relations with each other, and to strengthen and deepen their own unity, they should also be concerned with harmonising their policies in relation to other areas, taking into account the broader interests of the whole international community; particularly in working through the United Nations and elsewhere for the maintenance of international peace and security and for the solution of the problems that now divide the world.

33. In following this course, NATO can show that it is more than a defence organisation acting and reacting to the ebb and flow of the fears and dangers arising out of Soviet policy. It can prove its desire to cooperate fully with other members of the international community in bringing to reality the principles of the Charter of the United Nations. It can show that it is not merely concerned with preventing the cold war from deteriorating into a shooting one; or with defending itself if such a tragedy should take place, but that it is even more concerned with seizing the political and moral initiative to enable all countries to develop in freedom, and to bring about a secure peace for all nations.

34. Our caution in accepting without question the pacific character of any Soviet moves, our refusal to dismantle our defences before we are convinced that conditions of international confidence have been restored, will, particularly after the events in Hungary, be understood by all people of sincerity and good-will. What would not be understood is any unwillingness on our part to seek ways and means of breaking down the barriers with a view to establishing such confidence.

35. The coming together of the Atlantic nations for good and constructive purposes—which is the basic principle and ideal underlying the NATO concept—must rest on and grow from deeper and more permanent factors than the divisions and dangers of the last ten years. It is a historical, rather than a contemporary, development, and if it is to achieve its real purpose, it must be considered in that light and the necessary conclusions drawn. A short-range view will not suffice.

36. The fundamental historical fact underlying development is that the nation state, by itself and relying exclusively on national policy and national power, is inadequate for progress or even for survival in the nuclear age. As the founders of the North Atlantic Treaty foresaw, the growing interdependence of states, politically and economically as well as militarily, calls for an ever-increasing measure of international cohesion and cooperation. Some states may be able to enjoy a degree of political and economic independence when things are going well. No state, however powerful, can guarantee its security and its welfare by national action alone.

37. This basic fact underlies our report and the recommendations contained therein which appear in the subsequent chapters.

38. It has not been difficult to make these recommendations. It will be far more difficult for the member governments to carry them into effect. This will require, on their part, the firm conviction that the transformation of the Atlantic Community into a vital and vigorous political reality is as important as any purely national purpose. It will require, above all, the will to carry this conviction into the realm of practical governmental policy.

CHAPTER II

Political Cooperation

I. Introduction

39. If there is to be vitality and growth in the concept of the Atlantic Community, the relations between the members of NATO must rest on a solid basis of confidence and understanding. Without this there cannot be constructive or solid political cooperation.

40. The deepening and strengthening of this political cooperation does not imply the weakening of the ties of NATO members with other friendly countries or with other international associations, particularly the United Nations. Adherence to NATO is not exclusive or restrictive. Nor should the evolution of the Atlantic Community through NATO prevent the formation of even closer relationships among some of its members, for instance within groups of European countries. The moves toward Atlantic cooperation and European unity should be parallel and complementary, not competitive or conflicting.

41. Effective and constructive international cooperation requires a resolve to work together for the solution of common problems. There are special ties between NATO members, special incentives and security interests, which should make this task easier than it otherwise would be. But its successful accomplishment will depend largely on the extent to which member governments, in their own policies and actions, take into consideration the interests of the Alliance. This requires not only the acceptance of the obligation of consultation and cooperation whenever necessary, but also the development of practices by which the discharge of this obligation becomes a normal part of governmental activity.

42. It is easy to profess devotion to the principle of political—or economic—consultation in NATO. It is difficult and has in fact been shown to be impossible, if the proper conviction is lacking, to convert the profession into practice. Consultation within an alliance means more than exchange of information, though that is necessary. It means more than letting the NATO Council know about national decisions that have already been taken; or trying to enlist support for those decisions. It means the discussion of problems collectively, in the early stages of policy formation, and before national positions become fixed. At best, this will result in collective decisions on matters of common interest affecting the Alliance. At the least, it will ensure that no action is taken by one member without a knowledge of the views of the others.

II. Consultation on Foreign Policies

A. Scope and Character of Political Consultation

43. The essential role of consultation in fostering political cooperation was clearly defined by an earlier NATO Committee on the North Atlantic Community in 1951:

"... The achievement of a closer degree of coordination of the foreign policies of the members of the North Atlantic Treaty, through the development of the 'habit of consultation' on matters of common concern, would greatly strengthen the solidarity of the North Atlantic Community and increase the individual and collective capacity of its members to serve the peaceful purposes for which NATO was established... In the political field, this means that while each North Atlantic government retains full freedom of action and decision with respect to its own policy, the aim should be to achieve, through exchanging information and views, as wide an area of agreement as possible in the formulation of policies as a whole."

"Special attention must be paid, as explicitly recognised in Article 4 of the Treaty, to matters of urgent and immediate importance to the members of NATO, and to 'emergency' situations where it may be necessary to consult closely on national lines of conduct affecting the interests of members of NATO as a whole. There is a continuing need, however, for effective consultation at an early stage on current problems, in order that national policies may be developed and action taken on the basis of a full awareness of the attitudes and interests of all the members of NATO. While all members of NATO have a responsibility to consult with their partners on appropriate matters, a large share of responsibility for such consultation necessarily rests on the more powerful members of the Community."

44. These words were written five years ago. They hold true now more than ever before. If we can say that they have not been ignored by NATO we must also recognise that the practice of consulting has not so developed in the NATO Council as to meet the demands of political changes and world trends. The present need, therefore, is more than simply broadening the scope and deepening the character of consultation. There is a pressing requirement for all members to make consultation in NATO an integral part of the making of national policy. Without this the very existence of the North Atlantic Community may be in jeopardy.

45. It should, however, be remembered that collective discussion is not an end in itself, but a means to the end of harmonising policies. Where common interests of the Atlantic Community are at stake consultation should always seek to arrive at timely agreement on common lines of policy and action.

46. Such agreement, even with the closest possible cooperation and consultation, is not easy to secure. But it is essential to the Atlantic Alliance that a steady and continuous effort be made to bring it about. There cannot be unity in defence and disunity in foreign policy.

47. There are, of course, certain practical limitations to consultation in this field. They are sufficiently obvious in fact to make it unnecessary to emphasise them in words. Indeed the danger is less that they will be minimised or evaded than that they will be exaggerated and used to justify practices which unnecessarily ignore the common interest.

48. One of these limitations is the hard fact that ultimate responsibility for decision and action still rests on national governments. It is conceivable that a situation of extreme emergency may arise where action must be taken by one government before consultation is possible with the others.

49. Another limitation is the difficulty, and indeed the unwisdom, of trying to specify in advance all the subjects and all the situations where consultation is necessary; to separate by area or by subject the matters of NATO concern from those of purely national concern; to define in detail the obligations and duties of consultation. These things have to work themselves out in practice. In this process, experience is a better guide than dogma.

50. The essential thing is that on all occasions and in all circumstances member governments, before acting or even before pronouncing, should keep the interest and the requirements of the Alliance in mind. If they have not the desire and the will to do this, no resolutions or recommendations or declarations by the Council or any Committee of the Council will be of any great value.

51. On the assumption, however, that this will and this desire do exist, the following principles and practices in the field of political consultation are recommended:

a. members should inform the Council of any development which significantly affects the Alliance. They should do this, not merely as a formality but as a preliminary to effective political consultation;
b. both individual member governments and the Secretary General should have the right to raise for discussion in the Council any subject which is of common NATO interest and not of a purely domestic character;
c. a member government should not, without adequate advance consultation, adopt firm policies or make major political pronouncements on matters which significantly affect the Alliance or any of its members, unless circumstances make such prior consultation obviously and demonstrably impossible;
d. in developing their national policies, members should take into consideration the interest and views of other governments, particularly those most directly concerned, as expressed in NATO consultation, even where no community of views or consensus has been reached in the Council;
e. where a consensus has been reached, it should be reflected in the formation of national policies. When for national reasons the consensus is not followed, the government concerned should offer an explanation to the Council. It is even more important that where an agreed and formal recommendation has emerged from the Council's discussions, governments should give it full weight in any national actions or policies related to the subject of that recommendation.

B. Annual Political Appraisal

52. To strengthen the process of consultation, it is recommended that Foreign Ministers, at each Spring meeting, should make an appraisal of the political progress of the Alliance and consider the lines along which it should advance.

53. To prepare for this discussion, the Secretary General should submit an annual report:

a. analysing the major political problems of the Alliance;
b. reviewing the extent to which member governments have consulted and cooperated on such problems;

c. indicating the problems and possible developments which may require future consultation, so that difficulties might be resolved and positive and constructive initiative taken.

54. Member governments, through their Permanent Representatives, should give the Secretary General such information and assistance, including that of technical experts, as he may require in preparing his report.

C. Preparation for Political Consultation

55. Effective consultation also requires careful planning and preparation of the agenda for meetings of the Council both in Ministerial and permanent session. Political questions coming up for discussion in the Council should so far as practicable be previously reviewed and discussed; so that representatives may have background information on the thinking both of their own and of other governments. When appropriate, drafts of resolutions should be prepared in advance as a basis for discussion. Additional preparatory work will also be required for the annual political appraisal referred to in the preceding section.

56. To assist the Permanent Representatives and the Secretary General in discharging their responsibilities for political consultation, there should be constituted under the Council a Committee of Political Advisers from each delegation, aided when necessary by specialists from the capitals. It would meet under the chairmanship of a member of the International Staff appointed by the Secretary General, and would include among its responsibilities current studies such as those on trends of Soviet policy.

III. Peaceful Settlement of Inter-member Disputes

57. In the development of effective political cooperation in NATO, it is of crucial importance to avoid serious inter-member disputes and to settle them quickly and satisfactorily when they occur. The settlement of such disputes is in the first place the direct responsibility of the member governments concerned, under both the Charter of the United Nations (Article XXXIII) and the North Atlantic Treaty (Article I). To clarify NATO's responsibilities in dealing with disputes which have not proved capable of settlement directly and to enable NATO, if necessary, to help in the settlement of such disputes, the Committee recommends that the Council adopt a resolution under Article I of the Treaty on the following lines:

a. re-affirming the obligation of members to settle by peaceful means any disputes between themselves;
b. declaring their intention to submit any such disputes, which have not proved capable of settlement directly, to good offices procedures within the NATO framework before resorting to any other international agency; except for disputes of a legal character for submission to a judicial tribunal, and those disputes of an economic character for which attempts at settlement might best be made initially in the appropriate specialised economic organisation;
c. recognising the right and duty of member governments and of the Secretary General to bring to the attention of the Council matters which in their opinion may threaten the solidarity or effectiveness of the Alliance;
d. empowering the Secretary General to offer his good offices informally at any time to the parties in dispute, and with their consent to initiate or facilitate procedures of enquiry, mediation, conciliation, or arbitration, and
e. empowering the Secretary General, where he deems it appropriate for the purpose outlined in d. above, to use the assistance of not more than three Permanent Representatives chosen by him in each instance.

IV. Parliamentary Associations and the Parliamentary Conference

58. Among the best supporters of NATO and its purposes are those Members of Parliament who have had a chance at first hand to see some of its activities and to learn of its problems, and to exchange views with their colleagues from other parliaments. In particular, the formation of national Parliamentary Associations and the activities of the Conference of Members of Parliament from NATO countries have contributed to the development of public support for NATO and solidarity among its members.

59. In order to maintain a close relationship of Parliamentarians with NATO, the following arrangements are recommended:

a. that the Secretary General continue to place the facilities of NATO Headquarters at the disposal of Parliamentary Conferences and give all possible help with arrangements for their meetings;

b. that invited representatives of member governments and the Secretary General and other senior NATO civil and military officers attend certain of these meetings. In this way the Parliamentarians would be informed on the state of the Alliance and the problems before it, and the value of their discussions would be increased.

CHAPTER III

Economic Cooperation

I. Introduction

60. Political cooperation and economic conflict are not reconcilable. Therefore, in the economic as well as in the political field there must be a genuine desire among the members to work together and a readiness to consult on questions of common concern based on the recognition of common interests.

61. These common economic interests shared by the members of NATO call for:

a. cooperative and national action to achieve healthy and expanding economies, both to promote the well-being and self-confidence of the Atlantic peoples and to serve as the essential support for an adequate defence effort;

b. the greatest possible freedom in trade and payments and in the movement of manpower and long-term capital;

c. assistance to economically underdeveloped areas for reasons of enlightened self-interest and to promote better relations among peoples; and

d. policies which will demonstrate, under conditions of competitive co-existence, the superiority of free institutions in promoting human welfare and economic progress.

62. A recognition of these common NATO interests, and collective and individual efforts to promote them, need not in any way prejudice close economic relations with non-NATO countries. Economic, like political, cooperation is and must remain wider than NATO. At the same time, the NATO countries have an interest in any arrangements for especially close economic cooperation among groups of European member nations. It should be possible—as it is desirable—for such special arrangements to promote rather than conflict with the wider objectives of Article 2 of our Treaty, which are of basic importance to the stability and well-being, not only of the North Atlantic area, but of the whole non-Communist world.

II. NATO and other Organisations

63. While the purposes and principles of Article 2 are of vital importance, it is not necessary that member countries pursue them only through action in NATO itself. It would not serve the interests of the Atlantic Community for NATO to duplicate the operating functions of other international organisations designed for various forms of economic cooperation.[1] NATO members play a major part in all these agencies, whose membership is generally well adapted to the purposes they serve.

64. Nor do there now appear to be significant new areas for collective economic action requiring execution by NATO itself. In fact, the common economic concern of the member nations will often best be fostered by continued and increased collaboration both bilaterally and through organisations other than NATO. This collaboration should be reinforced, however, by NATO consultation whenever economic issues of special interest to the Alliance are involved, particularly those which have political or defence implications or affect the economic health of the Atlantic Community as a whole. This, in turn, requires a substantial expansion of exchange of information and views in NATO in the economic as well as in the political field. Such economic consultation should seek to secure a common approach on the part of member governments where the questions are clearly related to the political and security interests of the Alliance. Action resulting from such a common approach, however, should normally be taken by governments either directly or through other international organisations.

65. NATO, as such, should not seek to establish formal relations with these other organisations, and the harmonising of attitudes and actions should be left to the representatives of the NATO governments therein. Nor is it necessary or desirable for NATO members to form a "bloc" in such organisations. This would only alienate other friendly governments. There should, however, be consultation in NATO when economic issues of special political or strategic importance to NATO arise in other organisations and in particular before meetings at which there may be attempts to divide or weaken the Atlantic Alliance, or prejudice its interests.

III. Conflicts in Economic Policies of NATO Countries

66. NATO has a positive interest in the resolution of economic disputes which may have political or strategic repercussions damaging to the Alliance. These are to be distinguished from disagreements on economic policy which are normally dealt with through direct negotiations or by multilateral discussions in other organisations. Nothing would be gained by merely having repeated in NATO the same arguments made in other and more technically qualified organisations. It should however, be open to any member or to the Secretary General to raise in NATO issues on which they feel that consideration elsewhere is not making adequate progress and that NATO consultation might facilitate solutions contributing to the objectives of the Atlantic Community. The procedures for peaceful settlement of political disputes discussed in the previous chapter should also be available for major disputes of an economic character which are appropriate for NATO consideration.

IV. Scientific and Technical Cooperation

67. One area of special importance to the Atlantic Community is that of science and technology. During the last decade, it has become ever clearer that progress in this field can be decisive in determining the security of nations and their position in world affairs. Such progress is also vital if the Western world is to play its proper role in relation to economically underdeveloped areas.

68. Within the general field of science and technology, there is an especially urgent need to improve the quality and to increase the supply of scientists, engineers and technicians. Responsibility for recruitment, training and utilisation of scientific and technical personnel is primarily a national rather than an international matter. Nor is it a responsibility solely of national governments. In the member countries with federal systems, state and provincial governments play the major part, and many of the universities and institutes of higher learning in the Atlantic area are independent institutions free from detailed control by governments. At the same time, properly designed measures of international cooperation could stimulate individual member countries to adopt more positive policies and, in some cases, help guide them in the most constructive directions.

69. Certain activities in this connection are already being carried out by other organisations. Progress in this field, however, is so crucial to the future of the Atlantic Community that NATO members should ensure that every possibility of fruitful cooperation is examined. As a first concrete step, therefore, it is recommended that a conference be convened composed of one or at the most two outstanding authorities, private or governmental, from each country in order:

a. to exchange information and views concerning the most urgent problems in the recruitment, training and utilisation of scientists, engineers and technicians, and the best means, both long-term and short-term, of solving those problems;
b. to foster closer relations among the participants with a view to continued interchange of experience and stimulation of constructive work in member countries; and
c. to propose specific measures for future international cooperation in this field, through NATO or other international organisations.

V. Consultation on Economic Problems

70. It is agreed that the Atlantic Community has a positive concern with healthy and accelerated development in economically underdeveloped areas, both inside and outside the NATO area. The Committee feels, however, that NATO is not an appropriate agency for administering programmes of assistance for economic development, or even for systematically concerting the relevant policies of member nations. What member countries can and should do is to keep each other and the Organisation informed of their programmes and policies in this field. When required, NATO should review the adequacy of existing action in relation to the interests of the Alliance.

71. The economic interests of the Atlantic Community cannot be considered in isolation from the activities and policies of the Soviet bloc. The Soviets are resorting all too often to the use of economic measures designed to weaken the Western Alliance, or to create in other areas a high degree of dependence on the Soviet world. In this situation it is more than ever important that NATO countries actively develop their own constructive commercial and financial policies. In particular, they should avoid creating situations of which the Soviet bloc countries might take advantage to the detriment of the Atlantic Community and of other non-Communist countries. In this whole field of competitive economic co-existence member countries should consult together more fully in order to determine their course deliberately and with the fullest possible knowledge.

72. There has been a considerable evolution in NATO's arrangements for regular economic consultation. In addition, a number of economic matters have been brought before the Council for consideration on an ad hoc basis. No substantial new machinery in this field is called for. However, in view of the extended range of topics for regular exchange of information and consultation described above, there should be established under the Council a Committee of Economic Advisers. This group should be entrusted with preliminary discussion, on a systematic basis, of the matters outlined above, together with such tasks as many be assigned by the Council or approved by the Council at the Committee's request. It would absorb any continuing function of the Committee of Technical Advisers. Since its duties would not be full-time, member governments could be represented normally by officials mainly concerned with the work of other international economic organisations. Membership, however, should be flexible, the Committee being composed, when appropriate, of specialists from the capitals on particular topics under consideration.

CHAPTER IV

Cultural Cooperation

73. A sense of community must bind the people as well as the institutions of the Atlantic nations. This will exist only to the extent that there is a realisation of their common cultural heritage and of the values of their free way of life and thought. it is important, therefore, for the NATO countries to promote cultural cooperation among their peoples by all practical means in order to strengthen their unity and develop maximum support for the Alliance. It is particularly important that this cultural cooperation should be wider than continental. This, however, does not preclude particular governments from acting on a more limited multilateral or even bilateral basis to strengthen their own cultural relations within the broader Atlantic framework. The Committee welcomes the measures for cultural cooperation within the Atlantic Community which have been initiated by private individuals and non-governmental groups. These should be encouraged and increased.

74. To further cultural collaboration, the Committee suggests that member governments be guided by the following general principles:

a. government activities in this field should not duplicate but should support and supplement private efforts;
b. member governments should give priority to those projects which require joint NATO action, and thus contribute to a developing sense of community;
c. in developing new activities in the cultural field, NATO can most fruitfully place the main emphasis on inspiring and promoting transatlantic contacts;
d. there should be a realistic appreciation of the financial implications of cultural projects.

75. In order to develop public awareness and understanding of NATO and the Atlantic Community, the Council should work out arrangements for NATO courses and seminars for teachers.

76. NATO and its member governments should broaden their support of other educational and related activities such as the NATO Fellowship and Scholarship Programme; creation of university chairs of Atlantic studies; visiting professorships; government-sponsored programmes for the exchange of persons, especially on a transatlantic basis; use of NATO information materials in schools; and establishment of special NATO awards for students.

77. Governments should actively promote closer relations between NATO and youth organisations and a specialist should be added to the International Staff in this connection. Conferences under NATO auspices of representatives of youth organisations such as that of July, 1956, should be held from time to time.

78. In the interests of promoting easier and more frequent contacts among the NATO peoples, governments should review and, if possible, revise their foreign exchange and other policies which restrict travel.

79. In view of the importance of promoting better understanding and goodwill between NATO service personnel, it would be desirable, in cooperation with the military authorities, to extend exchanges of such personnel beyond the limits of normal training programmes. Such exchanges might, at first step, be developed by governments on a bilateral basis. In addition, member governments should seek the assistance of the Atlatnic Treaty Association and other voluntary organisations in the further development of such exchanges.

80. Cultural projects which have a common benefit should be commonly financed. Agreed cultural projects inititiated by a single member government or a private organisation, such as the recent seminar held at Oxford or the Study conference sponsored by the Atlantic Treaty Association on "The Role of the School in the Atlantic Community", should receive financial support from NATO where that is necessary to supplement national resources.

CHAPTER V

Cooperation in the Information Field

81. The people of the member countries must know about NATO if they are to support it. Therefore they must be informed not only of NATO's aspirations, but of its achievements. There must be substance for an effective NATO information programme and resources to carry it out. The public should be informed to the greatest possible extent of significant results achieved through NATO consultation.

82. NATO information activities should be directed primarily to public opinion in the NATO area. At the same time an understanding outside the NATO area of the objectives and accomplishments of the Organisation is necessary if it is to be viewed sympathetically, and if its activities are not to be misinterpreted.

83. The important task of explaining and reporting NATO activities rests primarily on national information services. They cannot discharge this task if member governments do not make adequate provisions in their national programmes for that purpose. It is essential, therefore, that such provision be made. NATO can and should assist national governments in this work. The promotion of information about, and public understanding of NATO and the Atlantic Community should, in fact, be a joint endeavour by the Organisation and its members.

84. One of NATO's functions should be to coordinate the work of national information services in fields of common interest. Governments should pool their experiences and views in NATO to avoid differences in evaluation and emphasis. This is particularly important in the dissemination of information about NATO to other countries. Coordinated policy should underline the defensive character of our Alliance and the importance of its non-military aspects. It should cover also replies to anti-NATO propaganda and the analysis of Communist moves and statements which affect NATO.

85. In its turn, the NATO Information Division must be given the resources by governments as well as their support, without which it could not discharge these new tasks—and should not be asked to do so.

86. In order to facilitate cooperation between the NATO Information Division and national information services, the following specific measures are recommended:

a. an Officer should be designated by each national information service to maintain liaison with NATO and to be responsible for the dissemination of NATO information material;
b. governments should submit to NATO the relevant information programmes which they plan to implement, for discussion in the Committee on Information and Cultural Relations. Representatives of national information services should take part in these discussions;
c. within the NATO Information Division budget, provision should be made for a translation fund so that NATO information material can be translated into the non-official languages of the Alliance, according to reasonable requirements of the member governments;
d. NATO should, on request, provide national services with special studies on matters of common interest.

87. The journalists' tours sponsored by NATO should be broadened to include others in a position to influence public opinion, such as trade and youth leaders, teachers and lecturers. Closer relations between private organisations supporting NATO and the NATO Information Division should also be encouraged.

CHAPTER VI

Organisation and Functions

88. The Committee considers that NATO in its present form is capable of discharging the non-military functions required of it. Structural changes are not needed. The machine is basically satisfactory. it is for governments to make use of it.

89. At the same time, certain improvements in the procedures and functioning of the Organisation will be required if the recommendations of this report are to be fully implemented. The proposals in this Chapter are submitted for this purpose.

A. Meetings of the Council

90. More time should be allowed for Ministerial Meetings. Experience has shown that, without more time, important issues on the agenda cannot be adequately considered. Decisions concerning some of them will not be reached at all, or will be reached only in an unclear form.

91. Efforts should be made to encourage discussion rather than simply declarations of policy prepared in advance. Arrangements for meetings should be made with this aim in view. For most sessions, the numbers present should be sharply restricted. In order to facilitate free discussion, when Ministers wish to speak in a language other than French or English, consecutive translation into one of these official languages should be provided by interpreters from their own delegations.

92. Meetings of Foreign Ministers should be held whenever required, and occasionally in locations other than NATO Headquarters. Ministers might also participate more frequently in regular Council meetings, even though not all of them may find it possible to attend such meetings at the same time. The Council of Permanent Representatives has powers of effective decision: in other words, the authority of the Council as such is the same whether governments are represented by Ministers or by their Permanent

Representatives. Thus there should be no firm or formal line between Ministerial and other meetings of the Council.

B. Strengthening the Links between the Council and Member Governments

93. It is indispensable to the kind of consultations envisaged in this report that Permanent Representatives should be in a position to speak authoritatively and to reflect the current thinking of their governments. Differences in location and in constitutional organisation make impossible any uniform arrangements in all member governments. In some cases it might be desirable to designate a high official in the national capital to be concerned primarily with NATO affairs. The purpose would be to help both in fostering NATO consultations whenever national policies impinge on the common interest of the Atlantic Community, and in translating the results of such consultation into effective action within the national governments.

94. To ensure the closest possible connection between current thinking in the governments and consultations in the Council, there might be occasional Council Meetings with the participation of specially designated officials or the permanent heads of foreign ministries.

C. Preparation for Council Meetings

95. Items on the agenda of Ministerial Meetings should be thoroughly examined by Permanent Representatives and relevant proposals prepared before Ministers meet. For this purpose it may be found desirable for governments to send senior experts to consult on agenda items before the meetings take place.

96. The preparation of questions for discussion in the Council should be assisted by appropriate use of the Council's Committees of Political and Economic Advisers. (Recommendations on the establishment of these Committees are set forth in Chapter II, paragraph 56, and Chapter III, paragraph 72.)

97. In the case of consultations on special subjects, more use should be made of senior experts from national capitals to assist permanent delegations by calling them, on an ad hoc basis, to do preparatory work. Informal discussions among specialists with corresponding responsibilities are a particularly valuable means of concerting governmental attitudes in the early stages of policy formation.

98. Member governments should make available to one another through NATO "basic position material" for background information. This would help the Alliance as a whole in the consideration of problems of common concern and would assist individual governments to understand more fully the reasons for the position adopted by any member country on a particular issue which might be its special concern, but which might also affect in varying degrees other members of NATO.

D. The Secretary General and the International Staff

99. To enable the Organisation to make its full contribution, the role of the Secretary General and the International Staff needs to be enhanced.

100. It is recommended that the Secretary General preside over meetings of the Council in Ministerial session, as he does now in other sessions. Such a change with respect to the conduct of the Council's business would follow naturally from the new responsibilities of the Secretary General, arising out of the recommendations of this report. It is also warranted by the Secretary General's unique opportunities for becoming familiar with the problems and the activities of the Alliance as a whole.

101. It would, however, still be desirable to have one Minister chosen each year as President of the Council in accordance with the present practice of alphabetical rotation. This Minister, as President, would continue to have especially close contact with the Secretary General during and between Ministerial Meetings, and would, as at present, act as the spokesman of the Council on all formal occasions. He would also preside at the formal opening and closing of Ministerial sessions of the Council.

102. In addition:

a. the Secretary General should be encouraged to propose items for NATO consultation in the fields covered by this report and should be responsible for promoting and directing the process of consultation;
b. in view of these responsibilities member governments should undertake to keep the Secretary General fully and currently informed through their permanent delegations of their governments' thinking on questions of common concern to the Alliance;
c. attention is also called to the additional responsibilities of the Secretary General, recommended in connection with the annual political appraisal (Chapter II, paragraph 52), and the peaceful settlement of disputes (Chapter II, paragraph 57).

103. The effective functioning of NATO depends in large measure on the efficiency, devotion and morale of its Secretariat. Acceptance of the recommendations in this report would impose on the Secretariat new duties and responsibilities. Governments must, therefore, be prepared to give the International Staff all necessary support, both in finance and personnel. If this is not done, the recommendations of the report, even if accepted by governments, will not be satisfactorily carried out.

ANNEX

Council Resolutions

1. Resolution on the Peaceful Settlement of Disputes and Differences between Members of the North Atlantic Treaty Organisation

Whereas the parties to the North Atlantic Treaty, under Article I of that treaty, have undertaken "to settle any international disputes in which they may be involved by peaceful means in such a manner that international peace and security and justice are not endangered";

Whereas the parties have further undertaken to seek to eliminate conflicts in their international economic policies and will encourage economic collaboration between any or all of them;

Whereas NATO unity and strength in the pursuit of these objectives remain essential for continuous cooperation in military and non-military fields;

The North Atlantic Council:

Reaffirms the obligations of all its members, under Article I of the Treaty, to settle by peaceful means any dispute between themselves;

Decides that such disputes which have not proved capable of settlement directly be submitted to good offices procedures within the NATO framework before member governments resort to any other international agency except for disputes of a legal character appropriate for submission to a judicial tribunal and those disputes of an economic character for which attempts at settlement might best be made initially in the appropriate specialised economic organisations;

Recognises the right and duty of member governments and of the Secretary General to bring to its attention matters which in their opinion may threaten the solidarity or effectiveness of the Alliance;

Empowers the Secretary General to offer his good offices informally at any time to member governments involved in a dispute and with their consent to initiate or facilitate procedures of enquiry, mediation, conciliation, or arbitration;

Authorises the Secretary General where he deems it appropriate for the purpose outlined in the preceding paragraph to use the assistance of not more than three permanent representatives chosen by him in each instance.

2. *Resolution on the Report of the Committee of Three on Non-military Cooperation in NATO*

Whereas the North Atlantic Council at its meeting in Paris on May 5th established a Committee composed of the Foreign Ministers of Italy, Canada and Norway to advise the Council on ways and means to improve and extend NATO cooperation in non-military fields and to develop greater unity within the Atlantic Community;

Whereas the Committee of Three has now reported on the task assigned to it and has submitted to the Council a number of recommendations on such ways and means to improve and extend NATO cooperation in non-military fields;

The North Atlantic Council:

Takes note of the Report of the Committee of Three; and

Approves its recommendations; and

Invites the Council in Permanent Session to implement in the light of the comments made by governments the principles and recommendations contained in the Report; and

Invites the Secretary General to draw up for consideration by the Council such further specific proposals as may be required for the implementation of these recommendations and to report periodically on the compliance with these recommendations by governments.

Authorises the Committee of Three to publish their report.

---

[1] The outstanding instances are the Organisation for European Cooperation and Development (OECD) (which includes all NATO countries and four others); the General Agreement on Tariffs and Trade (GATT); the International Monetary Fund (IMF); the International Bank for Reconstruction and Development (IBRD); the International Finance Corporation (IFC); and the various other United Nations agencies including the Economic Commission for Europe. Several NATO members participate actively in the Colombo Plan for promoting economic development in Asia. Most members are taking an active part in technical assistance programmes and are also participating in discussions of proposals for the creation of a Special United Nations Fund for Economic Development (SUNFED).

7

The Future Tasks of the Alliance (Harmel Report)

Report of the Council
Annex to the Final Communiqué of the Ministerial Meeting

December 14, 1967

1. A year ago, on the initiative of the Foreign Minister of Belgium, the governments of the fifteen nations of the Alliance resolved to "study the future tasks which face the Alliance, and its procedures for fulfilling them in order to strengthen the Alliance as a factor for durable peace". The present report sets forth the general tenor and main principles emerging from this examination of the future tasks of the Alliance.

2. Studies were undertaken by Messrs. Schütz, Watson, Spaak, Kohler and Patijn. The Council wishes to express its appreciation and thanks to these eminent personalities for their efforts and for the analyses they produced.

3. The exercise has shown that the Alliance is a dynamic and vigorous organisation which is constantly adapting itself to changing conditions. It also has shown that its future tasks can be handled within the terms of the Treaty by building on the methods and procedures which have proved their value over many years.

4. Since the North Atlantic Treaty was signed in 1949 the international situation has changed significantly and the political tasks of the Alliance have assumed a new dimension. Amongst other developments, the Alliance has played a major part in stopping Communist expansion in Europe; the USSR has become one of the two world super powers but the Communist world is no longer monolithic; the Soviet doctrine of "peaceful co-existence" has changed the nature of the confrontation with the West but not the basic problems. Although the disparity between the power of the United States and that of the European states remains, Europe has recovered and is on its way towards unity. The process of decolonisation has transformed European relations with the rest of the world; at the same time, major problems have arisen in the relations between developed and developing countries.

5. The Atlantic Alliance has two main functions. Its first function is to maintain adequate military strength and political solidarity to deter aggression and other forms of pressure and to defend the territory of member countries if aggression should occur. Since its inception, the Alliance has successfully fulfilled this task. But the possibility of a crisis cannot be excluded as long as the central political issues in Europe, first and foremost the German Question, remain unsolved. Moreover, the situation of instability and uncertainty still precludes a balanced reduction of military forces. Under these conditions, the Allies will maintain as necessary a suitable military capability to assure the balance of forces, thereby creating a climate of stability, security and confidence.

In this climate the Alliance can carry out its second function, to pursue the search for progress towards a more stable relationship in which the underlying political issues can be solved. Military security and a policy of detente are not contradictory but complementary. Collective defence is a stabilising factor in world politics. It is the necessary condition for effective policies directed towards a greater relaxation of tensions. The way to peace and stability in Europe rests in particular on the use of the Alliance constructively in the interest of detente. The participation of the USSR and the USA will be necessary to achieve a settlement of the political problems of Europe.

6. From the beginning the Atlantic Alliance has been a cooperative grouping of states sharing the same ideals and with a high degree of common interest. Their cohesion and solidarity provide an element of stability within the Atlantic area.

7. As sovereign states the Allies are not obliged to subordinate their policies to collective decision. The Alliance affords an effective forum and clearing house for the exchange of information and views; thus, each Ally can decide its policy in the light of close knowledge of the problems and objectives of the others. To this end the practice of frank and timely consultations needs to be deepened and improved. Each Ally should play its full part in promoting an improvement in relations with the Soviet Union and the countries of Eastern Europe, bearing in mind that the pursuit of detente must not be allowed to split the Alliance. The chances of success will clearly be greater if the Allies remain on parallel courses, especially in matters of close concern to them all; their actions will thus be all the more effective.

8. No peaceful order in Europe is possible without a major effort by all concerned. The evolution of Soviet and East European policies gives ground for hope that those governments may eventually come to recognise the advantages to them of collaborating in working towards a peaceful settlement. But no final and stable settlement in Europe is possible without a solution of the German question which lies at the heart of present tensions in Europe. Any such settlement must end the unnatural barriers between Eastern and Western Europe, which are most clearly and cruelly manifested in the division of Germany.

9. Accordingly the Allies are resolved to direct their energies to this purpose by realistic measures designed to further a detente in East-West relations. The relaxation of tensions is not the final goal but is part of a long-term process to promote better relations and to foster a European settlement. The ultimate political purpose of the Alliance is to achieve a just and lasting peaceful order in Europe accompanied by appropriate security guarantees.

10. Currently, the development of contacts between the countries of Western and Eastern Europe is mainly on a bilateral basis. Certain subjects, of course, require by their very nature a multilateral solution.

11. The problem of German reunification and its relationship to a European settlement has normally been dealt with in exchanges between the Soviet Union and the three Western powers having special responsibilities in this field. In the preparation of such exchanges the Federal Republic of Germany has regularly joined the three Western powers in order to reach a common position. The other Allies will continue to have their views considered in timely discussions among the Allies about Western policy on this subject, without in any way impairing the special responsibilities in question.

12. The Allies will examine and review suitable policies designed to achieve a just and stable order in Europe, to overcome the division of Germany and to foster European security. This will be part of a process of active and constant preparation for the time when fruitful discussions of these complex questions may be possible bilaterally or multilaterally between Eastern and Western nations.

13. The Allies are studying disarmament and practical arms control measures, including the possibility of balanced force reductions. These studies will be intensified. Their active pursuit reflects the will of the Allies to work for an effective detente with the East.

14. The Allies will examine with particular attention the defence problems of the exposed areas, e.g. the south-eastern flank. In this respect the present situation in the Mediterranean presents special problems, bearing in mind that the current crisis in the Middle East falls within the responsabilities of the United Nations.

15. The North Atlantic Treaty area cannot be treated in isolation from the rest of the world. Crises and conflicts arising outside the area may impair its security either directly or by affecting the global balance. Allied countries contribute individually within the United Nations and other international organisations to the maintenance of international peace and security and to the solution of important international problems. In accordance with established usage the Allies, or such of them as wish to do so, will also continue to consult on such problems without commitment and as the case may demand.

16. In the light of these findings, the Ministers directed the Council in permanent session to carry out, in the years ahead, the detailed follow-up resulting from this study. This will be done either by intensifying work already in hand or by activating highly specialised studies by more systematic use of experts and officials sent from capitals.

17. Ministers found that the study by the Special Group confirmed the importance of the role which the Alliance is called upon to play during the coming years in the promotion of detente and the strengthening of peace. Since significant problems have not yet been examined in all their aspects, and other problems of no less significance which have arisen from the latest political and strategic developments have still to be examined, the Ministers have directed the Permanent Representatives to put in hand the study of these problems without delay, following such procedures as shall be deemed most appropriate by the Council in permanent session, in order to enable further reports to be subsequently submitted to the Council in Ministerial Session.

8

Declaration on Atlantic Relations

This declaration was approved and published by the North Atlantic Council in Ottawa on June 19, 1974 and signed by Heads of NATO Governments in Brussels on June 26, 1974

1. The members of the North Atlantic Alliance declare that the Treaty signed 25 years ago to protect their freedom and independence has confirmed their common destiny. Under the shield of the Treaty, the Allies have maintained their security, permitting them to preserve the values which are the heritage of their civilisation and enabling Western Europe to rebuild from its ruins and lay the foundations of its unity.

2. The members of the Alliance reaffirm their conviction that the North Atlantic Treaty provides the indispensable basis for their security, thus making possible the pursuit of detente. They welcome the progress that has been achieved on the road towards detente and harmony among nations, and the fact that a Conference of 35 countries of Europe and North America is now seeking to lay down guidelines designed to increase security and cooperation in Europe. They believe that until circumstances permit the introduction of general, complete and controlled disarmament, which alone could provide genuine security for all, the ties uniting them must be maintained. The Allies share a common desire to reduce the burden of arms expenditure on their peoples. But States that wish to preserve peace have never achieved this aim by neglecting their own security.

3. The members of the Alliance reaffirm that their common defence is one and indivisible. An attack on one or more of them in the area of application of the Treaty shall be considered an attack against them all. The common aim is to prevent any attempt by a foreign power to threaten the independence or integrity of a member of the Alliance. Such an attempt would not only put in jeopardy the security of all members of the Alliance but also threaten the foundations of world peace.

4. At the same time they realise that the circumstances affecting their common defence have profoundly changed in the last ten years: the strategic relationship between the United States and the Soviet Union has reached a point of near equilibrium. Consequently, although all the countries of the Alliance remain vulnerable to attack, the nature of the danger to which they are exposed has changed. The Alliance's problems in the defence of Europe have thus assumed a different and more distinct character.

5. However, the essential elements in the situation which gave rise to the Treaty have not changed. While the commitment of all the Allies to the common defence reduces the risk of external aggression, the contribution to the security of the entire Alliance provided by the nuclear forces of the United States based in the United States as well as in Europe and by the presence of North American forces in Europe remains indispensable.

6. Nevertheless, the Alliance must pay careful attention to the dangers to which it is exposed in the European region, and must adopt all measures necessary to avert them. The European members who provide three-quarters of the conventional strength of the Alliance in Europe, and two of whom possess nuclear forces capable of playing a deterrent role of their own, contributing to the overall strengthening of the deterrence of the Alliance, undertake to make the necessary contribution to maintain the common defence at a level capable of deterring and if necessary repelling all actions directed against the independence and territorial integrity of the members of the Alliance.

7. The United States, for its part, reaffirms its determination not to accept any situation which would expose its Allies to external political or military pressure likely to deprive them of their freedom, and states its resolve, together with its Allies, to maintain forces in Europe at the level required to sustain the credibility of the strategy of deterrence and to maintain the capacity to defend the North Atlantic area should deterrence fail.

8. In this connection the member states of the Alliance affirm that as the ultimate purpose of any defence policy is to deny to a potential adversary the objectives he seeks to attain through an armed conflict, all necessary forces would be used for this purpose. Therefore, while reaffirming that a major aim of their policies is to seek agreements that will reduce the risk of war, they also state that such agreements will not limit their freedom to use all forces at their disposal for the common defence in case of attack. Indeed, they are convinced that their determination to do so continues to be the best assurance that war in all its forms will be prevented.

9. All members of the Alliance agree that the continued presence of Canadian and substantial US forces in Europe plays an irreplaceable role in the defence of North America as well as of Europe. Similarly the substantial forces of the European Allies serve to defend Europe and North America as well. It is also recognized that the further progress towards unity, which the member states of the European Community are determined to make, should in due course have a beneficial effect on the contribution to the common defence of the Alliance of those of them who belong to it. Moreover, the contributions made by members of the Alliance to the preservation of international security and world peace are recognised to be of great importance.

10. The members of the Alliance consider that the will to combine their efforts to ensure their common defence obliges them to maintain and improve the efficiency of their forces and that each should undertake, according to the role that it has assumed in the structure of the Alliance, its proper share of the burden of maintaining the security of all. Conversely, they take the view that in the course of current or future negotiations nothing must be accepted which could diminish this security.

11. The Allies are convinced that the fulfilment of their common aims requires the maintenance of close consultation, cooperation and mutual trust, thus fostering the conditions necessary for defence and favourable for detente, which are complementary. In the spirit of the friendship, equality and solidarity which characterise their relationship, they are firmly resolved to keep each other fully informed and to strengthen the practice of frank and timely consultations by all means which may be appropriate on matters relating to their common interests as members of the Alliance, bearing in mind that these interests can be affected by events in other areas of the world. They wish also to ensure that their essential security relationship is supported by harmonious political and economic relations. In particular they will work to remove sources of conflict between their economic policies and to encourage economic cooperation with one another.

12. They recall that they have proclaimed their dedication to the principles of democracy, respect for human rights, justice and social progress, which are the fruits of their shared spiritual heritage and they declare their intention to develop and deepen the application of these principles in their countries. Since these principles, by their very nature, forbid any recourse to methods incompatible with the promotion of world peace, they reaffirm that the efforts which they make to preserve their independence, to maintain their security and to improve the living standards of their peoples exclude all forms of aggression against anyone, are not directed against any other country, and are designed to bring about the general improvement of international relations. In Europe, their objective continues to be the pursuit of understanding and cooperation with every European country. In the world at large, each Allied country recognises the duty to help the developing countries. It is in the interest of all that every country benefits from technical and economic progress in an open and equitable world system.

13. They recognise that the cohesion of the Alliance has found expression not only in cooperation among their governments, but also in the free exchange of views among the elected representatives of the peoples of the Alliance. Accordingly, they declare their support for the strengthening of links among Parliamentarians.

14. The members of the Alliance rededicate themselves to the aims and ideals of the North Atlantic Treaty during this year of the twenty-fifth Anniversary of its signature. The member nations look to the future, confident that the vitality and creativity of their peoples are commensurate with the challenges which confront them. They declare their conviction that the North Atlantic Alliance continues to serve as an essential element in the lasting structure of peace they are determined to build.

Adopted and published in
Ottawa on June 19, 1974

Signed in Brussels
on June 26, 1974

9
The Montebello Decision

Annex to the Final Communiqué of the Autumn Ministerial Meeting of the NATO Nuclear Planning Group (NPG) Montebello, Canada.

October 27, 1983

At Montebello, Nuclear Planning Group (NPG) Ministers declared that the policy of the Alliance is to preserve the peace through the maintenance of forces at the lowest level capable of deterring the Warsaw Pact threat.

Consistent with this policy the Alliance since 1977 has been conducting analyses aimed at assuring that nuclear weapons in NATO's armoury are held to the minimum number necessary for deterrence, taking account of developments in conventional as well as nuclear forces.

On the basis of the initial results of these analyses, the Alliance decided in December 1979 that, unless obviated by successful negotiation with the Soviet Union, the deployment of longer-range weapons (Pershing II and cruise missiles) was essential to restoring the balance and maintaining the integrity of NATO's deterrent posture. The Alliance remains committed to the dual-track decision and its implementation.[1] At the same time Ministers decided to reduce the NATO stockpile by 1,000 warheads. This withdrawal has been completed. Moreover, Ministers mandated further analysis to determine whether the withdrawal of weapons beyond the 1,000 then decided could be accomplished safely, in a manner consistent with the maintenance of deterrence at the lowest possible level of weapons.

With the Alliance analysis now complete, the Nuclear Planning Group has decided on 27th October, 1983 to withdraw 1,400 warheads during the next several years. This Ministerial decision, taken together with the already accomplished withdrawal of 1,000 warheads will bring to 2,400 the total number of warheads to be removed from Europe since 1979. Moreover, this reduction will not be affected by any deployment of Longer-Range INF (LRINF) since one warhead will be removed for each Pershing II or Ground-Launched Cruise Missile (GLCM) warhead deployed.

The detailed implementation of this decision as to the precise composition of the stockpile is a matter for the responsible military authorities to determine and a programme to effect this will be worked out and implemented over the next five to six years. In this context, appropriate consideration will be given to short-range systems. NATO's military authorities should report their findings at a future NPG meeting.

Recognising that for this minimum level stockpile to make the most effective contribution to deterrence, both the delivery systems and the warheads must be survivable, responsive and effective, Ministers accordingly identified a range of possible improvements. Ministers established broad criteria which will remain valid for the next decade, including the continuing importance of strengthening conventional forces. The Alliance must, however, take account at all times of changes to Soviet capabilities during this period.

Contrary to the impression that NATO has been fuelling an arms build-up by adding to its nuclear armoury, this sustained programme of reductions will have reduced NATO's nuclear stockpile to the lowest level in over 20 years. Ministers urged the Soviet Union to follow the example set by the Alliance, to halt and reverse its build-up of nuclear forces, and to join NATO in the search for a safer future.

---

[1] Greece has expressed its views in the minutes of the NPG at Montebello.

10

Declaration by the Foreign Ministers at the North Atlantic Council Meeting in Brussels

December 9, 1983

We, the representatives of the sixteen member countries of the North Atlantic Alliance, reaffirm the dedication of the Allies to the maintenance of peace in freedom.

Our Alliance threatens no one. None of our weapons will ever be used except in response to attack. We do not aspire to superiority, neither will we accept that others should be superior to us. Our legitimate security interests can only be guaranteed through the firm linkage between Europe and North America. We call upon the Soviet Union to respect our legitimate security interests as we respect theirs.

We are determined to ensure security on the basis of a balance of forces at the lowest possible level. Faced with the threat posed by the Soviet SS-20 missiles, the Allies concerned are going forward with the implementation of the double-track decisions of 1979. The ultimate goal remains that there should be neither Soviet nor United States land based long-range INF missiles. The deployment of US missiles can be halted or reversed by concrete results at the negotiating table. In this spirit we wish to see an early resumption of the INF negotiations which the Soviet Union has discontinued[1].

We urge the countries of the Warsaw Pact to seize the opportunities we offer for a balanced and constructive relationship and for genuine detente. In all arms control negotiations progress must be made among the states participating, in particular in:

— the Strategic Arms Reductions Talks (START);
— the Intermediate-range Nuclear Forces Talks (INF);
— the negotiations on Mutual and Balanced Force Reductions (MBFR);
— the endeavours for a complete ban on chemical weapons in the Committee on Disarmament.

We are also resolved to use the forthcoming Stockholm Conference as a new opportunity to broaden the dialogue with the East, to negotiate confidence building measures and enhance stability and security in the whole of Europe.

We shall continue to do our utmost to sustain a safe and peaceful future. We extend to the Soviet Union and the other Warsaw Pact countries the offer to work together with us to bring about a long-term constructive and realistic relationship based on equilibrium, moderation and reciprocity. For the benefit of mankind we advocate an open, comprehensive political dialogue, as well as co-operation based on mutual advantage.

[1] Denmark and Greece reserve their positions on this paragraph; Spain, not having been a party to the double-track decision of 1979, reserves its position on this paragraph.

11
Washington Statement on East-West Relations

Issued by the Foreign Ministers at the North Atlantic Council Meeting, Washington

May 31, 1984

1. At their meeting in December 1983 the Ministers of Foreign Affairs of the member countries of the Alliance, on the initiative of the Foreign Minister of Belgium, decided that the Council should undertake an appraisal of East-West relations with a view to achieving a more constructive East-West dialogue.

2. The appraisal has confirmed the continuing validity of the balanced approach contained in the Harmel Report of 1967. To ensure the security of members of the Alliance, the most appropriate long-term policies are the maintenance of adequate military strength and political solidarity and, on that basis, the pursuit of a more stable relationship between the countries of East and West through dialogue and cooperation. These elements are complementary: dialogue can only be fruitful if each party is confident of its security and is prepared to respect the legitimate interests of others: military strength alone cannot guarantee a peaceful future. Experience points to the continuing need for full, consistent and realistic implementation of the two main tasks of the Alliance set out in the Harmel Report.

3. In pursuit of this approach the Allies sought to alleviate sources of tension and to create a propitious climate for expanded cooperation. Steps such as the Berlin Quadripartite Agreement, improvements in relations between the two German states with positive results for individuals, the Strategic Arms Limitation Talks (SALT) I accords including the Anti-Ballistic Missile Treaty, and the Final Act of the Conference on Security and Cooperation in Europe (CSCE) were the fruits of this policy. However, progress towards the expansion of human contacts and human freedoms remains unsatisfactory. Individuals have nonetheless benefited from increased opportunities for contacts and communication.

4. At the same time, the Soviet Union engaged in a massive military build-up. This poses a continuing threat to Alliance security and vital Western Interests. The Soviet Union has sought to exploit any apparent weakness which it has perceived on the part of the Alliance. Further, Allied restraint has not been met with reciprocal restraint by the Soviets. Instead they have pursued a relentless campaign to breach the solidarity of the Alliance. Soviet willingness to threaten or use military power for political ends has been exemplified most notably in the invasion of Afghanistan and pressure on Poland[1].

5. Notwithstanding continuing fundamental differences between countries in East and West, the Allies remain convinced that there exist areas where common interests should prevail. These include the need to safeguard peace, to build confidence, to increase security, to improve mechanisms for dealing with crises, and to promote prosperity. To this end, the Allies remain determined to build upon these and other areas of common interest in pursuing their efforts to promote more constructive dialogue and cooperation with the members of the Warsaw Pact with a view to achieving genuine détente.

6. The Allies support the continuation and strengthening of the CSCE process which represents an important means of promoting stable and constructive East-West relations on a long-term basis. They insist on the implementation of the Helsinki Final Act and the Madrid concluding document in all their parts. While important agreements have been reached within the CSCE framework, much remains to be done. Any improvement in East-West relations would be incomplete if individuals were not able to benefit from greater respect for human rights and increased human contacts.

7. The Allies will continue to be guided by the awareness of a common history and traditions of all European peoples. Given the continuing division in Europe and particularly Germany, the Alliance continues to support the political aim of the Federal Republic of Germany to work towards a state of peace in Europe in which the German people regains its unity through free self-determination.

8. Neither side must seek unilateral advantage, military superiority or dominance over other states. Mutual respect for each other's security on the basis of equality of rights, non-use of force as called for in the United Nations Charter and other current international agreements, restraint, and respect for international rules of conduct are essential for strengthening confidence and cooperation.

9. The Allies respect the sovereignty and independence of states everywhere and genuine non-alignment. This is reflected in their political, economic and aid relations with other countries. Responsible Soviet behaviour world-wide would be an important contribution to a durable improvement in East-West relations.

10. The Allies recognise that, as members of the Alliance, their vital security interests can be affected by developments outside the Treaty area. They will engage in timely consultations on such developments. They underline the responsibility of all states to prevent the transfer of East-West differences to the regions of the Third World. They would like to see the benefits of peace, stability, human rights and freedom from interference which they themselves have enjoyed for over 35 years secured in other areas of the world as well.

11. On a basis of unity of purpose and assured security, the Allies reaffirm their offers to improve East-West relations, made most recently in the Declaration of Brussels of 9 December 1983. They propose that particular efforts be devoted to the following:

a. dialogue, cooperation and contacts at all levels on the full range of questions between East and West—including political and security problems, human rights and bilateral matters—aimed at increasing mutual understanding, identifying common interests, clarifying objectives, expanding areas of agreement and resolving or isolating areas of disagreement;

b. mutually advantageous trade and economic cooperation with Warsaw Pact members on commercially sound terms which are consistent with Allies' broad security concerns, which include avoidance of contributing to Soviet military strength;

c. achieving security at the lowest possible level of forces through balanced, equitable and verifiable agreements on concrete arms control, disarmament and confidence building measures.

To these ends, the Allies concerned will continue in particular:

i. to emphasise the readiness of the United States to resume bilateral negotiations on Intermediate-Range Nuclear Forces (INF) and Strategic Arms Reductions (START) with the Soviet Union at any time without preconditions and to call on the Soviet Union to return to the negotiating table[2];

ii. to work for progress at the Mutual and Balanced Force Reductions (MBFR) negotiations where they have recently made new proposals to break the impasse on conventional force reductions;

iii. to urge the world-wide elimination of chemical weapons which is the objective of the United States draft Treaty tabled at the Conference on Disarmament;

iv. to press at the Stockholm Conference (CDE) for agreement on concrete measures, as proposed by the Allies, designed to build confidence and ensure the openness of military activities in the whole of Europe, thus reducing the risk of surprise attack and the threat of war. In order to give further effect and expression to the existing duty of all participating states to refrain from the threat or use of force in their mutual relations, agreement would be necessary on the above concrete measures in accordance with the Madrid mandate.

12. The purpose of the Alliance is exclusively defensive: none of its weapons will ever be used except in response to attack. The Alliance does not aspire to superiority, but seeks a stable balance of forces. Defence and arms control are integral parts of the security of the Alliance. The legitimate security interests of all countries must be respected on a reciprocal basis. The cohesion and security of the Alliance, based on a firm linkage between its European and North American members, and reinforced by close consultations, remain the foundation for the protection of their common interests and values. In the course of carrying out their appraisal, the Allies have confirmed their consensus on the conduct of East-West relations and their commitment to a constructive East-West dialogue.

13. Peace and stability require a united effort: the Allies look to the Soviet Union and the other Warsaw Pact countries to join in an endeavour which would be of benefit to the world at large. The Allies are prepared to do their part and are ready to examine any reasonable proposal. A long-term, constructive and realistic relationship can then be brought about.

---

1 Greece and Spain reserve their positions on this paragraph.

2 Greece reserves its position on this sub-paragraph.

12

Statement on the Ministerial Meeting of the North Atlantic Council at Halifax, Canada

May 30, 1986

At Halifax, we have reviewed all aspects of East-West relations. We conclude that obstacles to agreement, however serious, should not prevent both sides from building on areas of common interest. We remain ready to co-operate where common ground exists. We will continue our efforts to narrow differences elsewhere.

We remain united in our resolve to maintain adequate forces and to seek a more constructive relationship with the countries of the East. However, the conventional imbalance in Europe and the sustained build-up and modernization of all categories of Soviet military power continue to be of concern. In order to preserve peace and to prevent any kind of war, we will maintain the Alliance's strategy of deterrence.

We are determined to pursue our efforts for progress in arms control and disarmament. We aim at a lower and more balanced level of armaments. We support US efforts to achieve deep reductions in Soviet and US nuclear forces. We seek a treaty totally eliminating chemical weapons. Reductions in conventional forces are also crucial in order to correct the present conventional imbalance between the Alliance and the Warsaw Pact. Beyond this, we aim at conventional stability throughout Europe. We have today made a separate statement on conventional arms control.

In all negotiating fora in which they are engaged, the participating Allies have presented detailed proposals directed at enhancing stability and security. We now await an equally constructive response at the negotiating table from the Soviet Union and the other members of the Warsaw Pact. Public statements alone are not enough.

Adequate verification measures are the key to progress in all the present negotiations and essential for building trust and openness. Any agreement should enhance confidence of compliance and strengthen the existing treaty regime. We are prepared to accept comprehensive verification measures, on a fully reciprocal basis, including systematic on-site inspections.

But the development of peaceful and realistic East-West relations requires more than arms control. The human dimension remains crucial: this embraces respect for human rights and encouragement of individual contacts. Moreover, a more co-operative East-West relationship, including political dialogue, trade, and cultural exchanges, in which all states participate on equal terms, is needed.

We reaffirm the importance each of us attaches to the CSCE process in all its aspects. At Stockholm we are pressing for agreement on a substantial set of confidence and security building measures by September 1986. We are determined to further the CSCE process at the Vienna CSCE Follow-up meeting in November, which should be opened at a political level.

We underline the importance of the continued observance of the Quadripartite Agreement on Berlin and, particularly in view of the current situation, of maintaining freedom of circulation in the city.

Terrorism is a serious concern to us all. It poses an intolerable threat to our citizens and to the conduct of normal international relations. We are resolved to work together to eradicate this scourge. We urge closer international cooperation in this effort.

The purpose of our Alliance is to enable our peoples to live in peace and freedom, free from any threat to their security. We seek a productive East-West dialogue. This will enhance stability in our relations with the members of the Warsaw Pact. We call upon the Soviet Union and the other Eastern European countries to join us in this endeavour.

13

Brussels Declaration on Conventional Arms Control

December 11, 1986

1. At Halifax we agreed on the objective of strengthening stability and security in the whole of Europe, through increased openness and the establishment of a verifiable, comprehensive and stable balance of conventional forces at lower levels. In pursuit of this objective we set up a High Level Task Force; we have today reviewed its first report. We have instructed it to continue in being and to provide further regular reports to the Council.

2. Arms control should enhance, and not diminish, security in Europe. We reiterate our commitment to the maintenance of an effective and credible deterrent posture. Therefore our approach to arms control will remain consistent with the need, at each step of the negotiating process, to retain the means to implement Alliance and national strategies.

3. While maintaining effective deterrence involving both nuclear and conventional forces, we seek to establish a stable relationship of conventional forces in Europe. Reductions in nuclear weapons which are the subject of discussions between the US and the USSR in Geneva would increase the importance of eliminating conventional disparities.

4. We are therefore ready to open East-West discussions with a view to the establishment of a new mandate for negotiating on conventional arms control covering the whole of Europe from the Atlantic to the Urals.

5. For such negotiations to succeed, there must be recognition of the facts about the current situation, and a common understanding on philosophy, objectives and methods.

The Facts

6. Statements by Eastern spokesmen sometimes imply that the present military situation in Europe is stable and balanced. It is not. On the contrary, it is marked by asymmetries and disparities which vary from region to region but which are detrimental to Western security and which are a source of potential instability. The relevant factors include:

— the armaments, equipment types, deployments, numbers, mobility and readiness of the armed forces involved;
— the information, predictability and confidence about them;
— considerations of geography.

The Philosophy

7. Military forces should exist to prevent war and to ensure self-defence, not for the purpose of initiating aggression and not for purposes of political or military intimidation.

The Objectives

8. These should be:

— the establishment of a stable and secure level of forces, geared to the elimination of disparities;

— a negotiating process which proceeds step-by-step, and which guarantees the undiminished security of all concerned at each stage;

— focus on the elimination of the capability for surprise attack or for the initiation of large scale offensive action;

— further measures to build confidence and to improve openness and calculability about military behaviour;

— the application of the measures involved to the whole of Europe but in a way which takes account of and seeks to redress regional imbalances and to exclude circumvention;

— an effective verification regime (in which detailed exchanges of information and on-site inspection will play a vital part) to ensure compliance with the provisions of any agreement, to guarantee that limitations on force capabilities are not exceeded.

The Methods

9. We propose that distinct negotiations take place:

— to build upon and expand the results of the Stockholm Conference on confidence and security building measures;

— to eliminate existing disparities, from the Atlantic to the Urals, and establish conventional stability at lower levels, between the countries whose forces bear most immediately upon the essential security relationship in Europe, namely those belonging to the Alliance and the Warsaw Pact.

10. In the light of the foregoing therefore, we are ready to initiate discussion on enhancing conventional stability in the whole of Europe.

14

Statement on the Ministerial Meeting of the North Atlantic Council at Reykjavik

June 12, 1987

1. Our meeting has taken place at a time when developments in East-West relations suggest that real progress may be possible particularly in the field of arms control. We welcome these developments and will work to ensure that they result in improved security and stability. We note some encouraging signs in Soviet internal and external policies. In assessing Soviet intentions, we agree that the final test will be Soviet conduct across the spectrum from human rights to arms control.

We reaffirm the validity of the complementary principles enunciated in the Harmel report of 1967. The maintenance of adequate military strength and Alliance cohesion and solidarity remains an essential basis for our policy of dialogue and cooperation — a policy which aims to achieve a progressively more stable and constructive East-West relationship.

2. Serious imbalances in the conventional, chemical and nuclear field, and the persisting build-up of Soviet military power, continue to preoccupy us. We reaffirm that there is no alternative, as far as we can foresee, to the Alliance concept for the prevention of war — the strategy of deterrence, based on an appropriate mix of adequate and effective nuclear and conventional forces, each element being indispensable. This strategy will continue to rest on the linkage of free Europe's security to that of North America since their destinies are inextricably coupled. Thus the US nuclear commitment, the presence of United States nuclear forces in Europe[1] and the deployment of Canadian and United States forces there remain essential.

3. Arms control and disarmament are integral parts of our security policy; we seek effectively verifiable arms control agreements which can lead to a more stable and secure balance of forces at lower levels.

4. We reiterate the prime importance we attach to rapid progress towards reductions in the field of strategic nuclear weapons. We thus welcome the fact that the US and the Soviet Union now share the objective of achieving 50% reductions in their strategic arsenals. We strongly endorse the presentation of a US proposal in Geneva to that effect and urge the Soviet Union to respond positively.

We reviewed the current phase of the US-Soviet negotiations in Geneva on defence and space systems which aim to prevent an arms race in space and to strengthen strategic stability. We continue to endorse these efforts.

5. We note the recent progress achieved at the Geneva Conference on Disarmament towards a total ban on chemical weapons. We remain committed to achieving an early agreement on a comprehensive, worldwide and effectively verifiable treaty embracing the total destruction of existing stockpiles within an agreed timeframe and preventing the future production of such weapons.

6. Recognising the increasing importance of conventional stability, particularly at a time when significant nuclear reductions appear possible, we reaffirm the initiatives taken in our Halifax Statement and Brussels Declaration aimed at achieving a comprehensive, stable and verifiable balance of conventional forces at lower levels. We recall that negotiations on conventional stability should be accompanied by negotiations between the 35 countries participating in the CSCE, building upon and expanding the confidence and security building measures contained in the Helsinki Final Act and the Stockholm Agreement. We agreed that the two future security negotiations should take place within the framework of the CSCE process, with the conventional stability negotiations retaining autonomy as regards subject matter, participation and procedures. Building on these agreements we took the decisions necessary to enable the High Level Task Force on Conventional Arms Control, which we established at the Halifax Ministerial, to press ahead with its work on the draft mandates to be tabled in the CSCE meeting and in the Conventional Stability mandate talks currently taking place in Vienna.

7. Having reviewed progress in the negotiations between the United States and the Soviet Union on an INF agreement the Allies concerned call on the Soviet Union to drop its demand to retain a portion of its SS-20 capability and reiterate their wish to see all long-range landbased missiles eliminated in accordance with NATO's long-standing objective.

They support the global and effectively verifiable elimination of all US and Soviet land-based SRINF missiles with a range between 500 and 1,000 km as an integral part of an INF agreement.

They consider that an INF agreement on this basis would be an important element in a coherent and comprehensive concept of arms control and disarmament which, while consistent with NATO's doctrine of flexible response, would include:

— a 50% reduction in the strategic offensive nuclear weapons of the US and the Soviet Union to be achieved during current Geneva negotiations;
— the global elimination of chemical weapons;
— the establishment of a stable and secure level of conventional forces, by the elimination of disparities, in the whole of Europe;
— in conjunction with the establishment of a conventional balance and the global elimination of chemical weapons, tangible and verifiable reductions of American and Soviet land-based nuclear missile systems of shorter range, leading to equal ceilings.

8. We[2] have directed the North Atlantic Council in Permanent Session, working in conjunction with the appropriate military authorities, to consider the further development of a comprehensive concept of arms control and disarmament. The arms control problems faced by the Alliance raise complex and interrelated issues which must be evaluated together, bearing in mind overall progress in the arms control negotiations enumerated above as well as the requirements of Alliance security and of its strategy of deterrence.

9. In our endeavour to explore all opportunities for an increasingly broad and constructive dialogue which addresses the concerns of people in both East and West, and in the firm conviction that a stable order of peace and security in Europe cannot be built by military means alone, we attach particular importance to the CSCE process. We are therefore determined to make full use of the CSCE follow-up meeting in Vienna.

The full implementation of all provisions agreed in the CSCE process by the 35 participating states, in particular in the field of human rights and contacts, remains the fundamental objective of the Alliance and is essential for the fruitful development of East-West relations in all fields.

Recalling our constructive proposals, we shall persist in our efforts to persuade the Eastern countries to live up to their commitments.

We will continue to work for a substantive and timely result of the conference.

10. Those of us participating in the MBFR talks reiterate our desire to achieve a meaningful agreement which provides for reductions, limitations and effective verification, and call upon the Warsaw Pact participants in these talks to respond positively to the very important proposals made by the West in December 1985 and to adopt a more constructive posture in the negotiations.

11. In Berlin's 750th anniversary year we stress our solidarity with the City, which continues to be an important element in East-West relations. Practical improvements in inner-German relations should in particular be of benefit to Berliners.

12. It is just 40 years since US Secretary of State Marshall delivered his far-sighted speech at Harvard. The fundamental values he expressed, which we all share, and which were subsequently embodied in the Marshall Plan, remain as vital today as they were then.

13. We reiterate our condemnation of terrorism in all its forms. Reaffirming our determination to combat it, we believe that close international cooperation is an essential means of eradicating this scourge.

14. Alliance cohesion is substantially enhanced by the support of freely elected parliamentary representatives and ultimately our publics. We therefore underline the great value of free debate on issues facing the Alliance and welcome the exchanges of views on these issues among the parliamentarians of our countries, including those in the North Atlantic Assembly.

15. We express our gratitude to the government of Iceland, which makes such a vital contribution to the security of the Alliance's northern maritime approaches, for their warm hospitality.

16. The Spring 1988 meeting of the North Atlantic Council in Ministerial Session will be held in Spain in June.

---

[1] Greece recalls its position on nuclear matters.

[2] In this connection France recalled that it had not been a party to the double-track decision of 1979 and that it was not therefore bound by its consequences or implications.

15

Conventional Arms Control: The Way Ahead

Statement issued under the Authority of the Heads of State and Government participating in the meeting of the North Atlantic Council in Brussels

March 2, 1988

At Halifax in 1986, our governments issued a clear call to strengthen stability in the whole of Europe through conventional arms control negotiations. At Brussels later that year they elaborated the basic purposes and methods for such negotiations.

The military confrontation in Europe is the result, not the cause, of the painful division which burdens this continent. While seeking to overcome this division in other ways, we also seek security and stability in Europe at the lowest possible level of armaments. Both arms control and adequate defence programmes can contribute towards this goal.

A. The present realities

1. The Soviet Union's military presence in Europe, at a level far in excess of its needs for self defence, directly challenges our security as well as our hopes for change in the political situation in Europe. Thus the conventional imbalance in Europe remains at the core of Europe's security concerns. The problem is to a large extent a function of the Warsaw Pact's superiority in key conventional weapon systems. But it is not only a matter of numerical imbalances. Other asymmetries are also important, for example:

— the Warsaw Pact, based on the Soviet Union's forward-deployed forces, has a capability for surprise attack and large-scale offensive action; the Allies neither have, nor aspire to, such a capability;

— the countries of the Warsaw Pact form a contiguous land mass; those of the Alliance are geographically disconnected;

— the Warsaw Pact can generate a massive reinforcement potential from distances of only a few hundred kilometres; many Allied reinforcements need to cross the Atlantic;

— the Warsaw Pact's military posture and activities are still shrouded in secrecy, whereas those of Allied countries are transparent and under permanent public scrutiny.

2. These asymmetries are compounded by the dominant presence in Europe of the conventional armed forces of the Soviet Union. They represent 50% of all the active divisions in Europe between the Atlantic and the Urals. This Soviet conventional superiority and its military presence in other Eastern European countries serve a political as well as a military function. They cast a shadow over the whole of Europe.

3. Conventional arms control is not merely a technical corrective to a self-contained problem. It should be seen in a coherent political and security framework.

B. A political and security framework

4. We reiterate our conviction that military forces should only exist to prevent war and to ensure self defence, not for the purpose of initiating aggression and not for the purposes of political or military intimidation. Our ability to prevent every kind of war, nuclear or conventional, rests on our capacity and determination to deter any form of aggression. All the Allies' military resources are designed to contribute to that objective. This approach is shared alike both by those Allies who belong to the integrated military organisation and by those who do not.

5. The relationship between nuclear and conventional forces is complex. The existence of a conventional imbalance in favour of the Warsaw Pact is not the only reason for the presence of nuclear weapons in Europe. The countries of the Alliance are, and will remain, under the threat of Soviet nuclear forces of varying ranges. Although conventional parity would bring important benefits for stability, only the nuclear element can confront a potential aggressor with an unacceptable risk; therefore, for the foreseeable future deterrence will continue to require an adequate mix of nuclear as well as conventional forces.

6. Hence the determination of our nations to ensure defence preparedness as a means of achieving the stability we seek. We will continue to ensure that our military forces are effective and up-to-date, in particular by:

— continued compliance with the principle of shared risks and responsibilities and acceptance of the priorities essential to the strengthening of our defence capabilities;
— provision of adequate defence expenditure, together with efforts to obtain the greatest return on our defence investment;
— closer cooperation designed to remedy key deficiencies and, in this context, support for recent legislative and other initiatives designed to foster cooperation in the area of conventional armaments, especially research, development, production and procurement;
— helping to meet the needs of the less advantaged Allies in strengthening their conventional defences, thus redressing important existing deficiencies.

7. It will be important that defence and arms control policies remain in harmony in order to ensure their complementary contribution to the security of the countries of the Alliance. In framing their negotiating proposals for conventional stability, the Allies will ensure that the continued requirement for deterrence and defence is not prejudiced; accordingly they will neither make nor accept proposals which would involve an erosion of the Allies' nuclear deterrent capability.

8. Security in Europe involves not just military, but also political, economic and, above all, humanitarian factors. We look forward to a Europe undivided, in which people of all states can freely receive ideas and information; enjoy their fundamental human rights; and determine their own future. Allied forces are stationed outside their national territory to protect these values and to uphold the solidarity of our free Alliance. They cannot therefore be equated with Soviet forces stationed in Eastern Europe. A just and lasting peaceful order in Europe requires that all states enjoy relations of confidence with their own citizens; trust them to make political or economic choices of their own; and allow them to receive information from and exchange ideas with citizens of other states.

9. Conventional arms control talks should be guided by a coherent political vision which reflects these values. It was their adherence to this vision which enabled the

Allies to secure a successful outcome to the Stockholm Conference. It is these same considerations that have led the Allies to decide that both the negotiations which they have now proposed, on conventional stability, as well as those on confidence and security building measures, will be undertaken within the framework of the CSCE process.

10. Those on confidence and security building will involve all 35 CSCE signatory states and will have as their objective to build upon and expand the results of the Stockholm Conference; the agreement reached there marked a significant step towards reducing the risk of war in Europe. Fully implemented over time, it would create more transparency and contribute to greater confidence and predictability of military activities in the whole of Europe. The momentum generated by Stockholm must be maintained.

11. At the same time we are conscious of the specific responsibility of the 23 members of the two military alliances in Europe whose forces bear most directly on the essential security relationship in Europe. Hence our decision that distinct and autonomous negotiations on conventional stability should take place between the 23 States.

12. The adoption of mandates for both of the negotiations must be part of a balanced outcome to the Vienna CSCE Follow-up Meeting, which necessitates substantial progress in all areas of the Helsinki Final Act.

C. The Allies' objectives

13. In accordance with the principles of our approach to conventional arms control, as set out in the Brussels Declaration, our objectives in the forthcoming conventional stability negotiations will be:

— the establishment of a secure and stable balance of conventional forces at lower levels;
— the elimination of disparities prejudicial to stability and security;
— and, as a matter of high priority, the elimination of the capability for launching surprise attack and for initiating large-scale offensive action.

14. This latter capability is the most worrying in relation to the seizure of territory by an aggressor. Its essential ingredient is the forward deployment of conventional forces capable of rapid mobility and high firepower. Tanks and artillery are among the most decisive components, though other elements of combat capability could prove to be similarly significant. Manpower is also important. But not all items of equipment are appropriate for limitation, if only for technical reasons, and manpower alone is an imprecise guide to offensive capability.

15. Our aims will be to establish a situation in Europe in which force postures as well as the numbers and deployments of weapon systems no longer make surprise attack and large-scale offensive action a feasible option. We shall pursue this aim on the basis of the following criteria:

— we need to enhance stability in the whole of Europe from the Atlantic to the Urals; and to do so in a way which, while safeguading the security of all Allies, takes account of the concentrations of Warsaw Pact forces and the particular problems affecting the Central, Southern and Northern regions;
— in seeking to eliminate the ability to conduct large-scale offensive action, we shall focus on the key weapon systems;
— we shall propose provisions dealing with stationed forces, taking account of the weight of forward-deployed Soviet conventional forces; we shall also take into consideration capabilities for force generation and reinforcement;

— equal number or percentage reductions by both sides would not eliminate the disparities which threaten stability in Europe. Our proposals will concentrate instead on results and residual entitlements;
— our goal is to redress the conventional imbalance. This can be achieved through a set of measures including, inter alia, reductions, limitations, redeployment provisions and related measures as well as the establishment of equal ceilings;
— this outcome will require highly asymmetrical reductions by the East and will entail, for example, the elimination from Europe of tens of thousands of Warsaw Pact weapons relevant to surprise attack, among them tanks and artillery pieces;
— reductions of combat-decisive equipment and modification of the Soviet forward deployment posture will only be part of our approach to reducing the risk of conflict. As a concurrent element in any effort to enhance stability and security, we shall also propose measures to produce greater openness of military activities throughout Europe, safeguard the maintenance of lower force levels, and support a rigorous, effective and reliable monitoring and verification regime;
— this monitoring and verification regime will need to include the exchange of detailed data about forces and deployments; and the right to conduct sufficient on-site inspections to provide confidence that agreed provisions are being complied with.

D. The way ahead

16. Early agreement on a conventional stability mandate, as part of a balanced outcome to the Vienna Follow-up Meeting of the Conference on Security and Cooperation in Europe, would be an important step forward. We seek the elimination of the conventional imbalances which so threaten stability and security in Europe. We also seek enhanced respect for human rights and fundamental freedoms on which lasting security and stability ultimately depend.

Greece recalls its position on nuclear matters.

16

Declaration of the Heads of State and Government participating in the meeting of the North Atlantic Council in Brussels

March 3, 1988

A time for reaffirmation

We, the representatives of the sixteen members of the North Atlantic Alliance, have come together to re-emphasise our unity, to assess the current state of East-West relations, to review the opportunities and challenges which lie ahead, and in so doing:

— to reaffirm the common ideals and purposes which are the foundation of our partnership;
— to rededicate ourselves to the principles and provisions of the Washington Treaty of 1949;
— to reassert the vital importance of the Alliance for our security, and the validity of our strategy for peace.

The purposes and principles of our Alliance

2. Our Alliance is a voluntary association of free and democratic equals, united by common interests and values. It is unprecedented in its scope and success. Our security is indivisible. Our Alliance is dedicated to preserving peace in freedom and to collective self-defence, as recognised by the United Nations Charter. None of our weapons will ever be used except in response to attack.

3. Our concept of a balanced security policy as set out in the Harmel Report has successfully stood the test of time. It remains valid in its two complementary and mutually reinforcing approaches: political solidarity and adequate military strength, and, on that basis, the search for constructive dialogue and cooperation, including arms control. The ultimate political purpose of our Alliance is to achieve a just and lasting peaceful order in Europe.

4. The security in freedom and the prosperity of the European and North American Allies are inextricably linked. The long-standing commitment of the North American democracies to the preservation of peace and security in Europe is vital. The presence in Europe of the conventional and nuclear forces of the United States provides the essential linkage with the United States strategic deterrent, and, together with the forces of Canada, is a tangible expression of that commitment. This presence must and will be maintained.

Likewise, a free, independent and increasingly united Europe is vital to North America's security. The credibility of Allied defence cannot be maintained without a major European contribution. We therefore welcome recent efforts to reinforce the

European pillar of the Alliance, intended to strengthen the transatlantic partnership and Alliance security as a whole.

The Atlantic Alliance cannot be strong if Europe is weak.

5. Our aim will continue to be to prevent any kind of war or intimidation. By maintaining credible deterrence the Alliance has secured peace in Europe for nearly forty years. Conventional defences alone cannot ensure this; therefore, for the foreseeable future there is no alternative to the Alliance strategy for the prevention of war. This is a strategy of deterrence based upon an appropriate mix of adequate and effective nuclear and conventional forces which will continue to be kept up to date where necessary.

6. While seeking security and stability at lower levels of armaments, we are determined to sustain the requisite efforts to ensure the continued viability, credibility and effectiveness of our conventional and nuclear forces, including the nuclear forces in Europe, which together provide the guarantee of our common security. Taking into account the structure of the Alliance, each of us undertakes to play his part in this joint endeavour in a spirit of solidarity, reaffirming our willingness to share fairly the risks, burdens and responsibilities as well as the benefits of our common efforts.

7. We seek a just and stable condition of peace in which the sovereignty and territorial integrity of all states are respected and the rights of all individuals, including their right of political choice, are protected.

We want gradually to overcome the unnatural division of the European continent, which affects most directly the German people. We will continue to uphold the freedom and viability of Berlin and to support efforts to improve the situation there.

The search for improved and more stable relations with the Soviet Union and the other countries of Eastern Europe is among our principal concerns. We call upon these countries to work with us for a further relaxation of tensions, greater security at lower levels of arms, more extensive human contacts and increased access to information. We will continue the effort to expand cooperation with the East wherever and whenever this is of mutual benefit.

East-West relations: the way ahead

8. We have noted encouraging signs of change in the policies of the Soviet Union and some of its allies. This creates the prospect for greater openness in their relations with their own peoples and with other nations. We welcome such progress as has been already achieved in certain areas. But we look beyond pronouncements for tangible and lasting policy changes addressing directly the issues dividing East and West.

9. However, we have to date witnessed no relaxation of the military effort pursued for years by the Soviet Union. The Soviet Union persists in deploying far greater military forces than are required for its defence. This massive force, which the Soviet Union has not refrained froim using outside its borders, as is still the case in Afghanistan, constitutes a fundamental source of tension between East and West. The steady growth of Soviet military capabilities, as it affects every region of the Alliance, requires our constant attention.

10. We will continue to be steadfast in the pursuit of our security policies, maintaining the effective defences and credible deterrence that form the necessary basis for constructive dialogue with the East including on arms control and disarmament matters.

To meet our security needs in the years to come will require ever greater efficiencies in the application of our scarce resources. We are therefore determined to expand our practical cooperation in the field of armaments procurement and elsewhere. In this context we recognise the challenges to our industrially less advanced Allies and the need to address them through mutual assistance and cooperation.

11. Arms control is an integral part of our security policy. We seek negotiations not for their own sake but to reach agreements which can significantly reduce the risk of conflict and make a genuine contribution to stability and peace. We shall work together vigorously and on the basis of the closest consultation to this end.

12. Our representatives to the North Atlantic Council continue actively the further development of a comprehensive concept of arms control and disarmament as directed in the Statement of our Ministers at Reykjavik in June 1987.

13. The recently concluded INF agreement between the US and the Soviet Union is a milestone in our efforts to achieve a more secure peace and lower levels of arms. It is the impressive result of the political courage, the realism and the unity of the members of the Alliance. The treaty's provisions on stringent verification and asymmetrical reductions provide useful precedents for future agreements. We look forward to its early entry into force.

14. Consistent with their security requirements, the fifteen Allies concerned will make use of all possibilities for effectively verifiable arms control agreements which lead to a stable and secure balance of forces at a lower level. For them, the comprehensive concept of arms control and disarmament includes:

— a 50% reduction in the strategic offensive nuclear weapons of the US and the Soviet Union to be achieved during current Geneva negotiations;
— the global elimination of chemical weapons;
— the establishment of a stable and secure level of conventional forces, by the elimination of disparities, in the whole of Europe;
— in conjunction with the establishment of a conventional balance and the global elimination of chemical weapons, tangible and verifiable reductions of American and Soviet land-based nuclear missile systems of shorter range, leading to equal ceilings.

15. Recognising the urgency and central importance of addressing the conventional force imbalances in Europe, we have adopted a separate statement on conventional arms control.

16. The resolution of East-West differences will require progress in many fields. Genuine peace in Europe cannot be established solely by arms control. It must be firmly based on full respect for fundamental human rights. As we continue our efforts to reduce armaments, we shall press for implementation on the part of the governments of the Soviet Union and of other Eastern countries of all of the principles and provisions of the Helsinki Final Act and of the Madrid Concluding Document. We support the continuation and strengthening of the CSCE process. It represents an important means of promoting stable and constructive relations on a long term basis between countries of East and West, and, moreover, enhances closer and more fruitful contacts between peoples and individuals throughout Europe. We call upon all participating states to make every effort for an early conclusion to the CSCE follow-up meeting in Vienna with a substantial and balanced final document.

17. We agree that the speedy and complete withdrawal of Soviet troops from Afghanistan and the effective restoration of that country's sovereignty would be of major significance. It is against these criteria that we shall assess General Secretary Gorbachev's recent statements.

18. We hope that at their forthcoming summit in Moscow President Reagan and General Secretary Gorbachev will be able to build upon the progress achieved at their Washington meeting last December. We strongly support the efforts of the United States. These fully accord with our consistent policy to seek, through high-level dialogue, early and substantial progress with the Soviet Union on a full range of issues, including greater respect for human rights, arms control, a lessening of regional tensions, and improved opportunities for bilateral contacts and cooperation.

19. Reflecting upon almost four decades of common endeavour and sacrifice and upon the results achieved, we are confident that the principles and purposes of our Alliance remain valid today and for the future. We are united in our efforts to ensure a world of more secure peace and greater freedom. We will meet the opportunities and challenges ahead with imagination and hope, as well as with firmness and vigilance. We owe no less to our peoples.

Greece recalls its position on nuclear matters.

17

Conventional Arms Control

Statement issued by the North Atlantic Council meeting in ministerial session at NATO Headquarters, Brussels

December 9, 1988

1. In their statement "Conventional Arms Control: The Way Ahead", the Heads of State and Government participating in the meeting of the North Atlantic Council in March 1988 emphasised that the imbalance in conventional forces remains at the core of Europe's security concerns. We shall be presenting specific proposals at the negotiating table to redress this imbalance.

2. We look forward to the early commencement of the two negotiations we have proposed: one on conventional stability between the 23 members of the two military Alliances in Europe and one on confidence and security-building measures among all 35 signatories of the Helsinki Final Act.

3. In these negotiations we will be guided by:
— the conviction that the existing military confrontation is the result, not the cause, of the painful division of Europe;
— the principle of the indivisible security of all our nations. We shall reject calls for partial security arrangements or proposals aimed at separate agreements;
— the hope that the new thinking in the Soviet Union will open the way for mutual agreement on realistic, militarily significant and verifiable arrangements which enhance security at lower levels.

Towards stability

4. The major threat to stability in Europe comes from those weapons systems which are capable of mounting large-scale offensive operations and of seizing and holding territory. These are above all main battle tanks, artillery and armoured troop carriers. It is in these very systems that the East has such a massive preponderance. Indeed, the Soviet Union itself possesses more tanks and artillery than all the other members of the Warsaw Pact and the Alliance combined. And they are concentrated in a manner which raises grave concerns about the strategy which they are intended to support as well as their role in maintaining the division of Europe.

5. The reductions announced by the Soviet Union are a positive contribution to correcting this situation. They indicate the seriousness with which the conventional imbalances which we have long highlighted as a key problem of European security are now also addressed by the Soviet government. We also welcome the declared readiness of the Soviet Union to adjust their force posture. The important thing is now to build on these hopeful developments at the negotiating table in order to correct the large asymmetries that will still remain and to secure a balance at lower levels of forces. For this, it will be necessary to deal with the location, nationality and the state of readiness of forces, as well as their numbers. Our proposals will address these issues in the following specific ways:

— We shall propose an overall limit on the total holdings of armaments in Europe. This limit should be substantially lower than existing levels, in the case of tanks close to a half. This would mean an overall limit of about 40,000 tanks.
— In our concept of stability, no country should be able to dominate the continent by force of arms. We shall therefore also propose more than a fixed proportion, such as 30 percent, of the total holdings in Europe of the 23 participants in each equipment category. In the case of tanks, this would result in an entitlement of no more than about 12,000 tanks for any one country.
— Limiting numbers and nationality of forces would not by itself affect the stationing of forces on other countries' territory. Stationed forces, particularly those in active combat units, are especially relevant to surprise attack. We shall propose limits on such forces.
— Our proposal will apply to the whole of Europe. In order to avoid undue concentration of these weapon categories in certain areas of Europe, we shall propose appropriate sub-limits.

6. To buttress the resulting reductions in force levels in the whole of Europe, we shall propose stabilising measures. These could include measures of transparency, notifications and constraint applied to the deployment, movement and levels of readiness of conventional armed forces, which include conventional armaments and equipment.

7. Finally, we shall require a rigorous and reliable regime for monitoring and verification. This would include the periodic exchange of detailed data about forces and deployments, and the right to conduct on-site inspections.

Towards transparency

8. Greater transparency is an essential requirement for real stabilty. Therefore, within the framework of the CSCE process, the negotiations on confidence and security-building measures form an essential complement to those on conventional stability. We are encouraged thus far by the successful implementation of the Stockholm Document and we consider that the momentum must be maintained.

9. In order to create transparency of military organisation, we plan to introduce a proposal for a wide-ranging, comprehensive annual exchange of information concerning military organisation, manpower and equipment as well as major weapon deployment programmes. To evaluate this information we will propose modalities for the establishment of a random evaluation system.

10. In addition, in order to build on the success of the Stockholm Document and to create greater transparency of military activities, we will propose measures in areas such as:

— more detailed information with regard to the notification of military exercises,
— improvements in the arrangements for observing military activities,
— greater openness and predictability about military activities,
— a strengthening of the regime for ensuring compliance and verification.

11. Finally, we shall propose additional measures designed to improve contacts and communications between participating states in the military field; to enhance access for military staffs and media representatives; and to increase mutual understanding of military capabilities, behaviour and force postures. We will also propose modalities for an organised exchange of view on military doctrine tied to actual force structures, capabilities and dispositions in Europe.

A vision for Europe

12. We will pursue these distinct negotiations within the framework of the CSCE process, because we believe that a secure peace cannot be achieved without steady progress on all aspects of the confrontation which has divided Europe for more than four decades. Moreover, redressing the disparity in conventional forces in Europe would remove an obstacle to the achievement of the better political relationship between all states of Europe to which we aspire. Conventional arms control must therefore be seen as part of a dynamic process which addresses the military, political, and human aspects of this division.

13. The implementation of our present proposals and of those we are making for further CSBMs will involve a quantum improvement in European security. We will wish to agree and implement them as soon as possible. In the light of their implementation we would then be willing to contemplate further steps to enhance stability and security in Europe, for example:

— further reductions or limitations of conventional armaments and equipment;
— the restructuring of armed forces to enhance defensive capabilities and further reduce offensive capabilities.

Our vision remains that of a continent where military forces only exist to prevent war and to ensure self defence, not for the purpose of initiating aggression or for political or military intimidation.

18

The Alliance's Comprehensive Concept of Arms Control and Disarmament

Adopted by the Heads of State and Government at the meeting of the North Atlantic Council in Brussels

May 29-30, 1989

At Reykjavik in June 1987, Ministers stated that the arms control problems facing the Alliance raised complex and interrelated issues that needed to be evaluated together, bearing in mind overall progress in arms control negotiations as well as the requirements of Alliance security and of its strategy of deterrence. They therefore directed the Council in Permanent Session, working in conjunction with the appropriate military authorities, to "consider the further development of a comprehensive concept of arms control and disarmament".

The attached report, prepared by the Council in response to that mandate, was adopted by Heads of State and Government at the meeting of the North Atlantic Council in Brussels on 29th and 30th May 1989.

I. Introduction

1. The overriding objective of the Alliance is to preserve peace in freedom, to prevent war, and to establish a just and lasting peaceful order in Europe. The Allies' policy to this end was set forth in the Harmel Report of 1967. It remains valid. According to the Report, the North Atlantic Alliance's "first function is to maintain adequate military strength and political solidarity to deter aggression and other forms of pressure and to defend the territory of member countries if aggression should occur". On that basis, the Alliance can carry out "its second function, to pursue the search for progress towards a more stable relationship in which the underlying political issues can be solved". As the Report observed, military security and a policy aimed at reducing tensions are "not contradictory, but complementary". Consistent with these principles, Allied Heads of State and Government have agreed that arms control is an integral part of the Alliance's security policy.

2. The possibilities for fruitful East-West dialogue have significantly improved in recent years. More favourable conditions now exist for progress towards the achievement of the Alliance's objectives. The Allies are resolved to grasp this opportunity. They will continue to address both the symptoms and the causes of political tension in a manner that respects the legitimate security interests of all states concerned.

3. The achievement of the lasting peaceful order which the Allies seek will require that the unnatural division of Europe, and particularly of Germany, be overcome, and that, as stated in the Helsinki Final Act, the sovereignty and territorial integrity of all states and the right of peoples to self-determination be respected, and that the rights of all individuals, including their right of political choice, be protected. The members of the Alliance accordingly attach central importance to further progress in the Conference on

Security and Cooperation in Europe (CSCE) process, which serves as a framework for the promotion of peaceful evolution in Europe.

4. The CSCE process provides a means to encourage stable and constructive East-West relations by increasing contacts between people, by seeking to ensure that basic rights and freedoms are respected in law and practice, by furthering political exchanges and mutually beneficial cooperation across a broad range of endeavours, and by enhancing security and openness in the military sphere. The Allies will continue to demand full implementation of all the principles and provisions of the Helsinki Final Act, the Madrid Concluding Document, the Stockholm Document, and the Concluding Document of the Vienna Meeting. The last document marks a major advance in the CSCE process and should stimulate further beneficial changes in Europe.

5. The basic goal of the Alliance's arms control policy is to enhance security and stability at the lowest balanced level of forces and armaments consistent with the requirements of the strategy of deterrence. The Allies are committed to achieving continuing progress towards all their arms control objectives. The further development of the Comprehensive Concept is designed to assist this by ensuring an integrated approach covering both defence policy and arms control policy: these are complementary and interactive. This work also requires full consideration of the interrelationship between arms control objectives and defence requirements and how various arms control measures, separately and in conjunction with each other, can strengthen Alliance security. The guiding principles and basic objectives which have so far governed the arms control policy of the Alliance remain valid. Progress in achieving these objectives is, of course, affected by a number of factors. These include the overall state of East-West relations, the military requirements of the Allies, the progress of existing and future arms control negotiations, and developments in the CSCE process. The further development and implementation of a comprehensive concept of arms control and disarmament will take place against this background.

II. East-West Relations and Arms Control

6. The Alliance continues to seek a just and stable peace in Europe in which all states can enjoy undiminished security at the minimum necessary levels of forces and armaments and all individuals can exercise their basic rights and freedoms. Arms control alone cannot resolve longstanding political differences between East and West nor guarantee a stable peace. Nonetheless, achievement of the Alliance's goal will require substantial advances in arms control, as well as more fundamental changes in political relations. Success in arms control, in addition to enhancing military security, can encourage improvements in the East-West political dialogue and thereby contribute to the achievement of broader Alliance objectives.

7. To increase security and stability in Europe, the Alliance has consistently pursued every opportunity for effective arms control. The Allies are committed to this policy, independent of any changes that may occur in the climate of East-West relations. Success in arms control, however, continues to depend not on our own efforts alone, but also on Eastern and particularly Soviet readiness to work constructively towards mutually beneficial results.

8. The immediate past has witnessed unprecedented progress in the field of arms control. In 1986 the Stockholm Conference on Disarmament in Europe (CDE) agreement created an innovative system of confidence and security-building measures, designed to promote military transparency and predictability. To date, these have been satisfactorily implemented. The 1987 INF Treaty marked another major step forward because it eliminated a whole class of weapons, it established the principle of asymmetrical reductions, and provided for a stringent verification regime. Other achievements include the establishment in the United States and the Soviet Union of nuclear risk reduction centres, the US/Soviet agreement on prior notification of ballistic missile launches, and the conduct of the Joint Verification Experiment in connection with continued US/Soviet negotiations on nuclear testing.

9. In addition to agreements already reached, there has been substantial progress in the START negotiations which are intended to reduce radically strategic nuclear arsenals and eliminate destabilising offensive capabilities. The Paris Conference on the Prohibition of Chemical Weapons has reaffirmed the authority of the 1925 Geneva Protocol and given powerful political impetus to the negotiations in Geneva for a global, comprehensive and effectively verifiable ban on chemical weapons. New distinct negotiations within the framework of the CSCE process have now begun in Vienna: one on conventional armed forces in Europe between the 23 members of NATO and the Warsaw Treaty Organisation (WTO) and one on confidence- and security-building measures (CSBMs) among all 35 signatories of the Helsinki Final Act.

10. There has also been substantial progress on other matters important to the West. Soviet troops have left Afghanistan. There has been movement toward the resolution of some, although not all, of the remaining regional conflicts in which the Soviet Union is involved. The observance of human rights in the Soviet Union and in some of the other WTO countries has significantly improved, even if serious deficiencies remain. The recent Vienna CSCE Follow-up meeting succeeded in setting new, higher standards of conduct for participating states and should stimulate further progress in the CSCE process. A new intensity of dialogue, particularly at high level, between East and West opens new opportunities and testifies to the Allies' commitment to resolve the fundamental problems that remain.

11. The Alliance does not claim exclusive responsibility for this favourable evolution in East-West relations. In recent years, the East has become more responsive and flexible. Nonetheless, the Alliance's contribution has clearly been fundamental. Most of the achievements to date, which have been described above, were inspired by initiatives by the Alliance or its members. The Allies' political solidarity, commitment to defence, patience and creativity in negotiations overcame initial obstacles and brought its efforts to fruition. It was the Alliance that drew up the basic blueprints for East-West progress and has since pushed them forward towards realisation. In particular, the concepts of stability, reasonable sufficiency, asymmetrical reductions, concentration on the most offensive equipment, rigorous verification, transparency, a single zone from the Atlantic to the Urals, and the balanced and comprehensive nature of the CSCE process, are Western-inspired.

12. Prospects are now brighter than ever before for lasting, qualitative improvements in the East-West relationship. There continue to be clear signs of change in the internal and external policies of the Soviet Union and of some of its Allies. The Soviet leadership has stated that ideological competition should play no part in inter-state relations. Soviet acknowledgement of serious shortcomings in its past approaches to international as well as domestic issues creates opportunities for progress on fundamental political problems.

13. At the same time, serious concerns remain. The ambitious Soviet reform programme, which the Allies welcome, will take many years to complete. Its success cannot be taken for granted given the magnitude of the problems it faces and the resistance generated. In Eastern Europe, progress in constructive reform is still uneven and the extent of these reforms remains to be determined. Basic human rights still need to be firmly anchored in law and practice, though in some Warsaw Pact countries improvements are under way. Although the WTO has recently announced and begun unilateral reductions in some of its forces, the Soviet Union continues to deploy military forces and to maintain a pace of military production in excess of legitimate defensive requirements. Moreover, the geo-strategic realities favour the geographically contiguous Soviet-dominated WTO as against the geographically separated democracies of the North Atlantic Alliance. It has long been an objective of the Soviet Union to weaken the links between the European and North American members of the Alliance.

14. We face an immediate future that is promising but still uncertain. The Allies and the East face both a challenge and an opportunity to capitalise on present conditions in order to increase mutual security. The progress recently made in East-West relations has given new impetus to the arms control process and has enhanced the possibilities of achieving the Alliance's arms control objectives, which complement the other elements of the Alliance's security policy.

III. Principles of Alliance Security

15. Alliance security policy aims to preserve peace in freedom by both political means and the maintenance of a military capability sufficient to prevent war and to provide for effective defence. The fact that the Alliance has for forty years safeguarded peace in Europe bears witness to the success of this policy.

16. Improved political relations and the progressive development of cooperative structures between Eastern and Western countries are important components of Alliance policy. They can enhance mutual confidence, reduce the risk of misunderstanding, ensure that there are in place reliable arrangements for crisis management so that tensions can be defused, render the situation in Europe more open and predictable, and encourage the development of wider cooperation in all fields.

17. In underlining the importance of these facts for the formulation of Alliance policy, the Allies reaffirm that, as stated in the Harmel Report, the search for constructive dialogue and cooperation with the countries of the East, including arms control and disarmament, is based on political solidarity and adequate military strength.

18. Solidarity among the Alliance countries is a fundamental principle of their security policy. It reflects the indivisible nature of their security. It is expressed by the willingness of each country to share fairly the risks, burdens and responsibilities of the common effort as well as its benefits. In particular, the presence in Europe of the United States' conventional and nuclear forces and of Canadian forces demonstrates that North American and European security interests are inseparably bound together.

19. From its inception the Alliance of Western democracies has been defensive in purpose. This will remain so. None of our weapons will ever be used except in self-defence. The Alliance does not seek military superiority nor will it ever do so. Its aim has always been to prevent war and any form of coercion and intimidation.

20. Consistent with the Alliance's defensive character, its strategy is one of deterrence. Its objective is to convince a potential aggressor before he acts that he is confronted with a risk that outweighs any gain—however great—he might hope to secure from his aggression. The purpose of this strategy defines the means needed for its implementation.

21. In order to fulfil its strategy, the Alliance must be capable of responding appropriately to any aggression and of meeting its commitment to the defence of the frontiers of its members' territory. For the foreseeable future, deterrence requires an appropriate mix of adequate and effective nuclear and conventional forces which will continue to be kept up to date where necessary; for it is only by their evident and perceived capability for effective use that such forces and weapons deter.

22. Conventional forces make an essential contribution to deterrence. The elimination of asymmetries between the conventional forces of East and West in Europe would be a major breakthrough, bringing significant benefits for stability and security. Conventional defence alone cannot, however, ensure deterrence. Only the nuclear element can confront an aggressor with an unacceptable risk and thus plays an indispensable role in our current strategy of war prevention.

23. The fundamental purpose of nuclear forces—both strategic and sub-strategic—is political: to preserve the peace and to prevent any kind of war. Such forces contribute to deterrence by demonstrating that the Allies have the military capability and the political will to use them, if necessary, in response to aggression. Should aggression occur, the aim would be to restore deterrence by inducing the aggressor to reconsider his decision, to terminate his attack and to withdraw and thereby to restore the territorial integrity of the Alliance.

24. Conventional and nuclear forces, therefore, perform different but complementary and mutually reinforcing roles. Any perceived inadequacy in either of these two elements, or the impression that conventional forces could be separated from nuclear, or sub-strategic from strategic nuclear forces, might lead a potential adversary to conclude that the risks of launching aggression might be calculable and acceptable. No single element can, therefore, be regarded as a substitute compensating for deficiencies in any other.

25. For the foreseeable future, there is no alternative strategy for the prevention of war. The implementation of this strategy will continue to ensure that the security interests of all Alliance members are fully safeguarded. The principles underlying the strategy of deterrence are of enduring validity. Their practical expression in terms of the size, structure and deployment of forces is bound to change. As in the past, these elements will continue to evolve in response to changing international circumstances, technological progress and developments in the scale of the threat—in particular, in the posture and capabilities of the forces of the Warsaw Treaty Organisation.

26. Within this overall framework, strategic nuclear forces provide the ultimate guarantee of deterrence for the Allies. They must be capable of inflicting unacceptable damage on an aggressor state even after it has carried out a first strike. Their number, range, survivability and penetration capability need to ensure that a potential aggressor cannot count on limiting the conflict or regarding his own territory as a sanctuary. The strategic nuclear forces of the United States provide the cornerstone of deterrence for the Alliance as a whole. The independent nuclear forces of the United Kingdom and France fulfil a deterrent role of their own and contribute to the overall deterrence strategy of the Alliance by complicating the planning and risk assessment of a potential aggressor.

27. Nuclear forces below the strategic level provide an essential political and military linkage between conventional and strategic forces and, together with the presence of Canadian and United States forces in Europe, between the European and North American members of the Alliance. The Allies' sub-strategic nuclear forces are not designed to compensate for conventional imbalances. The levels of such forces in the integrated military structure nevertheless must take into account the threat—both conventional and nuclear—with which the Alliance is faced. Their role is to ensure that there are no circumstances in which a potential aggressor might discount the prospect of nuclear retaliation in response to military action. Nuclear forces below the strategic level thus make an essential contribution to deterrence.

28. The wide deployment of such forces among countries participating in the integrated military structure of the Alliance, as well as the arrangements for consultation in the nuclear area among the Allies concerned, demonstrates solidarity and willingness to share nuclear roles and responsibilities. It thereby helps to reinforce deterrence.

29. Conventional forces contribute to deterrence by demonstrating the Allies' will to defend themselves and by minimising the risk that a potential aggressor could anticipate a quick and easy victory or limited territorial gain achieved solely by conventional means.

30. They must thus be able to respond appropriately and to confront the aggressor immediately and as far forward as possible with the necessary resistance to compel him to end the conflict and to withdraw or face possible recourse to the use of nuclear weapons by the Allies. The forces of the Allies must be deployed and equipped so as to enable them to fulfil this role at all times. Moreover, since the Alliance depends on reinforcements from the North American continent, it must be able to keep open sea and air lines of communication between North America and Europe.

31. All member countries of the Alliance strongly favour a comprehensive, effectively verifiable, global ban on the development, production, stockpiling and use of chemical weapons. Chemical weapons represent a particular case, since the Alliance's overall strategy of war prevention, as noted earlier, depends on an appropriate mix of nuclear and conventional weapons. Pending the achievement of a global ban on chemical weapons, the Alliance recognises the need to implement passive defence measures. A retaliatory capability on a limited scale is retained in view of the Soviet Union's overwhelming chemical weapons capability.

32. The Allies are committed to maintaining only the minimum level of forces necessary for their strategy of deterrence, taking into account the threat. There is, however, a level of forces, both nuclear and conventional, below which the credibility of deterrence cannot be maintained. In particular, the Allies have always recognised that the removal of all nuclear weapons from Europe would critically undermine deterrence strategy and impair the security of the Alliance.

33. The Alliance's defence policy and its policy of arms control and disarmament are complementary and have the same goal: to maintain security at the lowest possible level of forces. There is no contradiction between defence policy and arms control policy. It is on the basis of this fundamental consistency of principles and objectives that the comprehensive concept of arms control and disarmament should be further developed and the appropriate conclusions drawn in each of the areas of arms control.

IV. Arms Control and Disarmament: Principles and Objectives

34. Our vision for Europe is that of an undivided continent where military forces only exist to prevent war and to ensure self-defence, as has always been the case for the Allies, not for the purpose of initiating aggression or for political or military intimidation. Arms control can contribute to the realisation of that vision as an integral part of the Alliance's security policy and of our overall approach to East-West relations.

35. The goal of Alliance arms control policy is to enhance security and stability. To this end, the Allies' arms control initiatives seek a balance at a lower level of forces and armaments through negotiated agreements and, as appropriate, unilateral actions, recognising that arms control agreements are only possible where the negotiating partners share an interest in achieving a mutually satisfactory result. The Allies' arms control policy seeks to remove destabilising asymmetries in forces or equipment. It also pursues measures designed to build mutual confidence and to reduce the risk of conflict by promoting greater transparency and predictability in military matters.

36. In enhancing security and stability, arms control can also bring important additional benefits for the Alliance. Given the dynamic aspects of the arms control process, the principles and results embodied in one agreement may facilitate other arms control steps. In this way arms control can also make possible further reductions in the level of Alliance forces and armaments, consistent with the Alliance's strategy of war prevention. Furthermore, as noted in Chapter II, arms control can make a significant contribution to the development of more constructive East-West relations and of a framework for further cooperation within a more stable and predictable international environment. Progress in arms control can also enhance public confidence in and promote support for our overall security policy.

Guiding Principles for Arms Control

37. The members of the Alliance will be guided by the following principles:

— Security: Arms control should enhance the security of all Allies. Both during the implementation period and following implementation, the Allies' strategy of deterrence and their ability to defend themselves, must remain credible and effective. Arms control measures should maintain the strategic unity and political cohesion of the Alliance, and should safeguard the principle of the indivisibility of Alliance security by avoiding the creation of areas of unequal security. Arms control measures should respect the legitimate security interests of all states and should not facilitate the transfer or intensification of threats to third party states or regions.

— Stability: Arms control measures should yield militarily significant results that enhance stability. To promote stability, arms control measures should reduce or eliminate those capabilities which are most threatening to the Alliance. Stability can also be enhanced by steps that promote greater transparency and predictability in military matters. Military stability requires the elimination of options for surprise attack and for large-scale offensive action. Crisis stability requires that no state has forces of a size and configuration which, when compared with those of others, could enable it to calculate that it might gain a decisive advantage by being the first to resort to arms. Stability also requires measures which discourage destabilising attempts to re-establish military advantage through the transfer of resources to other types of armament. Agreements must lead to final results that are both balanced and ensure equality of rights with respect to security.

— Verifiability: Effective and reliable verification is a fundamental requirement for arms control agreements. If arms control is to be effective and to build confidence, the verifiability of proposed arms control measures must, therefore, be of central concern for the Alliance. Progress in arms control should be measured against the record of compliance with existing agreements. Agreed arms control measures should exclude opportunities for circumvention.

Alliance Arms Control Objectives

38. In accordance with the above principles, the Allies are pursuing an ambitious arms control agenda for the coming years in the nuclear, conventional and chemical fields.

Nuclear Forces

39. The INF Agreement represents a milestone in the Allies' efforts to achieve a more secure peace at lower levels of arms. By 1991, it will lead to the total elimination of all United States and Soviet intermediate range land-based missiles, thereby removing the threat which such Soviet systems presented to the Alliance. Implementation of the agreement, however, will affect only a small proportion of the Soviet nuclear armoury, and the Alliance continues to face a substantial array of modern and effective Soviet systems of all ranges. The full realisation of the Alliance agenda thus requires that further steps be taken.

Strategic Nuclear Forces

40. Soviet strategic systems continue to pose a major threat to the whole of the Alliance. Deep cuts in such systems are in the direct interests of the entire Western Alliance, and therefore their achievement constitutes a priority for the Alliance in the nuclear field.

41. The Allies thus fully support the US objectives of achieving, within the context of the Strategic Arms Reduction Talks, fifty percent reductions in United States and Soviet strategic nuclear arms. United States proposals seek to enhance stability by placing specific restrictions on the most destabilising elements of the threat—fast flying ballistic missiles, throw-weight and, in particular, Soviet heavy ICBMs. The proposals are based on the need to maintain the deterrent credibility of the remaining United States strategic forces which would continue to provide the ultimate guarantee of security for the Alliance as a whole; and therefore on the necessity to keep such forces effective. Furthermore, the United States is holding talks with the Soviet Union on defence and space matters in order to ensure that strategic stability is enhanced.

Sub-Strategic Nuclear Forces

42. The Allies are committed to maintaining only the minimum number of nuclear weapons necessary to support their strategy of deterrence. In line with this commitment, the members of the integrated military structure have already made major unilateral cuts in their sub-strategic nuclear armoury. The number of land-based warheads in Western Europe has been reduced by over one-third since 1979 to its lowest level in over 20 years. Updating where necessary of their sub-strategic systems would result in further reductions.

43. The Allies continue to face the direct threat posed to Europe by the large numbers of shorter-range nuclear missiles deployed on Warsaw Pact territory and which have been substantially upgraded in recent years. Major reductions in Warsaw Pact systems would be of overall value to Alliance security. One of the ways to achieve this aim would be by tangible and verifiable reductions of American and Soviet land-based nuclear missile systems of shorter range leading to equal ceilings at lower levels.

44. But the sub-strategic nuclear forces deployed by member countries of the Alliance are not principally a counter to similar systems operated by members of the WTO. As is explained in Chapter III, sub-strategic nuclear forces fulfil an essential role in overall Alliance deterrence strategy by ensuring that there are no circumstances in which a potential aggressor might discount nuclear retaliation in response to his military action.

45. The Alliance reaffirms its position that for the foreseeable future there is no alternative to the Alliance's strategy for the prevention of war, which is a strategy of deterrence based upon an appropriate mix of adequate and effective nuclear and conventional forces which will continue to be kept up to date where necessary. Where nuclear forces are concerned, land-, sea-, and air-based systems, including ground-based missiles, in the present circumstances and as far as can be foreseen will be needed in Europe.

46. In view of the huge superiority of the Warsaw Pact in terms of short-range nuclear missiles, the Alliance calls upon the Soviet Union to reduce unilaterally its short-range missile systems to the current levels within the integrated military structure.

47. The Alliance reaffirms that at the negotiations on conventional stability it pursues the objectives of:

— the establishment of a secure and stable balance of conventional forces at lower levels;

— the elimination of disparities prejudicial to stability and security; and

— the elimination as a matter of high priority of the capability for launching surprise attack and for initiating large-scale offensive action.

48. In keeping with its arms control objectives formulated in Reykjavik in 1987 and reaffirmed in Brussels in 1988, the Alliance states that one of its highest priorities in negotiations with the East is reaching an agreement on conventional force reductions which would achieve the objectives above. In this spirit, the Allies will make every effort, as evidenced by the outcome of the May 1989 Summit, to bring these conventional negotiations to an early and satisfactory conclusion. The United States has expressed the hope that this could be achieved within six to twelve months. Once implementation of such an agreement is under way, the United States, in consultation with the Allies concerned, is prepared to enter into negotiations to achieve a *partial* reduction of American and Soviet land-based nuclear missile forces of shorter range to equal and verifiable levels. With special reference to the Western proposals on CFE tabled in Vienna, enhanced by the proposals by the United States at the May 1989 Summit, the Allies concerned proceed on the understanding that negotiated reductions leading to a level below the existing level of their SNF missiles will not be carried out until the results of these negotiations have been implemented. Reductions of Warsaw Pact SNF systems should be carried out before that date.

49. As regards the sub-strategic nuclear forces of the members of the integrated military structure, their level and characteristics must be such that they can perform their deterrent role in a credible way across the required spectrum of ranges, taking into account the threat—both conventional and nuclear—with which the Alliance is faced. The question concerning the introduction and deployment of a follow-on system for the Lance will be dealt with in 1992 in the light of overall security developments. While a decision for national authorities, the Allies concerned recognise the value of the continued funding by the United States of research and development of a follow-on for the existing Lance short-range missile, in order to preserve their options in this respect.

Conventional Forces

50. As set out in the March 1988 Summit statement and in the Alliance's November 1988 data initiative, the Soviet Union's military presence in Europe, at a level far in excess of its needs for self-defence, directly challenges our security as well as our aspirations for a peaceful order in Europe. Such excessive force levels create the risk of political intimidation or threatened aggression. As long as they exist, they present

an obstacle to better political relations between all states of Europe. The challenge to security is, moreover, not only a matter of the numerical superiority of WTO forces. WTO tanks, artillery and armoured troop carriers are concentrated in large formations and deployed in such a way as to give the WTO a capability for surprise attack and large-scale offensive action. Despite the recent welcome publication by the WTO of its assessment of the military balance in Europe, there is still considerable secrecy and uncertainty about its actual capabilities and intentions.

51. In addressing these concerns, the Allies' primary objectives are to establish a secure and stable balance of conventional forces in Europe at lower levels, while at the same time creating greater openness about military organisation and activities in Europe.

52. In the Conventional Forces in Europe (CFE) talks between the 23 members of the two alliances, the Western Allies are proposing:

- **reductions to an overall limit on the total holdings of armaments in Europe, concentrating on the most threatening systems, i.e. those capable of seizing and holding territory;**
- **a limit on the proportion of these total holdings belonging to any one country in Europe (since the security and stability of Europe require that no state exceed its legitimate needs for self-defence);**
- **a limit on stationed forces (thus restricting the forward deployment and concentration of Soviet forces in Eastern Europe); and,**
- **appropriate numerical sub-limits on forces which will apply simultaneously throughout the Atlantic to the Urals area.**

These measures, taken together, will necessitate deep cuts in the WTO conventional forces which most threaten the Alliance. The resulting reductions will have to take place in such a way as to prevent circumvention, e.g. by ensuring that the armaments reduced are destroyed or otherwise disposed of. Verification measures will be required to ensure that all states have confidence that entitlements are not exceeded.

53 These measures alone, however, will not guarantee stability. The regime of reductions will have to be backed up by additional measures which should include measures of transparency, notification and constraint applied to the deployment, storage, movement and levels of readiness and availability of conventional forces.

54. In the CSBM negotiations, the Allies aim to maintain the momentum created by the successful implementation of the Stockholm Document by proposing a comprehensive package of measures to improve:

- **transparency about military organisation,**
- **transparency and predictability of military activities,**
- **contacts and communication,**

and have also proposed an exchange of views on military doctrine in a seminar setting.

55 The implementation of the Allies' proposals in the CFE negotiations and of their proposals for further confidence and security-building measures would achieve a quantum improvement in European security. This would have important and positive consequences for Alliance policy both in the field of defence and arms control. The outcome of the CFE negotiations would provide a framework for determining the future Alliance force structure required to perform its fundamental task of preserving peace in freedom. In addition, the Allies would be willing to contemplate further steps to enhance stability and security if the immediate CFE objectives are achieved—for example, further reductions or limitations of conventional armaments and equipment,

or the restructuring of armed forces to enhance defensive capabilities and further reduce offensive capabilities.

56. The Allies welcome the declared readiness of the Soviet Union and other WTO members to reduce their forces and adjust them towards a defensive posture and await implementation of these measures. This would be a step in the direction of redressing the imbalance in force levels existing in Europe and towards reducing the WTO capability for surprise attack. The announced reductions demonstrate the recognition by the Soviet Union and other WTO members of the conventional imbalance, long highlighted by the Allies as a key problem of European security.

Chemical Weapons

57. The Soviet Union's chemical weapons stockpile poses a massive threat. The Allies are committed to conclude, at the earliest date, a worldwide, comprehensive and effectively verifiable ban on all chemical weapons.

58. All Alliance states subscribe to the prohibitions contained in the Geneva Protocol for the Use in War of Asphyxiating, Poisonous or Other Gases, and of Bacteriological Methods of Warfare. The Paris Conference on the Prohibition of Chemical Weapons reaffirmed the importance of the commitments made under the Geneva Protocol and expressed the unanimous will of the international community to eliminate chemical weapons completely at an early date and thereby to prevent any recourse to their use.

59. The Allies wish to prohibit not only the use of these abhorrent weapons, but also their development, production, stockpiling and transfer, and to achieve the destruction of existing chemical weapons and production facilities in such a way as to ensure the undiminished security of all participants at each stage in the process. Those objectives are being pursued in the Geneva Conference on Disarmament. Pending agreement on a global ban, the Allies will enforce stringent controls on the export of commodities related to chemical weapons production. They will also attempt to stimulate more openness among states about chemical weapons capabilities in order to promote greater confidence in the effectiveness of a global ban.

V. Conclusions:

Arms Control and Defence Interrelationships

60. The Alliance is committed to pursuing a comprehensive approach to security, embracing both arms control and disarmament, and defence. It is important, therefore, to ensure that interrelationships between arms control issues and defence requirements and amongst the various arms control areas are fully considered. Proposals in any one area of arms control must take account of the implications for Alliance interests in general and for other negotiations. This is a continuing process.

61. It is essential that defence and arms control objectives remain in harmony in order to ensure their complementary contribution to the goal of maintaining security at the lowest balanced level of forces consistent with the requirements of the Alliance strategy of war prevention, acknowledging that changes in the threat, new technologies, and new political opportunities affect options in both fields. Decisions on arms control matters must fully reflect the requirements of the Allies' strategy of deterrence. Equally, progress in arms control is relevant to military plans, which will have to be developed in the full knowledge of the objectives pursued in arms control negotiations and to reflect, as necessary, the results achieved therein.

62. In each area of arms control, the Alliance seeks to enhance stability and security. The current negotiations concerning strategic nuclear systems, conventional forces and chemical weapons are, however, independent of one another: the outcome of any one of these negotiations is not contingent on progress in others. However, they can influence one another: criteria established and agreements achieved in one area of arms control may be relevant in other areas and hence facilitate overall progress. These could affect both arms control possibilities and the forces needed to fulfil Alliance strategy, as well as help to contribute generally to a more predictable military environment.

63. The Allies seek to manage the interaction among different arms control elements by ensuring that the development, pursuit and realisation of their arms control objectives in individual areas are fully consistent both with each other and with the Alliance's guiding principles for effective arms control. For example, the way in which START limits and sub-limits are applied in detail could affect the future flexibility of the sub-strategic nuclear forces of members of the integrated military structure. A CFE agreement would by itself make a major contribution to stability. This would be significantly further enhanced by the achievement of a global chemical weapons ban. The development of confidence and security-building measures could influence the stabilising measures being considered in connection with the Conventional Forces in Europe negotiations and vice versa. The removal of the imbalance in conventional forces would provide scope for further reductions in the sub-strategic nuclear forces of members of the integrated military structure, though it would not obviate the need for such forces. Similarly, this might make possible further arms control steps in the conventional field.

64. This report establishes the overall conceptual framework within which the Allies will be seeking progress in each area of arms control. In so doing, their fundamental aim will be enhanced security at lower levels of forces and armaments. Taken as a whole, the Allies' arms control agenda constitutes a coherent and comprehensive approach to the enhancement of security and stability. It is ambitious, but we are confident that—with a constructive response from the WTO states—it can be fully achieved in the coming years. In pursuing this goal, the Alliance recognises that it cannot afford to build its security upon arms control results expected in the future. The Allies will be prepared, however, to draw appropriate consequences for their own military posture as they make concrete progress through arms control towards a significant reduction in the scale and quality of the military threat they face. Accomplishment of the Allies' arms control agenda would not only bring great benefits in itself, but could also lead to the expansion of cooperation with the East in other areas. The arms control process itself is, moreover, dynamic; as and when the Alliance reaches agreement in each of the areas set out above, so further prospects for arms control may be opened up and further progress made possible.

65. As noted earlier, the Allies' vision for Europe is that of an undivided continent where military forces only exist to prevent war and to ensure self-defence; a continent which no longer lives in the shadow of overwhelming military forces and from which the threat of war has been removed; a continent where the sovereignty and territorial integrity of all states are respected and the rights of all individuals, including their right of political choice, are protected. This goal can only be reached by stages: it will require patient and creative endeavour. The Allies are resolved to continue working towards its attainment. The achievement of the Alliance's arms control objectives would be a major contribution towards the realisation of its vision.

19

Declaration of the Heads of State and Government participating in the meeting of the North Atlantic Council in Brussels

May 30, 1989

I

NATO's 40 Years of Success

1. As our Alliance celebrates its 40th Anniversary, we measure its achievements with pride. Founded in troubled times to safeguard our security, it has withstood the test of four decades, and has allowed our countries to enjoy in freedom one of the longest periods of peace and prosperity in their history. The Alliance has been a fundamental element of stability and cooperation. These are the fruits of a partnership based on enduring common values and interests, and on unity of purpose.

2. Our meeting takes place at a juncture of unprecedented change and opportunities. This is a time to look ahead, to chart the course of our Alliance and to set our agenda for the future.

Time of Change

3. In our rapidly changing world, where ideas transcend borders ever more easily, the strength and accomplishments of democracy and freedom are increasingly apparent. The inherent inability of oppressive systems to fulfil the aspirations of their citizens has become equally evident.

4. In the Soviet Union, important changes are under way. We welcome the current reforms that have already led to greater openness, improved respect for human rights, active participation of the individual, and new attitudes in foreign policy. But much remains to be done. We still look forward to the full implementation of the announced change in priorities in the allocation of economic resources from the military to the civilian sector. If sustained, the reforms will strengthen prospects for fundamental improvements in East-West relations.

5. We also welcome the marked progress in some countries of Eastern Europe towards establishing more democratic institutions, freer elections and greater political pluralism and economic choice. However, we deplore the fact that certain Eastern European governments have chosen to ignore this reforming trend and continue all too frequently to violate human rights and basic freedoms.

Shaping the Future

6. Our vision of a just, humane and democratic world has always underpinned the policies of this Alliance. The changes that are now taking place are bringing us closer to the realisation of this vision.

7. We want to overcome the painful division of Europe, which we have never accepted. We want to move beyond the post-war period. Based on today's momentum of increased cooperation and tomorrow's common challenges, we seek to shape a new political order of peace in Europe. We will work as Allies to seize all opportunities to achieve this goal. But ultimate success does not depend on us alone.

Our guiding principles in the pursuit of this course will be the policies of the Harmel Report in their two complementary and mutually reinforcing approaches: adequate military strength and political solidarity and, on that basis, the search for constructive dialogue and cooperation, including arms control, as a means of bringing about a just and lasting peaceful order in Europe.

8. The Alliance's long-term objectives are:

— to ensure that wars and intimidation of any kind in Europe and North America are prevented, and that military aggression is an option which no government could rationally contemplate or hope successfully to undertake, and by doing so to lay the foundations for a world where military forces exist solely to preserve the independence and territorial integrity of their countries, as has always been the case for the Allies;

— to establish a new pattern of relations between the countries of East and West, in which ideological and military antagonism will be replaced with cooperation, trust and peaceful competition; and in which human rights and political freedoms will be fully guaranteed and enjoyed by all individuals.

9. Within our larger responsibilities as Heads of State or Government, we are also committed

— to strive for an international community founded on the rule of law, where all nations join together to reduce world tensions, settle disputes peacefully, and search for solutions to those issues of universal concern, including poverty, social injustice and the environment, on which our common fate depends.

II

Maintaining our Defence

10. Peace must be worked for; it can never be taken for granted. The greatly improved East-West political climate offers prospects for a stable and lasting peace, but experience teaches us that we must remain prepared. We can overlook neither the capabilities of the Warsaw Treaty countries for offensive military action, nor the potential hazards resulting from severe political strain and crisis.

11. A strong and united Alliance will remain fundamental not only for the security of our countries but also for our policy of supporting political change. It is the basis for further successful negotiations on arms control and on measures to strengthen mutual confidence through improved transparency and predictability. Military security and policies aimed at reducing tensions as well as resolving underlying political differences are not contradictory but complementary. Credible defence based on the principle of the indivisibility of security for all member countries will thus continue to be essential to our common endeavour.

12. For the foreseeable future, there is no alternative to the Alliance strategy for the prevention of war. This is a strategy of deterrence based upon an appropriate mix of adequate and effective nuclear and conventional forces which will continue to be kept up-to-date where necessary. We shall ensure the viability and credibility of these forces, while maintaining them at the lowest possible level consistent with our security requirements.

13. The presence of North American conventional and nuclear forces in Europe remains vital to the security of Europe just as Europe's security is vital to that of North America. Maintenance of this relationship requires that the Allies fulfil their essential commitments in support of the common defence. Each of our countries will accordingly assume its fair share of the risks, rôles and responsibilities of the Atlantic partnership. Growing European political unity can lead to a reinforced European component of our common security effort and its efficiency. It will be essential to the success of these efforts to make the most effective use of resources made available for our security. To this end, we will seek to maximise the efficiency of our defence programmes and pursue solutions to issues in the area of economic and trade policies as they affect our defence. We will also continue to protect our technological capabilities by effective export controls on essential strategic goods.

Initiatives on Arms Control

14. Arms Control has always been an integral part of the Alliance's security policy and of its overall approach to East-West relations, firmly embedded in the broader political context in which we seek the improvement of those relations.

15. The Allies have consistently taken the lead in developing the conceptual foundations for arms control, identifying areas in which the negotiating partners share an interest in achieving a mutually satisfactory result while safeguarding the legitimate security interests of all.

16. Historic progress has been made in recent years, and we now see prospects for further substantial advances. In our determined effort to reduce the excessive weight of the military factor in the East-West relationship and increasingly to replace confrontation by cooperation, we can now exploit fully the potential of arms control as an agent of change.

17. We challenge the members of the Warsaw Treaty Organisation to join us in accelerating efforts to sign and implement an agreement which will enhance security and stability in Europe by reducing conventional armed forces. To seize the unique opportunity at hand, we intend to present a proposal that will amplify and expand on the position we tabled at the opening of the CFE negotiations on 9th March ([1]). We will

- — register agreement, based on the ceilings already proposed in Vienna, on tanks, armoured troop carriers and artillery pieces held by members of the two Alliances in Europe, with all of the withdrawn equipment to be destroyed. Ceilings on tanks and armoured troop carriers will be based on proposals already tabled in Vienna; definitional questions on artillery pieces remain to be resolved;
- — expand our current proposal to include reductions by each side to equal ceilings at the level 15 per cent below current Alliance holdings of helicopters and of all land-based combat aircraft in the Atlantic-to-the-Urals zone, with all the withdrawn equipment to be destroyed;
- — propose a 20 per cent cut in combat manpower in US stationed forces, and a resulting ceiling on US and Soviet ground and air force personnel stationed outside of national territory in the Atlantic-to-the-Urals zone at approximately 275,000. This ceiling would require the Soviet Union to reduce its forces in Eastern Europe by some 325,000. United States and Soviet forces withdrawn will be demobilised;
- — seek such an agreement within six months to a year and accomplish the reductions by 1992 or 1993. Accordingly, we have directed the Alliance's High Level Task Force on conventional arms control to complete the further elaboration of this proposal, including its verification elements, so that it may be tabled at the beginning of the third round of the CFE negotiations, which opens on 7th September 1989.

18. We consider as an important initiative President Bush's call for an "open skies" regime intended to improve confidence among States through reconnaissance flights, and to contribute to the transparency of military activity, to arms control and to public awareness. It will be the subject of careful study and wide-ranging consultations.

19. Consistent with the principles and objectives set out in our Comprehensive Concept of Arms Control and Disarmament which we have adopted at this meeting, we will continue to use arms control as a means to enhance security and stability at the lowest possible level of armed forces, and to strengthen confidence by further appropriate measures. We have already demonstrated our commitment to these objectives: both by negotiations and by unilateral action, resulting since 1979 in reductions of over one-third of the nuclear holdings assigned to SACEUR in Europe.

Towards an Enhanced Partnership

20. As the Alliance enters its fifth decade we will meet the challenge of shaping our relationship in a way which corresponds to the new political and economic realities of the 1990s. As we do so, we recognize that the basis of our security and prosperity—and of our hopes for better East-West relations—is and will continue to be the close cohesion between the countries of Europe and of North America, bound together by their common values and democratic institutions as much as by their shared security interests.

21. Ours is a living and developing partnership. The strength and stability derived from our transatlantic bond provide a firm foundation for the achievement of our long-term vision, as well as of our goals for the immediate future. We recognise that our common tasks transcend the resources of either Europe or North America alone.

22. We welcome in this regard the evolution of an increasingly strong and coherent European identity, including in the security area. The process we are witnessing today provides an example of progressive integration, leaving centuries-old conflicts far behind. It opens the way to a more mature and balanced transatlantic partnership and constitutes one of the foundations of Europe's future structure.

23. To ensure the continuing success of our efforts we have agreed to
— strengthen our process of political consultation and, where appropriate, co-ordination, and have instructed the Council in Permanent Session to consider methods for its further improvement;
— expand the scope and intensity of our effort to ensure that our respective approaches to problems affecting our common security are complementary and mutually supportive;
— renew our support for our economically less-favoured partners and to reaffirm our goal of improving the present level of cooperation and assistance;
— continue to work in the appropriate fora for more commercial, monetary and technological cooperation, and to see to it that no obstacles impede such cooperation.

Overcoming the Division of Europe

24. Now, more than ever, our efforts to overcome the division of Europe must address its underlying political causes. Therefore all of us will continue to pursue a comprehensive approach encompassing the many dimensions of the East-West agenda. In keeping with our values, we place primary emphasis on basic freedoms for the people in Eastern Europe. These are also key elements for strengthening the stability and security of all states and for guaranteeing lasting peace on the continent.

25. The CSCE process encompasses our vision of a peaceful and more constructive relationship among all participating states. We intend to develop it further, in all its dimensions, and to make the fullest use of it.

We recognise progress in the implementation of CSCE commitments by some Eastern countries. But we call upon all of them to recognise and implement fully the commitments which all CSCE states have accepted. We will invoke the CSCE mechanisms—as most recently adopted in the Vienna Concluding Document—and the provisions of other international agreements, to bring all Eastern countries to:

— enshrine in law and practice the human rights and freedoms agreed in international covenants and in the CSCE documents, thus fostering progress towards the rule of law;
— tear down the walls that separate us physically and politically, simplify the crossing of borders, increase the number of crossing points and allow the free exchange of persons, information and ideas;
— ensure that people are not prevented by armed force from crossing the frontiers and boundaries which we share with Eastern countries, in exercise of their right to leave any country, including their own;
— respect in law and practice the right of all the people in each country to determine freely and periodically the nature of the government they wish to have;
— see to it that their peoples can decide through their elected authorities what form of relations they wish to have with other countries;
— grant the genuine economic freedoms that are linked inherently to the rights of the individual;
— develop transparency, especially in military matters, in pursuit of greater mutual understanding and reassurance.

26. The situation in and around Berlin is an essential element in East-West relations. The Alliance declares its commitment to a free and prosperous Berlin and to achieving improvements for the city especially through the Allied Berlin Initiative. The Wall dividing the city is an unacceptable symbol of the division of Europe. We seek a state of peace in Europe in which the German people regains its unity through free self-determination.

Our Design for Co-operation

27. We, for our part, have today reaffirmed that the Alliance must and will reintensify its own efforts to overcome the division of Europe and to explore all available avenues of cooperation and dialogue. We support the opening of Eastern societies and encourage reforms that aim at positive political, economic and human rights developments. Tangible steps towards genuine political and economic reform improve possibilities for broad cooperation, while a continuing denial of basic freedoms cannot but have a negative effect. Our approach recognises that each country is unique and must be treated on its own merits. We also recognise that it is essentially incumbent upon the countries of the East to solve their problems by reforms from within. But we can also play a constructive rôle within the framework of our Alliance as well as in our respective bilateral relations and in international organisations, as appropriate.

28. To that end, we have agreed the following joint agenda for the future

— as opportunities develop, we will expand the scope of our contacts and cooperation to cover a broad range of issues which are important to both East and West. Our goal is a sustained effort geared to specific tasks which will help deepen openness and promote democracy within Eastern countries and thus contribute to the establishment of a more stable peace in Europe;

— we will pursue in particular expanded contacts beyond the realm of government among individuals in East and West. These contacts should include all segments of our societies, but in particular young people, who will carry the responsibility for continuing our common endeavour;
— we will seek expanded economic and trade relations with the Eastern countries on the basis of commercially sound terms, mutual interest and reciprocity. Such relations should also serve as incentives for real economic reform and thus ease the way for increased integration of Eastern countries into the international trading system;
— we intend to demonstrate through increased cooperation that democratic institutions and economic choice create the best possible conditions for economic and social progress. The development of such open systems will facilitate cooperation and, consequently, make its benefits more available;
— an important task of our cooperation will be to explore means to extend Western experience and know-how to Eastern countries in a manner which responds to and promotes positive change. Exchanges in technical and managerial fields, establishment of cooperative training programmes, expansion of educational, scientific and cultural exchanges all offer possibilities which have not yet been exhausted;
— equally important will be to integrate Eastern European countries more fully into efforts to meet the social, environmental and technological challenges of the modern world, where common interests should prevail. In accordance with our concern for global challenges, we will seek to engage Eastern countries in co-operative strategies in areas such as the environment, terrorism, and drugs. Eastern willingness to participate constructively in dealing with such challenges will help further cooperation in other areas as well;
— East-West understanding can be expanded only if our respective societies gain increased knowledge about one another and communicate effectively. To encourage an increase of Soviet and Eastern studies in universities of our countries and of corresponding studies in Eastern countries, we are prepared to establish a Fellowship/Scholarship programme to promote the study of our democratic institutions, with candidates being invited from Eastern as well as Western Europe and North America.

Global Challenges

29. Worldwide developments which affect our security interests are legitimate matters for consultation and, where appropriate, co-ordination among us. Our security is to be seen in a context broader than the protection from war alone.

30. Regional conflicts continue to be of major concern. The coordinated approach of Alliance members recently has helped toward settling some of the world's most dangerous and long-standing disputes. We hope that the Soviet Union will increasingly work with us in positive and practical steps towards diplomatic solutions to those conflicts that continue to preoccupy the international community.

31. We will seek to contain the newly emerging security threats and destabilising consequences resulting from the uncontrolled spread and application of modern military technologies.

32. In the spirit of Article 2 of the Washington Treaty, we will increasingly need to address worldwide problems which have a bearing on our security, particularly environmental degradation, resource conflicts and grave economic disparities. We will seek to do so in the appropriate multilateral fora, in the widest possible cooperation with other States.

33. We will each further develop our close cooperation with the other industrial democracies akin to us in their objectives and policies.

34. We will redouble our efforts in a reinvigorated United Nations, strengthening its role in conflict settlement and peacekeeping, and in its larger endeavours for world peace.

Our "Third Dimension"

35. Convinced of the vital need for international cooperation in science and technology, and of its beneficial effect on global security, we have for several decades maintained Alliance programmes of scientific cooperation. Recognising the importance of safeguarding the environment we have also cooperated, in the Committee on the Challenges of Modern Society, on environmental matters. These activities have demonstrated the broad range of our common pursuits. We intend to give more impact to our programmes with new initiatives in these areas.

The Future of the Alliance

36. We, the leaders of 16 free and democratic countries, have dedicated ourselves to the goals of the Alliance and are committed to work in unison for their continued fulfilment.

37. At this time of unprecedented promise in international affairs, we will respond to the hopes that it offers. The Alliance will continue to serve as the cornerstone of our security, peace and freedom. Secure on this foundation, we will reach out to those who are willing to join us in shaping a more stable and peaceful international environment in the service of our societies.

---

[1] France takes this opportunity to recall that, since the mandate for the Vienna negotiations excludes nuclear weapons, it retains complete freedom of judgement and decision regarding the resources contributing to the implementation of its independent nuclear deterrent strategy.

Appendix II

Statistical Tables[1]

Note: Defence expenditures of NATO countries

The figures given in the following tables represent payments actually made or to be made during the course of the fiscal year. They are based on the NATO definition of defence expenditures. In view of the difference between this and national definitions, the figures shown may diverge considerably from those which are quoted by national authorities or given in national budgets. For countries providing military assistance, this is included in the expenditure figures. For countries receiving assistance, figures do not include the value of items received.

France is a member of the Alliance without belonging to the integrated military struture; the relevant figures are indicative only.

Iceland has no armed forces.

To avoid ambiguity, the fiscal year has been designated by the year which includes the most number of months: e.g. 1985 represents the fiscal year 1985/1986 for Canada and the United Kingdom (where the fiscal year begins in April) and the fiscal year 1984/1985 for the United States (where the fiscal year begins in October).

Key: e = estimate
.. = not available.

[1] Data as available in November 1989.

Table I: Area and population of NATO countries

Country	Area		Population (thousand)					Density of population (1988)	
	Sq. mile	Sq. km	1970	1975	1980	1985	1988	Sq. mile	Sq. km
Belgium	11781	30513	9651	9795	9847	9858	9884	839	324
Denmark	16629	43069	4929	5060	5125	5114	5140	309	119
France	211208	547026	50772	52699	53880	55170	55869	265	102
Germany	95976	248577	60651	61829	61566	61024	61122	637	246
Greece	50944	131944	8793	9046	9642	9934	10010	196	76
Iceland	39769	103000	205	218	228	241	247	6	2
Italy	116304	301225	53661	55441	56416	57128	57441	494	191
Luxembourg	998	2586	340	359	365	367	375	376	145
Netherlands	15770	40844	13039	13666	14150	14491	14765	936	361
Norway	149410	386975	3879	4007	4087	4153	4211	28	11
Portugal	35553	92082	8432	8737	9819	10185	10304	290	112
Spain	194897	504783	33876	35515	37386	38505	38996	200	77
Turkey	301382	780576	35605	40348	44737	50664	54176	180	69
United Kingdom	94227	244046	55632	56215	56314	56618	57002	605	234
Total Europe	1334848	3457246	339465	352935	363562	373452	379542	284	110
Canada	3851809	9976139	21324	22727	24070	25181	25950	7	3
United States	3615122	9363123	205052	215973	227757	239279	246329	68	26
North America	7466931	19339262	226376	238700	251827	264460	272279	36	14
Total NATO	8801779	22796508	565841	591635	615389	637912	651821	74	29

Table II: Defence expenditures of NATO countries

Part 1. Current prices and exchange rates

Country	Currency unit (million)	1970	1975	1980	1985	1986	1987	1988	1989e
	(1)	(2)	(3)	(4)	(5)	(6)	(7)	(8)	(9)
Belgium	Belgium franc	37388	70899	115754	144183	152079	155422	150647	155164
Canada	Canadian $	1999	3360	5787	10331	10971	11715	12335	12611
Denmark	Danish Kroner	2967	5355	9117	13343	13333	14647	15620	15813
France	French franc	32672	55872	111672	186715	197080	209525	215073	223868
Germany *	Deutsch mark	22573	37589	48518	58649	60130	61354	61638	63269
Greece	Drachma	14208	45936	96975	321981	338465	393052	479236	521209
Italy	1000 Lira	1562	3104	8203	18584	20071	23788	26590	..
Luxembourg	Lux. franc	416	836	1534	2265	2390	2730	3163	3142
Netherlands	Dutch guilder	3909	7119	10476	12901	13110	13254	13300	13583
Norway	Norw. kroner	2774	4771	8242	15446	16033	18551	18865	21117
Portugal	Escudo	12538	19898	43440	111375	139972	159288	193864	207738
Spain	Peseta	..	..	350423	674883	715306	852767	835353	912173
Turkey	Turkish lira	6399	32833	203172	1234547	1867990	2476869	3788920	6104534
United Kingdom	Pound sterling	2607	5571	11542	18352	18639	19269	19495	21239
United States	US $	79846	88400	138191	258165	281105	288157	293093	300325
NATO Europe	US $	..	..	113248	92711	120787	148358	157014	..
North America	US $	81754	91704	143141	265731	289000	296992	303116	310810
NATO total	US $	..	..	256388	358442	409787	445350	460130	..

* In addition to defence expenditures (NATO definition), the German authorities are obliged to incur large expenditures for Berlin owing to the exceptional situation of this city and the need in the interest of the free world to ensure its viability. These expenditures, which are not included in the figures given above since they do not come within the NATO definition, are forecast to be 16785 million DM in 1988.

Table II: Defence expenditures of NATO Countries

Part 2. 1980 prices and exchanges rates

Country	Currency unit (million)	1970	1975	1980	1985	1986	1987	1988	1989e
	(1)	(2)	(3)	(4)	(5)	(6)	(7)	(8)	(9)
Begium	Belgium franc	73305	96529	115754	114788	120475	122428	118100	118906
Canada	Canadian $	5336	5227	5787	7708	7931	8104	8189	8012
Denmark	Danish Kroner	8409	8226	9117	9197	9166	9373	9643	9454
France	French franc	83537	91618	111672	120263	120665	124430	123647	125071
Germany	Deutsch mark	37866	45932	48518	50191	49912	49908	49388	49679
Greece	Drachma	51337	94420	96975	127521	114304	116217	123806	117333
Italy	1000 Lira	6484	7236	8203	9134	9228	9766	10202	10398
Luxembourg	Lux. franc	797	1130	1534	1710	1771	2008	2313	2242
Netherlands	Dutch guilder	9426	9788	10476	11604	12045	12251	12227	12398
Norway	Norw. kroner	7145	7230	8242	10069	9888	10844	10453	11305
Portugal	Escudo	49184	50485	43440	41421	43218	43795	47890	46274
Spain	Peseta	. .	. .	350423	394029	376519	423790	392764	404598
Turkey	Turkish lira	74001	161276	203172	221393	250179	247004	255302	262999
United Kingdom	Pound sterling	11627	11462	11542	12940	12529	12265	11740	12123
United States	US $	174994	130923	138191	188074	200162	199517	196676	194647
NATO Europe	US $	. .	. .	112791	122529	121861	123847	122419	124369
North America	US $	179558	135393	143141	194666	206945	206449	203680	201499
NATO total	US $	. .	. .	255932	317195	328806	330296	326100	325868

Table III: Defence expenditures as % of gross domestic product

Part I. Based on current prices

Country	Average 1970-1974	Average 1975-1979	Average 1980-1984	Average 1985-1989	1985	1986	1987	1988	1989e
	(1)	(2)	(3)	(4)	(5)	(6)	(7)	(8)	(9)
Belgium	2.9	3.2	3.3	2.9	3.1	3.1	3.0	2.8	2.7
Denmark	2.4	2.4	2.4	2.1	2.2	2.0	2.1	2.2	2.1
France	3.9	3.8	4.1	3.9	4.0	3.9	3.9	3.8	3.7
Germany *	3.5	3.4	3.3	3.0	3.2	3.1	3.1	2.9	2.9
Greece	4.7	6.7	6.6	6.4	7.0	6.2	6.3	6.4	6.0
Italy	2.3	2.1	2.2	..	2.3	2.2	2.4	2.5	..
Luxembourg	0.8	1.0	1.2	1.2	1.1	1.1	1.2	1.3	1.2
Netherlands	3.1	3.2	3.2	3.0	3.1	3.0	3.1	3.0	2.9
Norway	3.3	3.1	2.9	3.2	3.1	3.1	3.3	3.2	3.3
Portugal	6.9	3.9	3.4	3.1	3.2	3.2	3.1	3.2	3.0
Spain	..	..	2.4	2.2	2.4	2.2	2.4	2.1	2.1
Turkey	4.4	5.7	4.9	4.3	4.5	4.8	4.3	4.1	3.9
United Kingdom	5.1	4.9	5.2	4.6	5.2	4.9	4.6	4.2	4.2
NATO Europe	..	..	3.6	..	3.5	3.4	3.4	3.2	..
Canada	2.1	1.9	2.1	2.1	2.2	2.2	2.2	2.1	2.0
United States	6.5	5.1	5.8	6.3	6.5	6.7	6.4	6.1	5.8
North America	6.1	4.8	5.5	5.9	6.2	6.3	6.1	5.7	5.4
NATO total	..	..	4.7	..	5.2	5.0	4.8	4.5	..

* These percentages have been calculated without taking into account the expenditures on Berlin (see note in Table II), if these expenditures were included, the percentages would be as follows:

1970: 3.8   1980: 4.1   1986: 3.9   1988: 3.7
1975: 4.4   1985: 4.0   1987: 3.9   1989: 3.7

Table III: Defence expenditures as % of gross domestic product

Part 2. Based on constant prices

Country	Average 1970-1974	Average 1975-1979	Average 1980-1984	Average 1985-1989	1985	1986	1987	1988	1989e
	(1)	(2)	(3)	(4)	(5)	(6)	(7)	(8)	(9)
Belgium	2.9	3.3	3.4	3.2	3.2	3.3	3.3	3.1	3.0
Denmark	2.5	2.4	2.4	2.2	2.2	2.1	2.2	2.2	2.1
France	3.9	3.8	4.1	3.9	4.0	3.9	3.9	3.8	3.7
Germany *	3.5	3.4	3.3	3.0	3.2	3.1	3.1	2.9	2.9
Greece	4.7	6.7	6.6	6.4	7.0	6.2	6.3	6.4	6.0
Italy	2.3	2.1	2.1	2.2	2.2	2.1	2.2	2.2	2.2
Luxembourg	0.8	1.0	1.2	1.2	1.1	1.1	1.2	1.3	1.3
Netherlands	3.5	3.2	3.3	3.3	3.3	3.3	3.3	3.2	3.2
Norway	3.6	3.0	2.9	2.9	3.0	2.8	3.0	2.9	3.0
Portugal	6.4	3.8	3.4	3.1	3.2	3.2	3.1	3.2	3.0
Spain	..	..	2.4	2.2	2.4	2.2	2.4	2.1	2.1
Turkey	2.8	4.5	4.4	3.9	4.1	4.2	3.9	3.8	3.7
United Kingdom	5.7	5.0	5.2	4.5	5.1	4.8	4.5	4.1	4.1
NATO Europe	..	..	3.6	3.3	3.5	3.4	3.4	3.2	3.2
Canada	2.4	2.0	2.1	2.1	2.2	2.2	2.2	2.1	2.0
United States	6.8	5.1	5.6	5.9	6.1	6.3	6.0	5.7	5.5
North America	6.4	4.9	5.3	5.6	5.7	5.9	5.7	5.4	5.2
NATO total	..	..	4.4	4.5	4.6	4.7	4.5	4.3	4.2

* These percentages have been calculated without taking into account the expenditures on Berlin (see note in Table II), if these expenditures were included, the percentages would be as follows:

1970: 3.8	1980: 4.1	1986: 3.9	1988: 3.7
1975: 4.4	1985: 4.0	1987: 3.7	1989: 3.7

Table IV: Gross domestic product per capita in US $ (1980 prices and exchange rates)

Country	1970	1975	1980	1984	1985	1986	1987	1988
	(1)	(2)	(3)	(4)	(5)	(6)	(7)	(8)
Belgium	8886	10378	11986	12275	12381	12617	12867	13269
Denmark	10784	11580	12941	14176	14779	15210	15076	15015
France	9457	10809	12335	12802	12986	13216	13406	13793
Germany	10276	11165	13216	13813	14122	14442	14717	15224
Greece	2882	3584	4164	4203	4319	4358	4341	4509
Italy	6244	6809	8081	8381	8580	8784	9028	9365
Luxembourg	10230	11254	12454	13749	14214	14763	14982	15635
Netherlands	9751	10893	11970	12025	12285	12474	12557	12821
Norway	9364	11374	14121	15607	16383	17002	17512	17587
Portugal	1861	2225	2555	2509	2570	2665	2775	2885
Spain	4455	5475	5674	5789	5898	6065	6375	6662
Turkey	984	1230	1272	1384	1419	1505	1580	1643
United Kingdom	7935	8759	9521	10099	10432	10743	11215	11654
NATO Europe	7112	7894	8864	9132	9314	9516	9732	10030
Canada	7897	9553	10934	11599	12038	12239	12567	12986
United States	10006	10611	11804	12586	12937	13194	13533	13921
North America	9808	10510	11721	12492	12851	13103	13442	13832
NATO total	8191	8950	10033	10522	10781	11008	11278	11619

Table V: Defence expenditures per capita in US $ (1980 prices and exchange rates)

Country	1970	1975	1980	1984	1985	1986	1987	1988
	(1)	(2)	(3)	(4)	(5)	(6)	(7)	(8)
Belgium	260	337	402	398	398	418	424	409
Denmark	303	288	316	316	319	318	324	333
France	389	411	490	518	516	516	529	524
Germany *	343	409	434	451	452	450	449	445
Greece	137	245	236	300	301	269	273	290
Italy	141	152	170	182	187	188	199	207
Luxembourg	80	108	144	162	159	164	185	211
Netherlands	364	360	372	403	403	416	420	417
Norway	373	365	408	427	491	480	525	503
Portugal	117	115	88	82	81	84	85	93
Spain	..	..	131	137	143	136	152	140
Turkey	27	53	60	54	57	64	61	62
United Kingdom	486	474	476	533	531	513	501	479
NATO Europe	..	..	310	327	328	325	328	323
Canada	214	197	206	256	262	267	270	270
United States	853	606	607	736	786	828	818	798
North America	793	567	568	690	736	775	766	748
NATO total	..	..	416	477	497	512	511	500

* These figures do not take in account the expenditures for Berlin (see note in Table II); if these expenditures were included, the figures would be as follows:

1970: 392 1980: 546 1985: 570 1987: 568
1975: 495 1984: 567 1986: 567

Table VI: Distribution of total defence expenditures by category

Part 1. Equipment and infrastructure expenditures

Country	Average 1970-1974	Average 1975-1979	Average 1980-1984	Average 1985-1989	1985	1986	1987	1988	1989e
	(1)	(2)	(3)	(4)	(5)	(6)	(7)	(8)	(9)
% devoted to equipment expenditures									
Belgium	10.7	11.7	13.8	12.0	12.7	12.9	13.1	12.0	9.6
Canada	7.3	9.0	17.8	19.7	18.5	20.2	21.4	20.1	18.3
Denmark	16.4	18.4	16.9	14.5	13.8	14.0	14.9	14.4	15.4
Germany	11.9	12.8	16.6	14.9	14.8	15.9	15.2	14.5	14.3
Greece	8.2	19.3	17.4	18.3	14.5	15.8	17.2	23.4	22.3
Italy	15.3	14.7	17.4	19.7	18.8	18.4	20.6	20.5	20.6
Luxembourg	1.5	1.9	1.8	3.6	4.0	3.1	3.9	2.8	4.3
Netherlands	12.8	18.0	20.5	20.1	23.4	20.3	17.8	20.4	19.2
Norway	15.2	16.0	19.4	23.1	24.9	20.2	20.4	21.3	29.8
Portugal	7.1	2.2	5.5	7.8	3.3	6.3	10.1	10.5	13.4
Spain	..	..	..	..	..	23.6	24.7	20.7	14.7
Turkey	3.9	19.2	9.1	18.8	13.6	17.9	21.1	22.5	20.2
United Kingdom	16.6	21.6	26.2	24.8	27.0	25.2	24.7	25.4	22.1
United States	21.4	17.6	21.9	25.5	25.7	25.8	26.5	24.5	25.0
% devoted to infrastructure expenditures									
Belgium	5.1	6.1	4.9	3.8	3.5	4.4	5.1	4.0	2.4
Canada	2.4	2.0	1.6	1.7	1.8	1.7	1.8	2.0	1.5
Denmark	2.8	2.0	2.5	2.8	3.8	2.6	2.1	2.3	3.7
Germany	6.3	6.4	5.3	5.8	6.0	5.9	5.7	5.3	5.8
Greece	10.7	6.4	3.5	4.0	3.1	3.5	3.8	4.9	5.0
Italy	1.4	1.7	2.1	2.5	2.5	3.2	2.2	2.4	2.5
Luxembourg	1.0	0.6	6.2	4.0	3.3	3.7	5.8	2.4	6.3
Netherlands	2.3	2.8	3.0	3.8	4.2	3.8	3.9	3.4	3.6
Norway	4.7	4.9	6.6	11.0	9.1	11.3	11.3	12.0	11.6
Portugal	2.7	3.8	5.9	6.0	5.7	5.8	5.7	6.7	6.1
Spain	..	..	..	..	..	..	4.0	3.2	4.0
Turkey	8.0	7.1	12.8	4.9	7.3	5.7	5.4	3.8	3.4
United Kingdom	2.1	1.6	2.9	4.0	3.8	3.9	3.6	4.2	4.5
United States	1.4	1.8	1.5	1.8	1.6	1.7	2.0	1.9	1.8

Table VI: Distribution of total defence expenditures by category

Part 2. Personnel and operating expenditures

Country	Average 1970-1974	Average 1975-1979	Average 1980-1984	Average 1985-1989	1985	1986	1987	1988	1989e
	(1)	(2)	(3)	(4)	(5)	(6)	(7)	(8)	(9)
% devoted to personnel expenditures									
Belgium	62.4	62.9	61.8	62.9	63.0	61.2	62.1	63.7	64.7
Canada	65.6	60.8	50.7	46.2	45.1	46.7	46.1	45.4	47.6
Denmark	58.9	58.0	54.6	56.1	53.8	56.1	55.2	58.0	57.3
Germany	50.5	49.8	46.6	48.6	46.1	48.5	49.2	49.7	49.9
Greece	66.8	57.6	54.6	60.4	59.6	61.8	61.7	57.9	61.3
Italy	59.9	61.9	59.1	57.5	55.6	57.7	59.0	57.8	57.6
Luxembourg	82.2	85.5	77.5	76.4	78.6	77.6	76.8	74.7	74.6
Netherlands	65.4	61.2	55.3	52.6	51.2	51.3	53.6	54.3	52.9
Norway	52.1	52.9	48.8	43.1	42.7	45.6	43.3	44.0	39.9
Portugal	50.8	68.8	66.6	66.4	69.3	66.2	65.7	66.4	64.5
Spain	..	..	..	..	..	..	49.7	54.5	55.4
Turkey	66.7	47.6	45.3	35.4	36.9	33.3	34.7	35.6	36.8
United Kingdom	48.8	44.6	37.4	38.8	35.0	39.0	39.0	40.7	40.4
United States			41.9	36.9	37.5	35.8	35.9	37.6	37.6
% devoted to other operating expenditures									
Belgium	20.9	18.8	18.8	20.7	19.9	21.5	20.3	20.4	21.4
Canada	24.0	27.3	29.0	31.5	34.0	30.5	29.9	31.6	31.4
Denmark	21.2	21.0	25.7	25.9	28.5	26.5	27.1	24.2	23.3
Germany	31.3	31.0	31.3	30.5	33.1	29.5	29.8	30.3	29.8
Greece	18.5	17.0	24.9	18.6	23.3	20.5	19.2	16.4	14.9
Italy	23.0	21.5	21.0	20.0	23.2	20.6	18.0	19.2	19.3
Luxembourg	11.1	9.1	10.2	11.8	10.4	11.1	10.3	16.9	11.4
Netherlands	18.9	17.3	20.3	22.0	20.5	23.8	23.9	20.1	21.8
Norway	28.0	26.6	26.7	25.3	25.4	26.6	26.5	26.2	22.0
Portugal	37.9	25.1	21.9	20.9	23.2	23.9	20.6	19.0	18.4
Spain	..	..	..	..	..	..	21.6	21.6	25.9
Turkey	22.6	23.7	30.1	39.7	41.8	42.6	38.3	37.5	38.5
United Kingdom	32.0	31.9	33.5	32.3	34.3	31.8	32.6	29.7	33.0
United States	44.1	36.8	34.5	35.7	35.1	36.6	35.5	35.8	35.5

Table VII: Armed forces

Part 1. Military strengths (thousands)

Country	1970	1975	1980	1985	1986	1987	1988	1989e
	(1)	(2)	(3)	(4)	(5)	(6)	(7)	(8)
Belgium	108	103	108	107	107	109	110	110
Denmark	42	34	33	29	28	28	30	31
France	571	585	575	563	558	559	558	554
Germany	455	491	490	495	495	495	495	495
Greece	178	185	186	201	202	199	199	201
Italy	522	459	500	531	529	531	446	450
Luxembourg	1	1	1	1	1	1	1	1
Netherlands	112	107	107	103	106	106	107	107
Norway	37	38	40	36	38	38	40	40
Portugal	229	104	88	102	101	105	104	105
Spain	..	..	356	314	314	314	304	308
Turkey	625	584	717	814	860	879	847	780
United Kingdom	384	348	330	334	331	328	324	322
NATO Europe	..	..	3531	3630	3669	3693	3565	3505
Canada	91	78	82	83	85	86	88	89
United States	3294	2146	2050	2244	2269	2279	2246	2242
North America	3385	2224	2132	2327	2354	2365	2334	2331
NATO total	..	..	5662	5957	6023	6058	5898	5836

Table VII: Armed forces

Part 2. Military and civilian personnel as % of labour force

Country	1970	1975	1980	1985	1986	1987	1988	1989e
	(1)	(2)	(3)	(4)	(5)	(6)	(7)	(8)
Belgium	3.0	2.8	2.8	2.7	2.7	2.7	2.8	2.8
Denmark	2.2	1.8	1.7	1.4	1.3	1.3	1.4	1.4
France	3.3	3.2	3.0	2.9	2.9	2.9	2.9	2.8
Germany	2.3	2.5	2.4	2.4	2.4	2.4	2.4	2.4
Greece	6.2	6.5	6.1	6.1	5.9	5.8	5.7	5.6
Italy	2.7	2.3	2.3	2.4	2.3	2.3	1.9	1.9
Luxembourg	0.9	0.8	0.8	0.9	0.8	0.8	0.8	0.9
Netherlands	2.9	2.7	2.6	2.4	2.5	2.6	2.5	2.5
Norway	2.9	2.8	2.6	2.3	2.3	2.3	2.4	2.3
Portugal	6.8	2.9	2.3	2.6	2.6	2.6	2.6	2.6
Spain	..	..	3.0	2.6	2.5	2.5	2.4	2.4
Turkey	4.6	3.9	4.5	4.7	5.0	5.0	4.8	4.4
United Kingdom	2.9	2.5	2.2	1.9	1.9	1.8	1.7	1.7
NATO Europe	..	..	2.8	2.8	2.8	2.7	2.6	2.6
Canada	1.5	1.2	1.0	1.0	1.0	1.0	1.0	0.9
United States	5.5	3.4	2.8	2.9	2.9	2.9	2.8	2.7
North America	5.1	3.2	2.7	2.7	2.7	2.7	2.6	2.5
NATO total	..	..	2.8	2.8	2.7	2.7	2.6	2.6

Appendix III
Appointments

1. Chairmen and Presidents of the North Atlantic Council
2. Permanent Representatives on the North Atlantic Council
3. Principal Officials of the NATO International Staff
4. Presidents and Chairmen of the NATO Military Committee
5. Major NATO Commanders
6. Directors of the International Military Staff

1
Chairmen and Presidents of the North Atlantic Council

Chairmen of the North Atlantic Council

1949–1950	Dean G. Acheson	(United States)
1950–1951	Paul van Zeeland	(Belgium)
1951–1952	Lester B. Pearson	(Canada)
1952–1953	Ole Bjorn Kraft	(Denmark)
1953–1954	Georges Bidault	(France)
	Pierre Mendes-France	(France)
1954–1955	Stephanos Stephanopoulos	(Greece)
1955–1956	Kristinn Gudmunsson	(Iceland)
	Gudmundur I. Gudmunsson	(Iceland)
1956	Gaetano Martino	(Italy)

Presidents of the North Atlantic Council[1]

1957	Gaetano Martino	(Italy)
	Giuiseppe Pella	(Italy)
1957–1958	Joseph Bech	(Luxembourg)
1958–1959	Joseph M.A.H. Luns	(Netherlands)
1959–1960	Halvard M. Lange	(Norway)
1960–1961	Marcello Mathias	(Portugal)
	Franco Nogueira	(Portugal)
1961–1962	Selim Sarper	(Turkey)
	Feredun Cemal Erkin	(Turkey)
1962–1963	The Earl of Home	(United Kingdom)
1963–1964	Dean Rusk	(United States)
1964–1965	Paul-Henri Spaak	(Belgium)
1965–1966	Paul Martin	(Canada)
1966–1967	Jens Otto Krag	(Denmark)
1967–1968	Maurice Couve de Murville	(France)
	Michel Debré	(France)
1968–1969	Willy Brandt	(Germany)
1969–1970	Emil Jonsson	(Iceland)
1970–1971	Aldo Moro	(Italy)
1971–1972	Gaston Thorn	(Luxembourg)
1972–1973	W.K.N. Schmelzer	(Netherlands)
	M. van der Stoel	(Netherlands)
1974	Sir Alec Douglas-Home	(United Kingdom)
	James Callaghan	(United Kingdom)
1974–1975	Dimitri S. Bitsios	(Greece)
1975–1976	Knut Frydenlund	(Norway)
1976–1977	José Manuel de Medeiros Ferreira	(Portugal)

1977–1978	Ihsan Sabri Caglayangil	(Turkey)
	Gündüz Okçün	(Turkey)
1978–1979	David Owen	(United Kingdom)
	Lord Carrington	(United Kingdom)
1979–1980	Cyrus R. Vance	(United States)
	Edmund Muskie	(United States)
1980–1981	C.F. Nothomb	(Belgium)
1981–1982	Mark MacGuigan	(Canada)
1982–1983	Uffe Ellemann-Jensen	(Denmark)
1983–1984	Claude Cheysson	(France)
1984–1985	Hans-Dietrich Genscher	(Germany)
1985–1986	Gein Hallgrimsson	(Iceland)
1986	Matthias A. Mathiesen	(Iceland)
1986–1987	Giulio Andreotti	(Italy)
1987–1988	Jacques Poos	(Luxembourg)
1988–1989	Hans van den Broek	(Netherlands)
1989-	Thorvald Stoltenberg	(Norway)

---

[1] In 1956, in accordance with the recommendations of the Committee of Three, it was decided that each year a Foreign Minister of one of the member countries would become President of the North Atlantic Council, and that the Secretary General would be Chairman at all working sessions of the Council.

2

Permanent Representatives on the North Atlantic Council

Belgium

1952–1976	André de Staercke
1976–1979	Constant Schuurmans
1979–1983	Michel Van Ussel
1983–1987	Juan Cassiers
1987–	Prosper Thuysbaert

Canada

1952–1953	Arnold D. Heeney
1953–1958	L. Dana Wilgress
1958–1962	Jules Léger
1962–1966	Georges Ingatieff
1966–1967	Charles Ritchie
1967–1972	Ross Campbell
1972–1976	Arthur R. Menzies
1976–1980	Joseph E. Ghislain Hardy
1980–1982	John G.H. Halstead
1982–1985	James Hutchings Taylor
1985–	Gordon Scott Smith

Denmark

1952–1954	Vincens Steensen-Leth
1954–1956	Jens Anthon Vestbirk
1956–1961	Mathias A. Wassard
1961–1966	Erik Schram-Nielsen
1966–1973	Henning Hjorth-Nielsen
1973–1983	Anker Svart
1983–1988	Otto Rose Borch
1983–	Ole Bierring

France

1952–1954	Hervé Alphand
1954–1955	Maurice Couve de Murville
1955–1956	Alexandre Parodi
1957–1958	Etienne de Crouy-Chanel
1958–1959	Geoffroy Chodron de Courcel
1959–1962	Pierre de Leusse
1962–1965	François Seydoux de Clausonne

1965–1967	Pierre de Leusse
1967–1968	Roger Seydoux de Clausonne
1968–1970	Jacques Kosciusko-Morizet
1970–1975	François de Tricornot de Rose
1975–1979	Jacques Tiné
1979–1981	Claude Arnaud
1982–1984	Jean-Marie Merillon
1985–1987	Gilles Curien
1987–	Gabriel Robin

Federal Republic of Germany

1955–1959	Herbert Adolph Blankenhorn
1959–1962	Gebhardt von Walther
1962–1971	Wilhelm Grewe
1971–1976	Franz Krapf
1976–1980	Rolf Friedemann Pauls
1980–1985	Hans-Georg Wieck
1985–1989	Niels Hansen
1989–	Hans Friedrich von Ploetz

Greece

1952	Panalyotis Pipinelis
1952–1956	Georges Exintaris
1956–1962	Michel Melas
1962–1967	Christos Palamas
1967–1972	Phaedon-Annino Cavalierato
1972–1974	Anghelos Chorafas
1974–1976	Byron Theodoropoulos
1976–1979	Eustache Lagacos
1979–1981	Nicolas Athanassiou
1981–1982	George Sekeris
1982–1986	Stylianos Vassilicos
1986–	Christos Zacharakis

Iceland

1952–1954	Gunnlaugur Pétursson
1954–1962	Hans G. Andersen
1962–1965	Pétur Thorsteinsson
1965–1967	Henrik Sv. Björnsson
1967–1971	Niels P. Sigurdsson
1971–1977	Tómas Á. Tómasson
1977–1979	Gudmundur I. Gudmundsson
1979–1984	Henrik Sv. Björnsson
1985–1986	Tómas Tómasson
1986–	Einar Benediktsson

Italy

1952–1954	Alberto Rossi Longhi
1954–1958	Adolfo Alessandrini

1958–1959	Umberto Grazzi
1959–1967	Adolfo Alessandrini
1967–1971	Carlo de Ferrariis Salzano
1971–1979	Felice Catalano di Melilli
1980–1983	Vincenzo Tornetta
1983–1984	Sergio Romano
1985–	Francesco Paolo Fulci

Luxembourg

1952–1953	Albert Wehrer
1953–1959	Nicolas Hommel
1959–1967	Paul Reuter
1967–1973	Lambert Schaus
1973–1977	Marcel Fischbach
1977–1984	Pierre Wurth
1984–1986	Jean Wagner
1986–	Guy de Muyser

Netherlands

1952–1956	Alidius W.L. Tjarda van Starkenborgh Stachouwer
1956–1958	Eelco N. van Kleffens
1958–1961	Dirk U. Stikker
1961–1970	Henry N. Boon
1970–1973	Dirk P. Spierenburg
1974–1978	Abraham F.K. Hartogh
1978–1981	Carl D. Barkman
1982–1989	Jaap G.N. de Hoop Scheffer
1989–	Adriaan Jacobovits de Szeged

Norway

1952–1955	Arne Skaug
1955–1963	Jens Boyesen
1964–1970	Georg Kristiansen
1970–1971	Knut Aars
1971–1977	Rolf Busch
1977–1984	Kjeld Vibe
1984–1989	Eivinn Berg
1989–	Bjørn Inge Kristvik

Portugal

1952–1958	Count de Tovar
1958–1961	Antonio de Faria
1961–1970	Vasco da Cunha
1970–1974	Albano Nogueira
1974–1979	João de Freitas-Cruz
1979–1985	José Manuel P. de Villas-Boas
1985–1989	António Vaz Pereira
1989–	José Gregório Faria

Spain

1982	Nuno Aguirre de Cárcer
1982	Javier Ruperez
1983–	Jaime de Ojeda

Turkey

1952–1954	Fatin Rüstü Zorlu
1954–1957	Mehmet Ali Tiney
1957–1960	Selim Sarper
1960	Haydar Görk
1960–1972	Muharrem Nuri Birgi
1972–1976	Orhan Eralp
1976–1978	A. Coskun Kirca
1978–1988	Osman Olcay
1988–1989	Tugay Özçeri
1989–	Ünal Ünsal

United Kingdom

1952–1953	Sir Frederick Hoyer Millar
1953–1957	Sir Christopher Steel
1957–1960	Sir Frank Roberts
1960–1962	Sir Paul Mason
1962–1966	Sir Evelyn Shuckburgh
1966–1970	Sir Bernard Burrows
1970–1975	Sir Edward Peck
1975–1979	Sir John Killick
1979–1982	Sir Clive Rose
1982–1986	Sir John Graham
6–	Sir Michael Alexander

United States

1952	Charles M. Spofford
1952–1953	William H. Draper Jr.
53–1955	John C. Hughes
1955–1957	George W. Perkins
1957–1961	W. Randolph Burgess
1961–1965	Thomas K. Finletter
1965–1969	Harlan Cleveland
1969–1971	Robert Ellsworth
1971–1973	David M. Kennedy
1973–1974	Donald Rumsfeld
1974–1976	David K.E. Bruce
1976–1977	Robert Strausz-Hupé
1977–1983	W. Tapley Bennett Jr.
1983–1987	David M. Abshire
1987–1989	Alton G. Keel Jr.
1989–	William H. Taft IV

3
Principal Officials of the NATO International Staff

Secretaries General

1952–1957	Lord Ismay	(United Kingdom)
1957–1961	Paul-Henri Spaak	(Belgium)
1961–1964	Dirk U. Stikker	(Netherlands)
1964–1971	Manlio Brosio	(Italy)
1971–1984	Joseph M.A.H. Luns	(Netherlands)
1984–1988	Lord Carrington	(United Kingdom)
1988–	Manfred Wörner	(Germany)

Deputy Secretaries General

1952–1956	Jonkheer van Vredenburch	(Netherlands)
1956–1958	Baron Adolph Bentinck	(Netherlands)
1958–1962	Alberico Casardi	(Italy)
1962–1964	Guido Colonna di Paliano	(Italy)
1964–1968	James A. Roberts	(Canada)
1969–1971	Osman Olcay	(Turkey)
1971–1978	Paolo Pansa Cedronio	(Italy)
1978–1981	Rinaldo Petrignani	(Italy)
1981–1985	Eric da Rin	(Italy)
1986–1989	Marcello Guidi	(Italy)
1989–	Amedeo de Franchis	(Italy)

Directors of the Private Office of the Secretary General

1952–1953	Peter Scott (Private Secretary)	(United Kingdom)
1953–1957	Gilles de Boisgelin (Private Secretary)	(France)
1957–1962	André Saint-Mleux	(France)
1962–1963	George Vest	(United States)
1963–1964	John Getz	(United States)
1965–1971	Fausto Bacchetti	(Italy)
1971–1984	Paul van Campen	(Netherlands)
1984–1986	Brian Fall	(United Kingdom)
1986–1987	David Brighty	(United Kingdom)
1987–1988	Kevin Tebbit	(United Kingdom)
1988–1989	Jürgen Staks	(Germany)
1989–	James Cunningham	(United States)

Assistant Secretaries General

Political Affairs

1952–1955	Sergio Fenoaltea	(Italy)

Appointments

1955–1956	Guiseppe Cosmelli	(Italy)
1956–1958	Alberico Casardi	(Italy)
1958–1960	Evelyn Shuckburgh	(United Kingdom)
1960–1966	Robin Hooper	(United Kingdom)
1966–1969	Joachim Jaenicke	(Germany)
1969–1975	Jörg Kastl	(Germany)
1975–1978	Ernst E. Jung	(Germany)
1978–1981	Hans Christian Lankes	(Germany)
1982–1986	Fredo Dannenbring	(Germany)
1986–	Henning Wegener	(Germany)

Economic and Financial Affairs

1952–1955	René Sergent	(France)
1955–1967	Didier Gregh	(France)

Defence Planning and Policy

1967–1969	Arthur Hockaday	(United Kingdom)
1969–1972	Kenneth Nash	(United Kingdom)
1972–1976	Colin Humphreys	(United Kingdom)
1976–1980	William Mumford	(United Kingdom)
1980–1984	David Nicholls	(United Kingdom)
1983–1986	James Moray Stewart	(United Kingdom)
1986–1988	Michael Bell	(United Kingdom)
1988–	Michael Legge	(United Kingdom)

Production, Logistics and Infrastructure

1952–1953	David Hopkins	(United States)
1953–1955	Lowel Weicker	(United States)
1956–1957	Murray Mitchell	(United States)
1957–1959	Ernest Meili	(United States)
1959–1960	Robert Fiske	(United States)
1960–1965	Johnson Garrett	(United States)
1966–1967	John Beith	(United Kingdom)

Defence Support

1967–1973	Arthur Tyler Port	(United States)
1973–1976	Gardiner Tucker	(United States)
1976–1977	Walter LaBerge	(United States)
1977–1980	John Walsh	(United States)
1981–1983	Vitalij Garber	(United States)
1984–1987	Robin L. Beard	(United States)
1987–	Mack Francis Mattingly	(United States)

Infrastructure, Logistics and Council Operations

1979–1984	David Collins	(Canada)
1984–1986	Cornelis De Laat de Kanter	(Netherlands)

Appointments

Infrastructure, Logistics and Civil Emergency Planning

1986–1989	Cornelis De Laat de Kanter	(Netherlands)
1989–	Lawrence E. Davies	(Canada)

Scientific Affairs

1958–1959	Norman Ramsay	(United States)
1959–1960	Frederic Seitz	(United States)
1960–1962	William Nierenberg	(United States)
1962–1964	William Allis	(United States)
1964–1966	John McLucas	(United States)
1966–1968	Rudi Schall (Acting)	(Germany)
1968–1973	Gunnar Randers	(Norway)
1973–1979	Nimet Özdas	(Turkey)
1980–1983	Robert Chabbal	(France)
1983–1988	Henry Durand	(France)
1988–	Jacques Ducuing	(France)

4

Presidents and Chairmen of the Military Committee

Chairmen of the NATO Military Committee in Chiefs-of-Staff Session

1949–1950	General Omar N. Bradley	(United States)
1951–1952	Lt. General Etienne Baele	(Belgium)
1952–1953	Lt. General Charles Foulkes	(Canada)
1953–1954	Admiral E.J.C. Quistgaard	(Denmark)
1954–1955	General Augustin Guillaume	(France)
1955–1956	Lt. General Stylianos Pallis	(Greece)
1956–1957	General Giuseppe Mancinelli	(Italy)
1957–1958	General B.R.P.F. Hasselman	(Netherlands)
1958–1959	Lt. General Bjarne Øen	(Norway)
1959–1960	General J.A. Beleza Ferras	(Portugal)
1960	General Rustu Erdelhun	(Turkey)
1960–1961	Admiral of the Fleet Earl Mountbatten of Burma	(United Kingdom)
1961–1962	General Lyman L. Lemnitzer	(United States)
1962–1963	Lt. General C.P. de Cumont	(Belgium)

Chairmen of the NATO Military Committee in Permanent Session

1958–1961	General B.R.P.F. Hasselman	(Netherlands)
1961–1963	General Adolf Heusinger	(Germany)

Presidents of the NATO Military Committee[1]

1963–1964	Air Chief Marshal Frank R. Miller	(Canada)
1964–1965	General Kurt Ramberg	(Denmark)
1965–1966	General Charles Ailleret	(France)
1966–1967	General Ulrich de Maizière	(Gemany)
1967	Vice Admiral Spyros Avgheris	(Greece)
1967–1968	Lt. General Odysseus Angelis	(Greece)
1968–1969	General Guido Vedovato	(Italy)
1969–1970	Admiral H.M. van den Wall Bake	(Netherlands)
1970–1971	Admiral F.H. Johannessen	(Norway)
1971–1972	General Venancio Deslandes	(Portugal)
1972	General Menduch Tagmach	(Turkey)
1972–1973	General Faruk Gürler	(Turkey)
1973	General Semih Sançar	(Turkey)
1973	Admiral of the Fleet Sir Peter Hill-Norton	(United Kingdom)
1973–1974	Field Marshal Sir Michael Carver	(United Kingdom)
1974–1975	General George S. Brown	(United States)
1975–1976	Lt. General Armand Crekillie	(Belgium)
1976–1977	General Jacques Dextraze	(Canada)

1977–1978	General Knud Joergensen	(Denmark)
1978–1979	General Jürgen Brandt	(Germany)
1979–1980	Admiral Giovanni Torrisi	(Italy)
1980–1981	General Cornelis de Jager	(Netherlands)
1981–1982	General Sverre Hamre	(Norway)
1982–1983	General N.V.T. de Melo Egidio	(Portugal)
1983–1984	Lt. General D. Alvaro De Lacalle Leloup	(Spain)
1984	Admiral Angel Liberal Lucini	(Spain)
1984–1985	General Necdet Ürüg	(Turkey)
1985	Field Marshal Sir Edwin Bramall	(United Kingdom)
1985–1986	Admiral of the Fleet Sir John Fieldhouse	(United Kingdom)
1986–1987	Admiral William J. Crowe Jr.	(United States)
1987–1988	Lt. General Maurice J.L. Gysemberg	(Belgium)
1988–1989	General Paul D. Manson	(Canada)
1989	Admiral S. Thiede	(Denmark)
1989–	General J. Lyng	(Denmark)

Chairmen of the NATO Military Committee[2]

1963–1964	General Adolf Heusinger	(Germany)
1964–1968	Lt. General C.P. de Cumont	(Belgium)
1968–1971	Admiral Sir Nigel Henderson	(United Kingdom)
1971–1974	General Johannes Steinhoff	(Germany)
1974–1977	Admiral of the Fleet Sir Peter Hill-Norton	(United Kingdom)
1977–1980	General Herman F. Zeiner Gundersen	(Norway)
1980–1983	Admiral Robert H. Falls	(Canada)
1983–1986	General Cornelis De Jager	(Netherlands)
1986–1989	General Wolfgang Altenburg	(Germany)
1989–	General Vigleik Eide	(Norway)

[1] On December 11, 1963, the Council approved the introduction of a President of the Military Committee, rotating annually among the nations.

[2] In addition to the introduction of a post of President, Military Committee, in December 1963 the Chairman of the Military Committee in Permanent Session also became Chairman of the Military Committee in Chiefs-of-Staff Session.

5

Major NATO Commanders

Supreme Allied Commanders Europe

Since the departure of General Dwight D. Eisenhower (US) in May 1952, the post of Supreme Allied Commander Europe (SACEUR) has been held as follows:

General Mathew B. Ridgway (US) — appointed May 1952
General Alfred B. Gruenther (US) — appointed July 1953
General Lauris Norstad (US) — appointed November 1956
General Lyman L. Lemnitzer (US) — appointed January 1963
General Andrew J. Goodpaster (US) — appointed July 1969
General Alexander M. Haig, Jr. (US) — appointed June 1974
General Bernard W. Rogers (US) — appointed June 1979
General John R. Galvin (US) — appointed June 1987

Supreme Allied Commanders Atlantic

The first Supreme Allied Commander Atlantic (SACLANT) was Admiral Lynde D. McCormick (US). The following officers have succeeded Admiral McCormick as SACLANT:

Admiral Jerault Wright (US) — appointed April 1954
Admiral Robert L. Dennison (US) — appointed December 1959
Admiral H.P. Smith (US) — appointed April 1963
Admiral Thomas H. Moorer (US) — appointed May 1965
Admiral Ephraim P. Holmes (US) — appointed June 1967
Admiral Charles K. Duncan (US) — appointed October 1970
Admiral Ralph W. Cousins (US) — appointed October 1972
Admiral Isaac C. Kidd (US) — appointed May 1975
Admiral Harry D. Train (US) — appointed October 1978
Admiral Wesley L. McDonald (US) — appointed September 1982
Admiral Lee Baggett Jr. (US) — appointed September 1985
Admiral Frank B. Kelso II (US) — appointed November 1988

Allied Commanders-in-Chief Channel

The first Allied Commander-in-Chief Channel (CINCHAN) was Admiral of the Fleet Sir Arthur J. Power (UK) — appointed in February 1952. Since then the post of CINCHAN has been held by the following British naval officers:

Admiral Sir John H. Edelsten — appointed June 1952
Admiral of the Fleet Sir George E. Creasey — appointed September 1954
Admiral Sir Guy Grantham — appointed May 1957
Admiral Sir Manley L. Power — appointed February 1959
Admiral Sir Alexander N.C. Bingley — appointed October 1961
Admiral Sir Wilfrid J. Woods — appointed February 1963

Appointments

Admiral Sir Varyl C. Begg — appointed August 1965
Admiral Sir John B. Frewen — appointed January 1966
Admiral Sir John Bush — appointed October 1967
Admiral Sir William O'Brien — appointed Febraury 1970
Admiral Sir Edward Ashmore — appointed September 1971
Admiral Sir Terence Lewin — appointed December 1973
Admiral Sir John Treacher — appointed October 1975
Admiral Sir Henry Leach — appointed March 1977
Admiral Sir James Eberle — appointed May 1979
Admiral Sir John Fieldhouse — appointed April 1981
Admiral Sir William Staveley — appointed October 1982
Admiral Sir Nicholas Hunt — appointed June 1985
Admiral Sir Julian J.R. Oswald — appointed May 1987
Admiral Sir Benjamin Bathurst — appointed April 1989

6

Directors of the International Military Staff

1967–1968	Lt. General Ezio Pistotti	(Italy)
1969–1971	Lt. General N.G. Palaiologopoulos	(Greece)
1971–1974	Lt. General Sir John Read	(United Kingdom)
1974–1977	Lt. General Gerhard Schmückle	(Germany)
1978–1981	Air Marshal Sir Alan Davies	(United Kingdom)
1981–1985	Lt. General T. Huitfeldt	(Norway)
1985–1988	Lt. General A.L. Moriau	(Belgium)
1988–	Lt. General C. Melillo	(Italy)

Appendix IV
Chronology

Appendix IV
Chronology 1945–1989

1945

26 June

The United Nations Charter is signed at San Francisco.

6 August

Explosion of Hiroshima atom bomb.

1946

16 March

Winston Churchill's "Iron Curtain" speech at Fulton, Missouri.

1947

19 January

Elections in Poland. The Soviet-sponsored Communist "Lublin-Committee" monopolises power.

4 March

France and the United Kingdom sign a 50-year Treaty of Alliance and Mutual Assistance at Dunkirk.

12 March

President Truman delivers his message to Congress urging the United States of America "to support free peoples who are resisting attempted subjugation by armed minorities or by outside pressure" (Truman Doctrine), and requesting the appropriation of direct financial aid to Greece and Turkey.

5 June

General of the Army, George C. Marshall, United States Secretary of State, speaking at Harvard, announces a plan for the economic rehabilitation of Europe. This speech initiated the action which led to the European Recovery Programme and the formation of the OEEC.[1]

5 October

Establishment of Cominform, the organisation for the ideological unity of the Soviet bloc, following rejection of Marshall Aid by the Soviet Union and its allies.

1948

22 January

Ernest Bevin, United Kingdom Secretary of State for Foreign Affairs, speaking in the House of Commons, proposes a form of Western Union.

---

[1] The OEEC (Organisation for European Economic Cooperation) was set up in 1948 to administer Marshall Aid and to organise European economic recovery. It was replaced by the OECD (Organisation for Economic Cooperation and Development) on 30 September 1961.

22 February
The Communist Party of Czechoslovakia gains control of the government in Prague through a coup d'état

17 March
The Brussels Treaty—a 50-year treaty of economic, social and cultural collaboration and collective self-defence—is signed by the Foreign Ministers of Belgium, France, Luxembourg, the Netherlands and the United Kingdom.

16 April
The Convention for European Cooperation is signed by the Foreign Ministers of 16 European countries and by the Commanders-in-Chief of the Western zones of occupation in Germany. The OEEC was set up under Article 1 of the Convention.

11 June
The United States Senate adopts Resolution 239, known as the "Vandenberg Resolution".

24 June
Beginning of the Berlin blockade by the Soviet Union.

28 June
Formal expulsion of Yugoslavia from Cominform.

6 July
Talks on North Atlantic defence begin in Washington between the United States, Canada and the Brussels Treaty Powers.

1 September
West German Constituent Assembly convened.

27–28 September
The Defence Ministers of the Brussels Treaty Powers decide to create a Western Union Defence Organisation.

25–26 October
The Consultative Council of the Brussels Treaty Powers announces "complete agreement on the principle of a defensive pact for the North Atlantic and on the next steps to be taken in this direction".

10 December
Negotiations on the drafting of the North Atlantic Treaty open in Washington between the representatives of the Brussels Treaty Powers, Canada and the United States.

1949

15 March
The negotiating powers invite Denmark, Iceland, Italy, Norway and Portugal to accede to the North Atlantic Treaty.

18 March
The text of the North Atlantic Treaty is published.

31 March
The Soviet Government presents a memorandum to the 12 prospective signatories of the North Atlantic Treaty claiming that the Treaty is contrary to the United Nations Charter and to the decisions of the Council of Foreign Ministers.

1949–1950

2 April
The 12 governments repudiate Soviet assertions regarding the North Atlantic Treaty in a common note.

4 April
The North Atlantic Treaty is signed in Washington by Belgium, Canada, Denmark, France, Iceland, Italy, Luxembourg, the Netherlands, Norway, Portugal, the United Kingdom and the United States.

8 April
Texts published of requests by the Brussels Treaty Powers, and by Denmark, Italy and Norway, for United States military and financial assistance.

5 May
The London Ten-Power Agreement sets up the Council of Europe.

9 May
The Berlin blockade is lifted.

10 August
Inaugural session of the Council of Europe at Strasbourg.

24 August
The North Atlantic Treaty enters into force.

17 September
First meeting of the North Atlantic Council in Washington.

20 September
Constitution of the Federal Republic of Germany.

22 September
Anglo-American-Canadian announcement that an atomic explosion has taken place in the USSR.

6 October
Mutual Defence Assistance Act is signed by President Truman.

1950

27 January
President Truman approves the plan for the integrated defence of the North Atlantic area, releasing $ 900,000,000 of military aid funds.

9 May
The French Government proposes the creation of a single authority to control the production of steel and coal in France and Germany, open for membership to other countries (Schuman Plan).

25 June
North Korean Forces attack the Republic of South Korea.

25 July
First meeting of Council Deputies in London; Ambassador Charles M. Spofford, United States Deputy Representative to the North Atlantic Council, is elected Permanent Chairman.

1 August
Announcement of decision by Turkish Government to make formal application for Turkey's accession to the North Atlantic Treaty.

2 October
Turkey accepts Council invitation to be associated with the military agencies of NATO in Mediterranean defence planning.

5 October
Greece accepts Council invitation to be associated with Mediterranean defence planning.

24 October
French Prime Minister, René Pleven, outlines his plan for a European unified army, including German contingents, within the framework of NATO.

28–31 October
The NATO Defence Committee discusses the methods by which Germany might participate in the defence of Western Europe, and refers the political and military aspects of the problem to the Council Deputies and Military Committee respectively for further study.

19 December
The North Atlantic Council appoints General Dwight D. Eisenhower (United States) to be Supreme Allied Commander Europe (SACEUR)[2]. Opening of discussions with the Federal Republic on a possible German contribution to the defence of Western Europe (Petersberg negotiations).

20 December
The Consultative Council of the Brussels Treaty Powers decide to merge the military organisation of the Western Union into the North Atlantic Treaty Organisation.

1951

15 February
Conference convened by French Government on the setting up of a European Army opens in Paris.

2 April
Allied Command Europe becomes operational with Supreme Headquarters Allied Powers Europe (SHAPE) located at Roquencourt, near Paris.

18 April
Setting up of the European Coal and Steel Community by Belgium, France, Italy, Luxembourg, the Netherlands, and the Federal Republic of Germany.

3 May
Incorporation of the Defence Committee and the Defence Financial and Economic Committee into the North Atlantic Council.

19 June
The Parties to the North Atlantic Treaty sign an agreement on the status of their forces.

8 July
Suspension of the Petersberg negotiations on the role of the Federal Republic of Germany in the defence of Western Europe.

---

[2] The list of appointments of subsequent SACEURs is given in Appendix III.

1951–1952

24 July
The Paris Conference approves an interim report to governments, recommending the creation of a European Army. General Eisenhower agrees to cooperate in working out the military problems.

1 September
Australia, New Zealand and the United States sign the Pacific Defence (ANZUS) Pact.

20 September
The member countries sign an agreement in Ottawa on the Status of NATO, National Representatives and International Staff (Civilian Status Agreement).

9–11 October
The Temporary Council Committee (TCC) holds its first session in Paris. (The TCC was set up by the Council to reconcile the requirements of collective security with the political and economic capabilities of the member countries. It set the pattern for a continuing process of appraising defence programmes).

17 October
Signature in London of the protocol to the North Atlantic Treaty on the accession of Greece and Turkey.

19 November
Inauguration of the NATO Defense College, Paris (transferred to Rome on October 10, 1966).

1952

30 January
Appointment of Vice-Admiral Lynde D. McCormick (United States) to be the first Supreme Allied Commander Atlantic (SACLANT)[3].

18 February
Greece and Turkey accede to the North Atlantic Treaty.

20–25 February
The North Atlantic Council meeting in Lisbon reorganises the structure of the Alliance and NATO becomes a permanent organisation with its headquarters in Paris.

21 February
The Council establishes a Channel Command, and appoints Admiral Sir Arthur John Power as the first Commander-in-Chief (CINCHAN)[3].

12 March
Lord Ismay (United Kingdom) is appointed Vice-Chairman of the North Atlantic Council and Secretary General of the North Atlantic Treaty Organisation.

4 April
Third anniversary of the signing of the Treaty. Lord Ismay takes office, and the North Atlantic Council assumes responsibility for the tasks hitherto performed by the Council Deputies, the Defence Production Board, and the Financial and Economic Board. The international staffs serving those agencies are amalgamated into one organisation, with headquarters in Paris.

---

[3] The list of appointments of subsequent SACLANTs and CINCHANs is given in Appendix III.

10 April
Allied Command Atlantic (ACLANT) becomes operational, with headquarters at Norfolk, Virginia.

16 April
NATO opens its provisional headquarters at the Palais de Chaillot, Paris.

28 April
First meeting of the North Atlantic Council in permanent session in Paris.

26 May
Signing in Bonn of the Convention on Relations between the Three Powers and the Federal Republic of Germany and the appended Conventions.

27 May
Signature in Paris of the Treaty setting up the European Defence Community by Belgium, France, Italy, Luxembourg, the Netherlands and the Federal Republic of Germany. Representatives of the North Atlantic Treaty Governments sign a Protocol to the Treaty giving guarantees to the members of the European Defence Community.

28 August
Signature in Paris by member nations of the Alliance of a Protocol on the Status of International Military Headquarters.

4 November
General Eisenhower is elected President of the United States.

1953

28 February
A Treaty of friendship and collaboration is signed in Ankara between Greece, Turkey and Yugoslavia.

5 March
The death of Stalin.

28 May
Dissolution of the Soviet Control Commission in Germany and its replacement by a High Commissioner of the USSR.

23 July
Korean Armistice signed at Panmunjon.

8 August
USSR announces its possession of the hydrogen bomb.

5 December
Conference in Bermuda of the Heads of Government of France, the United Kingdom and the United States, attended by Lord Ismay as observer for NATO.

1954

25 January – 18 February
Abortive Four-Power Conference in Berlin on German re-unification.

26 April
Opening of Geneva Conference convened by France, the United Kingdom, the Soviet Union and the United States, for the purpose of reaching a settlement of the Korean problem and promoting peace in Indo-China.

7 May
In their reply to a Soviet note of March 31, France, the United Kingdom and the United States reject the USSR's bid to join the North Atlantic Treaty Organisation.

17–18 June
Meeting at The Hague of the Constituent Conference of the Atlantic Treaty Association sponsored by the International Atlantic Committee.

21 July
Geneva Armistice Agreements and Declarations on Indo-China.

29 August
The French National Assembly decides against ratification of the Treaty setting up the European Defence Community (EDC).

6 September
Opening of Manila Conference which culminates in the signing of the treaties setting up SEATO (South-East Asia Treaty Organisation)[4].

28 September – 3 October
Meeting in London of the Conference of Nine to seek an alternative to the EDC. (Participating countries: Belgium, Canada, France, Federal Republic of Germany, Italy, Luxembourg, Netherlands, United Kingdom and the United States).

5 October
Signature by Italy, Yugoslavia, the United States and the United Kingdom of a Memorandum of Understanding embodying the settlement of the Trieste dispute.

20–22 October
Four-Power Conference in Paris attended by France, Federal Republic of Germany, United Kingdom and the United States. The decisions of the Conference of Nine are endorsed and a protocol adopted terminating the occupation regime in the Federal Republic.

23 October
The Paris Agreements are signed. The Federal Republic of Germany is invited to join NATO, and Italy and the Federal Republic of Germany also accede to the Western European Union (WEU).

1955

26 January
The USSR ends the state of war with Germany.

24 February
Signing of Baghdad Pact between Iraq and Turkey; Iran, Pakistan and the United Kingdom join the Pact later in the year.

---

[4] Member countries: Australia, France, New Zealand, Pakistan, Philippines, Thailand, United Kingdom and United States.

5 March
President Eisenhower undertakes to maintain United States forces in Europe for as long as is necessary.

17 April
Opening at Bandung of the first conference of the non-aligned countries of Asia and Africa.

5 May
The Federal Republic of Germany becomes a member of NATO.

7 May
The USSR renounces Franco-Soviet and Anglo-Soviet wartime treaties.

9–11 May
Ministerial meeting of the North Atlantic Council. A public ceremony marks the entry into NATO of the German Federal Republic.

14 May
The USSR concludes the Warsaw Treaty with Albania, Bulgaria, Czechoslovakia, East Germany, Hungary, Poland and Romania.

15 May
Signing of Austrian State Treaty ending the Four-Power occupation.

7 June
The Governments of France, the United Kingdom and the United States invite the USSR to take part in a Four-Power Conference in Geneva from 18–21 July.

16 July
Ministerial meeting of the North Atlantic Council to enable the Allies to exchange views before the Geneva Conference.

18–23 July
First Conference of NATO Parliamentarians (since November 1966, the North Atlantic Assembly) in Paris.

8 August
Opening in Geneva of the first conference on the peaceful uses of atomic energy.

8 September
Chancellor Adenauer visits Moscow.

25 October
Ministerial meeting of the North Atlantic Council. The Foreign Ministers of France, the United Kingdom and the United States submit to their colleagues proposals they intend to make at the Foreign Ministers' Conference in Geneva on 27 October.

27 October – 11 November
Abortive Four-Power Meeting of Foreign Ministers in Geneva.

15–16 December
Ministerial meeting of the North Atlantic Council. The Council decides to equip the forces of the Alliance with atomic weapons, and adopts the principle of strengthening air defence by achieving closer cooperation between the European NATO countries in this field.

30 December
The USSR signs a treaty with the régime in East Germany, granting it the prerogatives of a State.

1956

14 February
Opening of the Twentieth congress of the Soviet Communist Party. Khrushchev denounces Stalin in "secret" speech.

18 April
Dissolution of Cominform.

4–5 May
Ministerial meeting of the North Atlantic Council. Gaetano Martino (Italy), Halvard Lange (Norway) and Lester B. Pearson (Canada) are instructed to submit recommendations to the Council on how to improve and extend cooperation between the NATO countries in non-military fields and to develop greater unity within the Atlantic Community.

28 June
Anti-régime riots erupt at Poznan in Poland.

26 July
Egypt nationalises the Suez Canal.

17 August
The Communist Party is banned in the Federal Republic of Germany.

29 September
Franco-German Agreements on the Saar.

21 October
Wladyslaw Gomulka is appointed First Secretary of the Polish United Workers' (Communist) Party.

23 October
People's rebellion in Hungary starts.

29 October
Beginning of the Israeli Sinai campaign.
Soviet Marshal Rokossovsky ceases to be Defence Minister of Poland.

31 October
Franco-British intervention in the Suez Canal area.

4 November
Soviet suppression of Hungarian insurrection.

13 December
The North Atlantic Council approves the recommendations contained in the Report of the Committee of Three and adopts a resolution on the peaceful settlement of disputes and differences between member countries and a resolution on non-military cooperation in NATO.

1957

1 January
Political integration of the Saar with the Federal Republic of Germany.

23 March
The United States accedes to the Baghdad Pact as an associate member.

25 March
Signature of the Rome Treaties setting up EURATOM and the European Economic Community.

8 April
Re-opening of the Suez Canal.

2–3 May
Ministerial meeting of the North Atlantic Council in Bonn. The Council decides to intensify its efforts in favour of German reunification by means of free elections.

16 May
Paul-Henri Spaak (Belgium) succeeds Lord Ismay as Secretary General of NATO.

29 July
Signing in Berlin of a declaration by the governments of France, the Federal Republic of Germany, the United Kingdom and the United States, affirming the identity of their policies with regard to the reunification of Germany and to European security.

2 August
The Air Defence Commands of the United States and Canada are integrated in a North American Air Defense Command (NORAD), with headquarters at Colorado Springs (In 1981 NORAD became the North American Aerospace Defense Command).

29 August
Proposals approved by all the NATO countries are submitted to the London talks on disarmament.

14 September
The General Assembly of the United Nations condemns the Soviet intervention in Hungary.

4 October
The first Soviet Sputnik is launched.

7 October
Creation of the International Atomic Energy Agency with headquarters in Vienna.

23–25 October
President Eisenhower and Harold Macmillan, joined later by Paul-Henri Spaak, meet in Washington. A declaration of common purpose is issued by the President of the United States and the Prime Minister of the United Kingdom, underlining the interdependence of the countries of the free world.

16–19 December
Meeting of the North Atlantic Council at the level of Heads of Government in Paris. A solemn declaration reaffirms the principles and purposes of the Atlantic Alliance. The Council decides to promote closer cooperation in the political and economic fields and to increase scientific and non-military cooperation.

1958

1 January
Entry into force of the Treaty of Rome setting up the European Economic Community.

31 January
The first United States satellite "Explorer 1" is launched.

19 March
First meeting in Strasbourg of the European Parliamentary Assembly.

26–29 March
First meeting of NATO Science Committee.

27 March
Khrushchev replaces Marshal Bulganin at the head of the Soviet Government.

15–17 April
In compliance with decisions taken by the Heads of Government in December 1957, the Defence Ministers of the NATO countries meet in Paris. They reaffirm the defensive character of the NATO strategy.

5 May
Minsterial meeting of the North Atlantic Council in Copenhagen. The Council declares that it is in favour of negotiations with the Warsaw Treaty countries provided they offer real prospects of a settlement of outstanding questions.

13 May
The Algerian French rebel against the Metropolitan Government and form a "Committee of Public Safety".

1 June
General de Gaulle is invited to head the French Government.

7 August
The United States atomic submarine Nautilus establishes the first link between the Atlantic and the Pacific, passing beneath the North Pole.

10 November
Khrushchev announces that the USSR wishes to terminate the Four-Power Agreement on the status of Berlin. (The Plan was rejected by the Western Powers on December 31).

16–18 December
Ministerial meeting of the North Atlantic Council. The Council associates itself with the views expressed by the governemnts of France, the United Kingdom and the United States on Berlin and on the right of the Western Powers to remain there.

21 December
General de Gaulle is elected President of the French Republic.

1959

1 January
Overthrow of the Batista régime in Cuba by Fidel Castro.

24 March
Iraq withdraws from the Baghdad Pact.

2–4 April
Ministerial meeting in Washington marks the Tenth Anniversary of the signing of the North Atlantic Treaty.

4–10 June
An Atlantic Congress is held in London organised by the Conference of NATO Parliamentarians. In particular, it recommends the creation of the Atlantic Institute.

11–19 June
Four-Power Meeting of Foreign Ministers (France, the United Kingdom, the United States and the USSR) on the German question (Geneva Conference).

13 July
Resumption of the Geneva Conference.

5 August
Second adjournment of the Geneva Conference; the four Foreign Ministers issue a statement on disarmament.

19 August
The Baghdad Pact becomes the Central Treaty Organisation (CENTO)—full members: Iran, Pakistan, Turkey and the United Kingdom; associate member: United States. Its headquarters is set up in Ankara.

15–23 September
Khrushchev visits the United States and meets President Eisenhower at Camp David.

20 November
Austria, Denmark, Norway, Portugal, Sweden, Switzerland and the United Kingdom initial the Stockholm Convention establishing the European Free Trade Association (EFTA)[5].

15–22 December
Ministerial meeting of the North Atlantic Council. The meeting marked the inauguration of the new NATO Headquarters at the Porte Dauphine in Paris; it was largely devoted to discussing East-West negotiations, in preparation for a new summit meeting.

1960

25 January
NATO moves to new headquarters at the Porte Dauphine, Paris.

15 March
The United Nations Ten-Power Disarmament Committee starts negotiations in Geneva.

1 May
American U2 aircraft is shot down over Soviet territory.

2–4 May
Ministerial meeting of the North Atlantic Council in Istanbul. The member countries review the situation prior to the forthcoming summit meeting.

16 May
Abortive summit meeting in Paris (France, the United Kingdom, the United States and the USSR).

---

[5] Finland became an associate member of EFTA in 1961. Iceland joined in 1970. Denmark and the United Kingdom withdrew from EFTA on joining the EEC on January 1, 1973.

19 May
French, United Kingdom and United States Foreign Ministers report to the North Atlantic Council on the breakdown of the summit meeting.

27 May
Military coup d'état in Turkey.

27 June
The Communist states withdraw from the United Nations Ten-Power negotiations on disarmament in Geneva.

23 September
Khrushchev attends the General Assembly of the United Nations in New York.

10 November
Summit meeting in Moscow of the Communist leaders of 81 countries. Approval of Khrushchev's concept of peaceful co-existence.

14 December
Convention for the Establishment of the Organisation for Economic Cooperation and Development (OECD) in place of the OEEC signed by 18 European countries and the United States and Canada.

16–18 December
Ministerial meeting of the North Atlantic Council. The Council confirms its declaration of December 16, 1958, on Berlin.

1961

1 January
Inception of the Atlantic Institute with provisional headquarters set up in Milan.

17 February
In a note to the Federal Republic of Germany, the Soviet Union reverts to the Berlin question.

5 March
Paul-Henri Spaak leaves his post of Secretary General of NATO to resume participation in national politics. Alberico Casardi, Deputy Secretary General, replaces him provisionally.

12 April
Soviet Major Yuri Gagarin becomes the first man orbited in extra-terrestrial space.

14–15 April
The abortive landing of Cuban exiles in the Bay of Pigs.

21 April
Dirk U. Stikker (Netherlands) succeeds Paul-Henri Spaak as Secretary General of NATO.

8–10 May
Ministerial meeting of the North Atlantic Council in Oslo. The Council once more confirms its position on Germany, as expressed in its declaration of December 1958.

2–3 June
Meeting of Kennedy and Khrushchev in Vienna.

13 August
Erection of the Berlin Wall.

30 September
The Convention establishing the OECD comes into force[6].

17 October
Opening of the 22nd Congress of the Soviet Communist Party. Khrushchev withdraws the end-of-year limit for settlement of the Berlin question. De-Stalinisation is intensified.

13–15 December
Ministerial meeting of the North Atlantic Council in Paris. The Council reaffirms its position on Berlin, strongly condemning the building of the Wall, and approves the renewal of diplomatic contacts with the Soviet Union to determine whether a basis for negotiation can be found. It also announces the establishment of a mobile task force.

1962

8–20 January
The "Atlantic Convention" of citizens of NATO countries meets and endorses the "Declaration of Paris" in favour of strengthening the Alliance and the Atlantic Community.

20 February
Lt. Col. John Glenn, first American astronaut, carries out three orbits of the earth in his "Friendship" capsule.

14 March
The 18-nation Disarmament Conference opens in Geneva.

18 March
The Evian Agreements establish an independent Algeria.

29 March
Signing of the Convention for the Establishment of a European Organisation for the Development and Construction of Space Vehicle Launchers (ELDO)—member countries: Australia, Belgium, Federal Republic of Germany, France, Italy, Netherlands and United Kingdom.[7]

10 April
In a joint statement Macmillan and Kennedy appeal to Khrushchev for agreement on a test ban treaty.

18 April
Referendum in France approving Algerian independence.

4–6 May
The Foreign Ministers and Defence Ministers of the North Atlantic Council meeting in Athens review the circumstances in which the Alliance might be compelled to have recourse to nuclear weapons (Athens Guidelines).

---

[6] The Convention was signed by 20 countries. There are now 24 full members: 19 European, two North American, Australia, New Zealand and Japan. Yugoslavia has special status.

14 June
Signing of the Convention for the establishment of a European Space Research Organisation (ESRO)—member countries: Belgium, Denmark, France, Federal Republic of Germany, Italy, Netherlands, Spain, Sweden, Switzerland, and the United Kingdom.[7]

16-28 October
Partial blockade of Cuba by the US following revelation of Soviet construction of missile bases on the island; lifted following Soviet agreement to dismantle the bases and withdraw Soviet bombers.

20 October
China attacks India.

11 December
United States Defence Secretary McNamara announces in London the cancelling of the "Skybolt" air-to-ground nuclear missile.

13–15 December
Ministerial meeting of the North Atlantic Council in Paris examines the implications of the Cuban affair and approves the action taken by the United States. It also reaffirms its position on Berlin and disarmament.

18–20 December
President Kennedy and Prime Minister Macmillan confer at Nassau, Bahamas. They agree to contribute part of their strategic nuclear forces to NATO.

1963

14 January
President de Gaulle voices his opposition to United Kingdom entry into the European Economic Community.

16 January
Following a statement by the French Representative, the Council notes that insofar as the former Algerian Departments of France are concerned, the relevant clauses of the North Atlantic Treaty became inapplicable as of July 3, 1962.

21–22 January
Signature of Franco-German Treaty of Cooperation

28 January
The negotiations in Brussels for United Kingdom entry into the European Economic Community are broken off.

22–24 May
The Ministerial meeting of the North Atlantic Council in Ottawa is devoted largely to defence problems. The British V-bomber force and three American Polaris submarines are assigned to SACEUR who is to appoint a Deputy responsible to him for nuclear affairs.

10 June
President Kennedy announces that representatives of the United States, United Kingdom and the USSR will meet in Moscow in July to discuss a nuclear test ban treaty.

---

[7] ELDO and ESRO merged to become the European Space Agency (ESA) on May 31, 1975.

20 June
An agreement on a "hot line" between Washington and Moscow is signed in Geneva by the United States and the Soviet Union.

21 June
The Geneva Disarmament Conference is adjourned to July 30.

25 June
On a visit to Europe, President Kennedy solemnly reaffirms America's guarantee to defend Europe and the principle of equal partnership within the Alliance.

15–25 July
Talks in Moscow between the United States, United Kingdom and the Soviet Union lead to the initialling of an agreement banning nuclear tests in the atmosphere, in outer space and under water. (The Limited Test Ban Treaty was signed on August 5 and entered into force on October 10, 1963).

29 July
President de Gaulle announces that France will not sign the Moscow Treaty on a partial nuclear test ban.

21 September
The Soviet Union criticises China's intention to possess atomic weapons and announces that there have been more than 5,000 violations of the Soviet border by the Chinese.

11 October
Konrad Adenauer resigns from the Office of Chancellor of the Federal Republic of Germany. Ludwig Erhard succeeds him on October 17.

22–23 October
Operation "Big Lift": 14,500 American soldiers are flown from the United States to Germany in record time to demonstrate that the United States is able to reinforce NATO forces in Europe in an emergency.

22 November
President Kennedy is assassinated in Dallas, Texas. Vice-President Lyndon Johnson becomes President of the United States.

25 November
Extraordinary meeting of the North Atlantic Council to pay tribute to the memory of President John F. Kennedy.

16–17 December
Ministerial meeting of the North Atlantic Council in Paris. In a message to the Council, President Johnson renews United States pledges of "steadfast resolve" with regard to NATO.

1964

7 January
France recognises the Peking Government.

4 June

The North Atlantic Council authorises the implementation, as from July 1, 1964, of a reorganisation of the Standing Group, designed to allow a broader participation on the part of officers from non-standing group nations in the preparation of NATO military plans and policies.

1 August

Manlio Brosio (Italy) succeeds Dirk Stikker as Secretary General of NATO.

8–9 October

First meeting of the Defence Research Directors Committee, created to advise the Alliance on the applications of science in strengthening its defences, especially those aspects which call for international scientific cooperation.

15 October

Khrushchev is removed from office. He is replaced by Leonid Brezhnev as General Secretary of the CPSU and by Alexei Kosygin as Prime Minister.

16 October

Communist China explodes its first atomic bomb.

15–17 December

Ministerial meeting in Paris of the North Atlantic Council. The Ministers review the international situation, taking into consideration recent developments in the Soviet Union and China. Ministers hear a report by the Secretary General on the Watching Brief on Greek-Turkish relations conferred on his predecessor at the Hague in May 1964.

1965

6 April

World's first commercial satellite "Early Bird" is launched by the United States. Successfully tested as first global communications system for telephone, TV and telegraphic communications.

7 April

Soviet and East German authorities block land access to Berlin at intervals for one week when the Parliament of the Federal Republic of Germany holds plenary session in West Berlin's Congress Hall.

23 April

Soviet Union launches its first communications satellite.

11–12 May

The Ministerial meeting of the North Atlantic Council in London associates itself with the Declaration issued by France, the United Kingdom and the United States on May 12, 1965, that in the absence of a real solution of the German problem, based on the exercise in the two parts of Germany of the right of self-determination, the situation in Europe as a whole would remain unsettled.

31 May – 1 June

Meeting of the NATO Defence Ministers in Paris pays special attention to the defence problems of Greece and Turkey, and agrees to consider a proposal for improving consultation and extending participation in the planning of nuclear forces.

1 July
France breaks off discussions in Brussels on the Agriculture Fund of the European Economic Community; a six-month French boycott of the Communities begins.

9 September
At a Press Conference President de Gaulle announces that French military integration within NATO would end at the latest by 1969.

20 October
The North Atlantic Council approves the revised missions of the Major NATO Commanders and the Canada-US Regional Planning Group.

27 November
Special Committee of NATO Defence Ministers initiates year-long study to explore ways of improving Allied participation in nuclear planning.

14–16 December
The North Atlantic Council meeting in Ministerial session in Paris accepts in principle new procedures designed to improve the annual process of reviewing the defence efforts of member countries and agreeing upon their force contributions.

1966

7 March
President de Gaulle writes to President Johnson stating French intention to cease participation in NATO integrated military commands.

10 March
President de Gaulle announces France's intention of withdrawing from the integrated military structure of the Alliance and the consequent need for the removal from France of Allied military forces and military headquarters.

29 March
The French Government announces that French force assignments will end on July 1, 1966, and declares that the withdrawal of French elements entails the transfer of Allied facilities out of France by April 1, 1967.

7–8 June
Ministerial Session of the North Atlantic Council in Brussels. Ministers agree to examine the problems raised by the French decision.

16 June
The North Atlantic Council calls for proposals from the Military Committee for the organisation of a new common-funded, integrated International Military Staff.

21 June
The Belgian Chamber of Representatives approves the transfer of SHAPE to Belgium.

25 July
Defence Ministers meet in Paris. They adopt a NATO force plan for the period up to and including 1970. Ministers underline the importance of the defence of the flank regions.

13 September
The decision is made to transfer SHAPE to Casteau near Mons, Belgium.
The North Atlantic Council notes that the Channel Committee should be reorganised as an advisory and consultative body and that henceforth CINCHAN would be responsible directly to the Military Committee.

10 October
The NATO Defense College moves to its new headquarters in Rome.
Decision made to transfer AFCENT to Brunssum, Netherlands.

26 October
The North Atlantic Council decides to move the NATO Headquarters to Brussels.

27 October
China announces its first guided missile nuclear weapon test (its fourth atomic experiment).

10 November
The NATO Defence Planning Committee (DPC) decides to transfer the Military Committee from Washington to Brussels.

14 November
Harold Wilson, Prime Minister of the United Kingdom, announces his Government's determination to take Britain into the European Economic Community.

1 December
Formation of a "grand coalition" Government of the German Federal Republic with Kurt-Georg Kiesinger as Chancellor (Christian Democrat), and Willy Brandt (Social Democrat), as Vice-Chancellor and Foreign Minister.

5 December
The Defence Planning Committee approves the activation of the IBERLANT Command as the first NATO Command in Portugal.

8 December
Agreement reached at United Nations on the first international treaty governing space exploration.

14 December
The Defence Planning Committee establishes the Nuclear Defence Affairs Committee and the Nuclear Planning Group.

20 December
The Defence Planning Committee notes the organisation of the integrated International Military Staff as the executive agency of the Military Committee.

1967

18 January
NATO Defense College officially opened in Rome.

31 March
Official opening ceremony of SHAPE at Casteau near Mons, Belgium.

6–7 April
First meeting of the Nuclear Planning Group in Washington.

21 April
Military régime takes over power in Greece.

1 June
AFCENT officially opened at Brunssum, the Netherlands.

5 June
AFMED is dis-established and NAVSOUTH is established at Malta as principal subordinate command under the Commander-in-Chief Allied Forces, Southern Europe.

14 June
The North Atlantic Council meeting in Ministerial session in Luxembourg reviews the Middle East situation following the hostilities between Israel and its Arab neighbours. A resolution adopted by the Ministers invites the Council in permanent session to pursue its studies of the role which the Alliance could play in the field of technology.

16 October
Official opening of new NATO Headquarters in Brussels.

20–25 November
The North Atlantic Assembly, formerly NATO Parliamentarians Conference, holds its first conference in Brussels.

12 December
The Nuclear Defence Affairs Committee holds a meeting in Brussels to examine the Report of the Nuclear Planning Group on the year's work concerning strategic nuclear forces, antiballistic missiles, the tactical use of nuclear weapons, and national participation in nuclear planning.

13–14 December
Ministerial meeting of the North Atlantic Council approves the Harmel Report on the Future Tasks of the Alliance. The Defence Planning Committee adopts NATO's new strategic concept of flexible response and approves the establishment of a Standing Naval Force Atlantic (STANAVFORLANT).

1968

13 January
STANAVFORLANT is commissioned at Portland, England. Ships from the Netherlands, Norway, the United Kingdom and the United States participate in the activation ceremonies.

19 January
The United States and the Soviet Union agree on a draft nuclear non-proliferation treaty and table this at the Geneva Disarmament Conference.

10 May
The Ministerial Session of the Defence Planning Committee held in Brussels reaffirms the need for the Alliance to assure a balance of forces between NATO and the Warsaw Treaty countries. Ministers adopt a series of force goals for the period 1969–1973, and endorse the view put forward by the Nuclear Defence Affairs Committee that present circumstances do not justify the development of an anti-ballistic missile system in Europe.

24–25 June
Ministerial meeting of the North Atlantic Council in Reykjavik, Iceland. Current measures affecting access routes to Berlin are reviewed, and a Declaration on Mutual and Balanced Force Reductions is issued.

20–21 August
Soviet, Polish, East German, Bulgarian and Hungarian troops invade Czechoslovakia.

21 August
An open-ended working group is created under the authority of the North Atlantic Council to proceed with consultations and discussions concerning relations with Malta.

12 September
Albania renounces its membership of the Warsaw Treaty Organisation.

17 October
Signature in Prague of agreement authorising temporary stationing of Soviet troops in Czechoslovakia.

5 November
Richard Nixon is elected President of the United States.

13–14 November
Formation of the Eurogroup.

15–16 November
The North Atlantic Council denounces Soviet actions in Czechoslovakia as contrary to the basic principles of the United Nations Charter and gives a warning to the USSR.

21 November
Activation of MARAIRMED at Naples to improve NATO surveillance of the Mediterranean area.

1969

10–11 April
Commemorative session of the Council in Ministerial session in Washington to celebrate the 20th Anniversary of the signing of the North Atlantic Treaty.

28 May
Ministerial meeting of the Defence Planning Committee approves creation of naval on-call force in the Mediterranean (NAVOCFORMED).

6 November
The Council approves the setting up of a Committee on the Challenges of Modern Society to study the problems of the human environment on the basis of a proposal by President Nixon.

4–5 December
Ministerial meeting in Brussels. The Council issues a Declaration on East-West Relations.

8–10 December
First meeting of the Committee on the Challenges of Modern Society (CCMS).

1970

5 March
Non-Proliferation Treaty on Nuclear Weapons comes into force.[8]

20 March
First NATO communications satellite launched from Cape Kennedy.

16 April
Opening in Vienna of US-USSR negotiations on strategic arms limitations (SALT).

26–27 May
Ministerial meeting in Rome. Ministers issue a Declaration on Mutual and Balanced Force Reductions.

11 June
The Defence Planning Committee in Ministerial session discusses the continuing expansion of the Soviet presence in the Mediterranean and welcomes the activation of the naval on-call force for the Mediterranean.

12 August
Signing in Moscow of a Non-Aggression Treaty between the Federal Republic of Germany and the USSR.

2 November
Opening of second session of US-USSR SALT negotiations at Helsinki.

2–4 December
Ministerial meetings of the Council and Defence Planning Committee (DPC) in Brussels. President Nixon pledges that, given a similar approach by other Allies, the United States will maintain and improve its forces in Europe and not reduce them except in the context of reciprocal East-West action. The DPC adopts the study on "Alliance Defence in the '70s". Ten European countries adopt a special European Defence Improvement Programme.

7 December
Signing in Warsaw of a Treaty on normalisation of relations between the Federal Republic of Germany and Poland.

1971

2 February
Second NATO communications satellite launched from Cape Kennedy.

3–4 June
MInisterial meeting of the Council in Lisbon. Ministers renew study of the Berlin problem, and note first Soviet reactions regarding mutual and balanced force reductions.

20 August
The Defence Planning Committee directs that NAVSOUTH be transferred from Malta to Naples.

1 October
Joseph Luns (Netherlands) succeeds Manlio Brosio as Secretary General of NATO.

---

[8] By the end of 1970 the Non Proliferation Treaty had been signed by 58 countries. By January 1, 1989, 137 countries had signed the Treaty.

5–6 October
At a meeting of the Council, attended by Deputy Foreign Ministers, Manlio Brosio is appointed to conduct exploratory talks on MBFR with the Soviet and other interested governments.

8–10 December
Ministerial meetings of the Council and Defence Planning Committee in Brussels. Ministers reaffirm readiness to begin multilateral exploration of European security and cooperation as soon as Berlin negotiations are successfully concluded.

1972

21–29 February
Visit of President Nixon to Peking, leading to normalisation of relations between the United States and the People's Republic of China.

26 May
Signature in Moscow of interim agreement on strategic arms limitations (SALT) and on anti-ballistic missile systems (ABM).

30–31 May
At its Ministerial meeting in Bonn, the North Atlantic Council agrees to start multinational preparatory talks for a Conference on Security and Cooperation in Europe (CSCE). Multilateral explorations on mutual and balanced force reductions (MBFR) are proposed by the countries participating in NATO's integrated military structure.

3 June
Quadripartite Agreement on Berlin signed by Foreign Ministers of France, United Kingdom, United States and the USSR.

21 November
Opening of SALT II in Geneva.

22 November
Opening in Helsinki of multilateral preparatory talks on a CSCE.

7–8 December
Ministerial meeting in Brussels. Ministers review Western objectives at Helsinki and express resolve to maintain Alliance defences in face of increased Warsaw Treaty country forces.

21 December
Signature in East Berlin of the "Basic Treaty" between the Federal Republic of Germany and the German Democratic Republic.

1973

1 January
Denmark, Eire and the United Kingdom join the European Economic Community (EEC).

31 January – 29 June
Multilateral exploratory talks on MBFR in Vienna.

11 May
Inauguration of Standing Naval Force Channel (STANAVFORCHAN).

14–15 June
Ministerial Council meeting in Copenhagen. Ministers consider outcome of CSCE preparatory talks and express willingness to enter first phase at Helsinki on July 3. Importance of MBFR talks due to start in October in Vienna reaffirmed.

19 June
Start of talks between Nixon and Brezhnev in Washington.

25 June
Announcement of US-USSR agreement on the prevention of nuclear war.

3–7 July
First phase of CSCE in Helsinki.

18 September
Start of second phase of CSCE in Geneva.

6–24 October
Arab-Israeli Yom Kippur War.

30 October
Negotiations on Mutual and Balanced Force Reductions (MBFR) open in Vienna.

7 December
In the Defence Planning Committee in Brussels, Defence Ministers consider budgetary and balance of payments problems arising from the stationing of United States troops in Europe and the United States share in NATO civil and military programmes.

10–11 December
Ministerial meeting of the North Atlantic Council in Brussels. Ministers review world developments and current negotiations. Members of the integrated military structure of the Alliance recognise that a common Alliance effort is required to maintain United States forces in Europe at present level.

23 December
OPEC (Organisation of Petroleum Exporting Countries) announces doubling of the price of crude oil sold by the six Persian Gulf members.

1974

11–13 February
Energy conference in Washington (Canada, Norway, Japan, United States and the nine EEC countries).

25 April
Military coup d'Etat in Portugal.

14 June
Ministers attending the Defence Planning Committee meeting in Brussels note continued expansion of Warsaw Treaty forces, review progress of the European Defence Improvements Programme (EDIP), and reaffirm importance of standardization and specialisation of defence tasks.

18–19 June
Ministerial meeting of the Council in Ottawa observes the Twenty-fifth Anniversary Year of the Alliance. Ministers adopt and publish a Declaration on Atlantic Relations.

26 June
Meeting of Heads of Government in Brussels. Signature of the Declaration on Atlantic Relations.

23 July
Resignation of President Nixon. Gerald Ford becomes 38th President of the United States.

Konstantinos Karamanlis becomes Prime Minister of Greece following the resignation of the Military Government.

14 August
Withdrawal of Greek forces from integrated military structure of NATO (Greek forces were reintegrated on October 20, 1980).

23–24 November
President Ford and General Secretary Brezhnev, meeting in Vladivostok, agree on steps towards limitation of US-USSR strategic nuclear arms.

10–11 December
Ministerial meeting in Brussels of Defence Planning Committee. Ministers note strengthening of Warsaw Treaty forces, review improvements to NATO conventional forces, and discuss impact of inflation on defence costs.

12–13 December
Ministerial meeting of the North Atlantic Council in Brussels. Ministers review East-West relations and progress of CSCE and MBFR, discuss economic developments, and reaffirm importance of maintaining peace in the Middle East.

1975

23 May
Ministerial meeting in Brussels of Defence Planning Committee. Ministers review the strategic situation in the Mediterranean, the activities of the Eurogroup, and issue guidelines for future defence planning.

29–30 May
Meeting of the North Atlantic Council with Heads of State and Government in Brussels.

31 May
The European Organisation for the Development and Construction of Space Vehicle Launchers (ELDO) and the European Space Research Organisation (ESRO) merge and become the European Space Agency (ESA)—member countries: Belgium, Denmark, France, Federal Republic of Germany, Italy, Ireland, Netherlands, Spain, Sweden, Switzerland and the United Kingdom.

24–27 June
First civil defence seminar sponsored by NATO held in Battle Creek, Michigan. Attended by Belgium, Canada, Denmark, Federal Republic of Germany, Iceland, Italy, Netherlands, Norway, United Kingdom and United States.

21 July
Ending of second phase of CSCE in Geneva.

1 August
Signature of the Helsinki Final Act by Heads of State and Government of 35 States participating in the Conference on Security and Cooperation in Europe. Initiation of CSCE process including human rights provisions and confidence-building measures (e.g. advance notification of military manoeuvres), regular implementation reviews and follow-up meetings.

9–10 December

Defence Planning Committee Ministerial meeting in Brussels. Ministers note continued increase in Warsaw Treaty strength and capabilities, reaffirm importance of maintaining and strengthening NATO forces, and review current efforts to improve standardization and compatability of military equipment within the Alliance.

1976

21–22 January

At the meeting of the Nuclear Planning Group (NPG) in Hamburg, Ministers discuss continuing increase in Soviet strategic nuclear capabilities and review prospects for stabilisation through SALT.

2 February

Establishment of the Independent European Programme Group with the participation of all European member countries of NATO except Iceland (which has no military forces), to promote cooperation in the research, development and production of defence equipment.

20–21 May

Ministerial session of North Atlantic Council in Oslo. Ministers review East-West relations and progress towards implementation of Final Act of CSCE. Ministers of countries taking part in MBFR negotiations reaffirm their continuing resolve to press for achievement of Western objectives.

10–11 June

Defence Planning Committee Ministerial meeting in Brussels. Ministers reaffirm support for Eurogroup activities, express concern at continuing increase of Warsaw Treaty military strength and endorse NATO Force Goals for 1977–82.

14–15 June

At a meeting of the Nuclear Planning Group in Brussels, Ministers resume discussions on improving the effectiveness of NATO's theatre force posture.

7–8 December

Defence Planning Committee Ministerial meeting in Brussels. Ministers express concern at relentless growth in Warsaw Treaty country military strength, review national force contributions and agree need for further strengthening of NATO conventional defences.

9–10 December

Ministerial meeting of the North Atlantic Council in Brussels. Ministers express determination to enhance Allied cohesion and strength, and in the light of the provisions of the Helsinki Final Act, reject proposals by Warsaw Treaty countries to renounce first use of nuclear weapons and to restrict Alliance membership.

1977

24 January

Visit of Vice-President Mondale to North Atlantic Council following inauguration of Jimmy Carter as 39th President of the United States.

1977–1978

25 March
Defence Planning Committee meets in Ministerial session in Brussels to discuss a NATO airborne early warning (AEW) capability.

10–11 May
Council meeting in London with participation of Heads of State and Government. The Allies call for fresh studies of long-term trends in East-West relations and leaders of states participating in NATO's integrated military structure agree to initiate and develop a long-term defence programme.

17–18 May
Ministerial meeting of Defence Planning Committee in Brussels. Ministers review results of Heads of State and Government Council Meeting, and agree setting up of long-term defence programme (LTDP).

8–9 June
Meeting of Nuclear Planning Group in Ottawa. Ministers note continuing improvements in Soviet nuclear forces, including mobile intermediate range systems, and discuss current and potential improvements in NATO nuclear forces.

4 October
CSCE Follow-up Meeting in Belgrade (4 October 1977 – 9 March 1978).

11–12 October
Ministerial session of Nuclear Planning Group in Bari (Italy). Establishment of NPG high-level group on theatre nuclear force modernisation within the context of the long-term defence programme.

1978

11–13 April
20th Anniversary Commemoration Conference of the NATO Science Committee.

18–19 April
Meeting of Nuclear Planning Group in Frederikshavn, Denmark. Ministers note with concern increased Soviet capability in longer range theatre nuclear forces.

18–19 May
Meeting of Defence Planning Committee in Brussels. Ministers approve a wide-range of measures designed to enhance NATO's defence posture in selected priority areas and endorse submission of the long-term defence programme to Heads of State and Government.

23 May – 1 July
United Nations Special Session on Disarmament.

30–31 May
Meeting of the North Atlantic Council with participation of Heads of State and Government in Washington. The Allies note repeated instances of exploitation by the Soviet Union and some of its allies of situations of instability and regional conflict in the developing world. Leaders of states taking part in NATO's integrated military structure express support for the long-term defence programme.

31 October–11 December
CSCE Experts' Meeting on the Peaceful Settlement of Disputes, Montreux.

18 November
Third NATO communications satellite launched from Cape Canaveral, Florida.

5–6 December
Approval of Airborne Early Warning and Control System programme (AWACS).

1979

13 February–26 March
CSCE Experts' Meeting on Mediterrean Cooperation, Valletta.

4 April
30th Anniversary Commemorative Session of the North Atlantic Council.

11 April
Establishment of Special Group to study arms control aspects of theatre nuclear systems.

7–10 June
First direct elections to European Parliament.

18 June
SALT II agreement signed in Vienna by President Carter and General Secretary Brezhnev.[9]

26 September
Dissolution of the Central Treaty Organisation (CENTO) following withdrawal of Iran, Pakistan and Turkey.

23–24 October
10th Anniversary Meeting of the Committee on the Challenges of Modern Society held in Washington.

4 November
Seizure of the United States Embassy in Tehran and 53 hostages by Islamic revolutionaries. (Negotiations led to the release of the hostages on 20 January 1981).

11–14 December
Ministerial meetings of Defence Planning Committee and North Atlantic Council in Brussels, followed by Special Meeting (12 December) of Foreign and Defence Ministers. "Double-track" decision on theatre nuclear force modernisation including the deployment in Europe of US ground-launched Cruise and Pershing II systems and a parallel and complementary arms control effort to obviate the need for such deployments.[10]

27 December
Soviet Union invades Afghanistan

29 December
Special session of North Atlantic Council to discuss Soviet invasion of Afghanistan.

---

[9] The SALT II agreement was not ratified by the United States. New negotiations between the United States and the Soviet Union, aimed at achieving reductions in strategic arms (Strategic Arms Reduction Talks — START) began in Geneva on 30 June 1982).

[10] France did not participate in the Special Meeting of Foreign and Defence Ministers.

1980

24 January
Members of the Alliance participating in the 12 December 1979 Special Meeting establish the Special Consultative Group on arms control involving theatre nuclear forces. (The Special Group established in April 1979, to study arms control aspects of theatre nuclear systems, concluded its work on 11 December 1979).

18 February–3 March
CSCE Forum on Scientific Cooperation, Hamburg.

4 May
Death of President Tito of Yugoslavia.

31 August
Gdansk Agreements, leading to establishment and official recognition of Polish independent trade union "Solidarity".

12 September
Turkish military leadership takes over the administration of the country.

22 September
War breaks out between Iraq and Iran.

20 October
Re-integration of Greek forces into the integrated military structure of the Alliance.

11 November
Opening of CSCE Follow-up Meeting in Madrid.

9–12 December
Ministerial meetings of the Council and Defence Planning Committee reflect concern over the situation with regard to Poland and the continuing Soviet occupation of Afghanistan.

1981

1 January
Greece becomes the 10th member of the European Economic Community.

20 January
Ronald Reagan becomes the 40th President of the United States.

23 February
Abortive attempts by rebel civil guards to overthrow Spanish caretaker government.

30 March
Attempted assassination of President Reagan.

10 May
François Mitterand is elected as the first Socialist President of the Fifth French Republic.

13 May
Attempted assassination of Pope John Paul.

25 May
Gulf Cooperation Council established by Bahrein, Kuwait, Qatar, Oman, Saudi Arabia and United Arab Emirates.

6 October
Assassination of Egyptian President Sadat.

18 October
Andreas Papandreou becomes first Socialist Prime Minister of Greece.

19 October
Wojciech Jaruzelski replaces Stanislav Kania as leader of the Polish United Workers Party.

27 October
Soviet submarine grounded in Swedish territorial waters.

20 November
Permanent Representatives of Allied countries participating in the Special Consultative Group issue a statement welcoming the 18 November speech by President Reagan announcing new arms control initiatives including intermediate-range nuclear force negotiations (INF) and strategic arms reduction talks (START) and supporting the United States negotiating position.

30 November
The United States and the Soviet Union open Geneva negotiations on intermediate-range nuclear forces (INF).

2 December
Spain formally applies to join NATO.

10 December
Foreign Ministers and Representatives of member countries of the Alliance issue a Declaration condemning all acts of terrorism.

10–11 December
The North Atlantic Council, meeting in Ministerial Session, signs the Protocol of Accession of Spain to the North Atlantic Treaty.

11 December
Ministerial Declaration on Intermediate-Range Nuclear Force Modernisation and Arms Control.

13 December
Imposition of martial law in Poland.

1982

11 January
Special Ministerial Session of the North Atlantic Council issues a Declaration on Events in Poland.

18 February
30th Anniversary of the Accession of Greece and Turkey to the North Atlantic Treaty.

2 April – 14 June
The Falklands Conflict.

30 May
Spain becomes the 16th member of the North Atlantic Treaty Organisation.

6 June
Israel invades the Lebanon.

10 June
Summit Meeting of the North Atlantic Council in Bonn. Heads of State and Government issue the Bonn Declaration setting out the Alliance Programme for Peace in Freedom and publish documents on Arms Control and Disarmament and on Integrated NATO Defence.

30 June
Opening of Strategic Arms Reduction Talks (START) in Geneva.

2–3 October
Informal meeting of NATO Foreign Ministers at La Sapinière, Val David, Canada.

10 November
Death of Leonid Brezhnev. Yuri Andropov subsequently becomes General Secretary of the Communist Party of the Soviet Union.

2 December
Felipe Gonzáles becomes Prime Minister of Spain.

15 December
Frontier between Spain and Gibraltar opened for pedestrians for the first time since 1969.

1983

23 March
President Reagan announces a comprehensive research programme aimed at eliminating the threat posed by strategic nuclear missiles (Strategic Defense Initiative).

31 March
The North Atlantic Council issues a statement supporting the United States proposal for an interim agreement in the US-Soviet INF negotiations in Geneva limiting land-based LRINF missiles on launchers to equal ceilings.

22 July
Ending of martial law in Poland. New laws reinforce Government controls.

1 September
A South Korean airliner with 269 people on board is shot down by Soviet air defence off the coast of Sakhalin.

9 September
Conclusion of CSCE Follow-up Meeting in Madrid.

25 October – 11 November
Preparatory meeting in Helsinki for Stockholm Conference on Security and Confidence-Building Measures and Disarmament in Europe (CDE).

25 October
Military intervention in Grenada by United States and East Caribbean forces.

27 October
The Montebello Decision. Defence Ministers meeting in the NATO Nuclear Planning Group in Montebello, Canada announce their decision to withdraw a further 1,400 warheads from Europe, bringing the total of such withdrawals since 1979 to 2,400.

23 November
Deliveries of GLCM components to the United Kingdom mark the beginning of NATO's intermediate-range nuclear force deployments (INF).
Decision by the Soviet Union to discontinue the current round of negotiations in Geneva on intermediate-range nuclear forces (INF).

8 December
Conclusion of the current round of US-Soviet Geneva negotiations on Strategic Arms Reductions (START) without a date being set by the Soviet side for their resumption.

8–9 December
Foreign Ministers meeting in the Ministerial Session of the North Atlantic Council issue the Declaration of Brussels expressing their determination to seek a balanced and constructive relationship with the East and calling on the Soviet Union and other Warsaw Treaty countries to respond.

13 December
Formation of a civilian government in Turkey following parliamentary elections under a new constitution.

1984

17 January
Opening of the Stockholm Conference on Confidence and Security-Building Measures and Disarmament in Europe (CDE), within the framework of the CSCE process, in the presence of Foreign Ministers of the 35 participating States.

9 February
Death of President Yuri Andropov. Konstantin Chernenko subsequently becomes General Secretary of the Soviet Communist Party and President of the Supreme Soviet of the USSR.

21 March–30 April
CSCE Experts' Meeting on the Peaceful Settlement of Disputes, Athens.

4 April
Meeting of the North Atlantic Council in Brussels commemorating the 35th Anniversary of the signing of the North Atlantic Treaty.

18 April
At the Geneva Conference on Disarmament Vice-President George Bush presents a US draft treaty banning the development, production, stock-piling and use of chemical weapons and calling for systematic on-site inspection of chemical weapons facilities to ensure compliance.

29–31 May
Ministerial meeting of the North Atlantic Council in Washington DC. Foreign Ministers issue the Washington Statement on East-West Relations.

7–9 June
Summit meeting in London. Heads of State and Government of the seven major industrialised countries issue a declaration on East-West Relations and Arms Control.

12 June
Foreign Ministers of the seven countries of the Western European Union meeting in Paris decide to reactivate the WEU.

25 June
Lord Carrington (United Kingdom) succeeds Joseph Luns as Secretary General of NATO.

26 September
United Kingdom and People's Republic of China agree on transfer of Hong Kong to Chinese control on 1 July 1997.

16–26 October
CSCE Seminar on Economic, Scientific and Cultural Cooperation in the Mediterranean, Venice.

26–27 October.
Foreign and Defence Ministers of the member countries of the Western European Union publish the "Rome Declaration" announcing their decision to increase cooperation within the WEU.

31 October
Indian Prime Minister Indira Gandhi is assassinated and is succeeded by her son Rajiv Gandhi.

6 November
President Reagan is elected for a second term.

7 December
Presentation by the Secretary General of NATO of the first Atlantic Award to Per Markussen (Denmark), for his outstanding contribution over many years to the objectives of the Atlantic Alliance.

13–14 December
Ministerial meeting of the North Atlantic Council in Brussels. Foreign Ministers consult on meeting of Secretary of State Shultz and Foreign Minister Gromyko on 7–8 January in Geneva regarding possible resumption of arms control talks.

1985

11 March
Death of Konstantin Chernenko. Mikhail Gorbachev subsequently becomes General Secretary of the Communist Party of the Soviet Union.

12 March
The United States and the USSR begin new arms control negotiations in Geneva, encompasssing defence and space systems, strategic nuclear forces and intermediate-range nuclear forces.

22 April
Foreign and Defence Ministers of the seven countries of the Western European Union meet in Bonn to review progress towards the reactivation of the WEU decided upon at their 1984 Paris and Rome meetings.

26 April
The 1955 Treaty of Friendship, Cooperation and Mutual Assistance, establishing the Warsaw Treaty Organisation, is extended for 30 years by party leaders of the seven member states.

7 May–17 June
CSCE Experts' Meeting on Human Rights, Ottawa.

22 May
Ministerial meeting of the Defence Planning Committee in Brussels. Defence Ministers focus their attention on measures necessary to improve NATO's conventional forces.

6–7 June
Ministerial meeting of the North Atlantic Council in Estoril, Portugal. Foreign Ministers welcome the US-Soviet negotiations in Geneva on strategic nuclear weapons, intermediate-range nuclear weapons and defence and space systems.

22 June
Visit of Vice-President Bush to the North Atlantic Council.

30 June
39 American hostages are released after being held for 17 days by Lebanese Shiite Moslems in Beirut, following the hijacking of a TWA airliner.

2 July
Andrei Gromyko becomes President of the Supreme Soviet of the Soviet Union. Eduard Shevardnadze succeeds Gromyko as Foreign Minister.

30 July
Foreign Ministers of 35 countries meet in Helsinki to celebrate the 10th anniversary of the Conference on Security and Cooperation in Europe (CSCE).

3 October
Soviet leader Mikhail Gorbachev and French President François Mitterrand meet in Paris on the eve of the Gorbachev-Reagan Geneva Summit.

7 October
Palestinian guerrillas hijack an Italian cruise liner, the Achille Lauro, in the Mediterranean, taking 440 people hostage. An American citizen is murdered.

10 October
United States forces intercept a plane carrying the hijackers of the Achille Lauro from Egypt and force it to divert to Italy. The four hijackers are arrested.

15 October–25 November
CSCE Cultural Forum in Budapest.

12 November
Professor van der Beugel (Netherlands) becomes the second recipient of NATO's Atlantic Award for outstanding services to the Atlantic Alliance.

19–21 November
Geneva Summit meeting between United States President Ronald Reagan and Soviet leader Mikhail Gorbachev. They agree in principle on a reduction of strategic nuclear forces by 50 % and on an interim agreement on intermediate-range nuclear forces.

20 November
The NATO Council agrees to extend until 1991 its Science for Stability Programme of research cooperation designed to assist Greece, Portugal and Turkey in the development of their scientific and technological capabilities.

21 November
President Reagan reports on his Geneva talks with Soviet leader Mikhail Gorbachev at a special meeting of the North Atlantic Council with the participation of Heads of State and Government and Foreign Ministers.

3–5 December
Ministerial meeting of the Defence Planning Committee in Brussels. Defence Ministers welcome the results achieved by President Reagan in his talks with Soviet leader Gorbachev. They consider measures necessary to improve NATO's conventional defences and to increase arms cooperation and adopt the NATO Force Plan for 1986–1990.

12–13 December
Ministerial meeting of the North Atlantic Council in Brussels. Following the Geneva Summit meeting between President Reagan and Soviet leader Gorbachev, Foreign Ministers express cautious optimism over developments in East-West relations. The Foreign Ministers publish a statement outlining the main elements of a new Armaments Cooperation Improvement Strategy.

1986

1 January
Portugal and Spain become members of the European Economic Community (EEC).

12 March
In a referendum organised by Prime Minister Felipe González, Spanish voters support the continued membership of Spain in the Atlantic Alliance without participation in NATO's integrated military structure.

20 March
Following legislative elections in France, Centre Right party leader Jacques Chirac becomes Prime Minister under Socialist President François Mitterrand.

24–25 March
United States forces sink Libyan patrol boats and attack a missile site inside Libya following Libyan attacks on US forces in the Mediterranean.

15 April
In response to terrorist attacks attributed to Libya, United States forces attack targets in Tripoli and Benghazi.

15 April–26 May
CSCE Experts' Meeting on Human Contacts, Berne.

26 April
Nuclear accident at the Chernobyl power station in the Soviet Union.

28 April
Foreign and Defence Ministers of the seven member countries of the Western European Union, meeting in Venice, review progress towards revitalisation of the WEU.

5–6 May
Leaders of the seven most industrialised Western nations hold their annual Economic Summit in Tokyo and agree on concerted action against terrorism.

20 May
At a meeting of the North Atlantic Council, Spain presents proposals based on general principles governing future Spanish participation in the institutions of the Alliance.

22 May
Ministerial meeting of the Defence Planning Committee in Brussels focuses attention on measures required to improve NATO's conventional forces and adopts the NATO Force Goals for 1987–1992.

29–30 May
Foreign Ministers issue a Statement on the Ministerial meeting of the North Atlantic Council in Halifax, Canada, calling on the Soviet Union to join them in taking "bold new steps" to promote peace, security and a productive East-West dialogue. Ministers establish a High-Level Task Force on Conventional Arms Control.

9 July
The first ship financed and owned by NATO, the research vessel known as "The Alliance", is launched at La Spezia, Italy.

22 September
End of Stockholm Conference on Confidence and Security-Building Measures and Disarmament in Europe (CDE). Concluding document (dated 19 September) includes mandatory measures for notification, observation and on-site inspection of military manoeuvres of participating countries.

11–12 October
Reykjavik Summit Meeting between United States President Reagan and Soviet Leader Mikhail Gorbachev ends without agreement being reached.

13 October
At a special session of the North Atlantic Council attended by Foreign and Defence Ministers in Brussels, US Secretary of State Shultz briefs the Council on the outcome of the Reykjavik Summit.

21–22 October
Ministerial meeting of NATO's Nuclear Planning Group in Gleneagles, Scotland. Defence Ministers express support for President Reagan's arms control programme.

4 November
The third CSCE Follow-up Conference opens in Vienna, attended by Foreign Ministers from the 33 European states and the United States and Canada.

24 November
Prof. Karl Kaiser (Federal Republic of Germany) receives the third Atlantic Award from the Secretary General of NATO in a ceremony at NATO headquarters in Brussels.

11 December
NATO Foreign Ministers issue the Brussels Declaration on Conventional Arms Control calling for two distinct sets of negotiations: on conventional stability, aimed at eliminating existing disparities from the Atlantic to the Urals and establishing conventional stability at lower levels; and on further confidence and security-building measures.

19 December
Academician Andrei Sakharov, exiled in Gorki since January 1980, is allowed to return to Moscow.

1987

14 January
US arms control negotiators attend the North Atlantic Council in Brussels for consultation prior to opening the 7th round of the nuclear arms control talks in Geneva.

15 January
A unilateral cease-fire is declared by the Afghan régime. The Afghan resistance rejects proposals for national reconciliation and announces that the armed struggle will continue.

26 January
Spain resumes talks with its NATO partners in the second round of formal negotiations on the future role of Spanish forces within the Alliance to take place since the March 1986 referendum confirming Spanish membership of the Alliance outside the integrated military command structure.

29 January
MBFR talks resume in Vienna against the background of informal contacts to discuss prospective expanded talks on conventional stability in Europe within the framework of the 35 nation CSCE process.

8 February
Sino-Soviet border negotiations reopen in Moscow after an interruption of 8 years.

10 February
Representatives of the 16 NATO countries begin informal contacts with the 7 Warsaw Treaty countries with a view to discussing prospective new negotiations on reducing conventional forces and on conventional stability in Europe.

17 February
Talks open in Vienna between NATO and Warsaw Treaty countries on a mandate for negotiations on conventional forces in Europe from the Atlantic to the Urals.

23 February
US-Soviet negotiations in Geneva on defence and space systems are temporarily suspended while consultations take place between the US and its NATO allies on the US space-based missile defence research and development programme (SDI) and its conformity with the 1972 Anti-Ballistic Missile (ABM) Treaty.

26 February
Meeting of the North Atlantic Council attended by Deputy Defence Ministers reviews the status of current Alliance efforts to improve allied conventional defence through enhanced armaments cooperation including implementation of the Armaments Cooperation Improvement Strategy agreed by Ministers in December 1985.

28 February

Soviet leader Mikhail Gorbachev announces Soviet willingness to conclude a separate treaty eliminating intermediate-range nuclear weapons, not conditional upon progress in US-Soviet talks on defence and space systems.

4 March

US negotiators present a draft intermediate-range nuclear force treaty proposing major cuts in intermediate-range nuclear missiles at the US-Soviet negotiations in Geneva in accordance with principles agreed at Reykjavik in October 1986.

9 March

Representatives of five NATO INF-basing countries (Belgium, Federal Republic of Germany, Italy, Netherlands and United Kingdom) meet with US representatives in Washington as part of the ongoing process of consultation on verification aspects of a possible US-Soviet treaty eliminating intermediate-range nuclear weapons.

18 March

Talks began in Geneva between representatives of the European Communities and of COMECON on measures aimed at mutual recognition.

27 March

NATO's Special Consultative Group declares its support for the US draft INF Treaty tabled on March 4, incorporating the INF understandings reached between President Reagan and General Secretary Gorbachev at Reykjavik in October 1986.

NATO Secretary General Lord Carrington, following an emergency meeting of the North Atlantic Council, offers to use his good offices to help to resolve the dispute in the Aegean between Greece and Turkey.

16 April

US Secretary of State Shultz briefs the North Atlantic Council on the results of his recent visit to Moscow; Ministers and permanent representatives agree that the Council in permanent session should begin work immediately to consider the implications to allied security of a new Soviet offer for a phased elimination of shorter-range INF missiles.

14–15 May

At the meeting of the NATO Nuclear Planning Group in Ministerial Session in Stavanger, Norway, Ministers review the status of current arms control negotiations and the status of implementation of the December 1979 Double-Track and October 1983 Montebello decisions.

23 May

A single-engined Cessna plane from the Federal Republic of Germany, piloted by Matthias Rust, lands in Red Square, Moscow, after illegally penetrating Soviet airspace from Finland. The Soviet Defence Minister subsequently loses his post, along with other senior military officials.

26–27 May

At the meeting of the NATO Defence Planning Committee in Brussels, Ministers welcome recent developments suggesting the possibility of real progress in relations between East and West, particularly in the field of arms control, and underline their objective of achieving improved security and stability at lower levels of forces.

4 June

The parliament of the Federal Republic of Germany formally endorses by 232 to 189 a proposal calling for the elimination of intermediate-range (INF) and shorter-range (SRINF) missiles in Europe.

5 June

The Canadian Government announces its decision to redirect its commitment to the reinforcement of Europe from the Northern to the Central Region.

11–12 June

Meeting of the North Atlantic Council at Reykjavik. Foreign Ministers pay particular attention to the further development of a comprehensive concept of arms control and disarmament and confirm the need for separate negotiations on confidence and security-building measures among the 35 CSCE States; and on conventional stability in Europe among the 23 NATO and Warsaw Treaty countries, within the CSCE framework.

19 June

Chancellor of the Federal Republic Helmut Kohl proposes the formation of a joint Franco-German brigade as the first step towards a joint European fighting force.

20 July – 7 August

At United States-Soviet talks in Geneva aimed at speeding up progress towards a global ban on chemical weapons, experts from both sides accept invitations to visit each other's countries to observe procedures for destroying these weapons.

22 July

Soviet Leader Mikhail Gorbachev announces Soviet readiness to eliminate all intermediate-range nuclear weapons including those deployed in the Asian part of the Soviet Union in the context of a United States-Soviet INF treaty.

23 July

Soviet negotiators present a proposal at the United States-Soviet Geneva arms control negotiations accepting the principle of a "double-zero option" eliminating Soviet and US land-based intermediate range (LRINF and SRINF) missiles on a global basis.

27 July

At the resumption of the 23 nation exploratory talks at Vienna on conventional stability in Europe, Western negotiators present a draft mandate for formal negotiations covering the whole of Europe, aimed at achieving a stable and secure balance of conventional forces at lower levels.

20 August

Western European Union experts meeting in The Hague consider possible joint action in the Gulf to ensure freedom of navigation in the oil shipping lanes of the region.

24 August – 11 September

International Conference on the Relationship between Disarmament and Development in New York. The Conference adopts a Final Document addressing the philosophical relationship between disarmament and development, economic and social implications of military spending, and future action.

26 August

Chancellor Helmut Kohl announces that the Federal Republic of Germany will dismantle its 72 Pershing IA missiles in order to permit progress towards conclusion of an INF Treaty, subject to agreement being reached on outstanding verification issues, the ratification of the Treaty and the adherence by both sides to an agreed timetable for implementation.

28–30 August

A team of United States inspectors attends military manoeuvres near Minsk, the first such inspection to take place under the provisions of the September 1986 Stockholm Document.

7 September

East German leader Erich Honecker begins a five-day official visit to the Federal Republic of Germany, the first such visit by an East German Head of State and Party Leader.

10 September

The North Atlantic Council is briefed by Ambassador Nitze, senior arms control adviser to President Reagan, and by arms control negotiators from Geneva on recent developments in those negotiations and preparations for the forthcoming meeting between Secretary of State Shultz and Soviet Foreign Minister Shevardnadze.

14 September

At the Geneva arms control negotiations the US tables a new draft treaty eliminating all US and Soviet ground based nuclear missiles between the ranges of 500 and 5,500 kilometres and a draft Inspection Protocol calling for a stringent verification regime.

21 September

NATO Foreign Ministers, in New York to attend the United Nations General Assembly, pursue further consultations on nuclear arms control and voice their support for the prospective INF Treaty eliminating land-based intermediate-range nuclear weapons.

21 September

France and Italy announce measures to promote exchange of information and technical coordination between naval forces operating to protect shipping in the Gulf.

22 September

Resumption of Vienna CSCE Follow-up Meeting to address outstanding human rights issues and future handling of conventional disarmament initiatives.

2 October

US Vice-President George Bush, during consultations in several NATO countries, provides assurances to the North Atlantic Council that European concerns will be taken fully into account in US-Soviet arms control agreements.

3–4 October

Arms control negotiators from 45 countries participating in the Geneva Conference on Disarmament visit chemical weapons facilities at Shikhang in the Soviet Union.

5–7 October

A team of Soviet inspectors attends NATO exercises in Turkey, the first such inspection to take place in an Alliance country under the provisions of the September 1986 Stockholm Document.

14 October
The European Parliament adopts a resolution on measures to strengthen European cooperation on defence and emphasising the importance of the Atlantic Alliance.

15 October
Three warships from the Federal Republic of Germany are sent to the Mediterranean to replace vessels of NATO allies redeployed to protect shipping lanes in the Gulf.

18 October
Destruction of two Iranian oil platforms in the Gulf by US naval forces following attacks on convoys passing through the area.

24 October
At a meeting of the North Atlantic Council, Alliance Foreign Ministers hold consultations with US Secretary of State Shultz and the US negotiating team from Geneva, focussing on the meetings of Secretary Shultz with Soviet leaders in Moscow.

26 October
Meeting of Western European Union countries in the Hague to coordinate their military presence in the Gulf following attacks on shipping in the area.

28 October
At a meeting of the North Atlantic Council, the Netherlands, as the country holding the presidency of the Western European Union, presents the Western European Union "Platform on European Security Interests" adopted on 27 October, to the 16 members of the North Atlantic Alliance.

2 November
Delegations from NATO and the Warsaw Treaty countries, meeting in Vienna, agree to open talks on conventional arms reductions in 1988.

4 November
NATO Defence Ministers, in the Nuclear Planning Group meeting in Monteray, California, voice their support for the agreement in principle between the US and the Soviet Union on the global elimination of land-based INF missiles with a range between 500 and 5,500 kilometres.

9 November
Resumption, after an interval of 7 years, of formal negotiations in Geneva between the US and the Soviet Union on limitations on nuclear test explosions.

24–26 November
Meeting of Warsaw Treaty Defence Ministers approves the proposed INF Treaty between the US and the Soviet Union.

25 November
A special session of the North Atlantic Council in Brussels is briefed by US Secretary of State George Shultz on details of the proposed INF Treaty between the US and the Soviet Union.

Presentation of NATO's annual Atlantic Award to Pierre Harmel (Belgium), author of the 1967 Harmel Report.

30 November

In a referendum in Poland the government fails to obtain the required majority for its political and economic reform programme.

2 December

At the meeting of the Defence Planning Committee in Brussels, Defence Ministers look forward to the imminent successful conclusion of the US-Soviet INF negotiations, and register their satisfaction at the agreement which represents a major accomplishment for the Alliance.

8 December

US President Reagan and Soviet leader Mikhail Gorbachev, meeting at the beginning of their 3-day summit talks, sign the Washington INF Treaty, eliminating on a global basis land-based intermediate-range nuclear missiles.

9 December

The US and the Soviet Union reach agreement on measures allowing the monitoring of nuclear explosions at each other's test sites.

10 December

In a general statement at the end of their 3-day summit meeting in Washington, US President Reagan and Soviet leader Mikhail Gorbachev pledge deep cuts in strategic arms and instruct their negotiators in Geneva to work out an agreement in line with the 1972 ABM Treaty.

11 December

The North Atlantic Council meeting in Ministerial session in Brussels receives a detailed report by US Secretary of State Shultz on the Washington summit talks and welcomes the signature of the INF Treaty. The meeting marks the 20th anniversary of the Harmel report setting out the basis for the Alliance's policies of maintaining adequate military strength and political solidarity to deter aggression while pursuing the search for progress towards a more stable East-West relationship.

At a ceremony at NATO Headquarters in Brussels, the Secretary of State of the United States, and the Foreign Ministers of Belgium, the Federal Republic of Germany, Italy, the Netherlands and the United Kingdom sign bilateral agreements permitting on-site inspection of missile bases on their territory in accordance with the verification procedures established under the INF Treaty, signed in Washington on 8 December.[11]

17 December

Milos Jakes becomes General Secretary of the Communist Party in Czecholovakia. Gustav Husak remains President.

1988

22 January

Establishment of a Joint Security Council by the Governments of the Federal Republic of Germany and of France. The two Governments also sign an agreement relating to the formation of a joint Franco-German Army Brigade.

---

[11] The countries concerned subsequently exchanged notes with the Soviet Union, formerly agreeing on INF Treaty verification procedures involving the granting of inspection rights to the Soviet Union, accompanied by Soviet undertakings related to national sovereignty and laws.

2–3 March

Summit meeting of the North Atlantic Council in Brussels. A Declaration published by Heads of State and Government emphasises Allied unity and reasserts the common objectives and principles and the continuing validity of Alliance policies. A Statement on Conventional Arms Control is also issued under the authority of Heads of State and Government, calling for significant steps to bring about progress in eliminating conventional force disparities through negotiations on conventional stability.

15 March

United States Defence Secretary Frank Carlucci and Soviet Defence Minister Dimitri Yazov meet for the first time at the beginning of three days of talks in Berne, Switzerland, marking a further stage in efforts to achieve progress in current arms control negotiations and other military aspects of US-Soviet relations.

22 March

United States Secretary of State Shultz and Soviet Foreign Minister Shevardnadze open a new satellite communications link between Washington and Moscow during preparatory talks for the May 29, 1988 US-Soviet Summit Meeting.

15 May

Beginning of Soviet troop withdrawals from Afghanistan, in accordance with the agreements reached in April, in Geneva, between Afghanistan, Pakistan, the United States and the Soviet Union.

22 May

In Hungary Janos Kádár is removed as General Secretary of Socialist Workers' Party. He is replaced by Karoly Grosz.

26–27 May

Meeting in the Defence Planning Committee, Defence Ministers commission the Executive Working Group to conduct a review of roles, risks and responsibilities shared by member nations in the context of their efforts to sustain the credibility and effectiveness of collective security and defence; Ministers also accept the importance of retaining the United States 401st Tactical Fighter Wing in Southern Europe, invite Italy to identify a suitable site and agree that the relevant costs for its relocation be funded from NATO's common infrastructure budget.

31 May

During a five-day Summit meeting in Moscow, President Reagan and General Secretary Gorbachev exchange documents implementing the recently ratified December 1987 INF Treaty and sign bilateral agreements on nuclear testing and in other fields.

9–10 June

At the first Ministerial meeting of the North Atlantic Council to be held in Madrid, Foreign Ministers review the positive progress in East-West relations registered at the Moscow Summit meeting, and welcome the evolution of the Spanish contribution to the common defence.

24 June

Announcement of the formation of a NATO Composite Force to reinforce Northern Norway in periods of tension or hostility, to replace the Canadian CAST Brigade which will be reassigned to the Central Region in accordance with the plans of the Canadian Government.

28 June–1 July
The 19th CPSU Conference in Moscow sets in train a programme of political, constitutional and legal reforms.

1 July
Manfred Wörner, former Minister of Defence of the Federal Republic of Germany, succeeds Lord Carrington as Secretary General of NATO.

3 July
An Iranian airliner with 290 people on board enters the war zone over the Strait of Hormuz and is shot down by US naval forces, having been incorrectly identified as an attacking fighter aircraft.

6 July
Explosion and fire destroy the Piper Alpha oil rig off the coast of Scotland with large-scale loss of life. Naval vessels from NATO's Standing Naval Force in the Atlantic are involved in rescue operations.

20 August
Entry into force of a ceasefire in the Gulf war between Iran and Iraq, in the framework of UN Security Council Resolution 598.

30 September
Major reshuffle of Soviet leadership following Plenary meeting of CPSU Central Committee.

1 November
Gorbachev elected President of Praesidium of USSR Supreme Soviet. Henceforward he combines functions of Head of Party and Head of State.

7 November
George Bush is elected 41st President of the United States.

14 November
Portugal and Spain sign the Treaty of Accession to the Western European Union.

25 November
The members of the Alliance publish an assessment of the armed forces of NATO and of the Warsaw Treaty Organisation ("Conventional Forces in Europe: the Facts").

1–2 December
Ministerial meeting of the Defence Planning Committee. Publication of a report on Enhancing Alliance Collective Security—Shared Roles, Risks and Responsibilities in the Alliance.

5 December
Paul Nitze, Special Adviser on Arms Control to President Reagan, receives the 1988 Atlantic Award.

7 December
President Gorbachev, in the course of a major address to the UN General Assembly, announces unilateral Soviet conventional force reductions.

A major earthquake in Armenia devastates several cities and causes massive loss of life. Unprecedented international rescue and relief work begins immediately.

8 December
Meeting in the North Atlantic Council in Brussels, Alliance Foreign Ministers welcome Soviet reductions in conventional forces and changes in defence policy announced by President Gorbachev at the United Nations, and publish a major statement outlining the Alliance's proposals for forthcoming negotiations on conventional stability and further confidence and security-building measures.

15 December
General Mikhail Moïsseev replaces Marshal Akhromeïev as Chief of the Soviet General Staff.

1989

7–11 January
149 countries participate in an international Conference on Chemical Weapons in Paris focussing world-wide attention on their use and proliferation. The Conference reaffirms the importance of the commitments made under the 1925 Geneva Protocol and gives political impetus to the negotiations in Geneva for a global, comprehensive and effectively verifiable ban on chemical weapons.

18 January
President Gorbachev provides further details of intended reductions in Soviet armed forces referred to in his address to the United Nations on December 7, 1988, announcing cuts of 14.2% in Soviet defence expenditure and 19.5% in the production of arms and military equipment.

19 January
Conclusion of the Vienna CSCE Follow-up Meeting and adoption of a Concluding Document including mandates for new negotiations on Conventional Armed Forces in Europe (CFE) and new negotiations on Confidence and Security-Building Measures (CSBMs).

23–27 January
Future reductions in conventional forces and military budgets are announced by the German Democratic Republic, Poland, Hungary, Czechoslovakia, and Bulgaria. They are welcomed by Alliance countries as contributions to the reduction of conventional force imbalances in Europe.

29 January
Defence Ministers of the Warsaw Treaty countries publish comparative data on conventional forces in Europe.

2 February
Final Meeting of the Vienna negotiations on Mutual and Balanced Force Reductions.

11 February
The Central Committee of the Hungarian Communist Party endorses "gradual and steady" transition to a multi-party political system.

15 February
The Soviet Union completes the withdrawal of military forces from Afghanistan in accordance with the schedule announced by President Gorbachev.

6 March
Foreign Ministers of CSCE states meet in Vienna to mark the opening of new negotiations on Conventional Armed Forces in Europe (CFE) among the 23 members of NATO and the Warsaw Treaty Organisation and on Confidence and Security-Building Measures among all 35 CSCE participating States.

9 March
Formal negotiations open in Vienna on Conventional Armed Forces in Europe and on Confidence and Security-Building Measures.

27 March
Multi-candidate elections to the new USSR Congress of People's Deputies result in major set-backs for official Party candidates in many constituencies.

4 April
The fortieth anniversary of the signing of the North Atlantic Treaty is marked by a special session of the North Atlantic Council and other ceremonies at NATO and in capitals.

5 April
Agreements signed in Warsaw by Government and opposition negotiators on measures leading to political reforms in Poland including democratic elections and legalisation of the banned trade union movement "Solidarity".

17 April
Reregistration of Solidarity.

18 April-12 May
CSCE Information Forum, London. Participants, including diplomats and journalists, focus on the need to transform working conditions and professional rights for journalists in an era of "glasnost" and rapid technological change.

15-18 May
The visit of Soviet President Gorbachev to China and declarations by the Chinese and Soviet leadership on the normalisation of relations between their two countries, during the first Sino-Soviet meeting at summit level since 1959, are overshadowed by large-scale student-led protests against corruption and for democratic reform.

29-30 May
Summit Meeting of the North Atlantic Council in Brussels attended by Heads of State and Government.[12] Announcement by President Bush of major new initiatives for conventional force reductions in Europe. Adoption of the Alliance's Comprehensive Concept of Arms Control and Disarmament and Publication of a Summit Declaration.

---

[12] Postscript: The Alliance has held 10 meetings at summit level since the signature of the North Atlantic Treaty, viz: Paris: December 1957; Brussels: June 1974; Brussels: May 1975; London: May 1977; Washington: May 1978; Bonn: June 1982; and Brussels: November 1985, March 1988, May 1989, and December 1989.

30 May-23 June
First meeting of the Conference on the Human Dimension (CDH), in Paris. Participants examine proposals designed to improve the implementation of CSCE commitments in the humanitarian field and address specific human rights issues as well as the situation of minorities.

31 May
During a visit to the Federal Republic of Germany following the successful NATO Summit Meeting, President Bush outlines proposals for promoting free elections and pluralism in Eastern Europe and dismantling the Berlin Wall, as well as proposals for East-West cooperation in environmental matters and disarmament. He emphasises the continued solidarity of the North Atlantic Alliance and expresses cautious optimism over reforms in the Soviet Union and developments in some East European countries.

3-4 June
Chinese leaders use armed forces in Peking to suppress unarmed student-led popular demonstrations against corruption and in favour of democracy, causing large-scale loss of life and leading to major unrest in other cities, purges and infringements of basic rights throughout China.

4 and 18 June
Free elections for the Senate (upper house of the Polish parliament) and partial elections involving 35% of seats in the Sejm (lower house) result in major electoral success for Solidarity.

8-9 June
Ministerial Meeting of the Defence Planning Committee. Defence Ministers consider implications for defence planning of Western proposals for reduction of conventional forces in Europe, approve the 1989 Ministerial Guidance (including the target of a 3% real increase in defence expenditure in the absence of tangible improvement in the balance of forces) and review progress in the implementation of recommendations contained in the December 1988 report on equitable sharing of roles, risks and responsibilities within the Alliance.

16 June
Imre Nagy, leader of the 1956 Hungarian revolution who was hanged in 1958, is reburied with full honours in Budapest, amid continuing discussions between opposition groups and the communist leadership on power sharing and the preparation of multi-party elections scheduled for 1990.

15 and 18 June
European Parliamentary Elections.

19 June
Re-opening of Strategic Arms Reductions Talks (START) in Geneva after 7 month interval.

6 July
Death of János Kádár, Hungarian Party leader from 1957 to 1988. The judicial rehabilitation of Imre Nagy occurs on the same day.

9 August
A statement is issued by NATO's Secretary General on behalf of the Allies concerning the human rights situation in Bulgaria, calling upon the Bulgarian government to respond positively to apeals to meet its responsibilities under the CSCE documents.

24 August
Tadeusz Mazowiecki becomes Prime Minister of the first non-communist led government in Poland in 40 years.

25 September
Polish Foreign Minister Krzysztof Skubiszewski, addressing the UN General Assembly, denounces the August 1939 German-Soviet accords resulting in the partition of Poland, declaring them to be null and void.

18 October
Erich Honecker is replaced by Egon Krenz as leader of the German Democratic Republic as East German citizens demonstrate for political reform and large numbers of refugees continue to leave the German Democratic Republic through Prague and Budapest.

23 October
The new constitution adopted by the Hungarian Parliament on 18 October brings into being the Republic of Hungary as a "free, democratic, independent legal state".

9-10 November
Opening of the Berlin Wall. Following widespread demonstrations and demand for political reform, the government of the German Democratic Republic announces the lifting of travel restrictions to the West and sets up new crossing points.

Appendix V
Abbreviations in Common Use

ABM	Anti-Ballistic Missile
ACCHAN	Allied Command Channel
ACE	Allied Command Europe
ACLANT	Allied Command Atlantic
ACCS	Air Command and Control System
ACCSA	Allied Communications and Computer Security Agency
ADM	Atomic Demolition Munition
ADP	Automatic Data Processing
ADSIA	Allied Data Systems Interoperability Agency
AEW	Airborne Early Warning
AFCENT	Allied Forces Central Europe
AFNORTH	Allied Forces Northern Europe
AFSOUTH	Allied Forces Southern Europe
AGARD	Advisory Group for Aerospace Research and Development
ALCM	Air-Launched Cruise Missile
ALLA	Allied Long Lines Agency
AMF	ACE Mobile Force
ANCA	Allied Naval Communications Agency
AP	Allied Publication
APAG	Atlantic Policy Advisory Group
AQAP	Allied Quality Assurance Publication
ARFA	Allied Radio Frequency Agency
ASAT	Anti-Satellite Weapon
ASW	Anti-Submarine Warfare
ATA	Atlantic Treaty Association
ATCA	Allied Tactical Communications Agency
AWACS	Airborne Warning and Control System
BMD	Ballistic Missile Defence
BMEWS	Ballistic Missile Early Warning System
CAPS	Conventional Armaments Planning System
CBM	Confidence Building Measure
CCMS	Committee on the Challenges of Modern Society
CCPC	Civil Communications Planning Committee
CD	Conference on Disarmament
CDE	Conference on Security and Confidence Building Measures and Disarmament in Europe
CDH	Conference on the Human Dimension (CSCE)
CDI	Conventional Defence Improvements
CEAC	Committee for European Airspace Coordination
CENTAG	Central Army Group, Central Europe
CENTO	Central Treaty Organisation
CEOA	Central Europe Operating Agency
CEP	Civil Emergency Planning

CEPS	Central Europe Pipeline System
CFE	Negotiations on Conventional Armed Forces in Europe
CHANCOM	Channel Committee
CINCEASTLANT	Commander-in-Chief Eastern Atlantic Area
CINCENT	Commander-in-Chief Allied Forces Central Europe
CINCHAN	Allied Commander-in-Chief Channel
CINCIBERLANT	Commander-in-Chief Iberian Atlantic Area
CINCNORTH	Commander-in-Chief Allied Forces Northern Europe
CINCSOUTH	Commander-in-Chief Allied Forces Southern Europe
CINCUKAIR	Commander-in-Chief United Kingdom Air Forces
CINCWESTLANT	Commander-in-Chief Western Atlantic area
CIS	Communications and Information Systems
CMEA	Council for Mutual Economic Assistance (COMECON)
CNAD	Conference of National Armaments Directors
COCOM	Coordinating Committee of Western Nations on Technology Transfer
CONMAROPS	Concept of Maritime Operations
CPX	Command Post Exercise
CSBM	Confidence and Security-Building Measure
CSCE	Conference on Security and Cooperation in Europe
CST	Conventional Stability Talks
CSWG	Communications Systems Working Group
CUSRPG	Canada-US Regional Planning Group
DPC	Defence Planning Committee
DRC	Defence Review Committee
ECCM	Electronic Counter Counter Measures
ECM	Electronic Counter Measures
ECSC	European Coal and Steel Community
EDC	European Defence Community
EDIP	European Defence Improvement Programme
EDIS	European Defence Industry Study
EEC	European Economic Community
EFTA	European Free Trade Association
ELDO	European Launcher Development Organisation
EMP	Electro Magnet Pulse
ENTG	EURO/NATO Training Group
ESA	European Space Agency
ESRO	European Space Research Organisation
EUROGROUP	Acronym used for informal Group of NATO European Defence Ministers
EW	Electronic Warfare
EWG	Executive Working Group
FOFA	Follow-on Forces Attack
GLCM	Ground Launched Cruise Missile
HLG	High Level Group (NPG)
HLTF	High Level Task Force
IATA	International Air Transport Association
ICAO	International Civil Aviation Organisation
ICB	International Competitive Bidding
ICBM	Intercontinental Ballistic Missile
IEG	Information Exchange Group
IEPG	Independent European Programme Group

IISS	International Institute for Strategic Studies
IMS	International Military Staff
INF	Intermediate-Range Nuclear Forces
IRBM	Intermediate-Range Ballistic Missile
ISWG	Information Systems Working Group
LCC	Logistics Coordination Centre
LRINF	Longer Range INF
LRTNF	Long-Range Theatre Nuclear Forces
LTDP	Long Term Defence Programme
LTPG	Long Term Planning Guidelines
MARAIRMED	Maritime Air Forces Mediterranean
MAREQ	Military Assistance Requirements
MAS	Military Agency for Standardization
MBFR	Mutual and Balanced Force Reductions
MC	Military Committee
MCM	Mine Counter Measures
MCMG	Military Committee Meteorological Group
MEWSG	Multi-Service Electronic Warfare Support Group
MILREP	Military Representative (to the Military Committee)
MIRV	Multiple Independently-targetted Re-entry Vehicle
MLF	Multilateral Force
MNC	Major NATO Commander
MNF	Maritime Nuclear Forces
MOD	Ministry of Defence
MOU	Memorandum of Understanding
NAA	North Atlantic Assembly
NAAG	NATO Army Armaments Group
NAC	North Atlantic Council
NACISA	NATO Communications and Information Systems Agency
NACISC	NATO Communications and Information Systems Committee
NACISO	NATO Communications and Information Systems Organisation
NADC	NATO Air Defence Committee
NADEEC	NATO Air Defence Electronic Environment Committee
NADEFCOL	NATO Defense College
NADGE	NATO Air Defence Ground Environment
NAEW	NATO Airborne Early Warning
NAFAG	NATO Air Force Armaments Group
NAMFI	NATO Missile Firing Installation
NAMMA	NATO Multi-Role Combat Aircraft Development and Production Management Agency
NAMMO	NATO Multi-Role Combat Aircraft Development and Production Management Organisation
NAMSA	NATO Maintenance and Supply Agency
NAMSO	NATO Maintenance and Supply Organisation
NAPATMO	NATO PATRIOT Management Office
NAPMA	NATO Airborne Early Warning and Control Programme Management Agency
NAPMO	NATO Airborne Early Warning and Control Programme Management Organisation
NAPR	NATO Armaments Planning Review
NASMO	NATO Starfighter Management Office
NASPO	NATO Starfighter Production Organisation

NAVOCFORMED	Naval On-Call Force, Mediterranean
NCARC	NATO Conventional Armaments Review Committee
NCCIS	NATO Command, Control and Information System
NCEB	NATO Communications Electronic Board
NDAC	Nuclear Defence Affairs Committee
NEFMO	NATO European Fighter Aircraft Development, Production and Logistics Management Organisation
NEWAC	NATO Electronic Warfare Advisory Committee
NGO	Non-Governmental Organisation
NHMO	NATO HAWK Management Office
NHPLO	NATO HAWK Production and Logistics Organisation
NIAG	NATO Industrial Advisory Group
NICS	NATO Integrated Communications System
NICS COA	NICS Control Operating Authority
NISSPO	NATO Identification System Special Project Office
NMR	National Military Representative (to SHAPE)
NNA	Neutral and Non-Aligned
NNAG	NATO Naval Armaments Group
NORAD	North American Air Defence System
NORTHAG	Northern Army Group, Central Europe
NPG	Nuclear Planning Group
NPLO	NATO Production and Logistics Organisation
NPT	Non-Proliferation Treaty
NRSG	Network Rationalisation Sub-Group
NSC	NATO Supply Centre
NSG	NATO Standardization Group
NST	Nuclear and Space Talks
NSWP	Non-Soviet Warsaw Pact
NTM	National Technical Means
OECD	Organisation for Economic Cooperation and Development
OPEC	Organisation of Petroleum Exporting Countries
OTAN	Organisation du Traité de l'Atlantique Nord
PAPS	Phased Armaments Programming System (previously Periodic Armaments Planning System)
PBEIST	Planning Board for European Inland Surface Transport
PBOS	Planning Board for Ocean Shipping
PERM REP	Permanent Representative (on the North Atlantic Council)
PG	Project Group
PNET	Peaceful Nuclear Explosions Treaty
R & D	Research and Development
SAC	Strategic Air Command
SACEUR	Supreme Allied Commander Europe
SACLANT	Supreme Allied Commander Atlantic
SACLANTCEN	SACLANT Undersea Research Centre
SALT	Strategic Arms Limitation Talks
SAM	Surface to Air Missile
SATCOM	Satellite Communications
SCEPC	Senior Civil Emergency Planning Committee
SCG	Special Consultative Group
SCSG	Satellite Communications Sub-Group
SDI	Strategic Defence Initiative
SG	Sub-Group

SHAPE	Supreme Headquarters Allied Powers Europe
SLBM	Submarine Launched Ballistic Missile
SLCM	Sea-Launched Cruise Missile
SNF	Short-Range Nuclear Forces
SNLC	Senior NATO Logisticians Conference
SRINF	Shorter-Range INF
STANAG	Standardization Agreement
STANAVFORCHAN	Standing Naval Force Channel
STANAVFORLANT	Standing Naval Force Atlantic
START	Strategic Arms Reductions Talks
STC	SHAPE Technical Centre
STG	Study Group
TCC	Temporary Council Committee
TNF	Theatre Nuclear Forces
TSG	Tri-Service Group
TSGCEE	Tri-Service Group on Communications and Electronic Equipment
TTBT	Threshold Test Ban Treaty
UN	United Nations
UNCTAD	United Nations Conference on Trade and Development
UNESCO	United Nations Educational, Scientific and Cultural Organisation
WEU	Western European Union
WG	Working Group
WHO	World Health Organisation
WTO	Warsaw Treaty Organisation

ALPHABETICAL INDEX

Bold figures indicate the more important references; '*n*' relates to a footnote; '*bis*' means that the subject appears more than once on the page; '*passim*' implies that there are references throughout the specified group of pages, but not on every page.

Ministerial Meetings

NOTES: All meetings are listed by date and location.

* indicates that no reference to the meeting appears in the text. (Communiqués issued at the conclusion of all meetings held at Ministerial level are published at the time of the meeting and are subsequently reproduced in "NATO Final Communiqués" (Volumes 1, 2 and 3) and in annual booklets available from the NATO Information Service, 1110 Brussels).

Alphabetical index

Abbreviations used:

NAC — North Atlantic Council
DPC — Defence Planning Committee
NPG — Nuclear Planning Group

Ministerial meetings of the North Atlantic Council are normally attended by Foreign Ministers. On occasion they have also been attended by Defence and/or Finance Ministers. Summit Meetings of the North Atlantic Council (i.e. at the level of Heads of State and Government) are denoted in the following list by the initials HG.

Ministerial Meetings of the Defence Planning Committee and of the Nuclear Planning Group are attended by Defence Ministers of the countries concerned.

THE ATLANTIC ALLIANCE

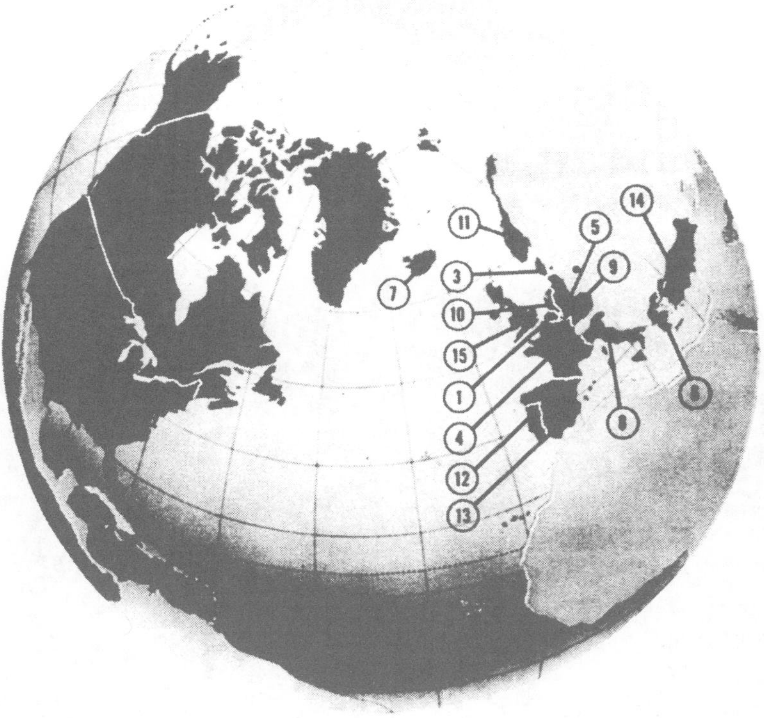

1) Belgium
2) Canada
3) Denmark
4) France
5) Federal Republic of Germany
6) Greece
7) Iceland
8) Italy
9) Luxembourg
10) Netherlands
11) Norway
12) Portugal
13) Spain
14) Turkey
15) United Kingdom
16) United States

Figure 18